EXPLORING WONDERLAND: JAVA PROGRAMMING USING ALICE AND MEDIA COMPUTATION

Wanda Dann
Carnegie Mellon University

Stephen Cooper
Purdue University

Barbara Ericson
College of Computing/GVU
Georgia Institute of Technology

D1568079

Prentice Hall

Boston Columbus Indianapolis New York San Francisco Upper Saddle River
Amsterdam Cape Town Dubai London Madrid Milan Munich Paris Montréal Toronto
Delhi Mexico City São Paulo Sydney Hong Kong Seoul Singapore Taipei Tokyo

**Library of Congress Cataloging-in-Publication
Data on File**

VP/Editorial Director, Engineering/Computer Science: Marcia J. Horton
Executive Editor: Tracy Dunkelberger
Editor in Chief: Michael Hirsch
Assistant Editor: Melinda Haggerty
Editorial Assistant: Allison Michael
Marketing Manager: Erin Davis
Senior Managing Editor: Scott Disanno
Production Liaison: Rose Kernan
Senior Operations Supervisor: Alan Fischer
Operations Specialist: Lisa McDowell
Design Manager: Kenny Beck
Interior Design: Macmillan Publishing Solutions
Cover Design: Kristine Carney
Cover Illustration/Photo: John William Banagan/Getty Images/Photographer's choice
Director, Image Resource Center: Melinda Patelli
Manager, Rights and Permissions: Zina Arabia
Manager, Visual Research: Beth Brenzel
Manager, Cover Visual Research & Permissions: Karen Sanatar
Composition Project Management: Macmillan Publishing Solutions
Printer/Binder: Courier-Kendalville

Prentice Hall
is an imprint of

www.pearsonhighered.com

10 9 8 7 6 5 4 3 2 1

ISBN-(10): 0-13-600159-9
ISBN-(13): 978-0-13-600159-1

To the memory of our friend and colleague Randy Pausch

Contents

Preface

A Brief History

In the Fall of 2005, Wanda Dann and Steve Cooper, originators of the Alice approach for introductory programming (in collaboration with Randy Pausch), met with Barb Ericson and Mark Guzdial, originators of the Media Computation (Media Comp) approach to introductory programming in Java. The focus of our meeting was an exploratory discussion of possible synergies resulting from combining the Alice approach with the Media Computation approach. For the Alice team, the gain would be a methodology for transitioning from Alice into Java (as taught in introductory computer science – CS1— courses) as well as the addition of material usually covered in CS1, such as string manipulation and arrays. For the Media Comp team, the gain would be a softening of the initial learning curve experienced by students just getting started programming with Java.

Factors that led us to considering a combination of these two approaches were obvious. Both approaches make heavy use of graphics and visualization. They both introduce objects early, and both use a problem-solving approach to teaching and learning programming. Previous studies have shown that students have found each approach highly motivating (*Evaluating the Effectiveness of a New Instructional Approach*, SIGCSE 2000 and *Tracking an Innovation in Introductory CS Education from a Research University to a Two-Year College* SIGCSE 2004) and each provides a real inspiration for students to learn programming. Another commonality is that both approaches are "non-traditional" and thus allow greater flexibility in the presentation of topics.

In the Spring of 2006, we received a National Science Foundation grant funding the development of a combined approach. Clearly, it was time to get serious about merging the two approaches into a single coherent course. The plan was for Cooper to pilot-test the combined course in a CS1 course at Saint Joseph's University in the Fall of 2006. Ericson would create a merged course for her summer workshops for high school teachers and work with Cooper and Dann to develop instructional materials and prepare a merged text-book. Guzdial would serve as a consultant. This meant that we were going to have a busy summer. Things got busier as we worked to resolve the differences between the two approaches. Media Comp makes heavy and early use of arrays (in particular, two-dimensional arrays). Alice, however, focuses on lists and defers arrays until the end of the course. Media Comp's Java examples are all presented using DrJava, while at Saint Joseph's University, jGrasp (`http://www.jgrasp.org`) was the Java IDE of choice. After much discussion, our general solution evolved into using the Media Comp approach and merging the Alice materials into it. This text presents the merged approach, with some modifications and additions made in response to findings from the pilot test.

Pilot Test Results

Cooper's experience with an Alice and Media Computation course at Saint Joseph's University was highly positive. Student evaluations of the course were extremely high.

Although the number of students in the course section was small (seven), all CS majors in this pilot group continued into CS2. In addition, three female mathematics majors switched their major to computer science. Furthermore, the students from this pilot test group did better in CS2 than did students in the control group, who had taken the traditional CS1 course. This last fact is remarkable considering that the CS2 course was taught (by another instructor) in a traditional manner, and in that the students who went through the combined Alice and Media Comp approach started out weaker in terms of math SAT scores, mathematics performance in high school, and previous programming experience.

High School Teacher Results

Ericson's experience with summer workshops for high school teachers was also positive. Teachers were able to learn computing concepts in Alice and then apply those concepts in Media Computation programs in Java. Alice helped the teachers learn computing concepts without having to also learn Java syntax at the same time. Additionally, showing the Alice code using the Java style option in Alice helped teachers make the transition to Java.

Teaching with Alice and Media Computation

In teaching a course using this combined Alice and Media Computation approach, it is important to note that Alice and Media Computation topics are alternated throughout the text and instructional materials. Generally, a particular topic is introduced first in an Alice animation problem-solving context, and then the same topic is illustrated in the context of a Media Computation problem in Java. One advantage of this book over other methods that transition to more traditional Java programs is that both approaches allow for open-ended assignments in the context of creating a movie. The Media Computation programs can be thought of as the special effects studio for Alice movies. Students can create sound clips in Java for their Alice movies, create advertisements in Java for Alice movies, and even blend live action and Alice movies using chromakey. Students find these types of assignments much more compelling than traditional Java assignments.

Teachers who have used Alice for six straight weeks and then tried to switch over to Java have reported that this approach is extremely challenging, from a pedagogy perspective. Students like Alice and want to continue programming in it. After six weeks with Alice, students have to be reminded of the concepts learned at the beginning of the course to help them make connections between what they learned in Alice and what they are learning in Java.

There is a real need for the instructor to *mediate the transfer* between Alice and Media Comp in Java. Our experience is that students "get" the concept by seeing very similar examples presented side by side in Alice and then in Java, and by the instructor making an effort to emphasize the similarities and explain the differences. Mediated transfer is the approach underlying this text and instructional materials. We strongly recommend that instructors follow this approach.

Book Topic Outline

In this textbook, we start by introducing Alice and the basic concepts for working in three dimensions in Chapter 1. We then explain how to design a program in Alice using storyboards and how to convert a storyboard into Alice code in Chapter 2. In Chapter 3 we introduce classes, objects, how to create object methods, and how to pass parameters in Alice. In Chapter 4 we transition to Java and explain how to declare object variables, create objects from classes, invoke methods on objects, create object methods, and pass parameters using a LOGO-style turtle. In Chapter 5 we deepen the students' understanding of variables in Java by explaining the differences between primitive variables and object variables, and we allow time to practice simple sequential programming in Java by teaching how to draw on pictures using standard Java classes. We also introduce the students to inheritance and interfaces in Chapter 5.

In Chapter 6 we transition back to Alice to introduce functions and conditionals. Chapter 7 introduces repetition (loops) in Alice. This includes for loops, nested for loops, while loops, and looping through all items in a list. In Chapter 8 we transition back to Java and modify all values in a sound using for-each loops, while loops, and for loops. This order is the reverse of how the loops were covered in Alice. We start with for-each loops in Java because research shows that people understand set operations like "for each item in a set" better than the general while or for loop. Chapter 8 also introduces conditionals in Java. In Chapter 9 we show how to modify small parts of a sound.

In Chapters 10-12 we deepen the students' understanding of loops and conditionals by using them to modify pictures in Java. Students profit from the repetition of these concepts in another context. We also found that while some students love manipulating pictures, others prefer manipulating sounds.

In Chapter 13 we create a complete class and a subclass in Java. Up until this chapter, we assume that students have been writing methods only in the provided existing classes. Our belief is that students have enough trouble learning the basics such as variables, loops, and conditionals, without adding the overhead of learning to write complete classes from the beginning. Chapter 14 also has students creating classes while working with strings, files, the random class, and reading from a network.

In Chapter 15 we introduce recursion in Alice. While recursion can be used to repeat a series of statements, we didn't want to overload the students by having them learn it earlier when we were teaching loops. In Chapter 16 we cover machine language, compilers, interpreters, searching, sorting, and recursion in Java. We also cover the limits of algorithms in Chapter 16. Some instructors may wish to cover some of these topics earlier, but we find that the students are more interested in these topics after they have had several weeks of experience creating and running programs of different sizes and complexities.

In Chapter 17 we use the material learned in Chapter 5 to make movies by using frame-based animation. This chapter doesn't teach new computing concepts, but it reinforces the need for parameters on methods and the reuse of methods. It also provides us the opportunity to merge Alice movies and live action. We definitely recommend covering this chapter because students find this topic very motivating.

In Chapter 18 we cover object-oriented analysis, inheritance, polymorphism, interfaces, and abstract classes. This chapter helps deepen the understanding of these advanced object-oriented concepts in the context of making a comic strip and drawing shapes.

Pilot Course Topic Outline

In the pilot test group, Cooper presented a subset of these topics in the order shown below. We hasten to add that it is not necessary to follow this sequence of topics. Topics in this book have been rearranged, based on our experience in the pilot test.

1. Introduction to virtual worlds in Alice (Chapter 1)
2. Building a world in Alice (Chapter 2)
3. Creating object-methods and using parameters in Alice (Chapter 3)
4. Introduction to Java (Chapter 4)
5. Creating object-methods and using parameters in Java using turtle graphics (Chapter 4)
6. Creating functions (non-void methods) in Alice (Chapter 6)
7. Using for loops and nested loops in Alice (Chapter 7)
8. Drawing on pictures in Java (Chapter 5)
9. 1-dimensional arrays, for loops and pictures in Java (Chapter 10)
10. Using nested for loops in Java (Chapter 11)
11. Conditionals in Alice (Chapter 7)
12. Conditionals in Java (Chapter 12)
13. Creating classes and subclasses in Media Computation (Chapter 13)
14. I/O in Java (Chapter 14)
15. Strings in Java (Chapter 14)
16. Recursion in Alice (Chapter 15)
17. Recursion, sorting and searching in Java (Chapter 16)

Dependency Chart

The book has been created for a typical semester-long course in introductory computer science at the university level (CS1). Of course, it can also be used for a high school Computer Science AP A course. High schools should either use this book for a full-year course, or pick and choose which chapters to cover.

Instructors wishing to create their own topic outline may find the following dependency chart helpful. The dependency chart illustrates which chapter topics depend on topics presented in previous chapters. It also shows which topics may be considered optional if you are pressed for time.

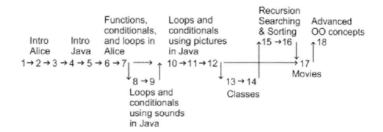

Technical Notes

Sound Sound can be used to provide a particularly good introduction to one-dimensional arrays. We recognize, however, that some schools have labs in which computers either lack sound cards, or do not allow their students to have headsets in class. (This was a problem faced by Cooper at Saint Joseph's University.) In this situation, we recommend instead that you skip the sound chapters (8 and 9) and introduce one-dimensional arrays using iteration through all pixels of a picture, as described in Chapter 10. Some students love manipulating sound, so if your students do have access to sound cards we recommend covering the sound chapters (8 and 9). We also find that the repetition of concepts using both pictures and sounds helps students better understand loops and conditionals as well as algorithms that work in both contexts.

Alice Animation Tips There are many tips towards building better animations in Alice. Though the animation tips are not necessary for teaching programming concepts, many students do find these tips great fun as they attempt to build more interesting virtual worlds. Thus, we include many such tips in Appendix A, and recommend that instructors allow students to explore these tips on their own.

Java IDEs The Java examples in the text are presented using DrJava (freely available from `http://www.drjava.org`). The authors like DrJava as an IDE particularly because it is free and allows students to try out their Java programs interactively (a main method is not required). There is, however, no dependence on using DrJava to teach the Media Computation part of this course. As long as the classpath can be set up to include the Media Comp libraries (bookClasses and the jar files in the bookClassess directory) the instructor can choose to use any Java IDE. To use DrJava you will also need to download the Java Development Kit (jdk) from Sun at http://java.sun.com.

Student and Instructor Resources

Students and instructors can find support materials at the Companion Website, www.pearsonhighered.com/wonderland.

Students can freely access the following materials:

- Pre-Setup Worlds: for Alice examples available in Alice chapters (no code)
- bookClasses: Java classes using in Media Computation Chapters
- mediasources: pictures, sounds, and video frames for Media Computation
- MediaTools: Squeak-based tools including sounds, pictures, and movies

- Glossary
- "Using Alice" Appendix

Instructor material is password-protected and includes the following:

- Solutions Manual for Alice Chapters
- PowerPoint Slides
- Example Syllabus
- Sample Tests
- Sample Lectures
- Post-Exercise Alice Worlds (Organized by chapter)
- bookClasses Solutions

Instructors are requested to contact their Pearson Education sales representative to access the materials.

The Solutions Manual and PowerPoint Slides are also available on the Instructor Resource Center located through the Publisher's web site, www.pearsonhighered.com.

In addition to this text, student and instructor resource materials (an appendix "using Alice," entitled a glossary, syllabi, lectures, assignments, exams, etc.) have been created to aid students and instructors in teaching this combined course. The materials are freely available from `http://home.cc.gatech.edu/TeaParty/31`. Instructors are requested to contact their Pearson Education sales representatives to obtain a key to access the materials. Because these materials include solutions and exams, we request that instructors maintain their protection. If instructors wish to make these materials available to their own students, we request that materials be placed in a password-protected area, where only their students have access.

Take a further look at Alice and Media Computation by visiting the author team web sites:

www.aliceprogramming.net
www.mediacomputation.org

Alice examples in this text have been created using Alice 2.2. You can freely download Alice 2.2 from `http://www.alice.org`. Alice 2.2 is being supported by the Alice Project and updates are posted at least twice a year. Alice 2.2 runs on both PC and Mac systems. The system requirements are:

Windows:

* Windows Vista, XP, or 2000
* Intel Pentium II or equivalent processor
* A VGA graphics card capable of high (16 bit) color and 1024×768 resolution (3D video card recommended)
* 512MB of RAM (1GB recommended)
* A sound card

Mac:

* Mac OS X 10.4+

* PowerPC or Intel processor

* A VGA graphic card capable of high (16 bit) color and 1024×768 resolution (3D video card recommended)

* 512MB of RAM (1GB recommended)

* A sound card

We hope that you will have the same enjoyment in teaching with Alice and Media Comp as we have had in creating this course and text, and in teaching this course ourselves.

STEPHEN COOPER
WANDA DANN
BARB ERICSON

Acknowledgment

The Alice and Media Computation project operates with support from the National Science Foundation under collaborative grant #0618531, to Saint Joseph's University, Georgia Institute of Technology, and Ithaca College. Any opinions, findings, and conclusions or recommendations expressed in this material are those of the author(s) and do not necessarily reflect the views of the National Science Foundation.

We wish to acknowledge the original development of Alice 2 by Randy Pausch and members of the Alice Team led by Dennis Cosgrove. We are also especially grateful for the updates contributed by Madelein Pitch and Aik Min Choong that are the significant modifications and bug fixes in the latest version, Alice 2.2.

The authors wish to thank the following individuals who have contributed their comments relative to the preparation of this text:

Kay Chen, *Bucks County Community College*
Mahmood Doroodchi, *Cardinal Stritch University*
Susan E. Crowe, *Fulton School District*
M. William "Bill" Dunklau, *Lakehill Preparatory School*
Michelle Venable-Foster, *South Gwinnett High School*
Rebecca Grasser, *Lakeland Community College*
Eugene Lemon, *Ralph J. Bunche High School*
Kelly Powers, *Dana Hall School*
Efstathios Mexas, *Water Johnson High School*
Regina Sikorski, *Northern Highlands Regional High School*
Robert H. Sloan, *University of Illinois, Chicago*
Wayne Summers, *Columbus State University*
John Osborne, *San Ramon Valley Unified School District*

List of Trademarks

Adobe, Macromedia Flash, Macromedia Sound Edit, Photoshop, and Quark are registered trademarks or trademarks of Adobe Systems Incorporated in the United States and other countries.

Apple, Final Cut Pro, and iMovie are trademarks or registered trademarks of Apple Computer, Inc.

AutoCAD is a registered trademark of Autodesk, Inc. in the USA and/or other countries.

DOOM is a registered trademark of Id Software, Inc.

DrJava is open-source software, ©2001–2003 by the JavaPLT group at Rice University (javaplt@rice.edu). All rights reserved.

Eudora is a registered trademark of QUALCOMM Incorporated in the United States and other countries.

Intel is a registered trademark of Intel Corporation or its subsidiaries in the United States and other countries.

Java and all Java-based trademarks and logos are trademarks or registered trademarks of Sun Microsystems, Inc. in the U.S. and other countries.

LEGO is a trademark of the LEGO Group of companies in the United States and other countries.

MasterCard is a registered trademark of MasterCard International, Incorporated in the United States and other countries.

Microsoft, Visual Basic, Visio, PowerPoint, Internet Explorer, Word, and Outlook are registered trademarks of Microsoft Corporation in the United States and/or other countries.

Netscape Navigator is a trademark of Netscape Communications Corporation.

Quicken is a trademark of Intuit, Inc., registered in the United States and other countries.

Squeak is licensed by MIT, ©2003 by Lucas Renggli and ©2003 by Software Composition Group, University of Berne.

Super Mario Brothers is a registered trademark of Nintendo of America, Incorporated in the United States and other countries.

Toyota Camry is a registered trademark of Toyota Motor Corporation.

VISA is a registered trademark of Visa International Service Association in the United States and other countries.

About the Authors

Wanda Dann is Director of the Alice Project and Associate Teaching Professor of Computer Science at Carnegie Mellon University. Wanda's research interests include visualization in programming and programming languages and innovative approaches to introductory programming. She received a Ph.D. in Computer Science at Syracuse University. With Steve, she has published multiple papers and journal articles, as well as Learning to Program with Alice (2006, Prentice-Hall). Dann is a distinguished contributor to professional Computer Science educator groups and has served as ACM's SIGCSE Technical Symposium publications editor and as ACM's SIGCSE Symposium chair. She was recently elected to serve as a member of the SIGCSE Executive Board and is the SIGCSE-CSTA liaison.

Stephen Cooper is a professor of Computer Graphics Technology at Purdue University. From 2007–2009, he served as a program manager in NSF's Division of Undergraduate Education, within its Education and Human Resources Directorate. Prior to coming to Purdue, Steve worked as an associate professor of Computer Science at Saint Joseph's University and as the Director of its Center for Visualization. His research areas lie in program visualization and semantics. He has been working with Alice and developing Alice-related curricular materials since 1998. With Wanda, he has written many technical papers on Alice, as well as Learning to Program with Alice (2006, Prentice-Hall). Along with Wanda and Barb, he wrote successful NSF grants (0618461, 0618380, 0618531, 0618562) from which this text is an output.

Barbara Ericson is a research scientist and the Director of Computing Outreach for the College of Computing at Georgia Tech. She has been working on improving introductory computing eduction since 2004.

She is currently the teacher education representative on the Computer Science Teachers Association board, the co-chair of the K-12 Alliance for the National Center for Women in Information Technology, and is on the Development Committee for the Advanced Placement Computer Science exams. She enjoys the diversity of the types of problems she has worked on over the years in computing including computer graphics, artificial intelligence, medicine, and object-oriented programming.

CHAPTER

1

Getting Started with Alice

Goals of this chapter:

- To introduce the Alice system, where animation of 3D objects takes place in a virtual world.
- To introduce the gallery of 3D models (classes).
- To introduce Alice objects as instances of the 3D model classes.
- To illustrate the six possible directions of motion for an object.
- To illustrate an object's orientation (the direction an object is facing and where the top of the object is located, relative to the world).
- To introduce the concept of the center of an object. An Alice object has a unique center set by the graphic artist when the 3D model is first created. The center of the ground in an Alice world is located at the position (0, 0, 0). The location of an object within the world is determined relative to the center of the ground.

1.1 Introduction to Alice

1.1.1 Why Is It Named Alice?

First of all, **Alice** is not an acronym: it isn't A.L.I.C.E. and it doesn't stand for anything. The team named the system "Alice" in honor of Charles Lutwidge Dodgson, an English mathematician and logician who wrote under the pen name Lewis Carroll. Carroll wrote *Alice's Adventures in Wonderland* and *Through the Looking Glass*. Just like the people who built Alice, Lewis Carroll was able to do complex mathematics and logic, but he knew that the most important thing was to make things simple and fascinating to a learner.

In the same way that Alice was hesitant when she first stepped through the looking glass, you may have some doubts about learning to program. Please take that first step, and we promise that **learning to program a computer will be easier than you might think**.

1.1.2 Installing Alice

We recommend that you use Alice 2.2 for the examples and exercises in this book. Alice is free, open source, and easy to use. Alice can be downloaded from http://www.alice.org/index.php?page=downloads/download_alice2.2. Alice does not require "installation" in the same way that many other software

1

applications do. All it really needs is a place on the machine's hard drive. As a result, the installation of Alice should succeed on machines where other software installations fail.

PC-only instructions: Download and extract the files within, as you would any other compressed (`.zip`) file. It will create an Alice folder within which you can run the Alice application (`Alice.exe`).

Mac-only instructions: Download the appropriate version of Alice based on your computer configuration—10.4+ for operating systems running Tiger or Leopard and 10.3 for operating systems running Panther. If you are unsure which operating system you are running, you can check by clicking on the Apple icon located in upper-left corner of the screen and clicking **About This Mac**. Your operating system version will be listed here. After downloading Alice, double-click the disk image (.dmg) to mount the Alice volume. Open the Alice volume (it should open automatically) and drag the Alice application to your desktop. If the file gets copied successfully, you can drag the Alice volume to the trash.

Linux-only instructions: Alice needs 250MB of free space. Please have opengl drivers and a Java Runtime Environment (`http://www.java.com/en/`). Download the file `Alice-2.0.0.tar.gz`. Open a terminal to the directory where you downloaded the file. Run the command: `tar xvfz Alice-2.0.0.tar.gz` then run: `cd Alice/Required`, then run: `./run-alice`

1.1.3 Starting Alice

Instructions for starting Alice and learning to use Alice are provided in the Appendix located on the web site of this textbook. We recommend that you sit at your computer and read the *Using Alice* instructions in that Appendix. As you read the instructions, follow along and do the same actions on your computer. After completing *Using Alice* in the Appendix located on the web site, return to this chapter.

1.2   Alice Concepts

Learning to program in Alice means that you will create virtual worlds on your computer and populate them with some really cool objects in creative scenes. Then, you will write **programs** (sort of like movie scripts or video game controllers) to direct your own production of animations in those worlds. In this section, we begin with an overview of the Alice software and the interface to help you get started. This section works hand-in-hand with the *Using Alice* exercises in Appendix posted to the web site.

1.2.1 Concept: Virtual World

Video games and simulations can be either two or three dimensional (**2D** or **3D**). You may have used a 2D graphic simulator in a driver education course. Pilots, as part of their training, use flight simulators. The advantage of simulation is obvious—when a fighter plane crashes under the hands of the novice pilot, neither the pilot nor the aircraft is actually in danger. A video game or simulation implemented in 3D is called

Figure 1.1
2D mock-up, front and back view

a **virtual world**. Using a virtual world lends a sense of reality to the simulator and increases its effectiveness.

To see the difference between 2D and 3D, compare the images in Figures 1.1 and 1.2. Figure 1.1 shows a movie set mock-up front and back. Clearly, the structure is 2D because it has width and height, but no depth. Figure 1.2 shows front and back camera shots of the tortoise and hare out for their daily exercise run. The tortoise and hare are objects in a 3D virtual world, having width, height, and depth, so camera shots captured from different angles show objects that give a sense of being real.

An Alice virtual world begins with a template for creating an initial scene. The templates are shown in the opening window when Alice is started. (The templates arc also displayed when you start a new world using File → New in the main menu bar at the top of the Alice interface.) The templates are illustrated in Figure 1.3, where we have selected an initial scene composed of a blue sky and a grassy-green ground surface.

1.2.2 Concept: Objects and 3D Models

Part of the fun of using Alice is to use your imagination to create new worlds. We begin with a simple scene and add **objects**. In the world shown in Figure 1.2, the objects added are a tree, fence, tortoise, and hare. Some objects provide a setting (trees, houses, starry skies, and such). Other objects (people, animals, space ships, and others) play the role of actors in your script (that is, they move around and perform various actions during the animation).

Figure 1.2
3D world with the tortoise and hare, front and back view

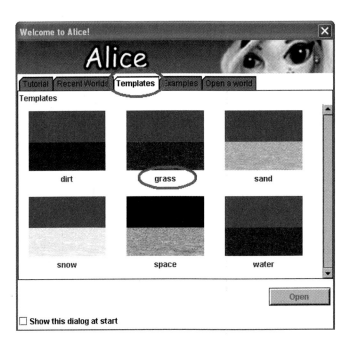

Figure 1.3
Selecting a template for an initial scene

To make it easy to create a new world and populate it with all kinds of objects, the Alice developers have provided a huge number of 3D models. In a way, a 3D model is like a blueprint used to design a house. The blueprint provides a model of what the house will look like, the location and size of each room in the house, and some instructions for the housing contractor to follow in actually building the house. Likewise, an Alice 3D model tells Alice how to create a new object in the scene. The 3D **model** provides instructions on how to draw the object, what color it should be, what parts it should have, its size (height, width, and depth), and many other details.

The installation of Alice on your computer includes a **Local Gallery** that contains a selection of 3D models. Additional models can be found in the **Web Gallery** (available from the downloads tab at http://www.alice.org). Easy access to the 3D models in a gallery collection is provided by the scene editor, shown in Figure 1.4. Examples and exercises in this book use models from both the Local and the Web Galleries. If you want to use a 3D model that does not appear in the Local Gallery, you can find it on the Web Gallery.

Alice is not a 3D graphics drawing program. This is why generous galleries of 3D models are provided. It is not possible, though, to think of everything someone may want for a virtual world. To help you build people objects of your own, custom builder tools (*hebuilder* and *shebuilder*) are available in the People folder of the Local Gallery. Details on using these tools are provided in Appendix A.

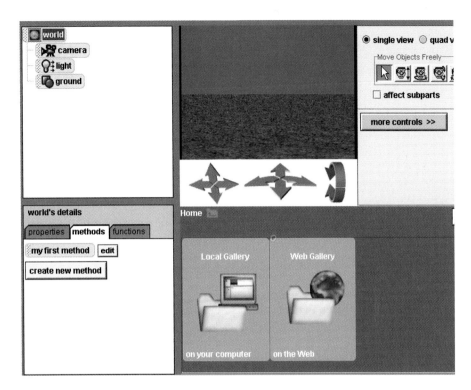

Figure 1.4
Scene editor with Local and Web Gallery folders

1.2.3 Concept: Three Dimensions and Six Directions

Objects in an Alice world are three dimensional. Each object has width, height, and depth, as illustrated in Figure 1.5. In this world, the astronaut has been added (People in the Local Gallery folder) to the space world template. The height is measured along an imaginary line running vertically from top to bottom, the width along an imaginary line running horizontally from left to right, and the depth along an imaginary line running from front to back.

In terms of these three dimensions, an object "knows" which way is *up* or *down* relative to itself. Also, the object "understands" the meaning of *left, right, forward,* and *backward*, as shown in Figure 1.6. This amounts to six possible **directions** in

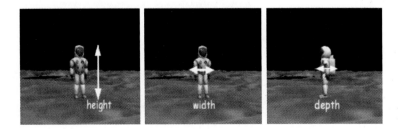

Figure 1.5
Three dimensions

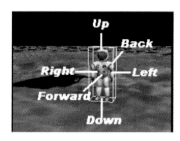

Figure 1.6
Object orientation: six directions

which an object may move. It is important to notice, for example, that directions are defined with respect to the individual object, not relative to the camera's point of view. The six directions relative to an object is defined as the object's **orientation**. Particularly important is the direction an object is facing.

On a PC, a mouse-click on an object in an Alice world causes a yellow **bounding box** to be displayed, as seen in Figure 1.6. The bounding box highlights the selected object. (This feature is not implemented in the Mac and Linux versions of Alice 2.0. The bounding box is available, however, on the Mac version of Alice 2.2.)

1.2.4 Concept: Center of an Object

Each object in Alice has a unique **center**. The center point isn't calculated. Instead, it is a feature of each object that is set by a graphic artist when the 3D model is first created. Usually, the center point of an object is at the center of its bounding box—or as near to the center of mass as the graphic artist could determine.

The center of an object provides a reference or **pivot point** for an object's roll and turn movements. So, an object like a tire or a bird will spin around its center. Figure 1.7 illustrates the center of a bird object. We used a wire frame display to show that the center of the bird is located in the interior of its body.

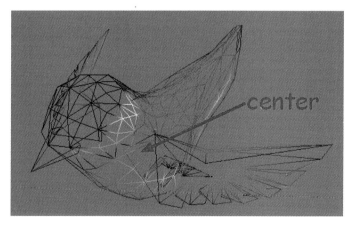

Figure 1.7
Center at the center of mass

Figure 1.8
Center of an object that stands on the ground

Not all objects, however, have their center located at their center of mass. Those that generally sit or stand on the ground or on a table have their center located at the bottom of their bounding box. For people objects, the center point is between their feet, as shown in Figure 1.8. This is because a person's feet are on the ground and having the center on the ground allows Alice to compute the distance of the person above the ground as zero (0) meters.

Other kinds of objects that do not have a center at the center of mass are those that are "held" in a specific location when used. For example, the center point of a baseball bat is where it would be held, as illustrated in Figure 1.9. The center is on the handle, so that when it is rotated, it will "swing" about that point.

1.2.5 Concept: Distance

Not only is the center of an object used as a pivot point, it is also used for determining distance from one object to another. One object's **distance** to another object is measured from its center. For example, the bird's distance downward to the ground in

Figure 1.9
Center of an object that is held

Figure 1.10
Distance downward to the ground is measured from the center

Figure 1.10 is measured from the bird's center. (In this illustration, we assume the bird is directly over the center point of the ground.)

1.2.6 Concept: Position

Another important thing to know about an object's center is that the center point is used by Alice as the **position** of the object in the world. Alice automatically puts the center of the ground at the center of the world. In Figure 1.11, a set of coordinate axes is positioned at the center of the ground. In the properties list for the ground (located

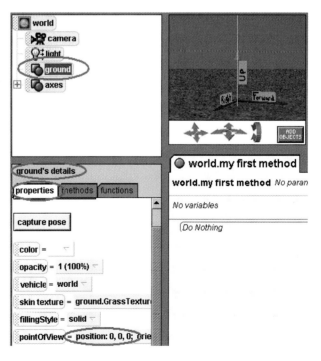

Figure 1.11
The center of the ground is located at the center of the world

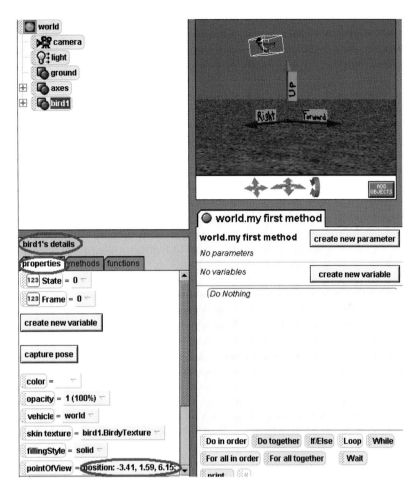

Figure 1.12
The bird's position relative to the center of the world

in the details panel at the lower left of Figure 1.11), you can see that the center of the ground is located at position (0, 0, 0).

Like the ground, any object in the world is located relative to the center of the world. The bird in Figure 1.12 is located at position (–3.41, 1.59, 6.15). That is, the center of the bird is 3.41 meters left, 1.59 meters above, and 6.15 meters forward of the center of the world.

1.2.7 Concept: Animation

In Alice, you will build virtual worlds and create animations by moving the objects in a world in the same way that objects are moved in a flight simulator or a video game. You will use many of the same techniques to give the illusion of motion as are used by animators to create animated cartoons for film studios such as Disney® and Pixar®. **Animation** is a fantasy of vision, an illusion. To generate this illusion, the filmmaker

Figure 1.13
A sequence of frames to create an animation

and artist collaborate to create a sequence of artwork frames (drawings or images) where each has a slightly different view of a scene. The scene is drawn with objects, and then redrawn with the objects positioned in a slightly different place. The scene is drawn again, and the objects are moved just a bit more, over and over and over! Figure 1.13 illustrates a sequence of frames in Alice.

In animation production, frames are photographed in sequence on a reel of film or captured by a digital video camera. The film is run through a projector or viewed on a monitor, displaying many pictures in rapid sequence and creating an illusion of motion. Alice creates a similar effect on your computer screen. There is no need to worry about being a great artist. Alice takes care of all the computer graphic work to create the sequence of frames. You act as the director to tell Alice what actions the objects are to perform. Alice creates (renders) the animation.

1.2.8 Java™ Syntax

In this book, programming concepts are first introduced in Alice and then applied in the context of Media Computation using Java. To help you make the transition from Alice to Java, we recommend that you set the Alice display style to show the code

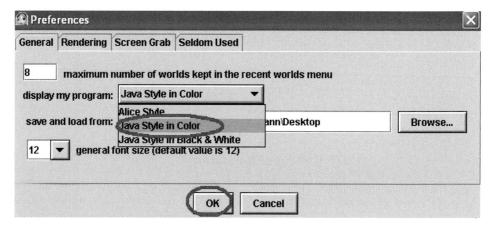

Figure 1.14
Select *Java Style in Color* to turn on the Java-style switch

using Java syntax. The style setting option can be found in the **Preferences** menu. To activate Java-style in Alice, first select **Edit** from the main menu bar at the top of the Alice interface and then select the **Preferences** menu item. In the **General** tab of the **Preferences** box, select the **Java Style in Color** option in **display my program:** and then click **OK**, as illustrated in Figure 1.14.

1.3 Concepts Summary

At the end of each chapter, we will present a summary. The purpose of a summary is to pull together the information and ideas presented in the chapter into a meaningful whole. The goal is to provide a quick review and study guide.

1.3.1 Using Alice

Alice is a 3D animation software tool that can be used to learn how to design and write computer programs. Alice allows you to quickly create cartoon-like animations of objects in a 3D virtual world. The objects are three dimensional, having width, height, and depth. We encourage you to experiment with the Alice system in much the same way as you would explore a new cell phone. You take it out of the box and try out all its cool features—sort of a "poke and prod" exploration. In the same way, you can learn how to use the Alice system.

The Appendix located on the web site provides a tutorial-style set of self-paced exercises with detailed instructions on how to start a new Alice world, where to find the galleries of 3D models, how to change the color of the ground, how to add objects to a new world, and how to properly position objects in a scene. If you have not already done so, go to the Appendix located on the web site and do these exercises now!

1.3.2 Virtual World

A video game or simulation implemented in 3D is called a **virtual world**. Using a virtual world lends a sense of reality to the simulator and increases its effectiveness. An Alice virtual world begins with a template for creating an initial scene, as shown in Figure 1.15.

1.3.3 Objects Have a Sense of Orientation and a Center Point

In an Alice virtual world, each object has an orientation that provides a sense of direction. That is, an object "knows" which way is up, down, left, right, forward, and backward relative to itself. Each object has a center point, which often corresponds to the center of mass of a real-world object. However, the center point of an object is used as a pivot point for turn and roll motions. For this reason, sometimes the center of an object will not be at the center of mass but will instead be at a location convenient for motion directions. For example, biped (two-legged) objects are likely to have a center that is located between their feet as the focal point of walking motions.

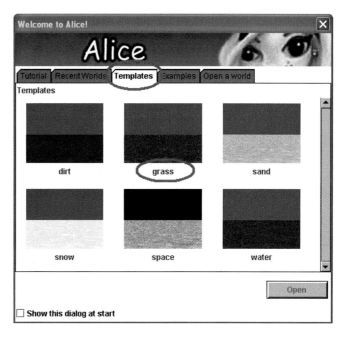

Figure 1.15
Selecting a template for the initial scene

1.3.4 Objects Have a Position in the World

An Alice world tracks the position (location) of an object in the world using the center of the object. In other words, the location of an object in the world is the same as the location of its center point. The distance from one object to another object therefore can be computed as the distance from the center point of one object to the center point of another object.

1.3.5 Computer Program

A computer program is a sequence of statements that tell the computer what to do. Importantly, a computer program is also a way to tell another human being what you want the computer to do. Learning to think about arranging a sequence of statements to carry out a task (how to design a program) is probably the most important part of learning to program.

Exercises

These exercises are to verify that you have learned and are comfortable using the Alice software. The goal in each exercise is to create an initial scene for a world. Alice will periodically prompt you to save your world. (Instructions on how to save a world are provided in the *Getting Started* exercises in the Appendix located on the web site.) The objects in each world are created from the 3D models in the Alice Galleries. Most models are located in the Local Gallery included in the Alice installation. If the model is not in the Local Gallery, lo ok for the model in the online Web Gallery (available at www.alice.org).

1. The tutorial in the Appendix located on the web site illustrates two different kinds of animations: movies and interactive. What is the difference between the two?

2. List three ways in which a class (3D model) is similar to a blueprint for constructing a house or other building.

3. List the six directions an Alice object can move.

4. Use a diagram to illustrate the distance between two Alice objects.

5. Is the center of an Alice object always located at its center of mass? Explain your answer.

6. *Island* Create an Island scene. Start by choosing a water world template. (Alternatively, start with a green grass world and change the ground color to *blue*.) Add an island object (from the Environments folder). Use the scene editor to position the island a bit to the right of the center of the scene. Now, add a goldfish to the scene. You may find that the goldfish is invisible because it is located behind the island or is not properly positioned. Use the scene editor and its quad view to arrange the goldfish so it looks like it is swimming in the water to the left of the island. Use the camera controls to zoom out so the island and the goldfish are both in the camera's view.

7. Add two snowmen (People folder) to a snowy scene. Use a snow template initial world. Then, create a snowman stack by using the scene editor's quad view to position one snowman on top of the other (vertically), as shown below.

8. Build a "wall" of four snowpeople by tipping them over on their sides and piling them on top of one another. (Use methods, mouse controls, and quad view.) Four

snowpeople (alternating between snowman and snowwoman) might be used to produce a wall that looks like this:

9. *Tea Party* As a tribute to Lewis Carroll, create a Tea Party for Alice Liddell and the white rabbit. In addition to Alice Liddell (People) and the white rabbit (Animals), the party should include a table (DiningTable in the Furniture folder in the Web Gallery) and three chairs (Furniture), a teapot, a toaster, and a plate (Kitchen). Use methods, the mouse, and quad view to properly position objects like the teapot and creamer on the table. The picture below is provided as an example. Use your imagination to make a better scene, if you wish.

10. *Soldiers on Deck* Add an aircraft carrier (Vehicle) and four toy soldiers (People) to a new world. Line up the soldiers for a formal ceremony—two on each end of the carrier deck, as shown.

Right-click on each soldier and use methods (from the popup menu) to move the arms of the soldiers to salute each other. Or, use the mouse controls in the Scene Editor to move the arms into position. (Use the *affect subparts* checkbox to allow the mouse to move their arms.) Raise the left arm of each soldier (at about a 45-degree angle with the horizontal plane). The result should be a scene where all four soldiers are saluting. This is not an animation—all you are trying to do is set up the scene.

Making It Work Tip: Watch Out for Subparts

If you check the *affect subparts* checkbox to allow the mouse to move subparts of an object, remember to uncheck the box before using the mouse for some other purpose!

CHAPTER

2

Program Design and Implementation

Goals of this chapter:

- To introduce a scenario as a problem statement that describes the overall animation in terms of what problem is to be solved, what lesson is to be taught, what game is to be played, or what simulation is to be demonstrated.

- To illustrate visual and textual storyboards.

- To use a visual storyboard sketch to represent the state of the animation—sort of a snapshot of the scene—showing the position, color, size, and other properties of objects in the scene.

- To relate a textual storyboard to a to-do list, providing an algorithmic list of steps that describe sequential and/or simultaneous actions.

- To introduce a program as a block of code that specifies the actions objects are to perform.

- To use *doInOrder* and *doTogether* blocks to structure a program so as to tell Alice which statements are to be executed in order and which are to be executed simultaneously.

- To illustrate the construction of a non-trivial animation from simple composition of *doInOrder* and *doTogether* blocks of code.

- To introduce the use of comments for documenting program code.

Introduction

In this chapter, we begin an introduction to programming. A program is a set of statements that tells the computer what to do. Each statement is an action to be performed. Writing a program to animate 3D objects in a virtual world is naturally all about objects and the actions objects can perform. From a practical viewpoint, writing a program is somewhat like working with word problems in math. We first read the word problem (a description of the situation) and decide how to go about solving it (what steps need to be done). Then, we solve the problem (write a solution) and test our answer to make sure it is correct. Similarly, we can use this problem-solving technique to help us create an animation program.

1. First read a scenario, also known as a problem statement. A **scenario** is a description of the story, game, or simulation.

2. Make a plan for creating the animation (design a **storyboard**).

15

3. Write the program **code**—the actual statements to the computer—using a formal computer language. This step is known as **implementation**.

4. Test the program by running it, that is, view the animation to see if the program is working as expected.

Section 2.1 begins with reading an example scenario and designing a storyboard. Visual storyboards were chosen because they are the design tool used by professional animators in film studios. Textual storyboards were chosen because they provide an algorithmic (step-by-step) structure. The lines of text in a textual storyboard are similar to pseudocode—a loose version of the statements that will eventually become program code.

Section 2.2 presents the basics of implementing and testing a simple program in Alice. The idea is to use a storyboard as a guide for writing the program (list of statements) in Alice's drag-and-drop editor. We can focus on a step-by-step solution because Alice will automatically take care of all the details of **syntax** (statement structure and punctuation). In an animation, some actions must take place in sequence and others simultaneously. This means the program code must be structured to tell Alice which actions to *doInOrder* and which to *doTogether*.

2.1   Scenarios and Storyboards

As described in this chapter's introduction, creating a computer program that animates objects in a virtual world is a four-step process: read the scenario (a description of the problem or task), design (plan ahead), implement (write the program), and test (see if it works). This section introduces the first two steps.

Reading the scenario and designing a plan of action are important steps in constructing programs for animation. A design is a "plan ahead" strategy and takes practice to master. While the programs presented in the first few chapters of this text are reasonably clear-cut, we think it is advisable to start building good designs early on. Then, when programs begin to get more complicated, the time invested in learning how to design good program solutions will pay great dividends.

2.1.1 Read the Scenario

Before we can discuss how to create a design, we need to read the scenario to find out what problem is going to be solved or what task is going to be performed. (Many computer scientists use the term **requirements specification** for describing the task to be performed. In Alice, the term *scenario* is easier to relate to the world scene, objects, and actions.) Cartoons and feature-length animated films begin with a scenario created by professional writers, sometimes called the "story." As used here, in addition to the traditional meaning, a story can be a lesson to teach, a game to play, or a simulation.

In an Alice world, a scenario gives all necessary details for setting up the initial scene and then planning a sequence of statements for the animation. That is, a scenario provides answers to the following questions:

1. What story is to be told?

2. What objects are needed? Some objects will play leading roles in the story, while other objects will be used to provide background scenery.

3. What actions are to take place? The actions in the story will eventually become the statements in the program.

2.1.2 Scenario Example

Let's consider an example scenario: After traveling through space, a robot-piloted craft has just made a breathless landing on the surface of a moon. The robot has already climbed out of the lunar lander and has set up a camera so earthbound scientists at the NASA center in Houston can view this historic event. Through the camera (the scene in our world), we can see the robot, the lunar lander, and some nearby rock formations. Suddenly, an alien peeks out from behind a rock and looks at the robot. The robot is surprised and rotates its head all the way around. The robot walks over to take a closer look, and the alien hides behind the rocks. Finally, the robot looks at the camera, signals danger, and says "Houston, we have a problem!"

From this scenario, we can answer the questions:

• What story is to be told? This scenario tells a humorous story about a robot's first encounter with an alien on a distant moon.

• What objects are to be used? The objects are the robot, a lunar lander, rocks, and an alien. The background scenery should depict a moon surface in a space world.

• What actions are to take place? The actions include the alien peeking out from behind a rock, the robot turning its head around and moving toward the alien, the alien hiding behind the rocks, and the robot sending a message back to earth.

2.1.3 Design

A **storyboard** is the design approach we will use to create a solution to a problem or plan a list of actions to perform a task, as specified in the scenario. At Pixar, Disney, and other major animation studios, animators break down a long scenario into sequences of many short scenarios. For each scenario, a storyboard is created to depict the sequence of scenes. The storyboard may consist of dozens of scene sketches, which are drawn by animation artists or generated by computer animation specialists using computer software.

The storyboard approach to design is not unique to computer programmers and animators. Playwrights, for example, break their plays down into individual acts and the acts into individual scenes! Engineers break down complicated systems (for example, jet airplanes and claw hammers) or devices (such as microcircuits) into component parts to make the problem more manageable.

2.1.4 Visual Storyboards

A **visual storyboard** breaks a scenario into a sequence of major scenes with transitions between scenes. Each sketch is a representation or a snapshot of a scene (state) in the animation. Each snapshot is associated with objects in certain positions, colors, sizes, and poses. When one or more transitions (changes) occur in the animation, the transition leads to the next scene (state).

The snapshots are numbered in sequence and labeled with necessary information. For short animations, the breakdown might be presented on one large sheet of paper. For more complex designs, a separate sheet of drawing paper can be used for each scene, allowing the animation artist to easily rearrange or discard scenes without starting over.

To create a visual storyboard, we borrow a technique from professional animators— a sequence of hand-drawn scenes. A visual storyboard template is shown in Figure 2.1. Each snapshot is labeled with a **scene number** and contains a sketch or picture showing where the objects are in the scene. The description tells what action is occurring. If sound is appropriate in the animation, the description will include a list of sounds that will be played during the scene. If a comic-book style is desired, text may be included to show the words or phrases that will be displayed in a text bubble. Sound and/or text are used only if needed.

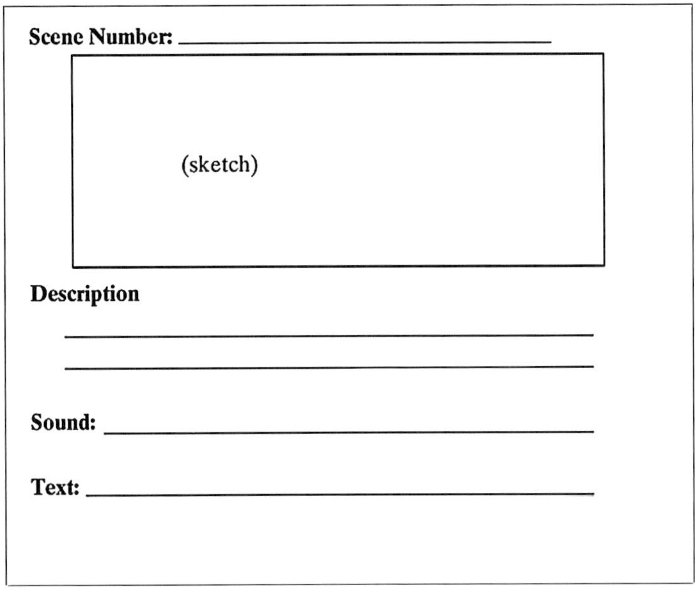

Figure 2.1
Storyboard template

For our purposes, preparing storyboard sketches is not intended to be a highly artistic task. Simple circles, squares, and lines can be used to represent the objects that will appear in the scene. If necessary, shapes can be labeled with the name of the object or color coded.

To illustrate the creation of a storyboard, the sample scenario for the robot's first encounter will be used. Figure 2.2 shows a simple scene where the alien peeks up from behind a rock. Simple sketches were used to create the lunar Lander, robot, and alien. Brown lines were drawn to create rocks in front of the alien. The grey squiggly lines represent the surface of the moon. Using simple figures, hand-sketched storyboards are quick and easy to create.

For illustrations in this book, we use Alice's scene editor to add objects to a world and then patiently arrange the objects in various poses. As each successive scene is created, a screen capture is made and copied to a document. Figure 2.3 illustrates screen captures in a storyboard for the beginning of the robot's first encounter animation. (We used the *spiderRobot* and the *alienOnWheels* from the SciFi folder in the Gallery.) Naturally, screen captures for a storyboard are fancier than hand-drawn sketches, but they take longer to put together.

2.1.5 Textual Storyboards

While professional animation artists use visual storyboards as part of their project development process, not everyone has the patience to make dozens of sketches. A **textual storyboard** is a good alternative. It looks something like a "to-do list" and allows us to prepare a planned structure for writing program code. To take advantage of the strengths of each, both visual and textual storyboards are used throughout this book.

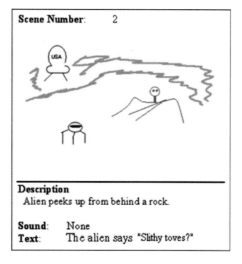

Figure 2.2
A hand-sketched visual storyboard

2.1.6 Textual Storyboard Example

A textual storyboard for the first encounter animation is shown next. Notice that a textual storyboard may summarize several scenes from a visual storyboard. For instance, the textual storyboard shown here summarizes Scene Number 1, Scene Number 2, and Scene Number 3 from the visual storyboard in Figure 2.3. This storyboard represents only the first few actions. It will be completed in the next section.

Scene Number: 1

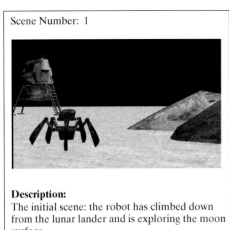

Description:
The initial scene: the robot has climbed down from the lunar lander and is exploring the moon surface.

Sound: None
Text: None

Scene Number: 2

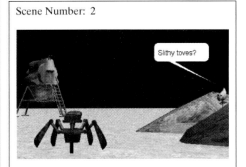

Description:
An alien peeks up from behind a rock.

Sound: None
Text: The alien says "Slithy toves?"

Scene Number: 3

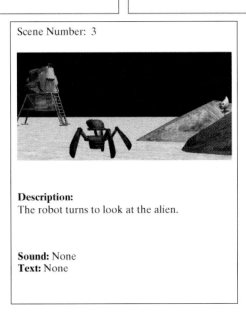

Description:
The robot turns to look at the alien.

Sound: None
Text: None

Figure 2.3
Screen captures of storyboard scenes

```
Do the following steps in order
  alien moves up
  alien says "Slithy toves?"
  robot's head turns around
  robot turns to look at alien
  Do the following steps together
    robot moves toward the alien
    robot legs walk
etc.
```

The lines of text in a textual storyboard provide an ordered list of actions. The lines are written in an outline format and indentation makes the storyboard easy to read. Notice that two lines (Do . . . in order and Do . . . together) in the above textual storyboard are in italics. These lines organize the actions—some actions are to be done in order (one at a time), others are to be done together (at the same time). The first four actions are performed in order (the alien moves up, the alien says "Slithy toves?", the robot's head turns around, and then the robot turns to look at the alien). The next action, where the robot moves toward the alien to take a closer look, is actually a composite of actions performed simultaneously (the robot moves forward at the same time as the robot's legs simulate a walking action).

In computing terminology, a textual storyboard is called an **algorithm**—a list of actions to perform a task or solve a problem. The actions in a textual storyboard are very close to (but not quite) actual program code, and so, they are often known as **pseudocode**.

2.1.7 Evaluate and Revise

Once a storyboard has been designed, it is a good idea to take an objective look to decide what might be changed. Evaluate the storyboard by answering these questions:

- Does the action flow from scene to scene, as the story unfolds?
- Do any transitions need to be added to blend one scene to the next?
- Did you overlook some essential part of the story?
- Is there something about the story that should be changed?

The important idea is that the storyboard is not final. We should be willing to review our plans and modify them, if necessary. In creating a program design, we go through the same kinds of cycles as an artist who has an idea to paint on a canvas. The painter often sketches a preliminary version of what the painting will look like. This is a way of translating the abstract idea into a more concrete vision. Then, the painter looks at the preliminary version and may change it several times before actually applying oils to the canvas. Likewise, an engineer who designs a bridge or an airplane (or anything else) goes through many design-modify-create phases before the final product is constructed. All creative people go through these design-modify-create cycles.

2.2 A First Program

In Section 2.1, you learned how to carefully read a scenario and design an animation to carry out a task, play a game, or create a simulation. Now you are ready to look at how an animation program can be written. This step is called **implementation**. We recommend that you read this section while sitting at a computer. Start up Alice and repeat the steps shown in the example in this section.

2.2.1 What Is a Program?

As you know, a program is a list of statements (actions) to accomplish a task. You can think of an Alice program as being somewhat like a script for a theatrical play. A theatrical script tells a story by describing the actions to be taken and the words to be delivered by actors on stage. In a similar manner, an Alice program describes the actions to be taken and the sound and text to be used by objects in a virtual world.

2.2.2 Create an Initial Scene

An ancient Chinese proverb advises that "The longest journey begins with a single step." Let's begin our journey by implementing the robot's first encounter animation described in Section 2.1. Recall that a robot-piloted spacecraft has just landed on a moon. The robot encounters an alien that curiously peeks out from behind the rocks. The surprised robot walks toward the alien to check it out and then sends a message back to earth: "Houston, we have a problem!"

The first step in implementing the animation program is to create the initial scene. A space template is selected and then a *spiderRobot, alienOnWheels,* and *lunarLander* (from the SciFi folder in the Gallery) are added to the world. Rocks (from the Nature folder in the Web Gallery) are added and positioned in front of the alien to hide the alien from view. The initial scene is shown in Figure 2.4.

Figure 2.4
First encounter initial scene

2.2.3 Example Worlds

The worlds for all examples in this book are available online at www. aliceprogramming.net. The worlds have all the objects for the world, properly positioned in the initial scene, but do not have the program code—the code is provided in the narrative of each chapter section. We recommend that you download the world for the example and, while sitting at a computer, reconstruct the program as you read the chapter. This experience will help you learn how to write programs and also will help you get started in creating your own animations.

2.2.4 Program Code Editor

Once the initial scene has been set up, the statements that make up the program code must be written. Alice provides a program code **editor**—the large yellow pane at the lower right of the main Alice window, as shown in Figure 2.5. The statements for a program are entered in the editor. (From now on, we refer to the program code editor as "the editor.")

2.2.5 *World.my first method*

As seen in Figure 2.5, the tab for the editing area is labeled *World.my first method*. A **method** is a segment of program code (a small number of statements) that defines how to perform a specific task. Alice automatically uses the name *World.my first method* for the first editing pane. Actually, any name can be made up and used for a method name. We will use the name *World.my first method* for this example. The

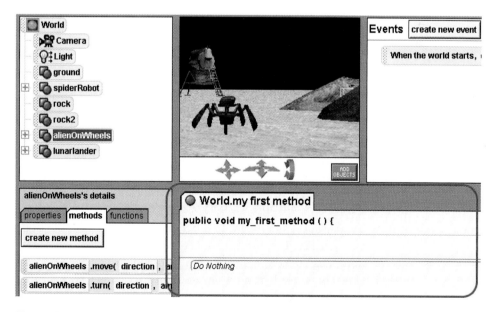

Figure 2.5
Program code editor (the large yellow pane)

robot world scenario is simple enough to be programmed in just one method, *World.my first method*. When the Play button is pressed, Alice will **execute** *World.my first method* by carrying out the statements that we write there.

2.2.6 What Statements Are Needed?

Let's take another look at the storyboard presented earlier.

```
Do the following steps in order
  alien moves up
  alien says "Slithy toves?"
  robot's head turns around
  robot turns to look at alien
  Do the following steps together
    robot moves toward the alien
    robot legs walk
  etc.
```

Actually, this storyboard is incomplete because (in the interests of space) we did not finish the story. The scenario described a sequence of actions: (a) the *alienOnWheels* moves up from behind the rocks, (b) the *alienOnWheels* says "Slithy toves?", (c) the *spiderRobot's* head turns around, (d) the *spiderRobot* turns to look at the *alienOnWheels*, (e) the *spiderRobot* moves toward the *alienOnWheels* to get a closer look, (f) the *alienOnWheels* hides behind a rock, (g) the *spiderRobot* looks at the camera, and (h) the *spiderRobot* says "Houston, we have a problem!" Let's complete the textual storyboard by adding the remaining actions, as shown next.

```
Do the following steps in order
  alien moves up
  alien says "Slithy toves?"
  robot's head turns around
  robot turns to look at alien
  Do the following steps together
    robot moves toward the alien
    robot legs walk
  alien moves down
  robot turns to look at the camera
  robot's head turns red (to signal danger)
  robot says "Houston, we have a problem!"
```

2.2.7 Translating a Storyboard to Program Code

To translate a storyboard to program code, begin with the first step of the storyboard and translate it to a statement. Then translate the second step to a statement, then the third, and so forth until the entire storyboard has been translated to statements. The statements used in program code are the same built-in methods you learned in the *Using Alice* exercises in the Appendix located on the web site. To display the *alienOnWheels'* available methods, first click the *alienOnWheels* object in the Object tree and then click the methods tab in the details area, as seen in Figure 2.6.

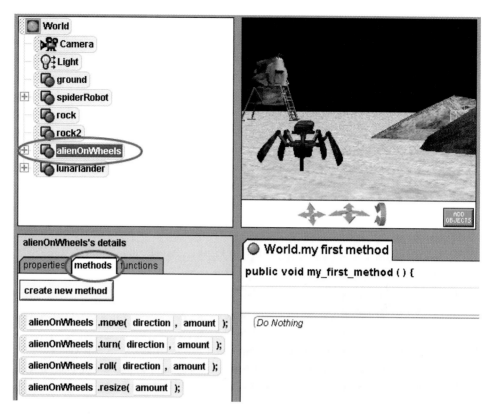

Figure 2.6
Built-in methods for writing program code

In our example, we want to translate the storyboard to program code. We begin with the first step, making the *alienOnWheels* peek up from behind the rocks. One of the *alienOnWheels'* methods is *move*—we can use this method to make the *alienOnWheels* move upward. The next step is to have the *alienOnWheels* say, "Slithy toves?" The *alienOnWheels* has a *say* method that can be used for this purpose. In a similar manner, each action in the storyboard will be translated to statements, using the built-in methods of the objects in the world.

2.2.8 Sequential versus Simultaneous Actions

From our storyboard, it is clear that the first four actions must occur one after another, in sequence. We can tell Alice to *do* these statements *in order*. Other actions occur simultaneously. For example, the *spiderRobot* moves forward at the same time as the *spiderRobot's* legs walk. Alice must be told to *do* these actions *together*. The doInOrder and doTogether statements are part of the Alice language. We call them *control statements*, because we use them to tell Alice how to carry out the statements in a program.

2.2.9 *doInOrder*

To tell Alice to do statements in sequential order, a **doInOrder** block is dragged into the editor, as shown in Figure 2.7.

The first four statements can now be placed within the doInOrder block. First, the *alienOnWheels* is selected in the Object tree. Then, the *alienOnWheels's* move method tile is selected and dragged into the doInOrder, as shown in Figure 2.8. The move method requires arguments—which *direction* and how far (*distance*) the *alienOnWheels* should move. (An **argument** is an item of information that must be supplied so Alice can execute the action.) In this example, the *alienOnWheels* is hidden behind the rocks and we want the *alienOnWheels* to move upward so the direction is *up*. The rocks are not very tall, so we will try a distance of 1 meter. (If this distance is not enough or is too much, we can adjust it later.) The method name and its arguments are the components of a statement.

The result is shown in Figure 2.9. The statement is

```
alienOnWheels.move (UP, 1);
```

In this statement, the *alienOnWheels* object is being sent a message to perform the action defined in the *move* method. The argument UP specifies the direction and the argument 1 specifies the number of meters to move.

The second statement is to have the *alienOnWheels* say, "Slithy toves?" Select *alienOnWheels* in the Object tree and drag in the *say* method tile. Select *other* as the argument, as shown in Figure 2.10. A popup dialog box provides a text area where you can enter the words you want to appear. Type "Slithy toves?" without the quotes, as illustrated in Figure 2.11, and then click OK.

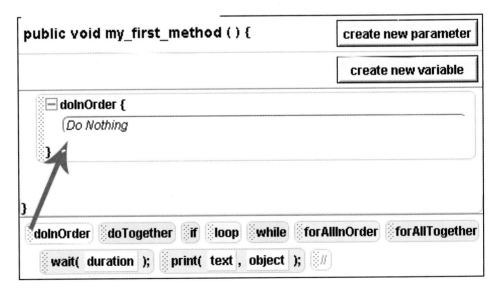

Figure 2.7
Dragging a *doInOrder* tile into the editor

World
Camera
Light
ground
spiderRobot
rock
rock2
alienOnWheels
lunarlander
ADD OBJECTS
alienOnWheels's details
properties
methods
functions
create new method
alienOnWheels .move(direction , amount);
alienOnWheels .turn(direction , amount);
alienOnWheels .roll(direction , amount);
alienOnWheels .resize(amount);
alienOnWheels .say(what);
alienOnWheels .think(what);
alienOnWheels .playSound(sound);
World.my first method
public void my_first_method ( ) {
doInOrder {
}
direction
UP
DOWN
LEFT
RIGHT
FORWARD
BACKWARD
amount
1/2 meter
1 meter
5 meters
10 meters
other...

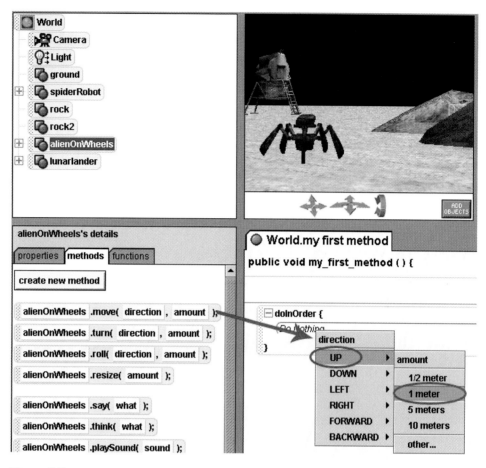

Figure 2.8
Adding a statement to *move* the object

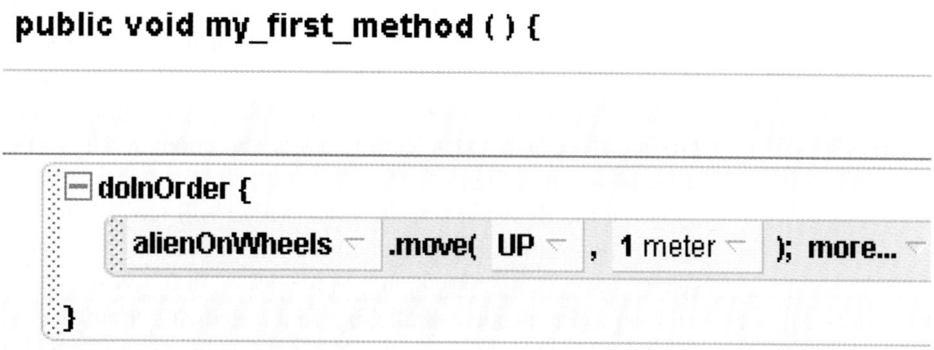

public void my_first_method ( ) {
doInOrder {
alienOnWheels .move(UP , 1 meter); more...
}

Figure 2.9
The completed *move* statement

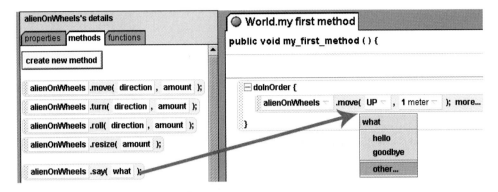

Figure 2.10
Adding a *say* statement for *alienOnWheels*

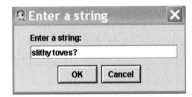

Figure 2.11
Entering a string

The first two statements are shown in Figure 2.12. When this program is run (it is perfectly fine to try out the effect of just one or two Alice statements by clicking on the Play button), the *alienOnWheels* will move up from behind the rocks and then say "Slithy toves?"

For the third statement, the *spiderRobot's* head is to turn around a full revolution (to express surprise). How can we turn the *spiderRobot's* head? Clicking the **+** next to *spiderRobot* in the Object tree causes its subparts to be displayed. Click on the **+** next to *spiderRobot's* neck in the Object tree. Then clicking on the *spiderRobot's* head in the Object tree allows access to statements for moving its head. Drag the turn method tile into the editor and select left as the direction and 1 revolution as the amount of turn, as shown in Figure 2.13.

In the fourth statement, the *spiderRobot* will turn to face the *alienOnWheels*. The *spiderRobot* turnToFace method tile is dragged into the editor and *alienOnWheels* is selected as the target argument, as illustrated in Figure 2.14.

The program code with the first four statements completed is shown in Figure 2.15. Note that the statements within the doInOrder method are enclosed in curly braces, { and }. One or more statements enclosed in curly braces is often referred to as a **block** of program code.

public void my_first_method ( ) {

```
doInOrder {
    alienOnWheels   .move( UP   , 1 meter   ); more...
    alienOnWheels   .say( Slithy toves?   ); more...
}
```

Figure 2.12
First two statements

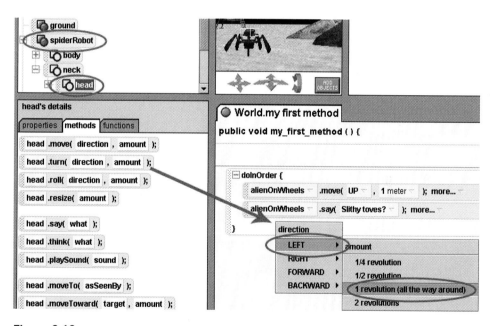

Figure 2.13
Adding a *turn* statement for *spiderRobot* head

2.2.10 *doTogether*

The next step in the storyboard requires two things to occur at once: the *spiderRobot* moving forward at the same time as its legs move up and down. A doTogether tile is dragged into the doInOrder, as shown in Figure 2.16. Notice the horizontal line (green in the editor) in Figure 2.16. A green line indicates where the doTogether tile will be dropped.

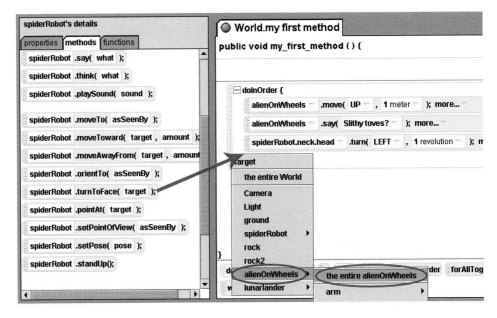

Figure 2.14
Adding a *turnToFace* statement

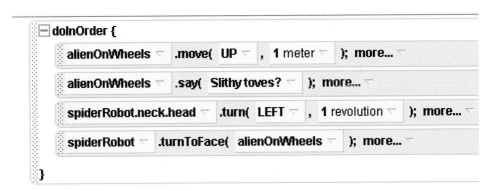

Figure 2.15
doInOrder with the first four statements

The result of this modification, illustrated in Figure 2.17, is that the doTogether block is nested within the doInOrder block. **Nesting** means that one block of code is written inside another block of code. Note that nesting the doTogether inside the doInOrder just happens to be the best way to animate this example. A doTogether does not have to be inside a doInOrder. These two coding blocks can work together or can work separately in many different combinations.

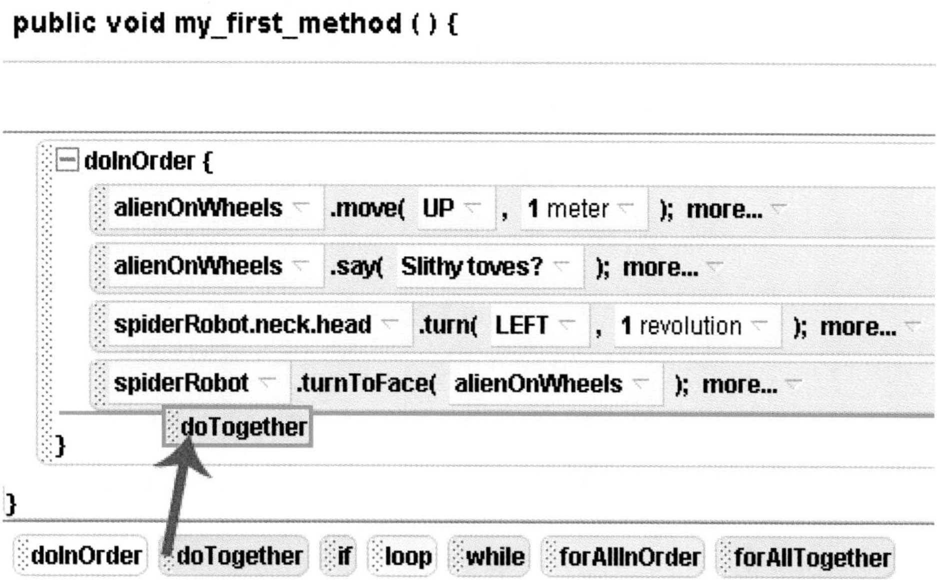

public void my_first_method ( ) {

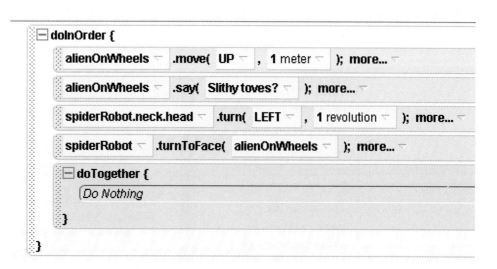

Figure 2.16
Adding a *doTogether* (inside the *doInOrder*)

public void my_first_method ( ) {

Figure 2.17
doTogether nested within a *doInOrder* block

Now, methods can be dragged into the doTogether block to simultaneously have the *spiderRobot* move forward and walk. The move forward statement is easy. Just add a *spiderRobot* move statement with forward as the *direction* and 1 meter as the *distance*, as illustrated in Figure 2.18.

The *spiderRobot* has several legs. To simplify our program, we will animate the walking action of just two legs (*backLeft* and *frontRight*). A leg walks by turning at a joint (similar to bending your knee). Let's begin by creating a statement to turn the *backLeftLegUpperJoint*. First select the *backLeftLegUpperJoint* subpart of the *backLeftLegBase* subpart of the *spiderRobot* in the Object tree and then drag the turn method tile into the doTogether block, as shown in Figure 2.19.

Note that pop-up menus allow you to select arguments for the *direction* and the *amount* of turn. Select FORWARD as the direction and other as the amount. When *other* is selected as the amount, a number pad (looks like a calculator) pops up on the screen. We chose 0.1 revolutions, clicking the buttons on the number pad to make our selection. How did we know to use *0.1* revolutions as the amount? Well, we didn't. We just tried several different amounts until we finally found one that worked to give the best bending motion for the leg joint. This is an example of a trial-and-error strategy. While we always recommend good planning strategies, trial and error is useful when first gaining a sense of distance and angle of a turn in an Alice virtual world.

Naturally, when a leg joint is turned in one direction, it must turn back again (to maintain balance). The two turn statements for the *backLeftLeg* are shown in Figure 2.20.

Using the same technique, statements are created to turn the *frontRightLeg*. The completed walking statements are shown in Figure 2.21.

2.2.11 Bugs

You will recall that the four problem-solving steps we are using to help us create an animation program are: read, design, implement, and test. Now that several lines of code have been written (implemented), it is a good idea to test whether what you have

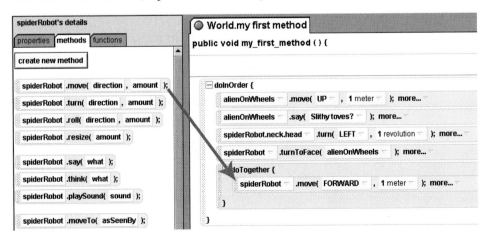

Figure 2.18
Adding a *move* statement inside the *doTogether* block

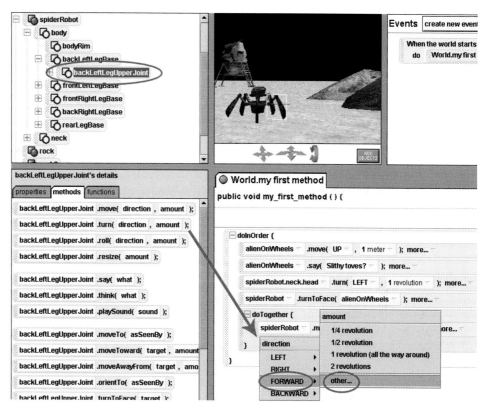

Figure 2.19
Dragging in a *turn* statement for the *backLeftLegUpperJoint*

spiderRobot.body.backLeftLegBase.backLeftLegUpperJoint ▿	.turn(FORWARD ▿ , 0.1 revolutions ▿); more... ▿
spiderRobot.body.backLeftLegBase.backLeftLegUpperJoint ▿	.turn(BACKWARD ▿ , 0.1 revolutions ▿); more... ▿

Figure 2.20
Statements to *turn* forward and backward

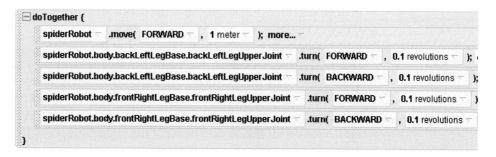

Figure 2.21
Statements to simulate a walking motion for the *spiderRobot*

written thus far works the way you thought it would. You do not have to wait until the entire program is completed. To test the code written thus far, click the PLAY button. The *alienOnWheels* pops up from behind the rocks and then says "Slithy toves?" The *spiderRobot's* head turns around and then the *spiderRobot* turns to face the *alienOnWheels*. So far so good, but when the *spiderRobot* moves forward, the legs do not walk. That is, the leg joints do not appear to turn at all!

The reason the leg joints do not turn is that the program has a **bug**. (Errors in computer programs are generally referred to as bugs. When we remove bugs from a program, we **debug** the program.) The problem is, in the code shown above, the leg joint turn statements are written inside a doTogether. Of course, if the joints turn both forward and backward at the same time, they effectively cancel each other and the *spiderRobot's* legs do not walk at all! To fix this problem, it is necessary to place the *backLeftLeg*-joint turn statements within a doInOrder block and also the *frontRightLeg*-joint turn statements within a doInOrder block, as illustrated in Figure 2.22.

Now the *spiderRobot's backLeft* and *frontRight* legs walk! There is one other useful observation to make. Animation statements, by default, require one second to run. Normally, within a doTogether block, each of the statements should take the same amount of time. Since it takes one second for the *spiderRobot* to move forward 1 meter, the walking action of each leg should also take one second. However, there are two steps in bending the leg joint (forward and then backward). Each step in bending the leg joint should require one-half second. To change the duration, click more . . . (at the far right of the statement where the duration is to be changed), select the duration menu item, and select 0.5 seconds, as shown in Figure 2.23.

2.2.12 Using a Property

We still need to complete the final four actions described in the storyboard (*alienOnWheels* moves down, the *spiderRobot* turns to face the camera, *spiderRobot's* head turns red, and *spiderRobot* says "Houston, we have a problem!"). You have already used a move, turnToFace, and say methods—so these will be easy to create. The only new statement is the one that requires the *spiderRobot's* head to turn red (a danger signal). To make this happen, we use the color **property** of the *spiderRobot's* head. To view the list of properties of the *spiderRobot's* head, select the *spiderRobot's* head in the Object tree and select the properties tab in the details area (lower left of the Alice window), as shown in Figure 2.24.

What we want to do is change the color of the *spiderRobot's* head after it turns to face the camera. Of course, the properties can be changed when the initial world is created. But, we want to change the color property while the animation is running. (The technical term for "while the animation is running" is "at runtime.") A statement must be created to set the color. Figure 2.25 demonstrates dragging in the color property tile to create a set statement. The color tile in the properties list for the *spiderRobot's* head is dragged into the doInOrder block. Then, the color red is selected from the popup menu of available colors.

The final code for the entire animation is listed in Figure 2.26.

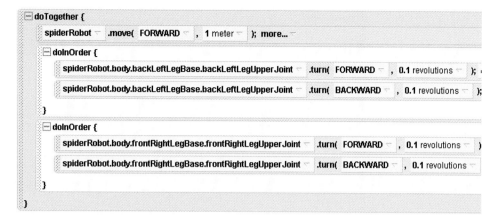

Figure 2.22
Revised statements for walking the *spiderRobot's* legs

Figure 2.23
Changing the *duration* of a statement

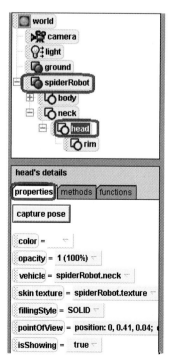

Figure 2.24
The properties of the *spiderRobot's* head

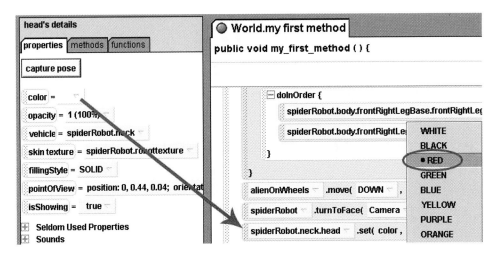

Figure 2.25
Changing the *color* of the *spiderRobot's* head

Figure 2.26
The program code for the entire first encounter animation

2.2.13 Comments

Now that we have written our first program, it is time to look at a useful component in programs—**comments**. Comments are NOT statements that cause some action to take place. This means that Alice can ignore comments when running a program. However, comments are considered good programming "style" and are extremely useful for humans who are reading a program. Comments help the human reader understand what a program does. This is particularly helpful when someone else wants to read your program code to see what you wrote and how you wrote it.

Comments in Alice are created by dragging the green // tile into a program and then writing a description of what a sequence of code is intended to do. Figure 2.27 illustrates *World.my first method* with a comment added. Where it is not obvious, a comment should be included at the beginning of a method to explain what the method does. This kind of comment is like writing a topic sentence in a paragraph—it summarizes what is going on.

Also, small sections of several lines of code that collectively perform some action can be documented using a comment. An additional comment has been added in Figure 2.28. This comment explains that this small section of the code is to have the *spiderRobot* move forward as its legs walk.

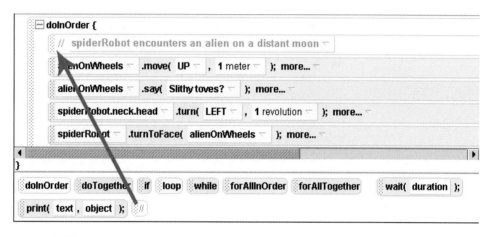

Figure 2.27
An overview comment for *World.my first method*

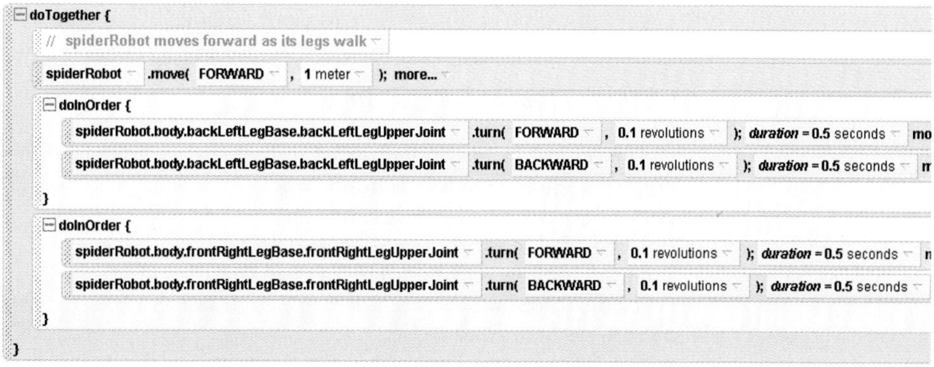

Figure 2.28
A comment for a small section of code

2.3 Concepts Summary

This chapter introduced the fundamental concepts of programming in Alice, using a problem-solving strategy.

2.3.1 Problem-Solving Strategy

1. First read a scenario, also known as a problem statement. A scenario is a description of a story, game, or simulation.

2. Make a plan for creating the animation (design a visual or a textual storyboard).

3. Write the program code, the actual statements to the computer, using a formal computer language. This step is known as implementation.

4. Test the program by running it. That is, play the animation to see if the program is working as expected.

2.3.2 Scenario to Storyboard

We began with reading the scenario and designing a storyboard. A scenario helps us set the stage—that is, it tells us what objects will be used and what actions they will perform. The example scenario used in this chapter was:

> After traveling through space, a robot-piloted craft has just made a breath-taking landing on the surface of a moon. The robot has already climbed out of the lunar lander and has set up a camera so earthbound scientists at the NASA center in Houston can view this historic event. Through the camera (the scene in our world), we can see the robot, the lunar lander, and some nearby rock formations. Suddenly, an alien peeks out from behind a rock and looks at the robot. The robot is surprised and rotates its head all the way around. The robot walks over to take a closer look and the alien hides behind the rocks. Finally, the robot looks at the camera, signals danger, and says "Houston, we have a problem!"

A storyboard breaks a scenario into a sequence of scenes that provide a sense of the order in which actions will take place. A storyboard can be either visual or textual. The textual storyboard used for the scenario in this chapter was

```
Do the following steps in order
  alien moves up
  alien says "Slithy toves?"
  robot's head turns around
  robot turns to look at alien
  Do the following steps together
    robot moves toward the alien
    robot legs walk
  alien moves down
  robot turns to look at the camera
  robot's head turns red (to signal danger)
  robot says "Houston, we have a problem!"
```

Once prepared, a storyboard is used as a guide for implementation (writing the program code).

2.3.3 Implementation: Sequential versus Simultaneous

To implement the program, each statement in the storyboard is translated into a statement of code by using Alice's drag-and-drop editor. Some statements in a program should take place in sequence (one after the other) and some statements occur simultaneously (at the same time). In Alice, a doInOrder construct is used to specify sequential execution. In the example program (Figure 2.29), the first four statements are being executed in sequence, as indicated by the doInOrder construct. Note that the statements within the doInOrder are enclosed in curly braces, { and }. One or more statements enclosed in curly braces is often referred to as a block of program code.

A doTogether construct is used to create a block of code in which all statements are executed at the same time, as illustrated in Figure 2.30.

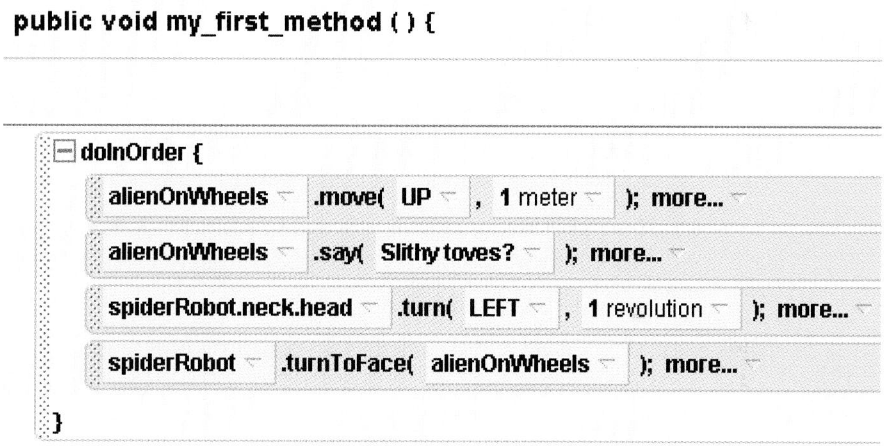

```
public void my_first_method ( ) {
```

```
doInOrder {
    alienOnWheels    .move( UP  , 1 meter  ); more...
    alienOnWheels    .say( Slithy toves?  ); more...
    spiderRobot.neck.head    .turn( LEFT  , 1 revolution  ); more...
    spiderRobot    .turnToFace( alienOnWheels  ); more...
}
```

Figure 2.29
A *doInOrder* block of code is executed sequentially

```
doTogether {
    spiderRobot    .move( FORWARD  , 1 meter  ); more...
    spiderRobot.body.backLeftLegBase.backLeftLegUpperJoint    .turn( FORWARD  , 0.1 revolutions  );
    spiderRobot.body.backLeftLegBase.backLeftLegUpperJoint    .turn( BACKWARD  , 0.1 revolutions  );
    spiderRobot.body.frontRightLegBase.frontRightLegUpperJoint    .turn( FORWARD  , 0.1 revolutions  )
    spiderRobot.body.frontRightLegBase.frontRightLegUpperJoint    .turn( BACKWARD  , 0.1 revolutions
}
```

Figure 2.30
A *doTogether* block of code is executed at the same time

2.3.3 Testing

Testing code (running the program) is an important step in finding and removing bugs (errors in the program). Alice's drag-and-drop editor automatically creates statements with all the semicolons, curly braces, dots, commas, and parentheses in all the right places. Still, it is possible to make an error by skipping important statements or selecting the wrong directions or amounts in menus. In Alice, the Play button is used to run the program. When the Play button is clicked, Alice automatically updates the program to include any changes we have made to the program. The Alice code is converted to code the computer can understand and then the animation is displayed. In viewing the animation as the program runs, we can look for errors.

2.3.4 Comments

Comments are used to document your program code, especially any new methods you write. Comments are used to describe the purpose of a method or a small section of a method that is not immediately obvious. Comments are considered good programming "style."

Exercises

1. Creating a computer program can be described as a four-step process using problem-solving techniques. List the four steps and give a brief description of each.

2. In what way does the design and implementation of a computer program follow the same process that an artist goes through when creating a painting?

3. How do you know whether a computer program has a "bug"?

4. Why do we add comments to a computer program?

5. Create a visual and a textual storyboard (two storyboards) for each of the following scenarios:

   (a) A child's game: Alice, the white rabbit, and the Cheshire cat enjoy a game of musical chairs in a tea party scene. One of the characters yells "Switch," and they all run around the table to stand beside the next chair. After the switch, a chair is tipped over and the character standing next to it is eliminated from the game (moves away from the table).

   (b) A video game: A jet fighter plane is returning to the carrier deck after a training mission. The plane makes a half-circle around the carrier to get into position for landing and then gradually descends. The carrier is in motion, so the plane has to continually adjust its descent to finally land on the deck. After the plane touches down on the carrier, it continues to move across the deck to finally come to a halt.

   (c) An Olympic simulation: An ice skater is practicing her skating routine for the Olympic trials. She will perform a sequence of jumps and spins while classical music is playing.

6. Create the example from the book.

   (a) The worlds used for chapter examples throughout this book can be found on the website. Each world has the initial scene already set up with the background scenery and the objects, as shown in the example. In this chapter, the example world is a first encounter, where a robot meets an alien on a distant moon. Start Alice. Then, copy the `FirstEncounter.a2w` world to your computer. In Alice, use **File|Open** to open the world. Follow along with the reading in the chapter and recreate the program as described in the chapter.

   (b) In the code presented in this chapter, only two legs (*backLeft* and *frontRight*) were animated in a walking action. Add code to animate a walking action for the other legs. Be sure to save the world.

7. *Snowpeople* Create a snowpeople world, as shown the following scene. Several snowpeople are outdoors on a snow-covered landscape.

A snowman is trying to meet a snowwoman who is talking with a friend (another snowwoman.) The snowman tries to get her attention. He turns to face the snowwoman and says "Ahem." She turns to look at the snowman and he blinks his eyes at her. She blushes (her head turns red). But, alas, she is not interested in meeting him. She gives him a "cold shoulder" and turns back to talk with her friend. He hangs his head in disappointment and turns away.

8. *Circling Fish* Create an island world with a fish in the water. (You may wish to reuse the island world created in an exercise for Chapter 1.) Position the fish and the camera point of view so the scene appears as illustrated. Write a program that has the fish swim around in a circle in front of the island. Next, have the fish swim around the island. You may wish to have the fish move **asSeenBy** the island (**asSeenBy** is described in Appendix A, Section 2). Finally, have the fish jump out of the water and then dive down into the water. The final scene should look somewhat like the initial scene, with the fish back in roughly the same position as where it started.

9. *Tortoise Gets a Cookie* Create a world having a tortoise (Animals), a stool (Furniture in the Local Gallery or Web Gallery), and a cookie (Kitchen/Food), as shown. Put the cookie on top of the stool. (Cookies are the tortoise's favorite snack food.) Position the tortoise and the stool side by side and then use a **move** method to move the tortoise 2 meters away from the stool. (This way, you know exactly how far the tortoise is from the stool.) Use a **turnToFace** method to be sure the tortoise is facing the stool. Write a program to move the tortoise to the stool to get the cookie. Have the tortoise show its thanks (for the cookie) by looking at the camera and waving an arm.

10. *Magnet Fun* Create a world where Mana (People) has a magnet (Objects) held out in her left hand. Add five metallic objects (Objects folder in Local or Web Galleries) of your choice to the world and, one by one, have Mana point the magnet at each object. As Mana points the magnet toward an object, have the object move to the magnet. Have the last object be very large (perhaps a car from the Vehicles folder) so when Mana points at it, she instead is pulled toward the object while saying something like "Whoa!" or "Yikes!"

Making It Work Tip: Refining Movement

See Appendix A, Section 2, for information on how to (1) use the vehicle property for help in making the magnet move in coordination with Mana's hand and (2) use the moveToward statement to make an object move toward another object. Also, you may wish to review the notion of center of an object, as described in Chapter 1, Section 2.

3

Classes, Objects, Methods, and Parameters

Goals of this chapter:

- To write your own method.
- To call (invoke) a method.
- To use parameters for communication with a method.
- To send an argument value to a method parameter.
- To declare a parameter as a value of a particular type. Types of values for parameters include object, Boolean ("true" or "false"), number, sound, color, string, and others.
- To create a new class by defining methods and then saving out a class with a new name.
- To define the concept of inheritance.
- To write an object method that accepts object parameters.

Introduction

When you created animation programs in earlier chapters, you may have started to think about more complicated scenarios with more twists and turns in the storyline, perhaps games or simulations. Naturally, as the storyline becomes more intricate, so does the program code for creating the animation. The program code can quickly increase to many, many lines—sort of an "explosion" in program size and complexity. Animation programs are not alone in this complexity. Real-world software applications can have thousands, even millions, of lines of code. How does a programmer deal with huge amounts of program code? One technique is to divide a very large program into manageable "pieces," making it easier to design and think about. Smaller pieces are also easier to read and debug. Object-oriented programming uses classes, objects, and methods as basic program components which help organize large programs into small manageable pieces. In this chapter and the next, you will learn how to write more intricate and impressive programs by using classes, objects (instances of classes), and methods.

3.1 Classes, Objects, and Methods

3.1.1 Classes

A **class** defines a particular kind of object. In Alice, classes are predefined as 3D models that are provided in the gallery. To make it easy to find the class you want, classes are categorized into groups such as Animals, People, Buildings, Sets and Scenes,

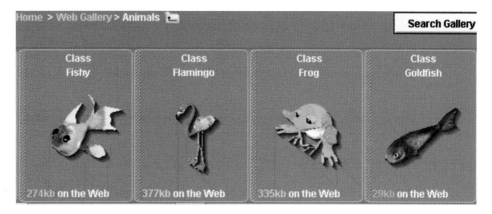

Figure 3.1
Classes of 3D Models in the Animals folder

Space, and so on. Figure 3.1 shows some of the classes in the Animals folder. Notice that the name of a class begins with a capital letter.

A class knows what each object of that class needs to keep track of and what it should be able to do, so the class creates the objects of that class. You can think of a class as an object factory. The factory can create many objects. A class is also like a cookie cutter. You can make many cookies from one cookie cutter and they will all have the same shape. When an object is created and displayed, we say an object is an **instance** of that class.

3.1.2 Objects

In Figure 3.2, *Person* and *Dog* are classes. Objects joe, stan, and cindy are instances of the *Person* class while spike, scamp, and fido are instances of the *Dog* class. Notice that the name of an object begins with a lowercase letter, while the name of a class begins with an uppercase letter. This naming convention helps us to easily distinguish the name of a class from the name of an object. All objects of the same class share some commonality. All *Person* objects have properties such as two legs, two arms,

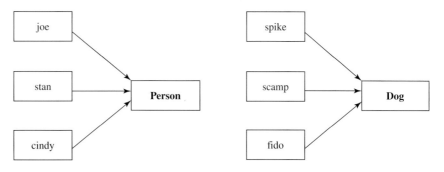

Figure 3.2
Organizing objects into classes

Figure 3.3
Objects of the *Lemur* class in Alice

height, and eye color. *Person* objects can perform walking and speaking actions.
All *Dog* objects have properties including four legs, height, fur color, and the ability
to run and bark. Although each object belongs to a class, it is still unique in its own
way. Joe is tall and has green eyes. Cindy is short and has blue eyes. Spike has brown
fur, and his bark is a low growl. Scamp has golden-color fur, and his bark is a high-
pitched yip.

In Figure 3.3, larry, lila, and louis are all instances of the *Lemur* class (Animals) in
Alice. We named the lemurs in this world, made them different heights, and changed
the color of lila. Although larry, lila, and louis are all objects of the same Lemur class
and have many common characteristics, they also differ in that larry is the tallest; lila
has rich, dark fur; and louis is the shortest.

3.1.3 Methods

A method is a coordinated sequence of statements that will be carried out when
requested. You have already used methods in your animations. Every object in an
Alice world has a repertoire of methods it knows how to do—*move, turn, turn to face*,
etc. These are actually **primitive** methods, built-in to the Alice software. The primitive
methods can be used to create a method of your own—to carry out a small piece of the
overall program. Each method performs its own job, but all the methods in a program
work together to create the overall animation.

As your animation programs grow larger, it will become increasingly important to use
many, many methods as a way of organizing the program. Methods divide a program
into small manageable pieces that work together to create a meaningful whole. Just as
paragraphs, sections, and chapters make a book easier to read, methods make a program
easier to read. Methods also provide a number of advantages. For example, once
a method is written, it allows us to think about an overall task instead of all the small
actions that were needed to complete the task. This is called **abstraction**.

Some methods need to be sent certain pieces of information to carry out an action. For example, a *move* method needs a *direction* (forward, backward, left, right, up, or down) and a *distance* (in meters). A **parameter** acts like a basket to receive information that we send to a method. In a way, you can think of a method as somewhat like a recipe—a sequence of statements that describe how to perform some action. Parameters hold onto the specific items of information.

In a recipe, a parameter could specify the amount of water. In a method, a parameter could specify the distance a spaceship is to move.

In Alice, you can define methods for an object acting alone or for two or more objects interacting with one another. This is similar to the way a director works with the cast of actors in a play. The director gives statements sometimes to a single cast member and at other times to several cast members to coordinate their actions. Methods that specifically reference more than one object are **world-level methods**. Methods that define behaviors for a single object may be considered **object methods**.

Section 3.2 presents an introduction to object methods. An advantage of object methods is that once new methods are defined, we can create a new class with all the new methods (and also the old methods) as available actions. This is a form of **inheritance**—the new class inherits methods from the old class.

3.2   Object Methods and Inheritance

The galleries of 3D models in Alice give us a choice of diverse and well-designed pre-written classes for creating objects that populate a scenic backdrop in a virtual world. When you add an instance of a 3D model class to an Alice world, it already "knows" how to perform a set of methods—*move, turn, roll*, and *resize* (to name a few). The 3D model class already defines these methods. After writing several programs, it is natural to think about extending the actions an object "knows" how to perform.

In this section, you will learn how to write new methods that define new actions to be carried out by an object acting alone (rather than several objects acting together). We call these object methods. Object methods are rather special, because we can save an object along with its newly defined method(s) as a new kind of 3D class model in Alice. Later instances of the new class still know how to perform all the actions defined in the original class but will also be able to perform all the actions in the newly defined methods. We say that the new class **inherits** all the properties and methods of the original class.

3.2.1 An Example with a Skater

Consider the *iceSkater* shown in the winter scene of Figure 3.4. (The *IceSkater* class is from the People collection, and the *Lake* class is from the Environments collection in the Alice gallery.)

We want the skater to perform typical figure-skating actions. She is dressed in a skating costume and is wearing ice skates, but this does not mean she knows how to

Figure 3.4
The *iceSkater*

skate. However, all Alice objects "know" how to perform simple methods such as *move, turn,* and *roll.* We can use a combination of these simple methods to "teach" the ice skater how to perform a more complex action. We begin with a method to make the skater perform a skating motion.

3.2.2 An Object Method

Skating movements are complex actions that require several motion statements involving various parts of the body. (Professional animators at Disney and Pixar may spend many, many hours observing the movement of various parts of the human body so as to create realistic animations.) To skate, a skater slides forward on the left leg and then slides forward on the right leg. Of course, the entire skater's body is moving forward as the legs perform the sliding movements. The steps in a skating action are put together as a sequence of motions in a storyboard, as shown next.

```
skate
doTogether
  Move skater forward 2 meters
  doInOrder
    slide on left leg
    slide on right leg
```

Notice that the storyboard breaks down the skating action into two pieces—slide on the left leg and slide on the right leg. The sliding motions can each be broken down into simpler methods. Breaking a complex action down into simpler actions is called **refinement**. Here we are using a design technique known as stepwise refinement. We first describe general actions and then break each action down into smaller and smaller steps (successively refined) until the whole task is defined in simple actions. Each piece contributes a small part to the overall animation; the pieces together accomplish the entire task.

The following diagram illustrates the refinement of the *slideLeft* and *slideRight* actions. The actions needed to slide on the left leg are to lift the right leg and turn the upper body slightly forward. Then, lower the right leg and turn the upper body backward (to an upright position). Similar actions are carried out to slide on the right leg.

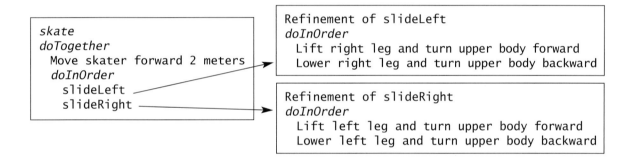

Nothing else needs to be refined. We are now ready to translate the design into program code. We could translate this design to statements in just the one method, but it would be lengthy and difficult to understand. Furthermore, you can quickly see that we have used stepwise refinement to break the skate task down into distinct pieces. So, we will demonstrate how to write several small methods and make them work together to accomplish a larger task.

Skate is a complex action that is designed specifically for the *iceSkater* and involves no other objects. Likewise, the *slideLeft* and *slideRight* actions are designed specifically for the iceSkater. The *slideLeft* and *slideRight* methods will be written as object methods because they involve only the ice skater. We begin with the *slideLeft* method. The *iceSkater* is selected in the Object tree and the **Create New Method** button is clicked in the details panel. In the New Method popup window, enter *slideLeft* as the name of the new method. The left side of Figure 3.5 illustrates this first step. Click the **OK** button. The code editor opens a new panel where the program code can be created. The right side of Figure 3.5 shows the method name and the new panel in the code editor.

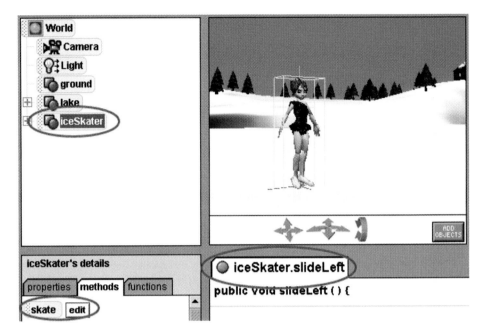

Figure 3.5
A *slideLeft* object method

To implement the *slideLeft* method, we enter statements in the editor. The idea is to translate the design into actual program statements. For example, to translate the design steps for sliding on the left leg, we use the following:

Design step	Statement
Lift the right leg	*turn* the rightLeg forward
Turn upper body forward (We inserted a short wait to allow time for forward movement)	*turn* the upperBody forward
Lower the right leg	*turn* the rightLeg backward
Turn the upper body backward	*turn* the upperBody backward

Figure 3.6 illustrates translating the textual storyboard into statements for sliding on the left leg. The statements for sliding forward on the right leg are similar. So, writing the *slideRight* method is rather easy. Figure 3.7 illustrates translating the textual storyboard into statements to slide forward on the right leg.

With the *slideLeft* and *slideRight* methods written, we are now ready to write the *skate* method. The *skate* method is really quite simple: *slideLeft* and then *slideRight,* while at the same time, the entire skater is moving forward. To create the *skate* method, the

public void slideLeft ( ) {

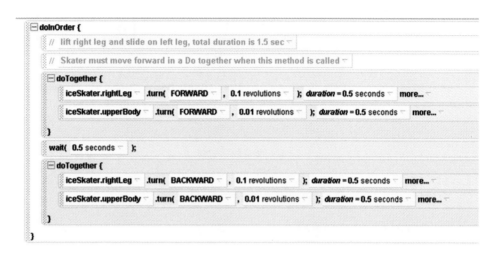

Figure 3.6
The *slideLeft* method

slideLeft and *slideRight* methods are dragged into the editor (using the same drag-and-drop technique as previously used to create statements for built-in methods, such as *move, turn,* and *roll*.) Figure 3.8 illustrates the *slideLeft* and *slideRight* method tiles dragged into the editor for the *skate* method. The *skate* method moves the skater forward, calls the *slideLeft* method, and then calls the *slideRight* method. Note that the calls to *slideLeft*

Figure 3.7
The *slideRight* method

public void skate ( ) {

```
doTogether {
    //  entire ice skater moves forward as legs slide
    iceSkater  .move(  FORWARD  ,  2 meters  );  duration = 3 seconds   more...
    doInOrder {
        //  slide on right leg
        iceSkater.slideRight (  );
        //  slide on left leg
        iceSkater.slideLeft (  );
    }
}
```

Figure 3.8
The *skate* method

and *slideRight* methods are enclosed in a *doInOrder* block nested within a *doTogether*. The *doTogether* block is needed to ensure that the statement that moves the skater forward is performed simultaneously with the left and right sliding motions. The duration of the forward movement of the skater is the sum of the durations of the left and right slides. Paying attention to the durations of the statements in a *doTogether* block will help synchronize the motions to begin and end at the same time.

If the Play button is clicked at this time, the animation will NOT run. Although the *skate* method has been defined, Alice has not been told to execute it. That is, Alice has not been told to **call** or **invoke** the method into action. To call the *skate* method into action, it is necessary to drag the *skate* method tile into *world.my first* method. When the *skate* method is called, the skater glides forward in a realistic motion. Figure 3.8 illustrates the completed *skate* method.

3.2.3 A Second Example—Using a Parameter

The forward skate motion is truly impressive! Building on this success, let's write a second method to make the ice skater perform a spin. Once again, we will need to write several methods that work together to complete a complex action.

A spin maneuver generally has three parts, the preparation for the spin, the spin itself, and the end of the spin (to finish the spin). In preparation for the spin, the skater's arms and legs change position to provide the strength needed to propel her body around. Then the skater spins around. After the spin, the arms and legs should be repositioned to where they were before the spin. A *spin* method is likely to have the skater turn several revolutions. We don't know exactly how many times the skater might turn. This is an example of a method where a parameter can be helpful. A parameter allows you to send information to a method when the method is called. You have been using parameters all along. Most built-in methods have parameters that allow you to send information to the method. For example, a *move* method has parameters that allow you to send in the direction, distance, and duration. We say that the each value is sent in as an argument to the parameters. A parameter, *howManyTimes,* is needed to receive the argument value that specifies the number of times the ice skater will spin around. The storyboard is shown next.

```
spin

Parameter: howManyTimes
doInOrder
  prepare to spin
  spin the skater around howManyTimes
  finish the spin
```

We can use refinement to design the simple steps for each part of the spin. The "prepare to spin" step can be written as a method (*prepareToSpin*) where the skater's arms move up and one leg turns. The "finish spin" step can also be written as a method (*finishSpin*) to move the arms and legs back to their original positions, prior to the spin. The following diagram illustrates refinements for the *spin* method.

```
prepareToSpin

doTogether
  move arms up
  raise and turn left leg
```

```
spin

Parameter: howManyTimes
doInOrder
  prepare to spin
  spin the skater around howManyTimes
  finish the spin
```

```
finishSpin

doTogether
  move arms down
  lower and turn left leg
```

Nothing else needs to be refined. We are now ready to translate the design into program code. Once again, object methods should be used, because we are defining a complex motion specifically for the ice skater.

Figure 3.9 illustrates the *prepareToSpin* method, where the ice skater raises her left leg as she lifts her arms.

Figure 3.10 presents the *finishSpin* method to reposition the skater's arms and leg to their original positions at the end of her spin.

Now that *prepareToSpin* and *finishSpin* have been written, the *spin* method can be created. A **Create New Parameter** button can be found in the upper right-hand corner of the editor. When the **Create New Parameter** button is clicked, a dialog box pops up. The name of a parameter is entered and its *type* is selected. The *type* of a parameter can be

public void prepareToSpin ( ) {

```
doTogether {
    // move arms up and raise the left leg
    iceSkater.upperBody.chest.leftShoulder.arm  .turn( BACKWARD , 0.5 revolutions ); more...
    iceSkater.upperBody.chest.rightShoulder.arm  .turn( BACKWARD , 0.5 revolutions ); more...
    iceSkater.leftLeg  .turn( LEFT , 0.2 revolutions ); more...
    iceSkater.leftLeg  .turn( BACKWARD , 0.25 revolutions ); more...
}
```

Figure 3.9
The *prepareToSpin* method to raise arms and one leg

public void finishSpin ( ) {

```
doTogether {
    // lowers arms and left leg after spin
    iceSkater.upperBody.chest.leftShoulder.arm  .turn( FORWARD , 0.5 revolutions ); more...
    iceSkater.upperBody.chest.rightShoulder.arm  .turn( FORWARD , 0.5 revolutions ); more...
    iceSkater.leftLeg  .turn( FORWARD , 0.25 revolutions ); more...
    iceSkater.leftLeg  .turn( RIGHT , 0.2 revolutions ); more...
}
```

Figure 3.10
The *finishSpin* method to lower arms and leg

a *Number,* **Boolean** ("true" or "false"), *Object,* or *Other* (for example, a color or sound).
The *howManySpins* parameter represents a number that will specify how many times the
skater is to turn around (one revolution is one complete spin around). The order in which
the methods are called is important so as to adjust the skater's arms and legs in preparation
for the spin and after the spin. The completed *spin* method is shown in Figure 3.11.

The code for the two examples (the *skate* and *spin* methods) is a bit longer than we
have written in previous chapters. It is important that the code is easy to understand,
because we have carefully broken down the overall task into smaller methods. The small
methods all work together to complete the overall action. Also, the methods have been
well documented with comments that tell us what the method accomplishes. Good design
and comments make our code easier to understand as well as easier to write and debug.

3.2.4 Creating a New Class

The iceSkater now has two object methods, *skate* and *spin*. (She also has several
smaller object methods that implement small pieces of the *skate* and *spin* methods.)

```
public void spin ( Number 123 howManySpins ) {
```

```
doInOrder {
    // skater spins around
    // howManySpins specifies the number of revolutions for the spin
    iceSkater.prepareToSpin ( );
    iceSkater  .turn( LEFT  , howManySpins revolutions  ); more...
    iceSkater.finishSpin ( );
}
```

Figure 3.11
The *spin* method

Writing and testing the methods took some time and effort to achieve. It would be a shame to put all this work into one world and not be able to use it again in another animation program we might create later. We would like to save the *iceSkater* and her newly defined methods so we can use them in another world (we won't need to write these methods again for another animation program). To do this, we must **save out** the *iceSkater* as a new 3D model (class).

Saving the *iceSkater* (with her newly defined methods) as a new class is a two-step process. The first step is to rename the *iceSkater*. This is an **Important Step**! We want Alice to save this new class with a different 3D filename than the original *IceSkater* class. To rename an object, right-click the name of the object in the Object tree, select **Rename** from the popup menu, and enter the new name in the box. In this example, we right-clicked *iceSkater* in the Object tree and changed the name to *cleverSkater*, as shown in Figure 3.12.

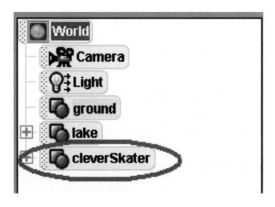

Figure 3.12
Renaming *iceSkater* as *cleverSkater*

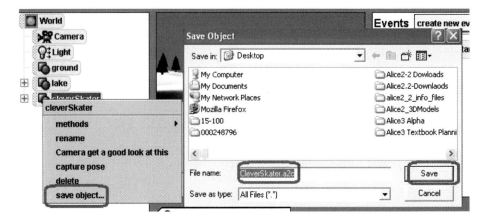

Figure 3.13
Save Object dialog box

The second step is to save out **cleverSkater** as a new class: right click *cleverSkater* in the Object tree and this time select *save object*. In the **Save Object** popup box, navigate to the folder/directory where you wish to save the new class, as in Figure 3.13, and then click the **Save** button.

The class is automatically named with the new name, beginning with a capital letter and a filename extension .a2c, which stands for "Alice 2 class" (just as the .a2w extension in a world filename stands for "Alice 2 world").

Once a new class has been created, it can be used in a new world by selecting Import from the File menu, as illustrated in Figure 3.14. When an instance of the *CleverSkater* class is added to a world, she will be just like an instance of the *IceSkater*

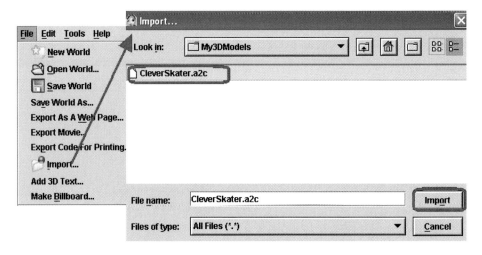

Figure 3.14
Importing a new object from a saved class

class, except that a *cleverSkater* object knows how to *skate* and *spin* in addition to all of the methods a standard gallery *iceSkater* object can perform.

3.2.5 Inheritance—Benefits

Creating a new class based on a previously defined class is a simple form of inheritance. Inheritance in most object-oriented languages is more complicated than in Alice. The basic idea is the same—adding functionality by defining new methods for a new kind of inherited class. Inheritance is considered one of the strengths of object-oriented programming because it allows you to write code once and reuse it in other programs.

Another benefit of creating new classes is the ability to share code with others in team projects. For example, if you are working on an Alice project as a team, each person can write object methods for an object in the world. Then, each team member can save out the new class. Objects of the new classes can then be added to a single team-constructed world for a shared project. This is a benefit we cannot overemphasize. In the "real world," computer professionals generally work on team projects. Cooperatively developed software is often the way professional animation teams at animation studios work.

3.2.6 Guidelines for Writing Object Methods

Object methods are a powerful feature of Alice. Of course, with power there is also some danger. To avoid potential misuse of object methods, we offer some guidelines.

1. Create many different object methods. They are extremely useful and helpful. Some classes in Alice already have a few object methods defined. For example, the *Lion* class has methods *startStance, walkForward, completeWalk, roar,* and *charge.* Figure 3.15 shows a thumbnail image for an object of the *Lion* class (from the Web Gallery), including its object methods and sounds.

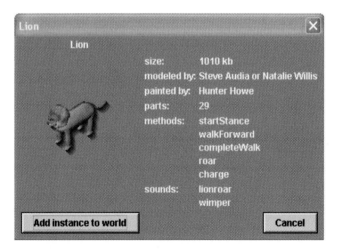

Figure 3.15
Class-level methods and sounds for the *Lion* class

2. Play a sound in an object method **ONLY IF** the sound has been imported for the object (instead of the world). If the sound has been imported for the object and the object's methods are saved out in a new class, the sound is saved out with the class. Then the sound can be played anywhere in any world where an object of this class is added. On the other hand, if the sound is imported for the world, the sound is not saved out with the new class and you cannot depend on the sound being available in other worlds.

3. Do not use statements for other objects from within an object method. Object methods are clearly defined for a specific class. We expect to save out the object's methods in a new class and reuse it in a later world. We cannot depend on objects of other classes being present in other programs in other worlds. For example, a *penguin* (Animals) is added to the winter scene, as in Figure 3.16. We write an object method named *skateAround*, where the *penguin* object is specifically named in two of the statements (circled in Figure 3.17). If the *cleverSkater* with the *skateAround* method is saved out as a new class and then a *cleverSkater* object is added to a later world where no penguin exists, Alice will open an Error dialog box to tell you about a missing object. The error would be that the *cleverSkater* cannot skate around a *penguin* that does not exist in the world!

Note: Possible exceptions to guideline #3 are the world and camera objects, which are always present.

3.2.7 An Object Method with an Object Parameter

What if you would like to write an object method where another object is involved? The solution is to use an object parameter in the object method. Let's use the same

Figure 3.16
The skater will skate around the penguin

public void skateAround ( ) {

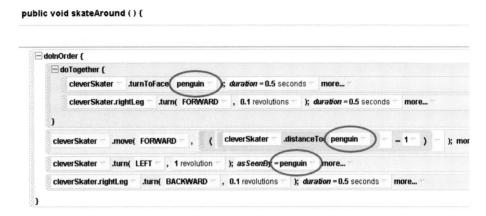

Figure 3.17
Bad example: statements specifying another object in an object method

example as above, where we want a *cleverSkater* to skate around another object. The *skateAround* method can be modified to use a parameter, arbitrarily named *whichObject*, as shown in Figure 3.18. The *whichObject* parameter is only a placeholder, not an actual object, so we do not have to worry about a particular object (like the penguin) having to be in another world. Alice will not allow the *skateAround* method to be called without passing in an object to the *whichObject* parameter. So, we can be sure that some sort of object will be there to skate around.

3.2.8 Testing
Once you have created and saved out a new class, it should be tested in a new world. The initial scene was shown in Figure 3.16. A sample test program is presented in

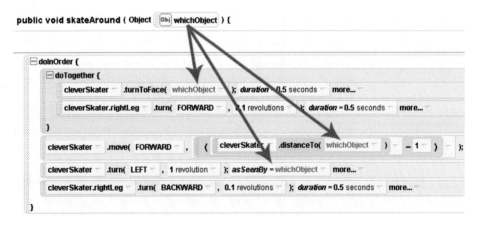

Figure 3.18
Using an object parameter in an object method

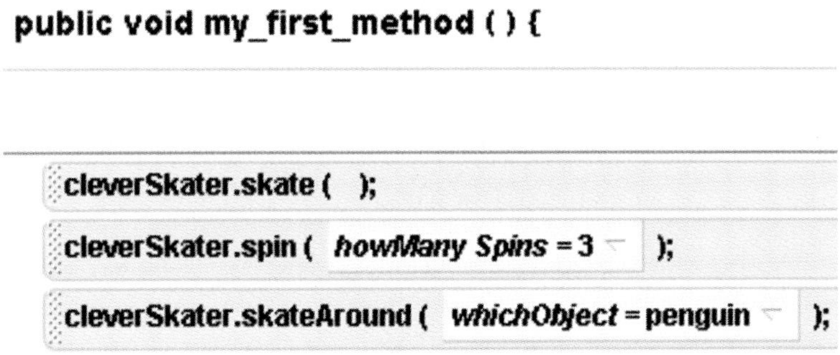

public void my_first_method ( ) {

cleverSkater.skate (   );

cleverSkater.spin (*howMany Spins* = 3 ▽   );

cleverSkater.skateAround (*whichObject* = penguin ▽);

Figure 3.19
A sample test program

Figure 3.19. In this test, we have called the *skate, spin,* and *skateAround* methods to test each method.

3.3   Concepts Summary

In this chapter, we looked at how to write your own methods and how to use parameters to communicate information to a method when it is called.

3.3.1 Methods

A method is an action defined as a named block of code in a class. In Alice, each 3D model class in the gallery defines two things: (1) how to draw an object of the class in an Alice virtual world and (2) which methods define actions the objects of that class can perform. You can write your own methods to define new actions for the objects in your Alice world. In this chapter, we wrote a *skate* method for the *iceSkater*. In designing the *skate* method, we found that the skating action was a complex task, and so, we broke the skating task down into two simpler tasks: *slideLeft* and *slideRight*. We broke a complex task down into small pieces and then each piece was broken down further until the entire task was completely defined by simple actions. The simple actions all work together to carry out the complex task.

An advantage of using methods is that it allows you, as the programmer, to think about a collection of statements as all one action—an example of abstraction. Also, methods make it easier to debug our code.

3.3.2 Parameters

When a method is "called on an object," what is actually happening is that an object is being sent a message to perform the statements in the method code. In some methods, additional items of information are needed in order to carry out the statements defined in the method. For example, sending a message to an *iceSkater* object to spin requires that we specify how many revolutions she should spin around.

When additional items of information are needed, a method is defined using parameters. A parameter acts as a placeholder for a value of a particular type that will be sent when the method is called. The values sent to a method are known as arguments. When an argument is sent to a method, the parameter represents the value of the argument in statements where the parameter is used in the method.

A parameter must be of a particular type. Parameter examples presented in this chapter included parameters of several different types, including object and number. Parameters allow you to write one method but use it several times with different objects, sounds, numbers, and other types of values.

3.3.3 A Form of Inheritance: Saving Out a New Class

In a way, object methods can be thought of as extending an object's behavior. Once new object methods are defined, a new class can be saved out. The new class has a different name and has all the new methods (and also the old methods of the original class) as available actions. It inherits the properties and actions of the original class but defines more things than the original class. A major benefit is that you can use objects of the new class over and over again in new worlds. This allows you to take advantage of the methods you have written without having to write them again.

Exercises

1. Is it possible for your Alice program to have more than one instance of the same class? Explain your answer.

2. What is another term commonly used for "calling" a method?

3. What is the relationship of an argument to a parameter when a method is called?

4. Why is it useful to test a method by sending in different arguments?

5. Create an even better *cleverSkater* than the one presented in Section 3.2. In addition to the *skate, spin,* and *skateAround* methods, create *skateBackward* and *jump* object methods. In *skateBackward*, the skater should perform similar actions to those in the *skateForward* method, but slide backward instead of forward. In a *jump* method, the skater should move forward, lift one leg, move upward (in the air) and back down to land gracefully on the ice, and then lower her leg back to its starting position. Save out your enhanced skater as *EnhancedCleverSkater*. Test your newly defined class by starting a new world with a frozen lake. Add an *enhancedCleverSkater* to the world. Also, add a penguin and a duck.

    (a) Call each of the methods you have written.

    (b) Call the *skateAround* method—to make the skater skate around the penguin and then the duck. (This will require two calls to the *skateAround* method.)

6. Create a world with a *comboLock* (Objects folder). Create four object methods—*leftOne, rightOne, leftRevolution,* and *rightRevolution*— that turn the dial one number left, one number right, one revolution left, and one revolution right, respectively. Then, create an object method named *open* that opens and another named *close* that closes the lock.

Making It Work Tip: Gentle Movements

One position on the dial is actually 1/40 of a revolution. Use the *endGently* style to make the motion more realistic. Rename *comboLock* as *TurningComboLock* and save it as a new class.

7. Starting with a basic chicken, create an object method *walk* that will have the chicken perform a realistic stepping motion consisting of a left step followed by a right step. Create a second method to make the chicken perform a *funkyChicken* dance, where the chicken walks and twists its body in all different directions! Save the chicken as a new class named *CoolChicken*. Create a new world and add a *coolChicken* to the world. In *my first method*, call the *walk* and *funkyChicken* methods. Play a sound file or use a *say* method to accompany the funky chicken dance animation.

8. Create a world with an *evilNinja* (People) and write object methods for traditional Ninja moves. For example, you can write *rightJab* and *leftJab* (where the Ninja jabs his hand upward with the appropriate hand), *kickLeft* and *kickRight* (where he kicks with the appropriate leg), and *leftSpin* and *rightSpin* (where he does a spin in the appropriate direction). Each method must contain more than one statement. For example, in the *kickLeft* method, the left lower leg should turn and the foot twist at the same time as the entire leg kicks out to the left. Save the Ninja as a new class named *trainedNinja*. Start a new world and add two *trainedNinja* objects. Create an animation where the two *trainedNinja* objects practice their moves, facing one another.

4 Working with Objects in Java

Goals of this chapter:

- To introduce an integrated development environment, DrJava.
- To create and name objects in Java.
- To declare object variables and primitive variables.
- To invoke methods on objects in Java.
- To create methods with parameters.

Introduction

You have been using Alice to create virtual worlds populated with 3D objects, such as ice skaters, penguins, robots, and aliens. In Alice, objects are instances of 3D models (pre-built classes) provided in the Galleries. To create a program that animates the objects, you followed a four-step problem-solving approach: (1) read the problem, (2) design a storyboard (visual or textual) solution, (3) implement the code, and (4) test the program to find and fix any bugs (errors).

Alice's drag-and-drop environment allowed you to create program code by dragging method tiles into the editor. You learned that methods define actions that an object can perform (or have performed on it). For example, an ice skater object has a *move* method that can be used to move her in a specified direction. Also, you learned that when a method is invoked (called), a message is sent to the object, asking it to perform the action defined in the method. Invoking a method may require that certain values be sent as arguments to the parameters. To move the skater, for example, "forward" was sent as an argument to the *direction* parameter and "1 meter" was sent as an argument to the *distance* parameter.

Alice's drag-and-drop editor made it easy to learn computing concepts, because you were able to concentrate on the concepts of design, objects, and program construction using methods and parameters without having to deal with syntax errors. Now that you have learned these fundamental concepts, you are ready to apply these concepts in a textual programming language where the syntax is under your control. In this chapter, we will use the object-oriented programming language **Java** to create objects, invoke methods on those objects, and create new methods for all objects of a class. Alice is specifically designed to allow you to create 3D movies and games and is limited in terms of creating other kinds of computer programs. With Java you are only limited by your imagination, experience, and the current state of computers.

4.1   Introduction to DrJava

We recommend that you program in Java using a tool named **DrJava**. DrJava is a simple text editor (tool for using the keyboard to enter program text) and interaction space so that you can try things out in DrJava and create new programs. DrJava is available for free under the DrJava Open Source License, and it is under active development by the JavaPLT group at Rice University.

If you don't wish to use DrJava, you can use this book with another development environment. Simply set the **classpath** (place to look for the classes that you are using in your program) to include the classes used in this book. Check your documentation for your development environment to see how to do this. We recommend using DrJava because it is free, easy to use, has an interactions pane for trying out Java statements, is written in Java so it works on all platforms, and it includes a debugger. Since it is free, you can use it just for the interactions pane and do your coding in another development environment if you prefer.

To install DrJava, you'll have to do the following. Additional detailed instructions are at `http://home.cc.gatech.edu/TeaParty/43`.

1. Make sure that you have Java 1.5 (also called 5.0) or above installed on your computer (be sure to get the development environment not just the run-time environment). If you don't have it you can download it from the Sun site at `http://www.java.sun.com`.

2. You'll need to install DrJava. You can download it from `http://drjava.org/`. Be sure to get a version of DrJava that works with the version of Java you are using!

3. Add the Java classes that come with the book to the extra classpaths for DrJava. Start DrJava (see the next section for how to do this), click Edit and then Preferences. This will show the Preferences window, seen in Figure 4.1. Click

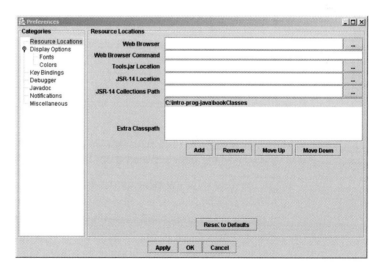

Figure 4.1
DrJava Preferences window

the Add button below the Extra Classpath text area and add the path to the directory where the classes that come with the book are, such as: `c:/intro-prog-java/bookClasses`. Also add the `jar` files that are in the bookclasses directory: `javazoom.jar`, `jmf.jar`, and `sound.jar`.

4.1.1 Starting DrJava

How you start DrJava depends on your platform. In Windows, you'll have a DrJava icon that you'll simply double-click. In Linux, you'll probably cd into your DrJava directory and type a command like `java -jar drjava-DATE-TIME.jar` where DATE-TIME are values for the release of DrJava that you are using. On the Macintosh, you'll probably have to type commands in your *Terminal* application where you cd to the correct directory then type `./DrJava`.

Common Bug: DrJava is Slow to Start

DrJava will take a while to load on all platforms. Don't worry—you'll see the logo shown in Figure 4.2 for a long time. This is called a **splash screen**, which is a small picture that displays while a program is loading. If you see the splash screen, DrJava will load.

Figure 4.2
DrJava splash screen

Common Bug: Making DrJava Run Faster

As we'll talk more about later, when you're running DrJava, you're actually running Java. Java needs memory. If you're finding that DrJava is running slowly, give it more memory. You can do that by quitting out of other applications that you're running. Your e-mail program, your instant messenger, and your digital music player all take up memory, sometimes lots of it! Quit out of those and DrJava will run faster.

Once you start DrJava, it will look something like Figure 4.3. There are three main areas in DrJava (the bars between them move so that you can resize the areas):

- The top-left window pane is the **Files Pane**. It has a list of the open files in DrJava. In Java each class that you create is usually stored in its own file. Java programs often consist of more than one class, thus more than one file. You can click on a file name in the Files pane to view the contents of that file in the top-right window pane (Definitions pane).

- The top-right part is the **Definitions Pane**. This is where you write *your* classes: a collection of related data and methods. This area is simply a text editor—think

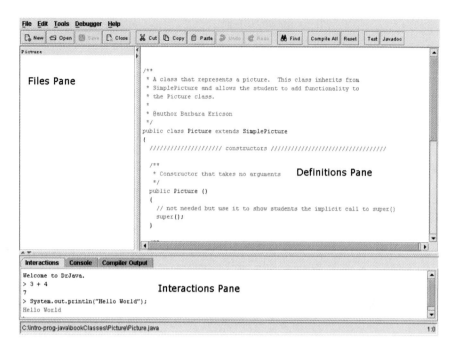

Figure 4.3
DrJava window (with annotations)

of it as Microsoft Word for your programs or the editor area in Alice. The computer doesn't actually try to interpret the names that you type up in the program area until you compile. Compiling means to translate the code that you write in your programs from something that you can understand to something the computer can understand. You can **compile** all the current files open in the Files pane by clicking the Compile All button near the top of the DrJava window.

- The bottom part is the **Interactions pane**. This is where you can literally **command** the computer to do something. You type your commands (statements) at the > prompt, and when you hit return, the computer will interpret your words (i.e., apply the meanings and encodings of the Java programming language) and do what you have told it to do. This interpretation will include whatever you typed and compiled in the Definitions pane as well.

Try typing the following (the items following the > prompt) in the Interactions pane. After you finish typing each line, press enter and the computer will respond as shown below.

```
> 3 + 4
7
> System.out.println("Hello World");
Hello World
```

As you can see, Java knows how to add numbers (using +) and how to print out a **string** (sequence of characters enclosed in double quotes) using System.out. println(*expression*).

There are other features of DrJava visible in Figure 4.3. The Open button will let you open a file, it will add the file name to the Files pane and show the code in that file in the Definitions pane. The Save button will save the file that is currently displayed in the Definitions pane.

Making It Work Tip: Exploring Help!

An *important* feature to already start exploring is HELP. If you click HELP and then click HELP again when a menu is displayed, you will see a HELP window. Start exploring it now so that you have a sense for what's there.   ◼

4.2   Working with Turtles

Dr. Seymour Papert, at MIT, used robot turtles in the late 1960s to help students think about how to specify a **procedure** (a sequence of statements). The original robot turtle had a pen in the middle of it that could be raised and lowered to leave a trail of its movements on the floor. As computer monitors with graphical displays became available in the late 1970s, he used a 2D virtual **turtle** on a computer screen.

With appreciation to Papert, we are going to create turtle objects that move around in a 2D world. The turtles know how to move forward, turn left, turn right, and turn by some specified angle. The turtles have a pen in the middle of them that leaves a trail to show their movements. The world keeps track of the turtles that are in it.

4.2.1   Defining Classes

How does the computer know what we mean by a world and a turtle? We have to define what we mean, which includes what worlds and turtles know and what they can do. We do this by writing class definitions for World and Turtle. In Alice, each class is predefined as a 3D model and made available in the Galleries. In Java, each class is usually defined in a file with the same name as the class and a file name extension of .java. Class names start with a capital letter (just like in Alice) and the first letter of each additional word is capitalized. So we define the class Turtle in the file Turtle.java. We define the class World in the file World.java.

We have predefined the classes Turtle and World for you so that you can practice creating objects and sending messages to objects in Java. Click the Open button in DrJava, find your bookClasses directory, and open Turtle.java and World.java. In DrJava, you can open more than one file at a time by holding down the control button (CTRL) while you click on the file names. Once you open Turtle.java and World.java, the result will look like what is in Figure 4.4. The class Turtle inherits from a class called SimpleTurtle (extends SimpleTurtle) just like the class CleverSkater inherited from the class IceSkater in Alice, as shown in Chapter 3.

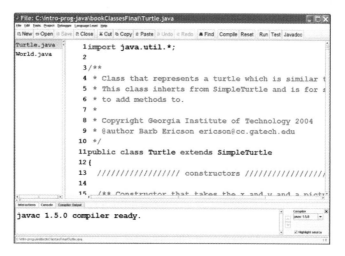

Figure 4.4
DrJava with Turtle.java and World.java open

4.2.2 Creating Objects

Object-oriented programs consist of code that works with objects. But how do we create those objects? A class knows what each object of that class needs to keep track of and what it should be able to do, so the class creates the objects of that class. You can think of a class as an object factory. The factory can create many objects. A class is also like a cookie cutter. You can make many cookies from one cookie cutter and they will all have the same shape.

In Alice, you can create objects by clicking the **Add Objects** button and then browse the gallery of classes. When you find a class that you want to create an object from, you can click on the class and drag an object of that class into the world. Or, you can click on the class and then click the **Add Instance to World** button, as shown in Figure 4.5. Notice that the class name for the ice skater is IceSkater. An object is an instance of a class and you can create many objects (instances) of a class. When you

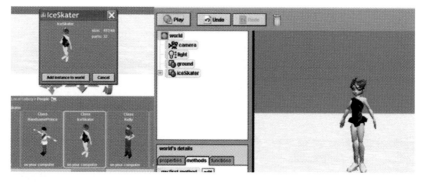

Figure 4.5
Creating an instance (object) of a class in Alice

create objects in Alice, they are automatically given a unique name and added to the world. You can see all the names for objects that are in the world in the Object tree. The ice skater object is named iceSkater, as shown in Figure 4.5. Class names start with an uppercase letter (IceSkater) and object names start with a lowercase letter (iceSkater) in both Alice and Java.

To create an object in Java, use the Java keyword new followed by the name of the class and then a list of items (the argument list) used to **initialize** (set the value of) the data for the object inside a pair of open and close parentheses.

```
new Class(argumentList)
```

This asks the class that defines the object to reserve space in memory for the data needed for that object and returns a **reference** to that space. A reference is a way to find the space the object is using again. In Alice, each new object had properties that were automatically initialized to default values. In Java, an object's properties are known as the object's **data**. The new object's data will be initialized based on the items passed in the argument list. There can be several ways to initialize a new object, and which one you are using depends on the order and types of things in the **argument** list.

In Alice, a world is created for you when you start Alice, and it is named world. In Java, if you want a world object, you will have to create it. One way to create an object of the class World is to use new World(). You don't *have* to pass any arguments to initialize the new world, but you must always include the open and close parentheses. Objects can initialize their data to default values. Type the following in the Interactions pane of DrJava (type the part after the >).

```
> new World()
A 640 by 480 world with 0 turtles in it.
> System.out.println(new World());
A 640 by 480 world with 0 turtles in it.
```

Making It Work Tip: Leaving Off a Semicolon in the Interactions Pane Prints the Result

If you type a Java statement or expression in the Interactions pane of DrJava and don't add a semicolon at the end of the statement or expression, it will print out the result of that statement or expression. In this case, it prints information about the newly created World object. If you do add a semicolon at the end, it will just execute the statement and not print out the result. If you want to add the semicolon and still print the result, use System.out.println(*expression*). Java statements usually end in a semicolon, just like English sentences usually end in a period. If you make a mistake when you are typing and get an error, you can use the up arrow to bring back what you just typed and fix it. ■

Making It Work Tip: If You Don't Have an Interactions Pane

If you aren't using DrJava, and the development environment that you are using doesn't have an interactions pane, you will need to edit the main method in the Test.java class. To try the previous example, it should look like the following code. You will need to compile and run this class to test out the code. Check the documentation that came with your IDE for the instructions on compiling a class and running it.

```
public class Test
{
  public static void main(String[] args)
  {
     System.out.println(new World());
  }
}
```

Common Bug: Finding Classes

You should have set your classpath to include the classes from the book. If you didn't do this, you will get the error message *Undefined Class* when you try to create a World object. Make sure that the full path (for example: `c:/intro-prog-java/bookClasses/`) to the directory that has the classes from the book is in your classpath. The classpath tells Java where to look for the compiled class definitions. Java needs to load the class definition before it can create an object of that class.

When you type the code in the **Interactions** pane, you will see a window appear with the title **World**, as shown in Figure 4.6. We have created an object of the `World` class which has a width of 640 and a height of 480. The world doesn't have any turtles in it yet. We would like to add a turtle to this world, but we have a problem. We don't have any way to refer to this `World` object. We need a way to refer to that object in memory, or else the object will just be garbage collected (the space will be recycled) after you close the window. Go ahead and close the window and let's try again, but this time, we will create a name that will let us refer to the `World` object again. Naming objects is also called declaring a **variable**. In Alice, objects are named automatically (the `World` object is called `world`. The `IceSkater` object is called `iceSkater`). In Alice if you create many objects of the `IceSkater` class, as in Figure 4.7, they will be

Figure 4.6
A window that shows a `World` object

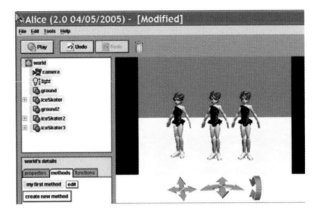

Figure 4.7
Notice that there is a unique name for each ice skater in the world

named iceSkater, iceSkater2, iceSkater3, and so on. In Java *you* must assign *unique* names for your objects.

When we declare a variable, we are associating a name with the memory location so that we can access it again using the name. To declare a variable in Java, you must give the type of variable, a name for it, and end it with a semicolon.

Type name;

The *Type* is the name of the class if you are creating a variable that refers to an object. So to create a variable that will refer to a World object, we need to say the type is World and give it a name. The first word in the variable name should be lowercase, but the first letter of each additional word should be uppercase. The name should describe what the variable represents. So, let's declare a variable that refers to an object of the class World using the name world (just like in Alice).

```
> World world;
> world
null
```

We declared a world variable in the code but didn't assign any value to it. Then we asked the **Interactions** pane of DrJava to print the value of that variable by just typing the name of the variable with no semicolon and pressing enter. By default, it has the value null, which is a Java keyword meaning that it doesn't refer to any variable yet.

You can also set the value of the variable when you declare it.

```
Type name = expression;
> World world = new World();
```

This says to create a variable with the name of world that will be of type World (will refer to an object of the class World). It will refer to the object created by the World class because of the code: new World().

To create a turtle object in this world, we will again use

```
new Class(parameterList)
```

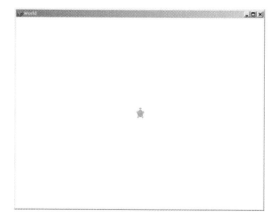

Figure 4.8
A window that shows a `Turtle` object in a `World` object

This time, we will ask the `Turtle` class to create the object in our `World` by passing a reference to the world that the turtle will live in. We will declare a variable so that we can refer to the `turtle` object again.

```
> Turtle turtle = new Turtle(world);
> turtle
No name turtle at 320, 240 heading 0.
```

Now a `turtle` object appears in the middle of the `world` object, as shown in Figure 4.8. This turtle doesn't know its name. It has a location of (320, 240) and a heading of 0, which is north. The default location for a new turtle is the middle of the `World` object. The default heading is 0 (north).

We can create another `turtle` object, and this time, we can say what location we want it to appear at in the world. To do this, we need to pass in the items used to initialize the new object. Separate the values with commas.

```
> Turtle turtle2 = new Turtle(30,50,world);
> turtle2
No name turtle at 30, 50 heading 0.
```

Notice that the second turtle appears at the specified location (30, 50), as shown in Figure 4.9. The top left of the window is location (0, 0). The *x* values increase going to the right, and the *y* values increase going down.

4.2.3 Sending Messages to Objects

In object-oriented programming, we invoke methods on objects. When we invoke (call) a method, we are actually sending a message to an object, asking that object to perform the action defined by the method. The structure of how you write a statement to invoke a method is referred to as the **syntax**—the words and characters that have to

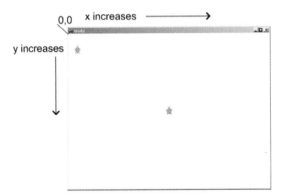

Figure 4.9
A window that shows two `turtle` objects in a `world` object

be there for Java to understand what's going on, and the order of those things. The full syntax for sending a message is

objectName.message(itemList);

The `objectName` is the name we are using for an object, `message` is what we want the object to do, and `itemList` is any additional item(s) of information that might be needed. The `.` and `()` are required even if there is no item list. Using `.` to send messages to objects is also called **dot notation**. Alice uses the same notation to ask objects to perform (execute) actions (methods), as shown in Figure 4.10. Alice also uses dot notation to access subparts (`cleverSkater.leftLeg`).

In the Java `turtle` class, methods have been written so that `turtle` objects can be sent a message asking them to go forward, turn left, turn right, turn by a specified angle, change their color, and set their name. So if we want the first `turtle` to go forward 20 steps, we would send the message `turtle.forward(20);`. If we want it to turn left, we would use `turtle.turnLeft();`. If we want it to turn right, we would use `turtle.turnRight();`. If we want it to turn left by an angle of 45 degrees, we would use `turtle.turn(-45);`. To turn the first turtle to the right 45 degrees, use `turtle.turn(45);`. Negative angles turn to the left, and positive angles turn that amount to the right.

```
> turtle.forward(20);
> turtle.turnLeft();
> turtle.forward(30);
> turtle.turnRight();
> turtle.forward(40);
> turtle.turn(-45);
> turtle.forward(30);
> turtle.turn(90);
> turtle.forward(20);
```

Figure 4.10
Using dot notation in Alice to invoke methods on objects

Figure 4.11
The result of messages to the first Turtle object

In Figure 4.11, we see the trail of the first turtle's movements. Notice that all of the messages were sent to the first `turtle` object that is referenced by the `turtle` variable. The messages only get sent to that object. Notice that the second `turtle` object didn't move. It didn't get any messages yet. To send a message to the second `turtle` object, we use the variable name that refers to that `turtle` object, which is `turtle2`.

```
> turtle2.turnRight();
> turtle2.forward(200);
> turtle2.turnRight();
> turtle2.forward(200);
```

In Figure 4.12, we see the trail of the second turtle's movement. Can you draw a square with a turtle? Can you draw a triangle with a turtle? Can you draw a pentagon with a turtle? How about a circle?

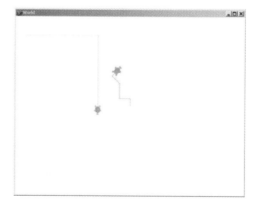

Figure 4.12
The result of messages to the second `turtle` object

4.2.4 Objects Control Their State

In object-oriented programming, we ask an object to do something by sending it a message. The object can refuse to do what you ask it to do. Why would an object refuse? An object *should* refuse when you ask it to do something that would cause its data to be wrong. The World that the turtles are in is 640 by 480. Try asking the Turtle object to go forward past the end of the world. What happens? First click the Reset button to reset the interactions pane. When you reset the interactions pane you get rid of any currently declared variables. Then create a new world and turtle.

```
> World world1 = new World();
> Turtle turtle1 = new Turtle(world1);
> turtle1
No name turtle at 320, 240 heading 0.
> turtle1.turnRight();
> turtle1.forward(400);
> turtle1
No name turtle at 639, 240 heading 90.
> world1.getWidth()
640
```

Remember that turtle objects are first created in the middle of the world (320, 240) facing the top of the world. When the turtle turned right, it was facing the right side of the window. If the turtle went forward 400 steps, it would be past the right edge of the window (320 + 400 = 720), because the x values increase to the right. Notice that the turtle stops when the middle of it reaches the limit of the window (639), as shown in Figure 4.13. This means your turtle will always have at least part of it in the world.

It may seem strange that turtle1 stopped when it reached 639, but the first pixel is at 0 and the last is 639. If we asked you to count 10 numbers starting at 0, you should end at 9. The number of items is the ending value minus the starting value plus 1. So 639 − 0 + 1 is 640, which means that a window with a width of 640 that starts with 0 must end at 639.

Figure 4.13
The turtle won't leave the world

4.2.5 Additional Turtle Capabilities

You may not want to see the turtle, but just the trail of its movements. To ask the turtle to stop drawing itself, send it the message hide(). To start drawing the turtle again send it the message show().

On the other hand, you may not want to see the trail. Ask the turtle to stop showing the trail by asking it to pick up the pen with the command penUp(). To start showing the trail again, send the turtle the message penDown().

You can ask a turtle to move to a particular location by sending it the message moveTo(x,y), where x is the x value that you want to move to and y is the y value that you want to move to.

You can ask a turtle to use a particular name by sending it the message setName *(name)* where name is the new name to use. If you print the variable that refers to a turtle, you will see the name printed. You can also get a turtle's name by sending it the message getName().

We can use these new messages to draw two squares with a turtle. First reset the Interactions pane and create a world and a turtle. Name the turtle Jane. Draw one square with an upper-left corner at (50, 50) and a width and height of 30. Draw another square at (200, 200) with a width and height of 30. We can use new Turtle(x,y,world) to create a turtle object that is located at (*x, y*). Let's turn off seeing the turtle when we draw the second square by sending it the message hide().

```
> World world1 = new World();
> Turtle turtle1 = new Turtle(50, 50,world1);
> turtle1.setName("Jane");
> turtle1.turnRight();
> turtle1.forward(30);
> turtle1.turnRight();
> turtle1.forward(30);
> turtle1.turnRight();
> turtle1.forward(30);
> turtle1.turnRight();
> turtle1.forward(30);
> turtle1.penUp() ;
> turtle1.moveTo(200,200);
> turtle1.hide();
> turtle1.penDown();
> turtle1.turnRight();
> turtle1.forward(30);
> turtle1.turnRight();
> turtle1.forward(30);
> turtle1.turnRight();
> turtle1.forward(30);
> turtle1.turnRight();
> turtle1.forward(30);
> turtle1
Jane turtle at 200,200 heading 0.
```

You can see the result of these commands in Figure 4.14.

Figure 4.14
Drawing two squares with a turtle

Making It Work Tip: Reuse the Previous Line in DrJava
You can use the up arrow on the keyboard to bring up previous lines you have typed in the Interactions pane in DrJava. This is easier than typing the same line in again.

4.3 Creating Methods

We had to send many messages to our `Turtle` object just to draw two squares. Do you notice any similarities in how we draw the squares? Each time we draw a square we turn right and go forward by 30 steps for a total of four times. It would be nice to name the list of steps for drawing a square and then just do the list of steps when a turtle is asked to draw a square. We did this in Alice by creating a new method. We can also create new methods in Java.

Methods in Java consist of named blocks of statements defined inside a class. Once we have defined a method and successfully compiled the class, *all* the objects of that class will respond to a message with the same name and parameters as the new method. So if we want `Turtle` objects to understand the message `drawSquare()`, we define a method `drawSquare()` in `Turtle.java`.

Computers Science Tip: Messages Map to Methods
When we send an object a message, it must map to a method that objects of that class understand. If objects of the class don't understand the message, you will get an error when you compile. Be sure that the items you are passing as input also match the parameter declarations, because if they aren't, you will get an error that says such a method does not exist. Make sure that you compile a new method before you try and use it. Compiling translates the code from something humans can read and understand into something the computer can execute.

You have seen how to declare variables in Java:

```
type name;
```

or

```
type name = expression;
```

To declare a method in Java, use the following syntax:

```
visibility type methodName(parameterList)
```

A **method declaration** has a visibility (usually the keyword `public`), the type of the thing being returned from the method, the method name, and the parameter list in parentheses. The body of a method is defined in a block of code. A **block** is all the Java statements between an open curly brace { and a close curly brace }. The block of commands that follow a method declaration are the ones associated with the name of the method (function) and are the ones that will be executed when the method is invoked.

Common Bug: Curly Braces Come in Pairs

Each open curly brace in your Java code must have a matching close curly brace. You should indent code inside of a pair of curly braces. Indentation doesn't matter to the compiler but makes your code easier to read and understand. Be careful not to mix up curly braces and parentheses.

To declare a method that will draw a square, we can use

```
public void drawSquare()
{
  // statements to execute when the method is executed
}
```

Notice that we started the open curly brace on a new line and lined it up with the close curly brace. This can help beginners line up the curly braces and help them check that they have a close curly brace for each open curly brace. Some people prefer to put the curly brace at the end of the previous line. This approach takes up less space on a page:

```
public void drawSquare() {
  // statements to execute when the method is executed
}
```

You can do it either way, Java doesn't care. The Java style guidelines use the second approach. This is also the approach used in Alice, as in Figure 4.15. Beginning programmers may find it easier to put the open curly brace on a new line and line it up with the close curly brace (the first way).

The visibility in this method declaration is `public`. **Visibility** means who can invoke the method (ask for the method to be executed). The keyword `public` means that this method can be invoked by any code in any class definition. If the keyword `private` is used, the method can only be accessed from inside the current class definition. You can think of this as a security feature. If you keep your journal on the Web

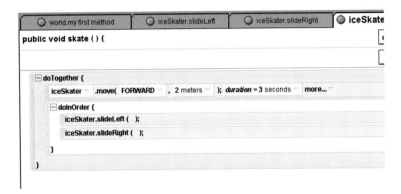

Figure 4.15
An Alice method

as a blog, it is public and anyone can read it. If you keep it in a notebook hidden in your room, it is private, and hopefully, only you can read it.

The **return type** in this method declaration is void. The return type is the type of the value or object being returned or the keyword void if nothing is returned from the method. The return type is required and is given before the method name. If you leave off a return type, you will get a compiler error. If your method returns a value, the return type must match the type of the value returned, or you will get a compiler error.

The method name in this declaration is drawSquare. By convention, method names start with a lowercase letter and the first letter of each additional word is uppercase: drawSquare. Another example method name is turnRight.

A method *must* have parentheses following the method name. If any items are to be sent to the method, they will be declared inside the parentheses separated by commas. To declare a parameter, you must give a type and name. The name can be used by the code in the body of the method to refer to the passed value.

We create a collection of statements by defining a block. Each statement in a block is executed one after the other, just like in the doInOrder construct in Alice.

Debugging Tip: Proper Method Declarations

All method declarations must be *inside* a class definition, which means that they are defined inside the open { and close } curly braces that enclose the body of the class definition. If you put a method declaration after the end of the class definition, you will get *Error: 'class' or 'interface' expected*. Methods cannot be defined inside of other methods. If you accidentally do this, you will get *Error: illegal start of expression* at the beginning of the inner method declaration.

Statements in a method end in a semicolon. (The semicolon at the end of a statement in a method is not optional in the Definitions pane of DrJava.) If you forget to put the semicolon at the end of a statement, you will get *Error: ';' expected*. All compiler errors will highlight the line of code that caused the error. If you don't see the error on that line of code, check the preceding line. You can double-click on an error in the Compiler Output area and it will place the cursor at that line of code and highlight it.

We can now define our first method in Java! Open Turtle.java by clicking on the OPEN button near the top of the window and using the file chooser to pick Turtle.java in the bookClasses directory. Type the following code into the definitions pane of DrJava before the main method (which starts with public static void main). A main method is executed when you click the Run button in DrJava. Main methods are used to begin execution of an object-oriented program and can be used instead of the Interactions pane to test your programs. When you're done adding the drawSquare method to the Turtle.java file, save the file and click the Compile All button shown near the top of the window in Figure 4.16.

Why do we have to compile the file before we can use the new method? Computers don't understand the Java source code directly. We must *compile* it, which translates the class definition from something people can read and understand into something a computer can read and understand.

Unlike some other computer languages, Java doesn't compile into **machine code**, which is the language for the machine it is running on. When we compile Java source code, we compile it into a language for a **virtual machine**, which is a machine that doesn't necessarily exist.

When we successfully compile a *ClassName*.java file, the compiler outputs a *ClassName*.class file which contains the instructions that a Java virtual machine can understand. If our compile is not successful, we will get error messages that explain what is wrong. We have to fix the errors and compile again before we can try out our new method. A successful compile of the Java class definition Turtle.java will produce a Turtle.class file.

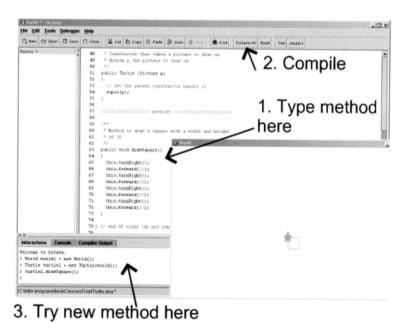

Figure 4.16
Defining and executing drawSquare()

When we execute a Java class the Java Virtual Machine will read the compiled code in the class file and map the instructions for the virtual machine to the machine it is currently executing on. This allows you to compile Java programs on one type of computer and run them on another without having to recompile.

Debugging Tip: Compile All

The Compile All button will compile all open files. If you have an empty file open named (Untitled), go ahead and close it. DrJava creates this for you so that you can start writing a new class definition. But we won't do that right away. Select the name of the file in the Files Pane and press the Close button to close a file.

Making It Work Tip: Copying and Pasting

Text can be copied and pasted between the Interactions pane and Definitions pane. To copy text, select it and click Copy (in the Edit menu), then click in the Definitions pane and click Paste (also in the Edit menu). You can also use keyboard shortcuts for copy (Control-c) and paste (Control-v). This means to hold the "Ctrl" key and then press the "c" key to copy and hold the "Ctrl" key and the v key to paste. You can copy entire methods in the Definitions pane by selecting the text in the method and then copying and pasting it. You can select a method name in the Definitions pane and paste it in the Interactions pane to send a message asking for that method to be executed. You can also try things out in the Interactions pane and later save them in a method in the Definitions pane.

Program 4.1: Draw a Square

```java
public void drawSquare()
{
  this.turnRight();
  this.forward(30);
  this.turnRight();
  this.forward(30);
  this.turnRight();
  this.forward(30);
  this.turnRight();
  this.forward(30);
}
```

Notice that in Program 4.1 we changed `turtle1.turnRight();` to `this.turnRight();`. The variable `turtle1` isn't defined inside the method `drawSquare()`. Variables names are known in a **context** (area that they apply). This is also known as the **scope** of a variable. The variables that we define in the Interactions pane are only known in the Interactions pane. They aren't known inside methods. We need some other way to reference the object that we want to turn. Object methods are passed a reference to the object the method was invoked on, even though it doesn't look like it from the method definition. So even through it looks like `drawSquare()` doesn't take any values, it is actually called using `drawSquare(Turtle this)` where `this` is a reference to whatever object the method was called on. We say that methods are *implicitly* passed the object the method was called on. You can use the keyword `this` to refer to the object the method was called on.

Also notice that some words are shown in boldface in Program 4.1 (`public`, `void`, and `this`). These are keywords or reserved words in Java. These words have special meaning in Java and can't be used as variable names.

Making It Work Tip: Try *Every* Program!

To really understand what's going on, type in, compile, and execute *every* program as you read through this book. *Every* one. None are long, and the practice will go a long way toward convincing you that the programs work, developing your programming skill, and helping you understand *why* they work.

The code in Program 4.1 creates a method with the name `drawSquare` that takes no parameters (other than the implicit `this` parameter) and whenever the method is invoked, it will execute the statements inside of the open and close curly braces. It is a `public` method. It doesn't return a value, so it uses the keyword `void` to indicate this. This method *must* be called on an object of the `Turtle` class. The word `this` is a keyword that refers to the object this method was invoked on. Since this method is defined in the `Turtle` class, the keyword `this` will refer to a `Turtle` object.

Once the method has successfully compiled, you can ask for it to be executed by sending a message to a `Turtle` object with the same name and parameter types as defined in the method. Click the Interactions tab in the Interactions pane (near the bottom of the window). This method doesn't take any parameters, so just finish with the open and close parentheses and the semicolon. When you compile a program, DrJava's Interactions pane will be reset. When the Interactions pane is reset, all the variables we previously defined in the Interactions pane will no longer be understood. We will need to create objects of the `World` and `Turtle` classes again. This time we will use slightly different variable names.

```
> World world1 = new World();
> Turtle turtle1 = new Turtle(world1);
> turtle1.drawSquare();
```

The first time you use a class in a program, the Java Virtual Machine loads the compiled class definition (in this example, the `Turtle.class` file) and creates an object that contains all the information about the class, including the code for the methods. Every time you instantiate a new object of that class, the object is given space in the memory where the object's own data is stored, and it is also given a reference to the object that defines its class, as shown by Figure 4.17. The object that

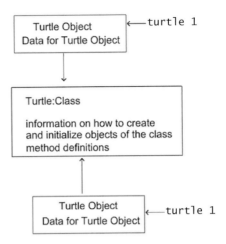

Figure 4.17
An object stores data for that object and has a reference to the class that created it

defines a class is an object of a class named `Class`. You can get the `Class` object using the method `getClass()`.

```
> world1.getClass()
class World
> turtle1.getClass()
class Turtle
```

The Java Virtual Machine will check for a method with the same name and parameter list in the object that defines the class (an object of the class `Class`). If it is found, it will execute that method. This means that the statements in the body of the method will be executed starting with the first statement. The object that the method was invoked on is implicitly passed to the method as well and can be referred to using the keyword `this`.

What if we want to draw a larger or smaller square? We could change each of the `this.forward(30);` lines to the new width and height and then compile. But, it would be easier to declare a variable in the method that would represent the width of the square and then use that variable name as the amount to go forward by like this: `this.forward(width);`. Then if we want to change the size of the square, we only have to change one line. You can declare a variable anywhere in the body of a method, but you *must* declare it before you use it. The name will be known and the value substituted for each occurrence of the name in the rest of the method. But the name will only be known inside the method in which it is declared. That is, a local variable (declared inside a method) has local scope and can only be used inside the method.

What type should we use to represent the width of the square? Thus far, we have only declared variables that refer to objects. But, just as Alice had some other types (Number, Boolean, and String), so too does Java. Java has types that represent integers (`int`), floating-point numbers (`double` or `float`), true and false values (`boolean`), and single characters (`char`). These types are called **primitive types** and are not objects in Java. Primitive types differ from object types in that, when you declare a primitive type, space is set aside for a value of that type and the name of the variable is mapped to that space. Since we were using the value 30, which is an integer value, we will declare the width to be of type `int`. The following are example declarations of primitive type variables.

```
> int numKids = 2;
> double price = 4.33;
> boolean isRaining = false;
> char startChar = 'a';
```

We can't have two methods with the same name and the same parameter list, so we need a new name for this method. We simply named it `drawSquare2` to show that it is the second version. We can copy the first method, paste it, rename it, and then change it to declare and use the `width` variable, as shown in Program 4.2.

Program 4.2: Draw Square Using a Variable for Width

```
public void drawSquare2()
{
    int width = 30;
    this.turnRight();
    this.forward(width);
    this.turnRight();
    this.forward(width);
    this.turnRight();
    this.forward(width);
    this.turnRight();
    this.forward(width);
}
```

Compile and run this method and check that you get the same results as with `drawSquare()`.

```
> World world = new World();
> Turtle turtle1 = new Turtle(world);
> turtle1.drawSquare2();
```

4.4   Passing Parameters to Methods

This is a bit better than the first version and a bit easier to change. But, you still have to recompile after you change the width to draw a larger or smaller square. Wouldn't it be nice if there were a way to tell the method what size you want when you ask for the method to be executed by sending a message that matches the method? Well there is! That is what the parameter list is for. We can make the width of the square a parameter.

Do you remember creating a method with a parameter in Alice, as shown in Figure 4.18? You had to specify the type of the parameter, and that type could be a number, Boolean, object, or string.

```
  world.my first method    cleverSkater.spin

public void spin ( Number  123 howManySpins ) {


  doInOrder {
    //  Skater spins around.
    //  howManyTimes specifies the number of revolutions for the spin.
    cleverSkater.prepareToSpin ( );
    cleverSkater  .turn( LEFT  , howManySpins revolutions  ); more...
    cleverSkater.finishSpin ( );
  }
}
```

Figure 4.18
A method that takes a parameter in Alice

You also have to specify the type of the parameter in Java. What type should we use for width? Well, in the second version, we used `int` because the turtle only takes whole steps, not fractional ones, so let's use that. What should we call this method? We could call it `drawSquare3(int width)`, but someone may think this means it draws a square with a width of 3. We could call it `drawSquareWithPassedWidth(int width)` but that is rather long, and you can tell it takes a passed width by looking at the parameter list. How about if we just call it `drawSquare(int width)`? You may think that isn't allowed, since we have a method `drawSquare()`. However, that method doesn't take any parameters and our new method does. Java allows you to use the same method name as another method as long as the parameter list is different. This is called **method overloading**.

Program 4.3: Draw Square with Width as a Parameter
```java
public void drawSquare(int width)
{
    this.turnRight();
    this.forward(width);
    this.turnRight();
    this.forward(width);
    this.turnRight();
    this.forward(width);
    this.turnRight();
    this.forward(width);
}
```

Type in the new method declaration and compile. Let's try this new method out.

```
> World world1 = new World();
> Turtle turtle1 = new Turtle(world1);
> turtle1.drawSquare(200);
```

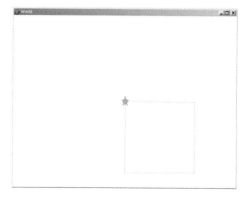

Figure 4.19
Showing the result of sending the width as a parameter to drawSquare

When you execute `turtle1.drawSquare(200);` you are asking the object named `turtle1` to execute a method named `drawSquare` that takes an integer parameter. The method `drawSquare` will use 200 for the parameter `width` everywhere it appears in the method `drawSquare`, with the result shown in Figure 4.19. The parameter name `width` is known throughout the body of the method. This is very similar to `drawSquare2()` but has the advantage that we don't need to change the method and recompile to use a different width.

An important reason for using parameters is to make methods more **general**. Consider method `drawSquare(int width)`. That method handles the *general* case of drawing a square. We call that kind of generalization **abstraction**. Abstraction leads to general solutions that work in lots of situations.

Making It Work Tip: Use Names that Make Sense

We called the first method drawSquare() and the second drawSquare2(). Does it matter? Absolutely not! Well, not to the computer, at any rate. The computer doesn't care what names you use—they're entirely for your benefit. Pick names that (a) are meaningful to you (so that you can read and understand your program), (b) are meaningful to others (so that others can read and understand it), and (c) are easy to type. Long names, like,

`drawARectangleWithEqualWidthAndHeight`

are meaningful, easy to read, but are a pain to type.

Does this mean that you can use "orange" as a method name? Yes, you can, but it may be confusing even for you and especially confusing for others. It helps to use method names that indicate what the method does.

When you evaluate a method by specifying its name with **input values** (also known as the arguments) inside parentheses, such as `turtle1.drawSquare(20);` or `new Turtle(20,30,world1)`, each parameter variable is set to a *copy* of the argument value. This is called **pass by value**. All arguments in Java are passed by making a copy of their value. Does this mean that we make a copy of the World object when we pass it as a parameter? No, we just make a copy of the reference to the object in the memory space, which means we make another reference to that `World` object.

4.5   Concepts Summary

This chapter introduced many concepts: declaring variables, creating objects, invoking object methods, creating new methods, and creating methods that take parameters.

4.5.1 Declaring Variables

To declare a variable (assign memory to it and give it a name) in Java, specify the type of the variable and a name.

```
type name;
```

You can also assign a value to the variable to the result of an expression when you declare it.

```
type name = expression;
```

When you declare a variable to be of an object type (using a class name for the type), space is allocated for a reference to an object and the name is associated with that space. Below is an example of declaring an object of the class `World`. Since we aren't assigning a value to it when we declare it, the value will be `null` (a Java keyword that means that the variable does not refer to an object yet).

```
> World world;
> System.out.println(world);
null
```

The type can also be one of the primitive types: `int`, `float`, `double`, `char`, or `boolean`. Below is an example of declaring an integer variable.

```
> int width = 3;
```

When you declare a variable to be one of the primitive types, space is allocated based on the type, and the value is stored in that space.

4.5.2 Creating Objects

To create an object, ask the class to create and initialize a new object. This is also called creating an **instance** of a class or **instantiating** an object.

```
new ClassName(parameterList)
```

Here is an example of creating an object of the class World:

```
> World world = new World();
```

4.5.3 Invoking Object Methods

You must invoke an `object` method on a reference to an object using dot notation.

```
objectReference.methodName(argumentList);
```

Here is an example of invoking an object method:

```
> turtle1.turnLeft();
```

The object that the method is invoked on will be implicitly passed to the method and can be referred to using the keyword `this` inside of the method. Object methods usually work with the data in the current object.

4.5.4 Creating New Methods

To create a method in a class, open the class definition file `ClassName.java`, and put the method before the closing curly brace at the end of the file.

To define a method use:

```
public returnType methodName(parameterList)
{
  statements in the body of the method
}
```

If the method doesn't return a value, use the keyword `void` as the return type. Each parameter in the parameter list has a type and name. Parameters are separated by commas. Method and parameter names start with a lowercase letter, but the first letter of each additional word is capitalized.

Here is an example method in the `Turtle` class:

```
public void drawSquare(int width)
{
  this.turnRight();
  this.forward(width);
  this.turnRight();
  this.forward(width);
  this.turnRight();
  this.forward(width);
  this.turnRight();
  this.forward(width);
}
```

4.6 Methods Summary

forward (int numberOfSteps)	Asks the `turtle` object that it is invoked on to move forward by the passed number of steps. No return value.
setPenDown(boolean value)	Asks the `turtle` object that it is invoked on to set the pen up or down depending on the passed value. If you pass in `false` for value, the pen is lifted and no trail will be drawn when the turtle moves. If you pass in `true`, the pen will be put down and the trail will be drawn.
hide()	Asks the `turtle` object that it is invoked on to stop showing itself. No return value.

`moveTo(int x, int y)`	Asks the `turtle` object that it is invoked on to move to the specified *x* and *y* location. No return value.
`penDown()`	Asks the `turtle` object that it is invoked on to put down the pen and draw the trail of future movements. No return value.
`penUp()`	Asks the `turtle` object that it is invoked on to pick up the pen so you don't see the trail of future movements. No return value.
`show()`	Asks the `turtle` object that it is invoked on to show (draw) itself. No return value.
`turn(int angle)`	Asks the `turtle` object that it is invoked on to turn by the specified angle (in degrees). A negative angle will turn that much to the left and a positive angle will turn that much to the right. No return value.
`turnLeft()`	Asks the `turtle` object that it is invoked on to turn left (degrees). No return value.
`turnRight()`	Asks the `turtle` object that it is invoked on to turn right (degrees). No return value.

Exercises

1. Some computer science concept questions:
   - What does a compile do?
   - What does method visibility mean?
   - What is a classpath?
   - What is a method?
   - What creates new objects?
   - What does "pass by value" mean?
   - What is scope?
   - What is a parameter?
   - When do you specify the value for a parameter?

2. Test your understanding of Java with the following:
   - What does `turtle1.forward()` do?
   - What does `turtle1.turn(-45)` do?
   - What does `turtle1.turn(45)` do?
   - What does `turtle1.penUp()` do?
   - What does `turtle1.hide()` do?

3. How do you create new objects in Java? How do you create a `World` object? How do you create a `Turtle` object?

4. What does this do? `System.out.println(new World());`

5. How many and what kind of variables (primitive or object) are created in the following code?

    ```
    > World worldObj = new World();
    > Turtle turtle1 = new Turtle(worldObj);
    > turtle1.forward(30);
    > Turtle turtle2 = new Turtle(worldObj);
    > turtle2.turnRight();
    > turtle2.forward(30);
    ```

6. How many and what kind of variables (primitive or object) are created in the following code?

    ```
    > double cost = 19.20;
    > double percentOff = 0.4;
    > double salePrice = cost * (1.0 - percentOff);
    ```

7. Write a method for Turtle to draw a rectangle. Pass in the width and height for the rectangle.

8. Write a method for Turtle to draw an equilateral triangle. Pass in the length of the sides.

9. Write a method for Turtle to draw a hexagon. Pass in the length of the sides.

10. Write a method for Turtle to draw a pentagon. Pass in the length of the sides.

11. Create a World object and a Turtle object and use the Turtle object to draw a star.

12. Create a World object and a Turtle object and use the Turtle object to draw an arrow.

13. Create a World object and a Turtle object and use the Turtle object to draw a pyramid.

14. Create a World object and a Turtle object and use the Turtle object to draw a flower.

15. Create a World object and a Turtle object and use the Turtle object to draw a house.

16. Create a World object and a Turtle object and use the Turtle object to draw your initials.

CHAPTER 5

Drawing in Java

Goals of this chapter:

- To introduce class methods.
- To introduce `String` methods.
- To use comments in Java programs.
- To use the Java API to explore classes and packages.
- To use Java classes to draw simple shapes (lines, ovals, rectangles, arcs) and text on pictures.
- To use the Java2D API for more complicated drawing.
- To introduce terms used to describe inheritance relationships.
- To introduce the concept of an interface.

Introduction

In the last chapter, you learned how to declare variables, create objects, invoke methods on objects, and create new methods while working with worlds and turtles in Java. In this chapter, you will practice doing all those things using another class: `Picture`. You will also learn how to use existing Java classes to draw on and modify pictures.

5.1 Working with Media

What if we want to create and manipulate pictures? Just as the `World` and `Turtle` classes were pre-defined and provided for your use in the last chapter, we also created a pre-defined class named `Picture`, which will allow you to work with digital picture objects.

5.1.1 Creating a Picture Object

How do you create a picture object? You may recall that the syntax for creating an object is

```
new Class(argumentList)
```

Try entering the following in DrJava's interactions pane.

```
> System.out.println(new Picture());
Picture, filename null height 100 width 200
```

It looks like we created a `Picture` object with a height of 100 and a width of 200, but why don't we see it? New objects of the class `Picture` aren't shown automatically.

You have to ask a `Picture` object to show itself using the message `show()`. It may seem strange to say that a picture knows how to show itself, but in object-oriented programming, we treat objects as intelligent beings that know how to do the things that we would expect an object to be able to do or that someone would want to do to it. We typically show pictures, so in object-oriented programming, `Picture` objects know how to show themselves (make themselves visible).

So let's ask the `Picture` object to show itself using dot notation (`object.message()`). Oops, we forgot to declare a variable to refer to the `Picture` object, so we don't have an object variable to use.

Let's try it again, and this time we will declare a variable that will hold a reference to the `Picture` object. The syntax for declaring a variable is

```
type name;
```
   or
```
type name = expression;
```

When you are declaring an object variable, the "type" is the name of the class. In this example, objects are of type `Picture`. What should the name be? Well, the name should describe what the object is, so let's use `picture1`.

```
> Picture picture1 = new Picture();
> picture1.show();
```

Now we can see the created picture in Figure 5.1.

Why doesn't it have anything in it? When you create a `Picture` object using new `Picture()` the default width is 200, the default height is 100, and the default is that all of the pixels in the picture are white. How can we create a picture from data in a file that came from a digital camera? We can use new `Picture(String fileName)` which takes an object of the `String` class that specfies the file name of a file from which to read the digital picture information. We haven't previously used objects of the `String` class, so let's pause to take a quick look at the `String` class, `String` objects, and some of the methods defined for `String` objects.

Strings and String Methods

An object of the **String** class consists of a sequence of characters. Also, the `String` class has many methods that can be invoked on a sequence of characters, such as turning all the

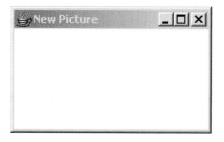

Figure 5.1
Creating a `Picture` object using `new Picture()`

characters to uppercase, turning all the characters to lowercase, or getting the number of characters (including spaces and punctuation) in the string. In the following Java statements, you can see that you can create a `String` object using `new String("chars")` just as you created new turtles. Or, you can create a new `String` object by specifying just the characters enclosed in a pair of double quotes (we call this a **literal**).

```
> String test = new String("this is a test");
> System.out.println(test.toUpperCase());
THIS IS A TEST
> String test2 = "Hi";
> System.out.println(test2.toLowerCase());
hi
> System.out.println(test.length());
14
```

We want to use a `String` object to specify the fully qualified file name of a file that contains the information in a picture from a digital camera. What is the **fully qualified file name** of a file? The full or complete name of a file is the path to the file as well as the base file name and extension. How can we get the full file name for a file? One way is to use another class we have created for you. The `FileChooser` class has a class method `pickAFile()` which will display a dialog window that will help you pick a file. A **class method** is one that can be invoked on the class by using the class name (it doesn't have to be invoked on an object of that class).

```
> System.out.println(FileChooser.pickAFile());
```

Common Bug: The File Chooser Window Doesn't Appear

If you don't see the window with the file chooser in it after typing in the code, try minimizing your DrJava window. Sometimes the file chooser, shown in Figure 5.2, comes up behind the DrJava window.

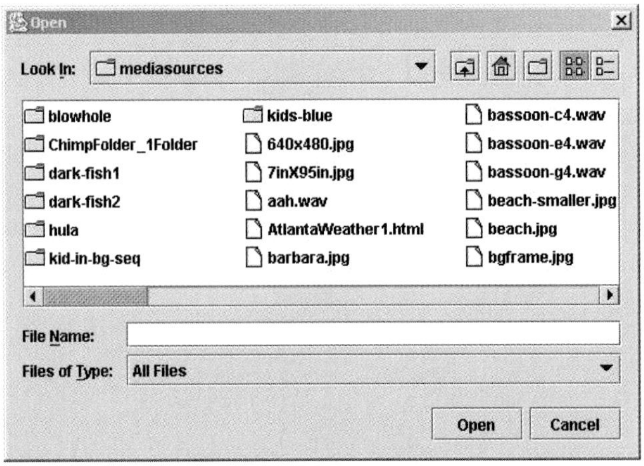

Figure 5.2
The file chooser

You're probably already familiar with how to use a file chooser or file dialog box, as shown in Figure 5.2

- Double-click folders/directories to open them.
- Click the top-right iconic button to see the details about the files, such as the types of files they are (if you put the cursor over the button and leave it there it will show Details). To create a picture, we want to pick a file with a type of JPEG Image. To create a sound, we would pick a file with a type of WAV Sound.
- Click the file name to select it and then click Open or double-click to select a file.

Once you select a file, what gets returned is the fully qualified file name as a string (a sequence of characters). If you click Cancel, pickAFile() returns **null** which is a predefined value in Java that means that it doesn't refer to a valid object.

Try it, type the following code after the > in the Interactions pane, select a file by clicking the mouse button when the cursor points to the desired file name, and then click the Open button.

```
> System.out.println(FileChooser.pickAFile());
C:\intro-prog-java\mediasources\flower1.jpg
```

What *you* get when you finally select a file will depend on your operating system. On Windows, your file name will probably start with C: and will have backslashes in it (that is, \). On Mac and Linux computers, the full path will be a bit different. The character between words (for example, the \ between intro-prog-java and mediasources) is known as a **path separator**.

No matter what your operating system, there are two important parts to a full file name:

1. Everything from the beginning of the file name to the last path separator is called the **path** to the file. The path describes exactly *where* on the hard disk (in which **directory***) a file exists. A directory (sometimes referred to as a "folder") is like a drawer of a file cabinet, and it can hold many files. A directory can even hold other directories.

2. The last part of the file (for example, flower1.jpg) is called the **base file name**. When you look at the file in the Finder/Explorer/Directory window (depending on your operating system), that's the part you see. The last three characters (after the period) are called the **file name extension**. The extension identifies the encoding of the file. You may not see the extension depending on the settings you have. But, if you show the detail view (by clicking the top-right iconic button on the file chooser), you will see the file types. Look for a file with an extension of .jpg or for files of type JPEG image.

Files that have an extension of **.jpg** or a type of JPEG Image are *JPEG* files. They contain pictures. (To be picky, they contain data that can be *interpreted* to be a *representation* of a picture—but that's close enough to "they contain pictures.") JPEG is a standard *encoding* (a representation) for any kind of image. The other kind of media files that we'll be using frequently are .wav files. The **.wav** extension means that these

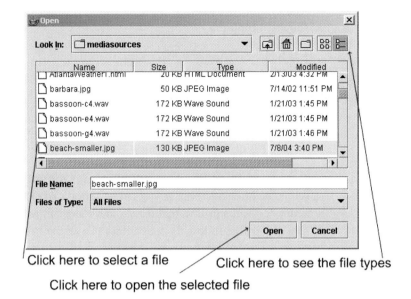

Click here to select a file   Click here to see the file types
Click here to open the selected file

Figure 5.3
File chooser with media types identified

are *WAV* files. They contain sounds. WAV is a standard encoding for sounds. There are many other kinds of extensions for files, and there are even many other kinds of media extensions. For example, there are also GIF (.gif) files for images and AIFF (.aif or .aiff) files for sounds. We'll stick to JPEG and WAV in this text, just to avoid too much complexity. Figure 5.3 shows some .jpg and .wav files in the file chooser.

5.1.2 Showing a Picture

So now we know how to get a complete file name: path and base name. This *doesn't* mean that we have the file itself loaded into memory. To get the file into memory, we have to tell Java how to interpret this file. *We* know that JPEG files are pictures, but we have to tell Java explicitly to read the file and make a Picture object from it (an object of the Picture class). So, to create a new object of the Picture class from a file name, use new Picture(fileName). The fileName is the complete name of a file as a string. We know how to get a file name using FileChooser.pickAFile().

```
> Picture p = new Picture(FileChooser.pickAFile());
> System.out.println(p);
Picture, filename
c:\intro-prog-java\mediasources\beach-smaller.jpg height 360
width 480
```

The result from printing the picture suggests that we did in fact make a Picture object from a given file name and with a given height and width. Also, recall that we can show a picture using the show() method. (See previous discussion about the show() method in Section 5.1.1.)

5.1.3 Variable Substitution

We can now pick a file, make a picture, and show it in two different ways.

1. We can do this all in one statement, because, the result from one method can be used as an argument for another method:

`new Picture(FileChooser.pickAFile()).show().`

In this statement, `FileChooser.pickAFile()` is written inside a set of parentheses as an argument to `new Picture()`. This will first invoke the `pickAFile()` class method of the class `FileChooser` because it is inside the parentheses. The `pickAFile()` method will return the fully qualified name of the selected file as a string. Next, it will create a new `Picture` object with the selected file name. And finally, it will ask the created `Picture` object to show itself. The result is shown in Figure 5.4.

2. The second way to accomplish the same action is to name each of the pieces by declaring variables. To declare a **variable** (a name for data) use type name; or type name=expression;. You can see this in Figure 5.5.

Try the following in the `Interactions` pane. Pick a file name that ends in `.jpg`.

```
> String fileName = FileChooser.pickAFile();
> Picture pictureObj = new Picture(fileName);
> pictureObj.show();
```

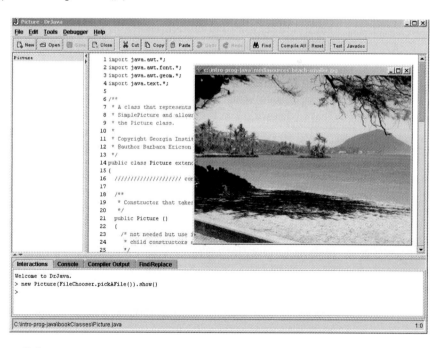

Figure 5.4
Picking, making, and showing a picture using the result of each method in the next method. The picture used is `beach-smaller.jpg`

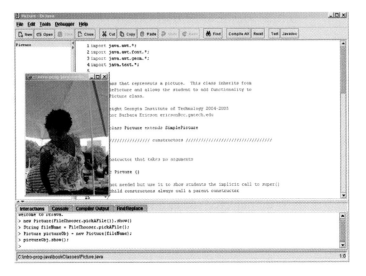

Figure 5.5
Picking, making, and showing a picture when naming the pieces. The picture shown
is `tammy.jpg`. Tammy is computer science graduate student at Georgia Tech

As you can see, we can name the file that we get from `FileChooser.pickAFile()`
by using (`String fileName =`). This says that the variable named `fileName` will be
of type `String` (will refer to an object of the `String` class) and that the `String` object
that it will refer to will be returned from `FileChooser.pickAFile()`. In a similar
fashion, we can create a variable named `pictureObj` that will refer to an object of the
`Picture` class we get from creating a `new Picture` object with the `fileName` using
`Picture pictureObj = new Picture(fileName)`. We can then ask that `Picture`
object to show itself by sending it the `show()` message using `pictureObj.show()`.
That's what we see in Figure 5.5.

This example shows that you can substitute a value, a name assigned to that value
(the variable name), and the method returning that value *interchangeably*. The computer cares about the values, not if it comes from a string, a name (a variable), or a
method (function) call.

Making It Work Tip: Java Conventions

By convention, all class names in Java begin with an uppercase letter, but all variable and
method names begin with a lowercase letter. This will help you tell the difference between
a class name and a variable or method name. So, `Picture` is a class name since it starts
with an uppercase letter, and `pictureObj` is a variable name since it starts with a lowercase
letter. If a name has several words in it, the convention is to uppercase the first letter of
each additional word, like `pickAFile()`. A **convention** is the usual way of doing something, which means that the compiler won't care, but other people will tar and feather you if
you don't do it this way because it will make your programs harder to understand.

Debugging Tip: Method Names Must be Followed by Parentheses!

In Java, all methods have to have parentheses after the method name both when you declare the method and when you invoke it. You can't leave off the parentheses if the method doesn't take any parameters. So, you always must type `pictureObj.show()` not `pictureObj.show`.

5.1.4 Primitive Variables versus Object References

When the type of a variable is `int`, `double`, or `boolean`, we call it a **primitive** variable. When a primitive variable is declared (like `int width = 30;`), memory (space) is reserved to represent that variable's value, and the name is used to find the address of that reserved space, as shown in Figure 5.6. If the type is `int`, 32 bits of space (4 bytes) are reserved. If the type is `double`, 64 bits of space (8 bytes) are reserved.

Binary Number System

Why does an integer need 32 bits of space and a double need 64 bits. What is a bit anyway? A **bit** is a binary digit that can only hold the value 0 or 1. A **byte** is a grouping of 8 bits, and computer memory is usually allocated as some number of bytes. When we group 8 bits, we can use the sequence of 0s and 1s to represent an integer using a binary number. **Binary numbers** are made up of only two digits (0 and 1). We usually work in the **decimal number** system, which has the digits 0 to 9. The value of a decimal number is calculated by multiplying each digit by a power of 10 and summing the result. The powers of 10 start at 0 and increase from right to left. The value of a binary number is calculated by multiplying each digit by a power of 2 and summing the result, as shown in Figure 5.7. The **octal number** system uses the powers of 8 and the digits 0 to 7. The **hexadecimal number** system uses powers of 16; the digits 0 to 9 plus the letters A (10), B (11), C (12), D (13), E (14), and F (15). So the code FF in hexadecimal is 15 times 16 (16^1) plus 15 times 1 (16^0), which is 255.

When the type of a variable is the name of a class (like `String`), this is called an **object variable** or **object reference**. Unlike primitive variables, object variables do

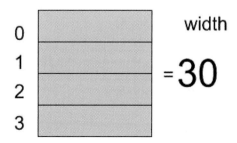

Figure 5.6
Primitive variables store the value in the memory associated with the *name*

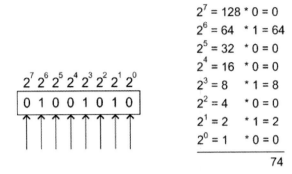

$$2^7 = 128 * 0 = 0$$
$$2^6 = 64 \ \ * 1 = 64$$
$$2^5 = 32 \ \ * 0 = 0$$
$$2^4 = 16 \ \ * 0 = 0$$
$$2^3 = 8 \ \ \ * 1 = 8$$
$$2^2 = 4 \ \ \ * 0 = 0$$
$$2^1 = 2 \ \ \ * 1 = 2$$
$$2^0 = 1 \ \ \ * 0 = 0$$
$$\overline{\hspace{4cm}}$$
$$74$$

Figure 5.7
Calculating the decimal value for a binary number

not reserve space for the value of the variable. This is because objects vary greatly in terms of the amount of space needed to store an object's information. How much space do you need for an object of the class `String`? How about an object of the class `Picture`? The amount of space you need for an object depends on the number and types of fields (data or properties) each object of that class has.

Object variables reserve space for a **reference** to an object of the given class. A reference allows the computer to *determine* the address of the actual object (it isn't just the address of the object). If the object variable is declared but not assigned to an object, the reference is set to `null`, which means that it doesn't refer to any object yet. Figure 5.8 shows one example. At the top of Figure 5.8, the String test

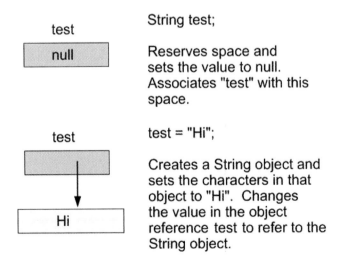

Figure 5.8
Object variables hold a reference to an object (or `null`)

is declared but not assigned a value. Because no value is assigned to *test,* it is automatically given the value `null`. Later in the code, *test* is assigned the value `Hi`. Now, memory is reserved for the object, the value `Hi` is stored in that memory, and the *test* variable is given a reference to that location in the memory.

5.2 Drawing Using the Graphics Class

Professional photographers have a problem: it is easy for people to scan pictures and print many copies of them. How can they allow people to see proofs of pictures but discourage people from using their pictures without paying for them? One way that professional photographers protect their images is to put some text on them. People can still scan the picture and make copies, but it is obvious that the picture is stolen. The text also hides some of the picture, so people are more likely to pay for pictures without the text. In the next section, you will learn how to draw many different things on your pictures using existing Java classes.

5.2.1 Drawing with Graphics Methods

Most modern programming languages with graphics capabilities provide ways to draw a variety of shapes and text. Java has a `Graphics` class that defines a number of methods that allow you to draw simple shapes and text. These graphics methods work similar to painting. First, you pick a color to paint with (using the class `Color`). Then you can paint several shapes using that color. If one shape is drawn over another, it will cover the shape underneath.

Packages

Java's `Graphics` class is in the `java.awt` package. A **package** is a collection of related classes. Java defines a large number of classes, and it would be overwhelming if they weren't grouped into packages. Some common packages are `java.lang`, which has the basics of the Java language in it; `java.awt`, which has the original graphics classes in it; and `java.io`, which contains classes used for input and output. The `Color` class is in the `java.awt` package. A **full class name** is the package name followed by a dot and then the class name. So the full name for the `Color` class is `java.awt.Color`, and the full name for the `Graphics` class is `java.awt.Graphics`.

Here is a list of some of the most useful methods in the `Graphics` class.

- `setColor(Color color)` sets the color to use for drawing.
- `drawLine(int x1, int y1, int x2, int y2)` draws a line from position (*x*1, *y*1) to (*x*2, *y*2) using the current color.
- `drawRect(int x1, int y1, int w, int h)` draws the outline of a rectangle with the upper-left corner at (*x*1, *y*1), a width of *w*, and a height of *h* using the current color.

- `fillRect(int x1, int y1, int w, int h)` draws a filled (solid) rectangle with the upper-left corner at $(x1, y1)$, a width of w, and a height of h using the current color.
- `drawOval(int x1, int y1, int w, int h)` draws the outline of an oval with the upper-left corner of the enclosing rectangle at $(x1, y1)$, where the width of the enclosing rectangle is w and the height of the enclosing rectangle is h using the current color.
- `fillOval(int x1, int y1, int w, int h)` draws a filled (solid) oval with the upper-left corner of an enclosing rectangle at $(x1, y1)$, where the width of the enclosing rectangle is w and the height of the enclosing rectangle is h using the current color.
- `drawArc(int x1, int y1, int w, int h, int startAngle, int arcAngle)` draws an outline of an arc that is part of an oval that fits in the enclosing rectangle at $(x1, y1)$, where the width of the enclosing rectangle is w and the height of the enclosing rectangle is h. The arc starts at the given `startAngle` and extends `arcAngle` degrees (where 0 degrees is at the 3 o'clock position on a clock and 45 degrees goes through the upper-right corner of the enclosing rectangle). The ending angle is the `startAngle` plus `arcAngle`.
- `fillArc(int x1, int y1, int w, int h, int startAngle, int arcAngle)` draws a filled arc that is part of an oval that fits in the enclosing rectangle at $(x1, y1)$, where the width of the enclosing rectangle is w and the height of the enclosing rectangle is h. The arc starts at the given `startAngle` and extends `arcAngle` degrees (where 0 degrees is at the 3 o'clock position on a clock and 45 degrees goes through the upper-right corner of the enclosing rectangle). The ending angle is the `startAngle` plus `arcAngle`.
- `drawPolygon(int[] xArray, int[] yArray, int numPoints)` draws the outline of a closed polygon using the x values in `xArray` and the y values in `yArray` using the current color.
- `fillPolygon(int[] xArray, int[] yArray, int numPoints)` draws a filled closed polygon using the x values in `xArray` and the y values in `yArray` using the current color.

Making It Work Tip: Use the Java API

Java is a large language, and it is nearly impossible to know every method for every class. We recommend that you use the application program interface (API) documentation to see the methods that are available for a class. If you look at the documentation for the Graphics class in the `java.awt` package, you will see *all* of the methods defined for that class. We are only showing some of the most commonly used methods here.

To view the API documentation, go to `http://java.sun.com/`. Find the specification for the version of the language that you are using. Click on the package in the top-left window frame, and then click on the class name in the bottom-left window frame. The documentation for that class will appear on the right. Scroll down to "Method Summary." As an example, Figure 5.9 shows the alphabetical listing of methods defined in the Graphics class which is in the `java.awt` package.

List of packages

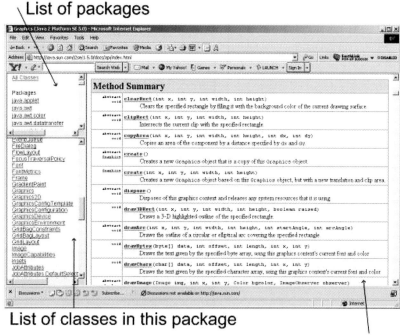

List of classes in this package

Documentation for the class: Graphics

Figure 5.9
Viewing the Java API for `java.awt.Graphics`

We can use methods defined in the `Graphics` class to add simple shap es to existing pictures. As an example, what would it look like if a mysterious red box washed up on the shore of a beach? We will need to get a `Graphics` object to use for the drawing. We can get a `Graphics` object from a `Picture` object by invoking the method `getGraphics()`on a `Picture` object.

Before we write code to create a `Graphics` object from a `Picture` object and then draw a box on it, we need to first figure out where to draw the box on the existing picture. We can use the picture explorer, which is a tool that allows you to explore digital pictures. Create the `Picture` object and then use `pictureObj.explore()` to see the picture explorer. Figure 5.10 shows an example of the picture explorer, which makes a copy of the current `Picture` object and shows it in a window. You can move the cursor and see the *x* value, *y* value, and color at the cursor location. In a picture, the *x* values increase from left to right and the *y* values increase from top to bottom.

```
> String fileName =
        "c:/intro-prog-java/mediasources/beach-smaller.jpg";
> Picture p = new Picture(fileName);
> p.explore();
```

Figure 5.10
Using the picture explorer to find the x and y values at the cursor

In Figure 5.10, we have picked a location for the bottom of the box by clicking the cursor at the desired location, which is (150, 250). The box will have a width of 50 and height of 50. Then, we determined the upper-left corner of the box by subtracting the height of the box from the bottom y value (250 − 50 = 200). So, the upper-left corner of the box will be located at (150, 200).

You can set the color using `graphicsObj.setColor(color)`. You can use any of the colors that have been predefined as constants in the `java.awt.Color` class, such as `Color.BLACK`, `Color.RED`, and `Color.GREEN`. The convention for constants in Java is to use all uppercase letters with an underscore between words, but Java also allows you to use lowercase names for color constants, such as `Color.black`. Figure 5.11 shows the output of Program 5.1, which adds a red box that is 50 pixels square.

Program 5.1: Adding a Box

```java
/**
 * Method to add a solid red rectangle to the current picture
 */
public void addBox()
{
  // get the graphics context from the picture
  Graphics g = this.getGraphics();
```

```
  // set the color to red
  g.setColor(Color.RED);

  // draw the box as a filled rectangle
  // upper left corner (150,200), height 50, width 50
  g.fillRect(150,200,50,50);
}
```

Making It Work Tip: Comments in Java

You may notice that there are some interesting characters in the addBox method. The /** and // are comments in Java. Comments were introduced in Chapter 3 in Alice. And, just like in Alice, we add comments to our Java programs to make them easier to read and understand. There are actually three kinds of comments in Java. The // starts a comment and tells the computer to ignore everything else till the end of the current line. You can use /* followed at some point by */ for a multi-line comment. The /** followed at some point by */ creates a JavaDoc comment. JavaDoc is a utility that pulls the JavaDoc comments from your class files and creates hyperlinked documentation from them. All of the Java class files written by Sun have JavaDoc comments in them, and that is how the Java API documentation was created.

You can execute the addBox() method using:

```
> String fileName = FileChooser.getMediaPath("beach-smaller.jpg");
> Picture p = new Picture(fileName);
> p.addBox();
> p.show();
```

Figure 5.11
A box washed up on the shore of the beach

Making It Work Tip: Saving Modified Pictures

When you change a picture in Java, you are not changing the original file from which the picture was read nor are you saving the picture that you have created. You can save the picture that you have created by using the `write()` method in the `Picture` class. Pass the `write()` method the full path name for the file, or use `FileChooser.getMediaPath(shortName)` to append the media directory to the short name.

Making It Work Tip: Setting the Media Directory

You can specify the directory that contains your media and use `FileChooser.getMediaPath (shortName)` to get the full path name for your picture and sound files. This will append the `shortName` to the media directory. You can set the directory using `FileChooser.pickMediaPath()`, which will allow you to pick the directory. You can also set the media directory using `FileChooser.setMediaPath(path)`. If you haven't set the media directory yet and you use `FileChooser.getMediaPath(shortName)`, it will ask you to pick the directory. The directory will stay defined until you change it. Once you have set the media directory, you can also just use the short name of the picture or sound file when you create a new `Picture` or `Sound` object, and it will automatically add the media directory to the short name.

```
> p.write("c:/intro-prog-java/mediasources/boxBeach.jpg");
> p.write(FileChooser.getMediaPath("boxBeach2.jpg"));
```

The `addBox()` method isn't very reusable. The only way to change it to work for other rectangles is to modify the color and rectangle information and then recompile. If we want this to work on any rectangle, then we will want to specify parameters to make the method more general. Program 5.2 shows a more reusable method for drawing a box.

Program 5.2: General Draw Box

```
/**
 * Method to draw a filled box on the current picture
 * @param color the color to draw the box with
 * @param topLeftX the top left x coordinate of the box
 * @param topLeftY the top left y coordinate of the box
 * @param width the width of the box
 * @param height the height of the box
 */
public void drawBox(Color color, int topLeftX, int topLeftY,
                    int width, int height)
{
  // get the graphics context for drawing
  Graphics g = this.getGraphics();

  // set the current color
  g.setColor(color);

  // draw the filled rectangle
  g.fillRect(topLeftX,topLeftY,width,height);
}
```

We could use this more general method to generate the same picture:

```
> Picture p =
  new Picture(FileChooser.getMediaPath("beach-smaller.jpg"));
> p.drawBox(java.awt.Color.RED,150,200,50,50);
> p.show();
```

The advantage of the method drawBox() over the method addBox() is that it can be used to draw any rectangle of any color on any picture. How would you find the top-left *x*, top-left *y*, width, and height to use on another picture? You can use the picture explorer.

How would you draw a simple face? You could draw an oval for the head. You could use filled ovals for the eyes. You could use arcs for the mouth and eyebrows. Program 5.3 shows one way to draw a face using drawing commands to create ovals and arcs. Figure 5.12 shows the results.

Program 5.3: An Example of Using Oval and Arc Drawing Commands

```
/**
 * Method to draw a face to demonstrate drawing
 * ovals and arcs
 */
public void drawFace()
{
  // get the graphics object to use for drawing
  Graphics graphics = this.getGraphics();

  // start with a black color
  graphics.setColor(Color.BLACK);

  // draw the oval for the face
  graphics.drawOval(130,50,380,380);

  // draw the ovals for the eyes
  graphics.fillOval(225,155,40,40);
  graphics.fillOval(375,155,40,40);

  // draw the arcs for the eyebrows
  graphics.drawArc(225,145,40,40,45,90);
  graphics.drawArc(375,145,40,40,45,90);

  // draw the arc for the mouth
  graphics.drawArc(190,85,255,255,-45,-90);
}
```

To try this, create a picture from the blank 640 by 480 file. Then invoke the method drawFace() on the picture.

```
> Picture p =
          new Picture(FileChooser.getMediaPath("640x480.jpg"));
> p.drawFace();
> p.show();
```

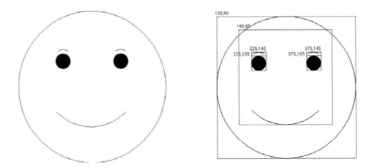

Figure 5.12
A drawn face (left) and the face with enclosing rectangles (right)

Making It Work Tip: Drawing Ovals and Arcs

Notice that to draw an oval or arc, you give the upper-left corner of the enclosing rectangle, not the upper-left corner of the oval or arc. The rectangles in the right half of Figure 5.12 show the starting points for the curves of the face, eyes, and smile. Arcs specify the starting angle but not the ending angle. The ending angle is the starting angle added to the arc angle. Graph paper and a protractor can help you plan your drawing.

5.2.2 Drawing Text (Strings)

In order to add text to an image, we can use the `java.awt.Graphics` method `drawString(String str, int x, int y)`. This will draw the passed string at the passed x and y position. However, the x and y values are not the top-left corner as is usual with the drawing methods. The x and y values give the leftmost starting point of the baseline of the string, which is the line on which you would write the string if you were using lined paper. Figure 5.13 shows font information including the baseline.

When you use the `drawString` method, the string will be drawn in the current color and **font**. The font specifies what the characters in the string will look like, what style will be used (bold, italic, plain), and how big the characters will be. You have

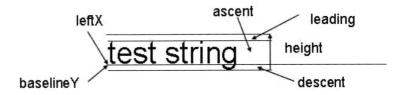

Figure 5.13
Font positioning information, including the baseline

seen that you can set the color using `setColor(Color colorObj)`. You can also set the font using `setFont(Font fontObj)`.

Making It Work Tip: Using `import` Statements

Both `Color` and `Font` are in the `java.awt` package, and so you must either use the full name of the class (`java.awt.Color` and `java.awt.Font`) or use an `import` statement. An **import statement** tells Java what package to look in for the class names you are using and allows you to use just the class name instead of the full name in your code. If you look at the `Picture` class, you will see `import` statements at the top of the file. But, when you use DrJava's Interactions pane, you will have to import classes before you can use the short name. You can use an `import` statement in one of two ways.

```
> import package.name.Class;
```

This will import just the named class. Or you can import all the classes in a package by using

```
> import package.name.*;
```

To create a Font object, specify the font name, style, and size: new `Font(String name, int style, int size)`. You can always use Dialog, DialogInput, Monospaced, Serif, or SansSerif for font names. You can get a list of all the available font names using

```
> import java.awt.*;
> GraphicsEnvironment env =
    GraphicsEnvironment.getLocalGraphicsEnvironment();
> String[] nameArray = env.getAvailableFontFamilyNames();
> for (int i=0; i < nameArray.length; i++)
    System.out.println(nameArray[i]);
```

Program 5.4 shows the `drawString()` method which can be used to draw a passed string on the current picture at the passed *x* and *y* baseline location.

Program 5.4: Drawing a String on a Picture

```
/**
 * Method to draw a string on the current picture
 * @param text the string to draw
 * @x the x location to start at
 * @y the y location of the baseline
 */
public void drawString(String text, int x, int y)
{
  // get the graphics object
  Graphics g = this.getGraphics();

  // set the color
  g.setColor(Color.BLACK);
```

```
    // set the font
    g.setFont(new Font("Arial",Font.BOLD,24));

    // draw the string
    g.drawString(text,x,y);
}
```

To use this program, you can use the picture explorer to determine where you want the baseline of the string to be and then use the `drawString()` method to draw the string on the picture. Barb's son, Matthew, took a picture of a kitten he saw while on a trip to Greece. Let's add a string that explains the picture near the bottom of the picture. Figure 5.14 shows the labeled picture.

```
> Picture p =
      new Picture(FileChooser.getMediaPath("kitten.jpg"));
> p.explore();
> p.drawString("Matt's picture of a kitten in Greece",67,283);
> p.explore();
```

The string isn't quite in the center of the picture. What if we want it to be in the center, as it is in Figure 5.15? How could we calculate the starting *x* position for the string such that the resulting string is centered? We know that the center of the picture horizontally is at half the width of the picture (`picture.getWidth() / 2`). If we subtract half the length of the string in pixels from the center of the picture, then the string would be centered. How do we calculate the length of the string in pixels? The length of the string depends on the number of characters in the string but also on the font used to draw the string.

To get information about the length of the string in the number of pixels drawn, we can use the `FontMetrics` class which is in package `java.awt`. To get a `FontMetrics` object, use `g.getFontMetrics()` where g is a `Graphics` object. The `FontMetrics` class contains methods for getting information about the display of a font. For example, we can get

Figure 5.14
Drawing a string on a picture

Matt's picture of a kitten in Greece

Figure 5.15
Drawing a string centered on a picture

the length in pixels of a string using the method `stringWidth(String str)`. We could get the height in pixels of a string drawn in the current font using the method `getHeight()`. We could get the length of the descent (part of a character like 'p' below the baseline) using `getDescent()`. Program 5.5 offers a method for centering a text string.

Program 5.5: Drawing a String Centered Horizontally on a Picture

```
/**
 * Method to draw a horizontally centered string
 * on the current picture
 * @param text the string to draw
 * @y the y location of the baseline
 */
public void drawHorizontalCenteredString(String text,
                                         int y)
{
  // get the graphics object
  Graphics g = this.getGraphics();

  // create the font object
  Font font = new Font("Arial",Font.BOLD,24);

  // set the color
  g.setColor(Color.BLACK);

  // set the font
  g.setFont(font);

  // get the font metrics
  FontMetrics fontMetrics = g.getFontMetrics();

  // get the width of the string
  int strWidth = fontMetrics.stringWidth(text);
```

```
        // calculate the center of the picture
        int center = (int) (this.getWidth() * 0.5);

        // draw the string centered in x
        g.drawString(text,
                     center - (strWidth / 2),
                     y);
    }
```

5.3   Using Graphics2D for Advanced Drawing

We have used the `java.awt.Graphics` object to draw simple shapes like lines, rectangles, ovals, arcs, and polygons. The `Graphics` object is like a painter who picks up a brush with the color you set and paints a shape with it. If you ask the painter to paint another shape over a previous one, the new shape will cover the original shape. But, what if we want to use a thicker "brush" when we draw? What if we want to treat our shapes as objects?

The `java.awt.Graphics` class is okay for simple drawing but lacks many advanced features. However, the class `java.awt.Graphics2D`, which is part of the Java 2D API, can be used for more advanced drawing. Some of the capabilities of a `Graphics2D` object are:

- You can set the width of the brush (pen). You can also set the style of the brush to make different types of dashed lines.
- You can rotate, translate, scale, or shear what you are drawing.
- You can fill a shape with more than just a solid color. You can fill a shape with a gradient or a texture.
- You can clip objects so that only the part visible inside the clipping area is drawn. This is like using a stencil.

5.3.1 Setting the Brush Width

To use these advanced features, you will need a `Graphics2D` object. To get a `Graphics2D` object, you must cast the `Graphics` object to a `Graphics2D` object using

`Graphics2D g2 = (Graphics2D) graphics`

To **cast** an object from one type to another means to change the type, like casting clay into a new form. You put the cast type inside parentheses in front of the value or variable to be cast. In Java, you can cast an object into another type if they are related via inheritance. You can **upcast**, which is changing the type to one of the classes the current class inherits from (like `Turtle` inherits from `SimpleTurtle`). You can also **downcast**, as in Figure 5.16, which means changing the type from one that is higher in the inheritance hierarchy to one that is lower in the inheritance hierarchy.

When one class inherits from another, the class that is doing the inheriting is called a **child class**, **subclass**, or **derived class**, while the class that it is inheriting from is

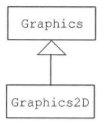

Figure 5.16
Showing the inheritance relationship between Graphics and Graphics2D

called the **parent class**, **superclass**, or **base class**. The class Graphics is the parent
class of the class Graphics2D. All Graphics objects are really Graphics2D objects
that have been upcast, so casting to Graphics2D is downcasting to the actual class.
Why do we need to do this casting? We know that an object keeps a reference to the
class that created it and thus knows what type it is. But the compiler doesn't know
what the type of a class truly is, so casting tells the compiler to change the type it is
using for an object when looking up methods and fields.

Now that you have a Graphics2D object (by casting a Graphics object), you can
set its brush options using setStroke(). Also, you can set the color, gradient, or texture to use for painting with the method setPaint(Paint p). Instead of methods that
draw shapes, the Graphics2D class has you create objects and either draw() them to
draw the outline or fill() them to fill with the current paint information. Program
5.6 is a simple program that draws a red "X" on the current picture using a brush
(stroke) with the specified width.

Program 5.6: Drawing an X on a Picture

```
/**
 * Method to add two crossed lines to a picture.
 * One line will go from the top left corner to the
 * bottom right corner. The other will go from the
 * bottom left corner to the top right corner.
 */
public void drawWideX(Color color, float width)
{
  // get the Graphics2D object
  Graphics graphics = this.getGraphics();
  Graphics2D g2 = (Graphics2D) graphics;

  // set the color and brush width
  g2.setPaint(color);
  g2.setStroke(new BasicStroke(width));

  // get the max x and y values
  int maxX = this.getWidth() - 1;
  int maxY = this.getHeight() - 1;
```

```
    // draw the lines
    g2.draw(new Line2D.Double(0,0,maxX,maxY));
    g2.draw(new Line2D.Double(0,maxY,maxX,0));
  }
```

You can use this program to add a wide red "X" to a picture, as shown in Figure 5.17.

```
> String fileName = FileChooser.getMediaPath("grayMotorcycle.jpg");
> Picture p = new Picture(fileName);
> p.drawWideX(java.awt.Color.RED,5);
> p.show();
```

Making It Work Tip: Creating and Drawing Shapes with Graphics2D

In Program 5.6, you may have noticed that we created a Line2D.Double object and then asked the Graphics2D object named g2 to draw this object. This is different from how we drew shapes using the Graphics class. With the Graphics2D class, you first create geometric objects and then either draw or fill them.

The Line2D.Double probably looks strange to you. This is actually the name of a class in the java.awt.geom package. Even though java.awt.geom and java.awt both start the same, they are different packages. If you imported all classes in the package java.awt using the wildcard *, you still wouldn't have imported the classes in the java.awt.geom package. You need at least two import statements if you are using classes from both of these packages.

5.3.2 Drawing with a GradientPaint Object

Instead of just filling with a solid color, you can fill with a blend of two colors (a **gradient**). You have to specify the two colors and the rectangular area where they transition from one color to another in the coordinates of the shapes you are drawing.

Figure 5.17
Drawing a red X on a picture

What if you want to add a sun that changes color from yellow at the top to red at the bottom to a picture? You can create a `java.awt.GradientPaint` object and set that change to be the paint using the method `setPaint(Paint p)`. A `GradientPaint` object is a kind of `Paint` object, because the class `GradientPaint` implements the `Paint` **interface**.

5.3.3 Interfaces

What is an interface? An **interface** is a boundary between two things. You use a user interface to communicate with the computer. You may be familiar with the USB interface. It allows several different types of devices to communicate with a computer. You can hook up a mouse, a camera, or a disk drive, and the computer will know how to communicate with the device because each uses the same interface. In Java, an interface is a special kind of class that only has **abstract methods** (methods that have just a method declaration but no code in the method's body) and perhaps some constants defined in it.

For example, Java provides an interface class named `java.lang.Comparable`. Other Java classes may implement the `Comparable` interface (actually define the methods declared in `Comparable`) to provide an abstraction for comparing objects of that class. The `String` class is a Java class that implements the `java.lang.Comparable` interface. You can compare two strings and find out if one is less than, equal to, or greater than another, because the `String` class provides the code for the `compareTo(Object o)` method. The `compareTo()` method returns an integer less than 0 if the string the method was invoked on is less than the passed string, an integer equal to 0 if the strings contain the same characters, and an integer greater than 0 if the string the method was invoked on is greater than the passed string. It compares the characters in the strings alphabetically. Take a look at the `java.lang.Comparable` interface for an example of an interface. Also, see `java.lang.String` for an example of a class implementing an interface.

```
> "bug".compareTo("apple")
1
```

Even though a class can only inherit from one parent class, a class can implement many interfaces. An object of a class that implements an interface is said to be of the interface type. So even though the class `GradientPaint` inherits from `java.lang.Object`, it implements the interface `java.awt.Paint`. So objects of `GradientPaint` can be passed to methods that expect objects of the type `Paint`. The classes `Color` and `TexturePaint` also implement the `Paint` interface, which is why they also can be passed to the method `setPaint(Paint p)`. Program 5.7 offers a specific example of how to use `GradientPaint` with an existing picture.

Program 5.7: Using a GradientPaint Object

```
/**
 * Method to add a gradient painted sun to the current picture
 * @param x the x location for the upper left corner of the
 * rectangle enclosing the sun
 * @param y the y location for the upper left corner of the
```

```
 * rectangle enclosing the sun
 * @param width the width of the enclosing rectangle
 * @param height the height of the enclosing rectangle
 */
public void drawSun(int x, int y, int width, int height)
{
  // get the graphics2D object for this picture
  Graphics g = this.getGraphics();
  Graphics2D g2 = (Graphics2D) g;

  // create the gradient for painting from yellow to red with
  // yellow at the top of the sun and red at the bottom
  float xMid = (float) (width / 0.5 + x);
  GradientPaint gPaint = new GradientPaint(xMid, y,
                                           Color.YELLOW,
                                           xMid, y + height,
                                           Color.RED);

  // set the gradient and draw the ellipse
  g2.setPaint(gPaint);
  g2.fill(new Ellipse2D.Double(x,y,width,height));
}
```

Figure 5.18 shows what happens when you use this program to add a sun to the beach.

```
> Picture p = new Picture(FileChooser.getMediaPath("beach.jpg"));
> p.drawSun(201,80,40,40);
> p.show();
```

Figure 5.18
A beach with a sun that is filled with a gradient from yellow to red

Figure 5.19
Clipping a picture using an ellipse

5.3.4 Clipping

You can create a shape and then use that shape as a stencil to limit what is shown when you draw other shapes or images. Only the area inside of the stencil will be seen. This is called **clipping**.

Let's create a stencil from an ellipse and then draw the beach using that stencil to clip the image of the beach. The only part of the beach that will be visible is the part inside the ellipse. Program 5.8 shows the method and Figure 5.19 shows the result.

Program 5.8: Clip an Image to an Ellipse

```
/**
 * Method to clip the picture to an ellipse
 * @return a new picture with the image clipped
 * to an ellipse
 */
public Picture clipToEllipse()
{
  int width = this.getWidth();
  int height = this.getHeight();
  Picture result = new Picture(width,height);

  // get the graphics2D object for this picture
  Graphics g = result.getGraphics();
  Graphics2D g2 = (Graphics2D) g;

  // create an ellipse to use for clipping
  Ellipse2D.Double ellipse =
      new Ellipse2D.Double(0,0,width,height);
```

```
// use the ellipse for clipping
g2.setClip(ellipse);

// draw the image
g2.drawImage(this.getImage(),0,0,width,
            height,null);

// return the result
return result;
}
```

To use this program try the following:

```
> Picture p = new Picture(FileChooser.getMediaPath("beach.jpg"));
> Picture p2 = p.clipToEllipse();
> p2.show();
```

5.4   Using Media Computation with Alice

Now that you know how to draw on digital pictures, you can use these drawing
techniques on pictures that you create in Alice. To take a picture in Alice, click the
Play button in the upper-left corner of the Alice window, and then click on
the **Pause** button to stop your animation. Click the **Take Picture** button to capture
and save a picture. Figure 5.20 shows the window that will appear telling you what
your picture is named and where it is being saved. You can rename the picture, move
it to your media directory, and then use the techniques you learned in this chapter to
draw on it.

You can use any of the drawing methods that we covered in this chapter on a picture
from Alice. Figure 5.21 shows what happens when you add a red scarf and your name
to picture with an Alice snowman.

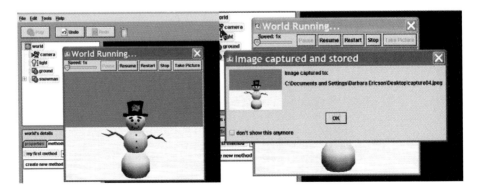

Figure 5.20
Saving a picture from an Alice animation

Figure 5.21
Drawing on a picture from Alice

Another way that you can apply what you have just learned is to modify pictures in Java and then use those pictures in Alice. To insert 2D pictures in an Alice world, click on File in the main menu and then select *Make Billboard* as shown in Figure 5.22. Then position your 2D picture in the Alice world. See Appendix A, Section 1, for instructions on using billboards in Alice.

You can also import pictures into Alice and then use them as the skin texture property for objects. For instance, Figure 5.23 shows what happens when you create a small picture (10 by 10) and draw a texture or gradient on it. Then, in Alice, select this picture as the ground object's texture map. See Appendix A, Section 8, for instructions on using texture maps.

5.5   Concepts Summary

In this chapter, we discussed packages using predefined Java classes, inheritance, and interfaces.

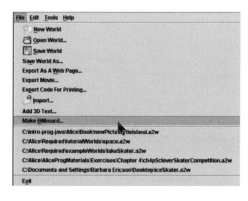

Figure 5.22
Making billboards from pictures

Figure 5.23
Using a `gradientPaint` object for the ground texture in Alice

5.5.1 Packages

A package is a group of related classes. Classes that are basic to the Java language, like the `System` class, are in the `java.lang` package. Classes that are used for graphics, like the `Color` class, are in the `java.awt` package. Classes that are used for input and output, like the `File` class, are in the `java.io` package.

The full name for a class is *packageName.ClassName*. You don't have to use the full name for any class in the package `java.lang`. You don't have to use the full name for classes in packages other than `java.lang` if you use an import statement. You can import a class by using the keyword `import` and then the full name of the class.

```
> import java.awt.Color;
```

You can also import all classes in a package.

```
> import java.awt.*;
```

When you use classes in packages other than `java.lang` in methods, you will either need to use the full class name or add import statements before the class definition.

```
import java.awt.*;
import java.awt.font.*;
import java.awt.geom.*;
import java.text.*;
/**
 * A class that represents a picture. This class inherits from
 * SimplePicture and allows the student to add functionality to
 * the Picture class.
 *
 * Copyright Georgia Institute of Technology 2004
 * @author Barbara Ericson ericson@cc.gatech.edu
 */
public class Picture extends SimplePicture
```

5.5.2 Predefined Java Classes

There is a large number of predefined classes in Java. The API contains the documentation for all the classes in a version of Java. The documentation tells you important information about each class, such as what methods it has. The documentation is organized by packages. There are classes for doing graphical user interfaces (in packages `javax.swing` and `java.awt`). There are classes for doing input and output (in package `java.io`). There are classes for doing work with databases (in package `java.sql`). There are classes for doing work with sound (in package `javax.sound`). There are classes for working with lists, sets, and maps (`java.util`).

It is easier and faster to build on what exists rather than write your own classes. Even if what you need isn't part of Java, someone else may have written something similar.

5.5.3 Inheritance

When one class inherits from another, it gets all the data (fields) and behavior (methods) from that class. This means that if `Graphics2D` inherits from `Graphics`, it understands the same public messages as `Graphics`. The API for a class shows what class it inherits from as well as all methods that are inherited and what class they are inherited from. The class that is being inherited from is called the superclass or parent class. The class that is inheriting is called the subclass or child class.

5.5.4 Interfaces

A Java class can inherit from only one class, but it can implement several interfaces. An interface defines how classes will communicate without worrying about what types they actually are. An object of a class that implements an interface can be declared with the interface name as the type. So if a `GradientPaint` object implements the `Paint` *interface* it can be passed as a parameter to methods that take objects of the type `Paint`. The API for a class shows what interfaces it implements.

5.6   Objects and Methods Summary

In this chapter we have talked about several kinds of objects.

`BasicStroke`	`java.awt`	An object that knows how to draw the outlines of shapes in different widths, with different kinds of joins between lines, and possibly using dashes.
`Ellipse2D.Double`	`java.awt.geom`	An object that represents an ellipse with coordinates that can be of the type `double`.
`Graphics`	`java.awt`	An object that knows how to draw or fill simple shapes.
`Graphics2D`	`java.awt`	An object that can handle more complicated drawing.
`Line2D.Double`	`java.awt.geom`	An object that represents a line with coordinates that can be of the type `double`.

5.6.1 Picture Methods

getGraphics()	Returns a Graphics object that can be used to draw on the current picture.
getImage()	Returns an Image object that can be used by drawImage methods in Graphics or Graphics2D.

5.6.2 Graphics Methods

drawArc(int x1, int y1, int w, int h, int startAngle, int arcAngle)	Draws the outline of an arc which is part of an oval that fits in an enclosing rectangle with an upper-left corner at ($x1$, $y1$), a width of w, and a height of h. The arc will start at the given startAngle and end at startAngle+arcAngle.
drawImage(Image image, int x, int y, ImageObserver observer)	Draws the passed image with the top-left corner at (x, y). The observer is the object to be notified as more of the image is drawn.
drawLine(int x1, int y1, int x2, int y2)	Draws a line from position ($x1$, $y1$) to ($x2$, $y2$).
drawOval(int x1, int y1, int w, int h)	Draws the outline of an oval that fits in an enclosing rectangle with an upper-left corner at ($x1$, $y1$), a width of w, and a height of h.
drawPolygon(int[] xArray, int[] yArray, int numPoints)	Draws the outline of a closed polygon with the points of the polygon given in the x and y arrays.
drawRect(int x1, int y1, int w, int h)	Draws the outline of a rectangle with the upper-left corner at ($x1$, $y1$), a width of w, and a height of h.
fillArc(int x1, int y1, int w, int h, int startAngle,int arcAngle)	Draws a filled arc which is part of an oval that fits in an enclosing rectangle with an upper-left corner at ($x1$, $y1$), a width of w, and a height of h. The arc will start at the given startAngle and end at startAngle+arcAngle.
fillOval(int x1, int y1, int w, int h)	Draws a filled oval that fits in an enclosing rectangle with an upper-left corner at ($x1$, $y1$), a width of w, and a height of h.
fillPolygon(int[] xArray, int[] yArray, int numPoints)	Draws a filled closed polygon with the points of the polygon given in the x and y arrays.
fillRect(int x1, int y1, int w, int h)	Draws a rectangle filled with the current color with an upper-left corner at ($x1$, $y1$), a width of w, and a height of h.
setClip(Shape clip)	Sets the shape to use as a stencil to limit what is shown.
setColor(Color colorObj)	Sets the color to draw with.
setFont(Font fontObj)	Sets the font to use for drawing strings.

5.6.3 Graphics2D Methods

draw(Object obj)	Draws the outline of the passed object.
getFontRenderContext()	Returns a FontRenderContext object that contains rendering hints and device information, such as the dots-per-inch.
fill(Object obj)	Draws the passed object filled with the current paint type.
setPaint(Paint paint)	Sets the color, gradient, or texture to use when painting.
setStroke(Stroke s)	Sets the brush (pen) to the one defined by the passed Stroke object.

Exercises

1. Define each of the following:
   - A constant
   - A package
   - Inheritance
   - An interface
   - A superclass
   - A primitive variable
   - An object variable
   - A subclass

2. Use the Java API to answer the following questions:
   - What method of the String class would help you check if a string ends with a certain sequence of characters?
   - What method of the String class would tell you the first position of a character in a String object?
   - What method of the String class would tell you the last position of a character in a String object?
   - What method of the String class removes extra spaces before and after the other characters?

3. Use the Java API to answer the following questions:
   - What methods of the String class are inherited?
   - What class does the String class inherit from?
   - What class does the Math class in package java.lang inherit from?
   - What class does the Integer class in package java.lang inherit from?
   - What interfaces are in the package java.lang?
   - Which classes implement the Comparable interface?
   - What interfaces does the String class implement?

4. Using the drawing tools presented in this chapter, draw a house—just go for the simple child's house with one door, two windows, walls, and a roof.

5. Create a method that will add a cartoon-style word balloon to your picture.

6. Use thick black lines to draw a picture frame around a picture and then add it to Alice as a billboard.

7. What is the decimal value for the binary number 1101? What is the decimal value for the octal value 23? What is the hexadecimal value for 1E3?

8. Draw a scarf on a snowman from Alice.

9. Create a new small picture using new `Picture(10,10)` and draw on this new blank picture using a `gradientPaint`. Write out the picture using `pictureObj.write(`"*fullName*`.jpg`"). Then import the picture into Alice by clicking **File** and then **Import**. Then select the ground in the Object tree and click on the **Properties** tab. Change the skin texture for the ground to the imported `gradientPaint` picture.

10. Modify the method `drawFace` to take the width and height of the desired face and calculate the positions based on the desired width and height.

11. Draw glasses on a picture of a person who doesn't normally wear glasses or on an Alice character.

12. Draw a hat on someone in a picture.

13. Draw a weight over someone in a picture.

14. Draw a string on a picture at the top of the picture and centered horizontally. You will need to use the `FontMetrics` class to get the height of the string in pixels in order to determine where the baseline should be so that the string is visible. You should also subtract the descent from the height.

15. Create another method that takes the text, x, y, font, and color to use when you draw a string. Rewrite the old `drawString()` method to call this new method.

16. Create a method that draws an "X" across the current picture using dashed lines.

17. Create a method that draws bars across the current picture using thick lines.

18. Write a method to clip an image to a triangle or star shape.

19. Create a movie poster for an Alice movie.

20. Add fire to an Alice picture using `gradientPaint`.

6 Functions and Conditionals

Goals of this chapter:

- To define a function as a block of program code that allows you to check certain conditions within a world while an animation is running.
- To compare a function to a method.
- To illustrate the use of a built-in function.
- To illustrate how to write your own function to compute and return a value.
- To use a conditional `if-else` statement as a block of program code that allows for the conditional execution of that code.
- To demonstrate that if the Boolean condition evaluates to `true`, the `if` part of the statement is executed and if the expression evaluates to `false`, the `else` part is executed.
- To illustrate a Boolean condition that invokes a built-in function.
- To illustrate using relational operators (<, >, >=, <=, ==, !=) in a Boolean expression.
- To show how to write your own function that returns a Boolean value and can be used in *If* statements.

Introduction

Before starting on this chapter, you may find it helpful to take a look back at what you have accomplished with Alice and Java. In the first three chapters of this book, you explored how to use the Alice programming environment to create objects from 3D models (prewritten classes) and designed Alice movie storyboards using the objects in a virtual world. You translated your first storyboard into actual program code using the drag-and-drop interface. Then, you used Alice to explore writing methods and using parameters to pass information into a method. Using Alice in the early stages of learning to program allowed you to concentrate on the concepts of design, classes, objects, and program construction using methods and parameters without having to deal with syntax errors that often plague beginning programmers.

After learning the fundamental concepts with Alice, you turned to exploring the same concepts in a textual programming environment where the syntax was under your control. Once again, you created objects, invoked methods on those objects, and created new methods for objects of a class. You were able to apply the concepts learned in Alice to your work with Java in the context of *turtle*-graphics and 2D drawings. This approach (learning the fundamental concepts in Alice and then applying those same concepts in the context of Media Computation using Java) is advantageous, because it helps you learn complex concepts in a meaningful context.

This Alice-to-Java approach will be used again in this and the next two chapters of this textbook. First, Alice will be used to introduce the fundamental concepts of functions, conditionals, and repetition. Later, these same concepts will be explored in Java using Media Computation.

In this chapter, we present the use of functions and explain how to write your own functions. A **function** is a named group of statements that computes and returns a value. One way of thinking about a function is to say that a function is a special kind of method. Like a method, it is a named group of statements that are executed when the function is invoked. A function is different from a method, however, in that it computes and returns a value when it is invoked. Why do we need functions? We need functions to get information about objects while the program is running (at runtime).

Also, in this chapter, we use conditional *if-else* statements to make decisions about whether (or not) to invoke a method. We will write our own Boolean function (which returns *true* or *false*) to be used as part of an execution control mechanism. In your Alice programs, you will use decisions to make animations execute in different ways depending on a condition, such as whether an object is visible or where an object is located.

6.1   Functions

Functions allow you to check certain conditions within a world while an animation is running. A function is similar to a method in that it is a collection of statements and (like a method) is invoked. In Alice, the purpose of a method is to perform an animation, but that of a function is to return a value. What difference does this make? Well, an animation performed by a method moves, turns, or performs some other action with objects in the world. We call this **changing the state** of the world. In an Alice function, however, objects do not move, turn, or perform some other action. So, functions leave the state of the world unchanged. Mathematicians say these are pure functions.

In writing program code, we often need some information about the objects in the world or information about the world itself. The most commonly used object data are the properties (such as *color* and *opacity*) that are listed in a properties list for the object. To get information about other properties (for example, *height* or *width*) we use a function to ask a question. The value returned by a function can be a number, an object, a Boolean (*true* or *false*), or some other type.

A function may receive values sent in as arguments (input), perform some computation on the values, and return (send back) a value as output. In some cases, no input is needed, but often values are sent in as arguments to the function parameters. The diagram in Figure 6.1 outlines the overall mechanism. An analogy of how a function works is that it is something like an ATM machine. You enter your bankcard and password as input and click on the button, indicating you would like to see your balance (another input). The ATM looks up your account information and then tells you your current balance (as output).

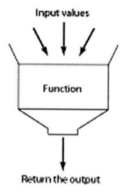

Figure 6.1
Overview of how a function works

6.1.1 Abstraction

As with object methods, one important benefit of a function is that it allows us to think about the overall process rather than all the nitty-gritty little details. When we use an ATM, for example, we think about getting the balance in our account—not about all the operations that are going on inside the machine. In the same way, we can call a function in our program to perform all the small actions, while we just think about what answer we are going to get. Like methods, functions are an example of abstraction—collecting lots of small steps into one meaningful idea to allow us to think on a higher plane.

6.1.2 Using a Built-in Function in a Method

Alice provides built-in functions that can be used to provide information for statements in a method. As an example, consider the world shown in Figure 6.2. In setting up this world, we put the *toyball* (Sports) on the ground next to a net (Sports) and then move it 1 meter away from the net (so we know the ball is exactly 1 meter from the net).

Figure 6.2
A world containing a *toyball* and a *tennisNet*

We want to bounce the ball over the tennis net. Do not be deceived. This is not as easy as it seems. The ball should move up and forward and then down and forward. But we cannot easily tell just by looking at the ball what its orientation is. That is, we don't know "which way is up" in terms of the ball's sense of direction.

Actually, we are thinking about the ball's up and down motion relative to the ground, so we need to align the ball's sense of direction with the ground. Orientation is done by using an *orientTo* method, as shown in Figure 6.3.

Having properly set up the initial scene, we can write a method to bounce the ball over the net. Since two objects are involved in this action, we will write a method named *ballOverNet*.

A textual storyboard would look like this:

```
ballOverNet
DoInOrder
  toyball turn to face the net
  DoTogether
    toyball move up
    toyball move forward
  DoTogether
    toyball move down
    toyball move forward
```

We know how far to move the ball forward, because we set up the world with the ball exactly 1 meter from the net. We do not know how far up to move the ball to clear the net. We can use a built-in function for the *tennisNet* to determine its height and then use that as the distance the ball moves up (and then back down). We don't have to

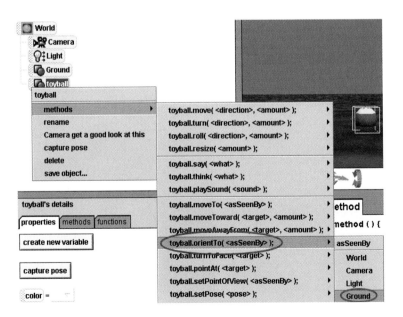

Figure 6.3
Using an *orientTo* method to orient the ball with the ground

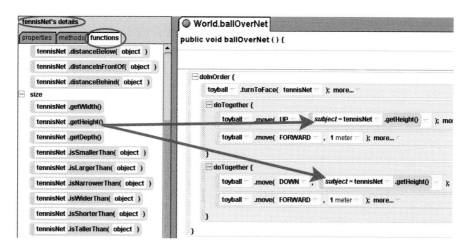

Figure 6.4
Dragging the built-in *getHeight* function into a method

think about what Alice is doing to figure out the height of the tennis net. We can just call the function and get the height. This is a two-step process:

1) Drag the *toyball's*, move tile into the editor and select 1 as a default distance.
2) Drag the *tennisNet*'s *getHeight* function tile on top of the 1.

Figure 6.4 illustrates dragging the *tennisNet*'s *getHeight* function onto the move up and move down statements.

6.1.3 The Need to Write Your Own Function

Sometimes when you want to invoke a function, none of the built-in functions will work for what you want to do. This is when you need to write your own function. It is helpful to illustrate with a simple example. Let's simulate rolling the ball forward. Once again, this is more challenging than it looks. Think about how the ball can be made to roll along the ground. The ball should appear to roll along the ground, not just glide along it. (A gliding motion is fine for an ice skater, but a ball should roll.) An obvious solution would be to use a simple *turn* statement.

Surprise—the *turn* statement simply rotates the ball in place! (It spins the ball around, but the ball does not move along the ground.) To actually roll, the ball must turn and also move in the same direction. A textual storyboard for a method to simulate a rolling action (*realisticRoll*) would be:

```
realisticRoll
  doTogether
  move ball forward 1 meter
turn ball forward 1 revolution
```

With this in mind, we can write an object method named *realisticRoll*, as in Figure 6.5.

public void realisticRoll ( ) {

```
doTogether {
    toyball  .move( FORWARD  ,  1 meter  ); more...
    toyball  .turn( FORWARD  ,  1 revolution  ); more...
}
```

Figure 6.5
The *move* and *turn* statements in a *doTogether*

Our testing of this code, however, is disappointing. The effect of moving and turning the ball at the same time is that the ball ends up at the same place it started. (The turning action prevents the ball from moving forward.)

Why is this? Well, the ball is moving relative to itself, not relative to the ground. A solution to this problem is to use *asSeenBy = ground* in the *move* statement. The code in Figure 6.6 moves and turns the ball forward 1 meter, simulating a real-life ball rolling on the ground.

We guessed that one revolution would look realistic. But when it is run, it is not quite right. We must now think about how many revolutions the ball needs to turn in covering a given distance in a forward direction. This presents a challenge, because the number of times the ball needs to turn is proportional to the ball's diameter. To cover the same forward distance, a small ball turns more times than a larger ball. In Figure 6.7, the larger ball covers the same distance in one revolution as the smaller ball covers in four revolutions.

Of course, the number of revolutions needed for the ball to roll, say, 10 meters could be found by trial and error. But then every time the ball changes size, you would have to figure it out all over again and change the code. A better way is to compute the number of revolutions. Alice does not have a function for this, so we will write our own.

public void realisticRoll ( ) {

```
doTogether {
    toyball  .move( FORWARD  ,  1 meter  ); asSeenBy = Ground
    toyball  .turn( FORWARD  ,  1 revolution  ); more...
}
```

Figure 6.6
The *toyball* rolls along the ground

Figure 6.7
Distance covered by a revolution is proportional to diameter

6.1.4 Writing a New Function

Since we are concerned only with the ball rolling, and no other objects are involved, we can write an object function. (An object function allows you save out the ball as a new class and reuse the function in future worlds.) To write your own object function, select the object in the Object tree. In the functions tab, click the **create new function** button, as in Figure 6.8.

A popup **New Function** box (Figure 6.9) allows you to enter the name of the new function and select its return type. Your new function is categorized by the type of information it returns. The types of functions include *Number, Boolean, Object,* and *Other* (such as String, Color, and Sound). In this section, we will write functions that return *Number* values. Examples and exercises later in the chapter use functions that return other types of values.

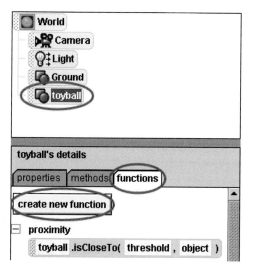

Figure 6.8
Creating a new function

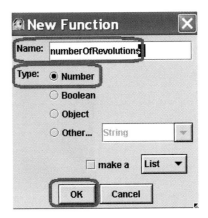

Figure 6.9
Enter a name and select a return type

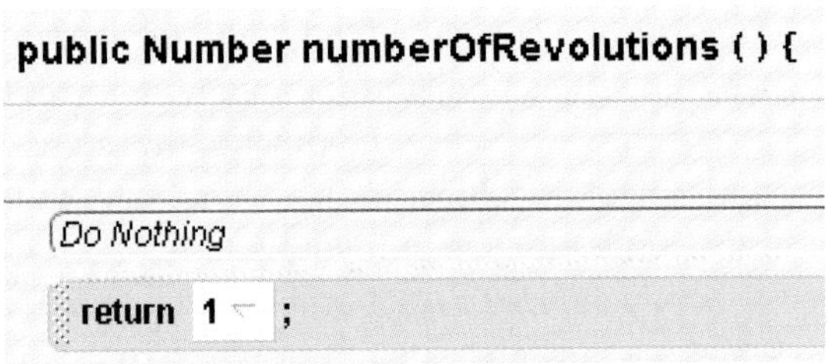

public Number numberOfRevolutions ( ) {

Do Nothing

return 1 ;

Figure 6.10
Editor panel for writing your own function

A click on the OK button creates an editor panel where you can write the code for the function, as shown in Figure 6.10.

6.1.5 The return Statement

Every function must have a *return* statement. The reason is that all functions return some information. When you first create a function, Alice automatically adds a *return* statement at the end, reminding you that your function must return some information. You cannot remove the *return* statement.

In our example, we want to ask the function: "How many revolutions does the ball have to make to move a given distance along the ground?" The number of revolutions depends on the distance traveled by the outside (circumference) of the ball in a single revolution, so we use the formula:

number of revolutions = distance / (diameter * π)

To use this formula, we need three pieces of information: the distance the ball is to roll, the diameter of the ball, and something named π. To provide this information,

- A parameter will be used to represent the distance the ball is to roll.
- The built-in function *toyball*'s *getWidth* will be invoked to get the diameter.

```
public Number numberOfRevolutions ( Number 123 distance ) {
```

```
Do Nothing
```

```
return   ( distance  /  ( 3.14  *  subject = toyball  .getWidth()  )  )  ;
```

Figure 6.11
The *toyBall.numberOfRevolutions* function

- The symbol π (also known as **pi**) is a constant value (does not change). Pi represents the ratio of the circumference of a circle to its diameter. We will use 3.14 as the constant value of pi.

The code shown in Figure 6.11 implements the function. The number of rotations is computed by dividing the distance the ball is to move (the *distance* parameter) by the product of the ball's diameter (*toyBall*'s *getWidth,* which is a built-in function) and pi (described above). The *Return* statement tells Alice to send back the computed answer.

The order of evaluation of the values in the function must be carefully arranged. Alice uses nested tiles and parentheses (one (inside) the other) to emphasize the order in which the values are evaluated. The innermost expression is computed first. In this example, *3.14* is multiplied by the *toyBall*'s width, and then that value is divided into the *distance*.

6.1.6 Invoking the Function

Now that the *toyBall* has a function named *numberOfRevolutions*, the function can be used to revise our *realisticRoll* method, as shown in Figure 6.12. An arbitrary distance of 10 meters is used for the *move* forward statement. The same value, 10 meters, is also used as the distance parameter for the *toyBall.numberOfRevolutions* function.

Although 10 meters was used as a test value in the previous example, we really should be testing our program by using lower distance values (for example, -2 and 0) and also with higher distance values (for example, 20). Using a range of values will reassure you that your program code works on many different values. One way to do this is to parameterize the *realisticRoll* method so it can be invoked with different test values, as illustrated in Figure 6.13.

```
public void realisticRoll ( ) {

  doTogether {
    toyball .move( FORWARD , 10 meters ); asSeenBy = Ground  duration = 3 seconds  more...
    toyball .turn( FORWARD , toyball.numberOfRevolutions( distance = 10 ) ); duration = 3 seconds
  }
}
```

Figure 6.12
Invoking the *numberOfRevolutions* function

Figure 6.13
A parameter for *rollDistance* allows testing with different distance values

6.2 Conditional Execution with `if-else` and Boolean Functions

We expect that you have written several methods as part of programs for exercises and projects in previous chapters. In some programs, you may want to control when a method gets invoked. You can do so with a program statement known as a control structure. You have been using control statements in Alice already. In methods, a *doInOrder* is a control structure used to make certain statements run sequentially and *doTogether* is a control structure used to make a block of statements run all at the same time. To control whether a block of statements is executed or a method is invoked, a conditional `if-else` statement is used. In this section, we look at the use of `if-else` statements in *Boolean* functions and how to make decisions about whether a method is or is not invoked.

As stated previously, an `if-else` is a control statement that makes a decision based on the value of a condition as a program is running. (For simplicity, we often refer to it as an **if statement** or just as a conditional statement.) Figure 6.14 illustrates the processing of an `if` statement. The statement checks to see whether a condition is *true*. If so, a block of code is executed. If the condition is *false*, a different block of code

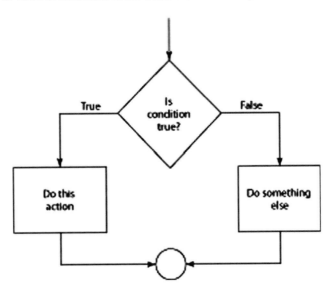

Figure 6.14
Describing the processing of a conditional `if-else` statement

is executed. One way to think about an *if* statement is that it provides a way of branching the program's execution through one of two possible paths.

6.2.1 Using a conditional *if-else* Statement in a Boolean Function

Execution control structures are a big part of game-type and simulation programs. The current conditions guide the actions of the objects in a game. In a basketball game, a method is invoked to increase a team's score only if the ball goes through the net. In a driver-training simulation, a method is invoked to move the car forward only if the car is still on the road.

As an example of using an *if* statement for conditional execution, consider the world shown in Figure 6.15. A *biplane* (Vehicle) and a *helicopter* (Vehicle) are flying in the same fly-space at approximately the same altitude near the *airport* (Buildings). One function of radar and software in the *control tower* (Buildings) is to check for possible collisions when two vehicles are in the same fly-space. If they are too close to one another, the flight controller can radio the pilots to change their flight paths.

First, let's write a function to check whether the *biplane* and *helicopter* are in danger of collision. The type of value the function will return is *Boolean*—*true* if the vertical distance between the two aircraft is less than some minimum distance, otherwise, *false*. Two parameters will be needed: the other aircraft object (*otherPlane*) and a minimum vertical distance (*minimumDistance*). A storyboard for *isTooClose* is

biplane.*isTooClose*

Parameters: *otherPlane, minimumDistance*
if the vertical distance to the other plane is less than
    minimumDistance
    return *true*
else
  return *false*

Figure 6.15
Fly-space collision danger

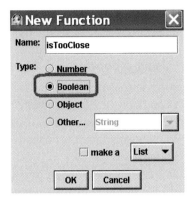

Figure 6.16
Creating a *Boolean* function

To translate the storyboard to program code, we create a new object function named *isTooClose*. (We have chosen to make this an object function for the biplane) The function should return *true* or *false*, so *Boolean* is selected as the type, as shown in Figure 6.16.

In the editor for the function, create the two parameters *otherPlane* (an object) and *minimumDistance* (a number). Then, drag an *if-else* tile into the editor, as in Figure 6.17. The condition selected from the popup menu for the *if* statement is *true*.

Although *true* was selected as the condition from the popup menu, it is acting as a placeholder. In this example the condition of the *if* statement should be "the vertical

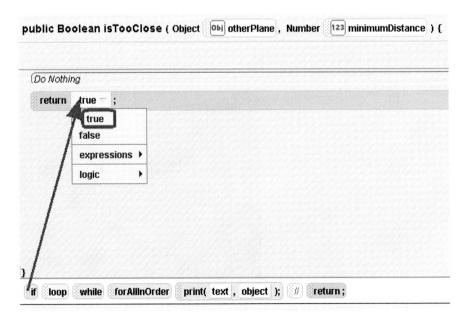

Figure 6.17
Dragging an *if* statement into a function and selecting *true* condition

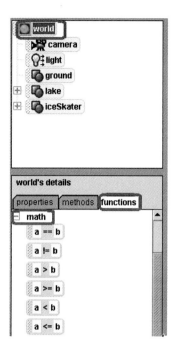

Figure 6.18
Relational operations in the built-in world functions

distance is less than the *minimumDistance*." To compare the vertical distance between the two aircraft to a minimum distance, we will use a built-in world-level function, the < (less than) operation. The < is one of six relational operators used in the World's built-in *math* functions, as shown in Figure 6.18.

A relational operator computes a *true* or *false* value based on the relationship between the two values. For example, == is "is equal to" and ! = is "is not equal to."

In this example, we want to check whether the distance between the two aircraft is less than a minimum distance. If this condition is *true*, the air traffic controller will tell the pilots to move the aircraft apart.

To create a conditional expression for the *if-else* statement, we drag a *less than* function $(a < b)$ from the world's functions into the editor and drop it on top of *true*, as in Figure 6.19. From the popup menu, we select 1 (for *a*) and *minimumDistance* (for *b*). (The vertical distance between the two aircraft is not an option in this popup menu as a choice for *a*, so we arbitrarily selected 1 as a placeholder. We will show you how to replace the 1 with the actual vertical distance in the next paragraph.)

We want to replace the placeholder (1) with the actual vertical distance between the two aircraft. Since we don't know whether the *helicopter* is above the *biplane* or the *biplane* is above the *helicopter*, we use an *absolute value* (abs) function. The absolute value of 4 is 4 and the absolute value of −4 is also 4. In other words, absolute value ignores a negative sign. To use absolute value, drag the *absolute value* function on top of the 1, as shown in Figure 6.20.

So we want to replace the value 1 with a *distanceAbove* function to determine the distance of the other plane above the biplane. Now the *biplane* is selected, and its

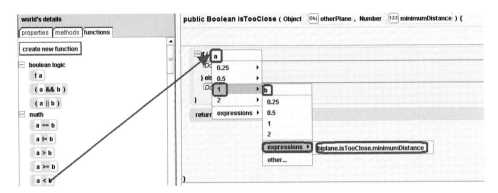

Figure 6.19
Creating a *less than* condition for an *if-else* statement

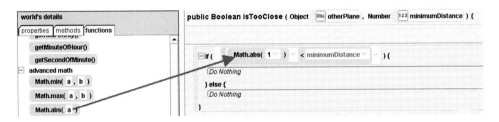

Figure 6.20
Drag the *absolute value* function on top of the 1

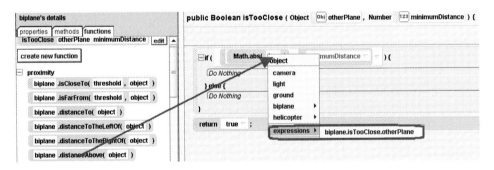

Figure 6.21
Creating an expression to compute the vertical distance

built-in *distanceAbove* method selected and dragged on top of the 1. Finally, the *otherPlane* parameter is selected, with the result as in Figure 6.21. The vertical distance can now be compared to *minimumDistance*. *return* statements and are dragged into the *if* and *else* parts of the *if-else* statement. If the vertical distance is less than *minimumDistance*, return *true*; otherwise return *false*. Figure 6.22 shows the completed *if-else* statement in the *isTooClose* function.

Once again, note that the nesting of tiles in a conditional expression creates an order of evaluation. First, Alice computes the *distanceAbove*, and then *absolute value* is applied to the result. For example, suppose the *biplane* is 500 meters above the ground,

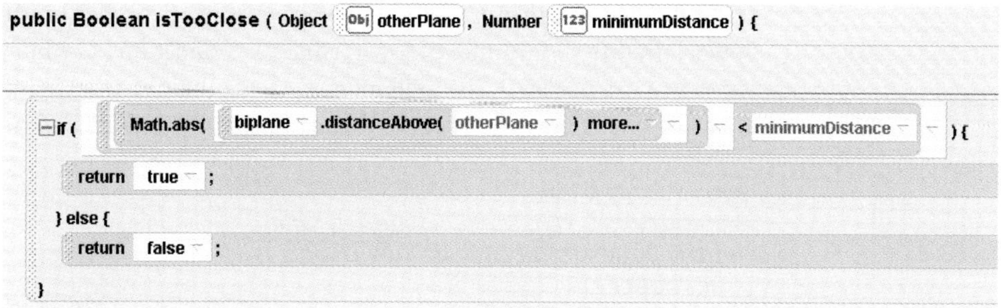

```
public Boolean isTooClose ( Object [Obj] otherPlane , Number [123] minimumDistance ) {

    ⊟if (   Math.abs(  biplane ⌄ .distanceAbove( otherPlane ⌄ ) more... ⌄  ) ⌄ < minimumDistance ⌄  ⌄ ){
        return   true ⌄ ;
    } else {
        return   false ⌄ ;
    }
}
```

Figure 6.22
The *isTooClose* function

and the other plane is 520 meters above the ground. Thus, the distance of the *biplane* above the *otherplane* is −20 meters (500 − 520). The absolute value of −20 is 20, so the vertical distance between the two aircraft is 20 meters.

6.2.2 Using a Conditional *if-else* Statement to Control Invoking a Method

Another common use of an *if-else* statement is to control whether a method is invoked. To show how this works, let's continue with the same example. The scenario for this world indicated that if the aircraft were too close, the flight controller should radio the pilots to change their flight path to avoid a collision. The storyboard could look like this:

```
if isTooClose
  avoidCollision
else
  < Do nothing >
```

The *isTooClose* function is invoked to check whether the biplane and the helicopter are too close to each other. If the function returns *true*, a method named *avoidCollision* is invoked. Otherwise, nothing is done (the method is not invoked). Let's pretend that the *avoidCollision* method is already written. That way, the previous storyboard can be implemented as shown in Figure 6.23 (10 is an arbitrary minimum distance).

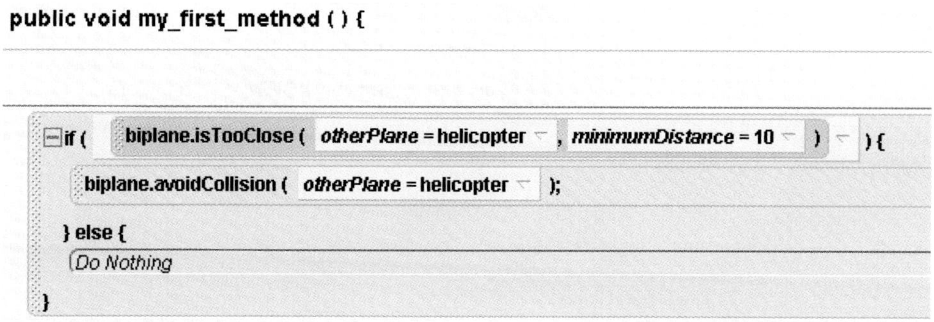

```
public void my_first_method ( ) {

    ⊟if (  biplane.isTooClose ( otherPlane = helicopter ⌄ , minimumDistance = 10 ⌄ ) ⌄ ){
        biplane.avoidCollision ( otherPlane = helicopter ⌄ );
    } else {
        (Do Nothing)
    }
}
```

Figure 6.23
Controlling a call to a method

In the *avoidCollision* method, the aircraft that is higher up should move up and the lower aircraft should move down. Since we don't know which aircraft is above the other, we can use an *if-else* statement to check their relative heights and move each one up or down, as needed. The storyboard for the *avoidCollision* method is

```
avoidCollision
Parameters: biplane, other plane
if biplane is above other plane
  doTogether
    biplane move up
    other plane move down
else
  doTogether
    biplane move down
    other plane move up
```

The translation of this storyboard to program code is shown in Figure 6.24. The condition for the *if-else* statement invokes a built-in function, *isAbove*, to determine which aircraft is above the other. The statements executed depend on the value returned. If the *biplane* is above the other plane, the *biplane* will move up and the other plane will move down. Otherwise, the *else* part kicks in, so the *biplane* will move down and the other plane will move up. Either way, the aircraft move away from one another.

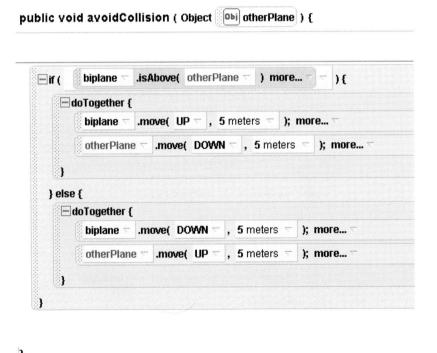

Figure 6.24
The *avoidCollision* method

An important part of any *if-else* statement is the condition. In these examples, the condition involved calls to functions (both built-in functions and our own function). One example (see Figure 6.24) used a *Boolean* expression with a relational operator. Regardless of how the condition is written, it must evaluate to *true* or *false*. The value of the condition determines whether the *if* part or the *else* part of the *if-else* statement is executed.

6.3 Summary

In Alice, a conditional *if-else* statement allows for conditional execution of a block of code (based on the value of a *Boolean* condition, *true* or *false*).

6.3.1 What is a Control Structure?

A control structure is a statement that tells the computer how to execute a small segment (a block of code) in a program. The *doInOrder* and *doTogether* statements are examples of control structures. In this chapter, we looked at another control structure, the conditional *if-else* statement which is used to make a decision about whether to execute the *if* part or execute the *else* part.

6.3.2 How Does an *if-else* Statement Work?

A *Boolean* condition is evaluated to determine whether the *if* part or the *else* part of the statement will be executed at runtime. If the condition is *true*, the *if* part is executed. But if the condition is *false* then the *else* part is executed. Only one of the two will be executed, the other will be skipped. Thus, an *if-else* statement allows us to control the flow of execution through one of two possible paths in our program code.

6.3.3 Built-In Functions versus Your Own Functions

Alice provides several built-in functions for objects of the classes in the gallery. Built-in functions, however, do not always meet the particular needs of a program. In this chapter, we looked at how to write your own functions that return different types of values. One of the example functions returned a *Boolean* value (*true* or *false*) and was used as the condition for an *if-else* control statement.

6.3.4 Using Parameters with Functions

Parameters can be used to allow a function to be used with different objects. As with object methods, you can write an object function and save it out with the object. This allows the function to be reused in another program.

6.3.5 Benefits of Using Functions

The benefit of using functions is that you can think about the task on a higher plane—a form of abstraction. Functions that compute and return a number value make program code much less cluttered and easier to read, because the computation is hidden in a function. Such functions will be useful in many situations. For example, we might want to write a function to return the number of visible objects on the screen in an arcade-style game. The function would be invoked to keep track of how many objects the user has eliminated (made invisible). When only a few objects are left, we might decide to speed up the game.

Exercises

1. What is the purpose of a conditional expression in an *if-else* statement?

2. What type of value is obtained by evaluating each of the following expressions?
   (a) *height* < *3*
   (b) (*5* + *1*) * *10*
   (c) *who* == *bunny*

3. Why must a function have a *return* statement?

4. Is it possible to have more than one *return* statement in the same function? Explain your answer.

5. Begin by creating the rolling ball world, as presented in Section 6.1. Add two objects/acrobats of your own choosing. (We used the *Pharaoh* and *Anabas* from the *Egypt* folder). Position them on top of the *ball* (*Sports*)—one on top of the other. In the world shown, we resized the *ball* to twice its size. Write a program for a circus act, where the acrobats move with the *ball*, staying on top of it, as the *ball* rolls. The acrobats should put their arms up half way, to help them balance as they move along with the rolling ball.

Making It Work Tip: Use Different Views to Check Your Work

Use the scene editor quad view to be certain the acrobats are standing directly on top of one another and are centered on the ball. Also, use pull-down menu methods to be sure that the acrobats and the ball all have the same orientation. (See Appendix A, Section 2 on how to use the *orientTo* statement to ensure that objects are synchronized for movement together.)

6. Create a new world with a *car* or *truck* (*Vehicles*). Write a program to make the four wheels of the car turn forward as the car moves forward. The code should be very similar to the code used to make a ball roll forward (see the *realisticRoll* method in Section 6.1).

7. It has been a hot, dry summer and a hive of bees is in desperate need of a new supply of pollen. One *bee* (*Animals/Bugs*) has ventured far from the hive to scout for new pollen sources. A natural place to look is near ponds in the area. Set up the initial scene with a *circle* (*Shapes*) flat on the ground and colored blue to look like a pond. Add plants, trees, and other natural scenery, including some *flowers* (*Nature*). Be sure the bee is located somewhere around the edge of the pond, as shown in the screen shot here.

Write a program to animate the *bee* scouting the edge of a pond for *flowers* that are in bloom. The bee is to fly around the perimeter of the pond (circle). Write a method to move the bee scout around the perimeter of the pond in which the circumference of the circle is used to guide the motion. (Yes, *asSeenBy* could be used—but that is not the point of this exercise.)

The formula for computing the circumference of a circle is $\pi \times$ the diameter of the circle. π is 3.14, and the diameter is the object's width. Write a function that computes and returns the circumference of the circle. Then have the bee fly around the perimeter of the pond by moving forward the amount of meters returned by the circumference function while turning left one revolution.

8. On spring break, a student is visiting the land of the Pharaohs. The student, for example, *randomGuy 1* (*People* folder), decides to climb one of the *pyramids* (*Egypt*) starting at the bottom and moving straight up the side. Set up an initial scene consisting of a person and a pyramid, as shown in the screen shot. Write a method to animate the *climb* so that the person's feet are always on the side of the pyramid.

   Begin by pointing the person at the pyramid and walking him/her up to the edge. Then, turn the person about 1/8 of a revolution so as to lean into the climb. (Play with this leaning movement until you get a reasonable angle for the person to climb the pyramid.) After reaching the top, the person should stand up straight.

   To determine how far the person must move to complete the climb, the *climb* method must invoke a function. The function computes the side length of the pyramid. The formula for computing the distance up the side of the pyramid is based on the Pythagorean theorem $(a^2 + b^2 = c^2)$. The value of c will provide a rough estimate of how far the person should move (in a diagonal direction) up the side of the pyramid. The formula is

$$\text{length of the pyramid side} = \sqrt{((\text{pyramid height})^2 + (\text{pyramid width}/2)^2)}$$

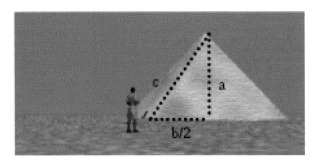

9. In this exercise, a *woman* (*People*) is learning how to make rolled cookies. Before she can cut out the cookies, she needs to roll the dough with her *rolling pin* (*Kitchen*). Create a function that determines how much the *rolling pin* is to

roll as she slides it along the table, flattening the dough. Use the function in a world that animates the *rolling pin* rolling across the table (*Furniture*).

10. Create a skater world, as illustrated next. Import an enhanced *CleverSkater* object, as designed and created in Chapter 3. (If you have not created the *EnhancedCleverSkater* class, an *iceSkater* can be used from the gallery, but you will have to write your own methods to make her skate forward and skate around an object.)

For this world, write a program to make the skater practice her turns on the ice. First, place the skater 1 meter from the second cone, facing forward. She then skates forward toward the first cone (a sliding step). When she gets close, she should skate halfway around the cone and end up facing the other way to skate back toward the other cone. Next, have the skater skate toward the other cone and, when close enough, make a turn around it. In this way, the skater should complete a path around the two cones.

Making It Work Tip: Check the Skater's Position

To find out whether the skater has gotten close enough to do a half-circle turn around the cone, you can use the *is within threshold of object* function for the *enhancedCleverSkater*. (The phrase *is within threshold of object* evaluates to *true* if the second object is within the specified distance of the first object.) Another possibility is to use the *distance* function and the relational operator *a* < *b* (available as a world-level function) to build the logical expression "Is the skater's distance to the cone less than 2 meters?" ■

11. This exercise is an extension of Exercise 10. Modify the world to have the skater complete a figure-eight around the cones.

12. Create an initial scene of a *troll* and a *dragon* (*Medieval*) as shown next. The *troll* is trying to frighten away the *dragon* from his favorite hunting grounds. The *troll* is to rant and rave while moving toward the *dragon* if the two are more than 5 meters apart. Use your own function to find out when the *troll* gets too close to the *dragon*. When the *troll* is less than 5 meters away from the *dragon*, have the *dragon* fly away. Run the world several times, each time positioning the *troll* in a different place in the world such that sometimes the *dragon* flies away and sometimes it doesn't.

13. A common use of animation is to prepare educational software for young children. This animation is taken from a classic children's story. The *prince* (*People*) is trying to find the woman whose foot fits the glass slipper. He has come to Cinderella's home, and *Cinderella* and the two *stepsisters* (*People*) are waiting to try on the shoe, as shown in an initial scene. This world will be interactive in that the user will click on one of the women in the scene. Write a function that returns *true* if the object clicked is *Cinderella* and *false* otherwise. If the shoe fits (it only fits *Cinderella*), the *prince* should move toward *Cinderella* and ask her to marry him. The glass slipper then appears on *Cinderella*'s foot. If one of the stepsisters is clicked, the shoe will not fit, and the *prince* should indicate that she is not the one for him.

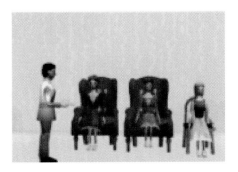

Making It Work Tip: Two Slippers Are Better Than One

To make this program easier to write, use two glass slippers: one the *prince* is holding and one on *Cinderella*'s foot. Make the glass slipper on *Cinderella*'s foot invisible. When the *prince* proposes marriage, make the shoe in the *prince*'s hand invisible and the one on *Cinderella*'s foot visible.

Common Bug: Illegal Characters

Do NOT use a "?" in the filename when saving a world.

14. *Phishy fish* (*Animals*) has just signed up at swim school to learn the latest motion, the *sineWave*. Your task is to write a method to teach her the *sineWave* motion. The initial scene with a fish and water is seen here.

Making It Work Tip: Creating Worlds

This world is provided on the Alice website. We recommend that you use the prepared world, as setting up the scene is time consuming. If you are an adventuresome soul, here are the statements for setting up the world on your own: Use pop-up methods to move the fish to the world origin (0, 0, and 0) and then turn the fish right one-quarter revolution. Because *Phishy* is partially submerged, set the opacity of the water to 30% so the fish can be seen in the water. Now, use camera controls to reposition the camera (this takes a bit of patience as the camera must be moved horizontally 180 degrees from its default position). Then, adjust the vertical angle to give a side view of the fish in the water. The fish should be located at the far left, and the water should occupy the lower half of the *World* view, as seen here.

Alice has a *sine* function that can be used to teach *Phishy* the *sineWave* motion. (The *sine* function is often used to determine the relationship between the lengths of the sides of a right triangle. For the purposes of this animation, that relationship is not really important.) If the *sine* function is computed over all angles in a full circle, the sine value starts at 0, goes up to 1, back through 0 to −1, and returns to 0.

Angle	Sine of the angle	Angle	Sine of the angle
0	0	225	−0.707
45	0.707	270	−1
90	1	315	−0.707
135	0.707	360	0
180	0		

This function is continuous, so if sine values are plotted some multiple of times, we will see the curve repeated over and over, as shown here.

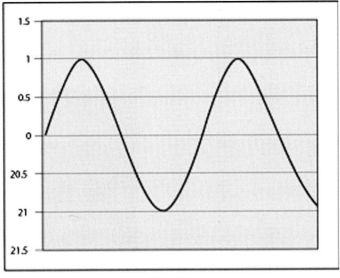

Sine wave

For the *sineWave* motion, *Phishy* is to move in the sine wave pattern. In the world provided on the Alice website, *Phishy* has been positioned at the origin of the world. In a 2D system, we would say she is at point (0,0). To simulate the sine wave pattern, she needs to move up to a height that is 1 meter above the water, then down to a depth of 1 meter below the surface of the water (−1 meter), back up to 1 meter above the water, and so on, at the same time as she moves to the right in the water. The Alice *sine* function expects to receive an angle expressed in radians (rather than degrees). Write a function, named *degreesToRadians*, which will convert the angle in degrees to the angle in radians. To convert from degrees to radians, multiply the angle degrees by π and divide by 180. The *degreesToRadians* function should return the angle in radians.

Now, write a method to have *Phishy* move in the sine wave pattern. Remember that in the world provided on the Alice website, *Phishy* already has been positioned at the origin of the world. So, *Phishy* is already at the position for 0 degrees.

Making It Work Tip: Smooth Swimming

One way to create the sine wave pattern is to use *moveTo* statements (Appendix A, Section 2). A *moveTo* statement should move *Phishy* to a position that is (*right, up*, 0), where *right* is the radian value and *up* is the *sin(radian value)*. After adding a *moveTo* statement, the built-in world-level function *(right, up, forward)* can be dropped onto the target of the *moveTo*, allowing individual specification of each coordinate. Use *moveTo* statements for angles: 45, 90, 135, 180, 225, 270, 315, and 360. For a smoother animation, make each *moveTo* statement have *style = abruptly*. Using *style = abruptly* seems counter-intuitive to making an animation run more smoothly. The reason is that animation statements begin slowly (gently) and end slowly (gently) by default. If we wish to have two statements appear to behave as a single statement, we do not want each statement to slow down as the statement starts/ends. Hence, we use the single *style = abruptly* option.

7

Repetition: Loops

Goals of this Chapter:

- To define the concept of a counted *for loop*.
- To count the number of times statements within a *for loop* are repeated.
- To introduce the possible values that can be used for a count.
- To illustrate the effects of nesting a *for loop* within a *doInOrder*.
- To illustrate the effects of nesting a *for loop* within a *doTogether* block of code.
- To nest a *for loop* within another *for loop*.
- To illustrate the use of a *while* statement as an indefinite *for loop*.
- To illustrate how to organize objects into a list.
- To create lists, where all the items in a list all have the same type (such as object).
- To iterate through a list sequentially or simultaneously.

Introduction

In this chapter, we look at control statements where statements and methods are repeated. In Section 7.1, examples are presented where an Alice ***for loop*** **statement** is used to execute a block of statements again and again. The *for loop* statement can be used when we know exactly how many times a block of code should be repeated (that is, a definite number of times). We use the word count to describe the number of times a *for loop* repeats. For this reason, a *for loop* statement is sometimes referred to as a **counted loop**.

In Section 7.2, the ***while*** **statement** is introduced for repeating a block of code where we do not know exactly how many times it should be repeated (an indefinite number of times). A *while* statement corresponds naturally to the way we say and think about certain actions in our everyday conversation. For example, we might say, "while I am driving, I will continue to keep my hands on the wheel and my eyes on the road," or perhaps something like, "while I am a member of the baseball team, I will practice batting." The *while* statement is intuitive — a way to think about actions that repeat while some condition remains true.

Section 7.3 will then explore a different aspect of programming—that of organizing objects or information of the same type into a group. Up to now, worlds typically contained only a few objects. Programs were written to make each individual object carry out specific actions, sometimes acting alone and sometimes coordinated with other objects. But what if you wanted to create an animation where 20 soldiers were marching in a parade, all performing the same marching steps? You could certainly create a marching method for a new class of soldier and then instantiate 20 soldiers in the world. To make each soldier perform the marching steps, though, you would have to drag the marching statement into the editor at least 20 times (once for each soldier)! One way to make this programming situation less tedious is to collect all the objects into an organizing structure. Then you can write program code either for all the objects as a group or for the individual objects, as before.

In programming, we call such an organizing structure a **data structure**. This chapter introduces a data structure known as a **list**. Section 7.3 begins with a demonstration of how to create a list. We then look at how to **iterate** through the list. (We have used the word "iterate" before—when we were talking about repetition.) To "iterate through a list" means to do the same thing repeatedly for all the items in a list.

Section 7.4 illustrates another use of lists, that of searching through a list to find an item that possesses a certain property. Searching through a list is similar to going shopping for a new pair of jeans. You walk down the aisle where all the jeans are hanging on the rack and look at each to find the pair with just the right size and color.

7.1 *for Loops*

As our worlds become more sophisticated, the code tends to become longer. One reason is that some animation statements and methods must be repeated to make the same action occur over and over. Perhaps you have already written programs where you needed to call (invoke) a method several times. In this section, we look at using a *for loop* statement to call a method repeatedly.

7.1.1 Using a *for loop* For Repeatedly Invoking a Method

Let's begin with a very simple world, shown in Figure 7.1. A *bunny* (Animals) has snuck into his neighbor's *garden* (Nature) and has spotted some nice broccoli shoots. We resized several *tree* (Nature) objects to a very small size to create the broccoli-like objects. The task is to write a program to animate the bunny hopping over to munch a few bites of broccoli.

Let's assume we have already written a method for the bunny named *hop*. A possible implementation of the *hop* method appears in Figure 7.2. (The sound statement is optional.) The *hop* method enables the bunny to hop forward by moving his legs up and down at the same time as he moves forward.

The bunny in our example world is eight hops away from the broccoli. One possible way to animate eight bunny hops is illustrated in Figure 7.3. In this program, a *doInOrder* block is placed in the *World.my_first_method*. Then, a *turn to face* statement is used to make the bunny turn to look at the broccoli. Finally, the call to the *bunny.hop* method is dragged into the editor eight times.

Of course, the code in Figure 7.3 will perform the task of making the bunny hop over to the broccoli. It was tedious, though, to drag eight *bunny.hop* statements into the

Figure 7.1
A bunny in the garden

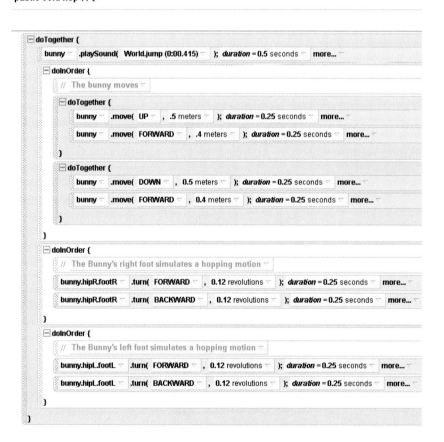

Figure 7.2
The *bunny.hop* method

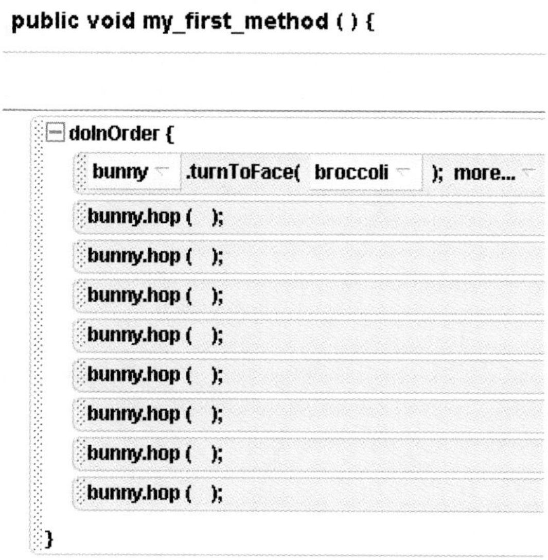

public void my_first_method ( ) {

dolnOrder {

bunny ⌄ .turnToFace(broccoli ⌄); more... ⌄

bunny.hop ( );

bunny.hop ( );

bunny.hop ( );

bunny.hop ( );

bunny.hop ( );

bunny.hop ( );

bunny.hop ( );

bunny.hop ( );

}

Figure 7.3
Eight hops

program. We want to look at a way to make our job easier by using a *for loop* statement. To create a *for loop* statement, drag the *for loop* tile into the editor. The popup menu offers a choice for the count (the number of times the *for loop* will execute), as shown in Figure 7.4. In this example, we selected other in the menu and then entered the number 8 using the popup number pad. Note that a *for loop* can execute only a whole number of times.

Next, a call to the *bunny.hop* method is placed inside the *for loop* statement, as shown in Figure 7.5. When the program is run, the bunny will turn to face the broccoli and then hop eight times. That is, the *for loop* will call the *bunny.hop* method eight times. The benefit of using a *for loop* is immediately obvious—the *for loop* is quick and easy to create. Although eight calls to the *bunny.hop* method is not a big deal, there are program situations where methods have to be repeated 20, 30, or even 100 times. It would be much easier to use a single *for loop* statement if the bunny had to hop 100 times!

In this simple example, we placed a single call to a method (*bunny.hop*) in the *for loop* statement. We could have dragged several statements and method calls into the block, and all would have been repeated. A *doInOrder* or *doTogether* block can be placed inside the *for loop* to control how the statements are repeated; otherwise Alice will assume the statements are to be done in order.

7.1.2 Nested Loops

The bunny hop example used only one *for loop* statement. Of course it is possible to have several *for loop* statements in the same program. In fact, a *for loop* statement can be nested inside another *for loop* statement. In this section, we take a look at a world where this is an appropriate way to write the program code.

public void my_first_method ( ) {
doInOrder {
bunny .turnToFace(broccoli); more...
}
end
1 time
2 times
5 times
10 times
infinity times
20 times
other...
Custom Number
8
7 8 9 ←
4 5 6 Clear
1 2 3 ±
0 . /
Okay Cancel
}
doInOrder doTogether if loop while forAllInOrder forAllTogether wait(duration); print(

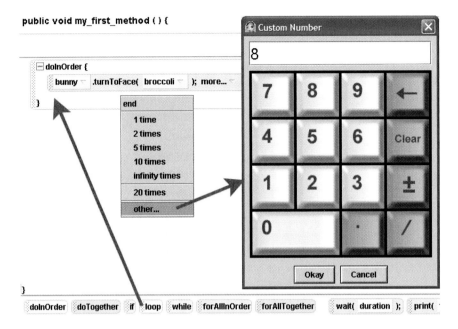

Figure 7.4
Selecting a count

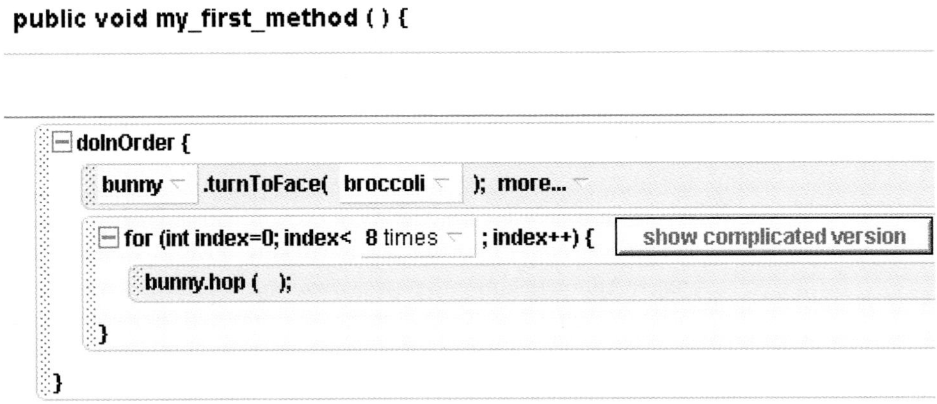

public void my_first_method ( ) {
doInOrder {
bunny .turnToFace(broccoli); more...
for (int index=0; index< 8 times ; index++) {
show complicated version
bunny.hop ( );
}
}

Figure 7.5
Using the *for loop* statement to invoke a method repeatedly

Consider an initial scene with a two-wheeled *Ferris wheel* (Amusement Park folder in Web gallery), as in Figure 7.6. An animation is to be written that simulates the running of this *Ferris wheel*. We want the entire double wheel to turn clockwise (roll right) while each of the individual wheels turn counterclockwise (roll left).

Figure 7.7 shows code for a *for loop* to roll the entire double wheel ten times. The *style = abruptly* parameter has been used to smooth out the rotating of the entire double wheel over each repetition. (We chose the *abrupt* style because the default style,

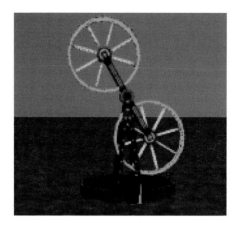

Figure 7.6
A Ferris wheel

```
for (int index=0; index< 10 times ; index++) {   show complicated version
    ferrisWheel.doublewheel .roll( RIGHT , 1 revolution ); style = BEGIN_AND_END_ABRUPTLY duration = 2 seconds
}
```

Figure 7.7
Rotating the double wheel 10 times

gently, slows down the animation statement as it begins and ends. Because we are repeating the statement within a *for loop*, we want to avoid having the wheel go through a repeated slowdown, speedup, slowdown, speedup kind of action.)

With the motion of the entire Ferris wheel accomplished, statements can now be written to rotate each of the inner wheels counterclockwise (roll left) while the outer double wheel is rotating clockwise (roll right). The code to rotate the inner wheels is presented in Figure 7.8.

Now the rotations can be combined. To increase the excitement of the ride, we will have the inner wheels rotate more frequently, perhaps twice as often as the outer wheel. So, each time the double wheel rotates one revolution clockwise, the inner wheels should rotate twice counterclockwise. Figure 7.9 shows the modified code.

```
for (int index=0; index< 2 times ; index++) {   show complicated version
    doTogether {
        ferrisWheel.doublewheel.wheel1 .roll( LEFT , 1 revolution ); style = BEGIN_AND_END_ABRUPTLY more...
        ferrisWheel.doublewheel.wheel2 .roll( LEFT , 1 revolution ); style = BEGIN_AND_END_ABRUPTLY more...
    }
}
```

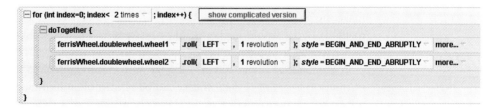

Figure 7.8
Rotating the inner wheels two times

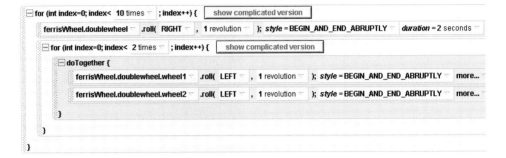

Figure 7.9
The complete code for the Ferris wheel

In previous programs you have seen that actions in a *doTogether* block need to be synchronized in duration. In this example the inner wheels need to rotate twice while the outer wheel rotates once. So, the duration of rotation for the outer wheel (*doublewheel*) is made to be twice the duration of rotation of the inner wheels (*doublewheel.wheel1* and *doublewheel.wheel2*). Each time the outer *for loop* runs once, the inner *for loop* runs twice. This means that the double wheel takes 2 seconds to complete its rotation, and the inner wheels require 1 second (the default duration) to complete their rotations, but rotate twice. In all, the inner wheels rotate 20 times counterclockwise as the outer wheel rotates 10 times clockwise.

Making It Work Tip: Optical Illusion

Instructions within a *doTogether* block can sometimes cancel each other out (in terms of the animated action we can observe). For example, in the First Encounter world described in Chapter 2, Section 2, turning the backLeftLegUpperJoint backward and forward at the same time made the animation look as though the leg was not turning at all. In the Ferris wheel example above, since the outer *for loop* is set to execute only 1 time and the inner *for loop* 2 times, the inner wheel will look as though it rotates only once. ∎

7.1.3 Invoking a Function to Compute the Count

In the examples presented here, the number of times a block of code was to execute a *for loop* was a specific number: 2, 8, or 10. But the count can also be a function that returns a number. For example, the code shown in Figure 7.10 uses a function to determine the count for a *for loop*. If the guy were 6 meters from the girl, the *for loop* would make the guy walk 6 times (assuming that the guy covers exactly 1 meter in his *walk* method). What would happen if the guy were 5.7 meters from the girl? The *for loop* only executes a whole number of times. So the guy would walk only 5 times.

A tremendous advantage of using the value returned from a function as the number of times to *for loop* is that objects can be repositioned in the initial scene, and it will not be necessary to modify the code to specify the count. The function will automatically compute the distance between the guy and the girl and the *for loop* will repeat only as many times as needed.

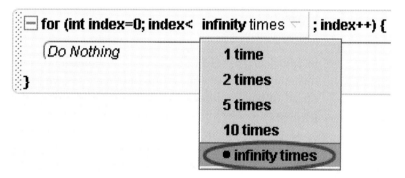

Figure 7.10
Invoking a function to determine a *for loop* count

Figure 7.11
Selecting *infinity* as the count

7.1.4 Infinite *for Loop*

One option in the popup menu for selecting a *for loop* count is *infinity*. (See Figure 7.11.) If *infinity* is selected, the *for loop* will continue on and on until the program stops.

Ordinarily, we advise that you avoid using an **infinite *for loop***. However, in animation programs an infinite *for loop* is sometimes useful. Consider an amusement park animation where a carousel is one of the objects in the scene, as in Figure 7.12. To make the carousel go around in the background, call the carousel's built-in method *carouselAnimation* in an infinite *for loop*, as shown in Figure 7.13.

7.2   *while*—A Conditional Loop

The *for loop* statement requires that the programmer specify the number of times the *for loop* is to be repeated. This could be a number, such as 10, or a function such as *boy.distanceToGirl*. The number of times a *for loop* should repeat might not be known

Figure 7.12
Carousel in infinite motion

```
⊟ for (int index=0; index<  infinity times ▽  ; index++) {        show complicated version

    carousel.carouselAnimation (   );

}
```

Figure 7.13
Loop *infinity* times

in advance. This is often the case in games and simulations, where objects move randomly. In this section, a form of looping known as the *while* statement will be introduced to handle situations where the programmer does not know (at the time the program is written) how many times a block of code should be repeated.

The *while* statement is a **conditional loop**. One way to think about a *while* statement is "while some condition is true perform code block." The code block performed inside the while statement can be a single action or several actions enclosed in a *doInOrder* or *doTogether* block. The condition used in a *while* statement is a Boolean condition (the same type of condition used in *If* statements). The Boolean condition acts like a gatekeeper at a popular dance club. If the condition is true, entry is gained to the *while* statement and the statements within the *while* statement are executed, otherwise the statements are skipped. Unlike the *If* statement, however, the *while* statement is repetitive. The diagram in Figure 7.14 illustrates how the *while* statement works as a loop.

If the condition is *true,* the statements are performed; then the condition gets checked again. If the condition is still *true*, the statements within the *while loop* are repeated. If the condition has become *false,* the *while loop* ends and Alice goes on to execute the next statement in the program. A *while* statement is useful for situations where we do not know how many times the loop should be repeated. All we need to know is the condition that determines whether the *while loop* will be repeated.

7.2.1 Chase Scene

Let's look at an example of a situation where we do not know (ahead of time) how many times a block of code should be repeated. This animation is a "chase scene"

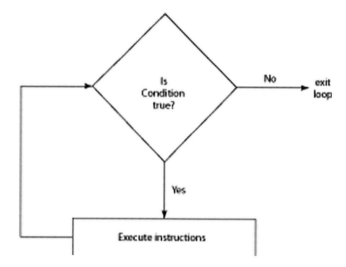

Figure 7.14
The *while* statement works as a loop

simulation. Chase scenes are common in video games and animation films where one object is trying to catch another. In this example, a shark is hungry for dinner. The *shark* is going to chase after and catch a fleeing *goldfish* (Animals). OK, so this is not an appetizing animation—but sharks have to eat, too! Figure 7.15 shows a very simple initial world.

7.2.2 Problem

Our task is to animate the shark chasing the goldfish, as it tries to get close enough (say, within 0.5 meters) to gobble the goldfish down for dinner. Naturally, as the shark chases it, the goldfish is not standing still. Instead, it is trying to escape by moving to a random position. Of course, we want the fish to look like it is swimming (not jumping all around on the screen), so we will move it to a random position that is close to the current position.

Figure 7.15
Chase scene

This animation is a simulation of a real-life scenario. When the world starts, the simulation should immediately begin. As you know, Alice automatically executes *World.my_first_method* when the world starts. Taking advantage of this automatic execution, the code for starting the simulation and keeping it in progress will be written in *World.my_first_method*.

7.2.3 Textual Storyboard Solution

The basic idea is that if the goldfish is more than 0.5 meters away from the shark, the shark is going to point at the goldfish and swim toward it. Meanwhile, the goldfish is moving away to a random position nearby. If the goldfish is still more than 0.5 meters away, the shark will change course and swim toward it and the goldfish will try to swim away. Eventually, when the shark finally gets within 0.5 meter of the goldfish, the chase is over and the shark can catch and eat the goldfish.

Let's plan for the chase animation using the *while* statement. Think about it like this: "while the goldfish is more than 0.5 meters in front of the shark, move the shark toward the goldfish and, at the same time, move the goldfish to a random position nearby. The condition in the *while* statement is "the goldfish is more than 0.5 meters in front of the shark." If this condition is true, the chase is on. A textual storyboard for the chase is shown here:

```
doInOrder
while the goldfish is more than 0.5 meters in front of the shark
  doInOrder
    shark point at the goldfish
    doTogether
      shark swim (toward the goldfish)
      goldfish flee (away from the shark)
shark eat (the goldfish)
```

In this example the condition of the *while* statement is "the goldfish's distance in front of the shark is greater than 0.5 meters." This condition must be *true* to allow entry into the *while loop*. After running the statements within the *while* statement, the condition will be evaluated again, and if the condition is still *true*, the statements within the *while* statement will run again. This process continues until the condition finally evaluates to *false* and the *while* statement ends. When the *while* statement ends, the shark eats the goldfish.

In the storyboard, the *shark swim, goldfish flee*, and *shark eat* steps will each require several statements. These actions will be written as methods. For now, let's pretend that these methods have already been written (we can write them next).

The only difficulty in translating the storyboard into code is in building the *while* statement. We dragged the *while* statement tile into the editor and selected *true* as the condition from the popup menu. The result is shown in Figure 7.16a. The *true* condition acts as a placeholder, but it is still necessary to create a Boolean expression to test the condition of whether the goldfish is more than 0.5 meters in front of the shark.

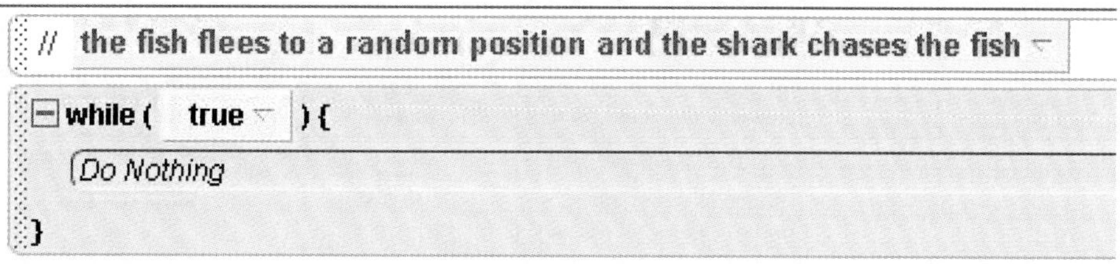

```
// the fish flees to a random position and the shark chases the fish  ▽

while (   true ▽ ) {

    Do Nothing

}
```

Figure 7.16a
A while statement with *true* as the placeholder condition

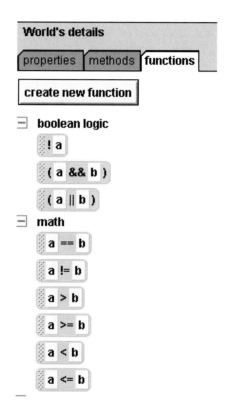

Figure 7.16b
Relational Operators

To create the conditional expression for the while statement, we need to use a relational operator, ">" (greater than). In Alice, the World's functions tab provides six relational operators in the **math** group of functions, as shown in Figure 7.16b.

We dragged the *a greater than b* (a > b) tile from the World's functions into the editor and dropped it on top of *true*, From the popup menu, we selected 1 (for *a*) and 0.5 (for *b*). Notice that the distance the goldfish is in front of the shark is not an option in this popup menu as a choice for *a*, so we arbitrarily selected 1 as a placeholder. To replace the placeholder 1, we clicked on the **goldfish** in the object tree, and then selected

Figure 7.17
Using the the goldfish's distanceInFrontOf to complete the condition

its functions tab, as illustrated in Figure 7.17. Next, we dragged the distanceInFrontOf tile and dropped it on top of the 1 and then selected shark as the target. The resulting code is illustrated in Figure 7.17.

Once the *while* statement condition is written, a *doInOrder* code block is created inside the *while* and statements are created to point the shark at the goldfish and then have the shark swim toward the goldfish at the same time as the goldfish moves to a nearby random position. The completed *chase,* implemented *in my_first_method,* is shown in Figure 7.18. Please note that specifying a *duration* of zero for the *shark.pointAt* statement causes the statement to occur instantaneously, without a gradual animation of the action.

Now, let's look at how to write the *shark.swim, goldfish.flee,* and *shark.eat* methods that are invoked from the *chase* code. First, let's create a storyboard and implementation for the shark's swim method. The *shark.swim* method moves the shark forward and the turns the torso of the shark right and left to simulate a swimming motion through water. Figure 7.19 illustrates *shark.swim.*

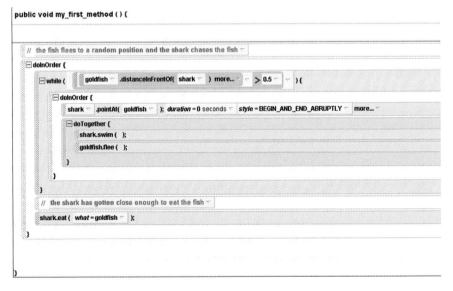

Figure 7.18
The *chase* code using a *while* statement

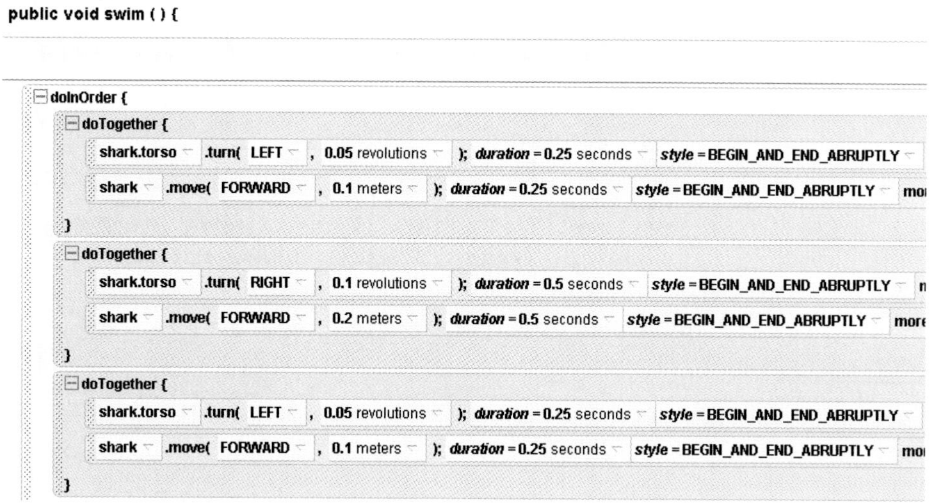

public void swim ( ) {

Figure 7.19
Storyboard and code for the *shark.swim* method

shark.swim

doInOrder
 turn torso left and move forward
 turn torso right and move forward
 turn torso left and move forward

A textual storyboard for the shark's eat method might look like this:

shark.eat

Parameter: *what*
doInOrder
 shark points at *what*
 shark opens jaw and moves forward
 shark closes jaw

The *shark.eat* method uses a parameter to specify *what* object in the scene is on the menu. In this example, *shark.eat* was invoked with the goldfish object as the argument. The shark moves forward 1 meter to completely swallow the goldfish. The opacity of the goldfish is faded to 0% so that the goldfish becomes invisible (disappearing into the shark's mouth). The complete implementation of the *shark.eat* method is shown in Figure 7.20.

A storyboard for the *goldfish.flee* method would look like this:

goldfish.flee
 doTogether
  wiggle tail
  randomMotion

In the storyboard design, the goldfish moves its tail to simulate a swim-like motion and then invokes a *randomMotion* method to move the fish to a nearby random

public void eat (Object `Obj` **what) {**

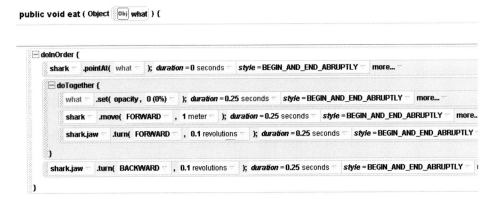

Figure 7.20
The *shark.eat* method

location. The World has a random number function that can be used to generate a random number. (See Appendix A, Section 6 for a description of the random number function and examples of how to use it.)

If the *random number* function is combined with a *move* statement, a form of random motion is created where an object can be made to move to a random location. Random motion is essential in many different kinds of games and simulations.

Making It Work Tip: Random Motion

We want the goldfish to swim in a random-like movement but we also want to restrict the movement to a nearby position. Otherwise, successive moves would make the goldfish jump around here and there on the screen — not at all like a goldfish swimming. Because Alice objects live in a three-dimensional world, you can write *move* statements to move the goldfish in any of six possible directions (*forward, backward, left, right, up*, and *down*). Combining the *random number* function with six *move* statements might be a bit clumsy. Let's try to make our work easier by taking advantage of negative numbers. If a negative number is used as the distance in a *move* statement, the object is to move in the opposite direction. For example, the statement shown below has a -1 meters argument for the distance. When executed, this statement will actually move the goldfish *right* 1 meter.

If we use both positive and negative distance values, only three *move* instructions are needed. We will use *up, left*, and *forward* directions. With this idea in mind, let's write a storyboard for a *randomMotion* method:

fish.randomMotion:
Parameters: *min, max*
Do together
    fish move up a random number distance
    fish move left a random number distance
    fish move forward a random number distance

```
public void randomMotion ( Number 123 min , Number 123 max ) {

    // randomly move to a position in 3D space
    doTogether {
        goldfish .move( UP , Random.nextDouble() minimum = min  maximum = max  more... ); more...
        goldfish .move( LEFT , Random.nextDouble() minimum = min  maximum = max  more... ); more...
        goldfish .move( FORWARD , Random.nextDouble() minimum = 0  maximum = max  more... ); more...
    }
```

Figure 7.21a
The *randomMotion* method

The *goldfish.randomMotion* storyboard contains a *Do together* block and three *move* statements. In each *move* statement, the random number function is invoked to generate a random distance. The parameters (*min* and *max*) are used to select the range of minimum and maximum values for the *random number* distance. In this example, we are going to use a *min* of −0.2 and a *max* of 0.2. So the *random number* function will return a value in the range of −0.2 to 0.2 for the move up and move left statements. Note that *min* for the *move forward* instruction is 0. This is because goldfish do not swim backwards.

Now we can translate the storyboard into program code. The code for the *randomMotion* method is shown in Figure 7.21a. Think about how this method works. In each *move* instruction, the *random number* question is invoked to get a random distance. Let's say the *random number* function returns a negative distance for the *move up* instruction; the goldfish will actually move *down*. A negative distance for the *move left* instruction will move the goldfish *right*. The distance for the *move forward* instruction will always be positive, so the goldfish will always move forward.

The *Do together* block executes the *move up, move right,* and *move forward* statements all at the same time. As a result the goldfish will move to some random location within a cube of space defined by the minimum and maximum random number distances.

Once the *randomMotion* instruction has been written, the *goldfish.flee* method can be implemented. The *goldfish.flee* method is shown in Figure 7.21b.

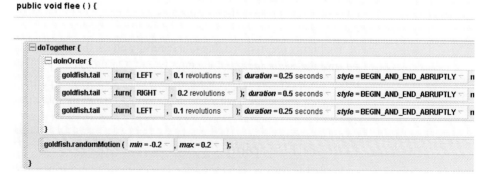

Figure 7.21b
The *goldfish.flee* method—fish swims to a random location

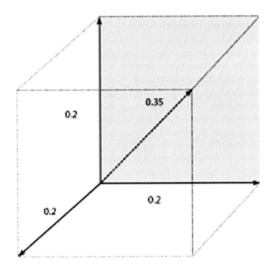

Figure 7.22
Maximum distance the goldfish can travel in one move

7.2.4 Infinite *while*

As a general rule, a *while* statement should contain statements that change conditions in the world so the *while* statement will eventually end. Otherwise, the *while loop* would continue to execute in a never-ending cycle—an infinite *while loop*. (An infinite *while loop* is often the cause of a program appearing to be "spinning its wheels.") In the shark chase example above, we avoided an infinite *while loop* by carefully planning the distance the shark and the goldfish move with each execution of the *while loop*. Although the goldfish is moving randomly, we set the maximum value to 0.2 meters in any one direction (forward, up/down, right/left). A bit of 3D geometry is needed to show that the total distance the goldfish travels must be less than .35 meters, as illustrated in Figure 7.22.

The goldfish, then, never moves more than 0.35 meters away from the shark, and the shark always moves 0.4 meters closer to the goldfish. You can confirm the 0.4 meters by checking the move statements in the *shark.swim* method. The shark's distance advantage guarantees that the shark is eventually going to catch up to the goldfish and the *while loop* will end.

We highly recommend that you carefully check the condition for a *while* statement to be sure the *while loop* will eventually end. On the other hand, there are some kinds of programs where an infinite *while loop* is desirable. This is particularly true in games and simulation animations, where an action should occur until the program shuts down.

7.3 Lists and Looping

A **list** is one of the most popular ways to organize information. We use lists in our everyday lives. For example, you might have a grocery list or a list of homework assignments. Programmers use lists to organize objects and information about objects

Figure 7.23
The rockettes

in their programs. Examples of specialized lists can be found in thousands of software applications. In Alice, a list (generally) contains items of a similar type. (For example, we might want a list of objects or a list of colors.) In this section we will look at how to create a list and then how to iterate through the list, to look for a particular item or to take some action with each item in the list.

7.3.1 Creating a List

In the initial scene shown in Figure 7.23, five *rockettes* (People) have been added to the world. The rockettes are famous for their holiday dance routines. We want to create an animation where the rockettes will perform the kick-step from one of their dances. In a kick-step routine, the dancers each perform a kick, one after the other down the line. Then, they all perform the same kick-step at the same time. This is an example of an animation where a list can be used to organize objects to act as a group.

Before a list can be used in a program, the list must be created. Five rockette dancers have been added to the scene and positioned to form a dance line. Just adding the objects to the world and then positioning them next to one another, however, is not enough to create a list.

To actually make a list, a list variable must be created (to give the list a name) and then the objects (already in the world) must be added to the list. To create a list variable, select the properties tab for the World and then click the **create new variable** button, as shown in Figure 7.24. (The list is created at the world level rather than at the object level because it will contain several different objects.)

When the **create new variable** button is clicked, a popup dialog box allows you to enter the list variable name, as shown in Figure 7.25. In this example, we used the name *dancers* and selected its Type as **Object**. The key action here is to check the box marked **make a List**. Then you can click the button labeled **new item** to add an object to the list. In the example shown in Figure 7.25, the **new item** button was clicked five times to enter each rockette. Finally, click the **Okay** button. The list variable name can now be used in statements where we want to have the dancers perform as a group.

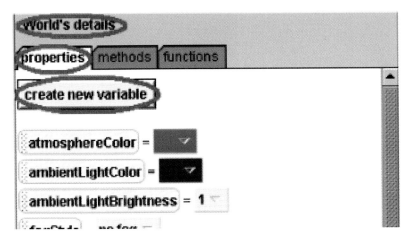

Figure 7.24
Creating a list variable

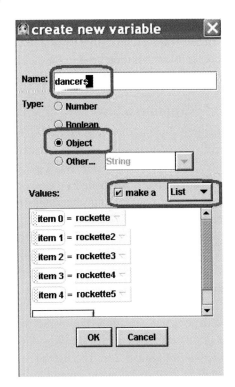

Figure 7.25
Naming a list and adding objects to the list

7.3.2 *forAllInOrder*—Iterating Sequentially Through a List

A useful operation that can be done with a list is to iterate sequentially through it. This means that each item in the list will be instructed to perform the same statement, one after the other. This is like a person walking down the street and placing mail in each mailbox. Iteration through a list is sometimes called "walking" or "traversing" a list.

Alice provides a special *forAllInOrder* statement that works with one item at a time from a list. As an example, let's have each rockette, from left to right, kick up her right leg as part of the dance routine. The storyboard is shown below. The *kickUpRightLeg* method consists of several simpler actions.

```
For all dancers in order
  item_from_dancers kickUpRightLeg
```

```
kickUpRightLeg
Parameter: whichRockette
doInOrder
  doTogether
    whichRockette right thigh turn back
    whichRockette right calf turn forward
  whichRockette right calf turn back
```

Now we can translate the textual storyboard design into a world-level method named *Rockette.kickUpRightLeg*, where the *whichRockette* parameter acts as a place-holder for an item from the *dancers* list. (At first glance, we might think the *kickUpRightLeg* method should be a object-level method. However, several different objects may be used in the *dancers* list.) The *kickUpRightLeg* method is shown in Figure 7.26.

An object parameter in a method requires that you perform more than one step to create statements that use the parameter. In this example, we want to move parts of the right leg (subparts) of the rockette. Alice has no way of knowing which kind of object is actually going to be sent in to *whichRockette* and also does not know whether the object has a right leg. (Suppose we had added a snowman to the list of *dancers*. Sending in a snowman to *whichRockette* would be a problem, because snowmen do not have right legs, or any legs for that matter!) What all this means is that we must use a *part named* function to specify the exact subpart of *whichRockette* is involved in the *turn* statements.

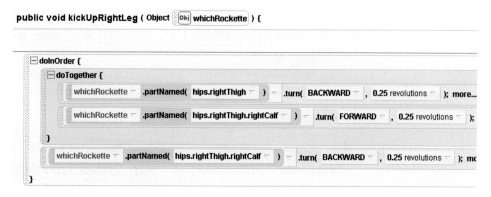

Figure 7.26
The *kickUpRightLeg* method

As an example, let's look at the steps we used to create the first turn statement in *kickUpRightLeg.*

1. Create a statement to turn one of the rockettes backward 0.25 revolutions.

2. Then, drag in the **part named** function for the rockette and drop it on top of the rockette tile. The result should look like this:

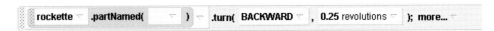

3. Click to the right of **part named** and enter the exact name of the part (Alice is case sensitive, so type it correctly). Now, we have this:

4. Now, drag the **whichRockette** parameter tile down to drop it on top of the rockette. The final statement should look like this:

Now that the *kickUpRightLeg* statement has been written, a *forAllInOrder* statement can be used to create the animation. The **forAllInOrder** tile is dragged into the editor, and the expression *World.dancers* is selected as the name of the list, as illustrated in Figure 7.27.

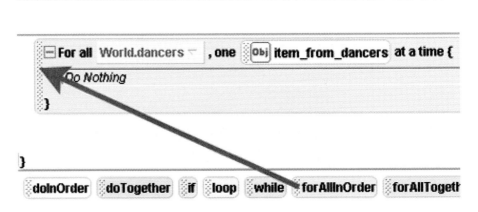

Figure 7.27
The *forAllInOrder* tile

public void my_first_method ( ) {

For all World.dancers ▽ **, one** [Obj] **item_from_dancers at a time {**

World.kickUpRightLeg(*whichRockette* = item_from_dancers ▽);

}

}

doInOrder   doTogether   if   loop   while   forAllInOrder   forAllTogeth

Figure 7.28
Calling *kickUpRightLeg* with *item_from_dancers* as the argument

A statement is written inside the *forAllInOrder* statement to invoke the *World.kickUpRightLeg* method, as illustrated in Figure 7.28.

When the program is run, each item from the *dancers* list is sent as an argument to the *kickUpRightLegs* method, one at a time. Each dancer kicks up her right leg one after the other, down the dance line. The screenshot in Figure 7.29 was captured after the first two rockettes have already kicked their right leg in the air and the third rockette has just started to do so.

7.3.2 *forAllTogether*—Iterating Simultaneously

Alice also provides a statement named *forAllTogether* to make all the objects of a list perform the same action at the same time. This is called "iterating through a list

Figure 7.29
Running the dance animation using *forAllInOrder*

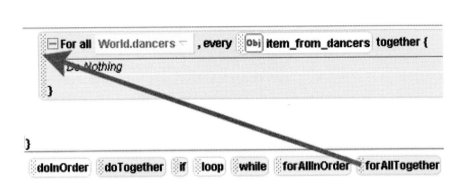

Figure 7.30
The *forAllTogether* tile

Figure 7.31
Calling *kickUpRightLeg* in a *forAllTogether* statement

simultaneously." One way to think of *forAllTogether* is that it is similar to a multi-way telephone conference call—everyone who is connected to the conference call is on the phone line at the same time and everyone can talk and interact at the same time.

In any dance group, the dancers perform some steps sequentially and others at the same time. Let's have all the rockettes kick up their right leg at the same time. To do so, drag the **forAllTogether** tile into the editor, as shown in Figure 7.30.

The *Rockette.kickUpRightLeg* method is invoked from within the *forAllTogether* statement. The resulting statement is shown in Figure 7.31.

Now, when the code is run, the dancers all kick up their right legs at the same time, as illustrated in Figure 7.32.

7.4   List Search

Internet search engines are a great invention for helping us locate Web pages. For instance, imagine you are looking for a video that tells the story of Caesar and Cleopatra. You connect to a search engine (such as Google™) and enter "Caesar and Cleopatra." In a few short seconds, a list of Web page links appears on your web

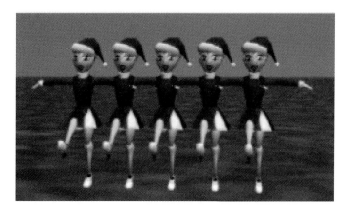

Figure 7.32
Running the dance animation using *forAllTogether*

browser. Now, you do a list search—you read through the items, one item at a time, and look for a Web page that has exactly what you want. A **list search** is a common list operation used in programming. Its purpose is to iterate through a list of items, one item at a time, and check each one to see if it has exactly what we are looking for. In this section we will explore how to do a list search in Alice.

7.4.1 Playing a Game Using a List Search

As an example of a list search, imagine a popular carnival game named "Whack A Mole." In this game, the player picks up a hammer and whacks at a mole-like puppet that pops up here and there out of a box. Points are scored each time the player whacks a mole.

Figure 7.33 shows the initial world for the game. A *WhackAMole* game booth has been added to a world. Twelve *moles* have been added and placed inside the game

Figure 7.33
Initial scene for WhackAMole game

booth, one below each hole (out of sight in Figure 7.33—except for the mole in a popped-up position). The *WhackAMole* game booth and *moles* are from the Amusement Park gallery. Finally, two *cylinders* (named *totalScore* and *playerScore*) have been added in the background to act as a primitive visual scoreboard. The *cylinders* are from the Shapes gallery. The *totalScore* cylinder, representing the total (or target) score, is grey and is positioned on the ground. The *playerScore* cylinder is yellow and is positioned so that its top is just under the surface of the ground (out of sight in Figure 7.33). The *playerScore* cylinder represents the current score. Of course, at the beginning of the game the player's score is zero—which is why the top of the *playerScore* cylinder is initially at ground level.

Making It Work Tip: Interactivity and Events

A game program must be **interactive**. That is, the person playing the game must be able to interact with the program as it is running. (Up to this point in the textbook, all Alice programs have been "movies" in that the animation is viewed passively and no interaction is involved.) The idea of this WhackAMole game is for a mole to randomly pop up and down in the game booth. The player tries to mouse-click on the mole before it goes back down. In an interactive game, a mouse-click is said to be an **event** (something that happens). Alice provides an Event editor that will allow us to specify the event and invoke a method that will respond to the event. The event editor is shown in Figure 7.33b. Alice automatically creates an event statement, *When the world starts*, do *World.my_first_method()*, in the Event editor with each new program you write. So, when you click the Play button, the world's *my_first_method* is invoked.

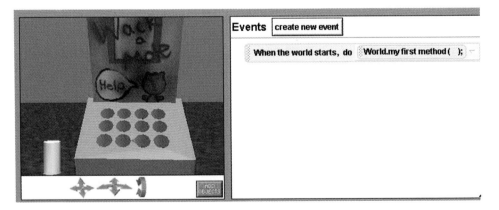

Figure 7.33b
Events editor

In this game, we want to respond when the player successfully clicks on a mole that pops up from the game booth. Each time the player succeeds, the *playerScore* cylinder should be raised, indicating an increase in the player's score. Once the entire *playerScore*

Figure 7.34
Scorekeeping columns at runtime

cylinder has been raised above ground level, it will then be the same height above ground as the *totalScore* cylinder. At this point, the player has won the game, and the moles should cease popping up and down. Figure 7.34 shows a screen capture of the game during execution. The top of the yellow *playerScore* cylinder is approaching the top of the grey *totalScore* cylinder, showing that the player is doing well in the game.

In designing a solution to this problem, two subtasks need to be considered. The first is to set up a *while loop* that continues to pop (raise and lower) moles randomly while the game is in progress. The second is to increase the player's score each time the player manages to actually click on one of the moles that pops up. In storyboard form,

```
Event:When the world starts
Response:World.myFirstMethod
  while the playerScore column is not yet completely above ground
    pop (and lower) a random mole

Event: User clicks mouse
Response:World.score
  If mouse was clicked on one of the moles
    doTogether
      move the playerScore column upward
      play a pop sound (sound is optional)
```

7.4.2 First Subtask—Game in Progress

When the world starts, the game should immediately begin. As you know, Alice automatically executes *World.my_first_method* when the world starts. Taking advantage of this automatic execution, the code for starting the game and keeping it in progress will be written in *World.my_first_method*.

A *while* loop can be used to provide continuous action in the game. As long as the yellow *playerScore* column has not yet moved up to the top level of the grey *totalScore*

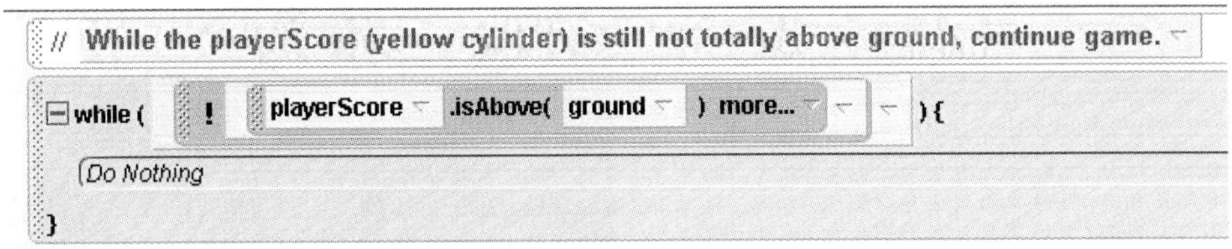

```
// While the playerScore (yellow cylinder) is still not totally above ground, continue game. ▽

while (    !    playerScore ▽ .isAbove( ground ▽ ) more... ▽  ▽  ){

    (Do Nothing

}
```

Figure 7.35a
While loop for continuous game action

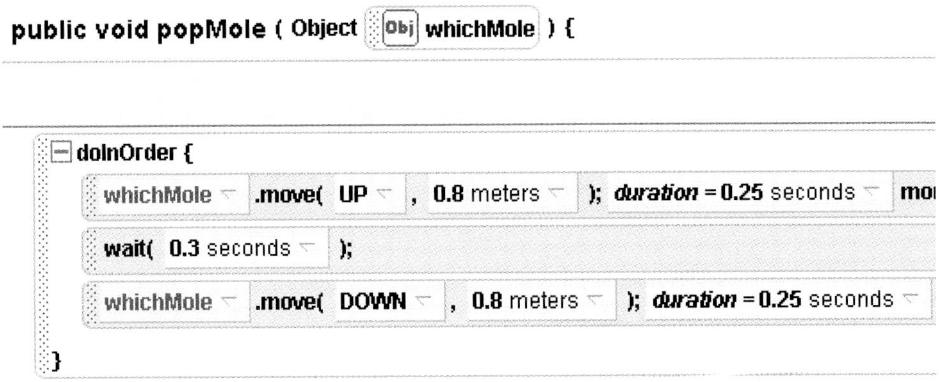

```
public void popMole ( Object  Obj whichMole ) {
```

```
doInOrder {

    whichMole ▽ .move( UP ▽ , 0.8 meters ▽ ); duration = 0.25 seconds ▽  mo

    wait( 0.3 seconds ▽ );

    whichMole ▽ .move( DOWN ▽ , 0.8 meters ▽ ); duration = 0.25 seconds ▽

}
```

Figure 7.35b
The *popMole* method

column (meaning that the player hasn't yet won the game), calls will be repeatedly made to a *popMole* method, as shown in Figure 7.35a.

Within the *while* loop, we need to invoke a method to pop up a mole. We have twelve moles, so we will create a method named *popMole* with an object parameter *whichMole* to represent the mole selected to pop up and then move back down. The method is illustrated in Figure 7.35b.

Of course, the first thing to do after this method is written is to test it. (We don't have to wait until the program is written!) Just invoke the method from *World.my_first_method*. Whichever mole is passed to *whichMole* is the mole that pops up. The popup action makes the mole move up, stay up for 0.3 seconds, and then move back down.

Now we need to figure out how to randomly select a mole object and pass it in to the *popMole* method. Our solution is to organize the moles into a list structure and then randomly select a mole from the list. A list of moles is created, as previously described in the rockettes example in Section 7.3. The name of the list variable in this WhackAMole game will be *moles*—not a very creative name, but it has the advantage of being obvious!

Now that the *popMole* method has been written (Figure 7.35) and the *moles* list created, the code for keeping the game in progress can be written in *World.my_first_method,* as in Figure 7.36. To send a random mole from the list to the *popMole* method each time it is invoked, we dragged the mole list into the parameter tile and then selected random

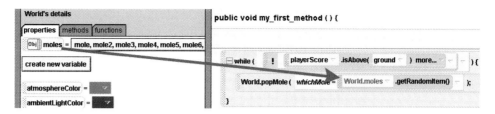

Figure 7.36
Repeatedly invoking *popMole*

item from list from the popup menu. When this code is run, a random mole from the list is passed as an argument to the *popMole* method each time the *while* statement is repeated.

Wait a second! When the code shown in Figure 7.36 is tested, it keeps playing and playing and playing. The *while* loop is supposed to end when the *playerScore* column moves up to the top of the *totalScore* column. Of course, the *playerScore* column does not move upward because we have not yet written the code to make that happen. Our program is not yet complete. We have one more step to accomplish.

7.4.3 Second Subtask—Scoring

A *score* method needs to be written to visually display the player's success in the game. Each time the player succeeds in clicking on a mole that pops up, the *playerScore* column should be raised. The *score* method is shown in Figure 7.37. The object clicked by the mouse will be sent to the *clicked* parameter. In this method, a *forAllInOrder* statement is used to iterate through the list of moles. Each mole is checked to determine whether it is the object clicked. This is where the list search takes place! If one of the

Figure 7.37
The *score* method

moles in the list is the object clicked, the player's score is increased (raising the *playerScore* column), and the clicked mole makes a popping sound.

Critical to the *score* method is capturing the user's mouse click and sending it to the *score* method as the *clicked* object. To capture the mouse-click event, we create a new event statement in the Event editor: *When mouse is clicked on something.* We selected anything as the argument for the event. (This allows the mouse to click on anything in the world, but we will check whether the clicked object is or is not a popped up mole.) To complete the statement, the World.score method tile is dragged into the editor and dropped on top of the to replace the default "do nothing" action. From the popup menu, we selected whatWasPicked() as the argument for the *clicked* parameter. The result is shown in Figure 7.38.

In response to the mouse being clicked on something (anything), the *score* method is invoked. This event notifies Alice the mouse has been clicked, and Alice can then determine what object is under the mouse cursor. The object under the mouse cursor will be passed to the *clicked* parameter for the *score* method.

Of course, it is possible that the player clicked too soon or too late and the object under the cursor was the top of the WhackAMole game booth (because the mole had disappeared back underneath). The player may move the cursor too quickly and click on the grass or the sky. In such situations, the search for a mole that has been clicked fails, so the player's score is not increased and no pop sound is made.

The important concept illustrated by the WhackAMole example is that of searching a collection of items to determine whether one of them has a particular property. Other techniques for searching can be used, but the overall idea is the same. In this example,

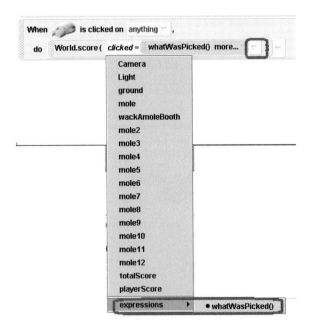

Figure 7.38
Creating the event

the collection of items is a list of moles. The search is conducted using a *forAllInOrder* statement to iterate through the list. The *forAllInOrder* statement goes through each mole in the list and checks whether one of them has been clicked by the player.

7.5   Summary

Control statements for repetition (*for loop* and *while* statement) were introduced in this chapter. In addition, a *list* data structure was used to organize multiple objects into a collection to allow sequential or simultaneous iteration of action statements on all objects in the list.

7.5.1 The *for loop* Statement

A *for loop* was introduced in this chapter as a control structure for repeating a block of code. A counted *loop (for loop)* allows you to specify exactly how many times a block of code will be repeated. The advantage of using *for loops* is immediately obvious. A *for loop* is fast and easy to write and also easy to understand. A code block within the *for loop* may consist of only a few statements, but can be repeated many, many times. For example, to make a bunny hop 30 times, we could do,

```
for (int index=0; index < 30; index++) {
  bunny.hop();
}
```

7.5.2 The *while* Statement

A *while* statement allows you to repeat a block of code as long as some condition remains true. For example, we could do,

```
while (bunny.distanceTo(broccoli) > 0.25) {
  bunny.hop();
}
```

Notice that a *while* statement uses a Boolean expression for conditional execution similar to the *if-Else* statement. A conditional *if-Else* statement, however, is executed only once. On the other hand, a *while* statement could execute many times before the condition becomes false and the *while* statement ends.

7.5.3 A List Data Structure

In programming, many different kinds of organizing structures can be used to create a collection of objects or information about objects. We use the term "data structure" for these organized collections of objects or information (data). Each kind of structure offers different capabilities or features. In Alice, lists are used as a collection of several items of the same type (such as *Object* or *Color*).

7.5.4 Repetition with a List

We looked at creating a list as well as iterating through a list (repeating actions with each item in a list). Alice provides two mechanisms for iterating through a list: sequentially (using *forAllInOrder*) and simultaneously (using *forAllTogether*). The *forAllInOrder* iteration is similar to "walking" (or traversing) through each item in the list, one at a time. The *forAllTogether* iteration is like setting up a multi-way telephone conference call—everyone is on the line at the same time. The *forAllInOrder* statement is similar to *doInOrder* in that actions are performed in sequence. And, the *forAllTogether* statement is similar to *doTogether* in that actions are performed simultaneously.

7.5.5 List Search

A common operation performed with lists is searching for an item in a list. A list search walks through each item in the list, one at a time, until we find the one we want. In this chapter we illustrated a list search using the WhackAMole game, in which we looked at each mole in the list to determine whether the user had successfully clicked on a popped-up mole.

7.5.6 Events

The WhackAMole game is interactive in that the player interacts with the program as the program is running. In an interactive game, a mouse-click is said to be an event (something that happens). Alice provides an event editor that allows you to specify the event and invoke a method that will respond to the event. In a game such as WhackAMole, the event commonly used is,

```
When mouse is clicked on <target> do <some action>
```

where *<target>* can be a specific object or anything in the world and *<some action>* is a call to a method that takes some action in response to an event.

Exercises

1. Give a reason for describing the *for loop* statement as a "counted loop."

2. If a block of program code is composed of nested *for loop* statements and the outer *for loop* count is 3 and the inner *for loop* count is 5, how many times does the inner *for loop* execute?

3. What distinguishes a *for loop* statement from a *while* statement, in terms of what is known about the number of times the block of code will be repeated?

4. Conditional expressions used in a *while* statement evaluate to the same type of value as a conditional expression used in what other conditional control statement?

5. If an Alice world contains six penguin objects, is it necessarily the case that six penguin are automatically considered to be a list of penguins? Explain your answer.

6. (a) Which control statement is used to iterate through a list of items in sequence?

   (b) Which control statement is used to iterate through a list of items simultaneously?

7. In what way is a "movie" animation different from an "interactive" animation?

8. What is meant by the term "event," as used in an Alice program?

9. This exercise is to complete the bunny example in this chapter. You will recall that the bunny has snuck into his neighbor's garden and is hopping over to take a bite of the tempting broccoli shoots. Code was presented to make the bunny hop eight times (in a *for loop*) over to the broccoli. Just as the bunny reaches the broccoli, Papa rabbit (*Hare* from Animals folder) appears at the garden gateway and taps his foot in dismay. The bunny hops a quick retreat out of the garden. Write a program to implement the bunny in the garden animation. Your code should use a loop not only to make the bunny hop over to the broccoli (see the initial scene in Figure 7.1) but also to hop out of the garden.

10. This exercise explores the use of nested *for loops*. Papa rabbit has been teaching the bunny some basic geometry. The lesson this morning is on the square shape. To demonstrate that the bunny understands the idea, the bunny is to hop in a square. Create a world with the bunny and the hop method, as described in Section 7.1. Use a *for loop* to make the bunny hop three times. When the *for loop* ends, have the bunny turn left one-quarter revolution. Then add another *for loop* to repeat the above actions, as shown in the storyboard here.

```
loop 4 times
   loop 3 times
      bunny.hop
   turn left 1/4 revolution
```

11. An old *saloon* (Old West) is being converted into a tourist attraction. Use 3D text to create a neon sign to hang on the front of the balcony. Then use a *for loop* to make the sign blink 10 times. (Appendix A, Section 1 provides instructions on using 3D text. Appendix A, Section 4 shows how to make an object visible or invisible.)

12. Exercise 6 in Chapter 3 asked you to create a new class of combination lock with four object methods—*leftOne, rightOne, leftRevolution*, and *rightRevolution*—that turn the dial 1 number left, 1 number right, 1 revolution left, and 1 revolution right, respectively. Also, the lock has a method named *open* that opens it, and another named *close* that closes it. The purpose of this exercise is to reuse the methods created in the previous exercise. Revise the previous world. Use a *for loop* statement to turn the dial left 25. Then use a *for loop* to turn the dial right and finally use a *for loop* to turn the dial back to the left 3 times. (The combination is 25, 16, 3.) Then, pop open the latch, close the latch, and return the dial to zero.

Making It Work Tip: Pausing the Action
Use *Wait* to make the lock pause between each turn of the dial.

13. Write a program that will make the *astronaut* (Space) perform a moonwalk. The *lunar lander* (SciFi) and *flag* (Objects) are used to decorate the Space template scene. To perform the moonwalk, the astronaut should turn right and then walk backward in a sliding sort of motion where one leg slides backward and then the other leg slides backward. The astronaut's entire body must move backward at the same time as the moonwalk leg motions are executed. Use a *for loop* to make the astronaut repeat the moonwalk steps 5 times.

14. Create a world with a *frog* (Animals) and a *ladybug* (Animals). Write an interactive program to allow the user to drag the ladybug around the scene. (Use a *let the mouse move objects* event.) As the ladybug is dragged around, make the frog chase after it by moving one hop at a time without colliding with the ladybug. If the user moves the ladybug within 2 meters of the frog, have the frog look at the camera and say "ribbit"—then end the animation.

15. Create a simulation of the *bumper car ride* (Amusement Park), where the cars move continuously around within the bumper arena. Add two bumper cars inside the arena. In this animation, each car should be moving forward a small amount until it gets too close to another car or to the wall, then turn the car a quarter of a revolution clockwise (to get a different direction) and continue moving forward. Use a *switch* (Controls) to stop and start the ride. As long as the switch is on, the ride should continue.

Making It Work Tip: Avoiding Collisions

To avoid a car driving through a wall of the arena, a simple form of collision detection is needed. One way to check for a possible collision is to use the *distance to* function to compute the distance of the car to the arena. Remember that *distance to* is measured "center-to-center." In this world, a measurement from the center of the car to the center of the arena is exactly what you need. (When a car gets too far from the center of the arena, it will collide with a wall.) It is also possible to write a function that returns whether two cars are about to collide with one another. What should be done in this case?

16. Create a world with a wind-up penguin. This is actually a *penguin* (Animals) with a *windUpKey* (Objects) positioned against its back. The key's *vehicle* property has been set to the penguin. In this world, make the penguin waddle (or walk) around the world continuously while its wind-up key turns.

17. A horse is in training for a circus act, in which the horse must jump through a large hoop (we used the *torus* from the Shapes folder). Create a world, as shown, with a horse facing the hoop. Write a program to use a *for loop* to have the horse trot forward several times and then jump through the hoop. When the horse gets close enough to the hoop to jump through it, have the horse jump through and then the world ends.

Your project must include a *trot* method that makes the horse perform a trot motion forward. A horse trots by turning the legs at the same time as the body moves forward. The leg motions can bend at the knee for a more realistic simulation, if desired. The loop invokes the *trot* method.

18. Create a water world with a *carrier* in the ocean and a *navy jet* (Vehicles) in the air, as shown. Write an interactive program to allow the user to use keyboard controls to land the jet on the deck of the carrier. Up, down, and forward controls are needed. Use a function to determine when the jet has landed (gotten close enough to the carrier's deck) and a *while* statement to continue the animation until the jet has landed.

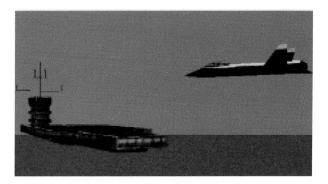

19. This exercise is to practice using *forAllInOrder*. Create an animation that simulates some sports fans doing "the wave"—a popular stadium activity. Create an initial scene where a *coach*, *student1*, *skaterGirl*, and *randomGuy2* (People) are standing on the field in the *stadium* (City). All four of these people have the same subpart structure. Then create a list made up of the people objects in the scene. Use the *forAllInOrder* statement to animate each person raising his or her arms to simulate "the wave."

20. This exercise is to practice using *forAllTogether*. Create a world with five *soldiers* (People) on the edge of the *carrier* (Vehicles). The idea is to make the soldiers walk "in step" from one end of the carrier to the other. An initial world

is shown below. Create a list variable, named *platoon*, made up of the five soldiers. Use the *forAllTogether* statement to conduct a military drill with the soldiers.

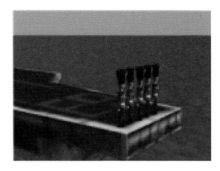

21. If you have a copy of the world that you created in Chapter 5, Exercise 13, you can revise that world. Otherwise build the world using the a *box* (Shapes) and *flowers* (Nature). Five flowers (your choice) are hidden inside the box.

(**Hint:** The flowers can be hidden inside the box by using the mouse to position them out of sight.)

Create a list, where each flower is one item of the list.

(a) Make each flower "grow" upward (out of the flowerbox) one at a time using *forAllInOrder*.

(b) When you have that working well, create a second version where all flowers grow out of the flowerbox at the same time, using *forAllTogether*.

22. One possible modification to the WhackAMole game is to play it until the user has whacked all of the moles. To make this adjustment, change the color of a mole in the list to red whenever it is whacked. Allow the mole to be raised only if it is not already red. The game ends when all moles have been whacked.

23. In this game, a *ghost* (Spooky) is out for a treasure hunt on Halloween night. The *haunted house* (Amusement Park) has been littered with *tombstones* (Spooky). Under each tombstone is a treasure. When the ghost gets close to a tombstone, the tombstone falls over and the treasure is revealed. The ghost's task is to visit all the tombstones and reveal all the treasures. Unfortunately, *skeletons*

(Spooky) are patrolling the grounds—walking back and forth near the tombstones to protect the treasures. If the ghost gets too close to a skeleton, he will vaporize and the game ends (and the ghost will have to wait until next Halloween night to find the treasures).

Create an animated game for the Halloween Treasure Hunt. Use a list to store 10 tombstones. The tombstones are all around the haunted house (screen shot shows only the front side). Allow the user to use the keyboard arrow keys to move the ghost around the grounds of Phantom Manor. Make the camera follow the ghost so he is always in sight. Do not worry about the ghost moving through an object—he is a ghost! As each tombstone gets visited, change its *opacity* property from *1* to *0*. If the ghost manages to visit all the tombstones (all of them have an opacity of 0), the game is over and the ghost has won. If the ghost encounters a skeleton at too close a range, the game is over and the ghost will vaporize into thin air.

24. A famous mathematical problem (the Monty Dilemma) goes something like this:

Suppose you're on a game show, and you're given the choice of three doors. Behind one door is a car, behind the others, toy monkeys. You pick a door, say number 1, and the host, who knows what's behind the doors, opens another door, say number 3, which has a toy monkey. He says to you, "Do you want to pick door number 2?" Is it to your advantage to switch your choice of doors?

One way to find an answer to this question is to create a simulation of the game where the objects are placed randomly behind the doors. Play the game 25 times where you do not switch and 25 times where you do switch. Keep track of your success rate when you switch and your success rate when you do not switch. Then you will know the answer to the question!

To set up the initial world, add three *doors* (Furniture), a *car* (Vehicles), and two *toy monkeys* (Animals) to a new world. Position the car and the two monkeys behind the three doors, as illustrated. Each door should be 2.5 meters to the left (or right) of its neighbor door. Make the door positioned in front of the car the vehicle for the car and then do the same for each monkey and its respective door. (When the door moves, the object behind will move with it.) Also create a 3D text object that asks the player to "Select a Door." Make the text object invisible by setting its *isShowing* property to *false*.

To program the game, make a list containing the three doors. When the animation begins, randomly pick two doors and swap them. Use a method called *swap* that takes two doors as parameters. Swap the two doors by having them move 2.5 meters in opposite directions.

Two doors should swap only if they are different (a door cannot swap places with itself). Repeat the swap ten times. (The idea is to make it difficult for the player to know what object is behind what door.)

Display the 3D text to ask the player to select a door. After the player clicks on one of the doors, pick another door that hides a monkey and open that door. Then ask the player whether he/she wants to switch the choice. If the object behind the door (selected by the player) is the car, the player has won. Open the door and declare the player a winner. Otherwise, the player has lost. Use sound or 3D text to indicate the win or loss.

25. Add a *rectangle* (Shapes) to a new world and change its color to blue. This will serve as a swimming pool. Add 7 *circles* (Shapes) to the world—5 yellow along the long side of the pool (each 1 meter apart), 1 green at the nearest side, and 1 red at the far edge. The yellow circles are lily pads that float back and forth across the pool. Add a frog, and place it on the green circle. The goal is to make the frog jump from lily pad to lily pad until it gets all the way across the pool. If the frog lands on the water (not on a lily pad) the frog sinks into the pool and the game is over. If the frog jumps all the way across the pool and lands on the red circle at the far edge, the player wins.

    Your program must place the 5 yellow circles in a list. Write a method that uses an infinite loop to repeatedly move each of the 5 yellow circles in the list across the pool and back at different speeds. (The easiest way to do this is to pass a random number to the method to specify the duration for the circle to move across the pool.) Create event handling methods that have the frog jump forward 1 meter if the player presses the ↑ key, move left if the player presses the ← key, and move right if the player presses the → key. Connect each event handling method to an event.

8
Modifying All Samples in a Sound

Goals of this chapter:

- To understand how we digitize sounds and the limitations of human hearing that allow us to digitize sounds.
- To use the formula that n bits result in 2^n possible patterns in order to figure out the number of bits needed to save sound values.
- To understand and use a one-dimensional array as a data structure.
- To use iteration (with for-each, `while`, and `for` loops) for manipulating sounds.
- To use conditionals (`if-else`) when m anipulating sounds.

Introduction

You have been learning about conditional (*if-else*) and loop (*for* and *while*) structures in Alice. In a conditional, a Boolean expression is evaluated to determine whether a block of code will or will not be executed. For example, in Alice, you used a conditional to decide which value to return from a function when testing whether two aircraft are too close to one another. You also used conditionals to determine which aircraft to move up and which aircraft to move down to avoid a collision. You have seen that loops allow you to repeat a block of code a counted number of times or while some condition is true. You have also used loops to make each element of a list do some action, either one at a time or at the same time.

Loops and conditionals are essential to computing, and it is time to apply the concepts learned in Alice to programming in Java. In this chapter, you will loop through values in a digital sound and change each one. You will conditionally modify sound values as well.

8.1 How Sound Is Encoded

There are two parts to understanding how sound is encoded and manipulated.

1. What are the physics of sound? How is it that we hear a variety of sounds?
2. How can we then map these sounds into numbers on a computer?

8.1.1 The Physics of Sound

Physically, sounds are waves of air pressure. When something makes a sound, it makes ripples in the air just like stones or raindrops dropped into a pond cause ripples

Figure 8.1
Raindrops causing ripples on the surface of the water, just as sound causes ripples in the air

on the surface of the water, as shown in Figure 8.1. Each drop causes a wave of pressure to pass over the surface of the water, which causes visible rises in the water and less visible, but just as large, depressions in the water. The rises are increases in pressure, and the lows are decreases in pressure. Some of the ripples we see are actually ones that arise from *combinations* of ripples—some waves are the sums and interactions from other waves.

We call these increases in air pressure **compressions** and decreases in air pressure **rarefactions**. It's these compressions and rarefactions that lead to our ability to hear. The shape of the waves, their frequency, and their amplitude all impact how we perceive sound.

The simplest sound in the world is a sine wave, as shown in Figure 8.2. In a sine wave, the compressions and rarefactions arrive with equal size and regularity. In a sine wave, one compression plus one rarefaction is called a **cycle**. The number of cycles that occur in a unit of time (for example, one second) is the frequency. The distance from the zero point to the greatest pressure (or least pressure) is called the **amplitude**.

Human perception of sound is not a direct mapping from the physical reality. The study of human perception of sound is called **psychoacoustics**. In general, amplitude is the most important factor in our perception of a sound's **volume**: If the amplitude rises, we perceive the sound as being louder. If the amplitude falls, we perceive the sound as being softer. When we perceive an increase in volume, we are perceiving an increase in

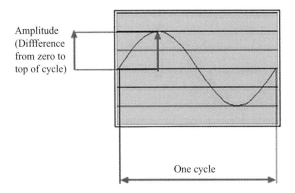

Amplitude
(Diffference
from zero to
top of cycle)

One cycle

Figure 8.2
One cycle of the simplest sound, a sine wave

the intensity of a sound. We measure the change in intensity of a sound in **decibels (dB).** That's probably the unit that you most often associate with volume. When decibels are used as an absolute measurement, it's in reference to the threshold of audibility at **sound pressure level (SPL)**: 0 dB SPL. Normal speech has an intensity of about 60 dB SPL. Shouted speech is about 80 dB SPL.

A second important factor in how we perceive a sound is the **frequency** of the sound, which is a measure of how often a cycle occurs. If a cycle is short, then there can be lots of them per second. If a cycle is long, then there are fewer of them. As the frequency increases, we perceive that the **pitch** increases (sounds higher). We measure frequency in **cycles per second (cps)** or **Hertz (Hz)**. Humans hear between 2 Hz and 20,000 Hz (or 20 kilohertz, abbreviated 20 kHz). Again, as with decibels, that's an enormous range! To give you a sense of where music fits into that spectrum, the note A above middle C, shown in Figure 8.3, is 440 Hz.

Figure 8.3
The note A above middle C is 440 Hz

What makes the experience of one sound different from another? Why is it that a flute playing a note sounds *so* different from a trumpet or a clarinet playing the same note? We still don't understand everything about psychoacoustics and what physical properties influence our perception of sound, but here are some other factors that lead us to perceive different sounds (especially musical instruments) as distinct.

- Real sounds are almost never single-frequency sound waves. Most natural sounds have *several* frequencies in them, often at different amplitudes. These additional frequencies are sometimes called **overtones**. When a piano plays the note C, for example, part of the richness of the tone is that the notes E and G are *also* in the sound, but at lower amplitudes. Different instruments have different overtones in their notes. The central tone, the one we're trying to play, is called the **fundamental**.

- Instrument sounds are not continuous with respect to amplitude and frequency. Some come slowly up to the target frequency and amplitude (like wind instruments), while others hit the frequency and amplitude very quickly and then the volume fades while the frequency remains pretty constant (like a piano).

- Not all sound waves are represented well by sine waves. Real sounds have funny bumps and sharp edges. Our ears can pick these up, at least in the first few waves. We can do a reasonable job synthesizing with sine waves, but synthesizers sometimes also use other kinds of wave forms, as shown in Figure 8.4, to get different kinds of sounds.

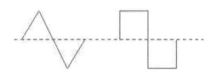

Figure 8.4
Some synthesizers using triangular (or **sawtooth**) or square waves

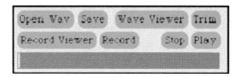

Figure 8.5
Sound editor main tool

8.1.2 Exploring Sounds

You can download the MediaTools application from `http://home.cc.gatech.edu/`
`TeaParty/43`. The MediaTools application contains tools for sound, graphics, and
video. Using the sound tools, you can actually observe sounds as they're coming into
your computer's microphone to get a sense of what louder and softer sounds look like
and of what higher and lower pitched sounds look like. Just start the MediaTools
(double-click `SqueakVM.exe` on Windows machines or `mediatools-v4-sa.image`
on Apple machines) and then click SoundTools.

The basic sound editor is shown in Figure 8.5. You can record sounds, open WAV
files (a type of sound file) on your disk, and view the sounds in a variety of ways. (You
will need a microphone on your computer to record sounds!)

To view sounds, click the Record Viewer button, then the Record button. (Hit the
Stop button to stop recording.) There are three kinds of views that you can display for
a sound.

The first is the **Signal view**, shown in Figure 8.6. In the signal view, you're looking at the sound raw—each increase in air pressure results in a rise in the graph, and
each decrease in sound pressure results in a drop in the graph. Note how rapidly the
wave changes! Try making some softer and louder sounds so that you can see how the
look of the representation changes. You can always get back to the signal view from
another view by clicking the Signal button.

The second view is the **Spectrum view**, shown in Figure 8.7. The spectrum view
is a completely different perspective on the sound. In the previous section, you read
that natural sounds are often actually composed of several different frequencies at
once. The spectrum view shows these individual frequencies. This view is also called
the **frequency domain**.

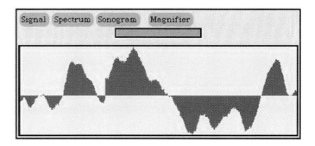

Figure 8.6
Viewing the sound signal as it comes in

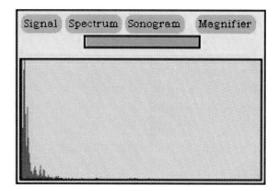

Figure 8.7
Viewing the sound in a spectrum view

Frequencies increase in the spectrum view from left to right. The height of a column indicates the amount of energy in that frequency in the sound. Natural sounds look like Figure 8.8 with more than one **spike** (rise in the graph). (The smaller rises around a spike are often seen as **noise**.)

The third view is the **Sonogram view**, shown in Figure 8.9. The sonogram view is very much like the spectrum view in that it is describing the frequency domain, but it presents these frequencies over time. Each column in the sonogram view, sometimes called a "slice" or "window (of time)," represents all the frequencies at a given moment in time. The frequencies increase in the slice from lower (bottom) to higher (top). The *darkness* of the spot in the column indicates the amount of energy of that frequency in the input sound at the given moment. The sonogram view is great for studying how sounds change over time, for example, how the sound of a piano key

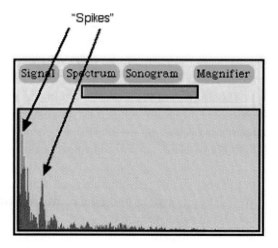

Figure 8.8
Viewing a sound in spectrum view with multiple "spikes"

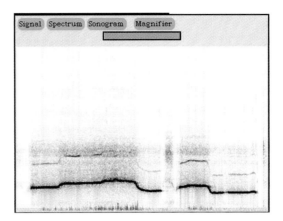

Figure 8.9
Viewing the sound signal in a sonogram view

being struck changes as the note fades, how individual instruments differ in their sounds, or how various vocal sounds differ.

Making It Work Tip: Explore Sounds!
You really should try these different views on real sounds. You'll get a much better understanding of sound and how our manipulations in this chapter are affecting the sounds.

8.1.3 Encoding Sounds

You just read about how sounds work physically and how we perceive them. To manipulate a sound on a computer and to play it back on a computer, we have to **digitize** the sound. To digitize sound means to take this flow of waves and turn it into numbers. We want to be able to capture a sound, perhaps manipulate it, and then play it back (through the computer's speakers) and hear what we captured, rendering it as exactly as possible.

The first part of the process of digitizing a sound is handled by the computer's hardware—the physical machinery of the computer. If a computer has a microphone and the appropriate sound equipment (like a SoundBlaster sound card on Windows computers), then it's possible, at any moment, to measure the amount of air pressure against that microphone as a single number. Positive numbers correspond to rises in pressure (compressions), and negative numbers correspond to drops in air pressure (rarefactions). We call this an **analog-to-digital conversion (ADC)**; we've moved from an analog signal (a continuously changing sound wave) to a digital value. By the way, playback systems on computers work essentially the same in reverse. The sound hardware does a **digital-to-analog conversion (DAC)**, and the analog signal is then sent to the speakers. The DAC process also uses numbers representing pressure. This means that we can get

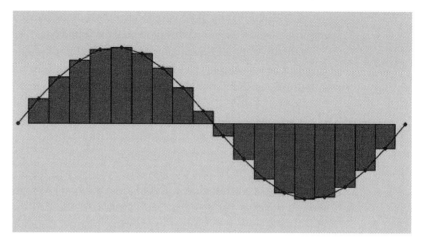

Figure 8.10
Area under a curve estimated with rectangles

an instantaneous measure of the sound pressure, but it's only one step along the way. Sound is a continuously changing pressure wave. How do we store that in our computer?

If you've had some calculus, you've got some idea of how we might do that. You know that we can get close to measuring the area under a curve with more and more rectangles whose height matches the curve, as Figure 8.10 shows. With that idea, it's pretty clear that if we capture enough of those microphone pressure readings we capture the wave. We call each of those pressure readings a **sample**—we are literally "sampling" the sound at that moment. But how many samples do we need? In integral calculus, you compute the area under the curve by (conceptually) having an infinite number of rectangles. While computer memories are growing larger and larger all the time, we still can't capture an infinite number of samples per sound.

Sampling Rate

Mathematicians and physicists wondered about these kinds of questions long before there were computers, and the answer to how many samples we need was actually computed long ago. In fact, a famous theorem known as the **Nyquist theorem** states that to capture a sound of at most n cycles per second, you need to capture $2n$ samples per second. This isn't just a theoretical result. The Nyquist theorem influences applications in our daily life. It turns out that human voices don't typically get over 4,000 Hz. That's why our telephone system is designed around capturing 8,000 samples per second, which is why playing music through the telephone doesn't really work very well.

So, by the Nyquist theorem, we know that the number of samples we need for a sound depends on the highest *frequency* you want to capture. Let's say that you don't care about any sounds higher than 8,000 Hz. We would need to capture 16,000 samples per second to completely capture and define a wave whose frequency is less than 8,000 cycles per second.

We call the rate at which samples are collected the **sampling rate**. You can capture and manipulate sounds with a sampling rate of 22 kHz (22,000 samples per second), and it will sound quite reasonable. If you use too low a sampling rate to capture a high-pitched sound, you'll still hear something when you play the sound back, but the pitch will sound strange.

Typically, each of these samples is encoded in two bytes (16 bits). Though a larger sample size is possible, 16 bits works perfectly well for most applications. CD-quality sound uses 16-bit samples. In 16 bits, the numbers that can be encoded range from −32,768 to 32,767.

These aren't magic numbers—they make perfect sense when you understand the encoding. These numbers are encoded in 16 bits using a technique called **two's complement notation**, but we can understand it without knowing the details of that technique. We've got 16 bits to represent positive and negative numbers. Let's set aside one of those bits (remember, a bit is just a 0 or 1) to represent whether we're talking about a positive (0) or negative (1) number. We call that the **sign bit**. That leaves 15 bits to represent the actual value. How many different patterns of 15 bits are there?

We could start counting:

```
000000000000000
000000000000001
000000000000010
000000000000011
. . .
111111111111110
111111111111111
```

That looks forbidding. Let's see if we can figure out a pattern. If we've got two bits, there are four patterns: 00, 01, 10, 11. If we've got three bits, there are eight patterns: 000, 001, 010, 011, 100, 101, 110, 111. It turns out that 2^2 is four, and 2^3 is eight. Play with four bits. How many patterns are there? $2^4 = 16$. It turns out that we can state this as a general principle:

2^n patterns can be represented in n bits

So, if you have n bits, there are 2^n possible patterns in those n bits. With 15 bits, $2^{15} = 32,768$. We said earlier that with 16 bits, the numbers that can be encoded range from −32,768 to 32,767. Why is there one more value in the negative range than the positive? Zero is neither negative nor positive, but if we want to represent it in bits, we need to define some pattern as zero. We use one of the positive range values (where the sign bit is zero) to represent zero, so that takes up one of the 32,768 patterns.

Sample Size

The **sample size** is a limitation on the amplitude of the sound that can be captured. If you have a sound that generates a pressure greater than 32,767 (or a rarefaction greater than −32,768), you'll only capture up to the limits of the 16 bits. If you were to look at the wave in the signal view, it would look like somebody took some scissors and *clipped* off the peaks of the waves. We call that effect **clipping** for that very reason. If you play (or generate) a sound that's clipped, it sounds bad—it sounds like your speakers are breaking.

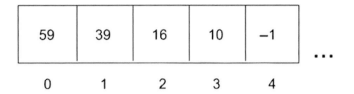

Figure 8.11
A depiction of the first five elements in a real sound array

There are other ways of digitizing sound, but the encoding we are using in this chapter is by far the most common. The technical term for this way of encoding sound is **pulse coded modulation (PCM).** You may encounter that term if you read further about audio or play with audio software.

What all this means is that a sound in a computer is a long list of numbers, each of which is a sample in time. There is an ordering in these samples: If you played the samples out of order, you wouldn't get the same sound at all. The most efficient way to store an ordered list of data items on a computer is with an array. An **array** is literally a sequence of bytes right next to one another in memory. We call each value in an array an **element**. In the previous chapter, you learned about lists, which also can be used to group objects of the same type. An array, like a list, can be used to hold a known number of objects of the same type.

We can easily store the samples that make up a sound in an array. Think of each two bytes as storing a single sample. The array will be large—for CD-quality sounds, there will be 44,100 elements for every second of recording. A minute long recording will result in an array with 26,460,000 elements.

Each array element has a number associated with it, called its **index**. The index numbers start at 0 and increase sequentially. The first one is 0, the second one is 1, and so on. It may sound strange to say the index for the first array element is 0, but this is basically a measure of the distance from the first element in the array. Since the distance from the first element to itself is 0, the index is 0. You can think about an array as a long line of boxes like the ones in Figure 8.11, with each box holding a value and each box having an index number on it.

You will soon learn how to read a file containing a recording of a sound turned into a sound object, view the samples in that sound, and change the values of the sound array elements. By changing the values in the array, you change the sound. Manipulating a sound is simply a matter of manipulating elements in an array.

8.2   Manipulating Sounds

Now that we know how sounds are encoded, we can manipulate sounds using Java programs. Here's what we'll need to do.

1. We'll need to get the filename for an existing WAV file, and make a new Sound object from it.

2. You will often get the samples of a sound as digital elements stored in an array. Sound sample objects are easy to manipulate and when you change them, they will automatically change the original sound.

3. To change the sound you will modify the value stored in the sample object.

4. You may then want to write the sound back out to a new file, in order to use it again.

8.2.1 Opening Sounds and Manipulating Samples

You have already seen how to pick a file with `FileChooser.pickAFile()` and you can make a **Sound object** (an object of the class Sound) using `new Sound(fileName)`. You can play a sound by invoking the `play()` method.

Here's an example of how to do all this in DrJava, as well as naming the file name and sound object. The example uses a sound file named `preamble.wav`.

```
> String fileName = FileChooser.pickAFile();
> Sound sound1 = new Sound(fileName);
> System.out.println(sound1);
Sound file: preamble.wav number of samples: 421110
> sound1.play();
```

What `new Sound(fileName)` does is to scoop up all the bytes from the file whose name is provided as input, dump the sound bytes into memory, and then place a big sign on the sound bytes saying, "This is a sound object (an object of the class Sound)." When you execute

```
Sound sound1 = new Sound(fileName)
```

you are saying, "Create an object variable called `sound1` that refers to the Sound object created from the information in the file with a file name given by the variable `fileName`." When you execute `sound1.play()`, you are saying, "Play the sound in that sound object over there (the one referred to by the variable `sound1`)." Also, when you use `sound1` as input to a method, you are saying "Use the sound object named `sound1` as input to this method."

You can get the samples from a sound by invoking the method `getSamples()`. When the method `getSamples()` is invoked on a Sound object, it returns an array of all the samples in the sound as `SoundSample` objects (objects of the class SoundSample).

To declare an array of any type, we use the syntax: `type[] name`. So to declare an array of type SoundSample, we use

```
SoundSample[] sampleArray
```

and assign to it the result of invoking the `getSamples()` method. For example,

```
> SoundSample[] sampleArray = sound1.getSamples();
```

When you execute the `getSamples()` method, it may take quite a while before it finishes—longer for longer sounds and shorter for shorter sounds.

To find out the number of items in an array, you can use the public field `length`. A **public field** is one that can be directly accessed from inside and outside the class using `objRef.field`. In the following example, the length of the `sampleArray` is displayed.

```
> System.out.println(sampleArray.length);
421110
```

As illustrated here, the method `getSamples()` creates an array of `SoundSample` *objects* out of the samples in the Sound object. An *object* is more than just a simple value—for example, a `SoundSample` object knows what Sound object it came from and what its index is.

How can we access and modify the individual objects (elements) in the array? You can access (get a reference to) the first element in an array using `arrayRef[0]`. You can access the second element in an array using `arrayRef[1]`. In general, you can access any element in an array at index *n* using `arrayRef[n]`. You can access the last element (the one at the length of the array minus one) in an array using `arrayRef[arrayRef.length -1]`. As an example, the following code accesses the first and last elements of `sampleArray`.

```
> SoundSample sample = sampleArray[0]; //first
> SoundSample sample2 = sampleArray[sampleArray.length-1]; //last
```

Once a `SoundSample` object is accessed, you can get the value of a `SoundSample` object by invoking the method `getValue()`, and you can set the value of a `SoundSample` object by invoking the method `setValue(value)`. The following code illustrates the use of `getValue()` and `setValue()` on the `SoundSample` object, which is called `sample`. Then, we access the second element in the array, which is `sampleArray[1]`, and set its value to 0.

```
> System.out.println(sample.getValue());
36
> sample.setValue(0);
> System.out.println(sample.getValue());
0
> sample = sampleArray[1];
> sample.setValue(0);
```

Now do you think you could hear any difference in the sound that we just changed? Remember that it has 421,110 values in it, and we just changed the first two values. You can play it and see if you hear any difference. You can also explore it and check that the first two values did change.

Once you've manipulated a sound, you can save it to a file with `write(String fileName)`, which takes a filename as input. Be sure that your file ends with the extension .wav if you're saving a sound so that your operating system knows what to do with it (what type of data is in it).

```
> sound1.write("c:/intro-prog-java/mediasources/preamble2.wav");
```

Common Bug: Saving a File Quickly—and How to Find it Again!

What if you don't know the whole path to a directory of your choosing? You don't have to specify anything more than the base name.

> sound1.write("new-preamble.wav")

The problem is finding the file again! In what directory did it get saved? This is a pretty simple bug to resolve. The default directory (the one you get if you don't specify a path) is wherever DrJava is. You can also use

FileChooser.getMediaPath("new-preamble.wav");

to get the full name of the media directory and base file name.

You'll probably figure out that, when playing sounds a lot, if you use play() a couple times in quick succession you'll mix the sounds. How do you make sure that the computer plays only a single sound and then waits for that sound to end? You use a method named blockingPlay(). BlockingPlay() works the same as play(), but it waits for each sound to end so that no other sound can interfere while it's playing.

8.2.2 Using the Explorer with Sounds

The sound explorer lets you explore a sound visually just as you explored a picture. To open a sound explorer on a sound object just execute soundObj.explore().

> sound1.explore();

This will open an explorer window on a copy of the sound, as shown in Figure 8.12.

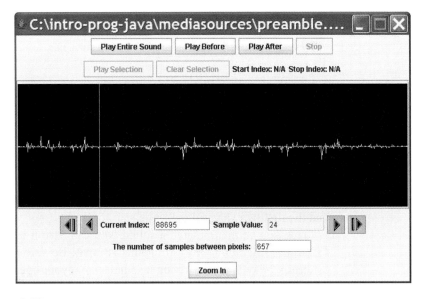

Figure 8.12
Using the explorer to explore a sound

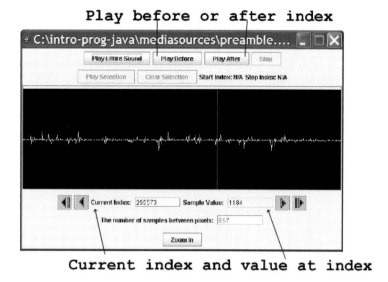

Figure 8.13
Using the sound explorer to see values and listen to parts of the sound

Just as you moved the cursor around a picture to find its *x*, *y*, and color values, you can move the cursor to different points on the sound wave to see the index and value of an individual sample at the cursor. It will show the current index with a blue line. Figure 8.13 shows how you can use the buttons at the top to play the entire sound or just the sound before or after the index. This can be useful to find the silences between words.

Figure 8.14
Zooming in on a sound to see every value in it

You can also click and drag to select a part of the sound wave. You can then play the section or clear it using the buttons below the Play buttons.

Sounds are very large, so you don't usually see every value in a sound in the explorer window. Figure 8.14 shows the Zoom in button at the bottom of the window that will show every value with a scroll bar to allow you to scroll through the sound. Above that button is a text area that tells you how many samples are being skipped in the current display of the sound wave. As you can see in Figure 8.13, there are 657 values being skipped between the values that are being shown. But when you zoom in as shown in Figure 8.14, you see all the values. You can click the Zoom Out button to see the entire sound again.

8.2.3 Introducing Loops

In the preamble.wav example (described in the previous section), you changed just two sample bytes in an array of 421,110 samples. How would you change all 421,110 sample sound bytes? To accomplish this task, we would need to change each element in the array, one at a time—421,110 times!

The problem of wanting to do something a great many times is a common one in computing: How do we get the computer to do something over and over again? We need to get the computer to *loop* or *iterate*. Java has reserved words especially for looping (iterating).

In Alice you used a forAllInOrder to loop through each element of a list. Each time through the loop, an object performs an action. Then the object that will perform the action changes to the next one in the list.

You can do something similar in Java using a for-each loop. It will execute the block of code in the body of a loop one time for each element in a collection of elements (for example, an array). The syntax of a for-each loop in Java is

```
for (Type variableName : collection)
    {
      //block of code - the body of the loop
    }
```

The first time through the loop, the variableName will refer to the first element of the array (the element at index 0). The second time through the loop, the variableName will refer to the second element of the array (the element at index 1).

Figure 8.15
Looping through all elements of a list in Alice

The last time through the loop, the `variableName` will refer to the last element of the array (the element at index (length −1)).

A method named `doubleValue()`, which loops through all the `SoundSample` objects in an array of `SoundSample` objects and sets the value of each sample to twice its original value is shown here.

```
public void doubleValue()
{
  SoundSample[] sampleArray = this.getSamples();
  int value = 0;

  // loop through all the samples in the array
  for (SoundSample sample : sampleArray)
  {
    value = sample.getValue();
    sample.setValue(2 * value);
  }
}
```

You can use the `for-each` loop whenever you want to process all the elements of an array, and you don't need to know the current index in the body of the loop.

Making It Work Tip: Keep Sounds Short

Longer sounds take up more memory and will process more slowly.

Common Bug: **Windows and WAV Files**

The world of WAV files isn't as compatible and smooth as one might like. WAV files created with other applications (such as Windows Recorder) may not play in DrJava, and DrJava WAV files may not play in all other applications (for example, WinAmp 2). Some tools, like Apple QuickTime Player Pro (`http://www.apple.com/quicktime`), are good at reading any WAV file and being able to export a new one that most any other application can read. Some WAV files are encoded using **MP3**, which means they are really MP3 files (another type of encoding for sound files). You can convert these using `Sound.convert(origFileName, convertedFileName)`, where `origFileName` and `convertedFileName` are the full names (including path information).

8.3 Changing the Volume of Sounds

What does doubling the value of each sample do? Earlier, we said that the amplitude of a sound is the main factor in the volume. This means that if we increase the amplitude, we increase the volume. Or if we decrease the amplitude, we decrease the volume.

Don't get confused here—changing the amplitude doesn't reach out and twist up the volume knob on your speakers. If your speaker's volume (or computer's volume) is turned down, the sound will never get very loud. The point is getting the sound itself louder. Have you ever watched a movie on TV where, without changing the volume on the TV, the sound becomes so low that you can hardly hear it? (Marlon Brando's dialogue in the movie *The Godfather* comes to mind.) That's what we're doing here. We can make sounds *shout* or *whisper* by tweaking the amplitude.

8.3.1 Increasing Volume

Here is the doubleValue() method again, but since it really increases the volume, let's call it increaseVolume instead.

Program 8.1: Increase the Sound's Volume

```java
public void increaseVolume()
{
  SoundSample[] sampleArray = this.getSamples();
  int value = 0;

  // loop through all the samples in the array
  for (SoundSample sample : sampleArray)
  {
    value = sample.getValue();
    sample.setValue(2 * value);
  }
}
```

Go ahead and type the above into your DrJava definitions pane before the last curly brace in the Sound.java class. Click **Compile All** to get DrJava to compile it. Then, in DrJava's **Interactions** pane, follow along with the example code below to get a better idea of how this all works.

To use the increaseVolume() method, you have to create a sound object first and then invoke this method on it. In the **Interactions** pane, we create a variable f which refers to a String object that holds the name of a file. Don't forget that you probably can't type this code in and have it work as-is: Your path names may be different than what is shown here! Adjust the path name assigned to String f, as needed. Then, create the variable s which refers to a Sound object created from the file using new Sound(f).

```java
> String f = "c:/intro-prog-java/mediasources/gettysburg10.wav";
> Sound s = new Sound(f);
```

Next, you can open an explorer window on a copy of the sound s to see what it looks like graphically using s.explore().

```java
> s.explore();
```

We next increase its volume using s.increaseVolume(). This implicitly passes the Sound object to the method increaseVolume(). So the code this.getSamples() in the method increaseVolume() means to get them from the implicitly passed Sound object (the one referred to by variable s). We loop through all values in the array `sampleArray` and change each value to two times the original value. We explore the changed sound so that we can compare the original and modified sounds.

```
> s.increaseVolume();
> s.explore();
```

Computer Science Idea: Changing Memory Doesn't Change the File

If you create another Sound object from the same file, will you get the original sound or the sound with volume increased? You will get the original sound. The Sound object s was created by reading the file data into memory. The change to the Sound object was done in memory, but the file wasn't changed. If you want to save your changes, write them out to a file using the method *soundObj*.`write(String fileName);`, where `soundObj` is the name of the Sound object and `fileName` is the full path name of the file. So to save the changed Sound object here, use `s.write("gettyLouder.wav");`. This will create a new file with the changed sound in it.

■

8.3.2 Did that Really Work?

Now, is it really louder, or does it just seem that way? We can check it in several ways. You could always make the sound even louder by evaluating `increaseVolume` on our sound a few more times—eventually, you'll be totally convinced that the sound is louder. But there are ways to test even more subtle effects.

   If you compare graphs of the two sounds using the sound explorer, you will find that the graph of the sound does have greater amplitude after increasing it using our method. Check it out in Figure 8.16.

   Maybe you're unsure that you're really seeing a larger wave in the second picture. You can use a sound explorer to check the individual sample values. You can actually already see that in Figure 8.16— see that the first value (index number 0) is 59 in the original sound and 118 in the second sound. You can also check the value at any index using the sound explorer. Just click on a location, and the value will be displayed for that location. To check the same location in the second explorer, just type in the desired index, and it will show the value at that index. Figure 8.17 shows that the louder sound really does have double the value of the same sample in the original sound.

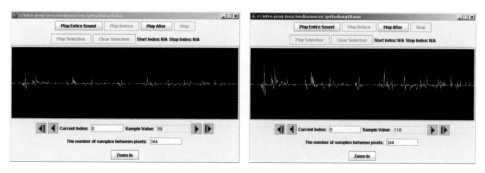

Figure 8.16
Comparing the graphs of the original sound (left) and the louder one (right)

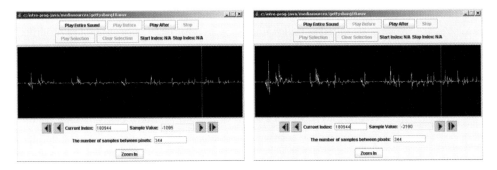

Figure 8.17
Comparing specific samples in the original sound (left) and the louder one (right)

Finally, you can always check for yourself from within DrJava. If you've been following along with the example,[1] then the variable s is the now louder sound. f should still be the filename of the original sound. Go ahead and make a new sound object which is from the *original* sound—named as sOrig (for *sound original*)—in the example code below. Check any sample that you want—it's always true that the louder sound has twice the value than the original sound.

```
> System.out.println(s);
Sound file:
c:/intro-prog-java/mediasources/gettysburg10-louder.wav number of
samples: 220568
> System.out.println(f);
c:/intro-prog-java/mediasources/gettysburg10.wav
> Sound sOrig = new Sound(f);
> SoundSample[] samples = s.getSamples();
> SoundSample sample = samples[0];
> System.out.println(sample.getValue());
118
> SoundSample[] origSamples = sOrig.getSamples();
> SoundSample origSample = origSamples[0];
> System.out.println(origSample.getValue());
59
> sample = samples[1];
> System.out.println(sample.getValue();
78
> origSample = origSamples[1];
> System.out.println(origSample.getValue());
39
> sample = samples[999];
> System.out.println(sample.getValue());
−80
> origSample = origSamples[999];
> System.out.println(origSample.getValue());
−40
```

[1]What? You haven't? You *should*! It'll make much more sense if you try it yourself!

You can see from the last value that even negative values become *more* negative. That's what's meant by "increasing the amplitude." The amplitude of the wave goes in *both* directions. We have to make the wave larger in both the positive and negative dimensions.

It's important to do what you just read in this chapter: *Doubt* your programs. Did that *really* do what we wanted it to do? The way you check is by *testing*. That's what this section is about. You just saw several ways to test:

- Looking at the result overall (like with the graphs created by the explorer).
- Checking pieces of the results (like with the explorer or MediaTools).
- Writing additional code statements that check the results of the original program.

8.3.3 Using a `while` Loop

A `for-each` loop is very useful if you want to loop through all the values in an array. But, how can you loop through just part of the values? You will need a way to tell Java when to stop the loop. A different loop that allows you to control when the loop stops is a `while` loop. A `while` loop executes the body of the loop, while a Boolean condition returns `true`. In order for the loop to stop, there must be some way for the Boolean condition to end up `false`.

In Alice, you used a `while` loop to check if a goldfish was too far in front of a shark to be eaten by the shark, (Figure 8.18). The Boolean condition was goldfish. distanceInFrontOf(shark) > 0.5. As long as this condition was true, the loop repeated, the goldfish fled, and the shark swam toward the goldfish. Once the distance of the goldfish in front of the shark fell to less than or equal to 0.5 meters, however, the loop stopped, and the shark ate the goldfish.

In a similar way, you can use a Boolean condition in Java to control a `while` loop instead of using a `for-each` loop to increase the volume in the sound.

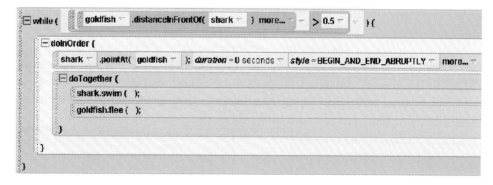

Figure 8.18
A `while` loop in Alice

Program 8.2: Increase the Sound's Volume with a while Loop

```java
public void increaseVolumeWhile()
{
  SoundSample[] sampleArray = this.getSamples();
  SoundSample sample = null;
  int index = 0;
  int value = 0;

  // loop through the samples
  while (index < sampleArray.length)
  {
    sample = sampleArray[index];
    value = sample.getValue();
    sample.setValue(2 * value);
    index++;
  }
}
```

Making It Work Tip: Shortcuts for Increment and Decrement

Adding one or subtracting one from a current value is something that is done frequently in programs. Programmers have to do lots of typing, so they try to reduce the amount of typing required for things they do frequently. Notice the statement index++; in Program 8.2. The statement index++; has the same result as the statement index = index + 1; and also can be written as ++index;. You also can use index--; or --index, which will have the same result as index = index - 1;.

Be careful when you are also assigning the result of these shortcut statements to a variable. If you do int x = index++; x will be assigned the original value of index, and then index will be incremented. If you do int x = ++index; the index will be incremented first, and then the value of index will be assigned to x.

Figuring Out How It Worked

Let's walk slowly through the code in increaseVolumeWhile() and consider how this program worked.

The very first statement, SoundSample[] sampleArray = **this**.getSamples(); creates an array named sampleArray. The array will hold SoundSample objects.

Recall our picture of the samples in a sound array. This is what this.getSamples()returns: An array of SoundSample objects.

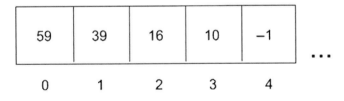

The second statement, `SoundSample sample = null;`, creates a variable named `sample` that will represent an individual sound byte. We initialized `sample` to **null** to tell Java that we do not, as yet, have a sound byte to assign to it.

Then, we declare two variables `index` and `value`, each initialized to zero.

```
int index = 0;
int value = 0;
```

The `index` will be used to access each element (a `SoundSample` object) in the array one at a time, and `value` will be used to represent the value of the accessed element.

Now that we have an array of `SoundSample` objects and variables to access and represent an individual object from the array, we can use a `while` loop to walk through each sample, one at a time. The name (variable) `sample` will refer to each `SoundSample` object in turn.

The variable `index` starts out with a value of 0. This is less than the length of the array `sampleArray`, so the body of the loop is executed. The variable `sample` is changed to refer to the first `SoundSample` object (the one at `index` 0).

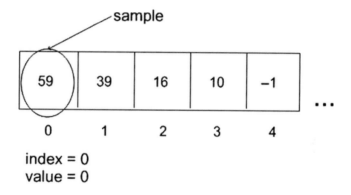

The variable `value` will take on the value of 59 when `value=sample.get Value()` is executed. The value stored at that `SoundSample` object will be set to `value` times 2 (59 * 2 or 118).

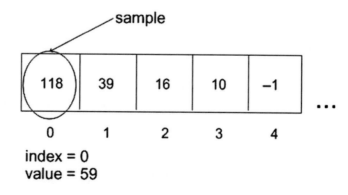

The value in variable index will be incremented by 1 (0 + 1 = 1). That's the end of the first pass through the body of the while loop. The loop will then start over. The test that index is less than the length of the array of samples will happen again. Since it is still less, the body of the loop will be executed (statements inside the open and close curly braces). The variable sample will be changed to refer to the second item in the array (the one at index 1).

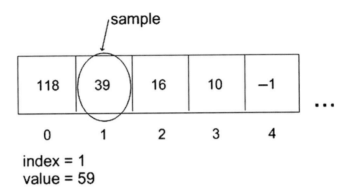

Again, the variable value is set to the value of the SoundSample object. The value of the SoundSample object is set to twice the amount held in the variable value.

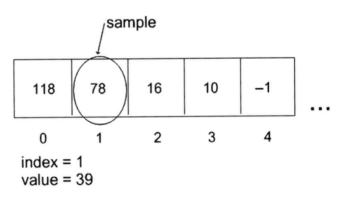

This is what it will look like after five times through the loop.

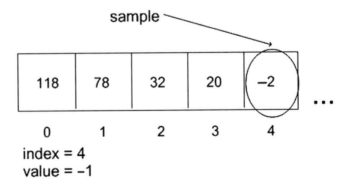

But really, the `while` loop *keeps* going through all the samples—tens of thousands of them! Thank goodness it's the *computer* executing this program!

What you have just read in this section is called **tracing** the program. We slowly went through how each step in the program was executed. We drew pictures to describe the data in the program. We used numbers, arrows, equations, and even plain English to explain what was going on in the program. This is the single most important technique in programming. It's part of **debugging**. Your program will *not* always work. Absolutely, guaranteed, without a shadow of a doubt—you will write code that does not do what you want. But the computer *will* do *SOMETHING*. How do you figure out what it *is* doing? You debug, and the most significant way to do that is by tracing the program.

8.3.4 Decreasing Volume

Decreasing the volume can be accomplished by reducing the sample values, as illustrated in Program 8.3.

Program 8.3: Decrease an Input Sound's Volume

```
/**
 * Method to decrease the volume (amplitude) of the sound.
 */
public void decreaseVolume()
{
  SoundSample[] sampleArray = this.getSamples();
  SoundSample sample = null;
  int value = 0;
  int index = 0;

  // loop through all the samples in the array
  while (index < sampleArray.length)
  {
    sample = sampleArray[index];
    value = sample.getValue();
    sample.setValue(value / 2);
    index++;
  }
}
```

- Our method is called on a Sound object. The Sound object is implicitly passed to the method and is accessed using the keyword `this`. You can leave off the `this` on `this.getSamples()` since it is understood to be invoked on the current object.

- The variable `sample` will refer to a different `SoundSample` object each time through the loop.

- Each time `sample` refers to a new `SoundSample` object, we will get the *value* of that `SoundSample` object. We put that in the variable `value`.

- We then set the `value` held by the `SoundSample` object to halve its current value.

We can use it like this.

```
> String f = FileChooser.pickAFile();
> System.out.println(f);
C:\intro-prog-java\mediasources\gettysburg10-louder.wav
> Sound sound1 = new Sound(f);
> System.out.println(sound1);
Sound file:
C:\intro-prog-java\mediasources\gettysburg10-louder.wav number of
samples: 220568
> sound1.play();
> sound1.decreaseVolume();
> sound1.play();
```

We can even do it again, and lower the volume even further.

```
> sound1.decreaseVolume();
> sound1.play();
```

8.3.5 Using a for Loop

One of the problems with using a `while` loop to repeat statements for each element in an array is that you might forget to declare the variable `index`. If you forget to declare the variable index, the method will not compile. Or you might forget to increment the variable index. If you did, the loop would never end until you hit Reset. Because of these problems, programmers typically use a `for` loop instead of a `while` loop when they want to execute a block of commands a known number of times. A `for` loop is equivalent to a `while` loop (means the same thing to the computer). The `for` loop is just less error prone for a programmer (though it can be harder for a beginner to understand).

In Alice, you used a `for` loop to have a bunny hop eight times, as Figure 8.19 shows. This `for` loop set the `index` equal to 0 and added one to it each time the body of the loop was finished executing. The `for` loop stopped when the `index` was no longer less than 8.

A `for` loop in Java is very similar to the Alice `for` loop:

for (*initialization*; *test*; *change*)

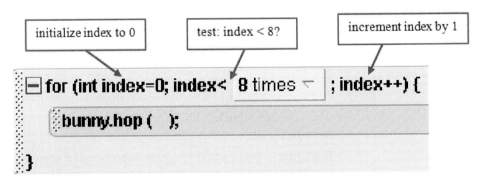

Figure 8.19
A `for` loop in Alice

The initialization area lets you declare and initialize variables for use in the loop, the test is where you test whether the loop should continue, and the change area is where you change the value of counters or indices used in the loop. For example, see the following new version of the method `decreaseVolume`, which has been modified to use a `for` loop instead of a `while` loop.

Program 8.4: Decrease an Input Sound's Volume Using a for Loop

```
/**
 * Method to halve the volume (amplitude) of the sound.
 */
public void decreaseVolumeFor()
{
  SoundSample[] sampleArray = this.getSamples();
  SoundSample sample = null;
  int value = 0;
  // int index = 0;

  // loop through all the samples in the array
  // while (index < sampleArray.length)
  for (int index = 0; index < sampleArray.length; index++)
  {
    sample = sampleArray[index];
    value = sample.getValue();
    sample.setValue(value / 2);
    // index++;
  }
}
```

In Program 8.4, we used a to-end-of-line comment `//` to comment out some lines of code to show the difference between the `while` and `for` loops. Notice what is different in the `for` loop: We don't declare and initialize the index *before* the loop, it is done in the *initialization* part of the `for` statement. We also don't increment the `index` as the last statement in the loop. This is moved to the change area in the `for` statement. So, we have replaced three lines of code with one line of code and made it more likely that we will remember to declare variables for use in the loop and to change them later.

Although a `for` loop is written more compactly than a `while` loop, what really happens during execution of a `for` loop *is the same thing* that happens during a `while` loop. The declarations and initializations written in the initialization part of a `for` loop statement actually are executed before the first test of the Boolean condition. Also, the changes of `index` variables are executed after each execution of the loop body and before the next test of the Boolean condition.

8.3.6 Making Sense of Methods

We want to write methods that do one and only one thing (considered a good design technique). Also, we want to write methods that can be reused. To write methods that can be reused, we need to make it possible for a method to work with many different input values (not just one built-in value). The way we can make this happen is to write a method that will take an input value (in Alice, an input value was known as a *parameter*).

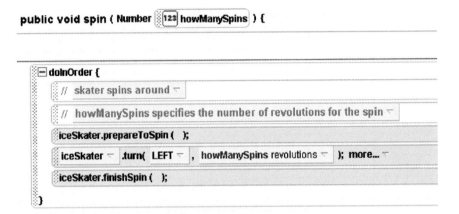

Figure 8.20
A spin method that accepts an input value for *howManySpins*

In Alice, you wrote a spin method for an *iceSkater*, where you passed an input value to a parameter named howManySpins, as shown in Figure 8.20.

If the spin method were invoked by passing in the value 3 (iceSkater.spin(3)), the *iceSkater* would spin around three times. The spin method could be invoked by passing in any other input value we want. For example, we could pass in 0.5, in which case the *iceSkater* would spin around one-half a revolution.

The same technique can be used to pass input values to a method in Java. For example, Program 8.5 contains a method to changeVolume of a soundSample object. It accepts a factor that is multiplied by each sample value. This method can be used to increase or decrease the amplitude (and thus, the volume).

Program 8.5: Change a Sound's Volume by a Given Factor

```java
/**
 * Method to change the volume (amplitude) of the sound
 * by multiplying the current values in the sound by
 * the passed factor.
 * @param factor the factor to multiply by
 */
public void changeVolume(double factor)
{
  SoundSample[] sampleArray = this.getSamples();
  SoundSample sample = null;
  int value = 0;

  // loop through all the samples in the array
  for (int i = 0; i < sampleArray.length; i++)
  {
    sample = sampleArray[i];
    value = sample.getValue();
    sample.setValue((int) (value * factor));
  }
}
```

Making It Work: Casting from a double to an int

The `factor` that is being passed in to the method `changeVolume` is declared to be of the type `double`, so you can make the volume smaller by passing in a `factor` that is less than one. Using a `factor` of 0.5 would halve the volume. But, what happens when you multiply 3 by 0.5? You end up with 1.5, but sound values only can be integer values, which means that we must throw away the amount past the decimal point. Casting to the type `int` using `(int)` will keep only the integer value.

This program is clearly more flexible than `increaseVolume()`. Does that make it better? Certainly it is for some purposes (for example, if you were writing software to do general audio processing), but for other purposes, having separate and clearly named methods for increasing and decreasing volume may be better. Of course, you could modify `increaseVolume()` and `decreaseVolume()` to call `changeVolume()` with the appropriate `factor`. Remember that software is written for humans—write software that is understandable for the people who will be reading and using your software.

We have reused the name `sample` several times in methods in the Sound class. *That's okay.* Names can have different meanings depending on their context. Variables declared in a method have meaning only inside that method. Methods can even use the same variable names as other methods. You can even use the same variable names that you use in your methods in the Interactions pane. This is a different **context** or **scope**, which means the area in which a variable name is known. If you create a variable in a method context (like `value` in Program 8.5), then that variable won't exist when you get back out to the Interactions pane.

8.4   Conditionally Modifying Sounds

In Alice, you wrote a function that used a conditional `if-else` statement to determine if a biplane was too close to another plane (shown again in Figure 8.21). If the biplane was too close to another plane, the function returned `true`, and if it wasn't too close, the function returned `false`. In this section, we will use a conditional `if/else` statement in Java to modify a sound.

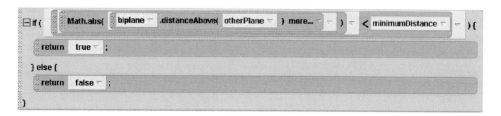

Figure 8.21
Using a conditional `if-else` statement in Alice

8.4.1 Generating Clipping

Earlier, we talked about *clipping*, which happens when the normal curves of a sound are broken by the limitations of the sample size. One way of generating clipping is to keep increasing the volume. Another way is to explicitly force clipping.

What if you *only* had the largest and smallest possible sample values? What if all positive values (including zero), were the *maximum* value (32,767) and all negative values were the minimum value (–32,768)? Try this program, particularly on sounds with words in them.

Program 8.6: Set Samples to Extreme Values

```java
/**
 * Method to set all the sample values to the
 * maximum positive value if they were positive or zero
 * and the minimum negative
 * value if they were negative.
 */
public void forceToExtremes()
{
  SoundSample[] sampleArray = this.getSamples();
  SoundSample sample = null;

  // loop through the sample values
  for (int i = 0; i < sampleArray.length; i++)
  {
    // get the current sample
    sample = sampleArray[i];

    // if the value was positive set it to the
    // maximum positive value
    if (sample.getValue() >= 0)
      sample.setValue(32767);

    // else, force to max negative value
    else
      sample.setValue(-32768);
  }
}
```

Here's how to run this program:

```
> Sound s = new Sound(FileChooser.getMediaPath("preamble.wav"));
> s.play();
> s.explore();
> s.forceToExtremes();
> s.play();
> s.explore();
```

Look at Figure 8.22 and see that all the values have been set to extremes. When you play the sound back, you'll hear a bunch of awful noises. That's clipping. The really

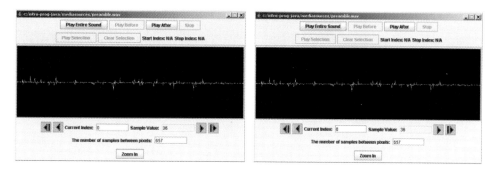

Figure 8.22
Comparing the original sound with one with all values set to extremes

amazing thing is that you can *still* make out the words in sounds that you manipulate with this method. Our ability to decipher words from noise is incredibly powerful.

In the clipping example of Program 8.6, the conditional `if-else` statement checked a single condition, `sample.getValue()` >=0. Sometimes we need to check multiple conditions. You can combine the results of two Boolean expressions using the symbols && (which means AND) and || (which means OR).

For example, if you want to check if a value is greater than some amount and less than another amount, you would use && to test both conditions. The following code illustrates checking whether the `value` represented by the variable x is greater than 1 and also is less that 10.

```
> int x = 3;
> if (x > 1 && x < 10) System.out.println("x is greater than 1 and
less than 10");
x is greater than 1 and less than 10
```

As a another example, if you want to check if just one of two (or more) Boolean expressions is true, you would use || as illustrated in the following code.

```
> int y = -4;
> if ( y < 0 || y > 2) System.out.println("y is either less than 0
or greater than 2");
y is either less than 0 or greater than 2
```

Lastly, it is possible to check for the opposite of some condition by negating a Boolean expression using ! (which means NOT). In the following code, the Boolean expression z!=0 is checking that z is not equal to 0.

```
> int z = 1;
> if (z != 0) System.out.println("z is not equal to 0");
z is not equal to 0
```

8.5 Using Media Computation with Alice

You can use the MediaTools application to record sounds. Just start the application and then click the **Sound Tools** window to see the sound tools, as shown in Figure 8.23.

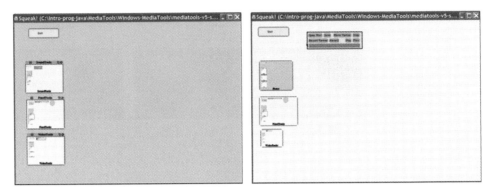

Figure 8.23
Showing the *Sound Tools* in the MediaTools

The green buttons at the top right of the visual display in the Mediatools window (as shown in Figure 8.24) are used to control recording a sound.

Click...

- **Record Viewer** to see what is being recorded.
- **Record** to start recording.
- **Stop** to stop recording.
- **Play** to play back the recorded sound.
- **Save** to save the recorded sound in a file, which will be saved in the MediaTools directory.
- **Quit** to quit.

Alice does not have a sound editor. You can use the MediaTools application, to record sounds that can then be imported into Alice. To import a sound into an Alice

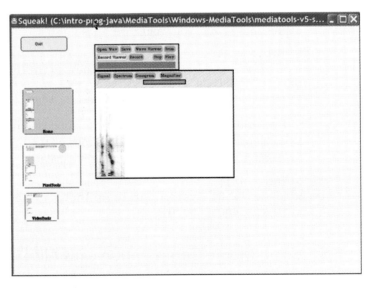

Figure 8.24
Recording a sound using the MediaTools application

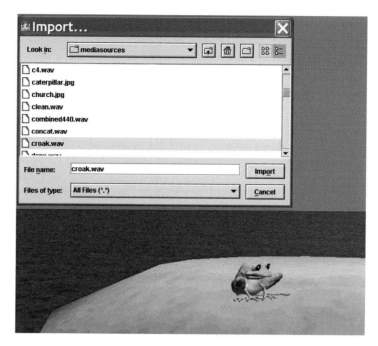

Figure 8.25
Importing a croak sound

world, click **File** and then **Import**. Pick the sound file to import and then click the **Import** button (see Figure 8.25).

Once a sound has been imported into an Alice world, you can ask any object to play it. Figure 8.26 shows what happens when you drag a **playSound** tile into a method and replace the sound with the imported sound (use the down arrow to change the sound).

You could create a world in Alice with two people in it (such as a teacher and student). Have the teacher ask the student, "Come here!" two times and each time make the sound louder. After the second time, have the student move forward toward the teacher, as in Figure 8.27. For more information on using sound in Alice, see Section A.1 in Appendix A.

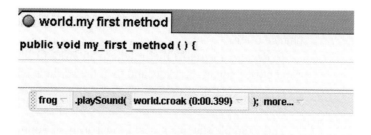

Figure 8.26
Playing an imported sound in Alice

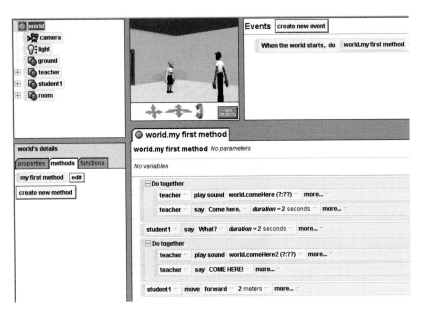

Figure 8.27
Using a louder sound in an Alice world

8.6 Concepts Summary

In this chapter, we worked with one-dimensional arrays, `for-each` loops, `while` loops, `for` loops, and conditionals.

8.6.1 Arrays

Arrays are used to store many pieces of data (elements) of the same type. They allow you to quickly access a particular element in the array using an index. If you couldn't use an array, you would have to create a separate variable name for each piece of data.

Arrays are similar to the lists we saw in Alice. Both lists and arrays can hold objects in an order. We tend to use arrays in Java when we have large amounts of data of the same type and the data is of a known size. We tend to use lists in Java when we don't know how many items the list will need to hold and/or when the contents of the list change often.

To declare a variable that refers to an array in Java, use the type followed by open [and close] square brackets and then the variable name.

```
SoundSample[] sampleArray;
```

This example statement declares an array of `SoundSample` objects. The value stored at each position in the example array `sampleArray` is a reference to a `SoundSample` object.

Arrays are objects, and you can find out how large an array is using

arrayReference.length

Notice that this statement isn't a method call, but instead, it accesses a *public field* named length. A public field is a variable that can be directly accessed on an object using objRef.fieldName.

You can access an element of an array using arrayReference[index], where the index values can range from 0 to arrayReference.length-1.

8.6.2 Loops

Loops are used to repeatedly execute a block of statements as long as some Boolean expression is true. Most loops have a variable that changes during each execution of the loop. The change in the variable should eventually cause the Boolean expression to become false and the loop to stop. Loops that never stop are called infinite loops.

We use three types of loops in this chapter: for-each, while, and for. The while loop is usually used when you don't know how many times a loop needs to execute, and the for and for-each loops are usually used when you do know how many times the loop will execute.

The for-each loop was introduced in Java 1.5 and loops through all the elements of an array or other collection of objects, one at a time. An example of a for-each loop is

```
SoundSample[] sampleArray = this.getSamples();
int value = 0;

// loop through all the samples in the array
for (SoundSample sample : sampleArray)
{
  value = sample.getValue();

  // do something to the value
  sample.setValue(value);
}
```

This example code declares a variable sample that is of the type SoundSample, and each time through the loop, the sample variable will refer to a different element of the array until all the elements have been processed.

The while loop has the keyword while followed by a Boolean expression and then a block of statements between open and close curly braces. If the Boolean expression is true, the body of the loop will be executed. If the Boolean expression is false, execution will continue after the body of the loop (after the close curly brace). If you just want to execute one statement in the body of the loop, then you don't need the open and close curly braces, but you should indent the statement.

```
while (Boolean expression)
{
  statement1;
  statement2;
  ...
}
```

The `for` loop does the same thing as a `while` loop, but it lets you declare the variables that you need for the loop, specify the Boolean expression to test, and specify how to change the loop variables all in one statement (the `for` statement). This means you are less likely to forget to do each of these things.

```
SoundSample[] sampleArray = this.getSamples();
SoundSample sample = null;
int value = 0;

// loop through all the samples in the array
for (int index = 0; index < sampleArray.length; index++)
{
  sample = sampleArray[index];
  value = sample.getValue();

  // do something to the value
  sample.setValue(value);
}
```

8.6.3 Conditional Execution

To conditionally execute one statement, use the `if` keyword followed by a Boolean expression inside of open and close parentheses. Put the statement that you only want executed if the Boolean expression is `true` on a new line and indent it. If the Boolean expression is `false`, execution will continue with the next statement.

```
if (Boolean expression)
    // statement to execute if the Boolean expression is true
    statement
// next statement
statement
```

To conditionally execute a block of statements, use the `if` keyword followed by a Boolean expression inside of open and close parentheses. Put the statements to be executed when the Boolean expression is `true` inside of open and close curly braces. Indent the statements to make it easier to visually see that these statements only will be executed if the Boolean expression is `true`. If the Boolean expression is `false`, execution will continue with the statement following the close curly brace.

```
if (Boolean expression)
{
    statements
}
```

If you want to execute one block of statements if a Boolean expression is `true` and another if it is `false`, use the `else` keyword as well. Put the statements that you want to execute when the Boolean expression is `true` inside of an open and close curly braces after the `if`(Boolean expression). Next, add the keyword **else** and put the statements that you want executed when the Boolean expression is false inside of open and close curly braces.

```
if (Boolean expression)
{
  statements
}
else
{
  statements
}
```

If multiple conditions must be checked you can connect Boolean expressions by using && (which represents AND) and | | (which presents OR). Also, you can negate a Boolean expression using ! (which represents NOT).

8.7   Objects and Methods Summary

In this chapter, we talked about several kinds of encodings of data (or objects).

Sound	Sound objects are encodings of sounds, typically coming from a WAV file.
SoundSample	An object that represents a sample in a sound. The value of a sample is between –32,768 and 32,767, representing the voltage that a microphone would generated at a given instant when recording a sound. The length of the instant is typically either 1/44,100 of a second (for CD-quality sound) or 1/22,050 of a second (for good enough sound on most computers). A SoundSample object remembers what sound it came from, so if you change its value, it knows to go back and change the right sample value in the sound.

Here are the methods used or introduced in this chapter.

FileChooser Methods

FileChooser.getMediaPath (String fileName)	Takes a file name as input and returns the full path name of the file with the media directory before the filename.
FileChooser.pickAFile()	Lets the user pick a file and returns the complete path name as a string.
FileChooser.setMediaPath (String directory)	Takes a directory as input and sets the directory name to be what is added to the passed filename using getMediaPath.

Sound Methods

blockingPlay()	Plays the Sound object it is invoked on, and makes sure that no other sound plays at the exact same time. (Compare two blockingPlay's with two play's right after each other.)
explore()	Makes a copy of the Sound object and shows it in the explorer
play()	Plays the Sound object it is invoked on.

write(String fileName)	Takes a file name (a string) and writes the sound in the Sound object it is invoked on to that file as a WAV file. (Make sure that the filename ends in ".wav" if you want the operating system to treat it right.)

SoundSample Methods

getValue()	Returns the value for the SoundSample object it is invoked on.
setValue(int value)	Sets the value for the SoundSample object it is invoked on to be the passed value.

Exercises

1. Define each of the following terms.
   - Clipping
   - Amplitude
   - Frequency
   - Rarefactions
   - WAV
   - Iteration
   - Conditionals
   - A sine wave

2. Modify Program 8.1 to use a for loop and call it increaseVolumeWithFor.

3. Create a method that finds the largest value in a sound and then determines the factor to multiply all the sound values by in order to make the sound as loud as possible. This is called normalizing a sound.

4. In Section 8.3.1, we walked through how Program 8.1 worked. Draw the pictures to show how Program 8.3 works in the same way.

5. Create a new method that will halve the volume of the positive values and double the volume of the negative values. You can use Program 8.6 as a starting point.

6. What is the output from the following code?

```
public void test1()
{
  int x = 0;
  while (x < 3)
  {
    x = x + 1;
    System.out.println(x);
  }
}
```

7. What is the output from the following code?
```java
public void test2()
{
  int x = 3;
  while (x > 0)
  {
    x = x + 1;
    System.out.println(x);
  }
}
```

8. What is the output from the following code?
```java
public void test3()
{
  int x = 2;
  while (x >= 2)
  {
    x = x + 1;
    System.out.println(x);
  }
  System.out.println("x is" + x);
}
```

9. What is the output from the following code?
```java
public void test4()
{
  for (int x = 2; x < 10; x++)
    System.out.println(x);
}
```

10. What is the output from the following code?
```java
public void test5()
{
  for (int y = -3; y < 0; y++)
    System.out.println(y);
}
```

11. What is the output from the following code?
```java
public void test6()
{
  for (x = 12; x > 0; x-)
    System.out.println(x);
}
```

12. What is the output from the following code?
```java
public void test7() {
  int x = 12;
  int y = 0;
  while (x < 10 || y < 1)
  {
    x = x + 1;
    y = y + 1;
    System.out.println(x + ", " + y);
  }
}
```

13. What is the output from the following code?

```java
public void test8() {
  int x = 12;
  int y = 0;
  while (x !< 10 || y < 1)
  {
    x = x + 1;
    y = y + 1;
    System.out.println(x + ", " + y);
  }
}
```

14. What is the output from the following code?

```java
public void test9()
{
  int x = 12;
  int y = 0;
  while (!(x < 10 || y < 1))
  {
    x = x + 1;
    y = y + 1;
    System.out.println(x + ", " + y);
  }
}
```

15. What is the output from the following code?

```java
public void test10()
{
  int x = 2;
  int y = 0;
  while (!(x < 10 && y < 1))
  {
    x = x + 1;
    y = y + 1;
    System.out.println(x + ", " + y);
  }
}
```

16. Write a method that will find the smallest value in a sound and print it out.

17. What happens if you increase a volume too far? Explore that by creating a Sound object, then increase the volume once, and again, and again. Does it always keep getting louder? Does something else happen? Can you explain why?

18. Instead of multiplying samples by a multiplier (like 2 or 0.5), try *adding* a value to them. What happens to a sound if you add 100 to every sample? What happens if you add 1,000 to every sample?

19. Use the method `changeVolume` to create three versions of a sound: one that is very quiet, one that is medium loud, and one that is very loud. Import the sounds into Alice and create a story that has a character use all three sounds in response to something.

20. Open up the **Sonogram** view and say some vowel sounds. Is there a distinctive pattern? Do "Oh's" always sound the same? Do "Ah's"? Does it matter if you switch speakers—are the patterns the same?

21. Get a couple of different instruments and play the same note on them into MediaTool application's sound editor with the **Sonogram** view open. Are all "C's" made equal? Can you *see* some of why one sound is different than another?

22. Try out a variety of WAV files as instruments, using the piano keyboard in the MediaTools application sound editor. What kinds of recordings work best as instruments?

CHAPTER 9

Modifying Samples Using Ranges

Goals of this chapter:

- To use ranges in iteration.
- To change more than one variable in a loop.
- To return a value from a Java method.

Introduction

In the last chapter, you learned about three different ways to loop through sound values using for-each, while, and for loops. You also learned how to conditionally execute code in Java using an if-else statement. In this chapter, we will use loops that work on parts of sounds. We will create clips of sounds, splice sounds together, reverse sounds, and mirror sounds. We will also learn how to return a value from a Java method.

9.1 Manipulating Different Sections of a Sound Differently

Manipulating all of the samples in a sound in the same way can be useful, but really interesting effects come from chopping up sounds and manipulating them differentially. How would you do that? We need to be able to loop through *portions* of the sound without walking through the whole thing. This turns out to be an easy thing to do, but we need to manipulate samples somewhat differently (that is, we have to use the for loop in a slightly different way).

Recall that each sample in a Sound object has an index number. In Chapter 8, we created an array of SoundSample objects and looped through the objects in the array and then modified the value in a SoundSample object using the methods getValue and setValue. We also can get an individual sample value directly from a Sound object using the index number with soundObj.getSampleValue(int index). Also, we can set the value in a Sound object with soundObj.setSampleValue(int index, int value) (with inputs of an index number and a new value).

Although we can manipulate samples by invoking setSampleValue() we still don't want to have to write code like:

```
sound.setSampleValue(0,12);
sound.setSampleValue(1,28);
```

Not for tens of thousands of samples! So we will continue to use a for loop. However, if we are not processing all the sound samples in the same way, the index value that we start at won't necessarily be 0, and the last index value won't necessarily be the length of the sound minus 1. That is, we want to select a **range** of samples from a sound by using a start index and an end index.

What if we want to *increase* the sound for the first half of the sound object and *decrease* it in the second half? How could we do that? First we will need to calculate the halfway point. We can determine that by dividing the length of the sound by 2. Since the length and 2 are both integers, the result will also be an integer, so no casting is needed (any values after the decimal point will be thrown away). We will need two loops. One loop will start at the beginning of sound (0) and loop to the halfway point. The second loop will start at the halfway point and loop to the end of the sound (*length* − 1). Program 9.1 defines a method increaseAndDecrease() to illustrate this idea.

Program 9.1: Increase the Volume then Decrease

```
/* *
 * Method to increase the first half of the sound
 * (double it) and then decrease the
 * second half (halve it).
 */
public void increaseAndDecrease()
{
  int half = this.getLength() / 2;
  int value = 0;

  // loop through the first half of the sound
  for (int i = 0; i < half; i++)
  {
    // get the current value
    value = this.getSampleValueAt(i);

    // set the value to 2x the original
    this.setSampleValueAt(i,value * 2);
  }

  // loop through the second half of the sound
  for (int i = half; i < this.getLength(); i++)
  {
    // get the current value
    value = this.getSampleValueAt(i);

    // set the value to half the original
    this.setSampleValueAt(i,(int) (value * 0.5));
  }
}
```

There are two loops in increaseAndDecrease(), each of which deals with one half of the sound.

- The first loop deals with the samples from 0 to halfway through the sound. Those samples all get multiplied by 2, to double their amplitude.
- The second loop goes from halfway through to the end of the sound. Here, we multiply each sample by 0.5, thus decreasing the sound by 50%.

9.2 Creating a Sound Clip

Sometimes a sound is too long and you want just part of it. This can happen when you record a sound. There may be silence before and after the actual sound. Or, you may want to pull one word out of a sound. You can **clip** a sound, which means to create a shorter segment from a longer sound (not to be confused with "clipping" that was used to create the awful sound we heard when we made all values in the sound the maximum negative or positive value back in Chapter 8).

What if we want to copy the sound of the word "This" from the sound file named thisisatest.wav and use it to create another sound? How can we tell where the word "This" ends in the sound? Open an explorer on the sound using sound.explore();. Click at the first flat area after the first non-flat area (silence should have values near 0). Click the Play Before button to play the part of the sound before the current index. You can use the arrow buttons to change the current index as well. In Figure 9.1, the explorer window shows us that the word "this" ends at an index around 8500.

So, to copy just part of a sound into another sound, we will need to create a new Sound object. One of the ways to make a new Sound object is to tell it how many samples it will have. To calculate the number of samples, we can subtract the starting value from the ending value and add 1 (end-start+1).

We can then create a new sound and loop copying from the source Sound object (from the start index to the end index) into the target Sound object (starting at the

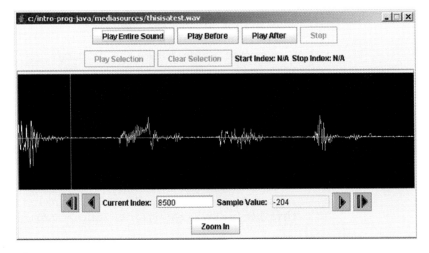

Figure 9.1
Exploring the Thisisatest sound to find the end of the first word

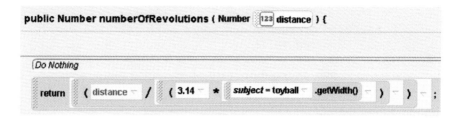

Figure 9.2
An Alice function using a method declaration

beginning of the target sound). This means we need two indices, one index for the source and one index for the target. We have to make sure to increment both the index in the source and the index in the target. If we forget to increment the source index, we will copy the same source sample over and over, and if we fail to increment the target index, we will copy to the same place in the target over and over.

Program 9.2 defines a method `clip(int start, int end)` in which a `for` loop is used to copy a part of one sound (from the `start` index to the `end` index) so as to create a new `Sound` object (`target`). Notice the `return` statement at the end of the `clip` method. We need to return our new `Sound` object from the method in order to be able to refer to it and play it whenever we want. A `return` statement consists of the keyword `return` followed by what we want to return.

You have seen the `return` statement before, in Chapter 6, where we created a *function* in Alice that returned the number of revolutions that a ball needs to roll in order to travel a given distance (passed as an input value). A *function* in Alice looks just like a *method* in Alice, except for two things.

(1) It has a `return` statement that returns a value.

(2) The type of value that will be returned (`Number`) is specified in the method declaration, as shown in Figure 9.2. The method declaration, `public Number numberOfRevolutions`, indicates that the type of value being returned is a number.

Alice makes a distinction between *methods* (named blocks of code that cause some action to occur) and *functions* (named blocks of code that return a value of some specific type). In Java, we call both of these named blocks of code *methods*, but we say that some methods have a return type of `void` (because they don't return a value) and some return a value of a specific type. Up to now in this textbook, all the Java methods were `void` methods. Program 9.2 illustrates our first method that returns a value. In this example, a `Sound` object is being returned, so the method declaration is

`public` **Sound** `clip(` **int** `start,` **int** `end)`

Program 9.2: Create a Sound Clip

```
/* *
 * Method to create a new sound by copying just part of
 * the current sound to a new sound
 * @param start the index to start the copy at (inclusive)
```

```
 * @param end the index to stop the copy at (inclusive)
 * @return a new sound with just the samples from start to
 * end in it
 */
public Sound clip(int start, int end)
{
  // calculate the number of samples in the clip
  int lengthInSamples = end - start + 1;

  Sound target = new Sound(lengthInSamples); // hold clip
  int value = 0;                    // holds the current sample value
  int targetIndex = 0;            // index in target sound

  // copy from start to end from source into target
  for (int i = start; i <= end; i++, targetIndex++)
  {
    value = this.getSampleValueAt(i);
    target.setSampleValueAt(targetIndex,value);
  }
  return target;
}
```

Notice that we said we would return a Sound object from this method by saying that the type of value returned is an object of the Sound class. At the end of the method, we use the keyword return followed by the variable that refers to the new Sound object. So in order to refer to this new Sound object again, we will need to declare a variable and set the value of that variable to refer to the returned Sound object.

```
> Sound test =
      new Sound(FileChooser.getMediaPath("thisisatest.wav"));
> test.explore();
> Sound s1 = test.clip(0,8500);
> s1.play();
> s1.explore();
```

Use the explorer on the original sound and then on the clipped sound. Change the number of samples between pixels (in the displayed picture in the explorer window) to be 100 in the clipped sound. Then compare the sample values. Check to be sure that the clipped sound does have the same values as the original, as shown in Figure 9.3.

9.3 Splicing Sounds

Splicing sounds is a term that dates back to when sounds were recorded on tape, so juggling the order of things on the tape involved literally cutting the tape into segments and then gluing it back together in the right order. That's "splicing". When everything is digital, it's *much* easier.

To **splice** sounds, we simply have to copy elements around in the array. It's easiest to do this with two (or more) arrays, rather than copying within the same array. Splicing lets you create all kinds of sounds, speeches, nonsense, and art.

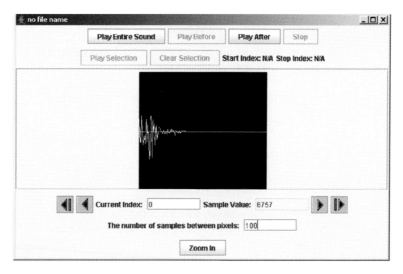

Figure 9.3
Exploring the sound clip

The easiest kind of splice to do is when the sounds are in separate files. All you need to do is copy each sound, in order, into a target sound. You need to keep track of the next index in the target sound. We often refer to the "target sound" as the "current sound" being created. Here's a method that creates the start of a sentence "It is ..." (readers are welcome to complete the sentence).

Program 9.3: Splice Words into a Single Sentence

```
/* *
 * Method to splice two sounds together with some silence
 * between them into the current (target) sound
 */
public void splice()
{
  Sound sound1 =
    new Sound(FileChooser.getMediaPath("it.wav"));
  Sound sound2 =
    new Sound(FileChooser.getMediaPath("is.wav"));
  int targetIndex = 0; // the starting place on the target
  int value = 0;

  // copy all of sound 1 into the current sound (target)
  for (int i = 0;
       i < sound1.getLength();
       i++, targetIndex++)
  {
    value = sound1.getSampleValueAt(i);
    this.setSampleValueAt(targetIndex,value);
  }
```

```
// create silence between words by setting values to 0
for (int i = 0;
     i<(int)(this.getSamplingRate() * 0.1);
     i++, targetIndex++)
{
  this.setSampleValueAt(targetIndex,0);
}

// copy all of sound 2 into the current sound (target)
for (int i = 0;
     i < sound2.getLength();
     i++, targetIndex++)
{
  value = sound2.getSampleValueAt(i);
  this.setSampleValueAt(targetIndex,value);
}
}
```

To test this, we need a "blank" Sound that the two sounds will be copied to. You can use the file sec3silence.wav for this. It holds 3 seconds of silence, which should be more than enough.

```
> String silence = FileChooser.getMediaPath("sec3silence.wav");
> Sound target = new Sound(silence);
> target.play();
> target.splice();
> target.play();
```

There are three loops in this method splice, each of which copies one segment into the current (target) sound—a segment being either a word or a silence between words.

- The method starts by creating Sound objects for the word "it" (sound1) and the word "is" (sound2).

- Notice that we set targetIndex (the index for the target sound) equal to 0 *before* the first loop. We then increment it in every loop, but we never again set it to a specific value. That's because targetIndex is always the index for the *next empty sample* in the target sound. Because each loop follows the previous one, we just keep tacking samples onto the end of the current sound (the target).

- In the first loop, we copy each and every sample from sound1 into the current sound this. We have the index i go from 0 to 1 before the length of sound1. We get the sample value at index i from sound1, then set the sample value at targetIndex in the current sound to that value. We then increment both i and targetIndex.

- In the second loop, we create 0.1 seconds of silence. The method getSamplingRate() gives us the number of samples in 1 second of the current sound, so 0.1 times that tells us the number of samples in 0.1 seconds. We don't get any source value here—we simply set the `targetIndex` sample to 0 (for silence), then increment the `targetIndex`.

- Finally, we copy in all the samples from `sound2`, just like the first loop where we copied in `sound1`.

The more common kind of splicing is when the words are in the middle of an existing sound, and you need to pull them out from there. The first thing to do in splicing like that is to figure out the index numbers that delimit the pieces you're interested in. Using the explorer, that's pretty easy to do.

- Open an explorer using `sound.explore()`.
- Click the mouse button to choose a current position and then play the sound before or after that current position.
- Alternatively, select part of the sound by clicking the mouse when the cursor points to a place to start and dragging the mouse to the end of an area of interest. This selection will highlight and you can play the selection.

Using exactly this process, Table 9.1 gives the ending points of the first few words in `preamble10.wav`. (assuming the first word starts at the index 0, though that might not always be true for every sound.)

Writing a loop that copies things from one array to another requires a little bit of juggling. You need to think about keeping track of two indices: where you are in the array that you're copying *from*, and where you are in the array that you're copying *to*. These are two different variables, tracking two different indexes. But they both increment in the same way.

Below is the method that changes the preamble from *We the people of the United States* to *We the UNITED people of the United States.* Be sure to set the media path before trying this on your computer.

Table 9.1 Word indices for `preamble10.wav`

Word	Ending index
We	15,730
the	17,407
People	26,726
of	32,131
the	33,413
United	40,052
States	55,510

Program 9.4: Splice the Preamble to have United People

```
/* *
 * Method to splice "We the" then "United" then
 * "people of the United States" into the current
 * (target) sound
 */
public void splicePreamble()
{
  String file = FileChooser.getMediaPath("preamble10.wav");
  Sound source = new Sound(file);
  int targetIndex = 0; // start copying to first sample value
  int value = 0;

  // loop copying the "We the" into the current sound
  for (int sourceIndex = 0;
      sourceIndex < 17407;
      sourceIndex++, targetIndex++)
  {
    value = source.getSampleValueAt(sourceIndex);
    this.setSampleValueAt(targetIndex,value);
  }

  // loop copying the "united" into the current sound
  for (int sourceIndex = 33414;
      sourceIndex < 40052;
      sourceIndex++,targetIndex++)
  {
    value = source.getSampleValueAt(sourceIndex);
    this.setSampleValueAt(targetIndex,value);
  }

  // copy the "people of the United States"
  for (int sourceIndex = 17408;
      sourceIndex < 55510;
      sourceIndex++, targetIndex++)
  {
    value = source.getSampleValueAt(sourceIndex);
    this.setSampleValueAt(targetIndex,value);
  }
}
```

```
> String silence = FileChooser.getMediaPath("sec3silence.wav");
> Sound target = new Sound(silence);
> target.play();
> target.splicePreamble();
> target.play();
```

The first loop copies the words "We the" into the current (target) sound. The second loop copies the word "united" into the current sound. The last loop copies the words

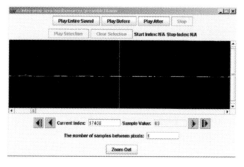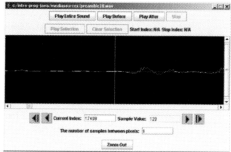

Figure 9.4
Comparing the original sound (left) to the spliced sound (right)

"people of the United States" into the current sound. Notice that the value of `targetIndex` is set to 0 at the beginning, so we start copying at the beginning of the current sound. In each loop we increment `targetIndex` but we never reset its value, so it always points to the next place in the current sound to copy to.

Figure 9.4 shows the original `preamble10.wav` file in the left sound explorer, and the new spliced one (saved with `write(String fileName)`) on the right.

Let's see if we can figure out what's going on mathematically. Recall Table 9.1. First, we copy the range from 0 to 17,406 to the target sound. This means we copied 17,407 samples ($17,406 − 0 + 1 = 17,407$). After the first loop, the value of `targetIndex` will be 17,407. Next, we copy the range from 33,414 to 40,051, which means we copy ($40,051 − 33,414 + 1 = 6,638$) 6,6638 samples. After the second loop, the value of `targetIndex` will be 24,045 ($17,407 + 6,638 = 24,045$). Next, we copy the range from 17,408 to 55,509, which is ($55,509 − 17,408 + 1 = 38,102$) samples. The total number of copied samples is ($17,407 + 6,638 + 38,102 = 62,147$). The value of `targetIndex` will be 62,147 after the last loop. You can add `System.out.println("Target index is" + targetIndex);` after each loop to check that this is correct.

Program 9.5: Splice Preamble and Show Target Index

```
/* *
 * Method to splice "We the" then "United" then
 * "people of the United States" into the current
 * sound
 */
public void splicePreamble()
{
  String file = FileChooser.getMediaPath("preamble10.wav");
  Sound source = new Sound(file);
  int targetIndex = 0; // start copying to first sample value
  int value = 0;

  // loop copying the "We the" into the current sound
  for (int sourceIndex = 0;
```

```
          sourceIndex < 17407;
          sourceIndex++, targetIndex++)
    {
      value = source.getSampleValueAt(sourceIndex);
      this.setSampleValueAt(targetIndex,value);
    }

    // print the value of the target index
    System.out.println("Target index is" + targetIndex);

    // loop copying the "united" into the current sound
    for (int sourceIndex = 33414;
         sourceIndex < 40052;
         sourceIndex++,targetIndex++)
    {
      value = source.getSampleValueAt(sourceIndex);
      this.setSampleValueAt(targetIndex,value);
    }

    // print the value of the target index
    System.out.println("Target index is" + targetIndex);

    // copy the "people of the United States"
    for (int sourceIndex = 17408;
         sourceIndex < 55510;
         sourceIndex++, targetIndex++)
    {
      value = source.getSampleValueAt(sourceIndex);
      this.setSampleValueAt(targetIndex,value);
    }

    // print the value of the target index
    System.out.println("Target index is" + targetIndex);
  }
```

We can also use the explorer to check that the last copied sample is at 62,146 by checking the value at 62,147. It should still be 0, as should all the values from that index to the end of the sound.

Each of the loops that copies part of the preamble sound into the current sound is very similar. To make a general splice method, we will pass in the Sound object to copy from, the starting index to use in that passed sound, the index to stop before in the passed sound, and the place to start the copy to in current sound.

Program 9.6: General Splice Method

```
/* *
 * Method to copy part of the passed sound into this sound at
 * the given start index
 * @param source the source sound to copy from
```

```
 * @param sourceStart the starting index to copy from in the
 * source (the copy will include this)
 * @param sourceStop the ending index (the copy won't include
 * this)
 * @param targetStart the index to start copying into
 */
public void splice(Sound source,
                     int sourceStart,
                     int sourceStop,
                     int targetStart)
{
  // loop copying from source to target
  for (int sourceIndex = sourceStart,
         targetIndex = targetStart;
       sourceIndex < sourceStop &&
         targetIndex < this.getLength();
       sourceIndex++, targetIndex++)
    this.setSampleValueAt(targetIndex,
      source.getSampleValueAt(sourceIndex));
}
```

■

This new object method can be used to splice "united" in the phrase "We the people of the United States" as shown next.

Program 9.7: Using the General Splice Method

```
/* *
 * Method to splice the preamble into the current sound so that
 * it says We the United people of the United States
 */
public void splicePreamble2()
{
  Sound preamble =
    new Sound(FileChooser.getMediaPath("preamble10.wav"));

  // first splice the "we the" into the current sound
  this.splice(preamble,0,17407,0);

  // now splice the "united" into the current sound
  this.splice(preamble,33414,40052,17407);

  /* now splice the "people of the United States" into
   * the current sound
   */
  this.splice(preamble,17408,55510,24045);
}
```

■

You can execute this new method using the following:

```
> String fileName = FileChooser.getMediaPath("sec3silence.wav");
> Sound target = new Sound(fileName);
> target.splicePreamble2();
> target.explore();
```

Compare the sound created using the `splicePreamble` method versus the sound created using the `splicePreamble2` method. They should result in exactly the same sound. Why should we try to write general methods? Take a look at `splicePreamble2`. It is much easier to read than `splicePreamble`. We want general methods because they are easier to reuse and make our programs smaller and easier to understand.

9.4 Reversing a Sound

In the splicing example, we copied the samples from the words just as they were in the original sound. We don't have to always go in the same order. We can reverse the words—or make them faster, slower, louder, or softer. For an example, here's a method that reverses a sound so that you can play it backward.

Program 9.8: Reverse a Sound

```
/* *
 * Method to reverse the current sound.
 */
public void reverse()
{
  Sound orig = new Sound(this.getFileName());
  int length = this.getLength();

  // loop through the samples
  for (int targetIndex = 0, sourceIndex = length - 1;
      targetIndex < length && sourceIndex > 0;
      targetIndex++, sourceIndex--)
    this.setSampleValueAt(targetIndex,
                          orig.getSampleValueAt(sourceIndex));
}
```

This method first creates another `Sound` object from the same file as the current `Sound` object. This makes a copy of the original sound. Also, the method saves the length of the current `Sound` object. Then it loops.

The loop initializes the value of `targetIndex` to 0 and the value of `sourceIndex` to the length of the sound minus 1. It loops while `targetIndex` is less than the length of the sound and the `sourceIndex` is greater than 0. It increments `targetIndex` by 1 after the body of the loop, and it decrements the value of `sourceIndex` by one each time through the loop.

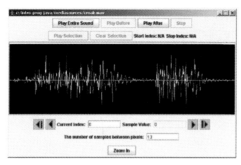 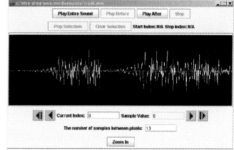

Figure 9.5
Comparing the original sound (left) to the reversed sound (right)

Why does it start `sourceIndex` at the length of the sound minus 1 and decrement it each time through the loop? Remember that the last valid index is at the length minus 1, which is why the `sourceIndex` starts with this value. So, we copy from the end of the source sound (*length* − 1) to the beginning of the target sound (0) during the first execution of the loop. The second time through the loop, we copy from the next to last sound sample in the source (*length* − 2) to the second position in the target (1). We will keep looping until the `targetIndex` equals the length of the sound.

Figure 9.5 illustrates invoking the `explore()` method to view the original sound, invoking the `reverse()` method on the original sound, and then invoking the `explore()` method on the reversed sound to allow us to see that the sound values have been reversed.

```
> Sound s = new Sound(FileChooser.getMediaPath("croak.wav"));
> s.play();
> s.explore();
> s.reverse();
> s.play();
> s.explore();
```

9.5   Mirroring a Sound

Once we know how to play sounds forward and backward, you can reverse only half of a sound, which is like creating a mirror image of the sound values.

Program 9.9: Mirror a Sound, Front to Back

```
/**
 * Method to mirror a sound front to back
 */
public void mirrorFrontToBack()
{
  int length = this.getLength(); // save the length
  int mirrorPoint = length / 2; // mirror around this
  int value = 0; // hold the current value
```

```
    // loop from 0 to mirrorPoint
    for (int i = 0; i < mirrorPoint; i++)
    {
      value = this.getSampleValueAt(i);
      this.setSampleValueAt(length - 1 - i,value);
    }
  }
}
```

To use this method try:

```
> Sound s = new Sound(FileChooser.getMediaPath("croak.wav"));
> s.explore();
> s.mirrorFrontToBack();
> s.explore();
```

The length of the sound in the file croak.wav is 8,808, so the mirror point is at 4,404. Figure 9.6 shows how to use the explorer to check the values on either side of the mirror point.

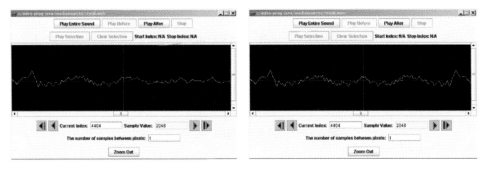

Figure 9.6
Comparing the mirror point in the original sound (left) to the mirrored sound (right)

9.6 Blending Sounds

In this example, we take two sounds—someone saying "Aah!" and a bassoon instrument sound of C in the fourth octave—and *blend* the two sounds. The way we do this is to first copy part of the first sound, "Aah!", then copy 50% of each sound, and then copy the rest of the second sound. Figure 9.7 shows the result. This is very much like mixing 50% of each sound at a mixing board.

Program 9.10: Blending Two Sounds

```
/* *
 * Method to overlap or blend two sounds. Start
 * by copying the first 20,000 samples from sound1 into
 * the current sound then copy the sum of half of sound1
 * and half of sound2 for the next 20,000 samples and
```

```
 *  end with the next 20,000 samples from sound2.
 */
public void blendSounds()
{
  Sound sound1 =
    new Sound(FileChooser.getMediaPath("aah.wav"));
  Sound sound2 =
    new Sound(FileChooser.getMediaPath("bassoon-c4.wav"));
  int value = 0;

  // copy the first 20,000 samples from sound1 into target
  for (int index=0; index < 20000; index++)
    this.setSampleValueAt(index,
                          sound1.getSampleValueAt(index));

  // copy the next 20,000 samples from sound1 and blend that
  // with the first 20,000 samples from sound2
  for (int index = 0; index < 20000; index++)
  {
    value = (int) ((sound1.getSampleValueAt(index + 20000) *
                   0.5) +
                   (sound2.getSampleValueAt(index) * 0.5));
    this.setSampleValueAt(index + 20000,value);
  }

  // copy the next 20,000 samples from sound2 into the target
  for (int index=20000; index < 40000; index++)
    this.setSampleValueAt(index + 20000,
                          sound2.getSampleValueAt(index));
}
```

Program 9.10 defines `blendSounds()`, a method to overlap or blend two sounds. There are loops in this method for each segment of the blended sound.

- We start by creating the `sound1` and `sound2` sounds for blending. The length of these sounds is over 40,000 samples, but we're just going to use the first 40,000 as an example.

- In the first loop, we simply get 20,000 samples from `sound1` and copy them into the current sound `this`. Notice that we're not using a separate index variable for the `target`—instead, we're using the same index variable, `index`, for both sounds, since we are copying from 0 to 19,999 from `sound1` into 0 to 19,999 in the current sound.

- In the next loop, we copy 20,000 samples from both `sound1` and `sound2` blended into the current sound. We get a sample from each of `sound1` and `sound2`, then multiply each by 0.5 and add the results together. The result is a sample that represents 50% of each. Notice that we are using one index variable here as well but adding 20,000 to the value of that for determining the index of `sound1` and the current sound. So, we blend values from `sound1` starting at index 20,000 and from

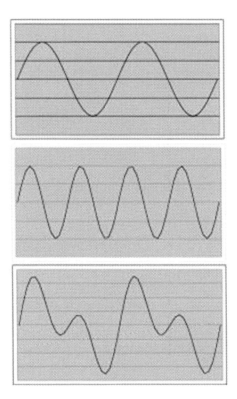

Figure 9.7
The top and middle waves are added together to create the bottom wave

sound2 starting at index 0, and the blended values go into the current sound starting at index 20,000.

- Finally, we copy another 20,000 samples from sound2. The result sounds like "Aah," first, then half of each, then just a bassoon note. Notice that we start the index at 20,000 for the next place to copy from sound2. This means we need to add 20,000 to that value for the index in the current sound (since there are already 40,000 values in the current sound).

The following code illustrates how to use the blendSounds() method to create a blended sound. First, create a sound using the file that has 3 seconds of silence. Then explore it to see what it looks like before the blending. Next, blend the two sounds into the silent sound. Finally, explore the new sound.

```
> String fileName = FileChooser.getMediaPath("sec3silence.wav");
> Sound target = new Sound(fileName);
> target.explore();
> target.blendSounds();
> target.explore();
```

Figure 9.8 shows the two source sounds and the resulting blended sound as they appear in the explorer window.

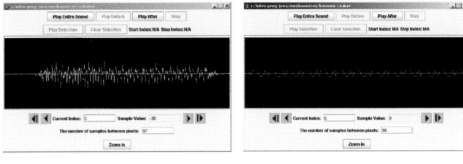

Figure 9.8
The original "Ahh" sound, the original bassoon note, and the blended sound

9.7   Creating an Echo

Creating an echo effect is similar to the splicing method used in Program 9.4 but involves actually creating sounds that didn't exist before. We do that by actually *adding* wave forms. What we're doing here is adding samples from a `delay` (number of samples away into the sound but multiplied by 0.6, so that they're fainter.)

Program 9.11: Make a Sound and a Single Echo of It

```
/* *
 * Method to add an echo to a sound
 * @param delay the number of samples before the echo starts
 */
public void echo(int delay)
{
  // make a copy of the original sound
  Sound s = new Sound(this.getFileName());
  int value = 0;

  // loop from delay to end of sound
  for (int i = delay; i < this.getLength(); i++)
  {
   /* get the value back by delay samples from the
    * copy of the sound and make it fainter
    */
```

```
        value = (int) (s.getSampleValueAt(i-delay) * 0.6);

        /* set the value at the current index to the sum
         * of the current value and the echo
         */
        this.setSampleValueAt(i,
                                this.getSampleValueAt(i) +
                                value);

    }
}
```

How it Works

The echo method takes a delay: the number of samples before the echo starts. Try this with different amounts of delay. With low values of delay, the echo will sound more like *vibrato*. Higher values (try 10,000 or 20,000) will give you a real echo.

- This method creates a copy of the current sound s. This is where we'll get the original, unadulterated samples for creating the echo. (You could try this without creating a copy to get some interesting layered echoes.)
- Next we declare a variable value to hold a value of a sample.
- Our loop starts with the index i being set to the passed delay and continues through the rest of the sound.
- The echoed sound is delay samples back, so i-delay is the sample we need. We multiply it by 0.6 to make it softer in volume.
- We then add the echoed sample to the current sample at i and set it in the current Sound object.

Try this method on sounds with words in them, as shown in Figure 9.9.

```
> String fileName = FileChooser.getMediaPath("thisisatest.wav");
> Sound sound = new Sound(fileName);
> sound.explore();
> sound.echo(20000);
> sound.explore();
```

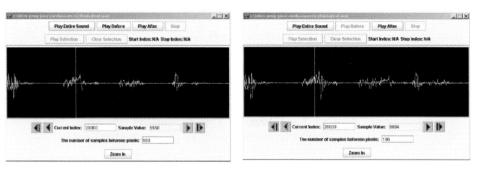

Figure 9.9
The original "This is a test" sound (left), and the sound with an echo (right)

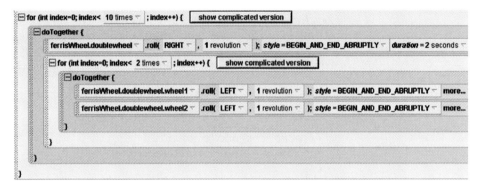

Figure 9.10
A nested loop in Alice

9.7.1 Creating Multiple Echoes

It is possible to set the number of echoes that you create in a sound. You can generate some amazing effects in this way. To create multiple echoes, you will need to use a nested for loop (a for loop inside of another for loop). You have seen nested for loops in Alice, where you used a nested for loop to turn the double wheel clockwise (roll right) and the individual wheels of a ferris wheel counterclockwise (roll left), as illustrated in Figure 9.10. We use the same nested for loop technique in Program 9.12 to define a method echo(**int** delay, **int** numEchoes) that allows you to specify multiple echoes in a sound.

Program 9.12: Creating Multiple Echoes

```
/* *
 * Method to create multiple echoes of the current sound
 * @param delay the number of samples before the echo starts
 * @param numEchoes the number of echoes desired
 * @return a new sound with the echoes in it
 */
public Sound echo(int delay, int numEchoes)
{
    int soundLength = this.getLength();
    Sound echoSound = new Sound(numEchoes * delay + soundLength);
    int value = 0;
    int echoIndex = 0;
    int echoValue = 0;
    double echoAmplitude = 1; // to start

    // copy the original sound
    echoSound.splice(this,0,soundLength,0);
```

```
/* loop starting with 1 to create the first echo at the
 * right place and end when = the number of echoes
 */
for (int echoCount = 1; echoCount <= numEchoes; echoCount++)
{
  // decrease the volume (amplitude) of the echo
  echoAmplitude = echoAmplitude * 0.6;

  // echo the whole sound
  for (int i = 0; i < soundLength; i++)
  {
    echoIndex = i + (delay * echoCount);
    echoValue = (int)(this.getSampleValueAt(i) *
                   echoAmplitude);
    echoSound.setSampleValueAt(echoIndex,echoValue +
            echoSound.getSampleValueAt(echoIndex));
  }
}
return echoSound;
}
```

To try out this method, create a Sound object, and then invoke this method on the Sound object. Be sure to save the resulting sound.

```
> Sound sound = new Sound(FileChooser.getMediaPath("croak.wav"));
> Sound echo = sound.echo(8000,5);
> echo.play();
```

9.8   How Sampling Keyboards Work

Sampling keyboards are keyboards that use recordings of sounds (e.g., pianos, harps, trumpets) to create music by playing those sound recordings in the desired pitch. Modern music and sound keyboards (and synthesizers) allow musicians to record sounds in their daily lives and turn them into virtual instruments by shifting the frequency of the original sounds. How do the synthesizers do it? It's not really complicated. The interesting part is that it allows you to use any sound you want as an instrument.

Sampling keyboards use huge amounts of memory to record lots of different instruments at different pitches. When you press a key on the keyboard, the recording *closest* in pitch to the note you pressed is selected, then the recording is shifted to exactly the pitch you requested.

This first method works by creating a sound that *skips* every other sample. You read that right—after being so careful to treat all the samples the same, we're now going to skip half of them! In the mediasources directory, you'll find a sound named c4.wav. This is the note C, in the fourth octave of a piano, played for one second. It makes a good sound to experiment with, although really, any sound will work.

Program 9.13: Double the Frequency of a Sound

```
/* *
 * Method to double the frequency of a sound by taking
 * every second sample. The result will be a higher
 * sound.
 */
public void doubleFreq()
{
// make a copy of the original sound
Sound s = new Sound(this.getFileName());

/* loop through the sound and increment target index
 * by one but source index by 2 and set target value
 * to the copy of the original sound
 */
for (int sourceIndex = 0, targetIndex = 0;
      sourceIndex < this.getLength();
      sourceIndex = sourceIndex+2, targetIndex++)
   this.setSampleValueAt(targetIndex,
                         s.getSampleValueAt(sourceIndex));

// clear out the rest of this sound
for (int i = this.getLength() / 2;
     i< this.getLength();
     i++)
   this.setSampleValueAt(i,0);
}
```

Figure 9.11 shows what happens when you use the double frequency method.

```
> Sound s = new Sound(FileChooser.getMediaPath("c4.wav"));
> s.explore();
> s.doubleFreq();
> s.explore();
```

This method starts like the other ones in this chapter by making a copy of the sound. Then it loops through the sound, but it increments the index that keeps the position in

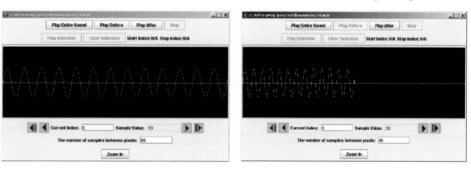

Figure 9.11
The original sound (left), and the sound with the frequency doubled (right)

the source sound `sourceIndex` by 2 and the index that keeps the position in the target sound `targetIndex` by 1. This will copy the sample value at `sourceIndex` = 0 to `targetIndex` = 0, then `sourceIndex` = 2 to `targetIndex` = 1, then `sourceIndex` = 4 to `targetIndex` = 2, and so on. Since the resulting sound will be half as long as it was, the second loop just fills the rest of the sound with zeroes.

Try it![1] You'll see that the sound really does double in frequency with the result that it sounds higher!

How did that happen? It's not really all that complicated. Think of it like this: The frequency of the original sound is really the number of cycles that pass by in a certain amount of time. If you skip every other sample, the new sound has just as many cycles, but has them in half the amount of time!

Now let's try the other way: Let's take every sample twice! What happens then?

To do this, we need to use a cast to "throw away" the fractional part of a floating-point number using a cast to integer. To cast a floating-point number to an integer number, use (**int**).

```
> System.out.println((int)0.5)
0
> System.out.println((int)1.5)
1
```

Here's the method that *halves* the frequency. The `for` loop moves the value of the variable `targetIndex` along the length of the sound. The `sourceIndex` is now being incremented–but only by 0.5! The effect is that we'll take every sample in the source twice. The `sourceIndex` will be 0.0, 0.5, 1.0, 1.5, and so on, but because we're using the (**int**) of that value, we'll take samples 0, 0, 1, 1, and so on.

Program 9.14: Halve the Frequency

```
/* *
 * Method to halve the frequency of a sound by taking
 * each sample twice. The result will be a lower
 * sound.
 */
public void halveFreq()
{
  // make a copy of the original sound
  Sound s = new Sound(this.getFileName());

  /* loop through the sound and increment target index
   * by one but source index by 0.5 and set target value
   * to the copy of the original sound
   */
  for (double sourceIndex=0, targetIndex = 0;
       targetIndex < this.getLength();
```

[1] You are now trying this out as you read, aren't you?

```
        sourceIndex=sourceIndex+0.5, targetIndex++)
      this.setSampleValueAt((int) targetIndex,
            s.getSampleValueAt((int) sourceIndex));
  }
```

This method first creates a copy of the sound. Then it loops through the sound incrementing the `sourceIndex` by 0.5 and the `targetIndex` by 1. We get a sample value from source at the *integer* value using (`(int)`) of the `sourceIndex`. We set the `target` at the *integer* value using (`(int)`) of the `targetIndex` to the sample value that we got from the copy of the sound. We then add 0.5 to the `sourceIndex`. This means that the `sourceIndex`, the first few times through the loop, will take on the values 0.0, 0.5, 1.0, 1.5, 2.0, 2.5, and so on. But the integer part of this sequence is 0, 0, 1, 1, 2, 2, and so on. The result is that we take each sample from the source sound *twice*.

Think about what we're doing here. Imagine that the 0.5 we use is actually 0.75 or 3.0. Would this work? The `for` loop would have to change, but essentially the idea is the same in all these cases. We are *sampling* the source data to create the target data. Using a *sample index* of 0.5 slows down the sound and halves the frequency. A sample index larger than one speeds up the sound and increases the frequency.

Let's try to generalize this sampling with the method in program 9.15. (Note that this one *won't* work right!)

Program 9.15: Changing the Frequency of a Sound: BROKEN!

```
/* *
 * Method to change the frequency of a sound by the
 * passed factor
 * @param factor the amount to increment the source
 * index by. A number greater than 1 will increase the
 * frequency and make the sound higher
 * while a number less than one will decrease the
 * frequency and make the sound lower.
 */
public void changeFreq(double factor)
{
  // make a copy of the original sound
  Sound s = new Sound(this.getFileName());

  /* loop through the sound and increment the target index
   * by one but increment the source index by the factor
   */
  for (double sourceIndex=0, targetIndex = 0;
      targetIndex < this.getLength();
      sourceIndex=sourceIndex+factor, targetIndex++)
```

```
  {
    this.setSampleValueAt(( int ) targetIndex,
         s.getSampleValueAt(( int ) sourceIndex));
  }
}
```

■

Here's how we could use this:

```
> s = new Sound(FileChooser.getMediaPath("c4.wav"));
> s.explore();
> s.changeFreq(0.75);
> s.explore();
```

That will work really well! But what if the `factor` for sampling is *MORE* than 1.0?

```
> String fileName = FileChooser.getMediaPath("Elliot-hello.wav");
> Sound hello = new Sound(fileName);
> hello.changeFreq(1.5);
You are trying to access the sample at index: 54759, but the last
valid index is at 54757.
```

Why? What's happening? Here's how you could see it: Print out the `sourceIndex` just before the `setSampleValueAt`. You'd see that the `sourceIndex` becomes *larger* than the source sound! Of course, that makes sense. If each time through the loop, we increment the `targetIndex` by 1, but we're incrementing the `sourceIndex` by *more than one*, we'll get past the end of the source sound before we reach the end of the target sound. But how do we avoid it?

Here's what we want to happen: If the `sourceIndex` ever gets equal to or larger than the length of the source, we want to reset the `sourceIndex`—probably back to 0. The key word here is *if*.

As we saw in Chapter 8, we can tell Java to make decisions based on a *test*. We use an `if` statement to execute a group of statements if a test evaluates to `true`. In this case, the test is `sourceIndex >= s.getLength()`. We can test on <, >, == (for equality); != (for inequality, not-equals); and even <= and >=. An `if` statement can take a block of statements, just as `while` and `for` do. The block defines the statements to execute if the *test* in the `if` statement is `true`. In this case, our block is simply `sourceIndex = 0;`. The block of statements is defined inside of an open curly brace { and a close curly brace }. If you just have one statement that you want to execute, it doesn't *have* to be in a block, but it is better to keep it in a block.

The method in Program 9.16 generalizes this and allows you to specify how much to shift the samples by.

Program 9.16: Changing the Frequency of a Sound

```
/* *
 * Method to change the frequency of a sound
 * by the passed factor
 * @param factor the amount to increment the source
```

```
 *  index by. A number greater than 1 will increase the
 *  frequency and make the sound higher
 *  while a number less than one will decrease the frequency
 *  and make the sound lower.
 */
public void changeFreq2(double factor)
{
  // make a copy of the original sound
  Sound s = new Sound(this.getFileName());

  /* loop through the sound and increment the target index
   *  by one but increment the source index by the factor
   */
  for (double sourceIndex=0, targetIndex = 0;
       targetIndex < this.getLength();
       sourceIndex=sourceIndex+factor, targetIndex++)
  {
    if (sourceIndex >= s.getLength())
    {
      sourceIndex = 0;
    }
    this.setSampleValueAt((int) targetIndex,
          s.getSampleValueAt((int) sourceIndex));
  }
}
```

■

We can actually set the factor so that we get whatever frequency we want. We call this factor the **sampling interval**. For a desired frequency f_0, the sampling interval should be:

$$samplingInterval = (sizeOfSourceSound)\frac{f_0}{samplingRate}$$

This is how a keyboard synthesizer works. It has recordings of pianos, voices, bells, drums, etc. By *sampling* those sounds at different sampling intervals, it can shift the sound to the desired frequency.

The last method of this section plays a single sound at its original frequency, then at two times, three times, four times, and five times the frequency. We need to use blockingPlay to let one sound finish playing before the next one starts. Try it with play, and you'll hear the sounds collide as they're generated faster than the computer can play them.

Program 9.17: Playing a Sound in a Range of Frequencies

```
/* *
 *  Method to play a sound 5 times and each time increase the
 *  frequency. It doesn't change the original sound.
 */
public void play5Freq()
```

```
{
  Sound s = null;

  // loop 5 times but start with 1 and end at 5
  for (int i = 1; i < 6; i++)
  {
    // reset the sound
    s = new Sound(this.getFileName());

    // change the frequency
    s.changeFreq.2(i);

    // play the sound
    s.blockingPlay();
  }
}
```

■

To use this method, try:

```
> Sound s = new Sound(FileChooser.getMediaPath("c4.wav"));
> s.play5Freq();
```

This method loops with the value of i starting at 1 and ending before it is 6. This will loop five times. Why start at 1 instead of 0? What would happen if we used a factor of 0 to change the frequency? We would end up with silence for the first sound.

When we double or halve the sound frequency, we are also shrinking and doubling the length of the sound (respectively). You might want a target sound whose length is *exactly* the length of the sound, rather than have to clear out extra stuff from a longer sound. You can do that with new Sound(int lengthInSamples). The statement new Sound(44000) returns a new empty sound of 44,000 samples.

9.9 Using Media Computation with Alice

The sound manipulation methods illustrated in this chapter can be used to create sound files for use in your Alice animations. For example, you can use Alice's rightmost mouse control, shown in Figure 9.12, to create copies of an object (like a frog). You can use the **resize Objects** controls to make one frog bigger and one frog smaller.

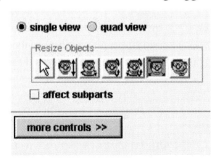

Figure 9.12
Alice mouse controls

Figure 9.13
An Alice world with three different sizes of frogs, each with its own sound

You can use the changeFreq2(**double** factor) method to make a higher and lower croak sound. You can import sounds into Alice, as shown in Chapter 8. With the three frogs shown in Figure 9.13, you can have the smallest frog play the highest sound, the medium sized frog play the original sound, and the largest frog play the lowest sound.

9.10 Concepts Summary

This chapter covered working with ranges in loops and how to return a value from a method.

9.10.1 Ranges in Loops

To limit the range of a loop, change the starting value and/or ending value for the loop index variable. For example, to create a new sound from just part of an original sound, you can change the start and end values for the loop. This was seen in Program 9.2.

```
// copy from start index to end index from source into target
for (int i = start; i <= end; i++, targetIndex++)
{
  value = this.getSampleValueAt(i);
  target.setSampleValueAt(targetIndex,value);
}
```

9.10.2 Returning a Value from a Method

When you declare a method you specify the visibility for the method, the type of value it returns, the name of the method, and the parameter list inside parentheses. This is followed by the body of the method, which is inside of a pair of curly braces.

Methods that do not return a value use the keyword void as the returnType. Java's void methods correspond to methods in Alice. If the method has a return type other than the keyword void, it must contain a return statement in the method that returns a value of that type. Java methods that return a value correspond to functions in Alice. Remember that a type is any of the primitive types or the name of a class.

```
visibility returnType name(parameterList)
{
  // statements in method
  // return a value
  return valueToReturn;
}
```

Here is an example of a public method declaration that doesn't return anything. The name of the method is mirrorFrontToBack, and it doesn't take any parameters.

public void mirrorFrontToBack()

Here is an example of a public method declaration that returns an object of the class Sound.

public Sound echo(**int** delay, **int** numEchoes)

Notice that it gives a return type of Sound. The body of the method must have the keyword return in it, and it must return an object that is an instance of the class Sound.

return echoSound;

9.11 Methods Summary

Here are the methods used or introduced in this chapter:

Sound Methods

blockingPlay()	Plays the Sound object it is invoked on and makes sure that no other sound plays at the exact same time. (Compare two blockingPlay's with two play's right after each other.)
getLength()	Returns the number of samples in the Sound object it is invoked on.
getSampleValueAt(int index)	Takes an index (an integer value) and returns the value of the sample at that index for the Sound object it is invoked on.
getSamplingRate()	Returns the number representing the number of samples in each second for the Sound object it is invoked on.
setSampleValueAt(int index, int value)	Takes an index and a value, and sets the value of the sample at the given index in the Sound object it was invoked on to the given value.

Exercises

1. What does each of the following mean?
   - Clip
   - Splice
   - Reverse
   - Mirror
   - Blend
   - Change frequency

2. What is the output from the following code?

```java
public void test1()
{
  for (int x = 5; x > 0; x--)
  {
     System.out.println(x);
  }
}
```

3. What is the output from the following code?

```java
public void test2()
{
  for (int x = 0; x < 10; x = x + 2)
  {
     System.out.println(x);
  }
}
```

4. What is the output from the following code?

```java
public void test3()
{
  for (int x = 1; x < 10; x = x + 2)
  {
     System.out.println(x);
  }
}
```

5. Would this compile? If not, what change do you need to make so that it will compile?

```java
public void test()
{
   System.out.println("In Test");
}
```

6. Would this compile? If not, what change do you need to make so that it will compile?

```java
public int test2(int x)
{
   System.out.println("In Test2");
}
```

7. Would this compile? If not, what change do you need to make so that it will compile?

```java
public void test3(int x)
{
    return "In Test3";
}
```

8. Would this compile? If not, what change do you need to make so that it will compile?

```java
public String test4(int x)
{
    return x * 4;
}
```

9. How many times will this loop execute?

```java
for (int i = 5; i <= 10; i++)
    System.out.println(i);
```

10. What does Alice mean by a *method* and a *function*? How do these compare to Java methods?

11. How many times will this loop execute?

```java
for (int i = 0; i < 10; i++)
    System.out.println(i);
```

12. Rewrite Program 9.1 so that two input values are provided to the method: the *sound* and a *percentage* of how far into the sound to go before dropping the volume.

13. Create a reversed sound and import both it and the original sound into Alice. Use both sounds in a story. Perhaps when the user presses the up arrow, an Alice character plays the original sound while she moves forward, and when the user presses the down arrow, the character moves backward and plays the reversed sound.

14. Create a sound with an echo and use it in an Alice animation.

15. Create sound clips that match your animation in Alice. You might play the theme music from *Jaws* when your shark moves forward.

16. Try using a stopwatch to time the execution of the methods in this chapter. Time from hitting return on the command until the next prompt appears. What is the relationship between execution time and the length of the sound? Is it a linear relationship, that is, do longer sounds take longer to process and shorter sounds take less time to process? Or is it something else? Compare the individual methods. Does normalizing a sound take longer than raising (or lowering) the amplitude a constant amount? How much longer? Does it matter if the sound is longer or shorter?

17. Make an audio collage. Make it at least five seconds long, and include at least two different sounds (sounds from different files). Make a copy of one of those different sounds and modify it using any of the techniques described in this chapter (for example, mirroring, splicing, and volume manipulations). Splice together the original two sounds and the modified sound to complete the collage.

18. Compose a sentence that no one ever said by combining words from other sounds into a grammatically correct new sound. Write a method named `audioSentence` to generate a sentence out of individual words. Use at least three words in your sentence! You can use the words in the `mediasources` folder or record your own words. Be sure to include a tenth (1/10) of a second pause between the words.

19. Write a method called `erasePart` to set all the samples in the second second of `thisisatest.wav` to zeros—essentially making the second second go silent. Play and return the partially erased sound.

20. We've seen a method that reverses a sound and a method that can process samples by index number. Write a method called `reverseLastHalf` that reverses just the second half of the current sound. For example, if the sound said "MarkBark" the returned sound should say "MarkkraB."

21. Write a method similar to Program 9.9 that mirrors from back to front.

Making It Work Tip:
Remember that zeroes for the sample values generate silence or pause.

Making It Work Tip:
Remember that the sampling rate is the number of samples per second. From there, you should be able to figure out how many samples need to set to zero to generate a 1/10 of a second pause. Be sure to access your sounds in your Media Folder using `getMediaPath` so that it will work for users of your program as long as they first execute `setMediaPath`.

Making It Work Tip:
Remember that `getSamplingRate()` tells you the number of samples in a single second in a sound.

10 Modifying Pictures Using Loops

Goals of this chapter:

- To review one-dimensional arrays.
- To introduce two-dimensional arrays (matrices).
- To write object methods.
- To do iteration with `for-each`, `while`, and `for` loops.
- To understand the scope of a variable name.

Introduction

In the last two chapters, you learned about three diffcrent ways to loop through sound values using `for-each`, `while`, and `for` loops. You learned how to conditionally execute code in Java using conditional `if-else` statements. Also, you learned how to return a value from a Java method.

In this chapter, we will use many of these same computing concepts to learn how pictures are represented on a computer and how they can be manipulated. We will use loops to modify pictures in the same way we used loops to modify sounds. We will write programs to change color values, make a negative, and convert color images to grayscale.

10.1 How Pictures Are Encoded

Pictures (images, graphics) are an important part of any media communication. In a computer, a picture is often digitized as a **bitmap (BMP)**, which is a format for saving image files. A bitmap is composed of **pixels** (short form of "picture element") in a **matrix** (a grid of vertical columns and horizontal rows). In Figure 10.1, a portion (the area inside the red box) of a picture is magnified 1000% to show that the picture is actually composed of pixels.

For our purposes, we will use pictures stored in a JPEG file. **JPEG** is an international standard for storing images with high quality but in a small amount of memory. JPEG is a **lossy compression** format. That means that a picture's bitmap is *compressed* (made smaller) but not with 100% of the quality of the original format. Typically, though, what gets thrown away is stuff that you don't see or don't notice anyway. For most purposes, a JPEG image works fine.

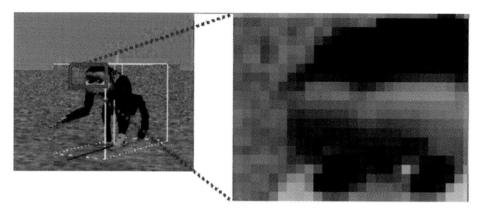

Figure 10.1
Selected portion of picture (left) blown up (right) to show the pixels

We want to write programs to manipulate JPEG images. But to do this, we need to understand more about how the images are stored and displayed. This means that we need to better understand arrays, matrices, pixels, and color.

10.1.1 Arrays

As we saw in Chapter 8, an **array** is a sequence of elements, each associated with an index number, as Figure 10.2 shows. The first element in an array is at index 0, the second at index 1, the third at index 2, and so on. The last element of the array will always be at the length of the array minus one. An array with five elements will have its last element at index 4.

The index of an element in the array is based on the distance from the beginning of the array to that element. The first item of the array is at the beginning of the array, so its index is 0, and the distance is 0. Why is the index based on the distance? Array values are stored one after the other in memory. This makes it easy to find any element of the array by multiplying the size of each element by the index and adding it to the address of the beginning of the array. If you are looking for the element at index 3 in an array where the size of each element is 4 bytes long and the array starts at memory location 26, the 3rd element is at (3 * 4 + 26 = 12 + 26 = 38).

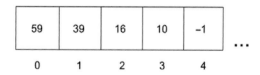

Figure 10.2
A depiction of the first five elements in an array

As seen in Chapter 8, to declare an array in Java, you specify the type and then use open and close square brackets followed by a name for the array:

```
> double[] grades;
> System.out.println(grades);
null
```

or you could have specified the square brackets after the variable name:

```
> double grades[];
> System.out.println(grades);
null
```

The above code declares an array of `double` with the name `grades`. Notice, though, that this just declared an array object reference. When the `System.out.println(grades)` statement is executed, Java prints out `null`. This is because Java actually *didn't create* an array, only an object named `grades` that can reference an array of `double` values.

How can you declare an array and actually create an array at the same time? One way to do this is to specify the values for the array, as illustrated in the following code:

```
> double[] gradeArray = {80.0, 90.5, 88.0, 92.0, 94.5};
```

Now, we have the `gradeArray` object, and it references an actual array of five values. Notice that all the values are of the same data type, `double`.

Although arrays are a great way to store lots of data of the same type, you still need a way to access an individual element of the array, so we use an index for that. You can access elements of an array in Java using `arrayName[index]`.

In the `gradeArray` example, use `gradeArray[0]` to access the first element. To access the second element, use `gradeArray[1]`. To access the third element, use `gradeArray[2]`. You can get the number of items in an array using `arrayName.length`. So, to access the last element in the `gradeArray`, you would use `gradeArray[gradeArray.length - 1]`. The following code illustrates how to access the length of an array and how to use an index to access an array element.

```
> System.out.println(gradeArray.length);
5
> System.out.println(gradeArray[0]);
80.0
> System.out.println(gradeArray[4]);
94.5
```

Making It Work Tip: Using Dot Notation for Public Fields

As you know, when a method is invoked, it *always* has a pair of parentheses after the method name even if there are no input parameters. For example, in the statement,

```
FileChooser.pickAFile();
```

the `pickAFile()` method does not have input parameters, but the call to `pickAFile()` has parentheses anyway. You may have noticed in the previous code that there are no parentheses following `gradeArray.length`. This is because an array's length is a **public**

field. A field is a variable that represents some item of information for an object of a class. A field can be private or public. If it is public, that means that it is publicly available (as if someone had posted it on a bulletin board that everyone could see). Because length is a public item of information, it does not have to be accessed by invoking a method. Public fields can be accessed using dot notation, as in *objectName.fieldName*. ◼

10.1.2 Matrix Representation

Picture encoding is actually more complex than sound encoding. A sound is inherently linear—it progresses forward in time. It can be represented using a one-dimensional array of sound samples. A picture, however, has two dimensions: a width and a height. Also, a picture is composed of hundreds of thousands of pixels arranged in a grid of vertical columns and horizontal rows. To digitally represent a picture in a computer program, we use a two-dimensional array—a **matrix**. A matrix is a collection of elements arranged in both a horizontal and vertical sequence.

For one-dimensional arrays, as in the gradeArray, an element can be accessed at index *i*, which is array[i]. For two-dimensional arrays, you need two indices to access an element, one to specify the row *r*, and another to specify the column *c*. This is given as matrix[r] [c]. This is called **row-major order**.

As an example of row-major order, consider the game Battleship™. If you have played this game, then you had to specify both the row and column of your guess (B-3). This means row B and column 3, as shown in Figure 10.3. Have you ever gone to a play? Usually your ticket has a row and seat number. These are both examples of row-major, two-dimensional arrays.

Another way to specify a *location* in a two-dimensional array is **column-major order** which specifies the column first and then the row: matrix[c] [r]. This is how we normally talk about pictures. We use an *x* for the horizontal location and a *y* for the vertical location: matrix[x] [y]. Picture data in this textbook is represented as a column-major, two-dimensional array.

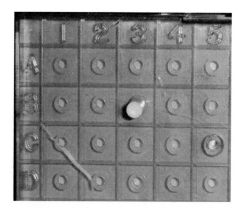

Figure 10.3
The top-left corner of a Battleship™ game board with a miss at B-3

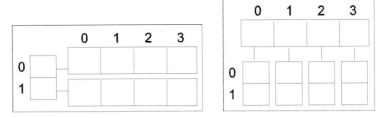

Figure 10.4
Picturing a 2D array as row-major or column-major

Just to be candid about what goes on inside the memory of the computer, let's take a look at what Java actually does when you create a two-dimensional array in your program. In the memory of the machine, Java actually creates a two-dimensional array as an array of arrays. When you have a two-dimensional array, the first index is the location in the outer array, and the second is the location in the inner array. You can think of the outer array as either the rows or the columns. So Java isn't really row-major or column-major. Figure 10.4 shows the same data in each format, illustrating the reality of the actual representation in the computer's memory.

Even though Java does some "fancy footwork" to represent a two-dimensional array (deep down in the computer's memory), it is much easier to think about two-dimensional arrays using a matrix visualization. It will help you understand how to write the program code, because it visually corresponds to the physical entity that we know in real life as a picture.

In Figure 10.5, you see an example matrix. Using column-major order for the **coordinates** (0, 0) (horizontal, vertical), you'll find the matrix element whose value is 15. The element at (1, 1) is 7, (2, 1) is 43, and (3, 1) is 23. We will often refer to these coordinates as (x, y) *(horizontal, vertical)*.

What is stored at each element in the picture is a *pixel*. It's literally a dot, and the overall picture is made up of lots of these dots. Have you ever taken a magnifying glass to view pictures in a newspaper or magazine, on a television, or even on your own computer monitor? Figure 10.6 was generated by capturing as an image the top-left

	0	1	2	3
0	15	12	13	10
1	9	7	43	23
2	6	13	15	16

Figure 10.5
An example matrix (two-dimensional array) of numbers

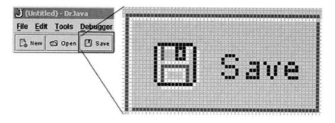

Figure 10.6
Upper-left corner of the DrJava window with a portion magnified 600%

part of the DrJava window and then magnifying it 600%. It's made up of many, many dots. When you look at the picture in the magazine or on the television, it doesn't look like it's broken up into millions of individual dots, but it is.

You can get a similar view of individual pixels using the picture explorer. The picture explorer allows you to zoom a picture up to 500%, so that each individual pixel is visible, as in Figure 10.7.

Our human sensory apparatus can't distinguish the small bits in the whole without using magnification or other special equipment. Humans have low visual *acuity*—we don't see as much detail as, say, an eagle. We actually have more than one kind of vision system in use in our brain and our eyes. Our system for processing color is different than our system for processing black and white (or **luminance**). We actually pick up luminance detail better with the sides of our eyes than the center of our eyes. That's an evolutionary advantage, because it allows you to pick out the sabertooth tiger sneaking up on you from the side.

The lack of resolution in human vision is what makes it possible to digitize pictures. Animals that perceive greater visual details than humans (such as eagles or cats) may actually see the individual pixels. Digitizing a picture breaks the picture up into smaller elements (pixels), but there are enough of them and they are small enough that

Figure 10.7
Image shown in the picture explorer: 100% image on left and 500% magnification on right (close-up of the branch over the mountain)

the picture doesn't look choppy when viewed from a normal viewing distance. If you *can* see the effects of the digitization (for example, if lines have sharp, jagged edges, or you see little rectangles in some spots), we call that **pixelization**—the effect when the digitization process becomes obvious.

10.1.3 Color Representations

Visible light is continuous, comprising any wavelength between 370 and 730 nanometers (0.00000037 and 0.00000073 meters). But our perception of light is limited by how our color sensors work. Our eyes have sensors that trigger (peak) around 425 nanometers (blue), 550 nanometers (green), and 560 nanometers (red). Our brain determines what color we "see" based on the feedback from these three sensors in our eyes. There are some animals with only two kinds of sensors, like dogs. Those animals still perceive color, but not the same colors nor in the same way as humans do. One of the interesting implications of our limited visual sensory apparatus is that we actually perceive two kinds of orange. There is a **spectral vision**—a particular wavelength that is natural orange. There is also a mixture of red and yellow that hits our color sensors just right so that we perceive it as the same orange.

Based on how we perceive color, as long as we encode what hits our three kinds of color sensors, we're recording our human perception of color. Thus, we can encode each pixel as a triplet of numbers. The first number represents the amount of red in the pixel. The second is the amount of green, and the third is the amount of blue. We can recreate any human-visible color by combining red, green, and blue light. We call this the **RGB color model**.

Type the following in the Interactions pane and press enter.

```
> ColorChooser.pickAColor();
```

You will see the color chooser shown in Figure 10.8. This will let you select a color. You can use the sliders to change the amount of red, green, and blue in your sample,

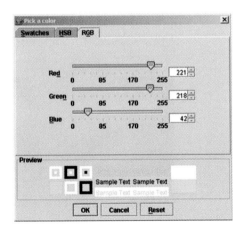

Figure 10.8
Picking a color using RGB sliders from Java

and the Preview section at the bottom will show the resulting color. What color is it when red = 0, green = 0, and blue = 0? What color is it when red = 255, green = 255, and blue = 255? Try to make brown, yellow, and orange.

Each color component (sometimes called a **channel**) in a pixel is typically represented with a single byte of 8 bits. Eight bits can represent 256 patterns (2^8): 0000000, 00000001, up through 11111111. We typically use these patterns to represent the values 0 to 255. Each pixel then uses 24 bits (8 bits for a red channel, 8 bits for a green channel, plus 8 bits for a blue channel) to represent a color. With 24 bits, there are 2^{24} possible patterns of 0's and 1's, which means that the standard encoding for color using the RGB model can represent 16,777,216 colors. We can actually perceive more than 16 million colors, but it turns out that it just doesn't matter. Humans have no technology that comes even close to being able to replicate the whole color space that we can see. We do have devices that can represent 16 million distinct colors, but those 16 million colors still don't cover the entire space of color (nor luminance) that we can perceive. So, the **24-bit RGB model** is adequate until technology advances.

There are computer models that use more bits per pixel. For example, there are 32-bit models that use the extra 8 bits to represent *transparency*—how much of the color "below" the given image should be blended with this color? These additional 8 bits are sometimes called the **alpha channel**. There are other models that actually use more than 8 bits for the red, green, and blue channels, but they are uncommon.

We actually perceive borders of objects, motion, and depth through a *separate* vision system. We perceive color through one system and **luminance** (how light/dark things are) through another system. Luminance is not actually the *amount* of light, but it is our *perception* of the amount of light. We can measure the amount of light (the number of photons reflected off the color) and show that a red and a blue spot each are reflecting the same amount of light, but we'll perceive the blue as darker. Our sense of luminance is based on comparisons with the surroundings—the optical illusion in Figure 10.9 highlights how we perceive gray levels. The two end quarters are actually the same level of gray, but because the two mid quarters end in a sharp contrast of lightness and darkness, we perceive that one end is darker than the other.

A triplet of (0, 0, 0) (red, green, blue) is black and of (255, 255, 255) is white. (255, 0, 0) is pure red, but (100, 0, 0) is red, too—just darker. (0, 100, 0) is a dark green,

Figure 10.9
The ends of this figure are the same colors of gray, but the middle two quarters contrast sharply, so the left looks darker than the right

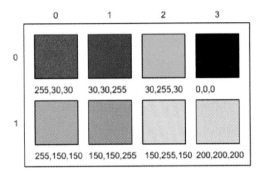

Figure 10.10
RGB triplets in a matrix representation

and (0, 0, 100) is a dark blue. When the red, green, and blue components are all the same value, the resultant color is gray. (50, 50, 50) would be a fairly dark gray, and (150, 150, 150) is a lighter gray.

Figure 10.10 is a representation of pixel RGB triplets in a matrix representation. In column-major order, the pixel at (1, 0) has color (30, 30, 255), which means that it has a red value of 30, a green value of 30, and a blue value of 255. Therefore, it's a mostly blue color, but not pure blue. The pixel at (2, 1) has pure green but also more red and blue (150, 255, 150), so it's a fairly light green.

The amount of memory needed to represent every pixel of even a small image is pretty large. As Table 10.1 demonstrates, a fairly small image of 320 pixels wide by 240 pixels high with 24 bits per pixel takes up 230,400 bytes—that's roughly 230 *kilobytes* (1,000 bytes) or 1/4 *megabyte* (million bytes). A computer monitor with 1,024 pixels across by 768 pixels vertically uses 32 bits per pixel and takes up over 3 megabytes just to represent the screen. Because of the large amounts of memory needed to store even a small picture, digitized images on disk and even in computer memory are usually stored in some kind of *compressed* form. This is why pictures are often stored in JPEG or GIF format—these formats compress the image into a smaller amount of memory.

Table 10.1   Number of bytes needed to store pixels at various sizes and formats

	320×240	**640×480**	**1,024×768**
24-bit color	230,400 bytes	921,600 bytes	2,359,296 bytes
32-bit color	307,200 bytes	1,228,800 bytes	3,145,728 bytes

Computer Science Idea: Kilobyte (kB) versus Kibibyte (KiB or K or KB)

We used the terms kilobyte and megabyte to describe the size of an image file. The term kilobyte has caused problems, because it has been interpreted differently by different groups. Computer scientists formerly used it to mean 2 to the 10th power, which is 1,024 bytes. Telecommunications engineers used it to mean 1,000 bytes. The

International Electrotechnical Commission (IEC) decreed in 1998 to call 1,024 bytes a kibibyte (KiB) and 1,000 bytes a kilobyte. Similarly, a mebibyte is defined to be 2 raised to the 20th power, and a megabyte is 1,000,000 bytes (one million bytes). A gibibyte is defined to be 2 raised to the 30th power, and a gigabyte is 1,000,000,000 (one billion bytes).

■

10.2   Manipulating Pictures

Now that you know more about pixels, color, and matrix representations, let's apply these concepts to manipulate a picture. You will create a picture object out of a JPEG file and then change the pixels in that picture. One way a picture can be altered is to change the colors associated with the pixels. To change the color, you manipulate the red, green, and blue components.

To create a picture object, use the syntax: new `Picture(fileName)`. The following code illustrates how to choose a JPG picture file (for example, `caterpillar.jpg`) and then create a `Picture` object (an object of the class `Picture`).

```
> String fileName = FileChooser pickAFile();
> System.out.println(fileName);
c:\intro-prog-java\mediasources\caterpillar.jpg
> Picture pictureObject = new Picture(fileName);
```

In the last statement of the code, what new `Picture(fileName)` does is scoop up all the bytes in the input filename, bring the bytes in to memory, reformat them slightly, and place a sign on them: "This is a picture object." When you execute `Picture pictureObject = new Picture(fileName)`, you are saying "The name `pictureObject` is referring to a `Picture` object created from the contents of the file."

Now that you have a `Picture` object, you can display the picture using the method `show()`. You could also explore a picture with the method `explore()`. These are both object methods, so they must be called on an object of the class that understands the method. This means that `show()` and `explore()` must be called on a `Picture` object (object of the `Picture` class) using dot notation, as in `pictureObject.show()`. The following code illustrates invoking the `show()` method to display the picture.

```
> pictureObject.show();
> System.out.println(pictureObject);
Picture, filename c:\intro-prog-java\mediasources\caterpillar.jpg
height 150 width 329
```

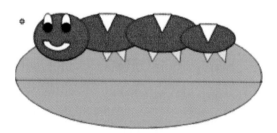

In the code, the `System.out.println(pictureObject)` statement causes Java to display information about the object: path and name of the file as well as its height and width. Clearly, a `Picture` object knows its own width and height. You can query a `Picture` object with the methods `getWidth()` and `getHeight()`.

```
> System.out.println(pictureObject.getWidth());
329
> System.out.println(pictureObject.getHeight());
150
```

How do you access an individual pixel in a `Picture` object? Remember that a `Picture` object represents the picture in a matrix. Each pixel is located in the matrix at an (x,y) coordinate position, where x is the horizontal location and y is the vertical location. The *x* coordinate starts at 0 at the top left of the picture and increases horizontally. The *y* coordinate starts at 0 at the top left of the picture and increases vertically. You can access any particular pixel in a picture using `getPixel(x,y)`, where *x* and *y* are the coordinates of the pixel desired. The `getPixel(x,y)` method returns an object of the class `Pixel` that knows what picture it is from and the *x* and *y* coordinate location of the pixel in that picture.

```
> Pixel pixelObject = pictureObject.getPixel(0,0);
> System.out.println(pixelObject);
Pixel red=252 green=254 blue=251
```

You can also get a one-dimensional array containing all the pixels in the picture using the method `getPixels()`. This just grabs all the pixels in the first row from left to right, followed by all of the pixels in the second row from left to right, and so on, until it has all of the pixels. The following code creates a one-dimensional array, `pixelArray`, containing all the pixels in the entire picture.

```
> Pixel [] pixelArray=pictureObject.getPixels();
> System.out.println(pixelArray[0]);
Pixel red=252 green=254 blue=251
```

Pixels know where they came from. You can ask them their *x* and *y* coordinates with `getX()` and `getY()`.

```
> System.out.println(pixelObject.getX());
0
> System.out.println(pixelObject.getY());
0
```

You can manipulate the red, green, and blue color components separately. For example, each pixel object knows how to get its red value `getRed()` and set its red value `setRed(redValue)`. (Green and blue work similarly.)

```
> System.out.println(pixelObject.getRed());
252
> pixelObject.setRed(0);
> System.out.println(pixelObject.getRed());
0
```

You can also manipulate all three color components at the same time. You can ask a pixel object for its color with getColor(), and you can ask the pixel object to set the color with setColor(color). When using the getColor() and setColor(color) methods, you are working with Color objects (objects of the class Color in package java.awt). A Color object knows its own red, green, and blue components. You can create a new Color object with

new Color(redValue,greenValue,blueValue)

The color values must be between 0 and 255. The following code illustrates the use of Color objects to get and set the color of a pixel in pixelObject.

```
> import java.awt.Color;
> Color colorObj=pixelObject.getColor();
> System.out.println(colorObj);
java.awt.Color[r=0,g=254,b=251]
> Color newColorObj=new Color(0,100,0);
> System.out.println(newColorObj);
java.awt.Color[r=0,g=100,b=0]
> pixelObject.setColor(newColorObj);
> System.out.println(pixelObject.getColor());
java.awt.Color[r=0,g=100,b=0]
```

In the code above, we specified color values (0 to 255 range) for red, green, and blue components. The Color class also has several colors predefined that you can use. If you need a color object that represents the color black, you can use Color.BLACK, and for yellow use Color.YELLOW. Other colors that are predefined are Color.BLUE, Color.GREEN, Color.RED, Color.GRAY, Color.ORANGE, Color.PINK, Color.CYAN, Color.MAGENTA, and Color.WHITE. You can also use lowercase names like Color.blue and Color.white. Notice that the predefined colors are actually public fields on the Color class and are not accessed by invoking class methods (no parentheses). Public class variables (fields) can be accessed using ClassName.fieldName.

Making It Work Tip: Importing Classes from Packages

You may have noticed the first statement in the previous code was an import statement:

import java.awt.Color;

When you start DrJava (or any other Java IDE), a default package of classes is available for you to use in writing your programs. A package is a group of related classes. By default, you always have access to the most commonly used classes, such as System and Math, in the java.lang package. An **import statement** tells Java that you want to use a class that is not available in the default package. **Color** is a Java class in the package java.awt. Java uses packages to group classes that you need for a particular purpose. To use classes in packages other than the default java.lang, you will need to *import* them. Importing a class or all classes in a package allows you to use the name of a class without fully qualifying it.

To fully qualify a name, use the package name followed by a period (dot) and the class name. The *fully qualified name* for the Color class is java.awt.Color. You can always use the fully qualified name instead of importing, but people don't usually want to type that much. To import all classes in the package java.awt, use import java.awt.*; . To import just the Color class from the package, java.awt use import java.awt.Color; . Importing doesn't make your class larger, it is just used to determine what class you want to use in your program.

Debugging Tip: Undefined Class Error

If you get the message Error: Undefined class Color, it means that you didn't import the class Color. You must either import classes that are in packages other than java.lang or fully qualify them.

Several pages ago, when we started with this example, we accessed the pixel at coordinate (0, 0) in our pictureObject, using code shown again here:

```
> Pixel pixelObject = pictureObject.getPixel(0,0);
> System.out.println(pixelObject);
Pixel red=252 green=254 blue=251
```

This code shows that the pixel at (0, 0) has red=252, green=254, and blue=251 color components. Over several paragraphs of code and explanations, we have manipulated this pixel so that if the following code is now executed,

```
> System.out.println(pictureObject.getPixel(0,0));
Pixel red=0 green=100 blue=0
```

you can see that the pixel at (0, 0) has red=0, green=100, and blue=0 color components. However, you may not immediately see a change in the color of the pixel in the picture display. This is because changing the color of a pixel in memory does not immediately update the picture being displayed. You won't see the change until the picture repaints.

Common Bug: Not Seeing Changes in the Picture

If you show your picture, and then change the pixels, you might be wondering, "Where are the changes?!?" Picture displays don't automatically update. If you ask the Picture object to repaint using pictureObject.repaint (), the display of the Picture object will update. Asking the picture to show itself again, pictureObject.show() will also repaint it. You can also use pictureObject.explore() to open a picture explorer for the picture.

We don't have to write new methods to manipulate pictures. We can do it in the Interactions pane using the methods just described. Please reset the Interactions pane by clicking the Reset button at the top of DrJava before you enter the following code.

```
> import java.awt.Color;
> String fName =
      "C:/intro-prog-java/mediasources/caterpillar.jpg";
> Picture picture = new Picture(fName);
> picture.explore();
> picture.getPixel(10,100).setColor(Color.BLACK);
> picture.getPixel(11,100).setColor(Color.BLACK);
```

```
> picture.getPixel(12,100).setColor(Color.BLACK);
> picture.getPixel(13,100).setColor(Color.BLACK);
> picture.getPixel(14,100).setColor(Color.BLACK);
> picture.getPixel(15,100).setColor(Color.BLACK);
> picture.getPixel(16,100).setColor(Color.BLACK);
> picture.getPixel(17,100).setColor(Color.BLACK);
> picture.getPixel(18,100).setColor(Color.BLACK);
> picture.getPixel(19,100).setColor(Color.BLACK);
> picture.explore();
```

Making It Work Tip: Reuse the Previous Line in DrJava

You can use the up arrow on the keyboard to bring up previous lines you have typed in the Interactions pane in DrJava. You can then use the left arrow key to get to a character to correct or change it, and then execute it by pressing the Enter key.

The result showing a small black line on the left side below the middle of the leaf appears in Figure 10.11. The black line is 100 pixels down, and pixels 10 through 19 from the left edge have been turned black.

10.3   Changing Color Values

The easiest thing to do with a picture is to change the color values of all its pixels by changing the red, green, and blue components. You can get radically different effects by simply tweaking those values. Many of Adobe® Photoshop®'s *filters* do just what we're going to be doing in this section.

The way we're going to be manipulating colors is by computing a *percentage* of the original color. For example, If we want to double the amount of red in the pricture, we're going to set the red channel for each pixel to 2 times (200%) whatever it is right now. If we want 50% of the amount of red in the picture, we're going to set the red channel to 0.50 times whatever it is right now. If we want to increase the red by 25%, we're going to set the red to 1.25 times whatever it is right now.

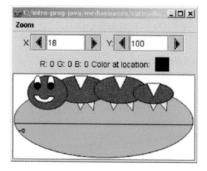

Figure 10.11
Exploring the caterpillar with the line

10.3.1 Using a `for-each` Loop

We can use the `getRed()` method to get the red value from a `Pixel` object, then we can multiply it by some amount to modify the red value, and then we can use `setRed()` to set the `Pixel` object's red component to the new value. We want to do this action for every pixel in a picture. We can use the `getPixels()` method to get a one-dimensional array of `Pixel` objects from a `Picture` object. Then, we need some way to repeat the statements that get the red value, change it, and then set the red value for each pixel in the array.

In Alice, you used a *forAllInOrder* to loop through each element of a list, as shown again in Figure 10.12. Each time through the loop, the object that was doing the action changed to the next one in the list.

As discussed in Chapter 8, we can do the same thing in Java by using a `for-each` loop to iterate through all the elements of an array one at a time. The syntax of a `for-each` loop is

```
for (Type variableName : array)
```

You can read this as "first declare a variable that will be used in the body of the loop" then "for each element in the array execute the body of the loop." The body of the loop can be either one statement or a block of statements inside an open curly brace { and a close curly brace }. The statements in the body of the loop are indented to show that they are part of the loop. A method that will loop through all the pixels in the current picture and set the red value in each to twice the original value is

```java
public void increaseRed()
{
Pixel[] pixelArray = this.getPixels();
int value = 0;
  // loop through all the pixels in the array
  for (Pixel pixelObj : pixelArray)
  {
  // get the red value
  value = pixel Obj.getRed();
  // double the red
  value = value * 2;
  // set the red value of the current pixel to the new value
  pixel Obj.setRed(value);
}
}
```

For all World.dancers ⌐ , one [obj] item_from_dancers at a time {

 rockette.kickUpRightLeg (*whichRockette* = item_from_dancers ⌐);

}

Figure 10.12
Looping through all elements of a list in Alice

Add the `increaseRed()` method to the `Picture.java` file before the last closing curly brace }. Then click the Compile All button in DrJava to compile the file. Once you have re-compiled the `Picture.java` file successfully, you can try out the `increaseRed()` method by typing the following in the interactions pane.

```
> String fName =
    "C:/intro-prog-java/mediasources/caterpillar.jpg";
> Picture pict = new Picture(fName);
> pict.explore();
> pict.increaseRed();
> pict.explore();
```

To compare the original picture with the changed picture, we used the picture explorer both before and after calling the `increaseRed()` method. This allows us to check that the amount of red was doubled. The `explore()` method makes a copy of the picture and then shows it in an explorer window, so the first `explore()` method will show the picture before it was changed, and the second `explore()` method will show it after the changes.

How does `increaseRed` really work? The `pict` variable is the name of a `Picture` object. And, when the statement `pict.increaseRed()` is executed, the Java runtime checks the `Picture` class to see if it has an `increaseRed()` method. If you have been following along and working with this example, you have added the `increaseRed()` method to the `Picture` class, so it does have this method, and it is invoked and executed.

Within the `increaseRed()` method, the first statement to be executed is

```
Pixel[] pixelArray = this.getPixels();
```

Although this looks like an ordinary kind of statement, it actually performs a magician's "pull a rabbit out of the hat" trick. Let's take a closer look to see what is hidden

- The `Pixel[] pixelArray` is a declaration of a variable `pixelArray` that references an array of `Pixel` objects. The = means that the variable `pixelArray` will be initialized to the result of the right-side expression, which is a call to `this.getPixels()`.

- Notice that the right-side expression uses `this`—a keyword that represents the current object on which the method was invoked. The `increaseRed()` method declaration doesn't have the keyword `static` in it, so it is an object method. An object method is always implicitly passed the object it was invoked on. What does "implicitly passed" mean? It means that, even though `increaseRed()` doesn't have any parameters listed, it is automatically passed the `Picture` object it was invoked on. So, calling the method without any parameters is like calling `increaseRed(Picture this)`. We don't see it there, but `this` is passed by the Java runtime and can be used (pulled out of a magician's hat) to refer to the current object.

- `this.getPixels()` invokes the method `getPixels()` on the current object. The `getPixels()` method returns a one-dimensional array of `Pixel` objects that are the pixels in the current `Picture` object.

So after execution of the first statement in the `increaseRed()` method, we have a variable `pixelArray` that refers to a one-dimensional array of `Pixel` objects. The `Pixel` objects came from the `Picture` object that was referred to as `pict` in the Interaction pane and as `this` in the method Definition of `increaseRed ()` in the Definitions pane.

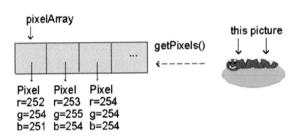

Now that we have an array of pixels, we are ready to begin working with the pixel values stored in each element of the array. First, we declare an int variable `value` and initialize it to 0.

`int value = 0;`

The `value` variable will be used to hold onto a copy of the red value of an individual pixel as we loop through the array. A `for-each` statement can be used to loop through the array.

`for (Pixel pixelObj : pixelArray)`

The first time through the loop, the `pixelObj` will refer to the first element of the array (the one at `index 0`). The second time through the loop, the `pixelObj` will refer to the second element of the array (the one at `index 1`). The last time through the loop, the `pixelObj` will refer to the last element of the array (the one at index (length − 1)). Each time through the loop, `value` receives a copy of the red component value

`value = pixel Obj.getRed();`

Then, the red component value is multiplied by a factor of 2 (to double the value).

`value = value * 2;`

Next, we modify the value in the `pixel` object by setting the red component to the computed value.

`pixel Obj.setRed(value);`

Note that the red, blue, and green components each have a maximum value of 255. But, if we try to set the red value to a value that is greater than 255, the value automatically will be set to 255.

A for-each loop is very useful for looping through all the elements in an array. But there are other loops in Java that you need to know about. A while loop can help you solve problems that a for-each loop can't solve.

10.3.2 Using while Loops

A while loop executes a statement or group of statements in a block (inside open and close curly braces). A while loop continues executing while a continuation test (a Boolean expression) is true. When the continuation test becomes false, the loop ends, and execution continues with the statement following the while loop.

In Alice, you used a while loop to check whether a goldfish was too far in front of the shark to allow the shark to eat it, and if that was true, the goldfish fled away from the shark, and the shark swam towards the goldfish. Once the distance between the goldfish and the shark decreased to less than or equal to 0.5 meters, the while loop ended, and the shark ate the goldfish. The code is shown again in Figure 10.13.

The same concept of a while loop is used in Java. The syntax for a while loop in Java is

```
while (test)
{
 /** commands to be done go here */
}
```

Let's talk through the pieces here.

- First comes the required Java keyword while.

- Then we have a required opening parenthesis.

- Then is the continuation test (a Boolean expression). While this test is true, the body of the loop will continue to be executed. When this test is false, the loop will finish, and the statement following the body of the loop will be executed.

- Next is the required closing parenthesis.

- Finally, we have the body of the loop, which is usually a block of statements to be executed each time the expression following the while keyword is true. The block

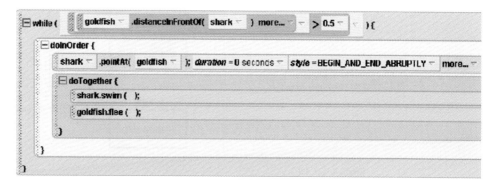

Figure 10.13
A while loop in Alice

of commands is enclosed by curly braces. If there is only one statement to be executed, you may leave off the curly braces, but you should still indent the statement to show it is in the body of the `while` loop.

Tell someone to clap their hands 12 times. Did they do it right? How do you know? In order to tell if they did it right, you would have to count each time they clapped, and when they stopped clapping, your count would be 12 if they did it right. A loop often needs a **counter** to count the number of times you want something done and a Boolean expression that stops the loop when that count is reached. You wouldn't want to declare the `count` variable inside the `while` loop, because you want it to change each time through the loop. Typically, you declare the `count` variable just before the `while` loop and then increment it just before the end of the block of statements you want to repeat.

Computer Science Idea: Flowcharts
Figure 10.14 shows a flowchart of a `while` loop. A flowchart is a visual representation of the execution of a method or function. It shows the order in which statements are executed and branches or conditional execution. Normal statements are shown in rectangles. Tests are shown in diamonds and have a *true* branch that is executed when the test is `true` and a *false* branch that is executed when the test is `false`. A flowchart can help you understand what a method is doing.

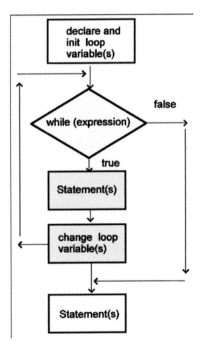

Figure 10.14
Flowchart of a `while` loop

A typical `while` loop will look like the following code.

```
int count = 0;
while (count < target)
{
  // commands to be done inside loop
  count = count + 1;
}
```

Debugging Tip: Loops and Variable Declarations

Declare any variables that you will need before you start the loop. A `while` loop may need some sort of counter or index declared outside the loop but changed inside the loop. If you forgot to change the counter or index, you will end up with a loop that never stops. This is called an **infinite loop**. Use the Reset button to stop if your code is in an infinite loop.

What if you want to write out the same sentence five times? You know how to print out a string using `System.out.println("some string");`. So, put this in the body of the loop. Start the count at 0, and increment it each time after the string is printed. When the count is 5, the string will have been printed five times, so stop the loop.

```
> int count = 0;
> while (count < 5)
{
    System.out.println("This is a test.");
    count = count + 1;
}
This is a test.
This is a test.
This is a test.
This is a test.
This is a test.
```

Now that we know how to get the computer to do thousands of commands without writing thousands of individual lines, let's do something useful with this concept. ■

10.3.3 Decreasing Red (Green, Blue)

A common desire when working with digital pictures is to shift the *redness* (or greenness or blueness—but most often, redness) of a picture. You might shift it higher to "warm" the picture or reduce it to "cool" the picture or to deal with overly-red digital cameras.

The `decreaseRedWhile()` method in Program 10.1 uses a `while` loop to decrease the amount of red by 50% in the current picture. After we multiply a red value by 0.5, we need to **cast** the value back to the integer. To cast a value means to change its data type. If the computer sees you using a `double` value (like 0.5), it assumes that the result should be a double. However, pixel color values must be integers, so we need to cast the result back to `int`.

Program 10.1: Decrease the Amount of Red in a Picture by 50%

```
/**
 * Method to decrease red by half in the current picture
 */
public void decreaseRedWhile()
```

```
{
  Pixel[] pixelArray = this.getPixels();
  Pixel pixel = null;
  int value = 0;
  int index = 0;

  // loop through all the pixels
  while(index < pixelArray.length)
  {
    // get the current pixel
    pixel = pixelArray[index];

    // get the value
    value = pixel.getRed();

    // decrease the red value by 50% (1/2)
    value = (int) (value * 0.5);

    // set the red value of the current pixel to the new value
    pixel.setRed(value);

    // increment the index
    index = index + 1;
  }
}
```

Go ahead and type this into your DrJava **Definitions** pane before the last curly brace in the `Picture.java` file. Click `Compile All` to get DrJava to compile the new method. Now that you have recompiled the `Picture` class, it is time to test the `decreaseRedWhile ()` method that we just wrote. In DrJava's **Interaction** pane, enter the code shown here.

```
> String fName =
    "C:/intro-prog-java/mediasources/caterpillar.jpg";
> Picture picture = new Picture(fName);
> picture.explore();
> picture.decreaseRedWhile();
> picture.explore();
```

In the code, we needed a `Picture` object—the one to get the pixels from. To create a `Picture` object, we passed in the file name. Then we explored the original picture using the picture explorer. Next, we invoked `decreaseRedWhile()` on the `picture` object. Finally, we explored it again to compare the original with the one that has had the red decreased.

Common Bug: Patience: Loops Can Take a Long Time
The most common bug with this kind of code is to give up and quit, because you don't think the loop is working. It might take a full minute (or two!) for some of the manipulations to work—especially if your source image is large.

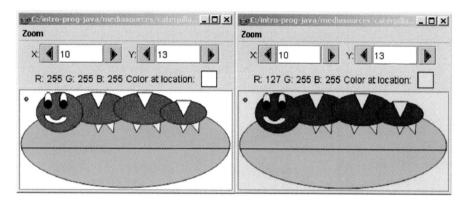

Figure 10.15
The original picture (left) and red-decreased version (right)

The original picture and its red-decreased version, as appears in Figure 10.15. Fifty percent is obviously a *lot* of red to reduce! The picture looks like it was taken through a blue filter.

Computer Science Idea: Changing Memory Doesn't Change the File

If you create another Picture object from the same file, will you get the original picture or the picture with red decreased? You will get the original picture. The Picture object picture was created by reading the file data into memory. The change to the Picture object was done in memory, but the file wasn't changed. If you want to save your changes, write them out to a file using the method pictObj.write(String fileName);, where pictObj is the name of the Picture object and fileName is the full path name of the file. So to save the changed Picture object, use picture.write ("c:/caterpillarChanged.jpg");. Be sure to add the ".jpg" extension so that the operating system knows what kind of file it is.   ∎

Computer Science Idea: The Most Important Skill Is Tracing

The most important skill that you can develop in programming is the ability to **trace** your program. This is also called **stepping** or **walking through** your program. To trace your program is to walk through it, line-by-line, and figure out what happens. Looking at a program, can you *predict* what it's going to do? You should be able to by thinking through what it does.   ∎

As an example of tracing, let's *trace* the decreaseRedWhile() method, as defined in Program 10.1, to see how it worked. We want to start tracing at the point where we just called decreaseRedWhile().

```
> String fileN =
        "C:/intro-prog-java/mediasources/caterpillar.jpg";
> Picture picture = new Picture(fileN);
> picture.explore();
> picture.decreaseRedWhile();
```

What happens now? The statement `picture.decreaseRedWhile()` really means invoking the `decreaseRedWhile()` method on the `Picture` object referred to by the variable `picture`. The `picture` object is implicitly passed to the `decreaseRedWhile()` method and can be referenced by the keyword `this`. (You may wish to review Section 10.3.1 where the use of the keyword `this` was explained.)

The first line executed in the `decreaseRedWhile()` method, defined earlier in Program 10.1.

```
Pixel[] pixelArray = this.getPixels().
```

The right-side expression, `this.getPixels()`, returns an array of pixels. So after execution of the first line, we have a variable `pixelArray` that refers to an array of `Pixel` objects. The `Pixel` objects came from the `Picture` object that was referred to as `picture` in the Interaction pane and as `this` in the method `decreaseRedWhile()`.

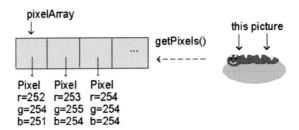

Next, the `decreaseRedWhile()` method is a declaration of a couple of variables that we will need in order to keep track of things in the loop. We will need something to represent the current `Pixel` object, so we declare a variable `pixel` of type `Pixel`. We start it off referring to nothing by using the defined value `null`. We also will need a variable to hold the current red value, we declare that as `int value = 0;`, which initializes the variable `value` to 0. Finally, we declare a variable to be an index into the array, `int index = 0;`. Remember that array elements are indexed starting with 0 and ending at the length of the array minus one.

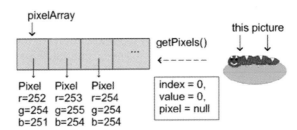

Variables that you declare inside methods are not automatically initialized for you, so you *should* initialize them when you declare them.

The loop `while(index < pixelArray.length)` tests whether the value of the variable `index` is less than the length of the `pixelArray`. If the test is `true`, the body of the loop will be executed. The body of the loop is all the code between the open and close curly braces following the test. If the test is `false`, execution continues after the body of the loop.

In the body of the loop, we have `pixel` = `pixelArray[index];`. This will set the `pixel` variable to refer to a `Pixel` object in the array of pixels with an index equal to the current value of `index`. Since `index` is initialized to 0 before the loop, the first time through this loop the pixel variable will point to the first `Pixel` object in the array.

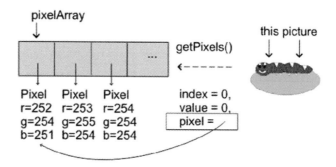

Next in the body of the loop is `value` = `pixel.getRed();`. This sets the variable `value` to the amount of red in the current pixel. Remember that the amount of red can vary from a minimum of 0 to a maximum of 255.

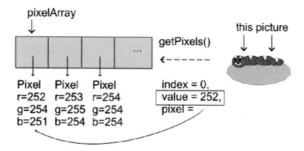

Next in the body of the loop is `value` = `(int) (value * 0.5);`. This sets the variable `value` to the integer amount that you get from multiplying the current contents of `value` by 0.5. The `(int)` is a cast to integer so that the compiler doesn't complain about losing precision (since we are storing a floating-point number in an integer number). Any digits after the decimal point will be discarded. This is called *casting* and is required whenever a larger value is being stored into a smaller variable's memory space. If the result of a multiplication has a fractional part, that fractional part will just be thrown away so the result can fit in an `int` memory space.

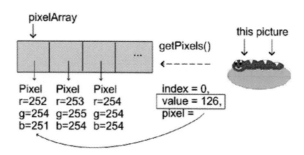

The next step in the body of the loop is `pixel.setRed(value);`. This changes the amount of red in the current pixel to be the same as what is stored in variable `value`. The current pixel is the first one, so we see that the red value has changed from 252 to 126 after this line of code is executed.

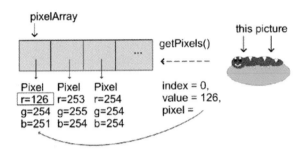

After the statements in the body of the loop are executed, the `index = index + 1;` will be executed, which will add one to the current value of `index`. Since `index` was initialized to 0, this will result in `index` holding the value 1.

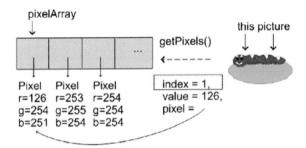

What happens next is very important. The loop starts over again. The continuation test will again check that the value in variable `index` is less than the length of the array of pixels, and since the value of `index` is less than the length of the array, the statements in the body of the loop will be executed again. The variable `pixel` will be set to the `pixel` object in the array of pixels at `index` 1. This is the second `Pixel` object in the array `pixelArray`.

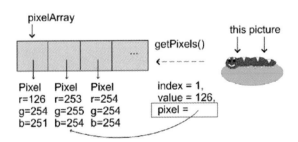

The variable `value` will be set to the red amount in the current pixel referred to by the variable `pixel`, which is 253.

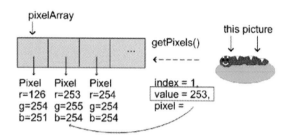

The variable `value` will be set to the result of casting to the integer, which is the result of multiplying the amount in `value` by 0.5. This results in (253 * 0.5) = 126.5, and after we drop the digits after the decimal, this is 126.

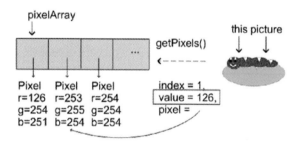

The red value in the current `pixel` object is set to the same amount as what is stored in `value`. So the value of red in the second pixel changes from 253 to 126.

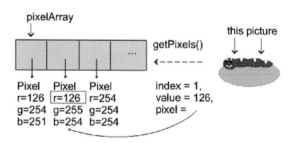

The variable `index` is set to the result of adding 1 to its current value. This adds 1 to 1, resulting in 2.

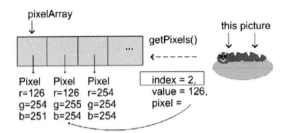

At the end of the loop body, we go back to the continuation test. The test will be evaluated, and if the result is true, the statement or statements in the loop body will be executed again.

These steps happen again and again. We keep going through all the pixels in the sequence and changing all the red values. Eventually, the continuation test evaluates to false, the loop ends, and execution goes on to the first statement after the body of the loop. In this example, we finally end up with the red-decreased picture, illustrated previously in Figure 10.15.

Making It Work Tip: Don't Just Trust Your Programs!

How do we know that it really worked? Sure, *something* happened to the picture, but did we *really* decrease the red by 50%?

It's easy to mislead yourself into believing that your programs worked. After all, you told the computer to do a particular thing. You shouldn't be surprised if the computer did what you wanted. But computers only follow the instructions you write—they can't figure out what you want. They only do what you actually tell them to do. It's pretty easy to get it *almost* right. The smart thing for you to do is actually check. You can print out the red, green, and blue values for particular pixels or use the picture explorer to compare the values.   ■

We can even get rid of a color completely. Figure 10.16 shows the result of running Program 10.2, which erases the blue component from a picture by setting the blue value to 0 in all pixels.

Program 10.2: Clear the Blue Component from a Picture

```
/**
 * Method to clear the blue from the picture (set
 * the blue to 0 for all pixels)
 */
public void clearBlue()
{
  Pixel[] pixelArray = this.getPixels();
```

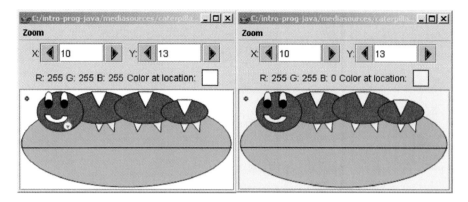

Figure 10.16
Original (left) and blue erased (right)

```
Pixel pixel = null;
int index = 0;

// loop through all the pixels
while (index < pixelArray.length)
{
  // get the current pixel
  pixel = pixelArray[index];

  // set the blue on the pixel to 0
  pixel.setBlue(0);

  // increment index
  index++;
  }
}
```

Compile the new method `clearBlue` and invoke it on a `Picture` object. Explore the picture object to check that all the blue values are indeed 0.

```
> String fName =
      "C:/intro-prog-java/mediasources/caterpillar.jpg";
> Picture picture = new Picture(fName);
> picture.explore();
> picture.clearBlue();
> picture.explore();
```

This method is similar to the `decreaseRedWhile()` method, except that it doesn't call the `getBlue()` method to get the current blue value, since we are simply setting all the blue values to 0.

10.3.4 Creating a Sunset

We can certainly do more than one color manipulation at once. What if you want to fake a sunset? You might try increasing the red, but that doesn't always work. Some of the red values in a given picture are pretty high. If you go past 255 for a color value, it will keep the value at 255.

Perhaps what happens in a sunset is that there is *less* blue and green, thus *emphasizing* the red without actually increasing it. Program 10.3 defines a method makeSunset() that emphasizes the red by decreasing the blue and green.

Program 10.3: Making a Sunset

```java
/**
 * Method to simulate a sunset by decreasing the green
 * and blue
 */
public void makeSunset()
{
  Pixel [] pixelArray = this.getPixels();
  Pixel pixel = null;
  int value = 0;

  int i = 0;
  // loop through all the pixels
  while (i < pixelArray.length)
  {
    // get the current pixel
    pixel = pixelArray[i];

    // change the blue value
    value = pixel.getBlue();
    pixel.setBlue((int) (value * 0.7));

    // change the green value
    value = pixel.getGreen();
    pixel.setGreen((int) (value * 0.7));

    // increment the index
    i++;
  }
}
```

Making It Work Tip: Using Short Variable Names for Loop Counters

Notice that instead of using index as the counter for the loop, we are using i. Again, programmers like to reduce the amount of typing, and so the simple variable name i is commonly used to represent the counter or index for a loop.

Compile the new method makeSunset() and invoke it on a Picture object. Explore the picture object to check that the blue and green values have been decreased.

```java
> String fName =
    "C:/intro-prog-java/mediasources/beach-smaller.jpg";
> Picture picture = new Picture(fName);
> picture.explore();
> picture.makeSunset();
> picture.explore();
```

Figure 10.17
Original beach scene (left) and at (fake) sunset (right)

What we see happening in Program 10.3 is that we're changing both the blue and green channels—reducing each by 30%. The effect works pretty well, as seen in Figure 10.17.

Computer Science Idea: Scope

Names in methods are *completely* separate from names in the Interactions pane and also from names in other methods. We say that they have different **scopes**. Scope is the enclosing context where a name is declared and can be accessed at runtime. Variables declared inside of a method have method scopes, and only apply inside that method. For example, a variable declared and named value in one method is not the same variable declared and named value in another method. Each method can only access its own value variable. That is why we can use the same variable names in several different methods.

Within a method, you can use any names you want. Names that you first define within the method (like pixel in the last example) or names that you use to stand for the input data (like fileName) *only* exist while the method is running. When the method is done, those variable names literally do not exist anymore.

This is really an advantage. Earlier, we said that naming is very important to computer scientists: We name everything from data to methods to classes. But if each name could mean one and only one thing *ever*, we'd run out of names. In natural language, words mean different things in different contexts (e.g., "What do you mean?" and "You are being mean!"). A method is a different context—names can mean something different than they do outside of that method.

In DrJava, variables declared inside the Interactions pane are known inside the Interactions pane until it is reset. This is why you get Error: Redefinition of 'picture' when you declare a variable that is already declared in the Interactions pane. However, variables declared inside the Interactions pane are not in scope in any methods you write in the Definitions pane. The *only* way to get any data (pictures, sounds, file names, or numbers) from the Interactions pane into a method is by passing it in as input to the method.

10.3.5 A General Method to Change All the Color Components

In the methods increaseRed() and decreaseRedWhile(), we changed just the red
color component. In the method makeSunset(), we changed just the blue and green
color components. We can write a more general method that changes all color components by some passed amount.

Program 10.4: Change all Pixel Colors by the Passed Amounts

```
/**
 * Method to change the color of each pixel in the picture
 * object by passed in amounts.
 * @param redAmount the amount to change the red value
 * @param greenAmount the amount to change the green value
 * @param blueAmount the amount to change the blue value
 */
public void changeColors(double redAmount,
                         double greenAmount,
                         double blueAmount)
{
 Pixel[] pixelArray = this.getPixels();
 Pixel pixel = null;
 int value = 0;

 int i = 0;
 // loop through all the pixels
 while( i < pixelArray.length)
 {
   // get the current pixel
   pixel = pixelArray[i];

   // change the red value
   value = pixel.getRed();
   pixel.setRed((int) (redAmount * value));

   // change the green value
   value = pixel.getGreen();
   pixel.setGreen((int) (greenAmount * value));

   // change the blue value
   value = pixel.getBlue();
   pixel.setBlue((int) (blueAmount * value));

   // increment i
   i++;
 }
}
```

We could use this method as shown here:

```
> String fName =
     "C:/intro-prog-java/mediasources/beach-smaller.jpg";
> Picture picture = new Picture(fName);
> picture.changeColors(1.0,0.7,0.7);
> picture.show();
```

This code would have the same result as makeSunset(). It keeps the red values the same, because the amount passed in for red is 1.0. It decreases the green and blue values by 30%, because the amount passed in is 0.7 for each. But, of course, makeSunset() could have been called with any combination of red, green, and blue factors. That's a pretty useful and powerful method. In programming, we often try to write methods that can be reused in a general purpose manner.

10.3.6 Using a for Loop

You may have had the problem that you forgot to declare the index variable before you tried to use it in your while loop. You also may have had the problem of forgetting to increment the index variable before the end of the loop body. This happens often enough that many programmers prefer to use a for loop when a loop is expected to iterate a set number of times. .

A for loop allows for declaration and/or initialization of variables before the loop body is first executed. The loop body contains a statement or block of statements that are executed with each iteration of the loop. A for loop continues executing the loop body while the continuation test (Boolean) is true. After each iteration of the loop and before the continuation test, one or more variables can be changed.

In Alice, you used a for loop to have a bunny hop eight times, shown again in Figure 10.18. This for loop set the index equal to 0 and incremented the index by one each time the body of the loop was finished executing. The loop stopped when the index was no longer less than 8.

We first introduced the for loop in Chapter 8, working with sound. For your convenience, the syntax and description of a for loop are repeated here

```
for (initialization; test; change)
{
 /* statements in body of the loop */
}
```

Let's talk through the pieces here.

• First is the required Java keyword for.

• Then we have a required opening parenthesis.

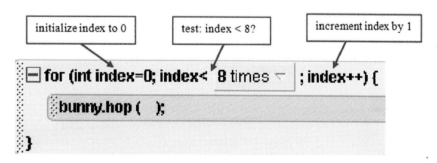

Figure 10.18
A for loop in Alice

- Next is the initialization where you can declare and initialize variables. Most often, a variable is declared and initialized for the purpose of controlling the number of times the loop iterates. For example, you can have `int i=0`, which declares a variable **i** of type `int` and initializes it to 0. You could initialize more than one variable here by separating the initializations with commas. You are not required to have any initializations here.

- Next is the required semicolon.

- Then we have the conditional test. This holds a Boolean expression that returns `true` or `false`. As long as this expression is `true`, the loop will continue to execute. When this test becomes `false`, the loop will end, and the statement following the body of the loop will be executed.

- Next is the required semicolon.

- The next step is the change area, where you usually increment or decrement variables, such as `i++` to increment **i**. The statements in the change area actually take place after each execution of the body of the loop.

- Finally, we have the required closing parenthesis.

If you just want to execute a single statement in the body of the loop, you can just write it on the next line. It is normally indented to show that it is part of the `for` loop. If you want to execute more than one statement in the body of the `for` loop, you will need to enclose the statements in a block (a set of open and close curly braces).

Common Bug: Change Loop Variables in More Than One Place

When you specify how to change the loop variables in the change area of the `for` loop, this will actually happen at the end of the body of the loop. So don't also change the loop variables in the loop, or you will change them twice and probably not get the desired result.

Compare the `for` loop flowchart in Figure 10.19 with the `while` loop flowchart previously shown in Figure 10.14. They look the same, because `for` loops and `while` loops *execute in the same way* even though the code looks different. Any code can be written using either loop structure. The syntax of the `for` loop just makes it easier to remember to declare a variable for use in the loop and to change it each time through the loop since all of that is written at the same time that you write the test. As an example, you could change the `clearBlue()` method to use a `for` loop by simply moving the declaration and initialization of the index variable `i` to the initialization area and the increment of `i` to the change area of a `for` loop statement. Program 10.5 defines a `clearBlueFor()` method, using a `for` loop instead of a `while` loop.

Program 10.5: Another Clear Blue Method

```
/**
 * Method to clear the blue from the picture (set
 * the blue to 0 for all pixels)
 */
```

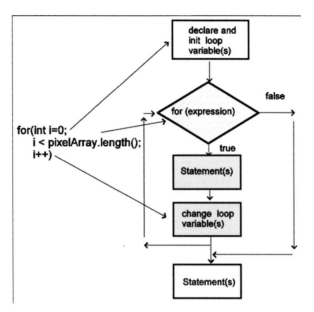

Figure 10.19
Flowchart of a for loop

```
public void clearBlueFor()
{
  Pixel [] pixelArray = this.getPixels();

  // loop through all the pixels
  for (int i=0; i < pixelArray.length; i++)
      pixelArray[i].setBlue(0);
}
```

10.3.7 Creating a Negative

Creating a *negative image* of a picture is much easier than you might think at first. Let's think it through. What we want is the opposite of each of the current values for red, green, and blue. It's easiest to understand at the extremes. If we have a red component of 0, we want 255 instead. If we have 255, we want the negative to have a zero.

Now let's consider a value somewhere in the middle of the 0 to 255 range. If the red component is slightly red (say, 50), we want something that is almost completely red—where the "almost" is the same amount of redness in the original picture. We want the maximum red (255), but 50 less than that. We want a red component of $255 - 50 = 205$. In general, the negative should be $255 - original$. We need to compute the negative of each of the red, green, and blue components, create a new negative color, and set the pixel to the negative color.

Program 10.6 defines a negate() method, and you can see from the image in Figure 10.20 that it really does work.

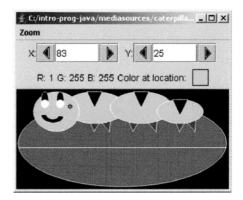

Figure 10.20
Negative of the image

Program 10.6: Create the Negative of the Original Picture

```java
/**
 * Method to negate the picture
 */
public void negate()
{
  Pixel[] pixelArray = this.getPixels();
  Pixel pixel = null;
  int redValue = 0, blueValue = 0, greenValue = 0;

  // loop through all the pixels
  for (int i = 0; i < pixelArray.length; i++)
  {
    // get the current pixel
    pixel = pixelArray[i];

    // get the current red, green, and blue values
    redValue = pixel.getRed();
    greenValue = pixel.getGreen();
    blueValue = pixel.getBlue();

    // set the pixel's color to the new color
    pixel.setColor(new Color(255 - redValue,
                             255 - greenValue,
                             255 - blueValue));
  }
}
```

10.3.8 Converting to Grayscale

Converting to grayscale is a fun program. It's short, not hard to understand, yet has such a nice visual effect. It's a really nice example of what one can do easily, yet powerfully, by manipulating pixel color values.

Recall that the resultant color is gray whenever the red component, green component, and blue component have the same value. That means that our RGB encoding supports

256 levels of gray from (0, 0, 0) (black), to (1, 1, 1), through (100, 100, 100), and finally, (255, 255, 255). The tricky part is figuring out what the replicated value should be.

What we want is a sense of the *intensity* of the color. It turns out that it's pretty easy to compute: We average the three component colors. Since there are three components, the formula for intensity is

$$\frac{(red\ +\ green\ +\ blue)}{3}$$

We can use the intensity as the value for each of the red, green, and blue color components to convert the picture to a grayscale image. This leads us to the simple grayscale() method defined in Program 10.7 and the resulting picture shown in Figure 10.21.

Program 10.7: Convert to Grayscale

```
/**
 * Method to change the picture to grayscale
 */
public void grayscale()
{
 Pixel[] pixelArray = this.getPixels();
 Pixel pixel = null;
 int intensity = 0;
 // loop through all the pixels
 for (int i = 0; i < pixelArray.length; i++)
 {
   // get the current pixel
   pixel = pixelArray[i];
   // compute the intensity of the pixel (average value)
   intensity = (int) ((pixel.getRed() + pixel.getGreen() +
               pixel.getBlue()) / 3);
   // set the pixel color to the new color
   pixel.setColor(new Color(intensity,intensity,intensity));
 }
}
```

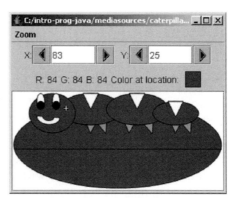

Figure 10.21
Color picture converted to grayscale

The grayscale() method actually uses an overly simply notion of grayscale. Let's revise it to take into account how the human eye perceives *luminance*. Remember that we consider blue to be darker than red, even if it's reflecting the same amount of light. So we *weight* blue lower, and red higher, when computing the average. Program 10.8 defines a grayscaleWithLuminance() method in which we weight the red, green, and blue components before computing the average for intensity.

Program 10.8: Convert to Grayscale with More Careful Control of Luminance

```
/**
 * Method to change the picture to grayscale with luminance
 */
public void grayscaleWithLuminance()
{
 Pixel[] pixelArray = this.getPixels();
 Pixel pixel = null;
 int luminance = 0;
 double redValue = 0;
 double greenValue = 0;
 double blueValue = 0;

 // loop through all the pixels
 for (int i = 0; i < pixelArray.length; i++)
 {
   // get the current pixel
   pixel = pixelArray[i];

   // get the weighted red, green, and blue values
   redValue = pixel.getRed() * 0.299;
   greenValue = pixel.getGreen() * 0.587;
   blueValue = pixel.getBlue() * 0.114;

   // compute the intensity of the pixel (average value)
   luminance = (int) (redValue + greenValue + blueValue);

   // set the pixel color to the new color
   pixel.setColor(new Color(luminance,luminance,luminance));
 }
}
```

10.4   Using Media Computation with Alice

You can capture a picture from an Alice world and use any of the methods in this chapter to modify the image. How about negating a picture from Alice, as in Figure 10.22?

Another way to use pictures with Alice is to modify a picture using any of the methods in this chapter. Then, import the picture into Alice as a billboard. See the Appendix for more information on using 2D graphic images as billboards in Alice.

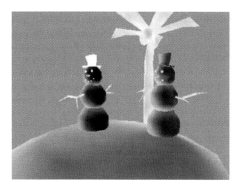

Figure 10.22
Negating a picture from Alice

10.5 Concepts Summary

In this chapter, we have introduced arrays, matrices, pixels, and colors in the context of writing programs to manipulate pictures. As with sound, we used three different kinds of loops to iterate through the array elements.

10.5.1 Arrays

Arrays are used to store many pieces of data of the same type. They allow you to quickly access a particular item in the array using an index. If you couldn't use an array, you would have to create a separate variable name for each piece of data.

To declare a variable that refers to an array, use the type, followed by open [and close] square brackets, and then the variable name.

```
Pixel[] pixelArray;
```

This declares an array of `Pixel` objects. The value stored at each position in the array is a reference to a `Pixel` object.

Arrays are objects, and you can find out how many elements an array can hold by accessing its `length`.

```
pixelArray.length
```

Notice that this isn't a method call (there are no parentheses). This accesses a public read-only field.

You can access an element of an array using `arrayReference[index]`, where the index values can range from 0 to `arrayReference.length-1`.

```
pixel = pixelArray[i];
```

10.5.2 Loops

Loops are used to execute a block of statements while a Boolean expression is `true`. Most loops have variables that change during the loop, which eventually cause the Boolean expression to be `false` and the loop to stop. Loops that never stop are called infinite loops.

We used three types of loops in this chapter: `for-each`, `while`, and `for`. The `while` loop is used most often when you don't know how many times a loop needs to execute, and `for` loops are used when you do know how many times the loop needs to execute. The `for-each` loop was introduced in Java 5 (1.5). It loops through all of the elements of an array, one at a time.

The `while` loop has the keyword `while` followed by a Boolean expression and then a block of statements between an open and close curly brace. If the Boolean expression is `true`, the body of the loop will be executed. If the Boolean expression is `false`, execution will continue after the body of the loop (after the close curly brace). If you just want to execute one statement in the body of the loop, then you don't need the open and close curly braces, but you should indent the statement.

```
while (Boolean expression)
{
 statement1;
 statement2;
}
```

The `for` loop does the same thing as a `while` loop, but it lets you declare the variables that you need for the loop, specify the Boolean expression to test, and specify how to change the loop variables all in one place. This means you are less likely to forget to do each of these things.

```
// loop through all the pixels
for (int index = 0; index < pixelArray.length; index++)
{
 // get the current pixel
 pixel = pixelArray[index];
 // do something to the pixel
}
```

10.6 Objects and Methods Summary

In this chapter, we talk about several kinds of encodings of data (or objects).

Color	An object that holds red, green, and blue values, each between 0 and 255.
Picture	Pictures are encodings of images, typically coming from a JPEG file (`.jpg`) or a bitmap (`.bmp`) file.
Pixel	A pixel is a dot in a `Picture` object. It has a color (red, green, and blue) and a position (*x*, *y*) associated with it. It remembers its own `Picture` object so that a change to the pixel changes the real dot in the picture.

Picture Methods

getHeight()	This method returns the height of the `Picture` object in pixels.
getPixel(int x, int y)	This method takes an *x* position and a y position (two numbers) and returns the `Pixel` object at that location in the `Picture` object it is invoked on.
getPixels()	Returns a one-dimensional array of `Pixel` objects in the `Picture` object it is invoked on.

getWidth()	This method returns the width of the Picture object in pixels.
write(String fileName)	This method takes a file name (a string) as input then writes the Picture object to the file as a JPEG. (Be sure to end the filename in .jpg or .bmp for the operating system to understand it well.)

Pixel Methods

getColor()	Returns the Color object for the Pixel object.
getRed(), getGreen(), getBlue()	Each method returns the value (between 0 and 255) of the amount of redness, greenness, and blueness (respectively) in the Pixel object.
getX(), getY()	This method returns the x or y (respectively) position of where that Pixel object is in the picture.
setColor(Color color)	This method takes a Color object and sets the color for the Pixel object.
setRed(int value), setGreen(int value), setBlue(int value)	Each method takes a value (between 0 and 255) and sets the redness, greenness, or blueness (respectively) of the Pixel object to the given value.

ColorChooser Methods

ColorChooser.pickAColor()	Displays a window with ways to pick a color. Find the color you want, and the method will return the Color object that you picked.

Exercises

1. What is meant by each of the following?

   - Pixel
   - Kilobyte
   - RGB
   - Loop
   - Flowchart
   - Infinite loop
   - Variable scope
   - Array
   - Matrix
   - JPEG

- Column-major order
- Pixelization
- Luminance

2. Why don't we see red, green, and blue spots at each position in our picture?

3. Why is the maximum value of any color value 255?

4. The color encoding we're using is RGB. What does that mean in terms of the amount of memory required to represent color? Is there a limit to the number of colors that we can represent? Can we represent *enough* colors in RGB?

5. Program 10.1 is obviously too much color reduction. Write a version that only decreases the red by 10% and one that reduces red by 20%. Which seems to be more useful? Note that you can always repeatedly reduce the redness in a picture, but you don't want to have to do it *too* many times, either.

6. Change any of the methods that used a `while` loop to use a `for-each` loop. Compile and run the changed method and make sure it still works.

7. Change any of the methods that used a `while` loop to use a `for` loop. Compile and run the changed method and make sure it still works.

8. Change a variable name in any of the given methods. Make sure you change all instances of the variable name to the new name. Compile and run the changed method and make sure it still works.

9. Write new methods (like Program 10.2) to clear red and green. For each of these, which would be the most useful in actual practice? How about combinations of these?

10. Write a method to keep just the blue color. This means to set all the green and red values to zero. Write a method to keep just the red color. Write a method to keep just the green color.

11. Write a new method to *maximize* blue (i.e., setting it to 255) instead of clearing it. Use Program 10.2 as a starting point. Is this useful? Would the red or green versions be useful?

12. Write a method that modifies the red, green, and blue values of a picture by different amounts. Try it out on different pictures to see if you get any nice results.

13. How do we get the height from a `Picture` object? How do we get the width from a `Picture` object?

14. Save a picture from Alice and make a grayscale of it.

15. How many pixels are in a picture with a width of 200 and a height of 100?

16. How many pixels are in a picture with a width of 640 and a height of 480?

17. How do you get an array of `Pixel` objects from a `Picture` object?

18. How do you get the red value from a `Pixel` object? How do you set the red value in a `Pixel` object?

19. Save a picture from Alice and try to fake a sunset on it.

20. There is more than one way to compute the right grayscale value for a color value. The simple method that we use in Program 10.7 may not be what your grayscale printer uses when printing a color picture. Compare the grayscale image using our simple algorithm with what your printer produces when you print the image. How do the two pictures differ?

11

Modifying Pixels in a Matrix

Goals of this chapter:

- To use nested loops for processing the elements in a matrix (a two-dimensional array).
- To initialize and change multiple variables in a `for` loop.
- To develop some tracing strategies, specifically, using print statements to watch what is happening as code executes.
- To break long methods into smaller pieces.
- To revisit returning a value from a method.
- To use method overloading.

Introduction

In the last chapter, you learned that a picture is represented by a matrix (a two-dimensional array). However, you modified a picture by first invoking the `getPixels()` method to copy all the pixels from the picture's matrix into a one-dimensional array. The conversion of a picture matrix into a one-dimensional array is convenient, because it allows you to use a simple loop to iterate through all the pixels and modify each one. Now that you have some experience in using loops to iterate through a one-dimensional array, you are ready to tackle a more challenging task: that of working directly with the two-dimensional array (matrix). In this chapter, you will use the two-dimensional array to modify a range of pixels in a picture. When you operate on a range of pixels, you can mirror, copy, blend, rotate, and scale pictures. You can also create an image collage.

11.1 Copying Pixels Using a Nested Loop

We can only get so far in our image processing before we need to know *where* a pixel is located in the picture's matrix. For example, if we want to copy just part of a picture to another picture, we will need to know the *x* and *y* coordinate values for the start pixel and the end pixel.

11.1.1 Looping Across the Pixels with a Nested Loop

Working with a picture's matrix means that we can't use a single `for` loop, because we need to keep track of the *x* and *y* values for a pixel. We have to use *two* `for` loops—one to move horizontally across the columns, and the other to move vertically down the rows so as to get every pixel. That is, one for loop for each dimension of the picture. To use two loops, one loop will be *nested* inside another; literally, inside its block.

You have worked with nested loops before. In Alice, you used a nested loop on a ferris wheel object. An outer loop was used to roll the large double wheel to the right (creating a clockwise motion for the large wheel) and an inner loop was used to make the smaller individual wheels roll left (creating a counterclockwise motion). The code showing nested for loops in this example is shown again in Figure 11.1.

One way to nest two loops to work on all pixels in a picture in Java is to have an outer loop that iterates through the columns and an inner loop that iterates through the rows. The code would look like this:

```java
// loop through the columns (x direction)
for (int x = 0; x < getWidth(); x++)
{
  // loop through the rows (y direction)
  for (int y = 0; y < getHeight(); y++)
  {
    // get the current pixel at this x and y position
    pixel = getPixel(x,y);

    // do something to the color
    // set the new color
    pixel. setColor(aColor);
  }
}
```

This code will process all the pixels (with increasing *y* values) from top to bottom in the first column, then all the pixels (with increasing *y* values) from top to bottom in the second column, then the next column, and so on until all the pixels are processed.

Alternatively, you could use nested loops where the outer loop iterates through the rows and the inner loop iterates through the columns. This arrangement of nested

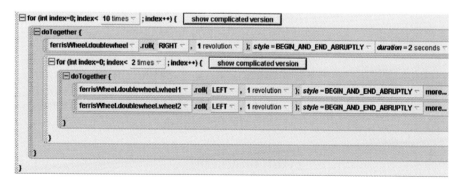

Figure 11.1
A nested loop in Alice

loops would process all the pixels (with increasing *x* values) in the top row and then all the pixels (with increasing *x* values) in the next row and so on. The code would look like this:

```
// loop through the rows (y direction)
for (int y = 0; y < getHeight(); y++)
{
  // loop through the columns (x direction)
  for (int x = 0; x < getWidth(); x++)
  {
    // get the current pixel at this x and y position
    pixel = getPixel(x,y);

    // do something to the color
    // set the new color
    pixel.setColor(aColor);
  }
}
```

Does it matter which way you process the pixels? Not if all you are trying to do is process all the pixels. Both of the above nested loop structures will process all the pixels in a picture.

As an example of nested loops, Program 11.1 is a rewrite of the clearBlue() method, first presented in Program 10.2. This new version, clearBlueNested(), uses nested for loops to access each pixel in the picture's two-dimensional array.

Program 11.1: Clear Blue Using Nested Loops

```
/**
 * Method to lighten the colors in the picture
 */
public void clearBlueNested()
{
    Pixel pixel = null;

    // loop through the columns (x direction)
    for (int x = 0; x < getWidth(); x++)
    {
      // loop through the rows (y direction)
      for (int y = 0; y < getHeight(); y++)
      {
        // get pixel at the x and y location
        pixel = getPixel(x,y);

        // clear the blue
        pixel.setBlue(0);
      }
    }
}
```

Let's assume that the method is called by the following statement:

```
picture.clearBlueNested();
```

Let's walk through (trace) how it would work.

1. The above statement, `picture.clearBlueNested()`, invokes the `clear-BlueNested()` object method on `picture`, which is an object of the `Picture` class. When invoked, the `clearBlueNested()` method is implicitly passed the current `Picture` object. Statements within the method could have used the keyword `this` to refer to the current `Picture` object, but it isn't required and is assumed if not present.

2. The first statement, `Pixel pixel = null;` declares the variable `pixel` as an object of the `Pixel` class. It is initialized to `null` (not referring to any object yet). This variable will be needed when we are looping through the pixels in the `picture` object. Although the `pixel` variable is not being used to control the `for` loop, we could have declared it inside the `for` loop, but then it would be re-declared each time through the loop. It is better to declare such variables once before the loop and change them each time through the loop.

3. The outer loop code `for (int x = 0; x < getWidth(); x++)` declares a loop control variable x of type `int`, which is initialized to 0, and then the condition x < `getWidth()` is checked to see if x is less than the width of the current `Picture` object. If this condition is true, then the body of the `for` loop will be executed. After the body of the loop has been executed one time, the value in x is incremented (by x++), and the continuation condition will be tested again.

4. The inner loop code, `for (int y = 0; y < getHeight(); y++)`, declares a loop control variable y of type `int`, which is initialized to 0. The condition y < `getHeight()` checks that y is less than the height of the current `Picture` object. If this condition is `true`, then the body of the `for` loop will be executed. After the body has executed the value in y will be incremented (by y++), and the continuation condition will be tested again.

5. The statement `pixel = getPixel (x,y);` sets the variable `pixel` to refer to the `Pixel` object at the given x and y location in the picture.

6. The statement `pixel.setBlue(0);` sets the current pixel's blue color component to be zero.

7. With each iteration of the inner `for` loop, the y value is incremented by 1 and then the value of y is compared to the height of the picture. If the value of y is less than the height, the statements in the body of the loop will be executed again. If the value of y is equal or greater than the height, execution of the inner loop ends. Execution then jumps to the next statement (in this example, the outer loop).

8. With each iteration of the outer `for` loop the x value is incremented by 1, and then the value of x is compared to the width of the picture. If the x value is less than the width of the picture, the commands in the loop body will be executed again. If the value of x is equal or greater than the width of the picture, the outer loop ends.

Now that you have an understanding of how nested loops can be used to access pixels in a picture's two-dimensional array, let's apply this technique to create some cool image effects.

11.1.2 Mirroring a Picture

Let's start out with an interesting effect that is only occasionally useful, but fun. Let's mirror a picture along its vertical axis. In other words, imagine that you have a mirror, and you position the mirror on the picture so that the left side of the picture shows up in the mirror. That's the effect that we're going to implement. We'll do it in a couple of different ways.

First, let's think through what we're going to do. We want to copy the pixel in the first column and first row $(0, 0)$ to the pixel in the last column and first row. Remember that the index for the last column is one less than the width, so we will copy the pixel from location $(0, 0)$ to location (width $- 1, 0$). We will copy the pixel in the second column and first row $(1, 0)$ to the second to last column and first row (width $- 2, 0$). In general, for each pixel, we will copy from the current (x, y) location to its mirrored location (width $- 1 - x$, y). We will continue to do this until we reach the middle of the picture (width/2). Once we pick a mirror point, we can just walk x halfway and copy from (x, y) to (width $- 1 - x, y$).

How do we pick a mirror point if we have an even number of pixels (the width of the picture is even)? The smallest even number of pixels is two. The `mirrorPoint` would be $(2/2 = 1)$. The first time through the loop this would copy from $(0, 0)$ to (width $-1 - 0, 0$), which is $(1, 0)$. Then x would increment, and the inner loop would stop since x isn't less than the `mirrorPoint`. Then the outer loop would continue with the next row. Figure 11.2 shows the outcome for a 2×2 matrix (top half of figure) and a 3×2 matrix (lower half of figure).

In the bottom half of Figure 11.2, the 3×2 matrix is an odd number of pixels (the width of the picture is odd). How do we pick a mirror point if we have an odd number of pixels? We don't want to copy the middle pixel. The `mirrorPoint` would be $(3/2 = 1)$. Remember that integer division results in an integer result, and the fractional part is thrown away. The first time through the loop this would copy from $(0, 0)$ to (width $- 1 - 0, 0$) which is $(2, 0)$. Then x would increment, and the inner loop would stop, since x wouldn't be less than the `mirrorPoint`.

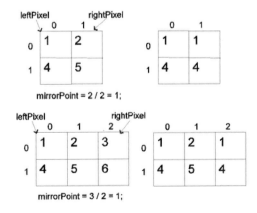

Figure 11.2
Mirror points in two types of matrices

Take a close look at Figure 11.2 to convince yourself that we'll actually reach every pixel (except the middle one if there are an odd number of pixels) using this scheme. The actual program code is shown in Program 11.2.

Program 11.2: Mirror Pixels in a Picture along a Vertical Line

```
/**
 * Method to mirror around a vertical line in the middle
 * of the picture based on the width
 */
public void mirrorVertical() {
{
    int width = this.getWidth();
    int mirrorPoint = width / 2;
    Pixel leftPixel = null;
    Pixel rightPixel = null;
    // loop through all the rows
    for (int y = 0; y < getHeight(); y++)
    {
      // loop from 0 to the middle (mirror point)
      for (int x = 0; x < mirrorPoint; x++)
      {
        leftPixel = getPixel(x, y);
        rightPixel = getPixel(width - 1 - x, y);
        right Pixel.setColor(leftPixel.getColor());
      }
    }
  }
}
```

Let's look at an example of how to use the vertical mirroring effect. The code below creates a picture from the file `caterpillar.jpg`, shows the picture, and invokes `mirrorVertical()`. Finally, `repaint()` is called to show the result of the mirror effect. Figure 11.3 shows the before and after effects.

```
>String fileName =
  "C:/intro-prog-java/mediasources/caterpillar.jpg";
> Picture picture = new Picture(fileName);
> picture.show();
> picture.mirrorVertical();
> picture.repaint();
```

Figure 11.3
Original picture (left) and mirrored along the vertical axis (right)

Can we mirror horizontally? Sure! Program 11.3 shows the code for `mirrorHorizontal`, which is a method that mirrors along a horizontal line in the middle of a picture based on its height.

Program 11.3: Mirror Pixels Horizontally, Top-to-Bottom

```java
/**
 * Method to mirror around a horizontal line in the middle
 * based on the height. It copies the top mirrored to
 * the bottom
 */
public void mirrorHorizontal()
{
  int height = this.getHeight();
  int mirrorPoint = height / 2;
  Pixel topPixel = null;
  Pixel bottomPixel = null;
  // loop through the columns
  for (int x=0; x < getWidth(); x++)
  {
    // loop from 0 to just before the mirror point
    for (int y=0; y < mirrorPoint; y++)
    {
      topPixel = getPixel(x,y);
      bottomPixel = getPixel(x,height - 1 - y);
      bottomPixel.setColor(topPixel.getColor());
    }
  }
}
```

The following code illustrates using the method. The `redMotorcycle.jpg` file is used to create a `Picture` object and `explore()` is used to view the picture both before and after calling `mirrorHorizontal()`.

```
> String fName =
  "C:/intro-prog-java/mediasources/redMotorcycle.jpg";
> Picture picture = new Picture(fName);
> picture.explore();
> picture.mirrorHorizontal();
> picture.explore();
```

As can be seen in the picture on the left side of Figure 11.4, the `mirrorHorizontal()` method copies from the top of the picture onto the bottom. You can see that we're getting the color from `topPixel`, which is from (x, y)—that will always be *above* `mirrorPoint` because smaller values of y are nearer the top of the picture. Contrast this to the right side of Figure 11.4, where the picture is mirrored from bottom to top (instead of top to bottom).

How can you copy from the bottom to the top to create an image similar to the one on the right side of Figure 11.4? The answer is to simply change the color at the top pixel to the color of the bottom pixel. The code for a bottom to top mirror effect is shown in Program 11.4.

Figure 11.4
A motorcycle mirrored horizontally, top to bottom (left) and bottom to top (right)

Program 11.4: Mirror Pixels Horizontally, Bottom-to-Top

```
/**
 * Method to mirror around a horizontal line in the middle
 * based on the height of the picture. It copies the bottom
 * to the top.
 */
public void mirrorHorizontalBottomToTop()
{
  int height = this.getHeight();
  int mirrorPoint = height / 2;
  Pixel topPixel = null;
  Pixel bottomPixel = null;
  // loop through the columns
  for (int x=0; x < getWidth(); x++)
  {
    // loop from 1 to just before the mirror point
    for (int y=0; y < mirrorPoint; y++)
    {
      topPixel = getPixel(x,y);
      bottomPixel = getPixel(x,height - 1 - y);
      topPixel.setColor(bottomPixel.getColor());
    }
  }
}
```

The following code shows how we produced the image on the right in Figure 11.4.

```
> String fName =
  "C:/intro-prog-java/mediasources/redMotorcycle.jpg";
> Picture picture = new Picture(fName);
> picture.show();
> picture.mirrorHorizontalBottomToTop();
> picture.repaint();
```

Mirroring Usefully

While mirroring is probably mostly used for interesting effects, occasionally it has some more serious (but still fun!) purposes. Mark Guzdial, Barb's husband, took a picture of the Temple of Hephaistos (Figure 11.5) in the ancient agora in Athens, Greece, while he was traveling to a conference. By sheer luck, Mark got the pediment dead horizontal. The Temple of Hephaistos had its pediment damaged. Mark wondered if he could "fix" it by mirroring the good part onto the broken part.

This time we don't want to mirror one-half of the picture onto the other half. We just want to mirror the pixels from the good side of the pediment on the left onto the bad side on the right. We also don't want to mirror all the pixels in the y direction. We just need the pixels from the top of the pediment to the bottom of the pediment. We can use the explorer to find out the locations for those pixels, as shown in Figure 11.5. The pediment starts at $x = 13$, and the middle is at $x = 276$. The highest part of the pediment is at $y = 27$, and it ends at $y = 97$.

How do we mirror just a small part of a picture? Well, we still need a mirror point. We will use 276 for that instead of half the width like we did in the method mirrorVertical(). Let's start by copying the mirrorVertical() method, change its name to mirrorTemple(), and set the mirror point to the value 276. We just want to copy from $x = 13$ to $x < 276$. We can start y at the top of the pediment 27 (instead of 0) and copy while it is less than 97 (instead of the height of the picture). Then we will copy from the pixel at (x, y) to a pixel at the mirror point plus the distance from the mirror point to the current x, which can be represented as (mirrorPoint + (mirrorPoint − x)). Program 11.5 defines the mirrorTemple() method.

Figure 11.5
Temple of Hephaistos from the ancient agora in Athens, Greece

Program 11.5: Mirror Part of a Picture Vertically

```
/**
 * Method to mirror part of the temple picture around a
 * vertical line at a mirror point
 */
public void mirrorTemple()
{
    int mirrorPoint = 276;
    Pixel leftPixel = null;
    Pixel rightPixel = null;
    // loop through the rows
    for (int y = 27; y < 97; y++)
    {
        // loop from 1 to just before the mirror point
        for (int x = 13; x < mirrorPoint; x++)
        {
            leftPixel = getPixel(x, y);
            rightPixel = getPixel(mirrorPoint +
                             (mirrorPoint - x), y);
            rightPixel.setColor(leftPixel.getColor());
        }
    }
}
```

To use this method, try the following code:

```
> String fileName =
  "C:/intro-prog-java/mediasources/temple.jpg";
> Picture picture = new Picture(fileName);
> picture.explore();
> picture.mirrorTemple();
> picture.explore();
```

The resulting picture is shown in Figure 11.6—it worked pretty well! Of course, it is possible to tell that it was digitally manipulated. For example, if you check the shadows, you can see that the sun must have been on the left and the right at the same time.

How Does That Work? Tracing the Program Code

The temple example is a good one to think about in terms of how well you understand what is going on in the computer as the program code is executed. If you really under-stand, you can answer questions like "What's *the first* pixel to be mirrored in this method?" and "How many pixels get copied, anyway?".

You may be able to figure out the answers by thinking through the program—pretend you're the computer and execute the program in your mind. This is often called **tracing** the program. Sometimes the code is too complex to trace the program in your mind. If so, you can insert several System.out.println() statements here and there throughout

Figure 11.6
The mirrored temple

the code to display the values of selected variables as the code executes. Using
println() allows you to watch how the values are changing with each iteration of the
loop.

As an example, we inserted a System.out.println() statement into the
mirrorTemple() method so it prints out: "Copying" the source pixel x location "to"
the target pixel x location.

```
/**
 * Method to mirror part of the temple picture around a
 * vertical line at a mirror point */
public void mirrorTemple()
{
  int mirrorPoint = 276;
  Pixel leftPixel = null;
  Pixel rightPixel = null;
  // loop through the rows
  for (int y = 27; y < 28; y++)
  {
    // loop from 13 to just before the mirror point
    for (int x = 13; x < 17; x++)
    {
      System.out.println("Copying color from " +
                  x + " to " +
                  (mirrorPoint + (mirrorPoint - x)));
      leftPixel = getPixel(x, y);
      rightPixel = getPixel(mirrorPoint + (mirrorPoint - x), y);
      rightPixel.setColor(leftPixel.getColor());
    }
  }
}
```

Notice that we also changed the ending values on the loops so that it won't take too long to finish. The previous code, therefore, will loop through the first four pixels. When we run this we get the following code.

```
> String fileName =
      "C:/intro-prog-java/mediasources/temple.jpg";
> Picture picture = new Picture(fileName);
> picture.mirrorTemple();
Copying color from 13 to 539
Copying color from 14 to 538
Copying color from 15 to 537
Copying color from 16 to 536
```

It starts copying at x = 13 and copies to *mirrorPoint + (mirrorPoint − x)*, which is 276 + (276 − 13) = 539. Next, it increments x and copies from x = 14 to 276 + (276 − 14) = 538. Each time through the loop, x will increment and the distance from the `mirrorPoint` to x will decrease.

We could also track how many pixels were processed. Just add a `count` variable that starts at 0 and then increment it each time we copy a pixel. After the loop finishes, we can print out the value of `count`, as shown in the following version of the code.

```
/**
 * Method to mirror part of the temple picture around a
 * vertical line at a mirror point
 */
public void mirrorTemple()
{
  int mirrorPoint = 276;
  Pixel leftPixel = null;
  Pixel rightPixel = null;
  int count = 0;
  // loop through the rows
  for (int y = 27; y < 97; y++)
  {
    // loop from 13 to just before the mirror point
    for (int x = 13; x < mirrorPoint; x++)
    {
      leftPixel = getPixel(x, y);
      rightPixel = getPixel(mirrorPoint + (mirrorPoint - x), y);
      rightPixel.setColor(leftPixel.getColor());
      count = count + 1;
    }
  }
  System.out.println("We copied " + count + " pixels");
}
```

When invoked, you will see the output: `We copied 18410 pixels`. Where did that number come from? You can calculate how many times you execute the commands in a for loop with *end − start* + 1. We copy 70 rows of pixels (y goes from 27 to 96 because of the <97, which is 96 − 27 + 1 = 70). We copy 263 columns of pixels (x goes from 13 to <276, which is 275 − 13 + 1 = 263). 70 * 263 is 18,410.

Making It Work Tip: Accessing Picture Files

In the program examples shown thus far in this chapter, we have been typing the full path name for each picture file. You may recall, however, that in Chapter 5 we illustrated the use of `FileChooser.getMediaPath()` to allow you to get the full path name. The `getMediaPath(fileName)` method generates a complete path for you by returning a string with the saved media directory name followed by the base file name. For example, to get the `temple.jpg` picture, we could have used:

```
> FileChooser.getMediaPath("temple.jpg")
  "C:/intro-prog-java/mediasources/temple.jpg"
> String fileName = FileChooser.getMediaPath("temple.jpg");
> Picture temple = new Picture(fileName);
```

The default media directory is "c:/intro-prog-java/mediasources/". If you wish to use a different media directory you should set the media directory first using,

```
FileChooser.pickMediaPath()
```

which will bring up a file chooser and allow you to pick the directory that your media is in. ∎

11.2 Copying and Transforming Pictures

We can copy from one picture to another. We're going to end up keeping track of a *source* picture that we take pixels from and a *target* picture that we're going to copy to. Actually, to copy the pixels, we simply make the pixels in the target the same color as the pixels in the source. Copying pixels requires us to keep track of multiple index variables: The (x, y) position in the source and the (x, y) position in the target.

What's exciting about copying pixels is that making some small changes in how we deal with the index variables leads to not only *copying* the image but *transforming* it. In this section, we're going to talk about copying, cropping, rotating, and scaling pictures.

11.2.1 Copying

To illustrate copying a picture, let's copy a picture of Barb's daughter, Katie, to a blank canvas. `KatieFancy.jpg` will be used as the source picture, and the target will be a paper-sized JPEG file (`7inx95in.jpg`) in the mediasources directory, which is 7 × 9.5 inches, so it will fit on a 9 × 11.5 inch piece of paper with one inch margins.

To select the target picture and verify its width and height, we could use the following code.

```
> String filename = FileChooser.getMediaPath("7inx95in.jpg");
> Picture targetPicture = new Picture(filename);
> targetPicture.show();
> System.out.println(targetPicture.getWidth());
504
> System.out.println(targetPicture.getHeight());
684
```

Program 11.6 defines a method copyKatie() that copies a picture of Katie to the current picture. The *current picture* is the targetPicture, as declared previously. To copy a picture, we need two *x* index variables (sourceX and targetX) and two *y* index variables (sourceY and targetY). We made sure that the sourceX and targetX variables (the source and target index variables for the *x* axis in the outer loop) were incremented together, and the sourceY and targetY variables (the source and target index variables for the *y* axis in the inner loop) were incremented together in the change area of each for loop.

Program 11.6: Copying a Picture to the Current Picture

```
/**
 * Method to copy the picture of Katie to the
 * upper left corner of the current picture
 */
public void copyKatie()
{
  String sourceFile =
    FileChooser.getMediaPath("KatieFancy.jpg");
  Picture sourcePicture = new Picture(sourceFile);
  Pixel sourcePixel = null;
  Pixel targetPixel = null;
  // loop through the columns
  for (int sourceX = 0, targetX=0;
      sourceX < sourcePicture.getWidth();
      sourceX++, targetX++)
  {
    // loop through the rows
    for (int sourceY = 0, targetY =0;
        sourceY < sourcePicture.getHeight();
        sourceY++, targetY++)
    {
    // set the target pixel color to the source pixel color
      sourcePixel = sourcePicture.getPixel(sourceX,sourceY);
      targetPixel = this.getPixel(targetX,targetY);
      targetPixel.setColor(sourcePixel.getColor());
    }
  }
}
```

Figure 11.7 shows the results of copying the picture of Katie to the top-left corner of the blank canvas.

To use this method, you can create a Picture object (targetPicture) from the file that has a blank paper-sized picture and then invoke copyKatie() on targetPicture, as in the code shown here.

```
> String fileName = FileChooser.getMediaPath("7inx95in.jpg");
> Picture targetPicture = new Picture(fileName);
> targetPicture.show();
```

Figure 11.7
Copying a picture to a canvas

```
> targetPicture.copyKatie();
> targetPicture.show();
```

The `copyKatie()` method copies a picture of Katie to the canvas (blank picture), as shown in Figure 11.7. Here's a trace of how it works.

- The first two lines are just setting up the source (`sourcePicture`).

- Then we declare two variables, `sourcePixel` and `targetPixel` to keep track of the target and source pixels.

- Next is the outer loop for managing the *x* index variables. The `for` loop declares both variables and initializes them to 0. You can have more than one variable declared and initialized in the initialization area of a `for` loop, just separate them with commas. Next the continuation test checks if the `sourceX` is less than the width of the source picture. Finally, in the change area, we increment both the `sourceX` and `targetX` variables each time after the statements in the body of the loop have been executed. You can change more than one variable in the change area as long as you separate the changes with commas. The `for` loop for looping through the columns is

```
for (int sourceX = 0, targetX=0;
     sourceX < sourcePicture.getWidth();
     sourceX++, targetX++)
```

- Inside the outer loop for the *x* variables is the inner loop for the *y* variables. It has a very similar structure, since its goal is to keep `targetY` and `sourceY` in sync in exactly the same way.

```
for (int sourceY = 0, targetY=0;
     sourceY < sourcePicture.getHeight();
     sourceY++, targetY++)
```

It's in the body of the *y* loop that we actually get the color from the source pixel and set the corresponding pixel in the target (current picture) to the same color.

Of course, we don't have to copy from (0, 0) in the source to (0, 0) in the target. We can easily copy to another location in the target picture. All we have to do is to change where the target *x* and *y* coordinates *start* and the rest of the code can stay exactly the same. Program 11.7 defines copyKatieMidway(), which specifies the target *x* and *y* start coordinates.

Program 11.7: Copy Elsewhere into the Current Picture

```
/**
 * Method to copy the picture of Katie to (100,100) in the
 * current picture
 */
public void copyKatieMidway()
{
  String sourceFile =
    FileChooser.getMediaPath("KatieFancy.jpg");
  Picture sourcePicture = new Picture(sourceFile);
  Pixel sourcePixel = null;
  Pixel targetPixel = null;
  // loop through the columns
  for (int sourceX = 0, targetX=100;
       sourceX < sourcePicture.getWidth();
       sourceX++, targetX++)
  {
    // loop through the rows
    for (int sourceY = 0, targetY = 100;
      sourceY < sourcePicture.getHeight();
      sourceY++, targetY++)
    {
      // set the target pixel color to the source pixel color
      sourcePixel = sourcePicture.getPixel(sourceX,sourceY);
      targetPixel = this.getPixel(targetX,targetY);
      targetPixel.setColor(sourcePixel.getColor());
    }
  }
}
```

Figure 11.8 shows the same picture of Katie copied to 100,100 in a blank page-sized picture.

To create the target picture shown in Figure 11.8, use a blank paper-sized picture file as the targetPicture, invoke the copyKatieMidway() method on the targetPicture, and then show the result. The picture of Katie will be copied and its the upper-left corner will be located at (100, 100).

```
> String fileName = FileChooser.getMediaPath("7inx95in.jpg");
> Picture targetPicture = new Picture(fileName);
> targetPicture.copyKatieMidway();
> targetPicture.show();
```

Figure 11.8
Copying a picture to the coordinates 100,100

Cropping

We don't have to copy a *whole* picture. **Cropping** is taking only part of a picture out of the whole picture. Digitally, that's just a matter of changing your start and end coordinates. To grab just Katie's face out of the picture, we need to figure out the upper-left corner of a rectangle enclosing her face and use that as the starting values for sourceX and sourceY. We also need to determine the bottom-right corner of the rectangle enclosing her face and use that as the stopping *x* and *y* values. We used the picture explorer to determine these values. The upper-left corner of the rectangle enclosing her face is at (70, 3), and the bottom-right corner is at (135, 80). Figure 11.9 shows the square cut-out of Katie's face after it has been copied.

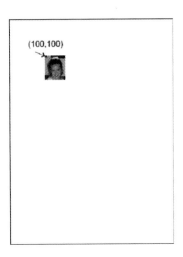

Figure 11.9
Copying part of a picture onto a canvas starting at location (100,100)

Program 11.8 defines a method named `copyKatiesFace()` that copies a portion of the picture of Kate within a rectangle having an upper-left corner at (70, 3) and a lower-right corner at (135, 80). The picture is copied to the target picture, starting at location (100,100) on the target canvas.

Program 11.8: Cropping a Picture onto a Canvas

```java
/**
 * Method to copy just Katie's face to the current picture
 */
public void copyKatiesFace()
{
  String sourceFile =
    FileChooser.getMediaPath("KatieFancy.jpg");
  Picture sourcePicture = new Picture(sourceFile);
  Pixel sourcePixel = null;
  Pixel targetPixel = null;

  // loop through the columns
  for (int sourceX = 70, targetX = 100;
    sourceX < 135; sourceX++, targetX++)
    {
    // loop through the rows
    for (int sourceY = 3, targetY = 100;
        sourceY < 80; sourceY++, targetY++) {
      {
      // set the target pixel color to the source pixel color
      sourcePixel = sourcePicture.getPixel(sourceX,sourceY);
      targetPixel = this.getPixel(targetX,targetY);
      targetPixel.setColor(sourcePixel.getColor());
      }
    }
  }
}
```

The following code shows how you can create the picture shown in Figure 11.9. First, create the target picture from the blank paper-sized picture file, then invoke the `copyKatiesFace()` method on it, and finally show the result. Just Katie's face is copied to the target picture with the upper-left corner at (100, 100).

```
> String fileName = FileChooser.getMediaPath("7inx95in.jpg");
> Picture targetPicture = new Picture(fileName);
> targetPicture.copyKatiesFace();
> targetPicture.show();
```

Try to copy part of another picture to the blank paper-sized picture file. What do you need to change and what can stay the same?

How Does That Work?

Let's look at a small example to see what's going on in the copying program. We start out with a source and a target and copy from x = 0, y = 0 to x = 3, y = 1.

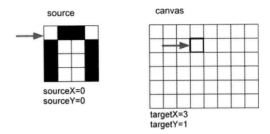

We then increment both the `sourceY` and `targetY` and copy again.

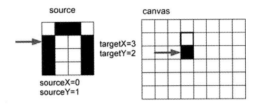

We continue down the column, incrementing both source and `targetY` index variables.

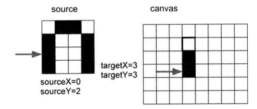

When done with that column, we increment both source and `targetX` index variables and move on to the next column, until we copy every pixel.

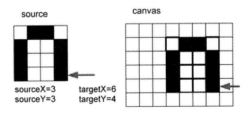

11.2.2 Creating a Collage

In the `mediasources` folder are a couple of images of flowers, as seen in Figure 11.10. Each one is 100 pixels wide.

Let's make a **collage** (an image made up of several images) by copying the pictures and using several of our effects to create different variations on the flowers. We'll copy

Figure 11.10
Flowers in the mediasources folder

them all into the blank image 7inx95in.jpg. All we really have to do is to copy the
pixel colors to the right places. Program 11.9 defines copyFlowersTop(), which
copies and applies effects to the flower pictures, lining them up near the top of the target canvas.

Program 11.9: Creating a Collage by Copying Flowers

```
/**
 * Method to copy flower pictures to create a collage.
 * All the flower pictures will be lined up near the
 * top of the current picture
 */
public void copyFlowersTop()
{
  // create the flower pictures
  Picture flower1Picture =
    new Picture(FileChooser.getMediaPath("flower1.jpg"));
  Picture flower2Picture =
    new Picture(FileChooser.getMediaPath("flower2.jpg"));
  // declare the source and target pixel variables
  Pixel sourcePixel = null;
  Pixel targetPixel = null;
  // copy the first flower picture to the top left corner
  for (int sourceX = 0, targetX = 0;
       sourceX < flower1Picture.getWidth();
       sourceX++, targetX++)
  {
    for (int sourceY = 0, targetY = 0;
         sourceY < flower1Picture.getHeight();
         sourceY++, targetY++)
    {
      sourcePixel = flower1Picture.getPixel(sourceX,sourceY);
      targetPixel = this.getPixel(targetX,targetY);
      targetPixel.setColor(sourcePixel.getColor());
    }
  }
```

```
// copy the flower2 picture starting with x = 100
for (int sourceX = 0, targetX = 100;
     sourceX < flower2Picture.getWidth();
     sourceX++, targetX++)
{
  for (int sourceY = 0, targetY = 0;
       sourceY < flower2Picture.getHeight();
       sourceY++, targetY++)
  {
    sourcePixel = flower2Picture.getPixel(sourceX,sourceY);
    targetPixel = this.getPixel(targetX,targetY);
    targetPixel.setColor(sourcePixel.getColor());
  }
}
// copy the flower1 negated to x = 200
flower1Picture.negate();
for (int sourceX = 0, targetX = 200;
     sourceX < flower1Picture.getWidth();
     sourceX++, targetX++)
{
for (int sourceY = 0, targetY = 0;
     sourceY < flower1Picture.getHeight();
     sourceY++, targetY++)
  {
    sourcePixel = flower1Picture.getPixel(sourceX,sourceY);
    targetPixel = this.getPixel(targetX,targetY);
    targetPixel.setColor(sourcePixel.getColor());
  }
}
// clear the blue in flower 2 picture and add at x=300
flower2Picture.clearBlue();
for (int sourceX = 0, targetX = 300;
     sourceX < flower2Picture.getWidth();
     sourceX++, targetX++)
{
  for (int sourceY = 0, targetY = 0;
       sourceY < flower2Picture.getHeight();
       sourceY++, targetY++)
  {
    sourcePixel = flower2Picture.getPixel(sourceX,sourceY);
    targetPixel = this.getPixel(targetX,targetY);
    targetPixel.setColor(sourcePixel.getColor());
  }
}
// copy the negated flower 1 to x=400
for (int sourceX = 0, targetX = 400;
     sourceX < flower1Picture.getWidth();
     sourceX++, targetX++)
{
  for (int sourceY = 0, targetY = 0;
       sourceY < flower1Picture.getHeight();
       sourceY++, targetY++)
```

```
        {
          sourcePixel = flower1Picture.getPixel(sourceX,sourceY);
          targetPixel = this.getPixel(targetX,targetY);
          targetPixel.setColor(sourcePixel.getColor());
        }
      }
    }
```

Figure 11.11 shows a sample collage. The code below shows how we created and saved the displayed collage.

```
> String fileName = FileChooser.getMediaPath("7inx95in.jpg");
> Picture targetPicture = new Picture(fileName);
> targetPicture.copyFlowersTop();
> targetPicture.show();
> targetPicture.write(FileChooser.getMediaPath("collage.jpg"));
```

The copyFlowersTop() method is long and repetitive, which makes it hard to read. One of the ways to improve it is to pull out pieces of code that perform the same task and make this into a new method. Each time we add a new picture to our canvas, the only things changing are the picture to be added and the targetX.

Program 11.10 defines a new more general method that is passed the picture to copy and the x location to start copying it to. The y location is at the top of the target picture canvas.

Program 11.10: General Copy Method

```
/**
 * Method that will copy all of the passed source picture into
 * the current picture object, starting with the left corner
 * given by xStart and the top of the picture in y.
 * @param sourcePicture the picture object to copy
 * @param xStart the x position to start the copy in the target
 */
public void copyPicture(Picture sourcePicture,
                        int xStart)
{
  Pixel sourcePixel = null;
  Pixel targetPixel = null;
  // loop through the columns
  for (int sourceX = 0, targetX = xStart;
       sourceX < sourcePicture.getWidth();
       sourceX++, targetX++)
  {
    // loop through the rows
    for (int sourceY =0, targetY = 0;
         sourceY < sourcePicture.getHeight();
         sourceY++, targetY++)
    {
      sourcePixel = sourcePicture.getPixel(sourceX,sourceY);
      targetPixel = this.getPixel(targetX,targetY);
```

```
        targetPixel.setColor(sourcePixel.getColor());
    }
  }
}
/**
 * Method to copy two flowers in a pattern to the
 * top of the current picture
 */
public void copyFlowersBetter()
{
  // create the flower pictures
  Picture flower1Picture =
    new Picture(FileChooser.getMediaPath("flower1.jpg"));
  Picture flower2Picture =
    new Picture(FileChooser.getMediaPath("flower2.jpg"));
  // copy the first flower picture
  this.copyPicture(flower1Picture,0);
  // copy the flower2 picture starting with x = 100
  this.copyPicture(flower2Picture,100);
  // copy the flower1 negated to x = 200 in the canvas
  flower1Picture.negate() ;
  this.copyPicture(flower1Picture,200);
  /* clear the blue in flower 2 picture and
   * add at x=300 in the canvas
   */
  flower2Picture.clearBlue();
  this.copyPicture(flower2Picture,300);
  // copy the negated flower 1 to x = 400
  this.copyPicture(flower1Picture,400);
}
```

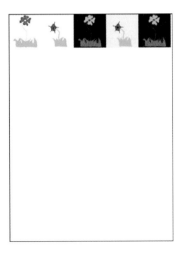

Figure 11.11
A Collage of flowers

The method `copyFlowersBetter()` is much easier to read and understand now. Also, we now have a method `copyPicture` that is easy to reuse.

We can even make a more general copy method, which takes both the starting *x* and starting *y* values for the target picture and copies the passed source picture into the current picture with the source picture's upper-left corner at the passed starting *x* and *y* values in the target, as shown in the following code.

```
/**
 * Method that will copy all of the passed source picture into
 * the current picture object, starting with the left corner
 * given by xStart, yStart
 * @param sourcePicture the picture object to copy
 * @param xStart the x position to start the copy into on the
 * target
 * @param yStart the y position to start the copy into on the
 * target
 */
public void copyPicture(Picture sourcePicture,
                        int xStart,
                        int yStart)
{
  Pixel sourcePixel = null;
  Pixel targetPixel = null;
  // loop through the columns
  for (int sourceX = 0, targetX = xStart;
       sourceX < sourcePicture.getWidth();
       sourceX++, targetX++)
  {
    // loop through the rows
    for (int sourceY = 0,
         targetY = yStart;
         sourceY < sourcePicture.getHeight();
         sourceY++, targetY++)
    {
      sourcePixel = sourcePicture.getPixel(sourceX,sourceY);
      targetPixel = this.getPixel(targetX,targetY);
      targetPixel.setColor(sourcePixel.getColor());
    }
  }
}
```

Notice that you can have two methods with the same names (`copyPicture`) and you don't have any trouble when you compile. As we pointed out in Chapter 4, Java allows you to have many methods with the same method name as long as the parameters are different. Having more than one method with the same name but different parameters is called **overloading**. The first `copyPicture` method took a `Picture` object and an `int`. The second `copyPicture` method took a `Picture` object and two `int` values. So the two methods have a different number of parameters. It doesn't really matter what you name the parameters. What matters is the types. Two methods with the same name are allowed if the number of parameters is different, the types of the parameters are different, or the order of the parameter types is different. A **method signature** is the method name and the parameter list. So the method signatures need to be different in order for a method to be overloaded. The return type is not part of the method signature. Having two methods with the same name and same parameter list but different return types is not allowed.

11.2.3 Blending Pictures

When we create collages by copying, any overlap typically means that one picture shows *over* another. The last picture painted on is the one that appears. But it doesn't have to be that way. We can *blend* pictures by multiplying their colors and adding them, just like we blended sounds in Chapter 9. Blending pictures gives us the effect of *transparency*.

We know that 100% of something is the whole thing. Using 50% of one and 50% of another would also add up to 100%. In Program 11.11, we blend a picture of the two sisters with an overlap of 50 columns (the width of Katie minus 150) of pixels onto the target picture canvas. Figure 11.12 shows the result.

Program 11.11: Blending Two Pictures

```
/**
 * Method to blend two sisters together onto the current
 * picture
 */
public void blendPictures()
{
  // create the sister pictures
  Picture katiePicture =
    new Picture(FileChooser.getMediaPath("KatieFancy.jpg"));
  Picture jennyPicture =
    new Picture(FileChooser.getMediaPath("JenParty.jpg"));
  // declare the source and target pixel variables
  Pixel katiePixel = null;
  Pixel jennyPixel = null;
  Pixel targetPixel = null;
  /* declare the target x and source x since we will need
   * the values after the for loop
   */
  int sourceX = 0;
  int targetX = 0;
  // copy the first 150 pixels of katie to the canvas
  for (; sourceX < 150; sourceX++, targetX++)
  {
    for (int sourceY=0, targetY=0;
         sourceY < katiePicture.getHeight();
         sourceY++, targetY++)
    {
```

```
      katiePixel = katiePicture.getPixel (sourceX,sourceY);
      targetPixel = this.getPixel(targetX,targetY);
      targetPixel.setColor(katiePixel.getColor());
    }
  }
  /* copy 50% of katie and 50% of jenny till
   * the end of katie's width
   */
  for (; sourceX < katiePicture.getWidth();
       sourceX++, targetX++)
{
  for (int sourceY=0,targetY=0;
       sourceY < katiePicture.getHeight();
       sourceY++, targetY++)
  {
    katiePixel = katiePicture.getPixel(sourceX,sourceY);
    jennyPixel =
      jennyPicture.getPixel(sourceX - 150,sourceY);
      targetPixel = this.getPixel(targetX,targetY);
      targetPixel.setColor(
        new Color((int) (katiePixel.getRed() * 0.5 +
                         jennyPixel.getRed() * 0.5),
                  (int) (katiePixel.getGreen() * 0.5 +
                         jennyPixel.getGreen() * 0.5),
                  (int) (katiePixel.getBlue() * 0.5 +
                         jennyPixel.getBlue() * 0.5)));
    }
  }
  // copy the rest of Jenny
  sourceX = sourceX - 150;
  for (; sourceX < jennyPicture.getWidth();
       sourceX++, targetX++)
  {
  for (int sourceY = 0, targetY = 0;
       sourceY < jennyPicture.getHeight();
       sourceY++, targetY++)
    {
    jennyPixel = jennyPicture.getPixel(sourceX,sourceY);
    targetPixel = this.getPixel(targetX,targetY);
    targetPixel.setColor(jennyPixel.getColor());
    }
  }
}
```

To try this out, create a picture object using the blank 640 × 480 file and invoke the method on that. Show the result.

```
> String fileName = FileChooser.getMediaPath("640x480.jpg");
> Picture picture = new Picture(fileName);
> picture.blendPictures();
> picture.show();
```

Figure 11.12
Blending the pictures of Katie and Jenny

Making It Work Tip: Optional Parts of the `for` Loop

In the `blendPictures()` method, we moved the declaration of `sourceX` and `targetX` outside the loops. This is because we wanted to be able to access the values after the first loop ends. If the variables are declared inside a loop, you can only access the values inside that loop.

The `sourceX` and `targetX` variables are declared and initialized before the first `for` loop is written. So, the initialization area in the `for` loop is empty. This is not a problem, because the initialization area of a `for` loop is optional (the `;` is not optional) in Java. In fact, the initialization area, continuation test, and change area are all optional. You could code a `for` loop as `for (;;)`, but that isn't terribly useful. It would execute the body of the loop forever. This is one way to create an infinite loop. ∎

11.2.4 Rotation

Transformations to an image occur by using the index variables differently or incrementing them differently, but otherwise keeping the same program. Let's rotate Katie 90 degrees to the left. What does that mean? Let's try it with something simple first. You can write some numbers in a table on a piece of paper and then rotate it left and then read the new table to see where the old numbers were moved to, as in Figure 11.13. Notice that the columns become the rows and the rows become the columns. But it isn't as simple as just using the source *x* for the target *y* and the source *y* for the target *x*.

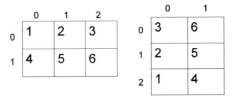

Figure 11.13
Rotating some numbers in a table to the left 90 degrees

The value at (0, 0) in the source moves to (0, 2) in the target. The value at (0, 1) in the source moves to (1, 2) in the target. The value at (1, 0) in the source moves to (0, 1) in the target. The value at (1, 1) in the source moves to (1, 1) in the target. The value at (2, 0) in the source moves to (0, 0) in the target. And, the value at (2, 1) in the source moves to (1, 0) in the target. So the first column values move into the bottom row, and the last column values move into the top row. Also notice that the target pixel's x coordinate is the same as the source pixel's y coordinate.

We will do the rotation by looping through the pixels in the usual way and getting the source pixel in the usual way, but the target x coordinate will be sourceY (the source y coordinate) and the target y coordinate will be the source width − 1 minus sourceX. Program 11.2 defines a method named copyKatieLeftRotation() that copies the picture of Katie but rotates her left 90 degrees on the target canvas. The result is shown in Figure 11.14.

Program 11.12: Rotating a Picture Left 90 Degrees

```java
/**
 * Method to copy the picture of Katie but rotate
 * her left 90 degrees on the current picture
 */
public void copyKatieLeftRotation()
{
    String sourceFile =
      FileChooser.getMediaPath("KatieFancy.jpg");
    Picture sourcePicture = new Picture(sourceFile);
    Pixel sourcePixel = null;
    Pixel targetPixel = null;
    // loop through the columns
    for (int sourceX = 0;
        sourceX < sourcePicture.getWidth();
        sourceX++)
    {
      // loop through the rows
      for (int sourceY = 0;
          sourceY < sourcePicture.getHeight();
          sourceY++)
      {
        // set the target pixel color to the source pixel color
        sourcePixel = sourcePicture.getPixel(sourceX,sourceY);
        targetPixel = this.getPixel(sourceY,
                sourcePicture.getWidth() - 1 - sourceX);
        targetPixel.setColor(sourcePixel.getColor());
      }
    }
}
```

The following code illustrates how you can create the picture shown in Figure 11.14. First create a Picture object from the blank paper-sized picture in 7inx95in.jpg and then invoke the copyKatieLeftRotation() method on it. Then, show the rotated picture.

Figure 11.14
Copying a picture, rotated to the left 90 degrees, to a blank picture

```
> String fileName = FileChooser.getMediaPath("7inx95in.jpg");
> Picture picture = new Picture(fileName);
> picture.copyKatieLeftRotation();
> picture.show();
```

How Does That Work?

Rotating starts with a source and target and even the same variable values as we used for copying. But, since we *use* the target x and y differently, we get a different effect. Now, as we increment the y variables, we're moving *down* the source, but *across* the target from left to right. As we increment the x variables, we're moving *across* the source but *up* the target.

To see how this works, let's trace through the copyKatieLeftRotation() method. The source picture's width is 200 pixels and its height is 300 pixels.

In the first iteration of the outer loop, sourceX is set to 0. Next, in the inner loop sourceY is set to 0. Then, in the body of the inner loop, sourcePixel is assigned the pixel at location (sourceX,sourceY)—the pixel at (0,0) in the source picture.

Next, the target pixel location is needed. As you know, the target x coordinate is equal to sourceY, thus, it is also 0. But, the target y coordinate is equal to the width of the source picture minus 1 minus the source x. So the target y coordinate is (200 − 1 − 0), which is 199. The last line in the inner for loop body copies the color of the source pixel at (0, 0) to the target pixel at (0, 199).

Now, sourceY is incremented by the inner loop to 1 and tested against the height of the source picture (300). Since it is less than the height, the body of the inner loop will be repeated. Now sourceX is 0 and the sourceY is 1. The target x coordinate is equal to sourceY, which means it is 1. The target y coordinate is equal to the width of the source picture minus 1 minus sourceX (200 − 1 − 0), which is 199. Thus, we copy the color of the source pixel at (0, 1) to the target pixel at (1, 199).

Over successive iterations, sourceY is incremented again and again by the inner loop until it finally becomes 300 and is tested against the height of the source picture (300). Since sourceY is not less than the height, the inner loop ends and the outer loop is back in control where it increments sourceX to 1. The inner loop starts all over again, setting sourceY back to 0. The inner loop iterates fully again, copying the next column from the source picture to the next to bottom row on the target canvas.

Overall, the nested loops work together to copy each column of pixels (left to right) from the source picture to a row of pixels on the target canvas (bottom up), where the bottom row's *y* coordinate is the width of the source picture minus one.

11.2.5 Scaling

A very common transformation for pictures is to scale them. **Scaling up** means to make them larger, and **scaling down** makes them smaller. It's common to scale a 1-megapixel or 3-megapixel picture down to a smaller size to make it easier to use on the Web or to send via e-mail. Smaller pictures require less disk space, and thus less network bandwidth, so they are faster to upload or download.

Scaling a picture requires the use of **sampling**. You may recall that sounds are sampled when they are digitized. To sample means to select part of the whole. To scale a picture *smaller* we are going to take *every other* pixel when copying from the source to the target. To scale a picture *larger* we are going to take *every pixel twice*.

Scaling the picture down is the easier method. We will use a picture of one of the graduates of the Computer Science doctoral program at Georgia Tech, Jakita N. Owensby (`jakita.jpg`). Her picture is 768 (width) by 768 (height). Program 11.13 defines a method `copyJakitaSmaller()` that scales down Jakita's picture. Instead of incrementing the `sourceX` and `sourceY` variables by 1, we simply increment by 2. We divide the amount of space by 2, since we'll fill half as much room—our width will be 768/2 and the height will be 768/2. The result is a smaller picture of Jakita on the blank 640 by 480 target canvas, as seen in Figure 11.15.

Figure 11.15
Scaling the picture of Jakita (a CS doctoral graduate) down

Program 11.13: Scaling a Picture Down (Smaller)

```
/**
 * Method to copy the picture of Jakita but smaller
 * (half as big) to the current picture
 */
```

```
public void copyJakitaSmaller()
{
  Picture jakitaPicture =
    new Picture(FileChooser.getMediaPath("jakita.jpg"));
  Pixel sourcePixel = null;
  Pixel targetPixel = null;
  // loop through the columns
  for (int sourceX = 0, targetX = 0;
       sourceX < jakitaPicture.getWidth();
       sourceX= sourceX + 2, targetX++)
  {
    // loop through the rows
    for (int sourceY=0, targetY = 0;
         sourceY < jakitaPicture.getHeight();
         sourceY= sourceY + 2, targetY++)
    {
      sourcePixel = jakitaPicture.getPixel(sourceX,sourceY);
      targetPixel = this.getPixel(targetX,targetY);
      targetPixel.setColor(sourcePixel.getColor());
    }
  }
}
```

■

To create the picture shown in Figure 11.15, first create a picture object p using the blank 640 × 480 file and then invoke the copyJakitaSmaller() method on it, as shown here.

```
> Picture p =
      new Picture(FileChooser.getMediaPath("640x480.jpg"));
> p.copyJakitaSmaller() ;
> p.show();
```

Scaling up the picture (making it larger) is a little trickier. We want to take every pixel twice. What we're going to do is to increment the source index variables by 0.5. Now, we can't access pixel 1.5 because pixels are numbered using whole number integers. But if we cast the value, for example: (int) 1.5, we'll get 1 again, and that will work. The sequence of 1, 1.5, 2, 2.5, ... will become 1,1,2,2, ... which in effect allows us to access every pixel twice. Program 11.14 defines a method named copyFlowerLarger() which scales up a picture named rose.jpg which is originally 320 × 240, as seen in Figure 11.16. The result will be a larger form of the picture, with a size of 640 × 480.

Program 11.14: Scaling the Picture Up (Larger)

```
/**
 * Method to copy a flower but scaled to 2x normal size
 * onto the target picture canvas
 */
public void copyFlowerLarger()
{
  Picture flowerPicture =
    new Picture(FileChooser.getMediaPath("rose.jpg"));
```

Figure 11.16
Scaling up a picture

```
Pixel sourcePixel = null;
Pixel targetPixel = null;
// loop through the columns
for (double sourceX = 0, targetX = 0;
    sourceX < flowerPicture.getWidth();
    sourceX = sourceX + 0.5, targetX++)
{
  // loop through the rows
  for (double sourceY=0, targetY = 0;
      sourceY < flowerPicture.getHeight();
      sourceY = sourceY + 0.5, targetY++)
  {
    sourcePixel =
        flowerPicture.getPixel((int) sourceX,(int) sourceY);
    targetPixel = this.getPixel((int) targetX,(int) targetY);
    targetPixel.setColor(sourcePixel.getColor());
  }
 }
}
```

The following code shows how to try this out: Create a target picture object using the blank 640 × 480 file and invoke the method on that. Show the result.

```
> String fileName = FileChooser.getMediaPath("640x480.jpg");
> Picture picture = new Picture(fileName);
> picture.copyFlowerLarger();
> picture.show();
```

How Does That Work?

We start from the same place as the original code for copying a picture but declare the sourceX and sourceY variables to be of type double so we can increment by 0.5. Say we are copying from the source picture starting at (0, 0) and copying to the target picture starting at (3, 1). First, we will copy the color of the pixel at (0, 0) in the source picture to (3, 1) in the target picture.

When we increment sourceY by 0.5, the actual value will be 0.5, but we cast it using (int), which truncates the value to 0, so we end up referring to the same pixel in the source. The targetY value was incremented by 1, however, and has moved on to the next pixel. So we will copy the color of the pixel at (0, 0) again, but this time to (3, 2) on the target canvas.

When we increment sourceY a second time by 0.5, it will now equal 1.0, so we now move on to the next pixel in the source and copy the color of the pixel at (0, 1) to (3, 3).

Again, when the sourceY is incremented by 0.5, the actual value will be 1.5, but the (int) of that is 1, so we will copy from (0, 1) to (3, 4).

Eventually, we cover every pixel. Notice that the quality of the end result is degraded—it's choppier than the original. Each pixel is copied four times: twice in the x direction and twice in the y direction.

Adding 0.5 works fine for scaling up by a factor of 2. What if we wanted to scale up by a factor of 3? Instead of adding 0.5, we could add 1/3 each time through the loop but what is 1/3? It is represented in a double as 0.3333333333333333. Casting this to int would give us 0 for the source. When we add the factor to sourceX, we would get 0.6666666666666666. This would also result in 0 when we cast to int. When we add the factor a third time, we would get 0.999999999999999, which is still less than one, and thus the cast to int would still result in 0. So, we would end up copying the source pixel four times instead of three times. So this approach won't work as a general algorithm. It will work for scaling up a picture by an even amount but not by an odd amount. ∎

You might want to be able to scale up a picture without always using the canvas picture as a target picture. One way to create a Picture object is to pass in a width and height: new Picture(width, height). This will create a blank picture of the passed width and height (both specified in pixels). new Picture(640,480) would create a picture object that is 640 pixels wide by 480 pixels tall—just like the canvas.

Program 11.15 defines a more general method, scaleUp(int numTimes), that will scale up the current picture object by some passed number of times. It creates a new Picture object of the desired width and height. It loops through all the source pixels and each source pixel is copied the passed number of times in both the x and y direction on the target picture's canvas. The hard part is determining the x and y values for the target picture's pixel locations. For example, if the passed in value for numTimes is 3, then the source pixel at (0, 0) should be copied to the target picture at locations (0, 0), (0, 1), (0, 2), (1, 0), (1, 1), (1, 2), (2,0), (2, 1), and (2,2). The source pixel at (1,0) should be copied to (0,3), (0,4), (0, 5), (1, 3), (1,4), (1,5), (2, 3), (2, 4), and (2, 5). In general, the target x and y is based on the source x and y times the number of times each pixel is copied plus the current x and y indices.

Since the scaleUp(int numTimes) method creates a picture object that it changes, we want to be able to return this object so that we can refer to it again. As was illustrated with sound files in Chapter 9, to return something from a method, we need to say what type of thing we are returning, and then we have to actually return it. Let's quickly review the syntax. First, you specify the type of thing that the method returns in the method declaration. Instead of the keyword void you use the type of thing that you are returning. Since this method will return an object of the Picture class, the type Picture is specified in the following method declaration.

```
public Picture scaleUp(int numTimes)
```

At the end of the method, use the keyword `return` followed by what you want to return. In this example, the return statement is

```
return targetPicture;
```

The compiler will check that the type of the thing you actually return matches the type you used in the method declaration. If it doesn't, you will get a compile-time error.

Program 11.15: General Scale Up Method

```java
/**
 * Method to create a new picture that is scaled up by the
 * passed number of times.
 * @return the new scaled up picture
 */
public Picture scaleUp(int numTimes)
{
  Picture targetPicture =
    new Picture(this.getWidth() * numTimes,
              this.getHeight()* numTimes);
  Pixel sourcePixel = null;
  Pixel targetPixel = null;
  int targetX = 0;
  int targetY = 0;
  // loop through the source picture columns
  for (int sourceX = 0;
      sourceX < this.getWidth();
      sourceX++)
  {
    // loop through the source picture rows
    for (int sourceY=0;
        sourceY < this.getHeight();
        sourceY++)
    {
      // get the source pixel
      sourcePixel = this.getPixel(sourceX,sourceY);
      // loop copying to the target y
      for (int indexY = 0; indexY < numTimes; indexY++)
      {
        // loop copying to the target x
        for (int indexX = 0; indexX < numTimes; indexX++)
        {
          targetX = sourceX * numTimes + indexX;
          targetY = sourceY * numTimes + indexY;
          targetPixel = targetPicture.getPixel(targetX,
                                                targetY);
          targetPixel. setColor(sourcePixel .getColor());
        }
      }
    }
  }
  return targetPicture;
}
```

Since the method `scaleUp()` returns a scaled `Picture` object, we should save a reference to the `Picture` object to be able to refer to it again, as shown in the following code.

```
> Picture p =
    new Picture(FileChooser.getMediaPath("flower1.jpg"));
> p = p.scaleUp(2);
> p.explore();
```

The code used the variable p to represent a `Picture` object containing the original picture from the `flower1.jpg` file. We then called the `scaleUp()` method which returns the new `Picture` object and we assigned the returned picture to the same variable p. You can reuse variables like p, but realize that you will no longer have a reference to the original `Picture` object. Of course, you could have declared a new `Picture` variable to hold the scaled picture, as illustrated in the following code.

```
> String fileName = FileChooser.getMediaPath("flower1.jpg");
> Picture origPicture = new Picture(fileName);
> Picture scaledPicture = origPicture.scaleUp(2);
> scaledPicture.show();
> origPicture.show();
```

If you scale a picture much larger than its original size, it will not look very good. Remember that we are just copying the original pixels several times, and not adding any additional detail.

11.3 Using Media Computation with Alice

You can also use Alice pictures with any of the methods in this chapter instead of the pictures in the mediasources directory. How about creating an Alice with two heads, as illustrated in Figure 11.17?

11.4 Concepts Summary

This chapter introduced two-dimensional arrays, nested loops, and working with multiple variables in a `for` loop. We also reviewed returning a value from a method and method overloading.

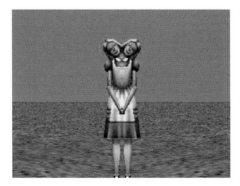

Figure 11.17
A two-headed Alice

11.4.1 Two-Dimensional Arrays

Pixels are stored in a two-dimensional array. A two-dimensional array is similar to seating in an auditorium. You can find your seat based on the row and chair number. You can access a location in a two-dimensional array by specifying an x (horizontal) and y (vertical) coordinate position, (x, y). All indices start with 0.

11.4.2 Nested Loops

To process all of the pixels in a picture and track the x and y location of each pixel, you need to use nested loops. Nested loops are loops inside of loops. You can either loop through the rows and then the columns (y and then x) or loop through the columns and then the rows (x and then y).

```
// loop through the rows (y direction)
for (int y = 0; y < this.getHeight(); y++) {
{
  // loop through the columns (x di rection)
  for (int x = 0; x < this.getWidth(); x++)
  {
    // get the current pixel at this x and y position
    pixel = this.getPixel(x,y);
    // do something to the color
    // set the new color
    pixel. setColor(aColor);
  }
}
```

To restrict the area that you are looping through, use different values for starting and stopping the loop. To loop through a rectangular area starting with the pixel at (startX, startY) at the upper-left corner of the rectangular area and ending with the pixel at (endX, endY) as the bottom-right corner of the rectangular area, use

```
// loop through the rows (y direction)
for (int y = startY; y <= endY; y++)
{
  // loop through the columns (x direction)
  for (int x = startX; x <= endX; x++)
  {
    // get the current pixel at this x and y position
    pixel = this.getPixel(x,y);
    // do something to the color
    // set the new color
    pixel.setColor(aColor);
  }
}
```

You can declare more than one variable in the initialization part of a for loop statement. This is useful when you copy from one picture to another. Use variables to represent the source picture x and y values, and use other variables to represent the target picture *x* and *y* values. You can change how the source and target pixel colors are used in order to rotate the picture.

```
// loop through the columns
for (int sourceX = 0, targetX = 0;
     sourceX < sourcePicture.getWidth();
     sourceX++, targetX++)
{
  // loop through the rows
  for (int sourceY = 0, targetY = 0;
       sourceY < sourcePicture.getHeight();
       sourceY++, targetY++)
  {
    sourcePixel = sourcePicture.getPixel(sourceX,sourceY);
    targetPixel = this.getPixel(targetX,targetY);
    targetPixel.setColor(sourcePixel.getColor());
  }
}
```

By changing the initial and ending values of `sourceX`, `sourceY`, `targetX`, and `targetY`, you can change what part of the source picture you want to copy and where you want it to go on the target picture. Using this technique, you can clip and create collages.

If you change the amount by which a loop variable is incremented or decremented, you can scale a picture up or down.

11.4.3 Returning a Value from a Method

To declare a method, you specify the visibility for the method, the type of thing it returns, the name of the method, and the parameter list inside parentheses. This is followed by the body of the method which is inside of an open and close curly brace.

```
visibility returnType name(parameterList)
{
  // statements in method
  // return a value
  return valueToReturn;
}
```

Methods that do not return any value use the keyword `void` as the return type. Methods that do return a value use the type of that value for the return type and then have a `return` keyword in them that is followed by the thing to return. Remember that a type is any of the primitive types or the name of a class.

Here is an example public method declaration that doesn't return anything. The name of the method is `mirrorVertical` and it doesn't take any parameters.

```
public void mirrorVertical()
```

Here is an example public method declaration that returns an object of the class `Picture`.

```
public Picture scaleUp(int numTimes)
```

Notice that it gives a return type of `Picture`. The body of the method must have the keyword `return` in it and it must `return` an object that is an instance of the class `Picture`.

11.4.4 Method Overloading

A class can have more than one method with the same name as long as the parameter list is different. The methods can take a different number of parameters, or the types of the parameters can be different, or the order of the types can be different. You can't have two methods with the same name and the same number of parameters with the same types in the same order.

```
public void copyPicture(Picture sourcePicture, int xStart)
public void copyPicture(Picture sourcePicture, int xStart,
                        int yStart)
```

Notice that there are two method declarations with the same name but one takes two parameters and one takes three. The compiler will check that a method exists that takes the same number and type of parameters. If the compiler can't find a method with the same number, type, and order of parameters, it will report that the method doesn't exist.

```
> p.copyPicture();
Error: No 'copyPicture' method in 'Picture'
```

11.5   Objects and Methods Summary

Here are the methods used or introduced in this chapter:

`new Picture(int width, int height)`	Creates a new `Picture` object with the given width and height. All pixels are white.
`getMediaPath(String fileName)`	Returns the full path name with the media directory followed by the passed file name. This is a class method on the `FileChooser` class. The default media directory is `c:/intro-prog-java/mediasources/`.
`setMediaPath(String directory)`	Sets the media directory to use when getting a full path using `getMediaPath(String fileName)`. This is a class method on the `FileChooser` class.

Exercises

1. What do the following mean?
   - Overloading
   - Nested Loop
   - Trace
   - Rotate
   - Scale

2. Modify any of the methods from the last chapter to use a nested loop. Run it to make sure it still works.

3. Take a picture of a person or an Alice character and mirror just their top part to their bottom part (two heads, with one at either end).

4. Take a picture of a person or an Alice character and mirror it so that the person looks like conjoined twins.

5. Create a new method that will blend two pictures with 10% from just the first picture, an 80% overlap, and then 10% from just the last picture. It helps if the two pictures are the same width and height.

6. Create a new method that will blend two pictures with 20% from just the first picture, a 60% overlap, and then 20% from just the last picture. It helps if the two pictures are the same width and height.

7. Create a movie poster for an Alice movie by blending Alice pictures, copying parts of Alice pictures, and adding text to the picture.

8. Modify Program 11.5 to be more general by passing in the start and stop x and y and the mirror point in x.

9. Convert the method `copyFlowerLarger()` from Program 11.14 to a method that can scale any picture up to twice the original width and height. It should return a new picture object created using
   `new Picture(`**`this`**`.getWidth() * 2,` **`this`**`.getHeight() * 2)`.

10. Write a method to flip a picture over so that things that were on the left are now on the right. You probably want to create a new picture and copy the pixels from a passed-in picture to the new picture. Return the new picture.

11. Modify Program 11.12 in this chapter to take the source picture, rotate it, and to create a new picture of just the needed size. Return the new picture.

12. Write a method to mirror a picture around a horizontal line from (0, height − 1) to (width − 1, height − 1). Be aware that this will double the height of the picture.

13. Write a method to mirror a picture around a vertical line from (width − 1, 0) to (width − 1, height − 1). Be aware that this will double the width of the picture.

14. Try to mirror a picture around a diagonal line from (0, 0) to (width − 1, height − 1). Try to mirror a picture around a diagonal line from (0, height − 1) to (width − 1, 0).

15. Write a method to rotate a picture to the right by 90 degrees.

16. Write a method to rotate a picture to the right by 180 degrees.

17. All of our copy methods copy rectangular areas. Try to write a copy method that copies a triangular area. Write one that copies a circular area.

18. We've seen that if you increment the source picture index by 2 while incrementing the target picture index by 1 for each copied pixel, you end up with the source being scaled down on the target. What happens if you increment the target picture index by 2 as well? What happens if you increment both source and target by 0.5 and use int to get the integer part?

19. Write a method named createCollage to create a collage of the same image at least four times onto the 7x95in.jpg blank JPEG. (You are welcome to add additional images, too.) One of those four copies can be the original picture. The other three should be modified forms. You can scale, crop, or rotate the image; create a negative of the image; shift or alter colors on the image; and make it darker or lighter.

    After composing your image, *mirror it.* You can do it vertically or horizontally (or otherwise), in any direction—just make sure that your four base images are still visible after mirroring.

    Your single method should make all of this happen—all of the effects and compositing must occur from the single function createCollage. Of course, it is perfectly okay to *use* other functions, but make it so that a tester of your program need only to call setMediaPath() and put all your input pictures in her mediasources directory. Create a Picture object from the blank paper-sized file, and then execute createCollage()—expect to have a collage generated and returned.

20. Think about how the grayscale algorithm works. Basically, if you know the *luminance* of anything visual (such as a small image or a letter), you can replace a pixel with that visual element in a similar way to create a collage image. Try implementing that. You'll need 256 visual elements of increasing lightness, all of the same size. You'll create a collage by replacing each pixel in the original image with one of these visual elements.

12 Conditionally Modifying Pixels

Goals of this chapter:

- To conditionally execute a statement or block of statements using `if`.
- To use a conditional with two possible results: `if` and `else`.
- To use a conditional with more than two possible results: `if`, `else if`, and `else`.
- To use the *not* operator.
- To combine Boolean expressions with *and* and *or*.

Introduction

A conditional statement is one that makes a decision based on the value of a condition (Boolean expression) as a program is running. We first introduced conditional (`if-else`) statements in Chapter 6 to build animations for simple games and simulations. Also, in Chapter 8, we used conditional statements to write programs that modified a sound. In this chapter, you will apply what you know about conditional statements to writing programs that modify pixels. Using conditionals will allow you to create image processing effects, such as simple edge detection, sepia-toned pictures, posterization of a picture, blurring a picture, and replacing the background on a picture.

12.1 Conditional Pixel Changes

So far, we have been processing all pixels in a picture the same way. But what if we want to process different pixels in different ways? For example, we might want to turn someone's hair a different color, get rid of "red-eye" in a picture, or even reduce the number of colors in a picture.

We need something that executes a block of code only if some condition is true. We know that we can write Boolean expressions using *equal* ($==$), *less than* ($<$), or *greater than* ($>$) and combinations of these operators. Boolean expressions always evaluate to either `true` or `false`. In Chapter 10, we used Boolean expressions with `while` loops to modify the color of all the pixels in a picture. For example, `while (index < pixelArray.length)` executes the loop while the expression (`index < pixelArray.length`) is `true`.

In Chapter 9, we also used Boolean expressions in conditional `if` statements to select a range of sound samples for creating a sound clip. The logic of an `if` statement instructs the program that if the Boolean expression evaluates to `true`, then execute

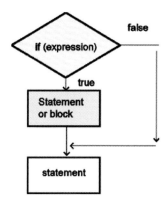

Figure 12.1
Flowchart of an if statement

the following statement or block of statements. If it is false, just skip the execution of that statement or block of statements. The if statement logic is illustrated as a flow-chart, shown in Figure 12.1.

In this section, we will use if statements as conditionals to modify the color of some pixels in a picture. We will check whether the color at the current pixel is close to a particular color and, if so, execute a statement or block of statements to modify the color of that pixel.

12.1.1 Comparing Colors

What does it mean to compare two colors? How can the computer tell if the color at the current pixel is "red"? You may remember from mathematics that the distance between two points (x_1, y_1) and (x_2, y_2) in a Cartesian coordinate system is

$$\sqrt{(x_1 - x_2)^2 + (y_1 - y_2)^2}$$

We can use a similar computation to figure out the distance between two colors. A color has three components (red, green, and blue). So, the Cartesian distance between two colors can be computed as points in a three-dimensional space where red, green, and blue are the three dimensions. The measure for two colors $(red_1, green_1, blue_1)$ and $(red_2, green_2, blue_2)$ is:

$$\sqrt{(red_1 - red_2)^2 + (green_1 - green_2)^2 + (blue_1 - blue_2)^2}$$

However, you won't have to code this. The Pixel class has an object method named colorDistance(Color color), which returns the distance between the color in the current Pixel object and the passed color.

12.1.2 Replacing Colors

Program 12.1 defines a method turnBrownIntoRed() that tries to replace the brown color pixels in a picture with red color pixels. The result is shown in Figure 12.2. We used the picture explorer to figure out roughly what the RGB values were for Katie's brown hair (red=42, green=25, blue=15). Then, we wrote a program to look for

Figure 12.2
Increasing reds in the browns

colors close to the brown color of Katie's hair and increased the redness of those pixels. The conditional if statement in the turnBrownIntoRed() method is the following.

```
// check if in distance to brown and if so double the red
if (pixel.colorDistance(brown) < 50.0)
    pixel.setColor(new Color((int) (pixel.getRed() * 2.0),
                                    pixel.getGreen(),
                                    pixel.getBlue()));
```

In this if statement, the condition pixel.colorDistance(brown) < 50.0 checks whether the current pixel's color is within 50 of the brown color of Katie's hair.

The trick in this program is in determining what "close enough" is for a color to match the brown color of Katie's hair. We played a lot with the "how close" value that we used for distance (here, 50.0) and the amount of redness increased (here, 100% increase).

Program 12.1: Color Replacement: Turn Brown into Red

```
/**
 * Method to turn the brown in a picture
 * into red
 */
 public void turnBrownIntoRed()
 {
   Color brown = new Color(42,25,15);
   Pixel[] pixels = this.getPixels();
   Pixel pixel = null;

   // loop through the pixels
   for (int i = 0; i < pixels.length; i++)
   {
     // get the current pixel
     pixel = pixels[i];
     // check if in distance to brown and if so double the red
```

```
        if (pixel.colorDistance(brown) < 50.0)
          pixel.setColor(new Color((int) (pixel.getRed() * 2.0),
                                          pixel.getGreen(),
                                          pixel.getBlue())));
    }
  }
```

To use this method to turn Katie into a redhead, first create a `Picture` object from the file `KatieFancy.jpg`. Then invoke the method `turnBrownIntoRed` on that `Picture` object and show or explore the result.

```
> String fileName = FileChooser.getMediaPath("KatieFancy.jpg");
> Picture picture = new Picture(fileName);
> picture.turnBrownIntoRed();
> picture.explore();
```

Notice that we used a simple `for` loop through the one-dimensional array of `pixels` for this method. We don't care where the pixels are in the two-dimensional array in this method. Of course, we could have used nested `for` loops instead to loop through all the pixels.

What this method is doing is looping through all the pixels in the current picture and for each pixel, checking if the distance between the color in the current pixel is less than 50 away from the color brown. If the distance between the current color and the defined brown is less than 50, the red value at the current pixel is doubled. If the distance is equal to or greater than 50, the pixel color is not changed. We indented the statement following the `if` to show that it is part of the statement and will not always be executed. Java doesn't care about the indentation, but it makes it easier for people to read and understand.

The approach used in `turnBrownIntoRed()` not only turned Katie's hair red, it also turned part of the couch and carpet red, too, as you can see on the left side of Figure 12.3. One thing we could do is use the picture explorer to figure out the coordinates around Katie's face and then just change the browns near her face. Program 12.2 revises the code, defining a method named `turnBrownToRedInRectangle()`. When executed, the effect isn't too good, although it's clear that it worked. The line of redness is too sharp and rectangular, as Figure 12.3 shows.

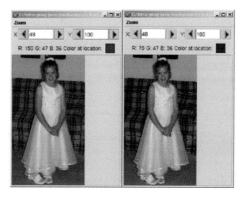

Figure 12.3
On left the couch color changes, on right the couch color doesn't change

Program 12.2: Color Replacement in a Rectangular Area

```
/**
 * Method to turn brown to red inside of
 * a rectangular area
 */
public void turnBrownToRedInRectangle()
{
  Color brown = new Color(42,25,15);
  Pixel pixel = null;
  // loop  through the x values
  for (int x = 63; x < 125; x++)
  {
    for (int y = 6; y < 76; y++)
    {
      // get the current pixel
      pixel = this.getPixel(x,y);
      // check if in dist to brown and if so double the red
      if (pixel.colorDistance(brown) < 50.0)
        pixel.setColor(new Color((int) (pixel.getRed() * 2.0),
                    pixel.getGreen(),
                    pixel.getBlue()));
    }
  }
}
```

■

The following code shows how you can try this method yourself. First create a `Picture` object from the file `KatieFancy.jpg`. Then invoke the method `turnBrownIntoRedInRectangle` on that `Picture` object and show the result.

```
> String fileName = FileChooser.getMediaPath("KatieFancy.jpg");
> Picture picture = new Picture(fileName);
> picture.turnBrownIntoRedInRectangle();
> picture.explore();
```

We put the values for the range of pixels that define the rectangle around Katie's head inside the `turnBrownIntoRedInRectangle()` method. This was convenient in because we didn't need to pass any values to specify the range. It makes the method less reusable. If we want to use this method to change a different picture, we would have to edit the method to change the range and then recompile. The method would be easier to reuse with other pictures if we declare parameters that will allow us to pass in the range when we invoke the method. We can also put in parameters that will allow us to pass in the distance to check for between brown and the current color. Program 12.3 illustrates a version of the method having parameters for the range (defined using upper-left and lower-right coordinates) and the distance between colors.

Program 12.3: Color Replacement with Passing in the Range

```
/**
 * Method to turn brown to red in a rectangular area
 * specified
```

```
 * by startX, endX-1, startY, endY-1
 * @param startX the starting location to check in x
 * @param endX the last pixel checked is one less than
 * this in x
 * @param startY the starting location to check in y
 * @param endY the last pixel checked is one less than
 * this in y
 */
 public void turnBrownToRedInRectangle(int startX, int endX,
                                       int startY, int endY,
                                       double distance)
 {
   Color brown = new Color(42,25,15);
   Pixel pixel = null;

   // loop through the x values
   for (int x = startX; x < endX; x++)
   {
     for (int y = startY; y < endY; y++)
     {
       // get the current pixel
       pixel = this.getPixel(x,y);

       /* check if in distance to brown is less than
        * the passed distance and if so double the red
        */
       if (pixel.colorDistance(brown) < distance)
         pixel.setColor(new Color((int) (pixel.getRed() * 2.0),
                                  pixel.getGreen(),
                                  pixel.getBlue()));

     }
   }
 }
```

Can you think of any other things that you could do to make this method easier to reuse? What if we want to change some color other than brown?

12.1.3 Reducing Red-Eye

Red-eye is a troublesome effect that you have likely seen in pictures of people. When taking a picture of someone, the flash from the camera sometimes bounces off the back of the subject's eyes. Reducing red-eye is a really simple matter. We find the pixels that are "pretty close" to red (a distance of 167 from red works well), then we change those pixels' color to a replacement color.

We probably don't want to change the whole picture. In Figure 12.4, we can see that Jenny is wearing a red dress—we don't want to wipe out that red, too. We'll fix that by only changing the *area* where Jenny's eyes are. Using the picture explorer, we find the upper-left and lower-right corners of a rectangular area that surrounds her eyes. Those points were (109, 91) and (202, 107).

Program 12.4 defines a method named removeRedEye() that has parameters for the upper-left corner (startX, startY) and the lower-right corner (endX, endY) of the

Figure 12.4
Finding the range of where Jenny's eyes are red

rectangular region around the subject's eyes. It also has a parameter that allows you to pass in the replacement color.

Program 12.4: Remove Red-Eye

```
/**
 * Method to remove red-eye from the current picture object
 * in the rectangle defined by startX, startY, endX, endY.
 * The red will be replaced with the passed newColor
 * @param startX the top left corner x value of a rectangle
 * @param startY the top left corner y value of a rectangle
 * @param endX the bottom right corner x value of a
 * rectangle
 * @param endY the bottom right corner y value of a
 * rectangle
 * @param newColor the new color to use
 */
public void removeRedEye(int startX, int startY, int endX,
                         int endY, Color newColor)
{
  Pixel pixel = null;

  /* loop through the pixels in the rectangle defined by the
     startX, startY, and endX and endY */
  for (int x = startX; x < endX; x++)
  {
    for (int y = startY; y < endY; y++)
    {
      // get the current pixel
      pixel = getPixel(x,y);
      // if the color is near red then change it
      if (pixel.colorDistance(Color.red) < 167)
        pixel.setColor(newColor);
    }
  }
}
```

Figure 12.5
After fixing red-eye

The following code shows how to try this method to replace the red with black—certainly other colors could be used for the replacement color.

```
> String fileName =
    "c:/intro-prog-java/mediasources/jenny-red.jpg";
> Picture jennyPicture = new Picture(fileName);
> jennyPicture.removeRedEye(109,91,202,107,
                            java.awt.Color.black);
> jennyPicture.explore();
```

The result was good, and we can check Figure 12.5 to see that the eyes really do now have all-black pixels.

12.2 Simple Edge Detection: Conditionals with Two Options

In a picture, an **edge** is an area in the picture where there is a big difference (contrast) in color between adjacent pixels. In typical pictures, edges characterize the boundaries of objects and are therefore useful for identifying objects in a scene. Locating the regions where an edge exists in a picture is known as **edge detection** and is a highly important technique in image analysis.

In this section, we will use a simple form of edge detection that looks for a big difference in the colors (high contrast) between one pixel and the pixel below it. One way to calculate the level of contrast is to average the red, green, and blue values in the top pixel and subtract this from the average of the red, green, and blue values in the bottom pixel. If the absolute value of the difference is less than than some specified amount, then there is low contrast. If the absolute value of the difference is greater than or equal to that specified amount, then there is high contrast.

We will compare each pixel in a picture to the pixel below it. If the contrast is low, we will make the pixel white, otherwise we will make the pixel black. This simple form of edge detection will result in a picture that looks like a pencil sketch.

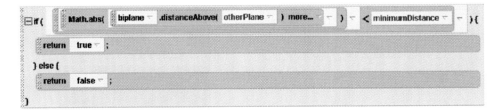

Figure 12.6
Using a conditional (`if-else`) statement in Alice

12.2.1 Conditionals with Two Options

In the `removeRedEye()` method presented in Section 12.1.3, we checked whether a pixel's color was close to red using the following conditional statement.

```
if (pixel.colorDistance(Color.red) < 167)
        pixel.setColor(newColor);
```

If the Boolean expression `pixel.colorDistance(Color.red) < 167` was `true`, the pixel's color was set to a new color. If the Boolean expression was `false`, however, the statement was skipped. That is, two options were available—either the color is replaced or it isn't.

But for edge detection, we need more options. We want to check for low contrast, and if the condition is `true`, set the color to white. If it is not, set the color to black. The way to create options is with a conditional `if-else` statement. You have seen conditionals with options in Alice, where we used a conditional `if-else` to avoid collision of two planes. One plane's distance above another was checked to determine if it was too close to the other plane. If it was too close, the function returned `true`, but if it wasn't too close, the function returned `false`. Figure 12.6 illustrates the code here, for your convenience.

Java also provides a conditional `if-else` statement. The logic of an `if-else` is the same as in Alice. The `if` part will execute the statement or block of statements following the `if` when the expression is `true` and the `else` part is skipped. But, if the Boolean expression is `false`, the statement or block of statements following the `if` will be skipped, and the statement or block of statements following the `else` will be executed. Figure 12.7 shows this in flowchart form.

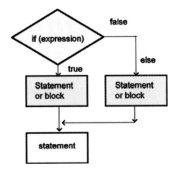

Figure 12.7
Flowchart of an `if` with an `else`

You can try out the logic of an `if-else` in DrJava's interaction pane. Be sure to use Shift-Enter after the `if` statement to let DrJava know that there will be a following `else`.

```
> int x = 30;
> if (x < 20) System.out.println("Yes, the value is less than
20");
else System.out.println("No, this value is not less than 20");
No, this value is not less than 20
```

As you can see, the statement following the `if` didn't execute, but the statement following the `else` did. Try the same thing, but this time give x a value less than 20.

```
> x = 15;
> if (x < 20) System.out.println(
    "Yes, the value is less than 20");
else System.out.println("No, this value is not less than 20");
Yes, the value is less than 20
```

Notice that this time the statement following the `if` did execute, but the statement following the `else` did not.

12.2.2 Simple Edge Detection

Program 12.5 defines a method named `edgeDetection()` in which a conditional `if-else` statement is used to check for low or high contrast. In the `edgeDetection()` method, we used two nested loops to iterate through the pixels in a picture. The outer loop loops through the pixels columnwise by incrementing y from 0 to less than picture height −1. Usually we have been looping while y is less than the height, so why stop at height −1? The reason is that we are comparing the value at a y position with the pixel below it, so the last y value that still has another row below it is at height −2.

The inner loop increments x from 0 to less than the picture width. The top pixel will be set to the pixel at the current x and y location, (x,y). The bottom pixel will be set to the pixel at the current x but y+1 location, (x, y+1). To determine the intensity of the top and of the bottom pixels, we invoke `getAverage()`, which is an object method defined in the `Pixel` class. The `getAverage()` method returns the average of a pixel's three color-component values. Then, we compare the absolute value of the difference between the two pixel's intensities to some passed amount. If the difference is less than the passed amount (low contrast), we change the top pixel color to white, otherwise we assume it is high contrast and set the top pixel color to black.

Program 12.5: Edge Detection

```
/**
 * Method to do a simple edge detection by comparing the
 * absolute value of the difference between the color
 * intensities (average of the color values) between a
```

```
 * pixel and the pixel below it. If the absolute value
 * of the difference between the color intensities is
 * less than a passed amount the top pixel color
 * will be set to white. Otherwise it is set to black.
 * @param amount if the absolute value of the differences
 * in the color average is less than this
 * set the color to white, else black
 */
 public void edgeDetection(double amount) {
   Pixel topPixel = null;
   Pixel bottomPixel = null;
   double topAverage = 0.0;
   double bottomAverage = 0.0;
   int endY = this.getHeight() - 1;

   /* loop through y values from 0 to height - 2
    * (since compare to below pixel) */
   for (int y = 0; y < endY; y++) {
   // loop through the x values from 0 to width
    for (int x = 0; x < this.getWidth(); x++) {
      // get the top and bottom pixels
      topPixel = this.getPixel(x,y);
      bottomPixel = this.getPixel(x,y+1);

      // get the color averages for the two pixels
      topAverage = topPixel.getAverage();
      bottomAverage = bottomPixel.getAverage();

      /* check if the absolute value of the difference
       * is less than the amount */
      if (Math.abs(topAverage - bottomAverage) < amount) {
        topPixel.setColor(Color.WHITE);

      // else set the color to black
      } else {
        topPixel.setColor(Color.BLACK);
      }
    }
   }
 }
```

You can execute this method and see the result shown in Figure 12.8 by entering the following code.

```
> String fileName = FileChooser.getMediaPath("butterfly1.jpg");
> Picture p = new Picture(fileName);
> p.explore();
> p.edgeDetection(10);
> p.explore();
```

Figure 12.8
Original picture and after edge detection

Making It Work Tip: Using Curly Braces

You may have noticed that the method edgeDetection() shows the starting curly braces at the end of the line instead of on a new line, as shown in the previous methods. Java doesn't care if the curly braces are at the end of a line or on a new line. Some programmers prefer one to another. It is often easier to see that you forgot a curly brace if it is by itself on a new line. However, the Java guidelines say to put the opening curly brace at the end of a line and the closing one on a new line.

You may also notice that we are using curly braces after the if and else even though there is only one statement to be executed and they aren't really needed. It is good practice to have them even if they aren't needed, because the code is easier to read and change.

12.2.3 Alternative Boolean Expressions

Sometimes, the way a problem is described makes a difference in how you think about and write your program code. For example, in the edge-detection example, we were very careful to describe the conditional like this: "If the contrast is low, we set the pixel to white, otherwise we assume the contrast is high, and the pixel is set to black." And we wrote the conditional if-else like this:

```
if (Math.abs(topAverage - bottomAverage) < amount) {
        topPixel.setColor(Color.WHITE);
    } else {
      topPixel.setColor(Color.BLACK);
    }
```

Alternatively, we could have stated the conditional: "If the contrast is NOT LOW, we make the pixel black, otherwise we make the pixel white." In essence, we are saying that if the condition Math.abs(topAverage - bottomAverage) < amount is false, we set the pixel to black, otherwise set it to white. But how do you execute a statement or block of statements if a condition is `false`? One way is to use an `if` but negate the condition using the `!` (*logical not*) operator. Basically, the `!` operator **negates** the Boolean condition . You can try out the `!` operator in Dr. Java's Interactions pane like this:

```
> !true
false
> !false
true
```

Using negation, we could have written the program code like this:

```
if (! Math.abs(topAverage - bottomAverage) < amount) {
    topPixel.setColor(Color.BLACK);
} else {
    topPixel.setColor(Color.WHITE);
}
```

Yet another way to describe this conditional is to say: "Test that the contrast IS HIGH, and if `true`, set the pixel to black, otherwise assume it is low, set the pixel to white." A HIGH contrast means that `Math.abs(topAverage - bottomAverage)` is greater than or equal to `amount`. To test greater than or equal to conditions, the conditional `if-else` could be written using a `>=` operator.

```
if (Math.abs(topAverage - bottomAverage) >= amount) {
    topPixel.setColor(Color.BLACK);
} else {
    topPixel.setColor(Color.WHITE);
}
```

12.3 Sepia-Toned and Posterized Pictures: Using Multiple Conditionals to Choose a Color

We handled the case of having two different ways to process the pixels using `if` and `else`. What if we have more than two ways that we want to process some pixels? For example, what if we wanted to do one thing if a value is less than some number, another thing if it is equal, yet a third if it is greater than the number? We could check for each of these conditions by writing an `if` statement for each condition, as shown here.

```
> int y = 10;
> if (y < 10) System.out.println("y is less than 10");
> if (y == 10) System.out.println("y is equal to 10");
y is equal 10
> if (y > 10) System.out.println("y is greater than 10");
```

This works but results in some unnecessary checking. Notice that *y* was equal to 10, so that was printed out, but it still executed the next statement, which checked if *y* was greater than 10. But can *y* be equal to 10 and greater than 10? What would have happened if *y* was less than 10? It would have printed out a string saying that *y* is less than 10, and still checked if *y* was equal to or greater than 10.

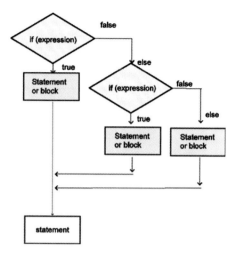

Figure 12.9
Flowchart of an if, else if, and an else

We need something to say that if the previous test was true, execute that, and then skip to the end of all the checks. We have seen a way to do this for two possibilities (true or false) using if and else. One way to handle three or more possibilities is with if, else if, and else, as illustrated in Figure 12.9. You can use as many else if statements as needed. You are not required to have a final else.

You can try out the logic of if . . . else if . . . else by entering the following in Dr.Java's **Interaction** pane.

```
> int y = 2;
> if (y < 10) System.out.println("Y is less than 10");
  else if (y == 10) System.out.println("y is equal to 10");
  else System.out.println("y is greater than 10");
y is less than 10
```

So far, we've done color modification by simply saying "This color replaces that color." We can be more sophisticated in our color swapping. We can look for a range of colors by using if, else if, and else and replace the color with some function of the original color or a specific color. The results are quite interesting.

For example, we might want to generate sepia-toned prints. Older prints sometimes have a sepia tone (brown and yellowish tint), caused by replacing the metallic silver in the old photographs with a pigment made from sepia (cuttlefish). We could just do an overall color change, but the end result isn't aesthetically pleasing. By looking for different kinds of color— highlights, middle ranges, and shadows— and treating them differently, we can simulate a sepia effect, as Figure 12.10 shows.

Program 12.6 defines a method named sepiaTint()in which we first convert the picture to gray, because older prints were in shades of gray, and also it makes it a little easier to work with. We then use if . . . else if . . . else to look for high, middle, and low ranges of color and change them separately. We want to make the shadows (darkest grays) a bit darker. We want to make most of the picture (middle grays) into a

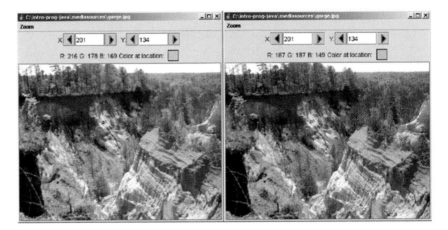

Figure 12.10
Original scene (left) and using our sepia-tone program

brownish color. We want to make the highlights (lightest grays) a bit yellow. Recall that yellow is a mixture of red and green, so one way to make things yellow is to increase the red and green. Another way is to reduce the amount of blue. The advantage to reducing the blue is that you don't have to worry about increasing a value past 255, which is the maximum.

Program 12.6: Convert a Picture to Sepia Tones

```
/**
 * Method to change the current picture to a sepia
 * tint (modify the middle colors to a light brown and
 * the light colors to a light yellow and make the
 * shadows darker)
 */
 public void sepiaTint()
 {
   Pixel pixel = null;
   double redValue = 0;
   double greenValue = 0;
   double blueValue = 0;

   // first change the current picture to grayscale
   this.grayscale();

   // loop through the pixels
   for (int x = 0; x < this.getWidth(); x++)
   {
     for (int y = 0; y < this.getHeight(); y++)
     {
       // get the current pixel and color values
       pixel = this.getPixel(x,y);
       redValue = pixel.getRed();
```

```
      greenValue = pixel.getGreen();
      blueValue = pixel.getBlue();

      // tint the shadows darker
      if (redValue < 60)
      {
        redValue = redValue * 0.9;
        greenValue = greenValue * 0.9;
        blueValue = blueValue * 0.9;
      }

      // tint the midtones a light brown
      // by reducing the blue
      else if (redValue < 190)
      {
        blueValue = blueValue * 0.8;
      }
      // tint the highlights a light yellow
      // by reducing the blue
      else
      {
        blueValue = blueValue * 0.9;
      }
      // set the colors
      pixel.setRed((int) redValue);
      pixel.setGreen((int) greenValue);
      pixel.setBlue((int) blueValue);
    }
  }
}
```

■

You can try this method out by entering the following code.

```
> Picture picture =
      new Picture(Picture.getMediaPath("gorge.jpg"));
> picture.show();
> picture.sepiaTint();
> picture.repaint();
```

Posterizing is a process of converting a picture to a smaller number of colors. Program 12.7 posterizes a picture by looking for specific ranges of color and setting the color to *one* value in that range. The result, seen in Figure 12.11, is that we reduce the number of colors in the picture.

Program 12.7: Posterizing a Picture

```
/**
 * Method to posterize (reduce the number of colors) in
 * the picture. The number of reds, greens, and blues
 * will each be 4.
 */
```

```java
public void posterize()
{
  Pixel pixel = null;
  int redValue = 0;
  int greenValue = 0;
  int blueValue = 0;

  // loop through the pixels
  for (int x = 0; x < this.getWidth(); x++) {
    for (int y = 0; y < this.getHeight(); y++) {

      // get the current pixel and colors
      pixel = this.getPixel(x,y);
      redValue = pixel.getRed();
      greenValue = pixel.getGreen();
      blueValue = pixel.getBlue();

      // check for red range and change color
      if (redValue < 64)
        redValue = 31;
      else if (redValue < 128)
        redValue = 95;
      else if (redValue < 192)
        redValue = 159;
      else
        redValue = 223;

      // check for green range
      if (greenValue < 64)
        greenValue = 31;
      else if (greenValue < 128)
        greenValue = 95;
      else if (greenValue < 192)
        greenValue = 159;
      else
        greenValue = 223;

      // check for blue range
      if (blueValue < 64)
        blueValue = 31;
      else if (blueValue < 128)
        blueValue = 95;
      else if (blueValue < 192)
        blueValue = 159;
      else
        blueValue = 223;

      // set the colors
      pixel.setRed(redValue);
      pixel.setGreen(greenValue);
      pixel.setBlue(blueValue);
    }
  }
}
```

Figure 12.11
Reducing the colors (right) from the original (left)

What's really going on here though is

1. setting up four *levels* for each of the color components (red, green, blue).
2. setting the *values* of the respective color component to the midpoint of its level.

To do this, we used `if . . . else if . . . else if . . . else` statements for each of the three color components. Although this process is actually rather simple, the program code is not easy to follow, because four levels for each of three color components results in twelve conditional statements needed to determine the level and set the color component values.

We can do this more generally and with fewer conditional statements if we mathematically compute the ranges for a desired number of levels and pick the midpoint relative to the range. We need to check whether the current value is in the range and, if so, to set it to the midpoint of the range.

How do we check whether a value is in a range? If we call the bottom of the range `bottomValue` and the top of the range `topValue`, then we could use this mathematical notation:

```
bottomValue <= testValue < topValue
```

However, in Java, this mathematical expression must be written as a Boolean expression like this:

```
if (bottomValue <= testValue && testValue < topValue)
```

The double ampersand (&&) is a logic operator that means *and*. If your mother says that you have to set the table *and* sweep the floor, how many jobs do you have to do? The answer is two (both of them). If she says that you can set the table *or* sweep the floor, how many jobs do you have to do then? The answer is one (just one of the two). Similarly, if in Java you have `if (expression && expression)`, both expressions must be true for the body of the `if` to be executed. On the other hand, if you have `if (expression ||`

expression), only one of the two expressions must be true for the body of the if to be executed. The double pipe || logic operator means *or*. (Note that the double pipe used for *or* || is not the same symbol as the double forward slash // used for comments.)

Program 12.8 defines a different posterize(int numLevels) method. (Recall that in Java you can overload methods. That is, you can have more than one method with the same name as long as they have different types and/or orders for the parameters.) This posterize method is more flexible than the previous one, because it allows you to pass in the number of levels to use for each color component. An increment is computed using

```
int increment = (int) (256.0 / numLevels);
```

Then a loop is used to iterate through the number of levels.

```
for (int i = 0; i < numLevels; i++)
```

With each iteration of the loop, the increment is used to compute the bottom, top, and middle values of the ith range.

```
bottomValue = i * increment;
topValue = (i + 1) * increment;
middleValue = (int) ((bottomValue + topValue - 1)/ 2.0);
```

Then a Boolean expression is used in an if statement to check whether each of the current pixel's color components are in this range. For example, the red component is checked by

```
if (bottomValue <= redValue && redValue < topValue)
        pixel.setRed(middleValue);
```

Program 12.8: Posterize by Levels

```
/**
 * Method to posterize (reduce the number of colors) in
 * the picture
 * @param numLevels the number of color levels to use
 */
public void posterize(int numLevels)
{
  Pixel pixel = null;
  int redValue = 0;
  int greenValue = 0;
  int blueValue = 0;
  int increment = (int) (256.0 / numLevels);
  int bottomValue, topValue, middleValue = 0;

  // loop through the pixels
  for (int x = 0; x < this.getWidth(); x++) {
    for (int y = 0; y < this.getHeight(); y++) {

      // get the current pixel and colors
      pixel = this.getPixel(x,y);
```

```
      redValue = pixel.getRed();
      greenValue = pixel.getGreen();
      blueValue = pixel.getBlue();

      // loop through the number of levels
      for (int i = 0; i < numLevels; i++)
      {
        // compute the bottom, top, and middle values
        bottomValue = i * increment;
        topValue = (i + 1) * increment;
        middleValue = (int) ((bottomValue + topValue - 1)
                              / 2.0);

        /* check if current values are in current range and
         * if so set them to the middle value
         */
        if (bottomValue <= redValue &&
            redValue < topValue)
          pixel.setRed(middleValue);
        if (bottomValue <= greenValue &&
            greenValue < topValue)
          pixel.setGreen(middleValue);
        if (bottomValue <= blueValue &&
            blueValue < topValue)
          pixel.setBlue(middleValue);
      }
    }
  }
}
```

Figure 12.12 shows a couple of examples. The original picture is on the far left, the picture in the middle has only two levels for each color component. The picture on the right has four levels for each color component.

Figure 12.12
Original picture (left) posterized to two levels (middle) and four levels (right)

12.4 Highlighting Extremes

What if we want to highlight the lightest and darkest areas of a picture? Would we highlight areas that are less than some amount from white *and* less than the same amount from black? Is there any color that is close to both white and black? No, we would want to replace the color at all pixels that have a distance from white **or** a distance from black less than some amount. We used the **&&** logic operator to mean *and* in the last program. In this example, we will use the **||** logic operator to mean *or*.

Program 12.9 highlights the extreme light and dark pixels in a picture by replacing the pixel color with a passed-in color. To determine whether a pixel is extremely light or dark, we compute its color distance to (a) white and (b) black. The color distances are each compared to some passed-in amount. If the color distance to white is less than the passed-in amount *or* if the color distance to black is less than the passed-in amount, then the pixel color is replaced.

Program 12.9: Highlight Extremes

```
/**
 * Method to replace the pixel colors in the current
 * picture object that have a color distance less than
 * the passed amount to white or black with the passed
 * replacement color
 * @param replacementColor the new color to use
 */
public void highlightLightAndDark(double amount,
                                  Color replacementColor) {
  Pixel pixel = null;

  // loop through all the pixels in the x direction
  for (int x = 0; x < getWidth(); x++) {

    // loop through all the pixels in the y direction
    for (int y = 0; y < getHeight(); y++) {

      // get the current pixel
      pixel = getPixel(x,y);

      // if the distance from white or black is less than the
      // passed amount use the replace color instead

      if (pixel.colorDistance(Color.white) < amount ||
          pixel.colorDistance(Color.black) < amount) {
        pixel.setColor(replacementColor);
      }
    }
  }
}
```

∎

You can try out the highlightLightAndDark() method by entering the following code. The result should look like the pictures displayed in Figure 12.13.

Figure 12.13
Original picture (left) and light or dark areas highlighted (right)

```
> String fileName = Picture.getMediaPath("butterfly1.jpg");
> Picture picture = new Picture(fileName);
> picture.explore();
> picture.highlightLightAndDark(50.0,java.awt.Color.yellow);
> picture.explore();
```

12.5   Combining Pixels: Blurring

When we make pictures larger (scale them up), we usually get rough edges. Sharp steps are visible in place of smooth lines, an effect we call **pixelation**. To reduce pixelation, we can **blur** the image by setting each pixel to an *average* of the pixels to either side of it.

12.5.1 `ArrayIndexOutOfBoundsException`

To blur an image, we need to loop through all pixels using nested `for` loops in the x and y dimensions. We have done this in many previous examples using code similar to the following:

```
for (int x = 0; x < this.getWidth(); x++) {
    for (int y = 0; y < this.getHeight(); y++) {
```

However, to blur an image, we want to compute the average of the pixels to either side of the pixel. Of course, we need to be careful not to try and access pixels beyond the allowed values of the two-dimensional array of pixels. To see what happens when you try to access pixels beyond the outer bounds of a two-dimensional array, try this in DrJava's Interactions pane:

```
> String fileName = FileChooser.getMediaPath("caterpillar.jpg");
> Picture p = new Picture(fileName);
```

```
> System.out.println(p.getWidth());
329
> System.out.println(p.getHeight());
150
> p.getPixel(330,160);
java.lang.ArrayIndexOutOfBoundsException: Coordinate out of
bounds!
  at sun.awt.image.ByteInterleavedRaster.getDataElements
    (Unknown Source)
  at java.awt.image.BufferedImage.getRGB(Unknown Source)
  at SimplePicture.getBasicPixel(SimplePicture.java:247)
  at Pixel.setValuesFromPictureAndLocation(Pixel.java:137)
  at Pixel.<init>(Pixel.java:57)
  at SimplePicture.getPixel(SimplePicture.java:270)
  at sun.reflect.NativeMethodAccessorImpl.invoke0(Native Method)
  at sun.reflect.NativeMethodAccessorImpl.invoke(Unknown Source)
  at sun.reflect.DelegatingMethodAccessorImpl.invoke
    (Unknown Source)
  at java.lang.reflect.Method.invoke(Unknown Source)
```

The `java.lang.ArrayIndexOutOfBoundsException` tells us that we tried to access an array element that was outside the allowed indices. If this happens when our program is executing, the program will stop and report the exception. This is called a **run-time exception,** because it is an error that happens when the program is running rather than at compile time.

So how do we check that the index values are acceptable? We know that the *x* indices range from 0 to width – 1 and the y indices range from 0 to height – 1. So we can use

```
x >= 0 && x < this.getWidth() && y >= 0 && y < this.getHeight()
```

to be sure that we stay within the indices of the two-dimensional array.

Program 12.10 defines a simple `blur()` method. The `blur()` method has a parameter that allows you to pass in the number of pixels (`numPixels`) to be used to compute the average. If you pass in 2, then each pixel will be assigned a color computed as the average of the colors of the current pixel, the two pixels to its left, plus the 2 pixels to its right, assuming this is possible within the borders of the two-dimensional array.

Program 12.10: A Simple Blur

```
/**
 * Method to blur the pixels
 * @param numPixels the number of pixels to average in all
 * directions so if the numPixels is 2 then we will average
 * all pixels in the rectangle defined by 2 before the
 * current pixel to 2 after the current pixel
 */
```

```java
public void blur(int numPixels)
{
  Pixel pixel = null;
  Pixel samplePixel = null;
  int redValue = 0;
  int greenValue = 0;
  int blueValue = 0;
  int count = 0;

  // loop through the pixels
  for (int x=0; x < this.getWidth(); x++) {
    for (int y=0; y < this.getHeight(); y++) {

      // get the current pixel
      pixel = this.getPixel(x,y);

      // reset the count and red, green, and blue values
      count = 0;
      redValue = greenValue = blueValue = 0;

      /* loop through pixel numPixels before x to
       * numPixels after x
       */
      for (int xSample = x - numPixels;
          xSample <= x + numPixels;
          xSample++) {
        for (int ySample = y - numPixels;
            ySample <= y + numPixels;
            ySample++) {

          /* check that we are in the range of acceptable
           * pixels
           */
          if (xSample >= 0 && xSample < this.getWidth() &&
          ySample >= 0 && ySample < this.getHeight()) {
            samplePixel = this.getPixel(xSample,ySample);
            redValue = redValue + samplePixel.getRed();
            greenValue = greenValue + samplePixel.getGreen();
            blueValue = blueValue + samplePixel.getBlue();
            count = count + 1;
          }
        }
      }
      // use average color of surrounding pixels
      Color newColor = new Color(redValue / count,
                                 greenValue / count,
                                 blueValue / count);
      pixel.setColor(newColor);
    }
  }
}
```

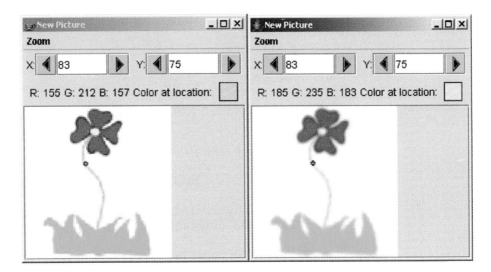

Figure 12.14
Making the flower bigger, and then blurring it to reduce pixelation

Here is how to use this method.

```
> Picture p = new Picture(
    FileChooser.getMediaPath("flower1.jpg"));
> p = p.scaleUp(2);
> p.explore();
> p.blur(2);
> p.explore();
```

Figure 12.14 shows the flower from the collage made bigger, then blurred. You can see the pixelation—the sharp, blocky edges—in the bigger version (left). With the blur, some of that pixelation goes away. The blur technique presented here is rather simple, but more careful blur techniques can be used to take into account regions of colors (so that edges between colors are kept sharp) and thus are able to reduce pixelation without removing sharpness.

12.6 Background Subtraction

Let's imagine that you have a picture of someone, and a picture of where they stood without them there, as seen in Figure 12.15. Could you *subtract* the background around the person (i.e., figure out where the colors are close) and then replace it with another another background? Say, of the moon?

Program 12.11 defines a method named swapBackground() that loops through the x and y dimensions of two pictures, oldBackground and newBackground. We call the colorDistance() method to find the color distance of current pixel of the newBackground picture to the corresponding pixel in the oldBackground picture. If the color distance is less than 15, the pixel in the oldBackground (oldPixel) is set to the color of the pixel in the newBackground (newPixel).

Figure 12.15
A picture of a child (Katie), and her background without her

Program 12.11: Subtract the Background and Replace it with a New One

```
/**
 * Method to replace the background in the current picture
 * with the background from another picture
 * @param oldBackground a picture with the old background
 * to replace
 * @param newBackground a picture with the new background
 * to use
 */
public void swapBackground(Picture oldBackground,
                 Picture newBackground)
{
  Pixel currPixel = null;
  Pixel oldPixel = null;
  Pixel newPixel = null;

  // loop through the columns
  for (int x = 0; x < getWidth(); x++)
  {
    // loop through the rows
    for (int y = 0; y < getHeight(); y++)
    {
      // get the current pixel and old background pixel
      currPixel = this.getPixel(x,y);
      oldPixel = oldBackground.getPixel(x,y);

      /* if the distance between the current pixel color
       * and the old background pixel color is less
       * than the 15 then swap in the new background pixel
       */
      if (currPixel.colorDistance(oldPixel.getColor()) < 15.0)
```

Figure 12.16
A new background, the moon (left), and Katie on the moon (right)

```
        {
          newPixel = newBackground.getPixel(x,y);
          currPixel.setColor(newPixel.getColor());
        }
      }
    }
  }
}
```

To test whether we can replace an old background with a new background, try

```
> String fileName = FileChooser.getMediaPath("kid-in-frame.jpg");
> Picture p = new Picture(fileName);
> fileName = FileChooser.getMediaPath("bgframe.jpg");
> Picture oldBg = new Picture(fileName);
> fileName = FileChooser.getMediaPath("moon-surface.jpg");
> Picture newBg = new Picture(fileName);
> p.swapBackground(oldBg,newBg);
> p.show();
```

This example shows that we can replace an old background with a new one, but the effect isn't as good as we would like (Figure 12.16). Katie's top color was too close to the color of the wall. And though the light was dim, the shadow is definitely having an effect here. In the next section, we will look at a different way to replace a background.

12.7 Chromakey

The way that a TV weather forecaster appears to be in front of a weather map that changes is that the weather forcaster is actually standing in front of a background of a fixed color (usually blue or green). The TV picture is fed into a computer before being broadcast, and a computer program is used to dynamically subtract that color and replace it with the weather map. Subtracting a color in this way is known as **chromakey**.

Figure 12.17
Mark in front of a blue sheet

You don't really want to do chromakey with a common color, like red—something that there's a lot of in your face. If you do, some of the person's face will be swapped. This is why moviemakers and weather reporters use blue or green backgrounds. To illustrate chromakey, Mark Guzdial took a blue sheet, attached it to an entertainment center, and took a picture of himself in front of it using a timer on a camera. The picture is shown in Figure 12.17.

Program 12.12 defines a method named chromakey that tests for a blue background and replaces blue pixels in the current picture with pixels from a new background image. Mark tried a new way to test for "blueness." If the blue value is greater than the sum of the red and green values, then the color is considered "blue." This is used in the conditional if statement:

```
if (currPixel.getRed() + currPixel.getGreen() <
        currPixel.getBlue())
```

Program 12.12: Chromakey: Replace All Blue with the New Background

```
/**
 * Method to do chromakey using a blue background
 * @param newBg the new background image to use to replace
 * the blue from the current picture
 */
 public void chromakey(Picture newBg)
 {
   Pixel currPixel = null;
   Pixel newPixel = null;

   // loop through the columns
   for (int x = 0; x < getWidth(); x++)
   {
     // loop through the rows
     for (int y = 0; y < getHeight(); y++)
```

```
      {
        // get the current pixel
        currPixel = this.getPixel(x,y);

        /* if the color at the current pixel is mostly blue
         * (blue value is greater than red and green
         * combined), then use new background color
         */
        if (currPixel.getRed() + currPixel.getGreen() <
            currPixel.getBlue())
        {
         newPixel = newBg.getPixel(x,y);
         currPixel.setColor(newPixel.getColor());
        }
      }
    }
  }
}
```

The effect is really quite striking, as Figure 12.18 shows. (Do note the "folds" in the lunar surface and the beach background, though. If you want to try this on a picture of your own, be sure to stretch the background fabric tightly to avoid such an effect.)

The really cool thing, also illustrated in Figure 12.18, is that this program works for any background that's the same size as the image. To put Mark on the moon and on the beach, try

```
> String fileName = FileChooser.getMediaPath("blue-mark.jpg");
> Picture mark = new Picture(fileName);
> fileName = FileChooser.getMediaPath("moon-surface.jpg");
> Picture newBg = new Picture(fileName);
> mark.chromakey(newBg);
> mark.explore();
> mark = new Picture(
  FileChooser.getMediaPath("blue-mark.jpg"));
> newBg = new Picture(FileChooser.getMediaPath("beach.jpg"));
> mark.chromakey(newBg);
> mark.explore();
```

Figure 12.18
Mark on the moon, and Mark on the beach

Program 12.13 defines a method named chromakeyBlue() that illustrates another way of writing this code, which is shorter but does the same thing. The difference is that this new method creates a one-dimensional pixel array to represent the picture. This allows us to write the code using a single for loop instead of two nested loops that are needed for working with a two-dimensional representation.

Program 12.13: Chromakey, Shorter

```
/**
 * Method to do chromakey using a blue background
 * @param newBg the new background image to use to replace
 * the blue from the current picture
 */
 public void chromakeyBlue(Picture newBg)
 {
   Pixel[] pixelArray = this.getPixels();
   Pixel currPixel = null;
   Pixel newPixel = null;

   // loop through the pixels
   for (int i = 0; i < pixelArray.length; i++)
   {
     // get the current pixel
     currPixel = pixelArray[i];

     /* if the color at the current pixel is mostly blue
      * (blue value is greater than green and red
      * combined), then use new background color
      */
     if (currPixel.getRed() + currPixel.getGreen() <
         currPixel.getBlue())
     {
       newPixel = newBg.getPixel(currPixel.getX(),
                                 currPixel.getY());
       currPixel.setColor(newPixel.getColor());
     }
   }
 }
```

Making It Work Tip: When Do You Need a Different Method Name?

Notice that we used a different name for the new, shorter method. We couldn't have used the same name and had both methods in our Picture class since the parameters are the same. Methods can be overloaded (use the same name) as long as the parameters are different (in number, order, or type).

Figure 12.19
Deleting the ground in Alice

12.8   Using Media Computation with Alice

To create an Alice world that can be used to create pictures for use with chromakey, first delete the ground in an Alice world by right-clicking **ground** in the Object tree and then selecting **delete**, as shown in Figure 12.19.

Then change the background color by clicking on **world** in the Object tree and selecting the **properties** tab in the **details** area. Click on the down arrow on the current **atmosphereColor** to change it, as in Figure 12.20.

Figure 12.21 shows the results of creating an Alice world in which Alice is standing against a green background. We then copied only the non-green pixels from a source picture to the current picture (a bridge in a pasture). You can do the same by writing your own method to copy only the non-green pixels to a digital picture. You might want to specify a region to copy and a starting top left location to copy to in the target picture.

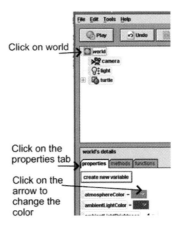

Figure 12.20
Changing the *atmosphereColor* in the world in Alice

Figure 12.21
Copying Alice characters onto digital pictures

12.9   Concepts Summary

We have covered Boolean expressions, conditionally executing code using `if` and `else`, combining Boolean expressions using *and* (**&&**) and *or* (**||**), and method overloading.

12.9.1 Boolean Expressions

A Boolean expression is one that evaluates to `true` or `false`. The values `true` and `false` are reserved words in Java. Here are some example Boolean expressions.

```
> int x = 20;
> System.out.println(x <= 30);
true
> System.out.println(x > 30);
false
> System.out.println(x == 20);
true
> System.out.println(x != 20);
false
```

Notice that to check for a variable having a value we use == not =. The = is used to assign a value to a variable, not to check for equality. To check for inequality, use !=.

12.9.2 Combining Boolean Expressions

You can combine Boolean expressions with the logic operators **&&** to represent *and* and **||** to represent *or*. When you use **&&**, both Boolean expressions must be `true` in order for it to return `true`. If the first Boolean expression isn't `true`, the second won't even be tested. This is called short-circuit evaluation. When you use **||**, only one Boolean expression must be `true` in order for it to return `true`. With **||**, if the first

Boolean expression is `true`, the second won't be evaluated. If the first Boolean expression is `false`, the second one will still be evaluated.

```
> int x = 3;
> int y = 5;
> System.out.println(x < 5 && y < 6);
true
> System.out.println(x > 5 && y < 6);
false
> System.out.println(x < 5 && y > 6);
false
> System.out.println(x > 5 && y > 6);
false
> System.out.println(x > 5 || y < 6);
true
```

12.9.3 Conditional Execution

To conditionally execute one statement, use the `if` keyword followed by a Boolean expression inside a pair of parentheses. Put the statement that you only want executed if the Boolean expression is `true` on a new line and indent it. If the Boolean expression is `false`, then execution will continue with the next statement.

```
if (Boolean expression)
   // statement to execute if the Boolean expression is true
   statement
// next statement
statement
```

To conditionally execute a block of statements, use the `if` keyword followed by a Boolean expression inside of an open and close parenthesis. Put the statements to be executed when the Boolean expression is `true` inside a pair of curly braces. Indent the statements to make it easier to visually see that these statements will only be executed if the Boolean expression is `true`. If the Boolean expression is `false`, execution will continue with the statement following the close curly brace.

```
if (Boolean expression)
{
   statements
}
```

If you want to execute one block of statements if the Boolean expression is `true` and another if it is `false`, use the `else` keyword as well. Put the statements that you want to execute when the Boolean expression is `true` inside a pair of curly braces after the `if (Boolean Expression)`. Next, add the keyword `else` and put the statements that you want executed when the Boolean expression is `false` inside a pair of curly braces.

```
if (Boolean expression)
{
   statements
}
```

```
else
{
  statements
}
```

If you have three or more options, use nested `if`s and `else`s.

```
if (Boolean expression)
{
  statements
}
else if (Boolean expression)
{
  statements
}
else
{
  statements
}
```

If you have four options, start with an `if (Boolean expression)`, followed by two `else if (Boolean expression)`, and a final `else`. The last `else` is optional.

Exercises

1. What are each of the following?
   - Conditional execution
   - Short-circuit evaluation
   - A Boolean expression
   - Chromakey
   - Sepia tint
   - Posterize
   - Edge detection
   - Blurring

2. Try doing chromakey (Program 12.13) in a range—grab something out of its background where the something is only in one part of a picture. For example, put a halo around someone's head, but don't mess with the rest of their body.

3. Try doing edge detection (Program 12.5) in a range. Change just part of a picture by passing in the start x, start y, end x, and end y.

4. Try doing a sepia tint on a picture from Alice. You might want to pass-in values for the lightest, medium, and darkest ranges.

5. Modify the general copy method `copyPicture` from Chapter 11 to stop looping if it is past the width of either the source picture or the current picture.

6. Write a method to copy all but the white pixels from one picture to another. Use this to put the robot in `robot.jpg` on the moon in `moon-surface.jpg`.

7. Start with a picture of someone you know, and make some specific color changes to it.

   - Turn the skin green.
   - Turn the eyes red.
   - Turn the hair orange.

   Of course, if your friend's skin is already green, or eyes red, or hair orange, you should choose different target colors.

8. Which of the following methods removes all the blue from every pixel of a picture that already has a blue value of more than 100?

   A.

   ```
   public void blueOneHundred()
   {
     Pixel p = null;
     for (int x = 0; x < 100; x++)
     {
       for (int y=0; y < 100; y++)
       {
         p = getPixel(x,y);
         p.setBlue(100);
       }
     }
   }
   ```

   B.

   ```
   public void blueChange()
   {
     Pixel[] pixelArray = getPixels();
     Pixel pixel = null;
     for (int i = 0; i < pixelArray.length; i++)
     {
       pixel = pixelArray[i];
       if (pixel.getBlue() > 0)
       {
         pixel.setBlue(100);
       }
     }
   }
   ```

   C.

   ```
   public void clearSomeBlue() {
       Pixel[] pixelArray = getPixels();
       Pixel pixel = null;
       for (int i = 0; i < pixelArray.length; i++)
       {
         pixel = pixelArray[i];
         if (pixel.colorDistance(Color.BLUE) > 100)
           pixel.setBlue(0);
       }
   }
   ```

D.

```java
public void setBlue() {
    Pixel[] pixelArray = getPixels();
    Pixel pixel = null;
    for (int i = 0; i < pixelArray.length; i++)
    {
      pixel = pixelArray[i];
      if (pixel.getBlue() > 100)
        pixel.setBlue(0);
    }
}
```

(a) A only

(b) D only

(c) B and C

(d) C and D

(e) None

(f) All

What do the other ones do?

9. What is the result of the following code?

```java
boolean value1 = true;
boolean value2 = false;
if (value1 && value2)
    System.out.println("first if is true");
if (value1 || value2)
    System.out.println("second if is true");
if (value1 && !value2)
    System.out.println("third if is true");
if (value1 || !value2)
    System.out.println("fourth if is true");
if (!value1 && value2)
    System.out.println("fifth if is true");
if (!value1 || value2)
    System.out.println("sixth if is true");
if (!value1 && !value2)
    System.out.println("seventh if is true");
if (!value1 || !value2)
    System.out.println("eighth if is true");
```

10. Write the method to turn the lightest areas of a picture gray to simulate a fog.

11. Write the method to turn the darkest areas of a picture green.

12. Try edge detection (Program 12.5) on an Alice picture. How well does it work?

13. Write a method to darken the lightest areas of a picture.

14. Write a method to turn the pixels with an average color<85 green, pixels with an average color<170 red, and the rest of the pixels blue.

15. Write another method to blur the picture from Program 12.10, but this time make a copy of the picture first and use the values from the copy to determine the new value for a pixel. To make a copy of a picture, just create a new picture passing in the old one `Picture copy = new Picture(oldPicture);`.

16. Write edge-detection methods similar to Program 12.5. Try comparing the current pixel intensity with the one on the right. Try comparing the current pixel to the average of the pixels to the right and below.

17. What would the output from the following code be?

```
int x = 30;
for (int i = x; i < 40; i++)
{
  if (i < 35)
    System.out.println("i is less than 35");
  else if (i == 35)
    System.out.println("i is 35");
  else
    System.out.println("i is greater than 35");
}
```

18. What would the output from the following code be?

```
boolean continues = true;
int count = 0;
int max = 20;
while (continues)
{
    System.out.println(count);
    count++;
    max++;
    if (count > 10 && max > 40)
        continue = false;
}
```

19. What would the output from the following code be?

```
boolean continues = true;
int count = 0;
int max = 20;
while (continues)
{
     System.out.println(count);
    count++;
    max++;
    if (count > 10 || max > 40)
        continues = false;
}
```

20. Write a method to do green or red chromakey as in Program 12.13.

CHAPTER 13
Creating Classes

Goals of this chapter:

- To define a class including the fields, constructors, and methods.
- To override an inherited method.
- To start using a debugger.
- To overload constructors.
- To create, initialize, access, and process an array.
- To create accessor and modifier methods.
- To introduce runtime exceptions.
- To create a main method.
- To create Javadoc comments.
- To introduce dynamic binding.

Introduction

We first looked at classes in Chapter 3 with Alice, where classes are predefined as 3D models in the Alice gallery. To create a new class in Alice, we have to modify an existing class. For example, we created new methods for an ice skater in Alice and then we saved the ice skater out as a new class named *CleverSkater*. This is the only mechanism in Alice 2.0 and 2.2 for creating new classes. In Java we can also create new classes that are based on existing classes and we can even create entirely new classes.

What classes should we create? A class usually defines a particular kind of object and so we create our own classes in order to be able to create new kinds of objects that we need to accomplish some task. We determine a type for those objects (classify them) and write a class definition for each type. A class definition contains information about the data that an object of that class needs to keep track of, or the information that the object "owns." In Alice, object data were known as *properties*. In Java, object data are known as **fields**. A class definition also contains special methods that are called for the purpose of initializing the data for each new object at the time each new object is first created. These special methods are known as **constructors** in Java. Also, a class definition contains methods that define the behaviors that objects of that class will need to know how to do. Up to now we have only written methods in Java, but now we will write an entire Java class. A class will have fields, constructors, and methods.

13.1   Identifying the Classes and Fields

The first problem we will use as an example for writing a Java class is: Create a slide show where we show pictures one after another and wait for some time between the pictures. One way to start identifying the classes that we will need to create is to underline the nouns in the problem description. If this example problem, the nouns are: *slide show*, *wait time*, and *picture*. Which of these should be a class, and which should be a field?

To decide whether a noun needs to be a class or a field, determine whether it has more than one piece of data associated with it. A slide show has pictures and a time to wait between pictures. A slide show has more than one piece of data associated with it. So slide show should be a class. Nouns that have other nouns associated with them are classes.

What about the time to wait between pictures? Well, the amount of time can be specified as a number. Simple data that can be represented by numbers or strings are usually fields. To determine which class the field belongs to, ask who owns the data, or who should know the data. A slide show should know how long to wait between pictures.

What about the pictures? A slide show will have more than one picture. We can reuse the `Picture` class (also used in Chapters 10–11) to represent each picture. A **UML diagram**, which shows the classes and the relationship between the classes is shown in Figure 13.1. It shows that we will need 2 classes, `SlideShow` and `Picture`. Each `SlideShow` object will have a `waitTime` field.

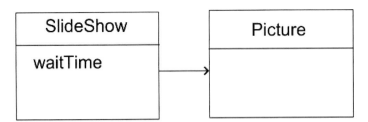

Figure 13.1
UML class diagram

Making It Work Tip: Class Names Should Be Singular

Although we can create many objects of the same class, a class name should be singular, not plural. We named this the `SlideShow` class, not the `SlideShows` class. We can create many `SlideShow` objects from this `SlideShow` class.   ■

13.2   Defining a Class

The computer doesn't know what we mean by a slide show, so we need to define it for the computer. We need to specify the name of the class, the data (fields) that objects of the class will have, how to initialize each object's fields when a new object of the class is created, and what methods the object will know how to do. We do this by creating a class definition. A class definition for a SlideShow class looks like this:

```
public class SlideShow
{
}
```

We could also write this as:

```
public class SlideShow {
}
```

This declares a public class named SlideShow. Public classes can be used by all other classes. By convention, class names start with an uppercase letter and the first letter of each additional word is uppercase. Notice the curly braces. They enclose a block of code that contains all fields, constructors, and methods for this class. All fields, constructors and methods must be inside the open { and close } curly braces for the class. We also indent the code inside the curly braces to make it visually obvious that the code is *inside* the class definition. This class *must* be saved in a file named SlideShow.java.

Debugging Tip: Naming Class Files

Each class that you define is usually saved in a separate file. The name of the file *must* exactly match the name of the class followed by the extension .java. So a class named SlideShow must be defined in a file SlideShow.java. A class named Turtle must be defined in a file Turtle.java not turtle.java or TurTLE.java. Case is important in Java!

You can create a new class in DrJava by clicking the **New** button. This will create a blank area in the definitions pane. Type your class definition there. When you are ready, you can save it to a file by clicking the **Save** button. Use the directory chooser to pick where to save the file and give it the same name as the class name. When you have saved the file, you will see SlideShow.java in the file pane, as in Figure 13.2 on the next page.

13.2.1 Defining Fields

Next, we want to add the fields that a slide show object will contain. Each slide show object needs to know the amount of time to wait between pictures and the pictures to show. So, we will need two fields: one for the amount of time to wait and one for the pictures.

To create a field, we need to decide what *type* to use for the field. The wait time can be an integer that represents the number of milliseconds to wait between pictures.

We declare fields by specifying the visibility, type, and name of the field.

visibility type name;

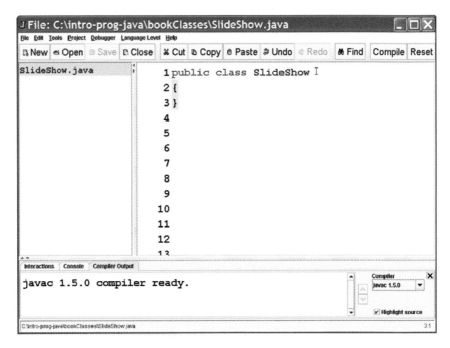

Figure 13.2
DrJava with the class definition for SlideShow

The *visibility* for fields is usually `private` so that an object can control its own data. Would you like objects of other classes to directly access and change a `SlideShow` object's data? You certainly wouldn't want this for your bank account! Objects are responsible for their data, and to be responsible they need to control who has direct access to their data. So you should nearly always make your fields `private`.

The *type* is a class name or one of the primitive types (`int`, `double`, `boolean`, etc.) Remember that you can declare an array by adding a pair of square brackets `[]` after the type. You can have arrays of either primitive values or of objects.

The *name* should be appropriate for what the field represents. The convention for field names is to start with a lowercase letter and uppercase the first letter of each additional word.

For the wait time, the declaration might look like this:

```
private int waitTime;
```

The declaration of a field can also specify an initial value for the field as the result of some expression.

```
visibility type name = expression;
```

For the wait time, the declaration might be written like this:

```
private int waitTime = 2000; // wait 2 seconds between pictures
```

Fields are *automatically* initialized if no other initialization is specified in the declaration. The default is to initialize object references to `null`, numbers to 0, and `boolean` variables to `false`.

Now that `waitTime` has been declared as a field, we need to declare a field for the pictures. We could create a variable for each `Picture` object and name them `picture1`, `picture2`, `picture3`, and so on, but we don't know how many pictures we will have in our slide show. We can use an array of pictures instead. That way we won't have to name each one. Remember that you can declare a variable that will refer to an array using either:

```
type[] name;
```

or

```
type name[];
```

So, the declaration for a pictures array might look like this:

```
private Picture[] pictureArray;
```

Debugging Tip: Use Square Brackets with Arrays
Be careful not to use curly braces {} in place of the square brackets [] when you declare an array!
∎

Program 13.1 shows a beginning definition for a `SlideShow` class with a declaration of a field of type `int` for the wait time, and a field which is an array of type `Picture` for the pictures.

Program 13.1: A SlideShow Class
```
public class SlideShow
{
  ////////////// fields //////////////
  private int waitTime = 2000; // wait 2 seconds
  private Picture[] pictureArray;
}
```
∎

We have now defined a class, `SlideShow`, and when an object of that class is created it will have two fields in it: `waitTime` and `pictureArray`. A `SlideShow` object will also have a reference to the object that defines the class (an object of the class named `Class`, as illustrated in Figure 13.3). Thus, it will know that it is an object of the class `SlideShow`. Every object has a reference to the class that created it.

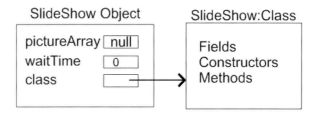

Figure 13.3
Showing a SlideShow object with a reference to its class

Each class you write in Java has a parent class even if none is specified. We could have explicitly named the parent class for SlideShow by using the extends keyword on the class definition followed by the name of a parent class, like this:

```
public class SlideShow extends Object
{
  ////////////// fields //////////////
  private int waitTime = 2000; // wait 2 seconds
  private Picture[] pictureArray;
}
```

If no parent class is specified the default parent class will be Object. Figure 13.4 shows a diagram of a SlideShow object with a reference to its class and a reference from the class to its parent class. The SlideShow class and its parent class form an **ancestor tree** of classes. In this example, there are only two classes in the ancestor tree but ancestor trees often consist of many classes (parent, grandparent, great grandparent. . . .)

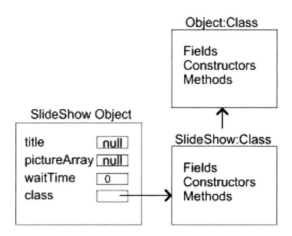

Figure 13.4
A slide show object and its ancestor class tree

What is the purpose of an ancestor class tree? Well, when an object is asked to invoke a method, it first looks in its own class definition for the method to execute. If it doesn't find it there, it will look in the parent class of the class that created it. If it doesn't find it there, it will look in the grandparent of the class that created it. It will keep looking up the ancestor class tree until it finds the method to execute. We know that the method must be somewhere in the ancestor tree or the code wouldn't have compiled. This process of looking up a method during run-time starting with the class that created the object is known as **run-time** or **late binding**.

The great thing about an ancestor class tree is that it allows methods to be defined in one class and used by objects of another class. We say that the methods are **inherited**. When one class inherits from another, it gets *all* the object methods and fields from that parent class. The parent class is the class the child class is inheriting from. In this example, Object is the **parent class** of SlideShow, and SlideShow is a **child class** of Object. A parent class is also known as a **superclass** or a **base class**. A child class is also known as a **subclass** or a **derived class**.

13.2.2 Inherited Methods

To illustrate inherited methods, let's compile the code in Program 13.1, create a slide show object, and print it out using System.out.println()? The code and an example of the output is shown here:

```
> System.out.println(new SlideShow());
SlideShow@2bd3a
```

From the output, it looks like a SlideShow object was created, but what are the strange numbers and letters after the '@'? To explain what the strange numbers and letters represent, we must first explain that when you call the method System.out.println and pass it any object, it will call the method toString() on that object. When the toString() method is invoked on a SlideShow object, first the runtime environment looks for that method in the SlideShow class. But, the SlideShow class (as written above) does not have a toString() method so it next checks the parent class of SlideShow which is Object. The Object class does have a toString() method and it is that method that is executed.

The Object class's toString() method prints out the class name followed by an unsigned hexadecimal representation of the **hash code** of the object. What does that mean? The hash code is usually based on the address of the object in memory and can therefore be used to tell whether two objects are the same object or different objects. For example, in the following code we create two different SlideShow objects:

```
> System.out.println(new SlideShow());
Slideshow@3ae941
> System.out.println(new SlideShow());
SlideShow@1e4853f
```

Notice that the hash codes for the two SlideShow objects shown previously are different because two distinct SlideShow objects were created.

When one class inherits from another, it gets *all* the object methods and fields from that parent class. So, since the Object class has a toString() method in it that prints out the class name and the hash code, and the class SlideShow inherits from the class Object, all SlideShow objects also know how to do this. As a second example, in the following code, we create only one new SlideShow object and the names show1 and show2 both reference the same object.

```
> SlideShow show1 = new SlideShow();
> SlideShow show2 = show1;
> System.out.println(show1);
SlideShow@676437
> System.out.println(show2);
SlideShow@676437
```

Notice that in this case we see the same hash code, which indicates that both show1 and show2 refer to the same SlideShow object.

Because each object keeps a reference to its class, you can get its class using the getClass() method (inherited from the Object class). This returns an object of the class named Class which represents the SlideShow class. Each class in the ancestry tree also knows its parent class (also known as a superclass), and you can get that by using the method getSuperclass(), as illustrated in the following code.

```
> SlideShow show1 = new SlideShow();
> Class showClass = show1.getClass();
> System.out.println(showClass);
class SlideShow
> Class parentClass = showClass.getSuperclass();
> System.out.println(parentClass);
class java.lang.Object
```

13.2.3 Overriding Inherited Methods

To change what happens when we print out a SlideShow object, we could create our own toString() method in our SlideShow class. Program 13.2 illustrates the SlideShow class in which we have now defined a toString() method. The method toString() returns a String object that contains information about relevant fields in the current object. Creating a method with the same **method signature** (method name and parameter list) as a method defined in a parent class is known as **overriding** a method. When the method is called at runtime, the overriding method will be executed *instead of* the method defined in the parent class. This works because when a method is invoked on an object, the runtime will look for the method starting with the class that created the current object. If the method isn't found there, it will next check the parent class of the class that created the object. It will keep looking upward in the classes of the ancestry tree until it finds the method. We know that the method must be there somewhere or else the code wouldn't have compiled.

Program 13.2: SlideShow Class with a Method

```
public class SlideShow
{

  ///////////// fields /////////////
  private int waitTime = 2000; // wait 2 seconds
  private Picture[] pictureArray;

  ////////// methods /////////////
  public String toString()
  {
    return "SlideShow object with a wait time of: " +
           this.waitTime;
  }
}
```

Now that we have written a `toString()` method that overrides the `toString()` method of the Object class, we can create a slide show object and print it out like this:

```
> System.out.println(new SlideShow());
SlideShow object with a wait time of: 2000
```

Making It Work Tip: The this Keyword

In the `toString()` method written for the SlideShow class, we used `this.waitTime`. The keyword `this` is how you can refer to the current object inside of a method. It is possible to have several objects of the same class and we want to print out the wait time of the current object. So we use `this.waitTime` to refer to that the current object. If we leave off the `this` the compiler will add it for us, but we find that writing `this` as part of our code helps us think about the intention of the program statement.

13.2.4 Default Field Initialization

When an object is created, *all* of the fields of the object are initialized. Object fields that aren't explicitly initialized by assignment statements in the declaration will be null, number fields will be 0, and `boolean` fields will be false. In Figure 13.5, we see that the

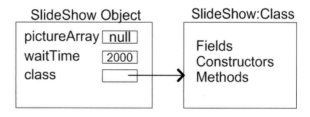

Figure 13.5
Showing a slide show object with the initialization of the fields

default for `pictureArray` is `null` since it is an object reference. If we hadn't set the wait time to 2000 in the declaration of the field `waitTime` the value would have been 0.

How do we set the values of the fields so that one slide show object is different from another? To set an object's fields to non-default values at the time an object is created, we write a *constructor*. A constructor is similar to a method, but the purpose of a **constructor** is to initialize the values of the fields when an object is created.

13.2.5 Declaring Constructors

A constructor is automatically called when a new object is created using the **new** operator. The constructor sets up an object, which usually means initializing the fields. You might say, "Wait a minute, we didn't define a constructor in the `SlideShow` class, so how could one have been called?" If the compiler doesn't see *any* constructors in the class definition it automatically creates a default constructor that doesn't take any parameters and uses the default value for each of the fields in the new object. A constructor that doesn't take any parameters is called the **no-argument constructor**.

To create a constructor use:

visibility ClassName (paramList)

Notice that the constructor declaration looks like a method declaration except *it doesn't have a return type* and the name of the constructor is the same name as the class name. Constructors usually have `public` visibility.

Common Bug: Constructors Don't Have a Return Type!

If you add a return type to a constructor, the compiler will think that you are creating a method. Constructors do **not** have a return type (not even `void`)! Constructors **must** use the name of the class, with the same upper and lower case letters.

When we write our own constructors, we will often write a constructor that has at least one parameter. In Program 13.3, we create a constructor for a `SlideShow` object that has the amount of time to wait between pictures as a parameter.

Program 13.3: SlideShow Class with a Constructor
```
public class SlideShow
{

  //////////// fields ////////////////
  private int waitTime = 2000; // wait 2 seconds
  private Picture[] pictureArray;

  //////////// constructors //////////
  public SlideShow(int theTime)
  {
    this.waitTime = theTime;
  }
```

```
/////////// methods //////////////
public String toString()
{
  return "SlideShow object with a wait time of: " +
         this.waitTime;
}
}
```

■

Now when we create a SlideShow object, we call the constructor with the word *new* in front of it and pass in the wait time. The following statement creates a new SlideShow object and then prints out information about the object:

```
> System.out.println(new SlideShow(5000));
SlideShow object with a wait time of: 5000
```

What happens now if we try to use the no-argument constructor?

```
> System.out.println(new SlideShow());
NoSuchMethodException: constructor SlideShow()
```

Notice that we got a compiler error (the error that you get may be somewhat different). In this example, the NoSuchMethodException says that there is no constructor that has no parameters in the class SlideShow. An **exception** is something that happens that is out of the ordinary sequence of a program's execution. In this case, the exception is an error.

What happened to the default no-argument constructor? Well, since we now have a constructor in the class SlideShow, the compiler will no longer add the default no-argument constructor for us. If we want one, we will need to add it ourselves.

In Program 13.4, we have added a no-argument constructor that leaves all the field values alone (allowing Java to use a default value for each field that is not explicitly initialized):

Program 13.4: SlideShow Class with Multiple Constructors

```
public class SlideShow
{
  ////////////// fields //////////////
  private int waitTime = 2000; // wait 2 seconds
  private Picture[] pictureArray;

  /////////// constructors //////////////
  public SlideShow() {}

  public SlideShow(int theTime)
  {
    this.waitTime = theTime;
  }

  /////////// methods //////////////
  public String toString()
```

```
      {
        return "SlideShow object with a wait time of: " +
                this.waitTime;
      }
  }
```

13.2.6 Using a Debugger

If your program runs but you aren't sure whether something is wrong, how do you figure out what your program is doing wrong? This is the process of **debugging**. Debugging is figuring out what your program is doing, how that differs from what you *want* it to be doing, and how to get it from where it is to where you need it to be.

In Chapters 8 and 10, we debugged our programs by adding print statements using `System.out.println()` that allowed us to trace what was happening as the program ran. We could use the same technique here: just add one of these print statements after we call the constructor and pass in a wait time. This should show that it was initialized to `2000`.

Another way to walk through your code with even more control is to use a **debugger**. A debugger is a tool that helps you walk through your program and see exactly what is happening. A debugger can save you *hours* of frustration, so it is worth spending some time learning to use one! Most integrated development environments (IDEs) have a debugger. To use the debugger in DrJava, you need to click on Debugger in the menu and then check the Debug Mode checkbox. This will modify the way the bottom of the DrJava window looks, as shown in Figure 13.6.

The debug mode adds some windows for debugging. You can peek ahead to Figures 13.8 and 13.9 to view the debug mode windows, but there is no need to worry about these for now. The most common thing to do in a debugger is set breakpoints. A **breakpoint** is a place in the code where you want to stop execution so you can see what is going on. Let's set a breakpoint in the constructor at the line that assigns the value of the wait time in the current object. Execution will stop *before* this line is executed.

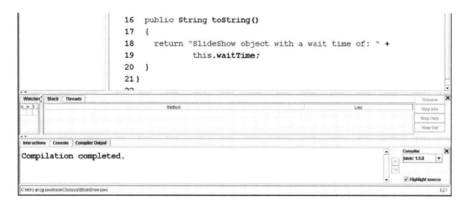

Figure 13.6
DrJava with debug mode turned on

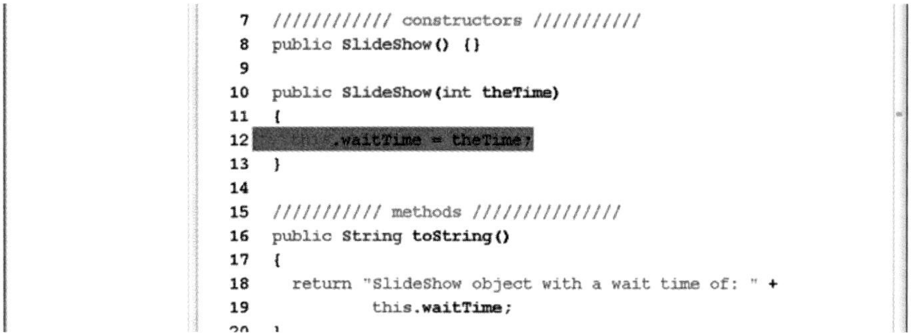

```
 7   /////////// constructors ///////////
 8   public SlideShow() {}
 9
10   public SlideShow(int theTime)
11   {
12        .waitTime = theTime;
13   }
14
15   /////////// methods ////////////////
16   public String toString()
17   {
18      return "SlideShow object with a wait time of: " +
19             this.waitTime;
20   }
```

Figure 13.7
A breakpoint highlighted in red

To set a breakpoint in DrJava you can right-click on a line of code and then click **Toggle Breakpoint** in the popup menu. You can also click on a line of code and then click **Debugger** and then **Toggle Breakpoint on Current Line**. In DrJava, once you set a breakpoint the line is highlighted in red, as shown in Figure 13.7; other IDEs may use another way to show a breakpoint. The key point is that *all* debuggers allow you to set breakpoints.

Now when you execute the following:

```
> System.out.println(new SlideShow(5000));
```

You will notice that the execution will stop and the breakpoint line will be highlighted in blue, as in Figure 13.8. The **Stack** tab will show the line number and the

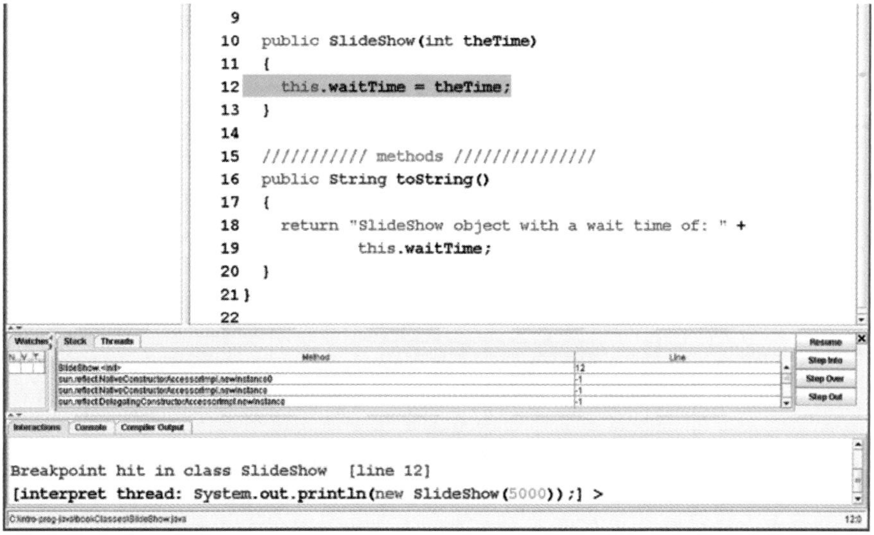

```
 9
10   public SlideShow(int theTime)
11   {
12        this.waitTime = theTime;
13   }
14
15   /////////// methods ////////////////
16   public String toString()
17   {
18      return "SlideShow object with a wait time of: " +
19             this.waitTime;
20   }
21 }
22
```

```
Watches  Stack  Threads                                                              Resume
                          Method                                      Line           Step Into
SlideShow <init>                                                      12
sun.reflect.NativeConstructorAccessorImpl.newInstance0               -1             Step Over
sun.reflect.NativeConstructorAccessorImpl.newInstance               -1
sun.reflect.DelegatingConstructorAccessorImpl.newInstance           -1             Step Out
```

```
Interactions  Console  Compiler Output

Breakpoint hit in class SlideShow   [line 12]
[interpret thread: System.out.println(new SlideShow(5000));] >
C:\drjo-prog-javabook\Classes\SlideShow.java                                         12:0
```

Figure 13.8
Execution stops at the breakpoint

method name where we have stopped. We have stopped at line 12 in the class SlideShow. The `<init>` is the name the debugger gives to constructors.

Now what do we want to do? At this point we can type things in the interactions pane to investigate the values of the variables and fields that are in scope.

```
> this.waitTime
2000
> this.pictureArray
null
> theTime
5000
```

From these we see that the `pictureArray` field did get assigned the default value of null and the waitTime field is set to 2000. And, we see the parameter `theTime` has a value of 5000. Let's let execution go forward by one step and then stop again. We do this by clicking the **Step Over** button.

We can check the value of the current object's wait time using the interactions pane, shown in Figure 13.9.

```
> this.waitTime
5000
```

We can let execution continue from here by clicking the **Resume** button. We can also stop debugging at anytime by clicking the **X** at the upper right of the debugging windows (to the right of the **Resume** button).

Figure 13.9
After clicking Step Over

13.3   Overloading Constructors

We can overload constructors, just as we overloaded methods. The parameter lists must be different. This can mean that they take a different number of parameters and/or that the types are different. In code presented in Figure 13.4, we defined two constructors. One takes no parameters and one takes an integer, which is the time to wait between pictures.

In Program 13.5, we add another constructor that has an array of pictures as a parameter.

Program 13.5: SlideShow Class with Three Constructors

```
public class SlideShow
{

  /////////////// fields ////////////////
  private int waitTime = 2000; // wait 2 seconds
  private Picture[] pictureArray;

  //////////// constructors ///////////////
  public SlideShow() {}
  public SlideShow(int theTime)
  {
    this.waitTime = theTime;
  }
  public SlideShow(Picture[] pictArray)
  {
    this.pictureArray = pictArray;
  }

  ////////// methods ///////////////
  public String toString()
  {
    return "SlideShow object with a wait time of: " +
           this.waitTime;
  }
}
```

We now have a third constructor that has a different parameter list than the previously defined constructors. To use the third constructor we need to pass in an array of Picture objects.

13.4   Working with Arrays

First, we need to create three pictures. You can use the following code to do this:

```
> Picture pict1 =
    new Picture(FileChooser.getMediaPath("beach.jpg"));
```

```
> Picture pict2 =
    new Picture(FileChooser.getMediaPath("church.jpp"));
> Picture pict3 =
    new Picture(FileChooser.getMediaPath("horse.jpg"));
```

Now, we can create an array of the three pictures. You may recall that we can declare an array using:

type[] name;

But this doesn't actually create an array object! It only declares a variable that will *refer* to an array object. To create an array object, you can initialize the elements of an array when you create it by listing the elements within curly braces, like this:

type[] name = {*elem1,elem2,elem3, . . .*};

So to create a SlideShow object and pass in an array of three pictures you can use the following:

```
> Picture[] pictArray = {pict1, pict2, pict3};
```

Alternatively, you can create an array and then separately fill in the pictures. To use this way of creating and initializing an array, we use:

new *type[numElements]*;

like this:

```
> Picture[] pictArray = new Picture[3];
```

Then, we can add the pictures to the array individually. Remember that the first index of an array is index 0.

```
> pictArray[0] =
    new Picture(FileChooser.getMediaPath("beach.jpg"));
> pictArray[1] =
    new Picture(FileChooser.getMediaPath("church.jpg"));
> pictArray[2] =
    new Picture(FileChooser.getMediaPath("horse.jpg"));
> System.out.println(new SlideShow(pictArray));
SlideShow object with a wait time of: 2000
```

The result (regardless of which array creation technique you use) is diagrammed in Figure 13.10. It doesn't matter whether you initialize the array when you create it or after you create it using the indices. In this example the values in the array are exactly the same. If you initialize the array when you create it, the array length is set to the number of items between the curly braces.

13.4.1 Displaying the Number of Pictures

It might be nice to change the toString method to also output the number of pictures in the slide show. Since this is something that objects of other classes might want to ask a SlideShow object, we should make getting the number of pictures in a slide show a public method.

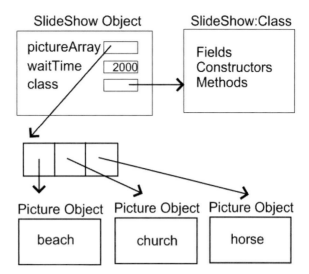

Figure 13.10
Showing a slide show object after the execution of a constructor that takes an array of pictures

Program 13.6 is the SlideShow class with a new method named getNumPicts().
This method first checks if there is a picture array yet. We can tell if there isn't one yet
by checking to see if pictureArray is null. If pictureArray doesn't reference a
valid array of pictures (is null) the method should return 0, otherwise it can return the
length of the picture array (pictureArray.length). We also modified the
toString() method to call this method (getNumPicts).

Program 13.6: SlideShow Class With More Information

```
public class SlideShow
{
  ///////////// fields ////////////////
  private int waitTime = 2000; // wait 2 seconds
  private Picture[] pictureArray;

  /////////// constructors //////////////
  public SlideShow() {}

  public SlideShow(int theTime)
  {
    this.waitTime = theTime;
  }

  public SlideShow(Picture[] pictArray)
  {
    this.pictureArray = pictArray;
  }
```

```
/////////// methods ///////////////
public int getNumPicts()
{
  // if no picture array then there are no pictures
  if (this.pictureArray == null)
  {
    return 0;
  }
  // else return the number of pictures in the array
  else
  {
    return pictureArray.length;
  }
}

public String toString()
{
  return "SlideShow object with a wait time of: " +
          this.waitTime + " and " +
          this.getNumPicts() + " pictures";
}
}
```

To try this out do the following:

```
> Picture pict1 =
    new Picture(FileChooser.getMediaPath("beach.jpg"));
> Picture pict2 =
    new Picture(FileChooser.getMediaPath("church.jpp"));
> Picture[] pictArray = {pict1, pict2};
> System.out.println(new SlideShow(pictArray));
SlideShow object with a wait time of: 2000 and 2 pictures
> System.out.println(new SlideShow(5000));
SlideShow object with a wait time of: 5000 and 0 pictures
```

Since we made the getNumPicts() method public, we can also invoke it directly on a SlideShow object from the interactions pane (which is outside the current class).

```
> SlideShow show1 = new SlideShow(pictArray);
> System.out.println(show1.getNumPicts());
2
```

13.4.2 Using **Step Into** in the Debugger

We can use the debugger again to check that things are working the way that we expect. Click **Debugger** and check the **Debug Mode** checkbox. Create a breakpoint at the first line in the constructor that takes an array of pictures, as shown in Figure 13.11. Create another breakpoint in the first line of the toString() method. You can set as many breakpoints as you want.

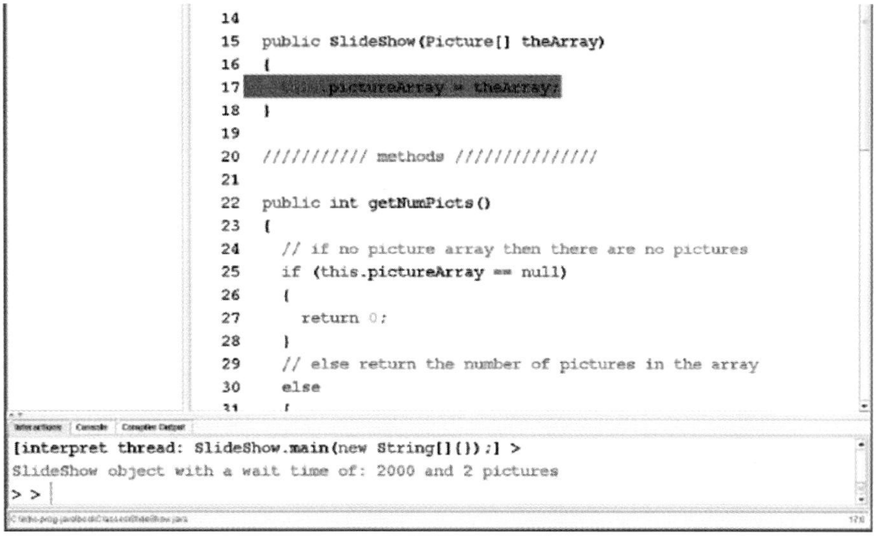

```
14
15   public SlideShow(Picture[] theArray)
16   {
17         pictureArray = theArray;
18   }
19
20   //////////// methods //////////////////
21
22   public int getNumPicts()
23   {
24      // if no picture array then there are no pictures
25      if (this.pictureArray == null)
26      {
27         return 0;
28      }
29      // else return the number of pictures in the array
30      else
31      {
```

```
Interactions  Console  Compiler Output
[interpret thread: SlideShow.main(new String[]{});] >
SlideShow object with a wait time of: 2000 and 2 pictures
> >
```

Figure 13.11
Breakpoint in the constructor that takes an array of pictures

Now let's execute this with the following code:

```
> Picture pict1 =
    new Picture(FileChooser.getMediaPath("beach.jpg"));
> Picture pict2 =
    new Picture(FileChooser.getMediaPath("church.jpp"));
> Picture[] pictArray = {pict1, pict2};
> SlideShow show1 = new SlideShow(pictArray);
> System.out.println(show1);
```

Execution will stop *before* the execution of the line that sets the current object's `pictureArray` field, as we see in Figure 13.12.

We can see that the current object fields have their default values by typing the following in the interactions pane. We can also check the values that were sent in to the parameters to the constructor.

```
> this.pictureArray
null
> this.waitTime
2000
> theArray
[LPicture;@fedfb6
```

We can use the **Step Over** button to execute the current line of code and then stop again after it has executed, as we see in Figure 13.13. If we do this, we can check the value of the current object's picture array again and see that it has been set to the value of the parameter.

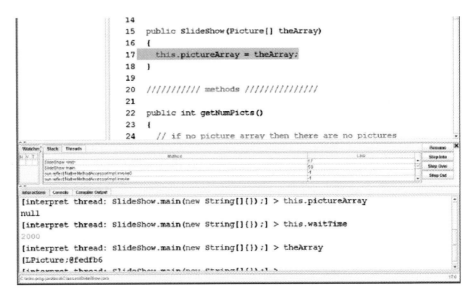

Figure 13.12
Execution stopped at the breakpoint

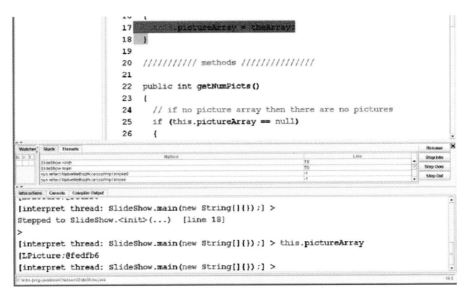

Figure 13.13
Execution stopped after step over

We can continue to click **Step Over** to execute each line of code and stop again. We can use the interactions pane to print out the values that have been changed. Or at this point we can click on **Resume** to let the program continue without stopping until the next breakpoint, or until it finishes.

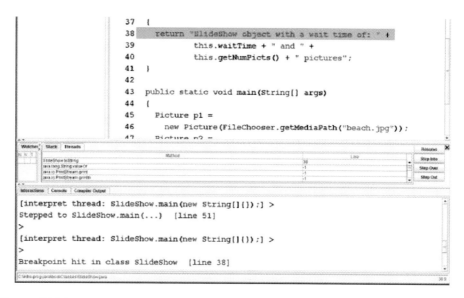

Figure 13.14
Execution stopped at the second breakpoint

Execution will stop at the second breakpoint in the method toString(), as Figure 13.14 shows. We can see from the Stack tab that it is stopped at line 38 in the method toString() in the class SlideShow. If, at this point, we want to see what happens when we execute this.getNumPicts() we can use Step Into instead of Step Over. Using Step Into will take us *into* a method which is invoked on the current line. If we use Step Over it will just execute the method and stop after it. We wouldn't get to see what happens *inside* the method.

After we use the Step Into button to step into the current line of code, execution will stop at the first line of the getNumPicts method (Figure 13.15). We can use the Step Over button to execute each line in this method and stop after each line to see what happened. Click on Resume to continue execution.

If you ever use Step Into when you meant to use Step Over, all you have to do is click Step Out. Clicking Step Out will finish execution of the current method and stop at the line following the line that called the current method.

13.4.3 Showing the Pictures

One of the things we would like to do with a slide show is show it. How can we do that? We may remember that in the Picture class, we have a method pictureObj.show()that can be used to show a picture. So we can just show one picture after another in the array of pictures. Also, we can hide the current picture before showing the next using pictureObj.hide().

Of course, we need to wait in between showing the pictures for the specified waitTime. To do this we could use the sleep method that is already defined as part of the java.lang.Thread class: Thread.sleep(amount). This will cause the

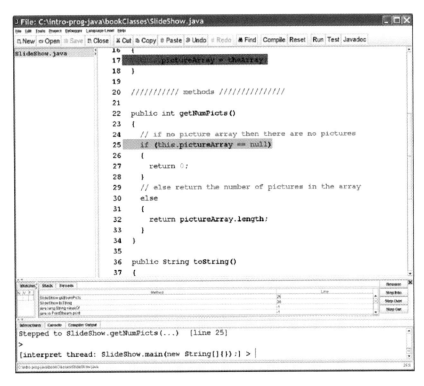

Figure 13.15
Execution stopped at the beginning of the getNumPicts method

current program to wait the specified amount of time before continuing with its execution. The amount of time is specified in milliseconds. There are 1,000 milliseconds in a second.

But, if we use `Thread.sleep(amount)` there is a possibility that the user will interrupt the program and an exception will occur. Some exceptions are known to occur so frequently that Java actually requires that you write your program code to either **catch** this kind of exception or **throw** it. To catch or throw an exception means to take care of it in some way so as to avoid freezing up the computer system when the exception occurs. We can add `throws Exception` to a method declaration to throw the exception. This can throw any object of the class `Exception` or of any child class of the `Exception` class. For this example, we write a method named `show()` that throws objects of the `Exception class`.

```
public void show() throws Exception
{
  for (Picture pictObj : this.pictureArray)
  {
    pictObj.show();
    Thread.sleep(this.waitTime);
    pictObj.hide();
  }
}
```

You can try this out with the following in the interactions pane:

```
> Picture pict1 =
    new Picture(FileChooser.getMediaPath("beach.jpg"));
> Picture pict2 =
    new Picture(FileChooser.getMediaPath("church.jpp"));
> Picture[] pictArray = {pict1, pict2};
> SlideShow show1 = new SlideShow(pictArray);
> show1.show();
```

13.5 Creating Accessors (Getters) and Modifiers (Setters)

So far, we have written constructors and methods in the SlideShow class that can be used to create a SlideShow object with a wait time and an array of pictures. Once a SlideShow object has been created, how can we access the data in an object's fields when we are writing code outside the class definition? In previous examples, we have used this to access the *public* length field of arrays (pictureArray.length). This makes use of **dot notation**:

(*objectRef.fieldName*)

What happens when we try using dot notation to access data in private fields of objects when we are writing code outside the class definition? The following is an example:

```
> System.out.println(show1.waitTime);
IllegalAccessException: Class
koala.dynamicjava.interpreter.EvaluationVisitor can not access a
member of class SlideShow with modifiers "private"
    at sun.reflect.Reflection.ensureMemberAccess(Unknown Source)
    at java.lang.reflect.Field.doSecurityCheck(Unknown Source)
    at java.lang.reflect.Field.getFieldAccessor(Unknown Source)
    at java.lang.reflect.Field.get(Unknown Source)
```

As can be seen in this example, trying to use dot notation to access the private field of an object from outside the class in which it is declared causes a compiler error. Fields that are declared to be private can only be accessed directly inside the same class definition. This means that objects of other classes won't be able to access this data directly using dot notation (*objectRef.fieldName*) in the interactions pane or in other classes.

13.5.1 Creating Accessors (Getters)

In order to let objects of other classes access the information in private fields, we need to create public methods that access the private fields. **Accessors** are public methods that return private field information. By convention, these are declared as:

public *type* get*FieldName*()

402   Chapter 13   Creating Classes

As an example, you could write a method that will return the value of the wait time like this:

```
public int getWaitTime() { return this.waitTime; }
```

Notice that in the `getWaitTime` method we put the code for the method on the same line as the method declaration. This is okay for short methods and is often used for accessor methods. We could also have written it as follows:

```
public int getWaitTime()
{
  return this.waitTime;
}
```

Should we create a method to return the array of pictures? If we return the array, we lose control over it, which means that we can't protect the array from being changed by other objects. A more protective accessor method could be written to return a single picture from the array, given the index where that picture is located in the array. The following code defines a `getPicture()` accessor that returns `null` if the `pictureArray` doesn't reference an array of pictures yet, or if the index isn't valid.

```
public Picture getPicture(int index)
{
  if (pictureArray == null ||
      index < 0 ||
      index > pictureArray.length)
    return null;
  else
    return this.pictureArray[index];
}
```

Computer Science Idea: Protecting Object Data

Objects should protect their data and make sure that it stays in a correct state. One of the ways that objects protect their data is by having private fields and providing public accessors that allow other classes to view the data. But accessors need to be careful that they don't allow objects of other classes to directly modify the data. ■

13.5.2 Creating Modifiers (Setters)

What if we want to change one of the pictures in the slide show? Since the `pictureArray` field is `private`, we can't directly modify it outside of the class definition. If we try to change it directly in the interactions pane of DrJava, we will get an `IllegalAccessException`, as illustrated here:

```
> show1.pictureArray[0] = new
Picture(FileChooser.getMediaPath("shops.jpg"));
IllegalAccessException:
Class koala.dynamicjava.interpreter.EvaluationVisitor can not
access a member of class SlideShow with modifiers "private"
```

```
at sun.reflect.Reflection.ensureMemberAccess(Unknown Source)
at java.lang.reflect.Field.doSecurityCheck(Unknown Source)
at java.lang.reflect.Field.getFieldAccessor(Unknown Source)
at java.lang.reflect.Field.get(Unknown Source)
```

But we might want a way to change a picture in the slide show. We can do this by asking the slide show object to change the picture at an index. The slide show object can refuse to change the picture and should refuse if the user passes null as the reference to the picture. Methods that modify fields are called **modifiers** or **mutators**. The Java convention is to declare a modifier method as follows:

```
public returnType setFieldName(type param1Name,
                               type param2Name, ...)
```

As an example, the setPicture() method shown here will try to replace the picture stored at a passed index to a passed new picture. If the passed picture object is null or the pictureArray is null, it won't try to replace the picture and will return false. Otherwise it will replace the picture and return true. Methods that modify a value can return a boolean to indicate whether the modification was successful or not.

```java
public boolean setPicture(int index, Picture pict)
{
  if (pict == null || this.pictureArray == null)
    return false;
  else
  {
    this.pictureArray[index] = pict;
    return true;
  }
}
```

Another modifier method is setPictureArray(), shown below. The setPicture Array() method can be used to assign an array of pictures to the pictureArray field. For example, if the no-argument constructor or the constructor that just takes the wait time was used to create a SlideShow object, the picture array will be null. We need some way to set it. One way is to pass in the picture array to use. The method only allows this if the picture array is currently null.

```java
public boolean setPictureArray(Picture[] theArray)
{
  if (this.pictureArray != null)
  {
    return false;
  }
  else
  {
    this.pictureArray = theArray;
    return true;
  }
}
```

The above modifier method examples have more than one return statement. Often times, such methods could easily be written with only one return statement as illustrated by this revision to the `setPictureArray()` method:

```java
public boolean setPictureArray(Picture[] theArray)
{
  boolean result = false;

  if (this.pictureArray == null)
  {
    this.pictureArray = theArray;
    result = true;
  }
  return result;
}
```

Which way is better? Both give the same result so the true test is which is easier for another person to understand and change? Beginners often think the first approach is better but the second approach may be easier to change.

Here is a method that will set the wait time. The wait time must be greater than 0.

```java
public boolean setWaitTime(int theTime)
{
  boolean result = false;
  if (theTime >= 0)
  {
    this.waitTime = theTime;
    result = true;
  }
  return result;
}
```

Why only change the wait time if it is greater than or equal to 0? You can't wait a negative number of milliseconds. The methods of a class should make sure that the fields are only set to valid values.

13.6 Creating a `main` Method

Up to now we have created objects and tried out new methods in the interactions pane. However, there is a special method named `main` that you can use to create objects and invoke methods. A `main` method is where execution starts when you click the Run button in DrJava (as well as other Java IDEs). A `main` method *must have* the following method declaration:

`public static void` main(String[] args)

The method must be a `public static` method named `main` and must take an array of `String` objects as a parameter. It doesn't matter if you name the array of strings `args` or some other name. The convention is just to use the name `args`. It must be a `public` method so that it can be called by objects of other classes. It must be static because no objects of the class exist when you start execution of the method. The first thing you usually do in a `main` method is create one or more objects of the class and then invoke a method or methods on the created objects.

Here is a `main` method that you can use to create a slide show:

```
public static void main(String[] args) throws Exception
{
    Picture p1 =
      new Picture(FileChooser.getMediaPath("beach.jpg"));
    Picture p2 =
      new Picture(FileChooser.getMediaPath("church.jpg"));
    Picture[] pictArray = {p1,p2};
    SlideShow show1 = new SlideShow(pictArray);
    System.out.println(show1);
    show1.show();
}
```

Notice that we added `throws Exception` to the end of the standard `main` method declaration statement. This is because the `show()` method can throw an exception, as we explained earlier in Section 13.4.3.

In DrJava you can execute the `main` method of the current class by clicking **Tools** and then **Run Document's Main Method**. It will show output in the interactions pane and in the console pane.

```
> java SlideShow
SlideShow object with a wait time of: 2000 and 2 pictures
```

If you are using the command-line tools from Sun you can invoke a `main` method on a class using:

```
java ClassName
```

As you may have noticed, this is what DrJava does when you ask it to run the document's `main` method.

13.7 Javadoc Comments

To conserve space in this textbook, we have only used comments to highlight the different parts of the `SlideShow` class definition: fields, constructors, and methods. However, we *strongly recommend* that you add Javadoc comments to your class definition. Javadoc is a utility from Sun that allows you to create *HTML* (HyperText Markup Language) documentation from special Javadoc comments in your source code. Comments make it easier to figure out what a class is for and what is happening in it.

You might think that you don't need to comment a class if you are the only one using it, but the point of creating a class is to make reusable pieces. Comments are notes in plain language that will help you *and* others understand and reuse the class. All the classes that are part of the Java language have Javadoc comments in them. The online Java API documentation was created by running the Javadoc utility on all the files that come with Java.

13.7.1 Class Comment

You *should* add a comment just before a class definition to explain the class and to give the author's name. Javadoc comments start with /** and end with */. They can take up several lines. Here is an example of a class comment:

```
/**
 * Class that defines a slide show. A slide show
 * has pictures and a time to wait between showing the
 * pictures
 * @author Barb Ericson
 */
public class SlideShow
```

Notice that a Javadoc comment is just before the class declaration. It tells something about the purpose of the class. It also should tell who the author or authors are. If there are multiple authors you just add another '@author' tag. The '@author' tag is just one of many special tags defined in Javadoc that will pull particular information out of the source code and format it in the HTML documentation.

13.7.2 Method Comments

You should add a comment before each method definition in the class. This comment should describe the purpose of the method, any parameters to that method, and what is returned from that method (if anything). Here is an example of a method comment:

```
/**
 * Method to set a picture at the passed index
 * @param index which one to change
 * @param thePict the picture to use
 * @return true if success else return false
 */
public boolean setPicture(int index, Picture thePict)
```

Notice that it has two @param tags because the method has two parameters. Also notice that it has a @return tag because it returns a value. Here is another method comment:

```
/**
 * Method to get the time to wait
 * between showing pictures
 * @return the time to wait in milliseconds
 */
public int getWaitTime()
```

Notice that this one has no @param tags in it. This is because it doesn't have any parameters. It does have the @return tag in it because it does return a value.

13.7.3 Constructor Comments

You can add Javadoc comments to constructors as well. They look like method comments. Of course you won't need any @return tags since constructors do not return a value.

13.7.4 Generating the Documentation

Once you add Javadoc comments to your class you can generate HTML documentation in DrJava by clicking the **Javadoc** button. This will generate all the HTML documentation for all classes that are in the same directory as all the open files.

Figure 13.16 shows a preview of the HTML documentation for just the current class. It was created by clicking **Tools** and then on **Preview Javadoc for Current Document**. This can be useful to check what the documentation looks like so far. It will also show you where you need to add documentation.

If you aren't using DrJava you can create the HTML documentation using the Javadoc utility that comes with Java. You can open a command prompt and go to the directory with the Java source in it and then type `javadoc *.java` to create the documentation. The `*` in `*.java` is a wildcard character that matches the file name of

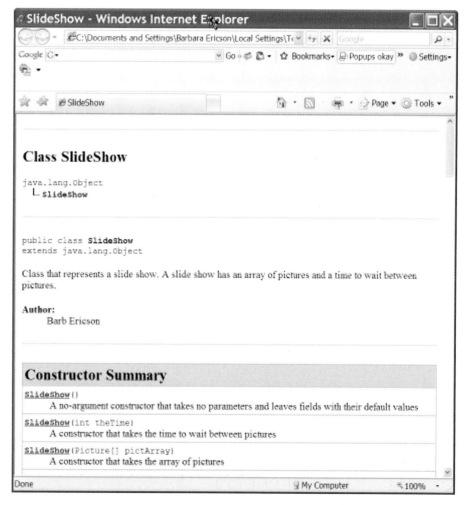

Figure 13.16
Showing the HTML documentation generated from Javadoc comments

any Java file. Using *.java means that documentation will be created for all the source files in the current directory. To create the documentation for just one Java file, use the actual name of the class instead of the *. For example, to create documentation for just the SlideShow class use javadoc SlideShow.java.

13.8   Reusing a Class Via Inheritance

A major reason for writing your programs using classes is that classes provide a way to reuse previously written program code. Reusing methods from class libraries allows professional programmers to implement new software applications faster and with fewer errors. As an example of reusing a class, let's write a class that reuses the Turtle class, first presented in Chapter 4.

Many children have a hard time with the concepts of left and right. Even some adults get these confused. Let's create a new class ConfusedTurtle that will turn right when asked to turn left and will turn left when asked to turn right. How can we do this? We can start by having the ConfusedTurtle class inherit from the Turtle class which inherits from SimpleTurtle. See Figure 13.17 for the UML class diagram that shows this inheritance.

In Section 13.2.1 we saw that you can specify the parent class when you declare a class using the extends keyword. If you don't specify the parent class the parent class will be Object. We don't want the parent class to be Object, so we create a class ConfusedTurtle that extends the Turtle class instead:

```
public class ConfusedTurtle extends Turtle
{
}
```

Now, Turtle is the parent class and ConfusedTurtle is the child class. So, the ConfusedTurtle class inherits all the object fields and methods from the class

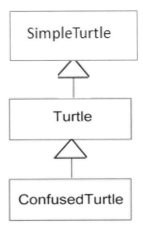

Figure 13.17
UML class diagram for ConfusedTurtle

Turtle, which inherits all the object fields and methods from the grandparent class, SimpleTurtle. If you review the SimpleTurtle class, you will find that it defines several methods, including turnLeft() and turnRight(). We want to override the method turnLeft() and have it turn right instead and then override the method turnRight() and have it turn left instead.

How can we override the turnLeft() method? We could just have it call the method turnRight() but we plan to override this method as well. What we really want to do is call the method in the parent class Turtle. Java gives us a way to do this using the keyword super. Usually the Java Virtual Machine (JVM) will start looking for a method in the class that created the current object. But if we use the keyword super to invoke a method, we will start looking for the method in the *parent* class of the current class. The following code defines turnLeft() and turnRight() for the ConfusedTurtle class by calling the opposite method of the parent (or grandparent) class.

```java
public class ConfusedTurtle extends Turtle
{
  /**
   * Method to turn right (but a confused
   * turtle will actually turn left)
   */
  public void turnRight()
  {
    super.turnLeft();
  }
}
  /**
   * Method to turn left (but a confused
   * turtle will actually turn right)
   */
  public void turnLeft()
  {
    super.turnRight();
  }
}
```

If we try to compile this we will get an error. The problem is that we haven't created any constructors yet. The compiler will try to add the no-argument constructor for us. But since ConfusedTurtle inherits from Turtle it will also add a call to super() which is a call to the parent's no-argument constructor. It does this to allow initialization of any private inherited fields. But, the Turtle class doesn't have a no-argument constructor either. This is because we always passed a World object (the 2D world the turtles move around in) when we created a new Turtle object (Section 4.2.2).

If we check the Turtle class, however, we don't see a constructor that takes a World object. But there is a constructor that takes a ModelDisplay object. This is because the World class constructor implements the ModelDisplay interface. (In other words, a World object can be used as a ModelDisplay object.) So, what we need to do is write a constructor for the ConfusedTurtle class that has a ModelDisplay object parameter. Then, we can call this constructor and pass in a World object.

The following code is the `ConfusedTurtle` class with the addition of a constructor that takes a `ModelDisplay` object. The first statement in the constructor is a call to the parent constructor using `super(modelDisplayObj)`. Note that if you are calling a superclass (parent) constructor, it *must* be the first line of code in the constructor. If the compiler doesn't find a call to the parent constructor as the first line of code in a child constructor, it will add a call to the parent's no-argument constructor.

```java
public class ConfusedTurtle extends Turtle
{
  /////////////// constructors ////////////////////////
  /**
   * A constructor that takes a ModelDisplay object
   * @param modelDisplayObj the thing that does the display
   */
  public ConfusedTurtle(ModelDisplay modelDisplayObj)
  {
    // use parent constructor
    super(modelDisplayObj);
  }
  /////////////// methods ////////////////////////
  /**
   * Method to turn right (but a confused
   * turtle will actually turn left)
   */
  public void turnRight()
  {
    super.turnLeft();
  }
  /**
   * Method to turn left (but a confused
   * turtle will actually turn right)
   */
  public void turnLeft()
  {
    super.turnRight();
  }
}
```

We'll name our new confused turtle Fred. To see how he works we can do the following in the interactions pane or in a main method:

```java
> World world = new World();
> ConfusedTurtle fred = new ConfusedTurtle(world);
> fred.forward();
> fred.turnLeft();
> fred.forward();
> fred.turnRight();
> fred.forward();
```

Notice that the `ConfusedTurtle` object still knows how to go forward. The only difference between it and a `Turtle` object is what happens when it is asked to turn left or right, as shown in Figure 13.18.

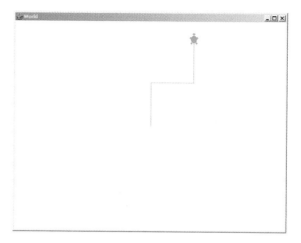

Figure 13.18
Result of commands to a confused turtle

What happens if we also override the `turn` method in the `ConfusedTurtle` class to actually turn (360 - the passed degrees)?

```
/**
 * Method to turn by the passed degrees
 * (a confused turtle will turn by 360- the
 * passed degrees)
 */
 public void turn(int degrees)
 {
   super.turn(360-degrees);
 }
```

We can try this out in the interactions pane with the following:

```
> World world = new World();
> ConfusedTurtle fred = new ConfusedTurtle(world);
> fred.turn(90);
> fred.forward();
> fred.turnLeft();
> fred.forward();
> fred.turnRight();
> fred.forward();
```

If we try this out in the interactions pane we will see that the `turn` method is doing what we expected but the `turnLeft()` and `turnRight()` methods are not, as Figure 13.19 illustrates. What happened? The overriding of `turnLeft()` and `turnRight()` methods was working fine until we did an override on `turn()`. This gives us a hint that the problem must have something to do with how `turnLeft()` and `turnRight()` perform a turn operation.

We have to remember that the Java Virtual Machine will *always* start looking for a method in the class that created the current object (unless we use `super.method()`).

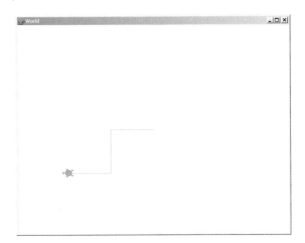

Figure 13.19
Result of overriding the turn method

When we call `turnLeft()` on a `ConfusedTurtle` object it will invoke the method in the `ConfusedTurtle` class. Figure 13.20 shows this diagrammatically. In that method we call `super.turnRight()`. This will start looking for the `turnRight()` method in the `Turtle` class but not find such a method. Then it will look in the parent class of `Turtle`, which is `SimpleTurtle`. As can be seen in Figure 13.20, the `turnRight()` method in `SimpleTurtle` contains the statement:

`this.turn(90);`

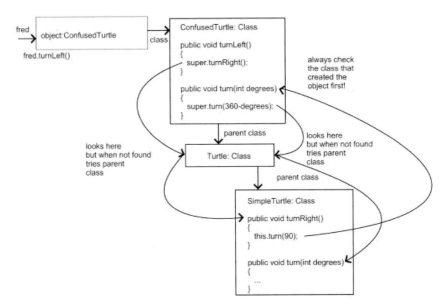

Figure 13.20
Diagram of the methods executed by `fred.turnLeft()`

Once again, the JVM starts looking for the turn method in the class that created the current object which was the ConfusedTurtle class (Figure 13.20). The turn(int degrees) method in the ConfusedTurtle class contains the line super.turn(360-degrees);. Now, the JVM starts looking for the turn method in the Turtle class but does not find it. It will then look in the parent class of the Turtle class and it finds it in SimpleTurtle. This will change the heading and redisplay the turtle, but not in the way we had expected.

Clearly, we have to revise the turnLeft() and turnRight() methods in the ConfusedTurtle class. To fix this problem we need to change the turnRight() method in the ConfusedTurtle class to call super.turn(-90) to make it turn left. We will also change the turnLeft() method in the ConfusedTurtle class to call super.turn(90) to make it turn right.

```java
/**
 * Class for a confused turtle. A confused turtle is like
 * a turtle but it turns right when asked to turn left and left
 * when asked to turn right.
 * @author Barb Ericson
 */
public class ConfusedTurtle extends Turtle
/////////////// constructors ///////////////////////////
  /**
   * A constructor that takes a ModelDisplay object
   * @param modelDisplayObj the thing that does the display
   */
  public ConfusedTurtle(ModelDisplay modelDisplayObj)
  {
    // use parent constructor
    super(modelDisplayObj);
  }
/////////////// methods ///////////////////////////////
  /**
   * Method to turn right (but a confused
   * turtle will actually turn left)
   */
  public void turnRight()
  {
    // turn left instead
    super.turn(-90);
  }
  /**
   * Method to turn left (but a confused
   * turtle will actually turn right)
   */
  public void turnLeft()
  {
    // turn right instead
    super.turn(90);
  }
```

```
/**
 * Method to turn by the passed degrees
 * (a confused turtle will turn by 360- the
 * passed degrees)
 */
public void turn(int degrees)
{
  super.turn(360-degrees);
}
}
```

Now if we try this out it should work correctly. The following code

```
> World world = new World();
> ConfusedTurtle fred = new ConfusedTurtle(world);
> fred.turn(90);
> fred.forward();
> fred.turnLeft();
> fred.forward();
> fred.turnRight();
> fred.forward();
```

should produce the output shown in Figure 13.21.

13.8.1 Dynamic (Runtime) Binding

As illustrated in the examples in this chapter, every object in Java keeps a reference to the class that created it. You can say that an object *knows what type it is*. When a method is invoked on an object, the Java Virtual Machine will always start looking for it in the class that created the object, unless you use `super.method()`, which will start looking for the method in the parent class of the class that contains the currently executing code.

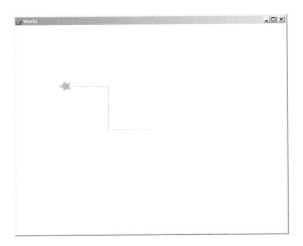

Figure 13.21
Result of fixing the methods `turnLeft()` and `turnRight()`

A class is considered to be a data type and an object created by that class is considered to be an object of that type. When you declare a variable, you can assign an object to it that is of the declared type, *or any child of the declared type*. So we can declare a variable of type `Turtle` and use it to reference an object of type `ConfusedTurtle`. When we invoke a method on an object variable, it will first look for that method in the class that created the object that the variable refers to. If we invoke the method `turnLeft()` on a variable that was declared to be of type `Turtle`, but was created by the class `ConfusedTurtle` the method in `ConfusedTurtle` will be executed. This is due to *dynamic* or *runtime* binding. The method that is executed depends on the type of the object when the program is running (sometimes called the **actual type**), not on the declared type of the variable. Objects always know what type they really are!

When we execute the following in the interactions pane, we will get the same result as before (Figure 13.21).

```
> World world = new World();
> Turtle fred = new ConfusedTurtle(world);
> fred.turn(90);
> fred.forward();
> fred.turnLeft();
> fred.forward();
> fred.turnRight();
> fred.forward();
```

13.9 Using Media Computation with Alice

Using the `SlideShow` class as a model, you could create a `ComicStrip` class that uses pictures captured from an Alice animation. In Java, you can create a `ComicStrip` class that defines fields, constructors, accessor and modifier methods. An object of the `ComicStrip` class will represent a comic strip such as the one shown in Figure 13.22. A comic strip object should have fields that represent a title, an author, and an array of four pictures. Methods can be written to display a title bar and the comic strip. A main class can be written to create a `ComicStrip` object and initialize its fields and then display the comic strip. In the title bar, the title should be displayed at the top left and the author should be displayed at the top right. Under the title bar, the pictures should be displayed in order (from index 0 to 3).

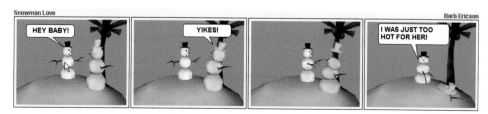

Figure 13.22
A comic strip created with pictures from Alice

13.10   Concepts Summary

In this chapter we have created classes with fields, constructors, and methods. We have shown how to create, initialize, and access an array. We have shown how to override an inherited method. We have shown how to use a debugger. We have shown how to use Javadoc comments to document a class. We explained how dynamic binding results in methods being invoked based on the class that created the current object.

13.10.1 Declaring a Class

To declare a class you use:

```
public class SlideShow
{
  // all fields, constructors, and methods
}
```

This will declare the class SlideShow, which will be a child of the class Object. You could have also declared this as:

```
public class SlideShow extends Object
{
  // all fields, constructors, and methods
}
```

The alternative code uses the extends keyword to explicitly say that this class inherits from the Object class. If no extends keyword is used, the class will automatically inherit from the class Object.

13.10.2 Fields

Fields are used to hold the object's data (properties). A field declaration looks very much like a local variable declaration except that it is inside the class definition and it should be preceded by the keyword private.

```
public class SlideShow
{
  ///////////// fields //////////////
  private int waitTime = 2000; // wait 2 seconds
  private Picture[] pictureArray;
}
```

Objects *should* protect their data from direct use by objects of other classes by making their data private. If not given an initial value, fields are automatically initialized to a default value (numbers are set to 0, Boolean values to false, and objects to null).

13.10.3 Constructors

To declare a constructor you will usually use the keyword public followed by the class name and then a parameter list.

```
public SlideShow()
```

The above constructor doesn't have parameters. This is called a no-argument constructor. In a no-argument constructor, the fields are initialized to default values; numbers are initialized to 0, object references to null, and boolean fields to false. A no-argument constructor will automatically be added by the compiler, if you don't have any constructors declared in your class. But if you declare any constructors, the no-argument constructor won't be automatically added. In addition, if you don't have a call to a superclass constructor in your constructor, one will be added that calls the superclass no-argument constructor.

A constructor is always called when a new object is created. It is used to initialize the fields in the new object. You can have several constructors as long as the parameter lists are different. In other words, you can overload constructors just as you can overload methods.

Here is a constructor that takes a wait time for the new SlideShow object:

```
public SlideShow(int theTime)
{
  this.waitTime = theTime;
}
```

13.10.4 Arrays

To create an array use the new keyword followed by a type and then the size in square brackets:

```
Picture[] pictArray = new Picture[3];
```

You can create arrays of primitive types too:

```
double[] gradeArray = new double[5];
```

You can also initialize the contents of the array when you create it by putting values inside of an open and close curly brace and separating the values with commas:

```
Picture[] pictArray = {pict1, pict2, pict3};
```

13.10.5 Using a Debugger

Most IDEs have debuggers. A debugger is a tool that helps you see exactly what is happening in a program. The main thing you do with a debugger is set breakpoints, which are places to stop the execution so you can see what is happening.

Once you have stopped at a breakpoint you can examine the values of variables and fields. You can use Step Over, which executes the current line of code and then stops again. You can use Step Into, which will go into any method call on the current line and then stop. You can use Step Out to let a current method finish executing and stop again in the method that called the current method. You can use Resume which will continue executing until another breakpoint or until execution of the program finishes.

13.10.6 Javadoc Comments

You *should* document your code to make it more reusable both by yourself and others. You should include at least a comment before the class definition and before each method.

A class comment should explain the purpose of the class and identify the author. Here is an example of a class comment:

```
/**
 * Class that defines a slide show. A slide show
 * has pictures and a time to wait between showing the
 * pictures
 * @author Barb Ericson
 */
public class SlideShow
```

A method comment should describe the purpose of the method. It can list any pre-conditions that should be true before the method is called and any post-conditions that will be true when the method has finished. It should also explain any parameters to the method and what is returned (if anything) from the method. Here is an example of a method comment:

```
/**
 * Method to set a picture at the passed index
 * @param index which one to change
 * @param thePict the picture to use
 * @return true if success else return false
 */
public boolean setPicture(int index, Picture thePict)
```

Exercises

1. What is the answer to each of the following?

    - What is a field?
    - What is a constructor?
    - What does override mean?
    - How do you specify the parent class of the class you are declaring?
    - If you don't specify a parent class is there still a parent class?
    - How do you overload a constructor?
    - What is the difference between override and overload?
    - How do you create an array?

2. What is the answer to each of the following?

    - How do you access elements of an array?
    - How do you initialize the elements of an array?
    - What is a Javadoc comment?
    - Can objects of a different class (in a different file) directly access private fields?

- Can objects of a different class (in a different file) directly access public fields?
- What is an accessor method?
- What is a modifier method?
- What does encapsulate mean?
- What does super.*method*() do?
- What does super() do?

3. Which of these is the correct class definition for a Teacher class?
   - public CLASS Teacher
   - public class Teacher
   - public class TEACHER
   - public class Teacher extends Object, Person

4. Which of these correctly defines a field in a class?
   - private INT count;
   - public INT count;
   - private int count = "HI";
   - private int count;

5. Which of these correctly defines a constructor in the class Student?
   - public STUDENT ()
   - PUBLIC student()
   - public void Student()
   - public Student()

6. What other methods do all classes inherit from the Object class?

7. Create a class ComicStrip and create a constructor that takes an array of Picture objects and displays them from left to right like a comic strip in a newspaper. You can use the scale method to scale the pictures to fit. You can create a new picture to use to display the cartoon on.

8. Edit the class Student from your bookClasses directory. Allow each student to also have a picture. Add the picture field, add a getter to get the picture for a student, and also add a setter to set the picture for a student. Add a show method that displays the picture for the student (if one exists).

9. What class does Turtle inherit from (in your bookClasses directory)? What class does Picture inherit from? What class does FileChooser inherit from? What class does World inherit from?

10. What methods did the class Turtle inherit from its parent class?

11. What methods did the class Picture inherit from its parent class?

12. How many constructors does the Turtle class have? How are they different?

13. How many constructors does the `Picture` class have? How are they different?

14. Add method comments for all the methods in the `SlideShow` class.

15. Add a `title` field to the `SlideShow` class and create constructors that take a title as well. Also create accessors and modifier methods for the title field. Modify the `show` method to show the title first before showing the first picture.

16. Create a class `Car` which has the manufacturer, model, year, and number of doors. An example car has a manufacturer of Toyota, a model of Camry, a year of 2009, and a number of doors of 4. Be sure to code all accessor and modifier methods.

17. Create a class `Book` which has a title, an author, an ISBN number, a price, and the year it was published. Be sure to code all accessor and modifier methods. You can use the information for this book as a test case.

18. Write the definition for a class `Address` which has line1, line2, city, state, and zip code. Be sure to code all accessor and modifier methods. Create an `Address` object with your address information in it.

19. Write the definition for a class `CreditCard` which has a number, an expiration date, and a name. Be sure to code all accessor and modifier methods.

20. Write a method in the `Turtle` class that takes an array of `Picture` objects. Use the `drop(Picture p)` method in `Turtle` to drop pictures at different locations in a circle.

CHAPTER 14
Creating and Modifying Text

Goals of this chapter:

- To manipulate strings.
- To read and write files.
- To handle exceptions.
- To use a dynamic array: `ArrayList`.
- To explain interfaces.
- To create a class method.
- To explain generics.
- To write programs that manipulate programs, leading to powerful ideas like interpreters and compilers.

Introduction

In this chapter, we will focus on text. Why text? One reason is the ever-present nature of the World Wide Web, which has leapt out of our desktop computer and into our lives. The World Wide Web is primarily text. Visit any Web page, then go to the menu of your Web browser and choose "View the source." What you will see is text. Every Web page is actually text. That text references pictures, sounds, and animations that appear when you view the page, but the page itself is defined as text. The words in that text use a notation called **HyperText Markup Language (HTML)**.

You first worked with text in Alice, where the "say" method lets you specify text as strings in text bubbles (similar to a comic strip text bubble). In Alice, you can't write programs to manipulate strings because Alice executes in a self-contained world that can't interact with data in files, or data from the Internet. Java, however, contains classes that make it easy to work with data in files and data on the Internet. Java has a class `String` that represents sequences of characters (text) and contains many methods for manipulating text. We will write programs that generate a form letter, work with delimited strings, read from files, write to files, read data from the Internet, generate random sentences, and modify a program. We will also map sound values to text and to pictures.

14.1 Text as Unimedia

Nicholas Negroponte, founder of the MIT Media Lab, said that what makes computer-based multimedia possible is the fact that the computer is actually **unimedia**. The computer really only understands one thing: zeros and ones. We can use the computer for multimedia because any medium can be encoded in these zeros and ones.

But he might as well have been talking about *text* as the unimedia. We can encode any medium as text, and what's even better than the zeros and ones, we can *read* the text much more easily than deciphering the zeros and ones! Later in this chapter, we map sounds to text and then back to sounds. But once we're in text, we don't have to go back to the original medium: We can map sounds to text and then to pictures, and thus create *visualizations* of sounds.

14.2 Strings: Character Sequences

Text is typically manipulated as a **string**. In Java, a string is a sequence of characters. Double quote marks are used to indicate the start and end of a string. For example, a string could be:

```
"Hello"
```

But, what if you want to have a string that has double quote marks within the string? If you want the string to *include* a double quote, you must use a backslash '\' in front of each included quote mark. The backslash is a special character that signals to Java that the character following it is to be treated differently than it otherwise would. For example, in the following `println` statement we want the double quote marks enclosing the word "Hi." to be treated as actual quote marks, not markers for the beginning and ending of a Java string. So, we put the backslash before the quote marks when we want them to be treated as quote marks that are part of the string rather than markers for the beginning and end of the string.

```
> System.out.println("He said, \"Hi.\"");
He said, "Hi."
```

Single quote marks are different. You can include single quote marks in strings without having to use the backslash.

```
> System.out.println("He won't go out!");
He won't go out!
```

Strings in Java are *not* just arrays of characters as they are in some other languages, like C. In Java, a String is an object of the `String` class. The String class has a field that is an array of characters and it also has many defined methods that can be used to access the string. A string array contains a sequence of characters. We can think about the characters of the string as being in boxes, each with its own index number. A particularly helpful accessor method is `charAt`. You can get a character from a string using the method `charAt(index)`.

```
> String hello = "Hello";
> System.out.println(hello.charAt(0));
H
> System.out.println(hello.charAt(4));
o
```

You can use a for loop to walk through all the characters of a string.

```
> String test = "Hello";
> for (int i = 0; i < test.length(); i++)
    System.out.println(test.charAt(i));
H
e
l
l
o
```

Notice that you *do* need the parentheses after length(). It is a method of the String class, *not* a public field as it is for Java arrays.

Strings are immutable. **Immutable** means that strings do not change. If you ask for a string to be converted to all uppercase letters you will get back a new string. Any method that modifies a string returns a new string.

```
> String test = "this is a test";
> String result = test.toUpperCase();
> System.out.println(test);
this is a test
> System.out.println(result);
THIS IS A TEST
```

What does it mean to compare strings? If we use stringRef1 == stringRef2 we are checking if the two string references refer to the same object in memory. Often what we really want to know is if the two strings contain the same characters. We can check this using the equals method.

```
> String str1 = new String("This is a test");
> String str2 = new String("This is a test");
> System.out.println(str1 == str2);
false
> System.out.println(str1.equals(str2));
true
```

14.2.1 Unicode

Java uses **Unicode** to represent each character. Unicode is an encoding for characters where two bytes are used for each character. Two bytes gives us 65,536 possible combinations. You can look up the codes at http://www.unicode.org/charts. Having that many possible combinations allows us to go beyond a simple Latin alphabet, numbers, and punctuation. We can represent Hiragana, Katakana, and other *glyph* (graphical depictions of characters) systems.

What this should tell you is that there are many more possible characters than can be typed at a standard keyboard. Not only are there special symbols, but there are invisible characters like tabs and backspace. We specify these in Java strings (and in many other languages, such as C) using **backslash escape sequences.** Backslash escape sequences consist of the backslash '\' followed by a character.

- \" allows for a double quote inside of a string.
- \t is the same as typing the tab key.
- \b is the same as typing the backspace key (which is not a particularly useful character to put in a string, but you can). When you print \b, it shows up as a box on most systems—it's not actually printable.
- \n is the same as typing the enter/return key. It is often called the *new-line* character.
- \uXXXX where XXXX is a code made up of 0-9 and A-F (known as a *hexadecimal* number) and prints the Unicode character represented by that hexadecimal code.

Here are some strings with backslash escapes in them. Try out a string with a backspace in it for yourself.

```
> System.out.println("A string with a tab \t in it");
A string with a tab     in it
> System.out.println("A string with a newline character \n in it");
A string with a newline character
in it
```

14.2.2 String Methods

The String class has many methods for working with String objects. These methods are useful for processing text. Some of the most commonly used String methods are:

- charAt(int position) returns the character at the given position in the string. The first character is at position 0, just as the first element of an array is at index 0.

```
> String str1 = "Bye";
> System.out.println(str1.charAt(0));
B
```

- compareTo(Object o) returns a negative number if this object is less than the passed object, 0 if this object is equal (has the same characters) to the passed object, and a positive number if this object is greater than the passed object.

```
> String str1 = "Bye";
> String str2 = "Hi";
> String str3 = new String("Bye");
> System.out.println(str1.compareTo(str2));
-6
> System.out.println(str2.compareTo(str1));
6
> System.out.println(str1.compareTo(str3));
0
```

- equals(String s) returns true if the string s has the same characters in the same sequence as the current string, otherwise it returns false. The equals method is case sensitive. For example, "School" does not equal "school".

- length() returns the number of characters in the string.

- substring(int n, int m) returns a new string which is a *substring* of the string starting at the *n*th character and preceding up to *but not including* the *m*th character. A substring includes part of the original string.

  ```
  > String str2 = "Do you go to school?";
  > String str3 = str2.substring(3,6);
  > System.out.println(str3);
  you
  ```

- substring(int n) returns a new string which is a substring of the string starting at the *n*th character and including the rest of the characters in the string.

  ```
  > str3 = str2.substring(6);
  > System.out.println(str3);
  go to school?
  ```

- startsWith(String prefix) returns true if the string starts with the given prefix, else it will return false.

  ```
  > String letter = "Mr. Guzdial requests the ";
  > letter = letter + "pleasure of your company ...";
  > System.out.println(letter.startsWith("Mr."));
  true
  > System.out.println(letter.startsWith("Mrs."));
  false
  ```

- endsWith(String suffix) returns true if the string ends with the given suffix, else it will return false.

  ```
  > String filename="barbara.jpg";
  > if (filename.endsWith(".jpg"))
      System.out.println("it is a picture");
  it is a picture
  ```

- indexOf(String str) returns the first index of the passed str, if it is found. If str isn't in the current string, it will return –1.

  ```
  > System.out.println(letter);
  Mr. Guzdial requests the pleasure of your company ...
  > System.out.println(letter.indexOf("Guzdial"));
  4
  > System.out.println(letter.indexOf("Mark"));
  -1
  ```

- indexOf(String str, int fromIndex) returns the first index of the passed str at or after the passed fromIndex, if it is found. If str isn't in the current string at or after the fromIndex, it will return –1.

  ```
  > String t = "That which is, is. That which is not, is not.";
  > System.out.println(t.indexOf("is",14));
  15
  ```

- `lastIndexOf(String str)` returns the last index of the passed `str`, if it is found. If `str` isn't in the current string, it will return –1.

  ```
  > String s = "It is a nice day, isn't it?";
  > System.out.println(s.lastIndexOf("it"));
  24
  ```

- `lastIndexOf(String str, int index)` returns the last index of the passed `str` found looking backward starting at `index`. If `str` isn't in the current string before the given `index`, it will return –1.

  ```
  > String s = "It is a nice day, isn't it?";
  > System.out.println(s.lastIndexOf("is",17));
  3
  ```

- `toUpperCase()` returns a new string with all the characters in uppercase.

  ```
  > System.out.println("Hello".toUpperCase());
  HELLO
  ```

- `toLowerCase()` returns a new string with all the characters in lowercase.

  ```
  > System.out.println("Hello".toLowerCase());
  hello
  ```

- `replace(String oldStr, String newStr)` returns a new string with the characters in the `oldStr` replaced with the characters in the `newStr` for all occurrences of the `oldStr`. This is new in Java 1.5.

  ```
  > System.out.println(letter);
  Mr. Guzdial requests the pleasure of your company ...
  > System.out.println(letter.replace("a","!"));
  Mr. Guzdial requests the pleasure of your company ...
  ```

- `replaceAll(String regex, Sting newStr)` will return a new string with all the matching substrings specified by the regular expression (`regex`) replaced with the characters in `newStr`. A **regular expression** can be just a string of characters, or it can also use special characters (such as * or \) to indicate that it will match any character, any digit, only uppercase characters, and so on. If you use just a string of characters, the `replaceAll` method works the same as the `replace` method.

  ```
  > System.out.println(letter);
  Mr. Guzdial requests the pleasure of your company ...
  > System.out.println(letter.replaceAll("a","!"));
  Mr. Guzdial requests the pleasure of your company ...
  ```

  To replace all digits (0–9) with a space, do:

  ```
  > String test = "This9 is a test7";
  > System.out.println(test.replaceAll("\\d"," "));
  This is a test
  ```

  To remove all non-digits, do:

```
> String input = "7a8c";
> System.out.println(input.replaceAll("\\D"," "));
78
```

In these two replace examples, \\d is a regular expression representing a digit and \\D is a regular expression representing a non-digit character.

- replaceFirst(String regex, Sting newStr) will return a new string with the first substring that matches the regular expression specified by regex replaced with the characters in newStr.

```
> System.out.println(letter);
Mr. Guzdial requests the pleasure of your company ...
> System.out.println(letter.replaceFirst("a","!"));
Mr. Guzdi!l requests the pleasure of your company ...
```

- trim() will return a new string with all white space (spaces and tabs) removed from the beginning and end of the string.

```
> String strWithSpaces = "   Janet Hund   ";
> System.out.println(strWithSpaces.trim());
Janet Hund
```

The String class methods can often be **cascaded**—one modifying the result of another, as shown in this example:

```
> String test ="This is a test of Something."
> System.out.println(test.substring(5).toUpperCase());
IS A TEST OF SOMETHING.
```

- split(String regex) will return an array of String objects. It will split the current string into many strings by breaking it wherever it matches the regular expression specified in regex.

```
> System.out.println(letter);
Mr. Guzdial requests the pleasure of your company
> String[] strArray = letter.split(" ");
> for (int i = 0; i < strArray.length; i++)
    System.out.println(strArray[i]);
Mr.
Guzdial
requests
the
pleasure
of
your
company
```

14.2.3 Processing Delimited Strings Using Split

Sometimes you get data for an object as a **delimited string**. A delimited string is a string with special characters (delimiters) that separate the string into different parts. As an example, there is a class in the bookClasses directory, Student.java, that defines a student object as having a name and an array of grades. You could use student objects for creating a gradebook application. What is needed is a quick and easy way to input the data for the student objects. If we read student data from a text file, the data may be represented in the file as a delimited string. In the strings below, the name is separated from the grades by ':', and the grades are separated from each other with a comma (',').

```
Jane Dorda        :88, 92, 95, 87, 93, 85
Mike Koziatek     :75, 92, 83, 81, 91, 87
Sharquita Edwards :91, 93, 95, 92, 94, 99
```

Program 14.1 defines a constructor for the Student class. This constructor takes a delimited string, the delimiter character that separates the name from the grades, and the delimiter character that separates the grades. It uses the delimiter characters to help **parse** (break up into parts) the delimited string and uses these parts to fill in the fields in a Student object. We use the split method of the String class to split the string into the name and grades, and then split again to split the grades up into an array of strings. We need to convert the grades that are in the array of strings into an array of doubles so that we can later do some mathematical computation on the grades, such as compute the average grade. To convert a string to a double, we use the method parseDouble(String doubleStr), which is a class (static) method defined in Java's Double class. Because it is a class method, it can be invoked on the class like this:

    Double.parseDouble("30.23")

Making It Work Tip: Converting Strings to Numbers

You often need to convert something from a string to a number. Remember that these are represented differently in the computer. Each of the wrapper classes (Integer, Float, Double, etc.) has a class (static) method to do this. A static (class) method can be called without having to create an object. For example, to convert a string to an integer, you can use Integer.parseInt(intStr). One important thing to remember is that each of these conversion methods can result in a runtime exception (error) if the passed string doesn't contain a valid number. ∎

Program 14.1: Constructor that Takes a Delimited String

```
/**
 * Constructor that takes a delimited string, the
 * name delimiter, and the grade delimiter.  It fills
 * in the fields from the delimited string.
 * @param delimString student information as a
 * delimited string
 * @param nameDelim what delimits the name field
 * from the grades
 * @param gradeDelim what delimits the grades
 */
public Student(String delimString,
               String nameDelim,
               String gradeDelim)
```

```
{
  // split string based on name delimiter
  String[] splitArray = delimString.split(nameDelim);
  this.name = splitArray[0].trim();

  // get the grade string and break it and convert to double
  String grades = splitArray[1];
  String[] gradeStrArray = null;
  if (grades != null)
  {
    gradeStrArray = grades.split(gradeDelim);
    this.gradeArray = new double[gradeStrArray.length];
    for (int i = 0; i < gradeStrArray.length; i++)
      this.gradeArray[i] =
        Double.parseDouble(gradeStrArray[i]);
  }
}
```

You can try this out using the following main method:

```
public static void main (String[] args)
{
  // test the constructor that takes a delimited string
  Student student =
    new Student("Susan Ericson:50,60,70,80,90,100",":",",");
  System.out.println(student);
}
```

Compile and run Student to test the new constructor.

```
> java Student
Student object named: Susan Ericson Average: 75.0
```

14.2.4 Strings Don't Have a Font

Strings don't have a *font* (characteristic look of the letters) or *style* (boldface, italics, underline, and other effects applied to a string) associated with them. Font and style information is added to strings in word-processors and other programs. Typically, these are encoded as **style runs**. A style run is a separate representation of the font and style information with indices into the string for where the changes should take place. For example, The **old** *brown* fox runs might be encoded as [[bold 0 6] [italics 8 12]]. When font and style information is added to a string, we say the string is **formatted.**

Most software that manages formatted text will encode strings with style runs as an *object*. Objects have data associated with them, perhaps in several parts (like strings and style runs). Objects know how to act upon their data, using *methods* that may be known only to objects of that type. If the same method name is known to multiple objects, it probably does the same thing, but maybe not in the same way.

14.3   Files: Places To Put Your Strings And Other Stuff

Files are large, named collections of bytes on your hard disk. Files typically have a **base name** and a **file suffix**. The file `barbara.jpg` has a base name of "barbara" and a file suffix of "jpg" that tells you the file is a JPEG picture.

Files are clustered into **directories** (sometimes called **folders**). Directories can contain files as well as other directories. There is a base directory on your computer that is referred to as the **root directory**. On a computer using the Windows operating system, the base directory will be something like `C:`. On an Apple computer it is usually `\User`. A complete description of what directories to visit to get to a particular file from the base directory is called a **path**. We have been using a path to select files for pictures.

```
> String filename = FileChooser.pickAFile();
> System.out.println(filename);
C:\intro-prog-java\mediasources\640x480.jpg
```

The path that is printed tells us how to go from the root directory to the file `640x480.jpg` in the `mediasources` directory. We start at `C:`, choose the directory `intro-prog-java`, then the directory `mediasources`.

We can represent the directory structure, shown in Figure 14.1, in a diagram known as a **directory tree**. We call `C:` the *root* of the tree. The tree has **branches** where there are sub-directories. Any directory can contain more directories (branches) or files, which are referred to as **leaves**. Except for the root, each **node** of the tree (branch or leaf) has a single *parent* branch node, though a parent can have multiple *child* branches and leaves.

We need to know about directories and files if we're going to manipulate files. If you're dealing with a big Web site, you are going to be working with a lot of files. If you are going to be dealing with video, you will have about 30 files (individual frames) for each second of video. You don't really want to write a line of code to open each frame! You want to write programs that will "walk" the directory tree structure to process Web or video files.

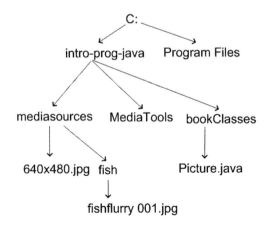

Figure 14.1
Diagram of a directory tree

14.3.1 Reading from Files

To read from a file we need a *class* that knows how to read from a file. In Java, the input and output classes are in the package `java.io`. A class in the java.io package that knows how to read from a character-based file is: `FileReader`. The class `FileReader` has a constructor that takes a file name as a string (an object of the `String` class).

When you read from a file you are moving data from secondary storage (disk) into memory. Reading from secondary storage is much slower than reading from memory. So it is better to read a block of data from the disk into memory, and then read from memory as you need the data, than to read a line at a time from the disk. This is called **buffering** the data. We will use a class to do this for us: `BufferedReader`. The class `BufferedReader` has a constructor which will take a `FileReader` object as a parameter.

Whenever we are working with files, things can go wrong. The file that we are trying to read from may not exist. The disk could go bad and stop working as we are reading from it. How do we deal with these problems? Java *requires* that the programmer write code to handle some exceptions (exceptional events) that can occur when a program is running. We first saw this when we needed to handle a `Thread.sleep` exception in Chapter 13. Now, we need to look at how to handle the kinds of exceptional events that occur when trying to read data from a file.

14.3.2 Handling Exceptions

In order to handle file read exceptions, you must have a deeper understanding of what happens in the computer when methods are invoked at runtime. As you already know, program execution begins in the `main` method of a class. The `main` method typically creates an object or objects and then calls at least one method. When it calls that other method, the `main` method probably isn't finished—the computer has to *remember* where it was in the `main` method so that it can come back to the exact same spot. A method that is called from the `main` method may call other methods—again, from somewhere in the middle of the method, so the computer has to keep track of where it was in those other methods, too. Each time a new method is called, a reminder of where the *calling* method stopped is added to the top of the *call stack* shown in Figure 14.2. A call stack is like a stack of cups. You can add to the top of the stack and remove from the top of the stack.

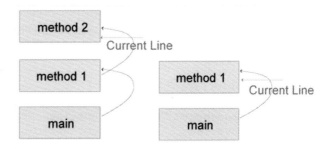

Figure 14.2
Showing a call stack before a method returns (left) and after (right)

The call stack keeps track of all the method calls between the original call to `main` and the currently executing method. When a method is done executing, it is removed from the top of the call stack, and execution continues from where the calling method paused. So a call stack is like a trail of bread crumbs, in that it shows how you got to the method that is currently executing.

To illustrate what happens to the call stack when an exception occurs, let's use the `getAverage` method in the Student class. The `getAverage` method computes and returns the grade average for the current student object. But, it first checks that the array of grades isn't null and has a length greater than 0. It does this to avoid a null pointer exception if there isn't an array of grades yet, or an ArithmeticException that would occur if you try to divide by zero.

```java
public double getAverage()
{
  double average = 0.0;
  if (this.gradeArray != null && this.gradeArray.length > 0)
  {
    double sum = 0.0;
    for (int i = 0; i < this.gradeArray.length; i++)
    {
      sum = sum + this.gradeArray[i];
    }
    average = sum / this.gradeArray.length;
  }
  return average;
}
```

If we were to change the `getAverage` method in the `Student` class to no longer check whether the `gradeArray` is null or has a length of zero, we would get a runtime exception if we tried to execute the following `main` method:

```java
public static void main (String[] args)
{
    Student student1 = new Student("Barb Ericson");
    System.out.println(student1);
}
```

When a runtime exception occurs, the current call stack is printed out. The following is the call stack printout that occurs in this example (your printout may be somewhat different):

```
> java Student
NullPointerException:
   at Student.getAverage(Student.java:136)
   at Student.toString(Student.java:152)
   at java.lang.String.valueOf(Unknown Source)
   at java.io.PrintStream.print(Unknown Source)
   at java.io.PrintStream.println(Unknown Source)
   at Student.main(Student.java:163)
   at sun.reflect.NativeMethodAccessorImpl.invoke0(Native Method)
```

```
at sun.reflect.NativeMethodAccessorImpl.invoke(Unknown Source)
at sun.reflect.DelegatingMethodAccessorImpl.invoke(Unknown
Source)
at java.lang.reflect.Method.invoke(Unknown Source)
```

From the call stack printout, we can see that a `NullPointerException` was encountered at line 136 in the `getAverage` method of the `Student` class. The `getAverage` method was called at line 152 of the method `toString` in the class `String`. We can continue following the call stack back to line 163 of the `main` method of the `Student` class.

Making It Work Tip: Viewing Line Numbers in DrJava

Line numbers are not ordinarily displayed as part of the program code in DrJava or other Java IDEs. To see the line numbers in the program in DrJava, click Edit, then Preferences, and then Display Options, and check the Show All Line Numbers checkbox in the Preferences window. Then click **ok**.

When an exception happens during execution of a method, an object of the class `java.lang.Exception`, or an object of one of the child classes of `java.lang. Exception` will be created. (Figure 14.3 shows the inheritance tree for some of the child classes of the Exception class.) The runtime environment will then look for a method in the call stack that handles this exception.

Some exceptions are **runtime exceptions** such as `ArrayIndexOutOfBounds Exception`. Methods are *not* required to handle runtime exceptions. Runtime exceptions are **unchecked exceptions**, meaning that they don't have to be checked for

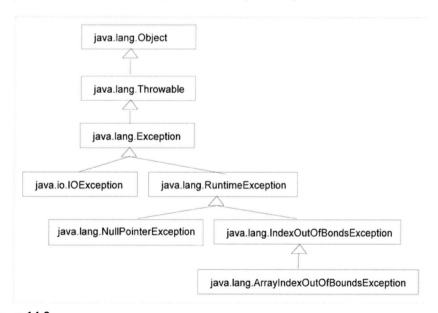

Figure 14.3
A depiction of the inheritance tree for some exception classes

in the code in order for the code to compile. If no method handles a runtime exception, execution will stop and information about the exception will be printed (including information about the call stack).

Other exceptions *must* be handled or the code will not compile. These are called **checked exceptions**. To handle checked exceptions in Java, you can either **catch** an exception or **throw** it. In Chapter 13, we threw the Thread.sleep exception. Throwing an exception means that we ask the runtime environment to throw the exception back to the caller of the method. A catch means we want to try to execute our code, but if an exception occurs we will catch the exception and do something about it. Of course, in order to be able to catch an exception some method somewhere has to throw it.

To catch an exception, you will use **blocks** of the types **try, catch**, and **finally**. A block is any number of statements inside an open curly brace and a close curly brace. The *try block* is a block of code that the runtime will *try* to execute. The statements in the try block are executed one after another until either you reach the end of the try block or an exception occurs.

If an exception occurs during the execution of a try block, it throws the exception to the *catch block* and the catch block will execute. A catch block will catch objects of the specified Exception class *and* objects of all classes that inherit from the specified class. You can have more than one catch block following a try block. If you do have more than one catch block, be sure to catch the most specific exception before you catch a more general one.

The *finally block* is optional. If a finally block is used, it is expected to do clean-up no matter what happens in the try and/or catch blocks. It will always execute regardless of whether an exception occurs or not. The general structure of a try – catch – finally code segment is:

```
try {
    // statements that can cause exceptions
} catch (Exception ex) {
    // what to do if an exception happens
} finally {
    // what to do no matter what happens above
}
```

Program 14.2 shows an example class that defines a method readAndPrintFile to read and print the contents of a file. Notice that because we are using classes from package java.io, we need to add an import statement before the class definition, so that we can use just the class name (FileReader) and not have to use the fully qualified name (java.io.FileReader).

Debugging Tip: Can't Resolve Class Names

If you get a compiler error that says it can't resolve a class name that you think should be part of the Java language, then you probably forgot to use an import statement and used just the class name. You can either use the full name for the class, packagename.ClassName, or you can use an import statement to import just the class (import java.io.BufferedReader), or import all classes in that package (import java.io.*). Import statements tell Java where to look for classes. They *don't* make your program any bigger by including code from other files. The import statements *must* go before the class declaration in the file.

Program 14.2: Sample Class to Read from a File

```java
import java.io.*;

/**
 * Class that allows you to easily read and print out the
 * contents of a file
 * @author Barb Ericson
 */
public class SimpleReader
{
  /**
   * Method to read a file and print out the contents
   * @param fileName the name of the file to read from
   */
  public void readAndPrintFile(String fileName)
  {
    String line = null;

    // try to do the following
    try {

      // create the buffered reader
      BufferedReader reader =
        new BufferedReader(new FileReader(fileName));

      // Loop while there is more data
      while((line = reader.readLine()) != null)
      {
        // print the current line
        System.out.println(line);
      }

      // close the reader

      reader.close();
    } catch(FileNotFoundException ex) {
      SimpleOutput.showError("Couldn't find " + fileName +
                             " please pick it.");
      fileName = FileChooser.pickAFile();
      readAndPrintFile(fileName);
    } catch(Exception ex) {
      SimpleOutput.showError("Error reading file" + fileName);
      ex.printStackTrace();
    }
  }
}
```

```java
    public static void main(String[] args)
    {
      SimpleReader reader = new SimpleReader();
      reader.readAndPrintFile("test.txt");
    }
}
```

In the try block of the method `readAndPrintFile`, a `BufferedReader` object, `reader`, is created to open the text file. If the file isn't found, the catch block

`catch(FileNotFoundException ex)`

takes over. This catch will show the error to the user (using a class that we developed, `SimpleOutput`, that makes it easy to show a dialog box to the user). Next it will use `FileChooser` to try to pick the file name. Then it will invoke the method again with the new file name.

Once the reader object is successful in opening the text file, a `while` loop is used to read one line at a time:

`line = reader.readLine`

If the line isn't null, it will be printed out. The `while` loop continues until the line that is returned is null. A null line will mean that we have reached the end of the current file. Once the end of the file is reached, it will close the `reader`, which will also close the file.

If some exception other than `FileNotFoundException` occurs during the execution of the try block, a second catch block will catch the exception:

`catch(Exception ex)`

In this catch block, an error message will be displayed to the user using `SimpleOutput` and the call stack will be displayed by the `Exception` object `ex` using the method `printStackTrace`.

Notice that we have two catch blocks and that the order of the catch blocks in the code is important. We catch `FileNotFoundException` *before* we catch `Exception`. The class `FileNotFoundException` is a child of the class `Exception`, so we can't switch the order or we would never reach the second catch block. Catching `Exception` first would also catch `FileNotFoundException` since it is a child of `Exception`.

The method `readAndPrintFile` does not contain a `finally` block (which is optional). Why not? Well, we could move the `reader.close()` into a finally clause because we always want to close the file even if there is an exception, but the close can also cause an exception. So let's leave it in the try block.

14.3.3 Working with an `ArrayList`

Now that we know how to read information from a text file, we can add a `static` method to the `Student` class that will read student information from a file and create new student objects. We don't know how many `Student` objects we will be creating. What size array should we use?

Take a look at the `ClassPeriod` class in bookClasses. Each class period has an array of `Student` objects, a teacher's name, and a period number. We created the array to hold up to 35 students. What if we have fewer than 35 `Student` objects in the array? Then we are wasting space. But, what if we have more than 35 students in the class period? Then we will get an `ArrayIndexOutOfBoundsException` if we try to add more than 35 `Student` objects to the array.

It would be nice to have an array that can grow or shrink as needed to fit the data that we put in it. Java does provide this capability as part of the **collection classes** in the `java.util` package. The collection classes are classes that represent data structures that hold collections of objects, such as lists, sets, and maps. A list holds objects in a fixed order and can hold duplicate objects. A set holds non-duplicate objects and doesn't preserve order. A map is used to map one piece of data with another, similar to how your phone maps contact names to phone numbers.

A `java.util.ArrayList` object has an array that can grow or shrink as needed. It stores items in an array, so it preserves the order of elements. It keeps elements in order and allows duplicate elements.

Here are some of the methods of the class `ArrayList`:

- `add(Object o)` will add the passed object (o) to the end of the list (next open position in the array).
- `add(int index, Object o)` will set the object at the given `index` to the passed object (o). If an object is at that index, it will be moved to (index+1). If an object was at (index+1), it will be moved to (index+2). So all objects at the passed index or above will change to the location specified by their (current index+1).
- `get(int index)` will return the object at the passed `index` in the array
- `set(int index, Object o)` will set the value at this `index` in the array to the passed object (o). If an object was at the specified index, it will be replaced with the passed object.
- `size()` returns the number of elements in the list
- `remove(int index)` removes the object at the passed `index`. Any objects with a current index value greater than this will change to (current index−1).

Let's use an `ArrayList` to hold the `Student` objects in a class period. We can change the field in the `ClassPeriod` class from an array of `Student` objects to a list of `Student` objects:

```
private List<Student> studentList = new ArrayList<Student>();
```

You may be wondering what the `<Student>` is doing after List? This is an example of using **generics** and it tells the compiler that the `List` named `studentList` can only hold `Student` objects. Generics were introduced in Java 5 (also known as 1.5) and they let you specify the type of data stored in a collection class, such as a `List`. If you try to add data that isn't of the specified type, you get an exception.

You may also be wondering, "Why is the type of the studentList field given as List instead of ArrayList?" We do this to make it easy to swap out one class for another. The type java.util.List is actually an **interface**. An interface is a special kind of class in Java that only defines public **abstract methods** and/or public class constants. An abstract method is a method that is declared with only the method signature. In other words, an abstract method doesn't have a block of code that defines what to do when the method is called. As an example of an interface with an abstract method, the following shows the java.lang.Comparable interface.

```
package java.lang;
public interface Comparable<T>
{
    int compareTo(T o);
}
```

As you can see, the method compareTo doesn't have a block of code that defines what to do when the method is called. Other classes can be written to **implement the interface**. To implement the interface, a class must fully define the abstract methods declared in the interface. So, any class that implements the Comparable interface must fully define the method compareTo. The compareTo method is expected to be invoked on the current object of the class and take another object of the class, passed in as an argument. When invoked, the compareTo method will return an integer that is 0 when the two objects have the same value, negative when the current object is less than the passed object, and positive when the current object is greater than the passed object. For example, the String class implements the Comparable interface. If you look up the String class API, you will find that one of the methods in the String class is compareTo.

What does it mean to compare two students and decide whether one is less than, equal to, or greater than the other? You have to decide what it means when you implement the method compareTo in the Student class. You may compare based on grades or names. The String class compares the characters in the two string objects alphabetically.

What is the purpose of writing an interface? Well, a class that *implements* an interface must override the abstract methods in the interface and provide code for them. Then, an object of a class that implements an interface can be declared to be of the interface type. For example, a String object can be declared to be of type Comparable because the String class implements the Comparable interface. So the purpose of using an interface is that it allows you to write general functions that only care about the methods defined in the interface. You will often implement the Comparable interface in classes you create. This will allow you to use general sorting programs that only care that the objects that are being sorted are of the type Comparable.

Look up the interface java.util.List in the API and see the abstract methods defined in that interface. Notice that an interface can inherit from another interface. What interface does List inherit from? When an interface inherits from another interface, it inherits all the methods and constants from the parent interface.

Since the class `ArrayList` implements the `List` interface, an `ArrayList` object can be declared to be of type `List`. Why should we declare it to be of type `List` instead of type `ArrayList`? There are actually several classes in Java that implement the interface `List`. If we change our minds about which actual class to use, and we have only specified the actual class one time (when we create the object) then it makes it easy to swap out the class for another class that implements the same interface.

Making It Work Tip: Use Interface Names Instead of Class Names

If you are declaring a variable for an object of a class that implements an interface, you should use the interface name as the type instead of the class name. This will let you use a different class in the future that implements the same interface. This is especially true for the collection classes in package `java.util`. Use `List` instead of `ArrayList`, `Set` instead of `HashSet`, and `Map` instead of `HashMap`.

So interfaces make it easy to plug classes together and to swap out one class for another that implements the same interface. Think of this like LEGO® blocks. All LEGO blocks have the same interface and will snap together. You can easily pull off one and replace it with another. Or, you can think of this like your computer's USB interface. The computer doesn't care what type of device you plug into the USB port. It only cares that the device understands the USB interface. So you can plug in a digital camera, a key drive, or a mouse.

Computer Science Idea: Decoupling Classes

One of the goals of object-oriented programming is to **decouple** classes. Decoupling means minimizing the number of changes you have to make to class A if you change class B and A refers to B. Interfaces let us decouple classes because one class can refer to an object of another class using the interface name as the type. This allows us to substitute class C for class B if classes B and C implement the same interface, without making many changes to class A.

Now that we have declared a variable `studentList` to be of type `List`, we also need to change the accessors and modifiers and any other methods that used the `students` array to work with the `studentList`. Here are the modified methods in the `ClassPeriod` class.

```
/**
 * Method to get a student based on the index
 * @return the student at this index
 */
public Student getStudent(int index)
{
  return this.studentList.get(index);
}
```

```
/**
 * Method to set the student at an index
 * @param studentObj the student object to use
 * @param index the index to set the student at
 */
public void setStudent(Student studentObj, int index)
{
  this.studentList.add(index,studentObj);
}

/**
 * Method to return the number of students in the period
 * @return the number of students in the period
 */
public int getNumStudents()
{
  int total = 0;
  for (int i = 0; i < this.studentList.size(); i++)
  {
    if (this.studentList.get(i) != null)
      total++;
  }
  return total;
}
```

Let's add another constructor to the ClassPeriod class that will take the teacher's name, the period number, and the name of a file that has student information in it. We will add a private method that will read the student information from the file and create the Student objects.

Program 14.3: Constructor that Takes a File Name

```
/**
 * Constructor that takes the teacher's name, period number,
 * and a file name that contains the student information
 * @param name the name for the teacher
 * @param num the period number
 * @param fileName the name of the file with the student
 * information
 */
public ClassPeriod(String name, int num, String fileName)
{
  this.teacherName = name;
  this.periodNumber = num;
  loadStudentsFromFile(fileName)
}
```

Now we need to create the loadStudentsFromFile method that takes the file name to read from. It will read student information from a file a line at a time and create the

Student objects. It will call the constructor that takes a delimited string to fill in the fields from the line. It will add each newly created Student object to the list of students.

Program 14.4: Loading the Student Information from a File

```java
/**
 * Method to read student information from a file and create
 * a list of student objects
 * @param fileName the name of the file to read from
 * @param nameDelim the delimter between the name and grades
 * @param gradeDelim the delimiter between the grades
 */
private void loadStudentsFromFile(String fileName)
{
  String nameDelim = ":";
  String gradeDelim = ",";
  String line = null;

  try {

    // open the file for reading
    BufferedReader reader =
      new BufferedReader(new FileReader(fileName));

    // loop reading from the file
    while ((line = reader.readLine()) != null)
    {
      studentList.add(new Student(line,nameDelim,gradeDelim));
    }

  } catch (FileNotFoundException ex) {
    fileName = FileChooser.pickAFile();
    loadStudentsFromFile(fileName);
  } catch (Exception ex) {
    System.out.println("Exception while reading from file " +
                       fileName);
    ex.printStackTrace();
  }
}
```

Here is a revised main method for the ClassPeriod class that will test the new constructor that takes a file name to read the student information from.

```java
/**
 * Main method
 * @param args the arguments to execution
 */
public static void main(String[] args)
{
  ClassPeriod period =
    new ClassPeriod("Ms. Clark",5,"student.txt");
```

```
    // print info about the class period
    System.out.println(period);

    // print info for each student
    for (int i = 0; i < period.studentList.size(); i++)
      System.out.println("Student" + i + " is " +
                            period.getStudent(i));
  }
```

Running this `main` method will result in:

```
Class Period 5 taught by Ms. Clark with 3 students
Student 0 is Student object named: Jane Dorda Average: 90.0
Student 1 is Student object named: Mike Koziatek Average: 84.84
Student 2 is Student object named: Sharquita Edwards Average: 94.0
```

14.3.4 Writing to a File

To read from a file, we used an object of the `FileReader` class, along with an object of the `BufferedReader` class to handle the buffering of the data in memory from the disk. We will do much the same thing when we write to a file. We will use a `BufferedWriter` which will buffer the data until there is enough to write to the file efficiently. We will use a `FileWriter` to handle the actual writing of the data to a file. The class `BufferedWriter` has a constructor which will take a `FileWriter` as a parameter.

Program 14.5 provides an example of writing text out to a file. (The content is rather silly, but it is easy to follow.) The method `newLine()` will print a new line that is correct for the operating system that the program is running on. Although we could use the special character \n, this isn't correct for all operating systems, so we use the `newLine()` method instead.

Program 14.5: Sample Class for Writing to a File
```java
import java.io.*;
  /**
   * Class that shows how to write to a file
   * @author Barb Ericson
   */
public class SimpleWriter
{

  /**
   * Method to write a silly file
   */
  public void writeSillyFile()
  {
    try {

      // try to open the buffered writer
      BufferedWriter writer =
        new BufferedWriter(new FileWriter("silly.txt"));
```

```
      // write out the file
      writer.write("Here is some text.");
      writer.newLine();
      writer.write("Here is some more.");
      writer.newLine();
      writer.write("And now we're done.");
      writer.newLine();
      writer.newLine();
      writer.write("THE END");
      writer.close();

    } catch (Exception ex) {
      System.out.println("Error during write of silly.txt");
    }
  }
  public static void main(String[] args)
  {
    SimpleWriter writer = new SimpleWriter();
    writer.writeSillyFile();
  }
}
```

Executing the `main` method of this class will create a text file with the following content:

```
Here is some text.
Here is some more.
And now we're done.
THE END
```

14.3.5 Generating a Form Letter

In Program 14.1, we used the `split` method of the `String` class to separate a delimited string into parts. We can also write methods that will *assemble* text. One of the classic structured texts that we're all too familiar with is spam or form letters. The really good spam writers (if that's not a contradiction in terms) fill in details that actually do refer to *you* in the message. How do they do that? It's pretty easy—spam writers have a method that takes in the relevant input and plugs it into the right places. Program 14.6 defines a method `writeLetter` that assembles passed information into a form letter.

Program 14.6: A Form Letter Generator

```
import java.io.*;
  /**
   * Class used to generate form letters
   * @author Barbara Ericson
   */
```

```java
public class FormLetterGenerator
{
  /**
   * Method to generate a form letter
   * @param title the person's title (Mr., Mrs., Dr.)
   * @param lastName the last name for the recipient
   * @param city the name of the city for the recipient
   * @param eyeColor the eye color of the recipient
   */
  public void writeLetter(String title, String lastName,
                           String city, String eyeColor)
  {
    String fileName = lastName + "Letter.txt";

    // try to open the file and write to it
    try {

      // create the buffered writer to use to write the file
      BufferedWriter writer =
        new BufferedWriter(new FileWriter(fileName));

      // write the beginning of the letter
      writer.write("Dear " + title + " " + lastName + ",");
      writer.newLine();
      writer.newLine();

      // write the body of the letter
      writer.write("I am writing to remind you of the offer");
      writer.newLine();
      writer.write("that we sent to you last week.");
      writer.write("Everyone in");
      writer.newLine();
      writer.write(city +
                   " knows what an exceptional offer this is!");
      writer.newLine();
      writer.write("(Especially those with lovely eyes of " +
                   eyeColor + "!)");
      writer.newLine();
      writer.write("We hope to hear from you soon.");
      writer.newLine();
      writer.newLine();

      // write the ending
      writer.write("Sincerely,");
      writer.newLine();
      writer.write("I. M. Acrook");

      // close the file
      writer.close();
    } catch (Exception ex) {
      System.out.println("Error writing to " + fileName);
    }
  }
}
```

```
  public static void main(String[] args)
  {
    FormLetterGenerator formGenerator =
      new FormLetterGenerator();
    formGenerator.writeLetter("Ms.","Ericson","Atlanta","brown");
  }
}
```

How It Works

The writeLetter method takes a title, a last name (family name), a city, and an eye color as input. It opens a file with a name created by appending Letter.txt to the last name. It writes out a bunch of text, inserting the parameter values into the right places. Then it closes the BufferedWriter, which closes the file.

When the main method is executed, it creates a file with the following contents.

```
Dear Ms. Ericson,

I am writing to remind you of the offer that we sent to you last
week.  Everyone in Atlanta knows what an exceptional offer this
is! (Especially those with lovely eyes of brown!) We hope to hear
from you soon.

Sincerely,
I. M. Acrook
```

14.3.6 Modifying Programs

Now let's start *using* files. Our first program will do something pretty interesting— let's write a program to *change* another program.

The following program is the one we will modify. This program creates a text balloon on a picture, similar to the comic-book style text balloons created in Alice animation programs.

```
import java.awt.*;
import java.awt.font.*;
import java.awt.geom.*;
/**
 * Class to create a cartoon out of a picture
 * @author Barb Ericson
 */
public class Cartoon
{

  /////////// fields ////////////////////
  private Picture picture;

  ////////// constructor ///////////////
```

```java
/**
 * Constructor that takes the picture
 * @param p the picture to use
 */
public Cartoon(Picture p) { this.picture = p; }

////////// methods //////////////////

/**
 * Method to add a word balloon that contains the message
 * @param message the text to show
 * @param xPos the top left for the word balloon
 * @param yPos the top left for the word balloon
 */
public void addWordBalloon(String message,int xPos,int yPos)
{
  // get the Graphics2D
  Graphics g = this.picture.getGraphics();
  Graphics2D g2 = (Graphics2D) g;

  // get the font information for the message
  Font font =  Font("Arial",Font.BOLD,24);
  FontRenderContext frc = g2.getFontRenderContext();
  Rectangle2D bounds = font.getStringBounds(message,frc);
  LineMetrics metrics = font.getLineMetrics(message,frc);
  float lineHeight = metrics.getHeight();
  float ascent = metrics.getAscent();

  // draw the ellipse for the word balloon
  double ellipseWidth = bounds.getWidth() * 1.5;
  double ellipseHeight = bounds.getHeight() * 2.0;
  g2.setColor(Color.WHITE);
  g2.fill(new Ellipse2D.Double(xPos,yPos,
                               ellipseWidth,
                               ellipseHeight));

  // draw the message centered in the ellipse
  float x0 = (float) ((ellipseWidth - bounds.getWidth()) / 2 +
                  xPos);
  float y0 = (float) ((ellipseHeight - lineHeight) / 2 +
                  yPos + ascent);
  g2.setColor(Color.BLACK);
  g2.setFont(font);
  g2.drawString(message,x0,y0);
}

public static void main(String[] args)
{
  Picture picture =
    new Picture(FileChooser.getMediaPath("horse.jpg"));
  Cartoon cartoon = new Cartoon(picture);
```

```
    cartoon.addWordBalloon("Just Horsing Around!",42,20);
    picture.explore();
  }
}
```

Run the `main` method for this class. It will create a cartoon by adding a word balloon containing the string *Just Horsing Around!* to a picture. It will display the text bubble on the picture.

Note that the string *Just Horsing Around!* is hard coded in the `main` method. What if we wanted to send in our own string of text to be displayed in the text bubble? To modify this file, we will read the `Cartoon.java` file, and replace the current word balloon text *Just Horsing Around!* with a different, passed in, string.

To do this, we will first open the program's text file (`Cartoon.java`) using a buffer, and then use a `while` loop to read a line at a time until we either reach the end of the file or find the text we want to replace. We look for the text to replace by using the `String` method `indexOf`. If we haven't reached the end of the file or found the text to replace, we just add the current line to a list of lines. We use an `ArrayList` object named `lineList` to hold the list of lines.

If we stopped the while loop because we found the text to be replaced, we will replace the text and add the modified line to the list of lines. Next, we use a second `while` loop that iterates through to the end of the file, adding each additional line to the list of lines.

At this point, we have reached the end of the file and we can close the input file. Then we open it again for output and write all the lines in the `lineList` to the file. The lines from the `lineList` overwrite the lines originally in the file and so now the program in the file has been changed. Finally, we can close the file again.

Program 14.7: A Program that Changes Another Program
```
import java.util.*;
import java.io.*;

  /**
   * Class to demonstrate using a program to modify another
   program
   * @author Barb Ericson
   */
public class FileModifier
{
  /**
   * Method to modify the first string in a method to
   * be the passed changed text
   * @param fileName the file name for the class to modify
   * @param textToChange the text to change
   * @param changedText the new text to use for the text to
   * change
   */
```

```java
public void modifyFile(String fileName,
                       String textToChange,
                       String changedText)
{
  List lineList = new ArrayList();
  String line = null;
  int pos = 0;

  // try the following
  try {

    // open the file to read from
    BufferedReader reader =
      new BufferedReader(new FileReader(fileName));

    /* loop while there are more lines in the file
     * and we haven't found the text to change yet
     */
    while((line = reader.readLine()) != null &&
          line.indexOf(textToChange) < 0)
    {
      lineList.add(line);
    }

    /* If we get here we either ran out of lines or we
     * found the text to change
     */
    if (line != null)
    {
      // get the position of the text to change
      pos = line.indexOf(textToChange);

      // modify the string
      lineList.add(line.substring(0,pos) +
                   changedText +
                   line.substring(pos +
                                  textToChange.length()));

      // loop till the end of the file adding the rest
      while ((line = reader.readLine()) != null)
      {
        lineList.add(line);
      }
    }

    // now close the file
    reader.close();

    // create a writer to write out the file
    BufferedWriter writer =
      new BufferedWriter(new FileWriter(fileName));

    // loop writing out the lines
    for (int i = 0; i < lineList.size(); i++)
```

```
      {
        writer.write((String) lineList.get(i));
        writer.newLine();
      }

      // close the writer
      writer.close();
    } catch (FileNotFoundException ex) {
      SimpleOutput.showError("Couldn't find file " + fileName);
      fileName = FileChooser.pickAFile();
      modifyFile(fileName,textToChange,changedText);
    } catch (Exception ex) {
      SimpleOutput.showError("Error during read or write");
      ex.printStackTrace();
    }
  }

  // Main method to run
  public static void main(String[] args)
  {
    FileModifier fileMod = new FileModifier();
    String file =
      "C:\\intro-prog-java\\bookClassesFinal\\Cartoon.java";
    fileMod.modifyFile(file,
                       "Just Horsing Around!",
                       "What's up, Wilbur?");
  }
}
```

After you execute the main method of this class, open Cartoon.java to verify that it did change the string. Here is what the main method looks like after it has been changed:

```
public static void main(String[] args)
{
  Picture picture =
    new Picture(FileChooser.getMediaPath("horse.jpg"));
  Cartoon cartoon = new Cartoon(picture);
  cartoon.addWordBalloon("What's up Wilbur?",42,20);
  picture.explore();
}
```

You should compile Cartoon.java and then run the main method to see the change. Figure 14.4 shows the output of the Cartoon class before and after the change.

This is how vector-based drawing programs work. When you change a line in AutoCAD or Flash or Illustrator, you're actually changing the underlying representation of the picture—in a real sense, a little program whose execution results in the picture you're working with. When you change the line, you're actually changing the program, which is then re-executed to show you the updated picture. Isn't that slow? Computers are fast enough that we just don't notice.

Figure 14.4
Original cartoon (left) and new cartoon after the class has been modified (right)

Being able to manipulate text is particularly important for gathering data on the Internet. Most of the Internet is just text. Go to your favorite Web page, then use the VIEW SOURCE option in the menu. That's the text that defines the page you're seeing in the browser. Later, we'll learn how to download pages directly from the Internet, but for now, let's assume that you've saved (*downloaded*) pages or files from the Internet onto your disk, and then we'll do searches from there.

For example, there are places on the Internet where you can grab sequences of nucleotides associated with things like parasites. A nucleotide can have only one of four possible values: *g*, *c*, *a* or *t*. DNA sequences are made up of nucleotides. A sample file has the parasite name followed by the DNA sequence for that parasite:

```
>Schisto unique AA825099
gcttagatgtcagattgagcacgatgatcgattgaccgtgagatcgacga
gatgcgcagatcgagatctgcatacagatgatgaccatagtgtacg
>Schisto unique mancons0736
ttctcgctcacactagaagcaagacaatttacactattattattattatt
accattattattattattattactattattattattattactattattta
ctacgtcgcttttttcactccctttattctcaaattgtgtatccttccttt
```

The parasite information is between the > and the end of the line. The DNA sequence for that parasite follows on several lines until > signals the beginning of the next parasite listing.

Let's say that we had a DNA subsequence (like *ttgtgta*) and we wanted to know which parasite it was part of. Program 14.8 defines a method `getNameForSequence` that opens the passed in file and loops through reading this file a line at a time until we find the sequence or the end of the file is encountered (in which case, the subsequence was not found). To search for the subsequence, however, we need to have the information all in one string because the DNA sequence often spans more than one line. To put the information all in one string, we append each line to a string and add a new line character \n to the string to help determine the end of each line from the input file. Once we find the sequence, we can look backward in the string for the last > character. Then we can look forward from that index to the next new line character (\n). The parasite information will be the characters between the two found indices.

Program 14.8: Finding a Subsequence in Parasite Nucleotide Sequences

```java
import java.io.*;

/**
 * Class that searches a file for a given sequence and reports
 * on the name where that sequence was found
 * @author Barb Ericson
 */
public class SequenceSearcher
{
  /**
   * Method to search for a given sequence and then
   * report on the name
   */
  public String getNameForSequence(String fileName, String seq)
  {
    String info = " ";
    String line = null;
    String name = null;

    // try the following
    try {

      // read from the file
      BufferedReader reader =
        new BufferedReader(new FileReader(fileName));

      // loop till end of file or find sequence
      while ((line = reader.readLine()) != null &&
             line.indexOf(seq) < 0)
      {
        // add to string with new line character
        info = info + line + "\n";
      }

      // if get here either end of line or we found the sequence
      if (line != null)
      {
        // look backward for the last >
        int firstIndex = info.lastIndexOf('>');

        // look forward from the > for the new line character
        int secondIndex = info.indexOf('\n',firstIndex);
```

```
      // get the name between the > and new line
      name = info.substring(firstIndex+1,secondIndex);
    }
  } catch (FileNotFoundException ex) {
    SimpleOutput.showError("Couldn't find file " + fileName);
    fileName = FileChooser.pickAFile();
    getNameForSequence(fileName,seq);
  } catch (Exception ex) {
    SimpleOutput.showError("Error during read or write");
    ex.printStackTrace();
  }
    return name;
}

public static void main(String[] args)
{
  SequenceSearcher searcher = new SequenceSearcher();
  String fileName = FileChooser.getMediaPath("parasites.txt");
  String seq = "ttgtgta";
  String name = searcher.getNameForSequence(fileName,seq);
  if (name == null)
    System.out.println("The sequence" + seq +
                       " wasn't found in " + fileName);
  else
    System.out.println("The sequence" + seq +
                       " was found in " + name);
  }
}
```

How It Works

The method getNameForSequence takes a file name to search and the sequence to search for. It will loop through the lines in the file until it finds the sequence to search for. Each line read from the file is appended to the string referred to by the variable info along with a new line character (\n). When the sequence that we are searching for is found, we look backward in the info string for the last >. Then we look forward from that index until we find the new line character. The name is the substring between the two found indices.

There are programs that wander the Internet, gathering information from Web pages. For example, Google's news page (http://news.google.com) isn't written by reporters. Google has programs that go out and snag headlines out of *other* news sites. How do these programs work? They simply download pages from the Internet and chop out the desired pieces.

For example, let's say that you wanted to write a function that would give you the current temperature by reading it off a local weather page. In Atlanta, a good place to find the current weather is http://www.ajc.com/weather—the weather page of the *Atlanta Journal-Constitution*. By viewing source, we can find where the current temperature appears in the page, and what the key features of the text are around it to grab just the temperature. Here's the relevant part of the page that Barb found one day:

```
<td ><img src="/shared-local/weather/images/ps.gif" width="48"
height="48" border="0"><font size=-2><br></font><font size="-1"
face="Arial, Helvetica, sans-serif">Currently<br> Partly sunny<br>
<font size="+2">54<b>&deg</b></font><font face="Arial, Helvetica,
sans-serif" size="+1">F</font></font></td> </tr>
```

You can see the word Currently in there, then the temperature (54) is just after the character > and just before the characters <b>&deg. Program 14.9 shows a program to chop out those pieces and return the temperature, given that the weather page is saved in a file named ajc-weather.html. This program won't *always* work. The page format might change and the key text we're looking for might move or disappear.

Program 14.9: Get the Temperature from a Weather Page

```java
import java.io.*;

/**
 * Class to find the temperature in a web page.
 * @author Barb Ericson
 */
public class TempFinder {

  /**
   * Method to find the temperature in the passed
   * file
   * @param fileName the name of the file to look in
   */
  public String getTemp(String fileName)
  {
    String seq = "<b[[[grt]]]&deg";
    String temp = null;
    String line = null;

    // try the following
    try {

      // read from the file
      BufferedReader reader =
        new BufferedReader(new FileReader(fileName));

      // loop till end of file or find sequence
      while ((line = reader.readLine()) != null &&
          line.indexOf(seq) < 0)
      {}

      // if there is a current line
      if (line != null)
      {
        // find the temperature
        int degreeIndex = line.indexOf(seq);
```

```
        int startIndex = line.lastIndexOf('>',degreeIndex);
        temp = line.substring(startIndex + 1, degreeIndex);
      }
    } catch (FileNotFoundException ex) {
      SimpleOutput.showError("Couldn't find file " + fileName);
      fileName = FileChooser.pickAFile();
      temp = getTemp(fileName);
    } catch (Exception ex) {
      SimpleOutput.showError("Error during read or write");
      ex.printStackTrace();
    }
    return temp;
  }

  public static void main(String[] args)
  {
    TempFinder finder = new TempFinder();
    String file = FileChooser.getMediaPath("ajc-weather.html");
    String temp = finder.getTemp(file);
    if (temp == null)
      System.out.println("Sorry, no temp was found in " + file);
    else
      System.out.println("The current temperature is " + temp);
  }
}
```

How It Works

The main method assumes that the file ajc-weather.html is stored in the media folder specified with getMediaPath. The method getTemp opens the file and reads a line at a time until it reaches the end of the file or finds the sequence. If we find the sequence, we save the position where we found it. Then we look backward from there for the index of the last >. The temperature is between these two indices.

If we run the main method of this class we get:

```
> java TempFinder
The current temperature is 54
```

14.4 Other Useful Classes

In every programming language, there's a way of extending the basic functionality of the language. In Java, we do this with classes. Java comes with an extensive library of classes that you can use to do a wide range of things, such as accessing the Internet, generating random numbers, and accessing files in a directory—a useful thing to do when developing Web pages or working with video. These classes are grouped into packages. We have been working with several classes from the java.io package, but there are many other useful classes and many more packages.

Let's get a list of the contents of a directory as our first example. The class we'll use is the java.io.File class. This is a class that represents a file or directory pathname.

There is a `list` method in the `File` class that will list all of the files and directories in a directory. It returns an array of `String` objects.

```
> import java.io.File;
> File dir = new File("C:\\intro-prog-java\\mediasources\\");
> String[] pathArray = dir.list();
> for (int i=0; i < 5; i++) System.out.println(pathArray[i]);
swan.jpg
MattScotland.jpg
twoSwans.jpg
kidsTree.jpg
redDoor.jpg
```

Program 14.10 uses the `list` method to add text to pictures in a directory. The added text inserts a copyright claim on each picture. The method `list` just returns the base filename and suffix. That's enough to make sure that we have pictures and not sounds or something else. But, it doesn't give us a complete path for storing a new `Picture` with the added text. To get a complete path, we can append the directory to the name we get from the method `list`. Then we can use the `drawString` method that we wrote in Chapter 5 to add a copyright string to each picture.

Program 14.10: Add Text to All Pictures in a Directory

```java
import java.io.*;

/**
 * Class to work with files in a directory
 */
public class DirectoryWorker
{
  /**
   * Method to add a string to every picture in directory
   * @param dir the name of the directory
   * @param text the text of the string to add
   */
  public void addStringToPictures(String dir, String text)
  {
    String name = null;

    // create the object that represents the directory
    File file = new File(dir);

    // Get the array of names in the directory
    String[] nameArray = file.list();

    // loop through the names
    for (int i = 0; i < nameArray.length; i++)
    {
      name = nameArray[i];

      // if this is a picture file
      if (name.indexOf(".jpg") >= 0)
```

```
    {
      // create the picture object
      Picture p = new Picture(dir + name);

      // add the text to the picture
      p.drawString(text, 5,
                   p.getHeight() - 50);

      // save the changed picture to a file
      p.write(dir + "titled-" + name);
    }
  }
}

  public static void main(String[] args)
  {
    DirectoryWorker worker = new DirectoryWorker();
    worker.addStringToPictures(
      "c:\\intro-prog-java\\mediasources\\",
      "Copyright 2009");
  }
}
```

How It Works

The method `addStringToPictures` takes a directory (a path name, as a string) and the text to add as input. It creates a `File` object using the directory path and then it gets a list of file names (and subdirectory names, if there are any) in that directory using the method `list`. It loops through the array of names, and if the current name has `.jpg` in it, it will create a `Picture` object from the current file and then draw a string on the picture. It will then write the changed picture back out, adding `titled-` in front of the name. It writes the changed picture to the same directory from which it read the original picture.

14.4.1 Another Fun Class: Random

Another fun and useful class is `Random` from the `java.util` package. It has a method `nextDouble()` that generates random numbers (evenly distributed) between 0.0 and 1.0. The following illustrates a sample generation of five random values.

```
> import java.util.Random;
> Random randomGen = new Random();
> for (int i = 0; i < 5; i++)
    System.out.println(randomGen.nextDouble());
0.9534889951932188
0.9713266979695472
0.2678907619250269
0.5310776290468512
0.9586483089727932
```

The Random class also has a method nextInt(int n) which generates a random number between 0 (inclusive) and n (exclusive). Because the random generator generates up to but not including n, if you wanted to generate random numbers from 0 to 10, you would use nextInt(11).

```
> for (int i = 0; i < 5; i++)
    System.out.println(randomGen.nextInt(11));
2
10
4
3
8
>
```

Random numbers can be fun when they're applied to tasks like picking random words from a list. Program 14.11 illustrates how to generate random sentences by randomly picking nouns, verbs, and phrases from arrays of Strings.

Program 14.11: Randomly Generate Language

```java
import java.util.Random;

/**
 * Class to generate sentences
 * @author Barb Ericson
 */
public class SentenceGenerator
{
  /////////// fields ////////////
  private String[] nounArray = {"Mark", "Adam", "Angela",
    "Larry", "Jose", "Matt", "Jim"};
  private String[] verbArray = {"runs", "skips", "sings",
    "leaps", "jumps", "climbs", "argues", "giggles"};
  private String[] phraseArray = {"in a tree", "over a log",
    "very loudly", "around the bush",
    "while reading the newspaper",
    "very badly", "while skipping",
    "instead of grading"};
  private Random randGen = new Random();

  ////////////// methods ////////////////////////////////////
  /**
   * Method to generate a random sentence
   * @return a random sentence
   */
  public String generateRandomSentence()
  {
    String sentence =
      nounArray[randGen.nextInt(nounArray.length)] + " " +
      verbArray[randGen.nextInt(verbArray.length)] + " " +
      phraseArray[randGen.nextInt(phraseArray.length)] + ".";
    return sentence;
  }
```

```java
public static void main(String[] args)
{
  SentenceGenerator sentenceGen = new SentenceGenerator();
  for (int i = 0; i < 5; i++)
    System.out.println(sentenceGen.generateRandomSentence());
}
}
```

```
> java SentenceGenerator
Jose runs around the bush.
Mark jumps while reading the newspaper.
Matt jumps very badly.
Angela skips very loudly.
Angela jumps while reading the newspaper.
```

How It Works

This class has arrays of nouns, verbs, and phrases. The method `generateRandom-Sentence` uses a random number generator (`randGen`) to randomly pick a noun, verb, and a phrase, and it returns the created sentence.

The basic process here is common in simulation programs. What we have here is a structure defined in the program: a definition of what counts as a noun, a verb, and a phrase, and a rule about how to put them together. A sentence is a noun, then a verb, and finally a phrase. The sentence gets filled in with random choices. The interesting question is how much can be simulated with a structure and randomness. Could we simulate intelligence like this? And what's the difference between a *simulation* of intelligence and a really thinking computer?

Imagine a program that reads input from the user, then generates a random sentence. Maybe there are a few *rules* in the program that searches for keywords and responds to those keywords, like:

```java
if (input.indexOf("mother") >= 0)
  System.out.println("Tell me more about your mother...");
```

Joseph Weizenbaum wrote a program like this many years ago called *Doctor* (later known as *Eliza*). His program would act like a Rogerian psychotherapist, echoing back whatever you said, with some randomness in it, but searching for keywords to seem like it was really "listening." It was meant as a joke, not a real effort to create a simulation of intelligence. To Weizenbaum's dismay, people took it seriously! They really started treating it like a therapist. Weizenbaum changed his research direction from *artificial intelligence* to concern over the ethical use of technology, and how easily people can be fooled by technology.

14.5   Networks: Getting Text from the Web

A **network** is formed whenever distinct computers communicate. Rarely does the communication take place with voltages over wires, the way that a computer encodes zeros and ones internally. It's too hard to maintain those voltages over distances.

Instead, zeros and ones are encoded in some other way. For example, a **modem** (literally *modulator–demodulator*) maps zeros and ones to different audio frequencies. When we hear these different tones, it sounds like a bunch of buzzing bees to us, but to modems, it's pure binary.

Like onions and ogres, networks have layers. At the bottom level is the physical substrate. How are the signals being passed? Higher levels define how data is encoded. What makes up a zero? What makes up a one? Do we send a bit at a time? A **packet** of bytes at a time? A packet of bytes is like a letter in an envelope in that it contains data and a header that gives the information needed to get the data from the source to the destination.

Higher-level layers define the **protocol** for communication. A protocol is a set of rules that guide how an activity is performed. How does my computer tell your computer that it wants to talk, and what it wants to talk about? How do we address your computer at all? By treating these as distinct layers, we can easily swap out one part without changing the others. For example, most people with a direct connection to a network use a wired connection to an **Ethernet** network, but Ethernet is actually a mid-level protocol that works over wireless networks, too.

Humans have protocols, too. If Steve walks up to you, holds out his hand, and says, "Hi, my name is Steve," you will most certainly hold out your hand and say something like "Hi, my name is Aisha" (assuming that your name is Aisha—if it wasn't, that would be pretty funny). There's an unwritten protocol for humans about how to greet one another. Computer protocols are about the same things, but they're written down to communicate the process exactly. What gets said isn't too different. One computer may send the message HELO to another to start a conversation (We don't know why the protocol writers couldn't spare the extra *L* to spell it right), and a computer may send BYE to end the conversation. (We even sometimes call the start of a computer protocol the **handshake**.) It's all about establishing a connection and making sure that both sides understand what's going on.

The **Internet** is a network of networks. If you have a device in your home so that your computers can talk to one another (e.g., a **router**), then you have a network. With just that, you can probably copy files between computers and share the same printer. When you connect your network to the wider Internet (through an **Internet Service Provider (ISP)**), your network becomes part of the Internet.

The Internet is based on a set of agreements about a whole bunch of things:

- *How computers will be addressed*: Currently, each computer on the Internet has a 32-bit number associated with it—four byte values, that are usually written like this separated by periods "101.132.64.15." These are called **IP addresses** (for Internet Protocol addresses).

  There is a system of **domain names** by which people can refer to specific computers without knowing their IP addresses. For example, when you access http://www.cnn.com, you are actually accessing http://64.236.24.20. (Go ahead and try it. It works!) There is a network of **domain name servers** that keep track of names like "www.cnn.com" and map them to addresses like "64.236.24.20." You can be connected to the Internet and still not be able to get to your favorite Web sites if your domain name server is broken—but it might work if you type in the IP address directly!

- *How computers will communicate*: Data will be placed in **packets** which have a well-defined structure, including the sender's IP address, the receiver's IP address, and a number of bytes per packet.

- *How packets are routed around the Internet*: The Internet was designed in the time of the Cold War. It was designed to withstand a nuclear attack. If a section of the Internet is destroyed (or damaged, or blocked as a form of censorship), the packet routing mechanism of the Internet will simply find a route around the damage.

    But the topmost layers of the network define what the data being passed around *means*. One of the first applications placed on top of the Internet was electronic mail. Over the years, the mail protocols have evolved to standards today like **POP (Post Office Protocol)** and **SMTP (Simple Mail Transfer Protocol)**. Another old and important protocol is **FTP (File Transfer Protocol)**.

    These protocols aren't super-complicated. When a communication ends, one computer will probably say "BYE" or "QUIT" to another. When one computer tells another computer to accept a file via FTP, it literally says "STO filename" (again, early computer developers didn't want to spare the two more bytes to say "STORE").

The *World Wide Web* is yet another set of agreements, developed mostly by Tim Berners-Lee. The Web is based on top of the Internet, simply adding more protocols on top of the existing ones.

- *How to refer to things on the Web*: A **resource** on the web is a web page or some other kind of file that can be downloaded. Resources on the Web are referenced using **URLs (Uniform Resource Locators)**. A URL specifies the protocol to use to address the resource, the domain name of the *server* that can provide the resource, and the *path* to the resource on that server. For example, a URL like `http://www.cc.gatech.edu/index.html` says "Use the HTTP protocol to talk to the computer at `www.cc.gatech.edu` and ask it for the resource named *index.html*."

    Not every file on every computer attached to the Internet is accessible via a URL! There are some preconditions before a file is accessible via a URL. First, an Internet-accessible computer has to be running a piece of software that understands a protocol that Web browsers understand, typically HTTP or FTP. We call a computer that is running such a piece of software a **server**. A browser that accesses a server is called a **client**. Second, a server typically has a **server directory** that is accessible via that server. Only files in that directory, or subdirectories within that directory, are available.

- *How to serve documents*: The most common protocol on the Web is **HTTP (HyperText Transfer Protocol)**. It defines how resources are served on the Web. HTTP is really simple—your browser literally says to a server things like `GET index.html` (just those letters!).

- *How those documents will be formatted*: Documents on the Web are formatted **using HTML (HyperText Markup Language)**.

You'll notice the term *HyperText* showing up frequently in reference to the Web. HyperText is literally non-linear text. It's a term invented by Ted Nelson to describe the kind of reading that we all do commonly on the Web, but that didn't exist before computers: Read a little on one page, then click a link and read a little over there, then click Back and continue reading where you left off. The basic idea of HyperText dates back to Vannevar Bush, who was one of President Franklin Roosevelt's science advisors. He wanted to create a device for capturing flows of thought, which he called a *Memex*. But not until computers came along would this be possible. Tim Berners-Lee invented the Web and its protocols as a way of supporting rapid publication of research findings with connections between documents. The Web is certainly *not* the ultimate HyperText system. Systems like the ones that Ted Nelson worked on wouldn't allow "dead links" (links that are no longer accessible), for instance. But for all its warts, the Web *works*.

A browser (like Internet Explorer®, Mozilla Firefox®, Safari, and so on) understands a lot about the Internet. It usually knows several protocols, such as HTTP, FTP, *gopher* (an early HyperText protocol), and *mailto* (SMTP). It knows HTML, how to format it, and how to grab resources referenced within the HTML, like JPEG pictures. For all of that, though, it's possible to access the Internet without nearly that much overhead. Mail clients (e.g., Outlook, Eudora, and Thunderbird) know some of these protocols without knowing all of them.

Java, like other modern languages, provides classes to support access to the Internet without all the overhead of a browser. Basically, you can write little programs that are clients. Java's class `java.net.URL` allows you to open URLs and read them as if they were files. It has a method `openStream` which returns an object of the class `java.io.InputStream`, which can be used to access a resource at a given URL. For example, we could create an input stream for the weather web page used in Program 14.9, located at `http://www.ajc.com`, like this:

```
String urlString = "http://www.ajc.com/";
URL url = new URL(urlStr);
InputStream inStr = url.openStream();
```

Although an `InputStream` object provides access to a resource file on a server at a given URL, the input stream is in bytes and we still need a way to read from that file so as to turn the bytes into characters. We have been using `FileReader` to read from files stored on our own computer. The class `FileReader` is a child of the more general class `InputStreamReader`, which is a child of the class `Reader`. The inheritance tree for the Reader class and some of its child classes is shown in Figure 14.5.

We can feed the input stream into an input stream reader by creating an object of the class `InputStreamReader` using the `InputStream` object. And, the class `InputStreamReader` is also a child of the class `Reader`. Finally, we can create a `BufferedReader` object by passing it an `InputStreamReader` object. The class `BufferedReader` has a constructor which takes a `Reader` object. Since `FileReader` and `InputStreamReader` both inherit at some point from the `Reader` class, they can both be used to create a `BufferedReader` object. This is because when a variable gives a class name as a type, *any* class that inherits from the given type can be used

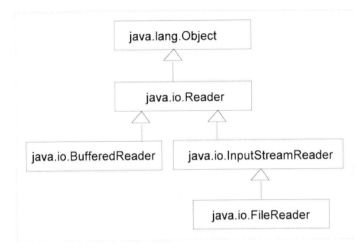

Figure 14.5
A depiction of the inheritance tree for some of the Reader Classes

instead. An object of a child class or even a grandchild class *is an object* of the inherited class, so this substitution is allowed. The code for creating the three objects that work together to read from a web file can be written like this:

```
// open a buffered reader on the input stream from url
BufferedReader reader =
    new BufferedReader(new InputStreamReader(inStr));
```

Program 14.12 defines another method for the TempFinder class. The additional method, named getTempFromNetwork, reads the temperature directly from the Internet. The Web site has changed since when we originally saved a page from it in ajc-weather.html. Now we will look for '&ordm', and we read from http://www.ajc.com.

Program 14.12: Get the Temperature from a Live Weather Page

```java
import java.io.*;
import java.net.URL;

/**
 * Class to find the temperature in a web page.
 * @author Barb Ericson
 */
public class TempFinder {

  /**
   * Method to find the temperature in the passed
   * file
   * @param fileName the name of the file to look in
   */
  public String getTemp(String fileName)
  {
    String seq = "<b[[[grt]]]&deg";
```

```java
    String temp = null;
    String line = null;

    // try the following
    try {

      // read from the file
      BufferedReader reader =
        new BufferedReader(new FileReader(fileName));

      // loop till end of file or find sequence
      while ((line = reader.readLine()) != null &&
             line.indexOf(seq) < 0)
      {}

      // if there is a current line
      if (line != null)
      {
        // find the temperature
        int degreeIndex = line.indexOf(seq);
        int startIndex = line.lastIndexOf('>',degreeIndex);
        temp = line.substring(startIndex + 1, degreeIndex);
      }
    } catch (FileNotFoundException ex) {
      SimpleOutput.showError("Couldn't find file " + fileName);
      fileName = FileChooser.pickAFile();
      temp = getTemp(fileName);
    } catch (Exception ex) {
      SimpleOutput.showError("Error during read or write");
      ex.printStackTrace();
    }
    return temp;
  }
  /**
   * Method to get the temperature from a network
   * @param urlStr the url as a string
   * @return the temperature as a string
   */

  public String getTempFromNetwork(String urlStr)
  {
    String temp = null;
    String line = null;
    String seq = "&ordm";
    try {
      // create a url
      URL url = new URL(urlStr);

      // open a buffered reader on the url
      InputStream inStr = url.openStream();
      BufferedReader reader =
        new BufferedReader(new InputStreamReader(inStr));
```

```java
        // loop till end of file or find sequence
        while ((line = reader.readLine()) != null &&
               line.indexOf(seq) < 0)
        {}

        // if there is a current line
        if (line != null)
        {
          // find the temperature
          int degreeIndex = line.indexOf(seq);
          int startIndex = line.lastIndexOf('>',degreeIndex);
          temp = line.substring(startIndex + 1, degreeIndex);
        }
    } catch (FileNotFoundException ex) {
      SimpleOutput.showError("Couldn't connect to " + urlStr);
    } catch (Exception ex) {
      SimpleOutput.showError("Error during read or write");
      ex.printStackTrace();
    }
    return temp;
  }

  public static void main(String[] args)
  {
    TempFinder finder = new TempFinder();
    String file = FileChooser.getMediaPath("ajc-weather.html");
    String temp = finder.getTemp(file);
    if (temp == null)
      System.out.println("Sorry, no temp was found in " + file);
    else
      System.out.println("The current temperature is " + temp);
    String urlString = "http://www.ajc.com/";
    temp = finder.getTempFromNetwork(urlString);
    if (temp == null)
      System.out.println("Sorry, no temp was found at " +
                         urlString);
    else
      System.out.println("The current temp " +
                         "from the network is " + temp);
  }
}
```

To run this `main` method, simply click Tools, then Run Document s Main Method. The output will look something like this:

```
> java TempFinder
The current temperature is 54
The current temp from the network is 82
```

How It Works

The method `getTempFromNetwork` is nearly identical to the last one, except that we're reading the string `weather` from the AJC website *live*. We use the class URL to gain the ability to read the Web page as an input stream (a stream of bits). We use `InputStreamReader` to convert the bits into characters. And we use `BufferedReader` to buffer the characters as we read them for more efficient reading. Notice that each object has a specific role to play, and we create several objects to work together to accomplish the task.

One way to make Web pages interactive is to write programs that actually generate HTML. For example, in an online search engine (e.g., Yahoo® or Google™), when you type a phrase into a text area then click the **Search** button, you are actually causing a program to execute on the server that executes your search and then *generates* the HTML (Web page) that you see in response. Java has increasingly been used to generate Web pages.

14.6 Using Text to Shift Between Media

As we said at the beginning of this chapter, we can think about text as the *unimedia*. We can map from sound to text and back again, and the same with pictures. And more interestingly, we can go from sound to text . . . to pictures! Why would we want to do any of this? Why should we care about transforming media in this way? We do it for the same reasons that we care about digitizing media at all. Digital media transformed into text can be more easily transmitted from place to place, checked for errors, and even corrected for errors. It turns out that very often when you are attaching binary files to an e-mail message, your binary file is actually converted to text first! In general, *choosing a new representation allows you to do new things.*

Mapping sound to text is easy. Sound is just a series of samples (numbers). We can easily write these out to a file. Program 14.13 adds a method to the Sound class that does this. We need to convert each sound sample number to a string. We use the String class method `valueOf` to do this. This is a class (`static`) method so it can be invoked using `String.valueOf` without needing to create an object on which to invoke the method.

Program 14.13: Write a Sound to a File as Text Numbers

```
/**
 * Method to write out the values in the sound to a file
 * as text
 * @param fileName the name of the file to write to
 */
public void writeSamplesAsText(String fileName)
{
  int value = 0;
```

```
// try the following
try {

  // try to open the buffered writer
  BufferedWriter writer =
    new BufferedWriter(new FileWriter(fileName));

  // loop through the samples
  for (int i = 0; i < this.getLength(); i++)
  {
    // get the int value
    value = this.getSampleValueAt(i);
    // write it as a string (text)
    writer.write(String.valueOf(value));
    // add the new line
    writer.newLine();
  }

  // close the writer
  writer.close();
} catch (Exception ex) {
  SimpleOutput.showError("Error during write");
  ex.printStackTrace();
}
}
```

To run this we can use the following `main` method in the Sound class.

```
public static void main(String[] args)
{
  Sound s = new Sound(FileChooser.getMediaPath("her.wav"));
  s.writeSamplesAsText(FileChooser.getMediaPath("her.txt"));
}
```

After we have compiled the Sound class we can run it using:

```
> java Sound
```

How It Works

First, we create a Sound object s, using the `FileChooser.getMediaPath` method. Then, we call the `writeSamplesAsText` method, passing in the file name to write to. We open the file for writing and then we loop though each sample in the Sound object s, converting it to a string and writing the string to a file. We use the `newLine` method of `BufferedReader` to add a new line after we write each sample value as a string.

What can we do with sound values written as text? We can manipulate the data as a series of numbers. Figure 14.6 shows how it looks in Excel. We can open Excel and open the file. We can tell it the delimiters are spaces and it will read the numbers into Column A. Once we have the data in Excel we can do modifications, such as multiplying each sample by 2.0.

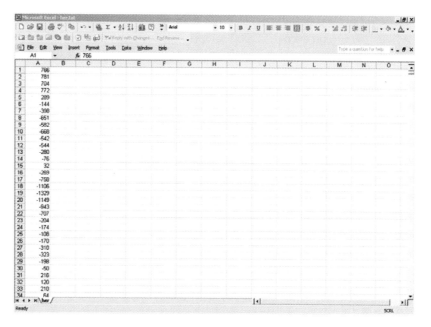

Figure 14.6
Sound-as-text file read into Excel

We can even use Excel to graph the numbers, and see the same kind of sound graph as we've seen in MediaTools (Figure 14.7). Select the column of numbers and then click Insert and Chart. You can just click the Finish button to use the defaults.

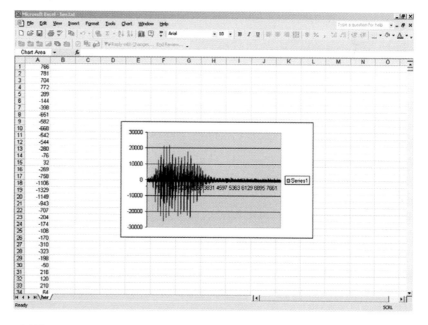

Figure 14.7
Sound-as-text file graphed in Excel

(You might get an error, though—Excel doesn't like to graph more than 32,000 points, and even at 22,000 samples per second, that's not a lot of samples.)

How do we convert a series of numbers back into a sound? Say that you do some modification to the numbers in Excel, and now you want to hear the result. How do you do it? The mechanics in Excel are easy: Simply copy the column you want into a new worksheet, save it as text, then get the pathname of the text file to use in Java.

The program itself is a little more complicated. When going from sound to text, we knew that we could use `getSampleValueAt(i)` to write out all the samples. But how do we know how many lines are in the file? We don't really know until we have read them all in. We have to watch out for two problems: (a) having more lines in the file than we can fit into the sound that we're using to read into, and (b) running out of lines before we reach the end of the sound.

So, for our text-to-sound example, we want to keep reading samples from the file and storing them into the sound *as long as* we have numbers in the file *and as long as* there is still room in the sound. We can use the method `Integer.parseInt` to convert the string number into an integer number. The following code illustrates how using `Integer.parseInt` works.

```
> System.out.println("1234" + 5);
12345
> System.out.println(Integer.parseInt("1234") + 5);
1239
```

In the above example, the first call to `System.out.println` appends the string `1234` with the number `5` translated to a string, and so results in the string `12345`. Whereas, in the second example, we convert the string into a number and then add `5` to the number, which prints the value `1239`.

Program 14.14 illustrates code for converting a file of text numbers into a Sound object. The `createSoundFromTextFile` method that we are writing does not work with a current Sound object. Instead, it creates a Sound object and so it needs to be a class (`static`) method.

Program 14.14: Convert a File of Text Numbers into a Sound

```
/**
 * Method to create a sound from a text file
 * @param fileName the name of the file to read from
 * @return the created sound object
 */
public static Sound createSoundFromTextFile(String fileName)
{
  String line = null;
  int value = 0;

  // create the sound to read into
  Sound s =
    new Sound(FileChooser.getMediaPath("sec3silence.wav"));
```

```
    // try the following
    try {

      // create the buffered reader
      BufferedReader reader =
        new BufferedReader(new FileReader(fileName));

      // loop reading the values
      int index = 0;
      while ((line = reader.readLine()) != null &&
             index < s.getLength())
      {
        value = Integer.parseInt(line);
        s.setSampleValueAt(index++, value);
      }

      // close the reader
      reader.close();
    } catch (FileNotFoundException ex) {
      SimpleOutput.showError("Couldn't find file " + fileName);
      fileName = FileChooser.pickAFile();
      s = createSoundFromTextFile(fileName);
    } catch (Exception ex) {
      SimpleOutput.showError("Error during read or write");
      ex.printStackTrace();
    }
    return s;
  }
```

How It Works

The method `createSoundFromTextFile` takes a filename as input that contains the samples as text. We open up a silent three-second sound to hold the sound. Next, we create a `BufferedReader` to read the file. We loop reading the file until *either* the end of the file is reached, or the index is equal to the length of the sound. In the body of the loop, we convert the string to an integer, and then set the sample value at the current index. We increment the current index. When we are done, we return the created Sound object.

But we don't *have* to map from sounds to text and back to sounds. We could map a sound to a picture instead! Program 14.15 defines a method `createPicture` that takes a sound and maps each sample to a pixel. All we have to do is to define our mapping: how we want to represent the samples. We chose a very simple one: If the sample is greater than 1,000, the pixel is red; less than −1,000 is blue; and everything else is green (Figure 14.8).

The `createPicture` method has to deal with the case where we might run out of samples before we run out of pixels. We added `i < this.getLength()` to the continuation test of the `for` loop using *and* (**&&**).

Figure 14.8
A visualization of the sound her.wav

Program 14.15: Creating a Picture from a Sound

```java
/**
 * Method to turn a sound into a picture
 * @return a created picture
 */
public Picture createPicture()
{
  int value = 0;
  Pixel pixel = null;

  // create a picture to write to
  Picture p =
    new Picture(FileChooser.getMediaPath("640x480.jpg"));

  // loop through the pixels
  Pixel[] pixelArray = p.getPixels();

  // loop through the pixels
  for (int i = 0; i < pixelArray.length &&
                  i < this.getLength(); i++)
  {

    // get this pixel
    pixel = pixelArray[i];

    // set the color based on the sample value
    value = this.getSampleValueAt(i);
    if (value > 1000)
      pixel.setColor(Color.RED);
```

```
    else if (value < -1000)
      pixel.setColor(Color.BLUE);
    else
      pixel.setColor(Color.GREEN);
  }
  return p;
}
```

∎

How It Works

In `createPicture()`, we open up a 640 × 480-pixel blank picture. We loop while `i` is less than the number of pixels in the picture and also less than the samples in the current sound. Each time through the loop, we get a sample value at `i` and figure out a mapping to a color, then set the pixel value to that color. Then we increment `i`. We `return` the created `Picture` object at the end of the method.

Think about how WinAmp does its visualizations, or how Excel or MediaTools graph, or how this program does its visualization. Each is just deciding a different way of mapping from samples to colors and space. It's just a mapping. It's all just bits.

Computer Science Idea: It's All Just Bits

Sound, pictures, and text are all just "bits." They're just information. We can map from one to the other as we wish. We merely have to define our representation.

∎

A really smart mathematician, Kurt Gödel, used the notion of encodings to come up with one of the most brilliant proofs of the twentieth century. He proved the *Incompleteness Theorem*, in which he proved that any powerful mathematical system *cannot* prove all mathematical truths. He figured out a mapping from mathematical statements of truth to numbers. This was long before we had ASCII, which maps numbers to characters. Once the mathematical statements were numbers, he was able to show that there are numbers representing true statements that could not be derived from the mathematical system. In this way, he showed that no system of logic can prove all true statements. By changing his encoding, he gained new capabilities, and thus was able to prove something that no one knew before.

14.7   Concepts Summary

In this chapter, we have learned about handling exceptions, reading and writing files, reading from the Internet, using `import` statements, manipulating `String` objects, and using `ArrayList` objects (dynamic arrays).

14.7.1 Exceptions

Exception handling is used to handle exceptional events. For example, if you try to read from a file and the file doesn't exist, you will get a FileNotFoundException. If you try to write to a file and the disk is full, you will get an IOException. If you try to invoke a method on an object reference that is null, you will get a NullPointerException. Each of these exceptions is defined in a class that inherits from java.lang.Exception, and each is an object. Every exception knows how to print the call stack (using the method printStackTrace()), which is helpful in figuring out where the exception occurred and how it got there.

There are two kinds of exceptions: checked and unchecked. The programmer must do something to handle checked exceptions. You can either catch exceptions or throw them. The programmer is not required to handle unchecked exceptions such as NullPointerException or ArrayIndexOutOfBoundsException.

To catch an exception use:

```
try {
  // statements that can cause exceptions
} catch (Exception ex) {
  // what to do if an exception happens
} finally {
  // what to do no matter what happens above
}
```

The finally block is optional. If a finally block is present, it will be executed both if an exception occurs and if an exception does not occur.

You can have more than one catch block. All Exception objects inherit from java.lang.Exception. When you catch an Exception object, you will also catch all objects that inherit from the type you specified.

14.7.2 Reading and Writing Files

The classes that handle reading and writing files are in the package java.io. Each class in the package is responsible for one task and the classes can be combined in different ways to solve different problems. Classes that work with character data are Reader and Writer classes. Classes that work with binary data are Stream classes. A stream is a series of bits.

To read files, we created a BufferedReader using a FileReader to buffer the data from the disk after it is read from the file. We used the readLine() method of BufferedReader to loop reading from the file until the returned String was null. Reading from a file can cause checked exceptions, so we enclosed the code in a try block and added catch blocks to catch the exceptions.

To write files, we created a BufferedWriter using a FileWriter to buffer the data in before writing it to the file. We used the write method to write String objects to the file and we used the newLine() method to force a new line in the file. Writing to a file can cause checked exceptions, so we enclosed the code in a `try` block and added `catch` blocks to catch the exceptions.

We also used the `File` class to get a list of the files in a directory.

14.7.3 Reading from the Internet

To create a program that reads directly from the Internet, we used the URL class from the `java.net` package. We created a URL object from a string representation of a URL. Then we used the `openStream()` method on the URL object to get back a `java.io.InputStream` object, which knows how to read from a stream of bytes. We used the `InputStream` object to create a `java.io.InputStreamReader` object, which knows how to turn the bytes into characters. We created a `java.io.BufferedReader` object from the `InputStreamReader` to handle the buffering of the data in memory. Then we were able to use the `readLine()` method of `BufferedReader` to read from the network.

14.7.4 Import Statements

Whenever we use classes from a package other than `java.lang`, we have to specify either the full name of the class or use an import statement before the class declaration. The full name of a class is the package name followed by a `.` and then the class name. The full name of the `BufferedReader` class is `java.io.BufferedReader`. If we want to refer to this in our code as just `BufferedReader`, we need an import statement before the class declaration. We can import this as:

```
import java.io.BufferedReader;
```

which imports just that class. Or we can use:

```
import java.io.*;
```

which allows us to use all the classes in that package. It doesn't include any code, it just tells the compiler where to look for the class. If you are using more than one class from a package, this second way is easier.

14.7.5 While Loops

Even though `for` loops and `while` loops are the same as far as the computer is concerned, people use them in different ways. Use a `for` loop when you know how many times the loop will execute and a `while` loop when you want to loop as long as a Boolean test is true. We used a `while` loop to read lines from a file until the line read was null, which indicates that we have reached the end of the file.

```java
// Loop while there is more data
while((line = reader.readLine()) != null)
{
  // print the current line
  System.out.println(line);
}
```

14.8   Methods Summary

String Methods

A `String` object in Java has a sequence of characters. The first character is at index 0. You can get the length of a string using the method `length()`. Here are the other methods we covered:

`charAt(int position)`	Returns the character at the given `position` in the string. The first character is at position 0, just as the first element of an array is at index 0.
`substring(int n, int m)`	Returns a new string which is a *substring* of the string starting at the *n*th character and preceding up to *but not including* the *m*th character. A substring includes part of the original string.
`substring(int n)`	Returns a new string which is a substring of the string starting at the *n*th character and including the rest of the characters in the string.
`startsWith(String prefix)`	Returns true if the string starts with the given `prefix`, else it will return false.
`endsWith(String suffix)`	Returns true if the string ends with the given `suffix`, else it will return false.
`indexOf(String str)`	Returns the first index of the passed `str`, if it is found. If `str` isn't in the current string it will return −1.
`indexOf(String str, int fromIndex)`	Returns the first index of the passed `str` at or after the passed `fromIndex`, if it is found. If `str` isn't in the current string at or after the `fromIndex`, it will return −1.
`lastIndexOf(String str)`	Returns the last index of the passed `str`, if it is found. If `str` isn't in the current string it will return −1.
`lastIndexOf(String str, int index)`	Returns the last index of the passed `str` found looking backwards starting at index. If `str` isn't in the current string before the given index it will return −1.
`toUpperCase()`	Returns a new string with all the characters in uppercase.
`toLowerCase()`	Returns a new string with all the characters in lowercase.
`replace(String oldStr, String newStr)`	Returns a new string with the character in the `oldStr` string replaced with the character in the `newStr` string for all occurrences of the `oldStr` string. This is new in Java 1.5.
`replaceAll(String regex, String newStr)`	Returns a new string with all the matching substrings specified by the regular expression (`regex`) replaced with the characters in `newStr`. A regular expression can be just a string of characters or it can also use special characters to indicate that it will match any character, any digit, only uppercase characters, etc.
`replaceFirst(String regex, String newStr)`	Returns a new string with the first substring that matches the regular expression specified by `regex` replaced with the characters in `newStr`. A regular expression can be just a string of characters or it can also use special characters to indicate that it will match any character, any digit, only uppercase characters, etc.

`split(String regex)`	Returns an array of `String` objects. It will split the current string into many by breaking it into new strings whenever it matches the regular expression specified in `regex`.
`trim()`	Returns a new string with all white space (spaces and tabs) removed from the beginning and end of the string.

ArrayList Methods

An `ArrayList` is a dynamic array (an array that can grow or shrink as needed). It is in the package `java.util`. It implements the `java.util.List` interface and thus an object of the class `ArrayList` can be referred to by a variable declared as type `List`. The methods that we covered are:

`add(Object o)`	Adds the passed object to the end of the list (next open position in the array).
`add(int index, Object o)`	Adds the passed object to the list at the given index. If another object is at that index it will be moved to (index+1). If an object was at (index+1) it will be moved to (index+2). So, all objects at the passed index or above will change to the location specified by their (current index+1).
`get(int index)`	Returns the object at this index in the list
`set(int index, Object o)`	Sets the value at this index in the list to the passed object. If an object was at the passed index it will be replaced.
`size()`	Returns the number of elements in the list
`remove(int index)`	Removes the object at the passed index. Any objects with a current index value greater than this will change to (current index –1).

File Methods

We have only covered one method of the `java.io.File` class. The method `list()` returns an array of `String` objects, which are the names of all the items in the directory represented by the `File` object.

Random Methods

We have covered two methods of the `java.util.Random` class. The method `nextDouble()` will return a double between 0 and 1.0 inclusive. The method `nextInt(int num)` will return an integer between 0 (inclusive) and `num` exclusive.

Exercises

1. Go to a page with a lot of text in it, like `http://www.cnn.com`, and use your browser's menu to **Save** the file as something like `mypage.html`. Edit the file using an editor like Window's Notepad. Find some text in the page that you can

see when you view the page, like a headline or article text. *Change it!* Instead of "protestors" rioting, make it "College students" or even "kindergarteners." Now Open that file in your browser. You've just rewritten the news!

2. Fill in the letter of the definition next to the appropriate phrase below. *(Yes, you will have one unused definition.)*

   ___ `Domain Name Server` ___ `Web Server` ___ `HTTP` ___ `HTML`
   ___ `Client` ___ `IP Address` ___ `FTP` ___ `URL`

   (a) A computer that matches names like `www.cnn.com` to their addresses on the Internet.

   (b) A protocol used to move files between computers, e.g., from your personal computer to a larger computer that acts as a Web server.

   (c) A string that explains how (what protocol) and on what machine (domain name) and where on that machine (path) a particular file can be found on the Internet.

   (d) A computer that offers files through HTTP.

   (e) The protocol on which most of the Web is built, a very simple form aimed at rapid transmission of small bits of information.

   (f) What a browser is (like Internet Explorer) when contacting a server like `www.yahoo.com`

   (g) The tags that go into Web pages to identify parts of the page and how they should be formatted.

   (h) A protocol that is used for transmitting e-mail between computers.

   (i) The numeric identifier of a computer on the Internet—four numbers between 0 and 255, like *120.32.189.12*

3. For each of the below, see if you can figure out the representation in terms of bits and bytes.

   (a) Internet addresses are four numbers, each between 0 and 255. How many bits are in an Internet address?

   (b) In the programming language Basic, lines can be numbered, each one between 0 and 65,535. How many bits are needed to represent a line number?

   (c) Each pixel's color has three components: Red, green, and blue, each of which can be between 0 and 255. How many bits are needed to represent a pixel's color?

   (d) A string in some languages can only be up to 1,024 characters. How many bits are needed to represent the length of a string?

4. Respond to the below Internet-related questions:

   (a) What's a Domain Name Server? What does it do?

   (b) What are FTP, SMTP, and HTTP? What are they each used for?

   (c) What is HyperText?

(d) What's the difference between a client and a server?

(e) How does knowing how to manipulate text help you in gathering and creating information on the Internet?

(f) What is the Internet?

(g) What is an ISP? Can you give an example of one?

5. You've used code to mirror pictures and you've seen code to mirror sounds. It should be pretty easy to use the same algorithm to mirror *text*. Write a function to take a string, then return the mirrored string with the front mirrored to the back.

6. Write a method in the `Picture` class to convert a `Picture` object into a `Sound` object using the average of the color values. Map all values from 0 to 84 to the maximum negative sound value, map all values from 85 to 169 to 0, and all values above 170 to the maximum positive value.

7. Read a file of text and modify each character, such as change 'a' to 'b' and 'b' to 'c' and so on. Write a class, `Encoder`, that encodes the text and another class, `Decoder`, to decode the text.

8. Modify the `Student` class to implement the `java.lang.Comparable` interface by adding `implements Comparable<Student>` to the class definition. This means that you will need to provide the method `compareTo(Student o)`, which should return 0 if the current student object is equal to the passed object, a negative number if the current student object is less than the passed object, and a positive number if the current student object is greater than the passed number. You can use the `compareTo` method of the `String` class to compare the student's names.

9. Write a program to read a list of words from a file and then output a new file with the letters scrambled using `Random`.

10. Write a program to ask the user for a word to check the spelling of, and then use a dictionary on the Internet to check the spelling. Tell the user whether the word is spelled correctly or not. You can use the class `SimpleInput` to get the word from the user, and the class `SimpleOutput` to tell the user whether the word is spelled correctly or not. Both `SimpleInput` and `SimpleOutput` are classes that come with the book.

11. Modify the `Student` class to use an `ArrayList` instead of an array to hold the grades. Change the method `getAverage` to walk through the `ArrayList`.

12. Read the nouns, verbs, and phrases for the `SentenceGenerator` class from files. Use an `ArrayList` instead of an array for each of these.

13. Extend the form letter recipe to take an input of a pet's name and type, and reference the pet in the form letter. `"Your pet "+petType+","+petName+" will love our offer!"` might generate `"Your pet poodle, Fifi, will love our offer!"`.

14. Imagine that you have a list of the genders (as single characters) of all the students in your class, in order of their last name. The list will look something like

"MFFMMMFFMFMMFFFM" where "M" is Male and "F" is Female. Write a function (below) `percentageGenders(string)` to accept a string that represents the genders. You are to count all of the "M"'s and "F"'s in the string, and print out the ratio (as a decimal) of each gender. For example, if the input string were "MFFF," then the function should print something like "There are 0.25 Males, 0.75 Females." (Hint: Better multiply something by 1.0 to make sure that you get floats, not integers.)

15. You worked late into the night on an assignment and didn't realize that you wrote a huge section of your term paper with your fingers on the wrong home keys!

    Where you meant to type: "This is an unruly mob." You actually typed: "Ty8s 8s ah 7hr7o6 j9b."

    Basically you swapped: 7 for U, 8 for I, 9 for O, 0 for P, U for J, I for K, O for L, H for N, and J for M. (Those were the only keystrokes that you got wrong—you caught yourself before you got much further.) You also never touched the shift key, so it's all lowercase letters that you care about.

    Knowing Java as you do, you decide to write a quick program to fix your text. Write a method `fixItUp` that takes a string as input and returns a string with the characters put the way that they ought to have been.

16. The government has data for baby names from 1879 up to the previous year at `http://www.ssa.gov/OACT/babynames`. Get the top 1,000 names for the year you were born and save it to a file. Write a method that will find the popularity of a passed name for that year for a given gender (some names are used for both boys and girls).

17. You can get historical weather data from `http://www.ndbc.noaa.gov/Maps/ northeast_hist.shtml`. Use this site to get data for a location and write methods to find the hottest and coldest date for that location.

18. In sleep research, a patient is hooked up to electrodes and data is recorded for the eight hours or so that the patient sleeps. This results in a large file of numbers. One way that researchers work with this data is to map it to sounds and then listen for repetitions. Find a file of large numbers on the Internet and see if you can map it to sound sample values in such a way that you can hear repetition.

19. Write a simple Eliza program. You can use the class `SimpleInput` to ask questions and the class `SimpleOutput` to show responses. Both `SimpleInput` and `SimpleOutput` are classes that come with the book.

20. Write a class `GraphicsInterpreter` that reads in a file of graphics *commands*. The class `GraphicsInterpreter` should have a method `interpret` that takes a filename as input (a `String`), reads the graphics commands from the file, and then returns a `Picture` with the graphics commands executed on it. The method `interpretCommands` starts out by creating a 640 × 480-pixel blank picture, then draws on that, and returns it.

There are two kinds of commands:

- line 10 20 300 400 should draw a line from (10,20) to (300,400). You can assume that those are single spaces between the coordinates.
- circle 100 200 10 draws a circle whose upper-left hand corner is (100,200) with a diameter for 10.

An input graphics command might look like:

```
circle 20 20 100
circle 300 20 100
line 210 120 210 320
line 210 320 310 320
line 20 350 400 350
```

The main method for GraphicsInterpreter might look like this:

```
public static void main(String[] args)
{
  GraphicsInterpreter interpreter =
    new GraphicsInterpreter();
  String fileName =
    FileChooser.getMediaPath("graphics-commands.txt");
  Picture p = interpreter.interpretCommands(fileName);
  p.show();
}
```

15 Repetition: Recursion

Goals of this chapter:

- To illustrate the use of recursion, in which a method calls itself.
- To demonstrate that recursion enables a method to be repeatedly called.
- To use a base case in a recursive method, to stop the recursive calls.
- To use an `if` statement to check a condition, where the decision to recursively call the method depends on the value of the conditional expression in the `if`.

Introduction

Chapters 8–14 provided you with lots of opportunities to learn more complex programming concepts in Java. You modified sound samples in various ways (changing volume, splicing, reversing, mirroring, blending, and echoes). Also, you modified pictures by manipulating the pixels (changing color values, copying, edge detection, sepia-toning, highlighting, blurring, and using chromakey). You worked with strings to shift between media. A really cool result was that you were able to take the products of your Java programs and use them in your Alice worlds. In this way, you can use Media Computation as a sound and video studio to create special effects for your Alice movies and games. In many of your Java programs, you have used some form of repetition (`for` and `while` loop statements).

In this chapter, Alice will be used to introduce a form of repetition known as **recursion**, in which a method (or a function) calls itself. This is an extremely powerful technique that greatly increases the types of problems that can be solved. Recursion is often used where we do not know (at the time the program is written) the number of times a block of code should be repeated. (This is also true for the `while` statement.)

In Alice, there are two major situations where we do not know (even at runtime, when the program first starts to run) the number of repetitions that will be needed to complete a particular task. The first situation where the number of repetitions is unknown is when random motion is involved. As you may recall, **random motion** means that an object is moving in a way that is somewhat unpredictable. The second situation is where the number of repetitions is unknown and when some complex computation is to be done that depends on an ability to break a problem down into smaller versions of the same problem (sub-problems) until some simplest problem is encountered. The solutions to the smaller sub-problems are then used cooperatively to solve the larger problem.

15.1   Introduction to Recursion

Recursion is a not a program statement with a special keyword that identifies it as part of the programming language. Instead, recursion is a well-known programming technique where a method calls itself. Recursion can be used to handle situations where the programmer does not know how many times the loop should be repeated. Examples in this section will show you how to use this technique.

15.1.1   A Game-Like Example

To illustrate recursion, we will use a simple version of a horse race in a carnival game (*Amusement Park*). The initial scene is shown in Figure 15.1. Unlike a traditional horse race, where horses run around an oval-shaped track and each horse breaks to the inside of the track, horses in a carnival game move straight ahead in a mechanical track. In a carnival game, you win a prize if you pick the right horse. In this example, we won't worry about picking the right horse. We will simply have the winning horse say, "I won!!!" This is not a realistic end to the game—but it will serve the purpose of signaling the end of the race.

The problem is how to make this simulate a real carnival game, where the horses move forward again and again until one of them finally reaches the finish line. At each move, the horses move forward different amounts. To keep the game honest, each horse must have an equal chance of winning the race. This means that over several runs of the game, each horse should win about the same number of times as the other horses.

A possible solution is to randomly choose one horse to move forward a short distance. If none of the horses has won (gotten to the finish line), we will once again randomly choose one of the horses to move forward. This action (a randomly chosen horse moves forward a short distance) will be repeated again and again until one of the horses eventually gets to the finish line and wins the race.

Figure 15.1
Initial scene for a three-horse race

An essential step is how to decide when the race is over. In this example, if one of the horses reaches the finish line, the horse wins the race and the game is over. An `if` statement can be used to check whether one of the horses has won. If so, the game is over. Otherwise (the `else` part), we randomly choose another horse to move forward and do it all again. A storyboard for this animation could look something like this:

```
race
If one of the horses has won
      the winner says, "I won!!!"
Else
      randomly choose a horse and move it forward a small amount
      do everything again
```

In the storyboard above, the line "do everything again" means that the entire method should be repeated. How do we write a program instruction to "do everything again"? We simply have the method call (invoke) itself! Let's modify the storyboard to show the recursive call:

```
race
If one of the horses has won
      the winner says, "I won!!!"
Else
      randomly choose a horse and move it forward a small amount
      call the race method
```

A close look at the modified `race` storyboard shows that the method is calling itself! This is known as recursion. A method that calls itself is said to be recursive. The effect of a recursive call is that the method will repeat. Repeated execution of a method may occur again and again until some condition is reached that ends the method. In this example, the condition that ends the recursive calls is "one of the horses has won."

Now, all we have to do is translate the storyboard into program code. To write the code for the race, we have three problems:

1. How to determine when the race is over.

2. How to randomly select one of the horses to move forward during each execution of the loop.

3. How to figure out which horse won the race and have it say, "I won!!!"

These problems can be solved using stepwise refinement, creating functions and/or methods to solve each, as shown in this diagram:

```
race

If one of the horses has won
    the winner says, "I won!!!"
Else
    randomly choose one horse and move it forward a small amount
    call the race method
```

| isRaceOver | moveRandomHorseForward | whichHorseWon |

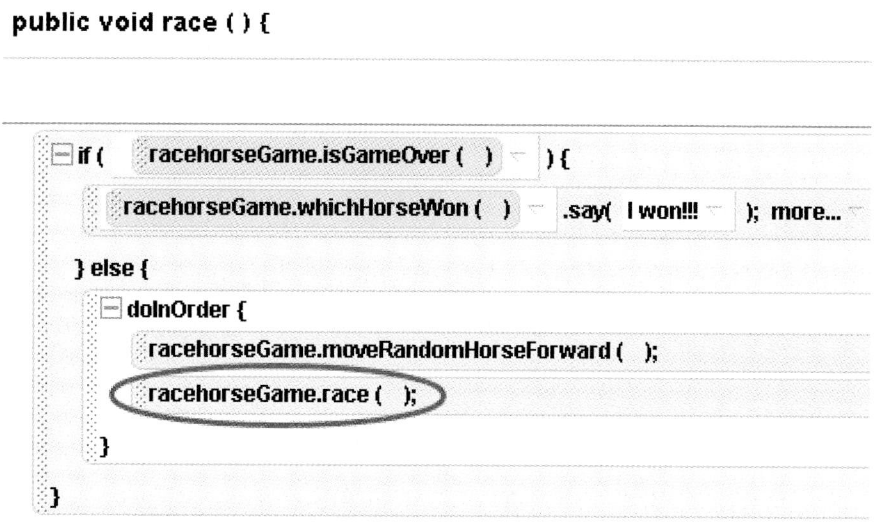

public void race ( ) {

```
if ( racehorseGame.isGameOver ( )  ) {
    racehorseGame.whichHorseWon ( )  .say( I won!!!  ); more...
} else {
    doInOrder {
        racehorseGame.moveRandomHorseForward ( );
        racehorseGame.race ( );
    }
}
}
```

Figure 15.2
The racehorseGame.race method uses recursion (calls itself)

For now, let's pretend that the functions isRaceOver and whichHorseWon along with the moveRandomHorseForward method have already been written. (We will write them next.) If the functions and method were already written, we could write the race method as shown in Figure 15.2. The f part checks to see whether the game is over. If so, the game ends with the winning horse saying "I won!!!" Otherwise, the else part kicks in and a horse is randomly selected to move forward a short distance. The last statement, racehorseGame.race, recursively calls the race method. The overall effect of the recursive call is repetition until some condition occurs that ends execution of the method.

Now that you have the overall idea of how recursion works, we can look further at the details of implementing isRaceOver, moveRandomHorse, and whichHorseWon.

15.1.2 Determining When the Race Is Over

Let's begin with the isRaceOver function. The race is over when one of the horses gets close enough to the finish line to be declared a winner. Either the race is over or it is not over, so the isRaceOver function should be a Boolean function (returns true or false). Within the isRaceOver function, we can make use of a built-in function. The question we will ask in the function is: "Is the finish line less than 0.5 meters in front of a horse?" The reason we have chosen 0.5 (rather than 0) is that Alice measures the distance between the horse and the finish line from the horse's center, not from the tip of its nose. In our example world, the horse's nose is approximately 0.5 meters in front of its center (a racehorseGame has very small horses), so we use a value of 0.5 rather than 0. (If you try this world, you may resize the racehorseGame and find that this distance needs a slight adjustment.)

```
public Boolean isGameOver ( ) {
```

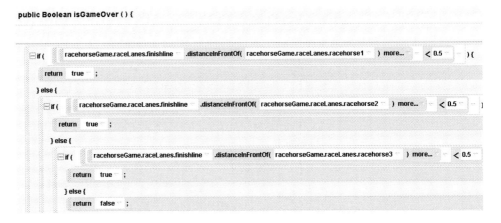

Figure 15.3
The isGameOver function

The function to determine if one of the horses has won is presented in Figure 15.3. A nested if-else control structure is used to check whether the game is over. If any one of the three horses is within the distance (0.5 meters) of the finish line, the function returns true. Otherwise, after all three horses have been checked and none is close enough to the finish line to end the game, the function returns false.

15.1.3 Random Selection

If the game is not over, we need to randomly choose a horse and move it forward a short distance. In this problem we need to give each horse a "fighting chance" to win the race. Let's use the world-level random selection function, choose true (probability of true) of the time. This function will return true some percentage of a total number of times (probability of true is a percentage). For example, saying "choose true 0.5 of the time" means that 50 percent of the time the function will return a true value, the other 50 percent of the time it will return a false value.

It seems reasonable to use a value of 0.33 (one-third) for probability of true, so that each horse will be chosen 33 percent (one-third) of the time. The other two-thirds of the time, that horse will not move. As shown in Figure 15.4, we start the random selection with the first horse, whose name is *racehorse1*. The *racehorse1* will be selected one-third of the time. But, what if *racehorse1* is not selected? Then the else-part takes over and a selection must be made from *racehorse2* or *racehorse3*. Once again, to decide which horse should move, choose true (probability of true) of the time is used. Figure 15.4 illustrates the code for the moveRandomHorseForward method.

15.1.4 Determining the Winner

Each time the race method is executed, one of the horses moves closer to the finish line. Eventually one of the horses will get close enough to the finish line to win the race. This is when we need to determine which horse is the winner. We want to ask the question, "Did a horse get close enough to the finish line to win the race?" Once again, we use the

```
public void moveRandomHorseForward ( ) {
```

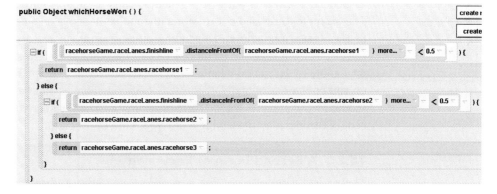

Figure 15.4
Randomly choose one horse and move it forward

distance (0.5 meters) of the finish line in front of the horse to check whether the horse is close enough to win. As in the isGameOver function, we can use a cascading (nested) if-else structure to ask first about *racehorse1*, then *racehorse2*, and so on. If *racehorse1* is not the winner, then we ask about *racehorse2*. If neither *racehorse1* nor *racehorse2* has won, we can assume that *racehorse3* was the winner.

The whichHorseWon function, as illustrated in Figure 15.5, returns the horse object that has won the game. Note that it is impossible for two horses to cross the finish line at once as only one horse moves at a time, and we check for a winner each time one of the horses moves forward. The winning horse simply says, "I won!!!" We admit it is not a very exciting end to a race, but at least it is easy to see which horse won.

15.1.5 Testing the Program

In any program where you are working with random numbers, it is especially important to do a lot of testing. Because of the random selection used in this program, different

Figure 15.5
The whichHorseWon function

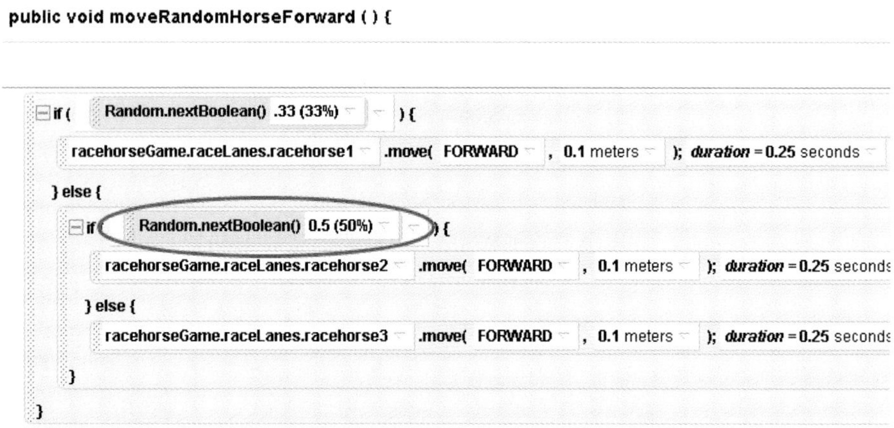

```
public void moveRandomHorseForward ( ) {

    if ( Random.nextBoolean() .33 (33%) ) {
        racehorseGame.raceLanes.racehorse1 .move( FORWARD , 0.1 meters ); duration = 0.25 seconds
    } else {
        if ( Random.nextBoolean() 0.5 (50%) ) {
            racehorseGame.raceLanes.racehorse2 .move( FORWARD , 0.1 meters ); duration = 0.25 seconds
        } else {
            racehorseGame.raceLanes.racehorse3 .move( FORWARD , 0.1 meters ); duration = 0.25 seconds
        }
    }
}
```

Figure 15.6
The corrected random-selection percentage

horses should win the race if the program is run several times. In this example, we ran the program 20 times and found the following very surprising results: *racehorse1* won 7 times; *racehorse2* won 3 times, and *racehorse3* won 10 times! Something is very wrong. The results for *racehorse1* are reasonable (it won about a third of the time). But *racehorse2* didn't win nearly enough, and *racehorse3* won far too often.

The problem is within the second (nested) random selection of which horse should move. We used 33% as the percentage of probability for choosing each horse. What we didn't think about was that if *racehorse1* was not selected, then we have only two choices: *racehorse2* or *racehorse3*. So, after *racehorse1* has been eliminated, we should select *racehorse2* to move 50 percent of the time to give *racehorse2* an equal chance with *racehorse3*. The modified code is presented in Figure 15.6. Now, each horse wins approximately one-third of the time!

15.2 Another Form of Recursion

The concept of recursion, where a method calls itself, was introduced in Section 15.1. The example illustrated a form of recursion that depends on a decision statement (if) that evaluates a condition. Depending on the results of that decision, a method may call itself. Each time the method is called, the same decision needs to be considered once more to determine whether another repetition will occur. This repetition may go on and on until, eventually, the tested condition changes and the method ends. In this section, we examine a second form of recursion. The goal here is to reinforce the concept of recursion by presenting a different kind of problem.

15.2.1 A Second Form of Recursion

The second form of recursion depends on an ability to break a problem down into smaller and smaller sub-problems. The solutions to the smaller sub-problems are used to cooperatively solve the larger problem. As an analogy, suppose you have an emergency situation where you need $60, but you have only $10. So, you ask your best friend to lend you the rest ($50). Your best friend has only $10, but he says he will ask another friend for the remaining amount ($40). The story continues like this

> You need $60 and have $10, so you ask a friend to borrow $50
> Friend has $10 and asks another friend to borrow $40
> Friend has $10 and asks another friend to borrow $30
> Friend has $10 and asks another friend to borrow $20
> Friend has $10 and asks another friend to borrow $10
> Friend loans $10

Collectively, each friend lends $10 back up the stream of requests, and the problem of borrowing enough money is solved. (Of course, you now have the problem of paying it back!) Notice that each friend has a problem similar to your problem—but the amount of money each friend needs to borrow is successively smaller. This is what we mean by breaking the problem down into smaller and smaller subproblems. When the smallest problem (the **base case**) is solved, the solution is passed back up the line, and that solution is passed back up the line, and so on. Collectively, the entire problem is solved. To illustrate this form of recursion in terms of designing and writing a program, it is perhaps best to look at an example world.

15.2.2 Towers of Hanoi Puzzle

The problem to be considered is the Towers of Hanoi, a legendary puzzle. In the ancient story about this puzzle, there are 64 disks (shaped like rings) and three tall towers. In the beginning, all 64 disks are on one of the towers. The goal is to move all the disks to one of the other towers, using the third tower as a spare (a temporary holder for disks). Two strict rules govern how the disks can be moved:

1. Only one disk may be moved at a time.

2. A larger disk may never be placed on top of a smaller disk.

Solving the puzzle with 64 disks is a huge task, and an animation showing a solution for 64 disks would take much too long to run! (In fact, assuming that it takes one second to move a disk from one tower to another, it would take many, many centuries to run!) However, we can use just four disks to illustrate a solution. Most people can solve the four-disk puzzle in just a few minutes, so this will allow you to test quickly for a correct solution.

In our solution to this puzzle, four disks (*torus* from *Shapes* folder) of varying widths have been placed on a *cone* (*Shapes*), as illustrated in Figure 15.7 on the next page. The cones in the world will play the same role as towers in the original puzzle. Initially, four disks are on the leftmost cone.

In setting up this world, careful positioning of cones and measurement of disks will make the animation easier to program. We positioned each cone exactly 1 meter from its nearest neighbor, as labeled in Figure 15.8 on the next page.

Figure 15.7
The Towers of Hanoi

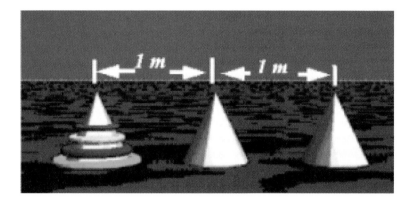

Figure 15.8
Each cone is 1 meter from neighboring cone

Each disk is placed exactly 0.1 meter in height above its neighbor, as illustrated in Figure 15.9.

To make it easier to describe our solution to the puzzle, let's give each disk an ID number and a name. The disk with ID number 1 is disk1, ID number 2 is disk2, ID number 3 is disk3, and ID number 4 is disk4. The smallest disk is disk1 at the top of the stack and the largest disk is disk4 at the bottom. Also, let's name the cones cone1, cone2, and cone3 (left to right from the camera point of view). The goal in the puzzle is to move all the disks from the leftmost cone, cone1, to another cone. In this example, we will move the disks to the rightmost cone (cone3).

A first attempt to solve the problem might be to use a while loop. The textual story-board might look something like this:

```
While all the disks are not on the target cone (cone3)
   Do
```

Unfortunately, it is not easy to figure out what needs to be done inside the "Do." The problem can be solved using a `while` loop, but it takes much thinking and insight into the problem. Recursion makes the problem much easier to think about and solve, so we will use recursion.

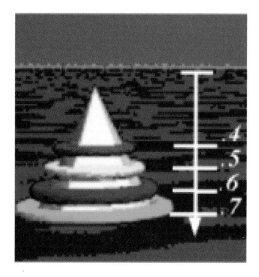

Figure 15.9
Each disk is 0.1 meter above its neighboring disk (measuring from top down)

15.2.3 Two Requirements

We want to solve this puzzle for four disks using the second form of recursion, where the problem is broken down into smaller and smaller sub-problems. To use this form of recursion, two requirements must be met.

The first requirement is that we must assume we know how to solve the problem for a smaller sub-problem. Let's assume that we do know a solution for solving the problem for three disks. If we know how to solve the problem of moving 3 disks, it would be quite easy to write a program to solve it for 1 more disk (four disks). The following steps would work:

1. Move the three disks (imagining the solution for the puzzle with only three disks is already known) from cone1 to cone2. See Figure 15.10-a.

2. Move the last disk, disk4, from cone1 to cone3. See Figure 15.10-b on the next page. (Remember that this move is now safe, as all of the three smaller disks are now located on cone2.)

Figure 15.10-a
After Step 1

Figure 15.10-b
After Step 2

Figure 15.10-c
After Step 3

3. Move the three disks (again, imagining the solution is already known) from cone2 to cone3. The final result is shown in Figure 15.10-c.

The second requirement is that we must have a base case. A base case is the simplest possible situation where the solution is obvious and no further sub-problems are needed. In other words, when we get down to the base case, we can stop breaking the problem down into simpler problems because we have reached the simplest problem. The obvious "base case" in the Towers of Hanoi puzzle is the situation where we have only one disk that still needs to be moved. To move one disk, we can just move it. We know that there are no smaller disks than disk 1. So, if it is the only disk to be moved, we can always move it to another cone!

15.2.4 The `towers` Method

Now that we have determined the necessary two requirements, we can write a method to animate a solution to the Towers of Hanoi puzzle. The method, named `towers`, will have instructions to move some number (`howmany`) of disks from a `source` cone (the cone where the disks are currently located) to a `target` cone (the cone where the disks will be located when the puzzle is solved). In the process of moving the disks from the source cone to the target cone, a spare cone (the cone that is neither source nor target) will be used as a temporary holder for disks on their journey from the source to the target.

To do its work, the `towers` method needs to know how many disks are to be moved, the source cone, target cone, and spare cone. To provide this information to the `towers` method, four parameters are used: `howmany`, `source`, `target`, and `spare`. Here is the storyboard:

```
towers
Parameters: howmany, source, target, spare
If howmany is equal to 1
  move it (disk 1) from the source to the target
Else
  Do in order
    call towers to move howmany-1 disks from source to spare
    (using target as spare)
    move it (disk # howmany) from the source to the target
    call towers to move howmany-1 disks from the spare to the
    target (using the source as the spare)
```

We know this looks a bit complicated; but it really is not too difficult. Let's break it down and look at individual pieces:

First, the `if` piece:

> if how many is equal to 1
> move it (the smallest disk) from the `source` to the `target`

This is simple. The `if` piece is the base case. We have only 1 disk to move, so move it! Second, the `else` piece:

> else

(1) call `towers` to move `howmany`-1 disks from `source` to `spare` (using `target` as spare)

(2) move it (disk # howmany) from the `source` to the `target`

(3) call `towers` to move `howmany`-1 disks from `spare` to `target` (using the `source` as the `spare`)

All this is saying is:

1. Move all but one of the disks from the `source` to the `spare` cone.

2. Now that only one disk is left on the `source`, move it to the `target` cone. This is ok, because all smaller disks are now located on the `spare` cone, after Step 1.

3. Now, move all the disks that have been temporarily stored on the `spare` cone to the `target` cone.

Notice that the `if` piece and the `else` piece in this storyboard each have a sub-step that says "move it" (move a disk) from the source cone to the target cone. Moving a disk from one cone to another is actually a combination of several moves, so we will need to use stepwise refinement to break down our design into simpler steps. The following diagram illustrates the stepwise refinement designed to call a `moveIt` method.

```
towers

Parameters: howmany, source, target, spare

If howmany is equal to 1
      move it (the smallest disk) from the source to the target
Else
    Do in order
        call towers to move howmany-1 disks from source to spare
        (using target as spare)

        move it (disk # howmany) from the source to the target

        call towers to move howmany-1 disks from the spare to the target
        (using the source as the spare)
```

```
moveIt
```

Exactly what does the `moveIt` method do? The `moveIt` method must lift a disk upward to clear the top of the cone it is currently on. Then, it must move that disk (forward or back) to a location immediately above the target cone. Finally, it must lower the disk down onto the target cone. Figure 15.11 illustrates a possible sequence of moves.

Note that the cone a disk is on (source) and the cone the disk is being moved to (target) changes with successive moves. This can be very confusing, so in writing the `moveIt` method, we will use different names for the three parameters because it needs to know: (1) which disk is to be moved (`whichdisk`—the disk ID number), (2) the source cone (`fromcone`), and (3) the target cone (`tocone`). A storyboard for `moveIt` could be:

```
moveIt
Parameters: whichdisk, fromcone, tocone
Do in order
    Lift the disk up above the top of the fromcone
    Move it (forward or back) to a location above the tocone
    Lower the disk down onto the tocone
```

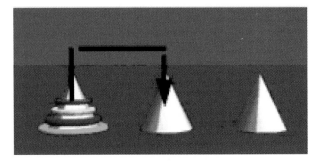

Figure 15.11
Moving a disk from source to target cone

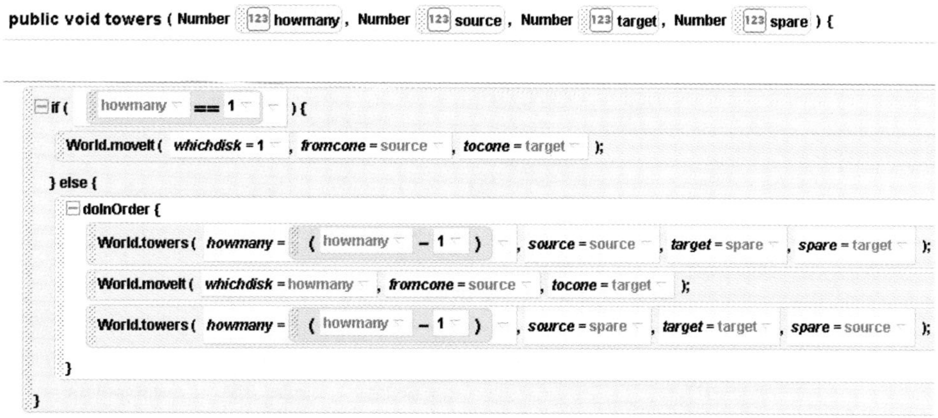

```
public void towers ( Number [123] howmany , Number [123] source , Number [123] target , Number [123] spare ) {

  ⊟if (   howmany ∨  == 1 ∨  ∨ ) {
      World.moveit (  whichdisk = 1 ∨ , fromcone = source ∨ , tocone = target ∨  );
  } else {
      ⊟doInOrder {
          World.towers (  howmany =  ( howmany ∨  - 1 ∨  )  ∨ , source = source ∨ , target = spare ∨ , spare = target ∨  );
          World.moveit (  whichdisk = howmany ∨ , fromcone = source ∨ , tocone = target ∨  );
          World.towers (  howmany =  ( howmany ∨  - 1 ∨  )  ∨ , source = spare ∨ , target = target ∨ , spare = source ∨  );
      }
  }
}
```

Figure 15.12
The towers method

Two methods are to be written: (1) the towers method and (2) the moveIt method. Let's start by writing the towers method, as shown in Figure 15.12.

15.2.5 The moveIt Method

The first step in the moveIt method is to lift the disk up above the cone it is currently on. How high should the disk be lifted? Each disk is at a different initial height on the cone, so it will be necessary to raise each disk a different amount. In our example world, we made each disk 0.1 meters in height, so we need to lift disk1 approximately 0.4 meters, disk2 approximately 0.5 meters, disk3 approximately 0.6 meters, and disk4 approximately 0.7 meters to "clear" the cone.

Now that we know the height to lift each disk, we can write the code to move a disk upward. Of course, the moveIt method needs to know which disk is to be moved. One possibility is to pass a parameter to the moveIt method that contains the ID number of the disk to be moved. If the disk ID is 1, move disk1, if the disk ID is 2, move disk2, and so on. We can use nested if statements to check on the ID number of the disk. When the correct disk is found, a move instruction can be used to lift it the appropriate amount. The storyboard (for the nested if statements) would look something like this:

```
If whichdisk is 1 then
  Move disk1 up 0.4 meters
Else
  If whichdisk is 2 then
    Move disk2 up 0.5 meters
Else
    If whichdisk is 3 then
      Move disk3 up 0.6 meters
    Else
      Move disk4 up 0.7 meters
```

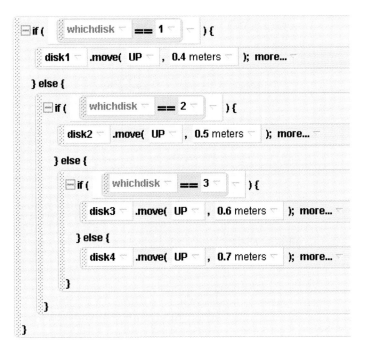

Figure 15.13
Nested If statements to select the disk to move upward

The code in Figure 15.13 will accomplish this task.

We thought about this for a while, realizing that the nested if statements might seem a bit awkward. We noticed that the distance each disk has to move up is 0.3 meters more than 0.1* the ID number (whichdisk). Thus, a nifty mathematical expression could be used to move a disk upward. Using an expression to compute the distance would allow the storyboard to be just one step:

```
move the appropriate disk up 0.3 + 0.1* whichdisk
```

Sometimes it is helpful to come up with an elegant idea like this one. We want to point out, however, that condensing the code into a more compact form may lead to other problems. In this case, using an expression to compute the distance leads us to a problem of how to write the statement. Notice that the one-statement storyboard uses the phrase "appropriate disk" because we don't know exactly which disk is to be moved. All we have is whichdisk—an ID number, not a name. Think of it like this: you have a name and a social security number. When someone talks to you, she says your name, not your social security number. Writing a move instruction is a similar situation. A move instruction uses the name of the object, not its ID number.

15.2.6 Conversion Function

"How is Alice to be told the name of the disk object to be moved when only the disk ID number is known?" One solution is to write a conversion method that takes the ID

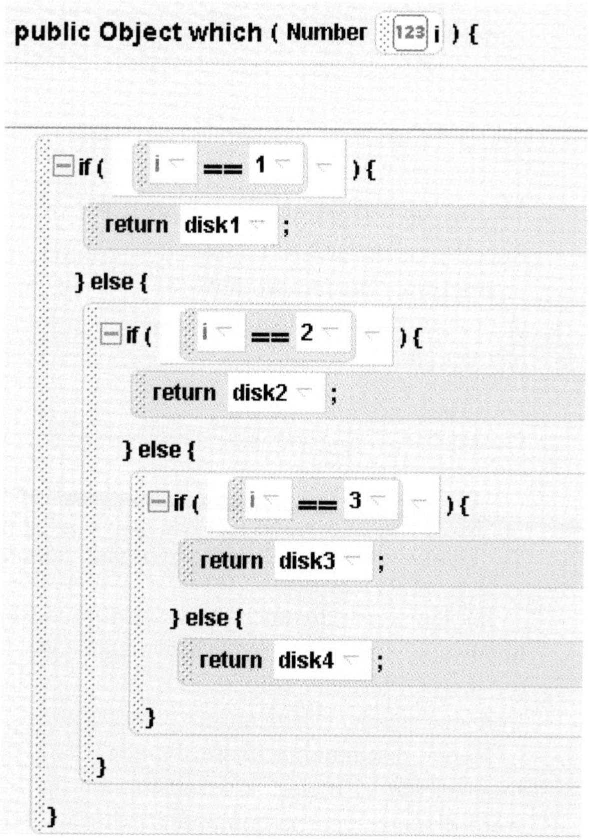

```
public Object which ( Number  123 i ) {

    if ( i == 1 ) {
        return disk1 ;
    } else {
        if ( i == 2 ) {
            return disk2 ;
        } else {
            if ( i == 3 ) {
                return disk3 ;
            } else {
                return disk4 ;
            }
        }
    }
}
```

Figure 15.14
A world-level conversion function

number as a parameter and returns the appropriate name of the disk object to move. Such a conversion method can be written using a function. The which function is illustrated in Figure 15.14. In this code, each if statement includes an instruction containing the keyword return. As you know, the return statement sends information back to the method that called it. For instance, suppose which ($i = 2$) is called; the information that will be returned is disk2. The which function provides a way to convert an ID number (the whichdisk parameter) to an object name. (We named the function which to make it easy to mentally connect the which function to the whichdisk parameter.)

An instruction can now be written in the moveIt method that calls the which function to determine which disk to move and uses a mathematical expression to compute the distance, as illustrated in Figure 15.15. In this instruction, which (i = whichdisk) is a call to the which function. When executed, which (i = whichdisk) will select the appropriate disk and return its name. That disk will then be moved upward the computed amount, as explained in the earlier expression.

Figure 15.15
Calling the function to determine which disk to move

15.2.7 Completing the movelt Method

Recall that the `moveIt` method is composed of a sequence of three movement instructions. So far, we have completed the first `move` instruction (highlighted in blue in the storyboard, below). Let's look at how to write the two remaining instructions.

```
moveIt
Parameters: whichdisk, fromcone, tocone
Do in order
    Lift the disk up above the top of the fromcone
    Move it (forward or back) to a location above the tocone
    Lower the disk down onto the tocone
```

For the second instruction, we want to move the disk `forward` or `backward` so as to position it immediately over the target cone. How far should the disk be moved? As previously illustrated (Figure 15.8), the cones are purposely positioned exactly 1 meter from one another. There are six possible moves, as shown in Table 15.1.

Notice that moving forward a negative (-1 meter) distance is the same as moving backward 1 meter. After examining the six cases in detail, we see that the forward distance can be computed using an expression (`tocone – fromcone`). For example, to move a disk from cone1 to cone3, move it 2 meters $(3-1)$ forward. With this insight, an instruction can be written to move the disk to the target cone, as shown in Figure 15.16.

The last step in the `moveIt` method is to move the disk downward onto the target cone. This instruction should simply do the opposite of what was done in Step 1. The complete `moveIt` method appears in Figure 15.17.

Now, with the `towers` and the `moveIt` methods completed, all that remains is to call the `towers` method when the world starts. A link in the Events editor can be used, as seen in Figure 15.18.

The second form of recursion (presented in this section) depends on the structure of a problem and its solution, breaking a problem down into smaller and smaller

Table 15.1 Six Disk Moves from Source Cone to Target Cone

Forward moves	Forward distance	Backward moves	Forward distance
from cone1 to cone2	1 meter	from cone2 to cone1	−1 meter
from cone1 to cone3	2 meters	from cone3 to cone1	−2 meter
from cone2 to cone3	1 meter	from cone3 to cone2	−1 meter

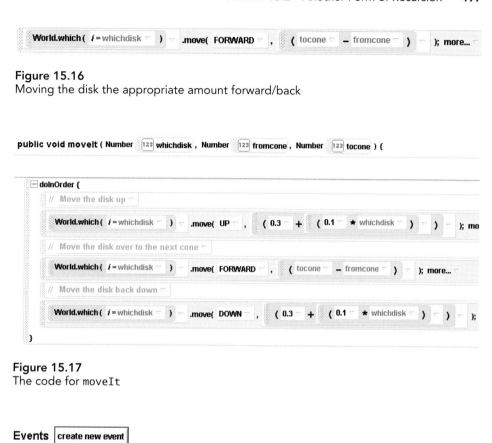

Figure 15.16
Moving the disk the appropriate amount forward/back

Figure 15.17
The code for moveIt

Figure 15.18
Calling the towers method

sub-problems. Many mathematicians (and computer scientists interested in logic) often prefer this form of recursion because it is easy to show that the program does end—and that it ends with the correct solution. For example, with the Towers of Hanoi, we reasoned that we could:

> move 4 disks, if we can move 3 disks and then 1 disk (we know how to move 1 disk)
>> move 3 disks, if we can move 2 disks and then 1 disk
>>> move 2 disks, if we can move 1 disk and then 1 disk
>>>> move 1 disk (base case—we know how to move 1 disk)

Clearly, the problem has been broken down into smaller and smaller sub-problems. We know that the program will end, because we know that eventually the problem size will get down to the base case, which is moving one disk.

15.3 Summary

This chapter introduced the concept of using recursion as a mechanism for repetition. Recursion is a powerful tool for building more complex and interesting worlds.

The horse race example in this chapter demonstrates a type of recursion where more executions of a section of program code are "generated" each time the result of the previous decision is true or false. The famous Towers of Hanoi puzzle is an example of a second type of recursion, where a complex problem is broken down into simpler and simpler versions.

15.3.1 A Comparison of Repetitions

In this text, we have presented three ways for accomplishing repetition in an Alice program: Loop, While, and recursion. You might ask, "Which one should I use, and when?"

The choice depends on the task being completed (the problem being solved) and why you need the repetition. If you know how many times the repetition needs to be performed (either directly or via a function), the Loop statement is generally easiest. In most programming that you do, you will want to avoid infinite loops. In animation programming, however, an infinite Loop statement can be used to create some background action that continues to run until the program is shut down.

Otherwise, use the While loop or recursion. Some programmers prefer While and others prefer recursion. Put two programmers in the same room and they are likely to disagree over this issue. The underlying difference between the two is how you think about solving a problem. We say, "Try both." Some problems are easier to solve with a While loop and others are easier to solve with recursion. With experience, you will discover which works best for you. The important thing is that you learn to write code that uses repetition.

Exercises

1. Give an explanation for the following statement: "Recursion is more appropriately described as a programming technique rather than as a control construct."

2. In what way(s) is a recursive method similar to a while loop?

3. A programmer who wishes to write a recursive method will use a statement that evaluates a condition to determine whether the method will call itself again. In Alice, what is the control construct that is used for the decision-making statement?

4. What is meant by a "base case" in a recursive method?

5. The horse race (*Amusement Park*) example presented in Section 15.1 randomly selected one horse at a time and moved it forward until one of the horses won the race. Another solution is to move all three horses forward at the same time, but to move each a random distance. Modify the horse race program to use this solution to the problem.

6. Use recursion to make the white rabbit (*Animal*) chase a butterfly (*Animals/Bugs*). The butterfly should fly to a random, nearby location (within 0.2 meters in any

direction). The white rabbit, however, must always remain on the ground (rabbits do not fly). Each time the butterfly moves, use turn to face to make the rabbit turn toward the butterfly and then move the rabbit toward the butterfly 0.5 meters. When the rabbit gets close enough, have him catch the butterfly in his net (*Objects*).

Making It Work Tip: Adapting the randomMotion Method

To move the butterfly to a random nearby location, you can adapt the randomMotion method presented in Chapter 7. It is necessary to keep the butterfly from flying too high or too low. (The butterfly could disappear below the ground or fly too high, so that the rabbit would never get close enough to catch it.) To limit the up-down direction of the butterfly's movement, use an if statement to check the butterfly's distance above the ground and then move the butterfly up or down accordingly. The butterfly's distance above the ground should always be within the range of 0 (ground level) and 1 (meter above the ground).

7. In the story of the Midas Touch, a greedy king was given the gift of having everything he touched turn to gold. This exercise is to create a simulation of the Midas Touch. In the initial scene shown below, a woman is facing a candy cane (Holidays). (Use turn to face to make this alignment.) Write a recursive method named checkCandy that checks whether the woman's right hand is very close to the candy cane. If it is, the woman should touch the candy cane. After she touches the candy cane, the candy cane turns to gold (color changes to yellow). If the woman is not yet close enough to the candy cane to be able to touch it, she moves a small distance forward and the checkCandy method is recursively called.

Making It Work Tip: Camera Range

It is possible that the woman will wander out of the range of the camera. There are two possible solutions. One is to make the camera point at the woman each time she moves. The other is to make the camera's vehicle be the woman.

9. Create the Towers of Hanoi puzzle as described Section 15.2. When you have it working, modify the event-trigger link that calls the `towers` method so that it moves the disks from cone1 to cone2 (instead of cone3).

10. In the Towers of Hanoi puzzle, we do not need to pass around the spare cone as a parameter. The spare cone is always

    6 - fromcone - tocone.

    Modify the towers method to use this new approach.

11. A popular child's riddle is, "Why did the chicken cross the road?" Of course, there are many answers. In this project, the chicken (*Animals*) has a real sweet-tooth and crosses the road to eat the gumdrops (*Kitchen/Food*) along the way.

Write a game animation where the player guides the chicken across the road to get to the gumdrops. Cars and other vehicles should move in both directions as the chicken tries to cross to where the gumdrops are located. Use arrow keys to make the chicken jump left, right, forward and back. Use the space bar to have the chicken peck at the gumdrop. When the chicken is close enough to the gumdrop and pecks, the gumdrop should disappear.

A recursive method is used to control the play of the game. If the chicken gets hit by a vehicle, the game is over (squish!). The game continues as long as the chicken has not managed to peck all the gumdrops and has not yet been squished by a vehicle. If the chicken manages to cross the road and peck at all the gumdrops along the way, the player wins the game. Signal the player's success by making 3D text "You Win" appear or by playing some triumphant sound.

12. In the world below, the row of skeletons (*Spooky*) is guarding the gate (*Spooky*). Every so often in this world, the row of skeletons is to reverse order. This project

is to animate the reversal using the second form of recursion. The storyboard goes something like the following:

```
reverse
If the row of skeletons not yet reversed is more than one then
    reverse the row of skeletons starting with the second
        skeleton (by recursively calling reverse)
    move the head skeleton to the end of the row
```

The base case is when there is just one skeleton in the row (that has not yet been reversed). Of course, a row of 1 skeleton is already reversed! The recursive case (for n skeletons, where n is larger than 1) says to first reverse the last $n-1$ skeletons and then move the first skeleton to the end of the row.

Implement the Skeleton Reversal storyboard given above. The program you write should be quite similar to the Towers of Hanoi program, including the `which` function.

13. Let us design a game where the goal is to click on an object that is appearing and then disappearing on the screen. If the user successfully clicks on the object while it is visible, some visual action should happen so the user will know he/she has managed to "click" the object with the mouse. In our sketch of a storyboard below, a cow (*Animals*) is the object and a windup key (*Objects*) is used to signal success. (Of course, you can creatively choose a different object and a different way to signal the fact that the user has clicked on the object.)

    We assume that the cow and wind-up key have been added to the world and both have been made invisible by setting their `isShowing` property to `false`. A storyboard for a method, `check`, will look something like this:

```
If the wind-up key is not visible
    Move the cow to a random location on the screen
    Make the cow visible
    Wait a short period of time, say 0.25 seconds
    Make the cow invisible
```

```
              Move the cow off the screen
                (perhaps by moving it down 10 meters so the user can
                no longer click on it)
              Recursively call check
      Else
              Have the cow say, "Thanks for playing"
```

When the user finally manages to click the mouse on the object, a method should be called that signals success. In our example, the wind-up key would become visible. Once the key is visible, the game ends.

Making It Work Tip: Moving the Object

The most challenging part of this project is to move the object to a random location on the ground (perhaps between −3 and 3 in the forward-back and right-left directions). Also, you will find it helpful to experiment with a Wait instruction to find out how long to wait while the object is visible (not too fast, not too slow) before making it invisible again. ■

CHAPTER
16 Speed

Goals of this chapter:

- To choose between compiled and interpreted programming languages, based on an understanding of machine language and how computers work.
- To recognize the categories of algorithms based on their complexity, and to avoid intractable algorithms.
- To understand some common searching and sorting algorithms and their complexity.
- To understand recursion and how it can be used to break a hard problem into simpler sub-problems.
- To consider processor choice based on an understanding of clock rates.
- To make decisions about computer storage options when aiming for optimizing speed.

Introduction

In the last chapter you were introduced to recursion in Alice. You saw how recursion can be used instead of iteration, as in the horse race, and how it can be used to break down a problem into smaller sub-problems, as in the Towers of Hanoi example. Recursion is an example of an advanced computer science concept.

In this chapter we will explore recursion in Java along with other advanced computer science topics such as how computers work, how compilers and interpreters work, how to compare algorithms, and how Java works. **Computer science** is the scientific study of computation, which includes how to program computers, the theoretical basis of computing, how to network computers, how to make computers more intelligent, and how to design interfaces between people and computers. We write programs to store, transform, and transfer information. But, learning to program computers is just a small part of what you can do in computer science. Fields in computer science include 3D graphics, artificial intelligence, robotics, human-computer interaction, theory, programming languages, compilers, networking, and databases. Jobs that require a computer science degree are projected by the U. S. Department of Labor, Bureau of Labor Statistics to be some of the fastest growing through 2016.

16.1   Focusing on Computer Science

At this point, you probably have a lot of questions about what you've been doing in this book.

- "Why is Photoshop so much faster on large pictures than the programs I'm writing in Java?"
- "How fast can we get our programs to go?"
- "Does it always take this long to write programs? Can you write smaller programs to do the same things? Can you write programs more easily than this?"
- "What does programming look like in other programming languages?"

The answers to most of these questions are known or studied in computer science. This part of the book is an introduction to some of those topics as a signpost to get you started in exploring computer science further.

16.2   What Makes Programs Fast?

Where does the speed go? You buy a really fast computer, and a photo editor like iMovie or Photoshop seems really fast on it. Colors change as quickly as you can change the slider. But larger pictures don't seem to process as quickly in Java as in Photoshop. Why?

16.2.1   What Computers Really Understand

In reality, computers do not understand Alice, Java, C, Visual Basic, Python, or any other language. The basic computer only understands one kind of language — **machine language**. Machine language instructions are just values in the bytes in memory, and they tell the computer to do very low-level activities. In a real sense, the computer doesn't even "understand" machine language. The computer is just a machine with lots of switches that make data flow this way or that. Machine language is just a bunch of switch settings that make other switches in the computer change. We *interpret* those data switchings to be addition, subtraction, loading data, and storing data.

Each kind of computer has its own machine language. Apple computers and computers that run Windows can't run one another's programs, not because of any philosophical or marketing differences, but because each kind of computer has its own **processor** (core of the computer that actually executes the machine language). They *literally* don't understand one another. That's why an .exe program from Windows won't run on a Macintosh, and a Macintosh application won't run on a Windows computer. Those executable files are (almost always) machine language programs.

Machine language looks like a bunch of numbers — it's not particularly user-friendly. **Assembly language** is a set of words (or near-words) that corresponds one-to-one with machine language. Assembly instructions tell the computer to do things like store numbers into particular memory locations or into special locations (variables or registers) in the computer, test numbers for equality or comparison, or add numbers together or subtract them. An assembler translates an assembly language program into machine code.

An **assembly program** (and the corresponding machine language generated by an **assembler**) to add two numbers together and store them somewhere might look like this:

```
LOAD #10,R0      ; Load special variable R0 with 10
LOAD #12,R1      ; Load special variable R1 with 12
SUM R0,R1        ; Add special variables R0 and R1
STOR R1,#45      ; Store the result into memory location #45
01 00 10
01 01 12
02 00 01
03 01 45
```

An assembly program that might make a decision could look like this:

```
LOAD R1,#65536   ; Get a character from keyboard
TEST R1,#13      ; Is it an ASCII 13 (Enter)?
JUMPTRUE #32768  ; If true, go to another part of the program
CALL #16384      ; If false, call func. to process the new line
05 01 255 255
10 01 13
20 127 255
122 63 255
```

Input and output devices are often just memory locations to the computer. Maybe when you store a 255 to location 65,542, suddenly the red component of the pixel at (101,345) is set to maximum intensity. Maybe each time that the computer reads from memory location 897,784, it's a new sample just read from the microphone. In this way, these simple load and store operations handle multimedia, too.

Machine language is executed very quickly. The computer on which this chapter is being typed has a 2 gigahertz (GHz) processor. What that means *exactly* is hard to define, but roughly, it means that this computer processes 2 *billion* machine language instructions *per second*. A 12-byte machine language program that corresponds to something like a = b + c executes on this mid-range computer in something like 12/2,000,000,000 of a second.

16.2.2 Compilers and Interpreters

Applications like Adobe Photoshop and Microsoft Word are typically **compiled**. That means that they were written in a computer language like C or C++ and then *translated* into machine language using a program called a **compiler**. Those programs then execute at the speed of that base processor.

However, programming languages like Python, Scheme, Squeak, Director, and Flash are actually (in most cases) **interpreted**. Interpreting a language means reading and executing the statements one at a time instead of translating all of them into another language first. Java can be interpreted, too, but in a subtly different way that is explained later (Section 16.2.3). Interpreted programs execute at a slower speed. It's the difference between *translating* and then doing instructions versus simply doing the instructions one at a time.

A detailed example might help. Consider this exercise:

> Write a class `GraphicsInterpreter` that reads in a file of graphics *commands*. `GraphicsInterpreter` will have a method `interpret-Commands` that takes a filename as input (a `String`), reads the graphics commands from the file, and then returns a `Picture` with the graphics commands executed on it. The method `interpretCommands` starts out by creating a 640 × 480-pixel blank picture, then draws on that, and returns it.

There are two kinds of commands:

- "line 10 20 300 400" should draw a line from (10,20) to (300,400). You can assume that those are single spaces between the coordinates.
- "circle 100 200 10" draws a circle where the enclosing rectangle has an upper-left-hand corner at (100,200) and a diameter of 10.

An input graphics command might look like:

```
circle 20 20 100
circle 300 20 100
line 210 120 210 320
line 210 320 310 320
line 20 350 400 350
```

Program 16.1 defines a class `GraphicsInterpreter` that is a solution to the exercise. The implementation reads a file, one line at a time, into a string. It's checked to see if it starts with "circle" or "line." Using `split`, it gets chopped into pieces, then each of the little strings (the numbers for the coordinates) is converted to an integer using `Integer.parseInt()`.

Program 16.1: Interpret Graphics Commands in a File

```java
import java.io.*;
import java.awt.Color;
import java.awt.Graphics;
import java.awt.Graphics2D;

/**
 * Class that reads in a file of graphics instructions, and
 * executes them, showing the result. Default picture size
 * is 640x480.
 *
 * Format of the file is a bunch of lines of the form:
 * Command X Y <parameters>
 * Commands are:
 * "line" with parameters of start and end X and Y and
 * "circle" with the upper-left corner of the enclosing
 * rectangle and the diameter of the circle
 *
```

```
 *  For example:
 *  line 10 10 50 70
 *  circle 10 20 30
 *
 *  Which draws a line from (10,10) to (50,70) and a
 *  circle at (10,20) with a diameter of 30.
 *
 *  @author Barb Ericson
 *  @author Mark Guzdial
 */
public class GraphicsInterpreter
{
  /**
   * Method to interpret the commands in the given file
   */
  public Picture interpretCommands(String fileName)
  {
    String line = null;

    Picture frame = new Picture(640,480);
    String [] params = null;
    int x1, y1, x2, y2, diameter;
    Graphics g = frame.getGraphics();
    g.setColor(Color.black);

    // try the following
    try {

      // read from the file
      BufferedReader reader =
        new BufferedReader(new FileReader(fileName));

      // loop till end of file
      while ((line = reader.readLine()) != null)
      {
        // what command is this?
        if (line.startsWith("line"))
        {
          // Get the parameters for drawing the line
          params = line.split(" ");
          // params[0] should be "line"
          x1 = Integer.parseInt(params[1]);
          y1 = Integer.parseInt(params[2]);
          x2 = Integer.parseInt(params[3]);
          y2 = Integer.parseInt(params[4]);

          // Now, draw the line
          g.drawLine(x1,y1,x2,y2);
        }
        else if (line.startsWith("circle"))
        {
          // Get the parameters for drawing the circle
          params = line.split(" ");
```

```
        // params[0] should be "circle"
        x1 = Integer.parseInt(params[1]);
        y1 = Integer.parseInt(params[2]);
        diameter = Integer.parseInt(params[3]);

        // Now, draw the circle
        g.drawOval(x1,y1,diameter,diameter);
      }
      else {
        System.out.println("Uh-oh! Invalid command! "+line);
        return frame;}
    }
  } catch (FileNotFoundException ex) {
    System.out.println("Couldn't find file " + fileName);
    fileName = FileChooser.pickAFile();
    interpretCommands(fileName);
  } catch (Exception ex) {
    System.out.println("Error during read or write");
    ex.printStackTrace();
  }
    return frame;
}
public static void main(String[] args)
{
  GraphicsInterpreter interpreter = new GraphicsInterpreter();
  String fileName =
    FileChooser.getMediaPath("graphics-commands.txt");
  Picture p = interpreter.interpretCommands(fileName);
  p.show();
}
}
```

This solution works. Figure 16.1 shows the result of executing this program with a graphics-commands.txt file containing:

```
circle 20 20 100
circle 300 20 100
line 210 120 210 320
line 210 320 310 320
line 20 350 400 350
```

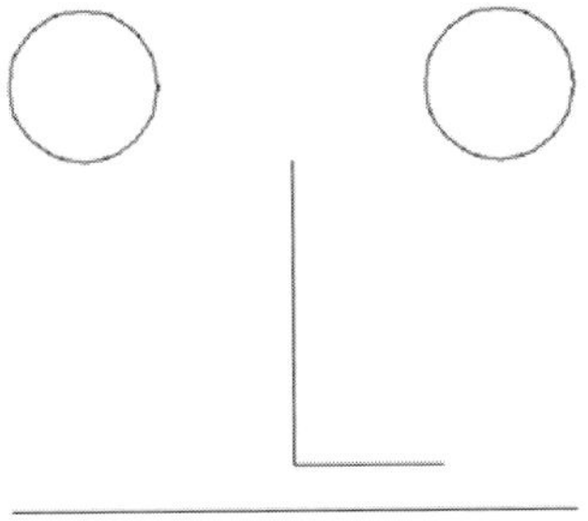

Figure 16.1
Results of running the GraphicsInterpreter

How It Works

The graphics commands are assumed to be in a file whose filename is passed to the method. In `interpretCommands`, we open a blank 640 × 480 frame for drawing, then get the graphics context for drawing on the frame. For each string `line` in the input file, we check to see if it starts with "line" or "circle." If it's a "line", we chop out the starting *x* and *y* coordinates and the ending *x* and *y* coordinates by using `split` on the string. Then we draw the line. If the command is a "circle," we get the two coordinates and the diameter, and draw the circle as an oval whose height and width are both the diameter. At the end, we return the resulting `Picture` object to the calling method (`main`) which calls `show` to display the picture.

What we've just done is implement a new language for graphics. We have even created an **interpreter** that reads the instructions for our new language and creates the picture that goes along with it. In principle, this is just what Postscript, PDF, Flash, and AutoCAD are doing. Their file formats specify pictures in just the way that our graphics language does. When they draw (**render**) the image to the screen, they are *interpreting* the commands in that file.

While we probably can't tell from such a small example, this is a relatively slow language. Consider the code in Program 16.2. Imagine that we compiled it and ran it — would it run faster than reading the list of commands and interpreting them? Both this program and Program 16.1 generate the exact same picture.

Program 16.2: Main with Drawing Commands

```java
import java.awt.*;
public class GeneratedDrawing
{
public static void main(String args[])
{
  Picture frame = new Picture(640,480);
  Graphics g = frame.getGraphics();
  g.setColor(Color.black);
  g.drawOval(20,20,100,100);
  g.drawOval(300,20,100,100);
  g.drawLine(210,120,210,320);
  g.drawLine(210,320,310,320);
  g.drawLine(20,350,400,350);
  frame.show();
} // end main()
} // end class
```

In general, we'd probably guess (correctly) that the direct instructions in Program 16.2 will run faster than Program 16.1 where the program reads a list of commands and interprets each command one at a time. Here's an analogy that might help. Say a student took French in college, but he says that he is really bad at it. Let's say that someone gave him a list of instructions in French. He could meticulously look up each word and figure out the instructions, and do them. What if he was asked to do the instructions again? He would have to look up each word again. What if they asked him to do it 10 times? He would do 10 lookups of all the words.

Now, let's imagine that he wrote down the English (his native language) translation of the French instructions. He can repeat doing the list of instructions as often as you like very quickly. Once the English version is created, it takes him no time to look up any words (though it probably depends on what he is being asked to do — brain surgery is *out*). In general, figuring out the language takes some time that is just over-head — just *doing* the instructions (or drawing the graphics) will always be faster.

Here's an idea: Could we *generate* the preceding program? Could we write a program that takes as input the graphics language we invented and then writes a Java program that draws the same pictures? This turns out not to be that hard. This would be a *compiler* for the graphics language. Program 16.3 implements a compiler for our graphics language.

Program 16.3: Compiler for New Graphics Language

```
import java.io.*;

/**
 * Class that reads in a file of graphics instructions, and
 * then generates a NEW Java Program that
 * does the same thing as the instructions. The default picture
 * size is 640x480.
 *
 * Format of the file is a bunch of lines of the form:
 * Command X Y <parameters>
 *
 * Commands are:
 * "line" with parameters of start and end X and Y and
 * "circle" with the upper-left corner of the enclosing
 * rectangle and the diameter of the circle
 *
 * For example:
 * line 10 10 50 70
 * circle 10 20 30
 *
 * Which draws a line from (10,10) to (50,70) and a
 * circle at (10,20) with a diameter of 30.
 *
 * @author Barb Ericson
 * @author Mark Guzdial
 */
public class GraphicsCompiler
{
  /** Method to write out the prologue for the new program:
   * All the imports, the class definition, main, etc.
   * @param file BufferedWriter to write the prologue to
   **/
  public void writePrologue(BufferedWriter file)
```

```java
{
  try {
    // Write out the prologue lines
    file.write("import java.awt.*;");
    file.newLine();
    file.write("public class GeneratedDrawing{");
    file.newLine();
    file.write(" public static void main(String args[]){");
    file.newLine();
    file.write("  Picture frame = new Picture(640,480);");
    file.newLine();
    file.write("  Graphics g = frame.getGraphics();");
    file.newLine();
    file.write("  g.setColor(Color.black);");
    file.newLine();}
  catch (Exception ex) {
    System.out.println("Error during write of prologue");
  }
}

/** Method to write out the epilogue for the new program:
 * Show the picture. Close the main and the class.
 * @param file BufferedWriter to write the epilogue to
 **/
public void writeEpilogue(BufferedWriter file){
  try {
    // Write out the epilogue lines
    file.write("  frame.show();"); file.newLine();
    file.write("  } // end main()"); file.newLine();
    file.write("} // end class"); file.newLine();}
  catch (Exception ex) {
    System.out.println("Error during write of epilogue");
  }
}

/**
 *Method to compile the commands in the given file
 * @param fileName the file to read from
 */
public void compileCommands(String fileName)
{
  String line = null;
  String [] params = null;
  int x1, y1, x2, y2, diameter;

  // try the following
  try {

    // read from the file
    BufferedReader reader =
      new BufferedReader(new FileReader(fileName));

    BufferedWriter writer =
      new BufferedWriter(new FileWriter(
    FileChooser.getMediaPath("GeneratedDrawing.java")));
```

```
        writePrologue(writer);
        // loop till end of file
        while ((line = reader.readLine()) != null)
        {
          // what command is this?
          if (line.startsWith("line"))
          {
            // Get the parameters for drawing the line
            params = line.split(" ");
            // params[0] should be "line"
            x1 = Integer.parseInt(params[1]);
            y1 = Integer.parseInt(params[2]);
            x2 = Integer.parseInt(params[3]);
            y2 = Integer.parseInt(params[4]);

            // Now, write the line that will LATER
            // draw the line
            writer.write("  g.drawLine("+x1+","+y1+",
                                  "+x2+","+y2+");");
            writer.newLine();
          }
          else if (line.startsWith("circle"))
          {
            // Get the parameters for drawing the circle
            params = line.split(" ");
            // params[0] should be "circle"
            x1 = Integer.parseInt(params[1]);
            y1 = Integer.parseInt(params[2]);
            diameter = Integer.parseInt(params[3]);

            // Now, draw the circle in
            writer.write("  g.drawOval("+x1+","+y1+",
                        "+diameter+","+
                        diameter+");");
            writer.newLine();
          }
          else {
            System.out.println("Uh-oh! Invalid command! "+line);
            return;}
        }
        writeEpilogue(writer);
        writer.close();

      } catch (FileNotFoundException ex) {
        System.out.println("Couldn't find file " + fileName);
        fileName = FileChooser.pickAFile();
        compileCommands(fileName);
      } catch (Exception ex) {
        System.out.println("Error during read or write");
        ex.printStackTrace();
      }
    }
```

```
  public static void main(String[] args)
  {
    GraphicsCompiler compiler = new GraphicsCompiler();
    String fileName =
      FileChooser.getMediaPath("graphics-commands.txt");
    compiler.compileCommands(fileName);
  }
}
```

How It Works

The main method calls the compiler (the method compileCommands does the compiling). The compiler accepts the *same* input as the interpreter (a filename to a file that contains our graphics commands). Then, as in the interpreter, the file containing the graphics command is opened for reading the commands one line at a time. Unlike the interpreter, however, the compiler doesn't open a Picture to write to but instead opens an output file named "GeneratedDrawing.java" in the current mediasources directory. The output file is named GeneratedDrawing.java because it will define a class named GeneratedDrawing. The writePrologue method is then called to write the start of the class and the beginning of a main method to the output file. At the beginning of the generated main method, we write out the code to create a Picture and a graphics context. Note that we're not really *making* the Picture here — we're simply writing out the Java commands that will make the Picture. The commands will be executed *later* when the output file containing the class GeneratedDrawing is compiled and its main method is executed.

The writePrologue method is a **helper method**, called from compileCommands. A helper method is one that helps another method by performing a subtask of the overall task. After writePrologue has completed its subtask, control returns to the compileCommands method.

Then, just like the interpreter, the compiler uses a while loop to read one line at a time from the input file and figure out which graphics command it is ("line" or "circle") and we figure out the coordinates from the input string. Then we write out the commands to do the drawing to the output file, GeneratedDrawing.java. Notice that we're reading the commands from the input file when executing the method compileCommands and we're writing the drawing commands to the class GeneratedDrawing that will be compiled and executed *later*. Just before the end of the method compileCommands, we call another helper method, writeEpilogue that performs the subtask of writing out commands to show the frame. Finally we close the file.

Now the compiler has a bunch of overhead, too. We still have to do the looking up of what the graphics commands mean. If we only have a small graphics program to run, and we only need it once, we might as well just run the interpreter. But what if we needed to run the picture 10 times, or 100 times? Then we pay the overhead of compiling the program *once*, and the next 9 or 99 times, we run it as fast as we possibly can. That will almost certainly be faster than doing the interpretation overhead 100 times.

This is what compilers are all about. Applications like Photoshop and Word are written in languages like C or C++ and then are *compiled* to *equivalent* machine language programs. The machine language program does the same thing that the C language says to do, just as the graphics programs created from our compiler do the same things as our graphics language says to do. But the machine language program runs *much* faster than we could interpret the C or C++ program.

Computer Science Idea: Compilers are Actually Programs

Compilers are one of the most magical things in computer science. Look again at the list of graphics commands that generated Figure 16.1. That's a program. Now look again at the Java program that GraphicsCompiler generated (the output of Program 16.3). Those are two *completely* different programs, but they *do* the same thing. A compiler writes an entirely new program in one language, given input in a different language. It's a program that writes programs.

16.2.3 The Special Case of Java

Originally, Java programs were designed to be *interpreted*. Java programs didn't originally compile to machine language for whatever computer they were being run on. Java programs compiled to a machine language for a *make-believe processor* — a *virtual machine*. The **Java Virtual Machine (JVM)** doesn't really exist as a physical processor. It's a definition of a processor. What good is that? It turns out that since machine language is *very* simple, building a machine language *interpreter* is pretty easy. It's just like our GraphicsInterpreter except that it reads in the bytes of a machine language program for a JVM, then just does what they say.

The result is that a JVM interpreter can be very easily made to run on just about any processor. That means that a program in Java is compiled *once* and then runs *everywhere*. Devices as small as wristwatches can run the same Java programs that run on large computers, because a JVM interpreter can run even on processors that live on your wristwatch. There's also an economic argument for virtual machines. Imagine that you're writing software for a programmable toaster oven. If the manufacturer decides to change the processor in the toaster oven, you have to recompile your traditional C or C++ programs to run on the new processor. But if both the old and new processor have JVM interpreters, then your Java programs will run on both without change or recompilation. Thus, a virtual machine can mean that you're less bound to a given processor, and a manufacturer has more flexibility to buy the least-expensive processor available.

On most computers today, Java *does* execute as machine language. Java *can* be compiled to machine language. But even when Java is compiled to JVM machine language, modern JVM interpreters are actually JVM *compilers*. When you tell Java on a Windows or Macintosh computer today "Go run this JVM machine language program," what it actually does is pause a moment, compile the JVM to native machine language, then run the native machine language. Computers are so fast today that you don't really notice the pause while it's compiling.

That's the first part of the answer to the question "Why is Photoshop faster than Java for large programs?" Photoshop is running in native machine code, while our Java programs are running on a JVM interpreter — which, even if it does compile to native machine language first, is still slightly slower than straight machine language.

Then why have an interpreter at all? There are many good reasons. Here are three:

- Do you like the Alice programming environment or the DrJava Interactions Pane? Did you even once ever create some example code just to *try* it? That kind of interactive, exploratory, trying-things-out programming is available with interpreters. Compilers don't let you easily try things out line-by-line and print out results. Interpreters are good for learners.

- Once a program is compiled to Java machine language, it can be used *anywhere,* from huge computers to programmable toaster ovens — as is! That's a big savings for software developers. They only ship one program, and it runs on anything.

- Virtual machines are safer than running machine language. A program running in machine language might do all kinds of non-secure things. A virtual machine can carefully keep track of the programs that it is interpreting to make sure that they only do safe things, like using only valid indices in arrays.

16.2.4 How Fast Can We Really Go?

The raw power of compiled vs. interpreted programs is only part of the answer of why Photoshop is faster. The deeper part, and one which can actually make interpreted programs *faster* than compiled programs, is in the design of the *algorithms.* There's a temptation to think, "Oh, it's okay if it's slow now. Wait 18 months, we'll get double the processor speed, and then it will be fine." There are some algorithms that are *so* slow they will never end in your lifetime, and others that can't be written at all. Rewriting the algorithm to be *smarter* about what we ask the computer to do can make a dramatic impact on performance.

An **algorithm** is a textual description of how to solve a problem, similar to the textual storyboards we used to design animation programs in Alice. A program (classes and methods in Alice and Java) are executable interpretations of algorithms. The same algorithm can be implemented in many different languages. There is always more than one algorithm to solve the same problem. Some computer scientists study algorithms and come up with ways to compare them and decide which ones are better than others.

We've seen several algorithms in different situations that are really doing the same things:

- Sampling to scale up or down a picture or to lower or raise the frequency of a sound

- Blending to merge two pictures or two sounds

- Mirroring sounds and pictures

All of these process data in the same way. It's just the data that changes — pixels for pictures, samples for sounds. We say that these are the same algorithms.

We can compare algorithms based on several criteria. One is how much *space* the algorithm needs to run. How much memory does the algorithm require? That can become a significant issue for media computation because so much memory is required to hold all that data. Think about how bad (unusable in normal situations) an algorithm would be that needed to hold *all* the frames of a movie in memory at the same time.

The most common criterion used to compare algorithms is *time*. How much time does the algorithm take? We don't literally mean clock time, but how many steps does the algorithm require? Computer scientists use **Big-Oh notation**, or $O(\ )$ to refer to the magnitude of the running time of an algorithm. The idea of Big-Oh is to express how much slower the program gets as the input data get larger. If the data get twice as large, an $O(n)$ algorithm would take twice as long to run, but an $O(n^2)$ algorithm would take *four* times longer to run. Big-Oh notation tries to ignore differences between languages, even between compiled versus interpreted, and focuses on the number of *steps* to be executed.

Think about our basic picture and sound processing examples such as `increaseRed` or `increaseVolume`. Some of the complexity of these programs is hidden in the provided methods like `getPixels()` and `getSamples()`. In general, though, we refer to these as being $O(n)$. The amount of time that the program takes to run is proportional linearly to the input data. If the picture or sound doubled in size, we'd expect the program to take twice as long to run.

When we figure out Big-Oh, we typically clump the body of the loop into one step. We think about those functions as processing each sample or pixel once, so the real time spent in those programs is the main loop, and it doesn't really matter how many statements are in that loop.

Unless there is another loop in that loop body, that is. Loops are multiplicative in terms of time. Nested loops multiply the amount of time that is needed to run the body. Think about this simple example:

```
> int count = 0;
> for (int x=0; x<5; x++)
    for (int y=0; y<3; y++)
      {count = count + 1;
       System.out.println("Ran "+count+" times: x="+x+" y="+y);}
```

When we run it, we see that it actually executes 15 times — five for the *x*'s, three for the *y*'s, and 5 * 3 = 15, as shown in the output created:

```
Ran 1 times: x=0 y=0
Ran 2 times: x=0 y=1
Ran 3 times: x=0 y=2
Ran 4 times: x=1 y=0
Ran 5 times: x=1 y=1
Ran 6 times: x=1 y=2
Ran 7 times: x=2 y=0
Ran 8 times: x=2 y=1
Ran 9 times: x=2 y=2
Ran 10 times: x=3 y=0
Ran 11 times: x=3 y=1
```

```
Ran 12 times: x=3 y=2
Ran 13 times: x=4 y=0
Ran 14 times: x=4 y=1
Ran 15 times: x=4 y=2
```

16.2.5 Making Searching Faster

Consider how you might look up a word in the dictionary. One way is to check the first page, then the next page, then the next page, and so on. That's called a **linear search**, and it's $O(n)$. It's not very efficient. The *best case* (fastest the algorithm could possibly be) is that the problem is solved in one step because the word we are seeking is on the first page. The *worst case* is n steps where n is the number of pages because the word could be on the last page or not even in the dictionary. The *average case* is $n/2$ steps which would be the case when the word is about halfway through.

Program 16.4 defines a `Searcher` class to implement this algorithm in method `linearFind` that performs a linear search of an array of strings.

Program 16.4: Linear Search of an Array of Strings

```java
/**
 * Class that demonstrates search algorithms
 * @author Mark Guzdial
 * @author Barb Ericson
 **/
public class Searcher
{

  /**
   * Implement a linear search through the list
   **/
  public static String linearFind(String target,
                                  String[] strArray)
  {
    for (int index=0; index < strArray.length; index++)
    {
      if (target.compareTo(strArray[index]) == 0)
      {return("Found it!"); }
    }
    return("Not found");
  }

  /** main for testing linearFind */
  public static void main(String[] args)
  {
    String[] searchMe = "apple","bear","cat","dog","elephant"};
    System.out.println(linearFind("apple",searchMe));
    System.out.println(linearFind("cat",searchMe));
    System.out.println(linearFind("giraffe",searchMe));
  }
}
```

When we run Program 16.4, we get what we would expect:

```
> java Searcher
Found it!
Found it!
Not found
```

The `linearFind` method in Program 16.4 uses the `compareTo` method on string objects because the class `String` implements the `java.lang.Comparable` interface. Because the method uses `compareTo`, we could make this search method more general by modifying the code to search an array of `Comparable` objects for a particular `Comparable` object. Program 16.5 shows a more general `linearFind` method that returns `true` if the target of the search is found and otherwise returns `false`.

Program 16.5: Linear Search of an Array of Comparable Objects

```
public static boolean linearFind(Comparable target,
                                 Comparable[] theArray)
{
  for (Comparable item : theArray)
  {
    if (target.compareTo(item) == 0)
      return true;
  }
  return false;
}
```

Now we can use this to search an array of any class that implements the `Comparable` interface. To illustrate, let's modify the `Picture` class to implement the `Comparable` interface by adding `implements Comparable` to the class declaration, like this:

```
public class Picture extends SimplePicture
  implements Comparable<Picture>
```

Note that we specified the type of object that can be compared by using a generic, (`Com.parable<Picture>`). The `Comparable` interface requires the implementing class to have a `compareTo` method that returns an integer. So add a method `compareTo` to the `Picture` class that returns a negative number if this picture is less than the passed picture object, 0 if they are equal, and a positive number if this picture is greater than the passed picture. To compare the pictures, we first compare the widths and if they do not have the same width, return the difference in widths. Otherwise, the two pictures have the same width so we then compare the heights. If the heights are different, return the height difference. Finally, if the width and height are the same, we compare the filenames.

```
public int compareTo(Picture p)
{
  // first compare the widths
  int diffWidth = this.getWidth() - p.getWidth();

  // if the difference in widths isn't zero return it
  if (diffWidth != 0)
    return diffWidth;
```

```
  // compare the heights
  int diffHeight = this.getHeight() - p.getHeight();

  // if the difference in heights isn't zero return it
  if (diffHeight != 0)
    return diffHeight;

  // else compare the fileNames
  return this.getFileName().compareTo(p.getFileName());
}
```

We can also override the `equals` method that we inherit from `Object` to call `compareTo`.

```
public boolean equals(Picture p)
{
  return (this.compareTo(p) == 0);
}
```

It is recommended that you override `equals` to match `compareTo` when you implement the `Comparable` interface. We can now use the `linearFind` method of the `Searcher` class to see if a slide show object contains a particular picture.

```
public boolean contains(Picture p)
{
    return Searcher.linearFind(p,this.pictureArray);
}
```

■

Dictionaries are already in sorted order so we can be smarter about how we search for a word, and do it in $O(logn)$ time ($logn = x$ where $2^x = n$). Split the dictionary in the middle. Is the word before, on the page, or after the page you're looking at? If after, look in the section from the middle to the end (that is, again split the book, but from the middle to end). If the word is on the page, you are done. If before, look from start to middle (split halfway between start and middle). Keep repeating until you find the word or it couldn't possibly be there. This is a more efficient algorithm. In the best case, it's in the first place you look. In the average and worst case, it's *logn* steps — keep dividing the *n* pages in half, and you'll have at most *logn* splits.

Program 16.6 defines a simple (not the best possible, but illustrative) implementation of this kind of a search, known as a **binary search**. Add it to the `Searcher` class. Then modify the `main` method as shown below.

Program 16.6: Simple Binary Search

```
/**
 * Method to use a binary search to find a target string in a
 * sorted array of strings
 */
public static String binaryFind(String target,
                                String[] strArray)
```

```
{
  int start = 0;
  int end = strArray.length - 1;
  int checkpoint = 0;

  while (start <= end)
  {
    // While there are more to search
    // find the middle
    checkpoint = (int)((start+end)/2.0);
    if (target.compareTo(strArray[checkpoint]) == 0)
    {
      return "Found it!";
    }
    else if (target.compareTo(strArray[checkpoint]) > 0)
    {
      start=checkpoint + 1;
    }
    else if (target.compareTo(strArray[checkpoint]) < 0)
    {
      end=checkpoint - 1;
    }
  }
  return "Not found";
}
/**
 * Main for testing binaryFind
 */
public static void main(String[] args)
{
  String[] searchMe = {"apple","bear","cat","dog","elephant"};
  System.out.println(binaryFind("apple",searchMe));
  System.out.println(binaryFind("cat",searchMe));
  System.out.println(binaryFind("giraffe",searchMe));
}
}
```

How It Works

We start with the low-end marker start at the beginning of the list, and end for the last index of the list (length of the list minus one). As long as there is *something* between start and end, we continue to search. We compute checkpoint as halfway between start and end. We then check to see if we found it. If so, we're done and we return. If not, we figure out if we have to move start up to checkpoint or end down to checkpoint and we continue searching. If we ever get through the whole loop, we didn't take the "Found it!" return, so we return that we didn't find it.

To trace what is happening as the code executes, you can insert a print statement just after assigning checkpoint and just before the first if statement:

```
System.out.println("Checking at: "+
  checkpoint+" start="+start+" end="+end);
```

Here's the same `main` running. With this additional print statement, we can see how the code narrows in on "apple" then "bear" and then never finds "giraffe."

```
Welcome to DrJava.
> java SearchMethods
Checking at: 2 start=0 end=4
Checking at: 0 start=0 end=1
Found it!
Checking at: 2 start=0 end=4
Found it!
Checking at: 2 start=0 end=4
Checking at: 3 start=3 end=4
Checking at: 4 start=4 end=4
Not found
```

16.2.6 Sorting Algorithms

Searching for something in a sorted array using binary search is much quicker than looking for something in an unsorted array. But, how do we sort data in an array? There is a group of algorithms called **sorting algorithms** that are used to order data in alphabetical or numerical order. One of the most commonly used algorithms in this group is known as a **selection sort**. The algorithm for doing a selection sort starts by assuming that the first element of an array (at index 0) has the smallest value, and then searches the rest of the array for anything smaller, keeping track of the index of the smallest element. Then it swaps the value at the first element with the value at the smallest index. It continues doing this for each element of the array except the last one (this one will be the largest after everything smaller is moved before it). Program 16.7 presents the `selectSort` method that has been defined in the class `ArraySorter`. The `ArraySorter` class has a field named a that is an array of integer values.

Program 16.7: Selection Sort on an Array of Integers

```
public void selectionSort()
{
  int maxCompare = a.length - 1;
  int smallestIndex = 0;
  int numSteps = 0;

  // loop from 0 to one before last item
  for (int i = 0; i < maxCompare; i++)
  {
    // set smallest index to the one at i
    smallestIndex = i;
    numSteps = 0;

    // loop from i+1 to the end looking for a smaller value
    for (int j = i + 1; j < a.length; j++)
```

```
      {
        numSteps++;
        if (a[j] < a[smallestIndex])
        {
          smallestIndex = j;
        }
      }
      System.out.println("#steps:"+numSteps);

      // swap the one at i with the one at smallest index
      swap(i,smallestIndex);
      this.printArray("after loop body when i = " + i);
    }
  }
```

We can try out the selection sort using the following method that creates an ArraySorter object named `sorter` and then calls the `selectionSort` method on the `sorter` object.

```
public static void testSelectionSort()
  {
    int[] testArray = {23, 14, 1, 89, 68, 32, 6};
    ArraySorter sorter = new ArraySorter(testArray);
    sorter.printArray("Before selection sort");
    sorter.selectionSort();
    sorter.printArray("After selection sort");
  }
```

We get the following output:

```
Before selection sort
23 14 1 89 68 32 6
#steps:6
after loop body when i = 0
1 14 23 89 68 32 6
#steps:5
after loop body when i = 1
1 6 23 89 68 32 14
#steps:4
after loop body when i = 2
1 6 14 89 68 32 23
#steps:3
after loop body when i = 3
1 6 14 23 68 32 89
#steps:2
after loop body when i = 4
1 6 14 23 32 68 89
#steps:1
after loop body when i = 5
1 6 14 23 32 68 89
After selection sort
```

Notice that this list has 7 elements in it and the number of steps is 6 the first time through the loop and then 5 the second time through the loop and then 4 and so on in successive loop iterations till the final time through the loop it is 1. We can generalize this concept in that for a list of n elements the selectionSort will execute $(n-1) + (n-2) + (n-3) + \ldots 2 + 1$ steps. This is a well known kind of problem and it means that there are $(n * (n-1)) / 2$ steps in this algorithm. This is a complexity of $O(n^2)$ since n^2 grows much faster than n as n gets really large.

Making It Work Tip: Adding N Numbers

You can look at the problem of adding up N numbers from 1 to N as the same thing as adding 1 and N and 2 and $N-1$ and 3 and $N-2$ etc., which is $(N+1) * N$ and then divide by 2 to get the answer for just the sum of 1 to N. This reduces to $(N+1)* N/2$. So to add up the numbers from 1 to 6 is 7*6/2 = 21 (as shown in Figure 16.2).

$$1 + 2 + 3 + 4 + 5 + 6$$
$$6 + 5 + 4 + 3 + 2 + 1$$

$$7 + 7 + 7 + 7 + 7 + 7$$
$$7 * 6 = 42 / 2 = 21$$

Figure 16.2
How to add N numbers

Another common sorting algorithm is **insertion sort**. Program 16.8 defines a method for using an insertion sort on an array of integers. In this algorithm the idea is to start at the next unsorted element in the array and insert it into the sorted part of the array at the correct location by shifting to the right any larger values. It starts with the second element in the array and inserts it into the sorted list that starts with the first element in the array. It loops through each additional element of the array inserting it into the proper place in the sorted section of the array.

Program 16.8: Insertion Sort on an Array of Integers

```
public void insertionSort()
  {
    int temp = 0;
    int pos = 0;

    // loop from second element on
    for (int i = 1; i < a.length; i++)
    {
      // save current value at i and set position to i
      temp = a[i];
      pos = i;

      // shift right any larger elements
      while (0 < pos && temp < a[pos - 1])
```

```
      {
        a[pos] = a[pos - 1];
        pos- -;
      }
      a[pos] = temp;
      this.printArray("after loop body when i = " + i);
    }
  }
```

We can test this method using the following:

```
  public static void testInsertionSort()
  {
    int[] testArray = {23, 14, 1, 89, 68, 32, 6};
    ArraySorter sorter = new ArraySorter(testArray);
    sorter.printArray("Before insertion sort");
    sorter.insertionSort();
    sorter.printArray("After insertion sort");
  }
```

We will get the following output:

```
Before insertion sort
23 14 1 89 68 32 6
after loop body when i = 1
14 23 1 89 68 32 6
after loop body when i = 2
1 14 23 89 68 32 6
after loop body when i = 3
1 14 23 89 68 32 6
after loop body when i = 4
1 14 23 68 89 32 6
after loop body when i = 5
1 14 23 32 68 89 6
after loop body when i = 6
1 6 14 23 32 68 89
After insertion sort
1 6 14 23 32 68 89
```

If we execute insertion sort on an array that is already sorted in ascending order, it will do $(n-1)$ comparisons and won't shift any values to the right. But, if we execute it on an array sorted in descending order, it will do as much work as a selection sort. On average, it will do about $(n * (n-1))/4$ steps which is $O(n^2)$; the same as the selection sort. ∎

The $O(n^2)$ complexity of both selection and insertion sort algorithms means that, on average, these two algorithms execute in about the same amount of time. There are smarter algorithms, however, like **mergesort** that have complexity $O(nlogn)$ which means that it can run faster than either selection or insertion sort. The mergesort algorithm is to break the array into two arrays and call mergesort on each new array. This will create two sorted arrays that just have to be merged back together in order. This uses recursion, which means that the method will call itself. An array that has only one element in it is considered sorted, and this is the point at which the recursion stops (the base case).

Program 16.9: Mergesort on an Array of Integers

```java
public void mergeSort()
{
  // check if there is only 1 element return
  if (a.length == 1) return;

  // otherwise create two new arrays
  int[] left = new int[a.length / 2];
  for (int i = 0; i < left.length; i++)
    left[i] = a[i];
  int[] right = new int[a.length - left.length];
  for (int i = left.length, j=0;
      i < a.length; i++, j++)
    right[j] = a[i];

  // create new ArraySorter objects
  ArraySorter sorter1 = new ArraySorter(left);
  sorter1.printArray("sorter1");
  ArraySorter sorter2 = new ArraySorter(right);
  sorter2.printArray("sorter2");

  // do the recursive call with the new sorters
  sorter1.mergeSort();
  sorter2.mergeSort();

  // merge the resulting arrays
  merge(left,right);
  this.printArray("After merge");
}

/**
 * Method to merge two sorted arrays
 * back into this object's array
 * @param left sorted left array
 * @param right the sorted right array
 */
private void merge(int[] left, int[] right)
{
  int leftIndex = 0; // current left index
  int rightIndex = 0; // current right index
  int i = 0; // current index in a

  // merge the left and right arrays into a
  while (leftIndex < left.length &&
        rightIndex < right.length)
  {
    if (left[leftIndex] < right[rightIndex])
    {
      a[i] = left[leftIndex];
      leftIndex++;
    }
}
```

```
      else
      {
        a[i] = right[rightIndex];
        rightIndex++;
      }
      i++;
    }

    // copy any remaining in left
    for (int j = leftIndex; j < left.length; j++)
    {
      a[i] = left[j];
      i++;
    }

    // copy any remaining in right
    for (int j = rightIndex; j < right.length; j++)
    {
      a[i] = right[j];
      i++;
    }
  }
}
```

You can test mergesort using the following:

```
public static void testMergeSort()
{
  int[] testArray = {23, 14, 1, 89, 68, 32, 6};
  ArraySorter sorter = new ArraySorter(testArray);
  sorter.printArray("Before merge sort");
  sorter.mergeSort();
  sorter.printArray("After merge sort");
}
```

This will give the following output:

```
Before merge sort
23 14 1 89 68 32 6
sorter1
23 14 1
sorter2
89 68 32 6
sorter1
23
sorter2
14 1
sorter1
14
sorter2
1
After merge
1 14
After merge
1 14 23
```

```
sorter1
89 68
sorter2
32 6
sorter1
89
sorter2
68
After merge
68 89
sorter1
32
sorter2
6
After merge
6 32
After merge
6 32 68 89
After merge
1 6 14 23 32 68 89
After merge sort
1 6 14 23 32 68 89
```

    With *selection sort* or *insertion sort* an array of 100 elements will require about 10,000 steps to sort. With *mergesort* an array of 100 elements would only take 460 steps to process. Those kinds of differences start to have huge real clock-time differences when you're talking about processing 10,000 customers to put them in order for reports . . .

16.2.7 Other Recursive Algorithms

Have you ever read the book *The Cat in the Hat Comes Back* by Dr. Seuss? In it the cat needs to clean up a mess and he does it by asking for help from the cat in his hat. The cat in his hat, named Little Cat A, asks for help from the cat in his hat, named Little Cat B. This continues on to Little Cat Z and the mess is finally all cleaned up. This is an analogy for the way recursion works.

    Recursion usually breaks a problem into easier sub-problems and stops when the simplest state is reached. You saw that in `mergesort` which broke the passed array into two parts and called `mergesort` on each part until the arrays had a length of 1 and then merged the sorted arrays back into one array. Each recursive call should get you closer to a stopping state (the base case).

    In Alice you used recursion to race horses in a carnival game. The `race` method had a test to see if a horse had won and if not it chose one horse to move a random small amount forward and called the `race` method again. The code for the `race` method is shown again in Figure 16.3. Recursion was also used to solve the Towers of Hanoi puzzle by breaking the puzzle down into simpler sub-problems.

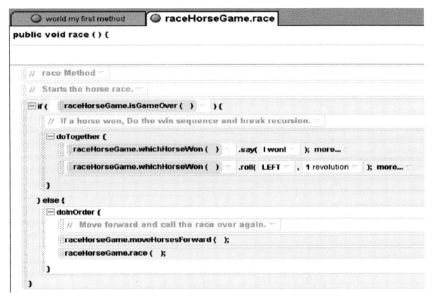

Figure 16.3
Recursion in Alice

We can apply the recursive technique to get a `Turtle` object to draw a tree. Turtles know how to go forward a given amount and they leave a trail when they move. In Program 16.10, we ask a Turtle to draw a tree and have it go forward a given amount and then create two new turtles at the same position, turn them slightly to the left and right, and then ask them draw a tree using a smaller amount to go forward. The turtles stop the recursion when the amount to go forward is 5 pixels or less. This recursive algorithm takes advantage of the branching nature of trees.

Program 16.10: drawTree method in the Turtle class

```java
public void drawTree(int branchLength)
  {
    // only continue if the branch is greater than 5
    if (branchLength > 5)
    {
      // move this turtle forward by the branch length
      this.forward(branchLength);

      // modify the length of the next branches
      branchLength = (int) (0.8 * branchLength);

      // get the current turtle values
      int x = this.getXPos();
      int y = this.getYPos();
      ModelDisplay display = this.getModelDisplay();
```

```
  // create a child to handle the left branch
  Turtle leftChild = new Turtle(x,y,display);
  leftChild.setHeading(this.getHeading());
  leftChild.turn(-30);
  leftChild.drawTree(branchLength);

  // create a child to handle the right branch
  Turtle rightChild = new Turtle(x,y,
                      this.getModelDisplay());
  rightChild.setHeading(this.getHeading());
  rightChild.turn(30);
  rightChild.drawTree(branchLength);
 }
 // don't show the turtle
 this.setVisible(false);
}
```

You can use the following to test the `drawTree` method.

```
> World w = new World(false);
> Turtle t = new Turtle(320,480,w);
> t.drawTree(100);
> w.setVisible(true);
```

The result is shown in Figure 16.4.

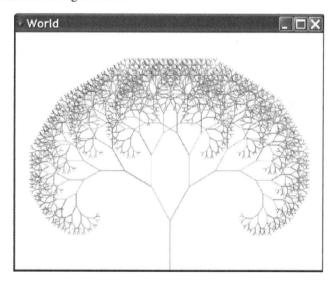

Figure 16.4
Using Turtle objects to draw a tree

Recursion is often used to navigate through directories and subdirectories in a computer's file system. In Java, the `java.io.File` class can represent a file or a directory. A directory can contain other directories and/or files. You can write a recursive method to write out the files in a directory and all sub-directories using recursion.

Barb added a listFiles method (see Program 16.11) to the DirectoryWorker class as a class (static) method.

Program 16.11: Method to List All the Files in a Directory and in All Sub-directories

```
public static void listFiles(File dir)
{
  File[] fileArray = dir.listFiles();
  for (File currFile : fileArray)
  {
    System.out.println(" File " +
                  currFile.getPath());
    if (currFile.isDirectory())
      listFiles(currFile);
  }
}
```

Because listFiles is a class method it can be called using DirectoryWorker. listFiles rather than being called on an instance of the class. You can test this with the following:

```
> File startDir =
new File("c:\\intro-prog-java\\mediasources\\students\\");
> DirectoryWorker.listFiles(startDir);
```

■

16.2.8 Algorithms that Never Finish or Can't Be Written

Here's a thought experiment: Imagine that you want to write a program that will generate hit songs for you. Your program will recombine bits of sounds that are some of the best riffs you've ever heard on various instruments — some 60 of them. You want to generate every combination of these 60 bits (some in, some out; some earlier in the song, some later). You want to find a combination that is less than 2 minutes 30 seconds (for optimal radio play time) and has the right amount of high and low volume combinations (and you've got a checkSound() function to do that).

How many combinations are there? Trying to solve this with 60 sound bits seems like a huge problem to start with. Let's solve an easier problem first. Let's say that you've got three sounds: *a*, *b*, and *c*. Your possible songs are the empty song (no bits at all), *a*, *b*, *c*, *bc*, *ac*, *ab*, and *abc*. Try it with two sounds or four sounds, and you'll see that the pattern is the same that we saw earlier with bits: For *n* things, every combination of include-or-exclude is 2^n. (If we don't want to use the empty song, it's $2^n - 1$.)

Therefore, our 60 sounds will result in 2^{60} combinations to run through our length and sound checks. That's 1,152,921,504,606,846,976 combinations. Let's imagine that we can do the checks in only a single instruction (unbelievable, of course, but we're pretending). On a 1.5-gigahertz computer, we can handle that many combinations in 768,614,336 seconds. Spell that out: That's 12,810,238 minutes, which is 213,504 hours, which is 8,896 days. That's 24 *YEARS* to run that program. Now, since **Moore's Law** says that technological innovations double computer process rates every 18 months, we could soon run that program in much less time. Only *12 YEARS!* If we cared about order, too (e.g., *abc* vs. *cba* vs. *bac*), the number of combinations would have 63 zeroes in it.

Finding the absolute optimal combination of just about anything is always expensive in terms of computer time. $O(2^n)$ is not an uncommon running time for these kinds of algorithms. But there are other problems that seem like they should be solvable in reasonable time, but aren't.

One of these difficult problems is the famous *Traveling Salesman Problem.* Imagine that you're a salesperson, and you're responsible for a bunch of different clients — let's say 30, half the size of the optimization problem. To be efficient, you want to find the shortest path on the map that will let you visit each client exactly once, and not more than once.

The best-known algorithm that gives an optimal solution for the Traveling Salesman Problem is $O(n!)$. That's *n factorial.* To calculate the factorial of a number *n* you multiply *n* by $(n - 1)$ then by $(n - 2)$ all the way down to 1. The factorial of 5 is $5 * 4 * 3 * 2 * 1 = 120$.

There are algorithms that take less time to run and give a good path but that path isn't guaranteed to be the shortest. For 30 cities, the number of steps to execute a $O(n!)$ algorithm that finds the shortest path is 30! or 265,252,859,812,191,058,636,308,480,000,000. Go ahead and run that on a 1.5-gigahertz processor — it won't get done in your lifetime.

The really aggravating part is that the Traveling Salesman Problem isn't some made-up, toy problem. There really are people who have to plan shortest routes. For example, shipping managers for shipping goods on truck, train, or airline routes. There are similar problems that are basically the same algorithmically, like planning the route of a robot on a factory floor. This is a big, hard problem.

Computer scientists classify problems into three kinds:

- Many problems (like sorting) can be solved with an algorithm whose running time has a complexity that's a polynomial, like $O(n^2)$. We call these **class P** (P for Polynomial) problems.

- Other problems, like optimization, have known algorithms (solutions to those problems) but the solutions are so hard and big that we know we just can't solve them in a reasonable amount of time even for reasonable amounts of data. We call these problems **intractable**.

- Still other problems, like Traveling Salesman, *seem* intractable, but maybe there's a solution in class P that we just haven't found yet. We call these **class NP**.

One of the biggest unsolved problems in theoretical computer science is either proving that class NP and class P are completely distinct (that is, we'll never solve Traveling Salesman optimally in polynomial time), or that class NP is within class P.

You might wonder, "How can we prove *anything* about algorithms?" There are so many different languages, and different ways of writing the same algorithm. How can we positively *prove* something is doable or not doable? It turns out that we can. In fact, Alan Turing proved that there are even algorithms that *can't be written!*

The most famous algorithm that can't be written is a solution to the *Halting Problem*. In this book, we've already written programs that can read other programs and write out other programs. We can imagine a program that can read one program and tell us things about it (for example, how many `print` statements are in it). Can we write a program that will input another program (for example, from a file) then tell us if the program will ever *stop*? Think about the input program having some complex `while` loops where it's hard to tell if the expression in the `while` loop is ever `false`. Now imagine a bunch of these, all nested within one another.

Alan Turing proved that such a program can never be written. He used proof by absurdity. He showed that if such a program (call it *H*) could ever be written, you could try feeding that program to itself as input. Now *H* takes input, a program, right? What if you modified *H* (call it *H2*) so that if *H* would say "This one halts!" *H2* would instead loop forever (that is, `while (true)`). Turing showed that such a setup would announce that the program would halt only if it loops forever, and would halt only if it announces that it would loop forever.

The really amazing thing is that Turing came up with this proof in 1936 — almost ten years before the first computers were ever built! He defined a mathematical concept of a computer called a **Turing machine** and he was able to make such proofs before physical computers were ever built.

Here's another thought experiment for you: Is human intelligence computable? Our brains are executing some process that enables us to think, right? Can we write down that process as an algorithm? And if a computer executes that algorithm, is it thinking? Is a human reducible to a computer? This is one of the big questions in the field of **artificial intelligence**.

16.2.9 Why Is Photoshop Faster than Our Programs in Java?

We can now answer the question of why Photoshop is faster than our programs in Java. First, Photoshop is compiled, so it runs at raw machine language speeds.

But the other part is that Photoshop has algorithms that are smarter than what we're doing. For example, think about the programs where we searched for colors, like in Chromakey or in making hair red. We know that the background color and the hair color were clumped next to one another. What if, instead of linearly searching all pixels, you just searched from where the color was what you were looking for, until you didn't find that color anymore — you reached the boundary. That would be a smarter search. That's the kind of thing that Photoshop does.

16.3   What Makes a Computer Fast?

Computers are getting faster all the time — Moore's Law promises us that. But that doesn't help us to compare computers that are all of the same Moore's Law generation. How do you compare advertisements in the paper and figure out which of the computers listed is *really* the fastest?

○ **Intel® Centrino® 2 processor technology with interrelated Intel® Core™2 Duo processor P8400**
Intel® PM45 chipset, Intel® Wi-Fi Link 5100 network connection (802.11a/b/g/n) and extended battery life.

○ **4GB DDR3 memory**
For multitasking power. 1066MHz frontside bus, 3MB L2 cache and 2.26GHz processor speed.

○ **Multiformat DVD±RW/CD-RW drive**
With double-layer support records up to 8.5GB of data or 4 hours of video using compatible DVD+R and DVD-R DL media; supports DVD-RAM; supports Labelflash direct-disc labels using compatible media.

○ **17" WXGA high-definition widescreen TFT-LCD display**
With UltraBright technology brings life to your movies and games.

○ **320GB SATA hard drive (7200 rpm)**
Offers spacious storage options and fast read/write times.

○ **NVIDIA GeForce 9800M GTS graphics**
Features 1GB of GDDR3 discrete video memory for lush images and vivid detail. 2 built-in speakers with high-definition audio support. HDMI v1.2 connector.

○ **Intel® Celeron® processor 585**
Features a 667MHz frontside bus, 1MB cache and 2.16GHz processor speed.

○ **2GB DDR2 memory**
For multitasking power, expandable to 4GB.

○ **Multiformat DVD±RW/CD-RW drive with double-layer support**
Records up to 8.5GB of data or 4 hours of video using compatible media.

○ **15.6" WXGA widescreen display with BrightView technology**
Supports high-definition video playback with 1366 x 768 resolution for movies and games with stunning clarity.

○ **160GB SATA hard drive (5400 rpm)**
Offers spacious storage options and fast read/write times.

○ **Intel® Graphics Media Accelerator 4500M**
With up to 797MB total available graphics memory. Altec Lansing audio for improved sound quality.

Figure 16.5
Sample computer advertisements

Simply being fast is only one criterion for picking a computer, of course. There are issues of cost, how much disk space you need, what kind of special features you need, and so on. But in this section we'll explicitly deal with what the various factors in the computer ads (see Figure 16.5 for some examples) mean in terms of computer speed.

16.3.1 Clock Rates and Actual Computation

When computer ads list that they have a "Some-brand Processor 2.26 GHz" or "Other-brand Processor 2.16 GHz," what they're talking about is the **clock rate**. The processor is the smarts of your computer — it's the part that makes decisions and does computation. It does all this computing work at a specific *pace*. Imagine a drill sergeant shouting, "Go! Go! Go! Go!" That's what the clock rate is — how fast does the drill sergeant shout "Go!"? A clock rate of 2.26 GHz means that the clock *pulses* (the drill sergeant shouts "Go!") 2.26 *billion* times per second.

That doesn't mean that the processor actually does something useful with every "Go!" Some computations have several steps to them, so it may take several pulses of the clock to complete a single useful computation. But *in general*, a faster clock rate implies faster computation. Certainly, for the same *kind* of processor, a faster clock rate implies faster computation.

Is there really any difference between 2.26 GHz and 2.16 GHz? Or is 1.0 GHz with processor X about the same as 2.0 GHz with processor Y? Those are much tougher questions. It's not really that much different than arguing over Dodge versus Ford trucks. Most processors have their advocates and their critics. Some will argue that processor X can do a particular search in very few clock pulses because of how well it's designed, so it's clearly faster even at a slower clock rate. Others will say that Processor Y is still faster overall because its average number of clock pulses per computation is so low — and how common is that particular search that X does so fast, anyway? It's almost like arguing about whose religion is better.

The real answer is to test drive the computer (like test driving a car). Try some realistic work on the computer that you're considering. Does it feel fast enough? If you can't do this yourself, you could check reviews in computer magazines — they often use realistic tasks (like sorting in Excel and scrolling in Word) to test the speed of computers.

16.3.2 Storage: What Makes a Computer Slow?

The speed of your processor is only one factor in what makes a computer fast or slow. Probably a bigger factor is where the processor goes to get the data that it works with. Where are your pictures when your computer goes to work on them? That's a much more complex question.

You can think about your computer storage as being in a hierarchy, from fastest to slowest.

- Your fastest storage is your **cache memory**. Cache is memory that is physically located on the same silicon chip (or very, very close to that) as your processor. Your processor takes care of putting as much as possible in the cache and leaving it there as long as it's needed. Cache is accessed far faster than anything else on your computer. The more cache memory that you have, the more things the computer can access very quickly. But cache (of course) is also your most expensive storage.

- Your **RAM** storage (whether it's called *DDR SDRAM* or any other kind of RAM) is your computer's main *memory*. RAM (an acronym for *Random Access Memory*) of 4 GB (gigibytes) means 4 *billion* bytes of information. It's where your programs reside when they're executing, and it's where your data is that your computer is directly acting upon. Things are in your RAM storage before they're loaded into the cache. RAM is less expensive than cache memory, and is probably your best investment in terms of making your computer faster.

- Your **hard disk** is where you store all your *files*. Your program that you're executing now in RAM started out as an `.exe` (executable) file on your hard disk. All your digital pictures, digital music, word processing files, spreadsheet files, etc., are stored on your hard disk. Your hard disk is your *slowest* storage, but it's also your largest. A hard disk of 320 GB means that you can store 320 *billion* bytes on it. That's a *lot* of space — and that's pretty small these days!

Movement between levels in the hierarchy means a huge speed difference. Some experts have said that if the speed of access of cache memory is like reaching for a paper clip on your desk, then getting something off the hard disk means traveling to Alpha Centauri — four light-years away from Earth. Obviously, we *do* get things off our disk at reasonable speeds (which really implies that cache memory is phenomenally fast!), but the analogy does emphasize how very different the levels of the hierarchy are in speed. The bottom line is that the more you have of the faster memory, the faster your processor can get the information that you want and the faster your overall processing will be.

You'll see advertisements occasionally mentioning the **system bus** (frontside bus). The system bus is a collection of wires that act like a highway on which data and addresses travel around your computer — from video or network to hard disk, from RAM to the printer. A faster system bus clearly implies a faster overall system, but a faster system bus might not influence (for example) the speed of a Java program. First, even the fastest bus is much slower than the processor — 400 million pulses per second versus 4 billion pulses per second. Second, the system bus doesn't usually influence the access to cache or memory, and that's where the majority of the speed is won or lost anyway.

There are things that you can do to make your hard disk as fast as possible for your computation. The speed of the disk isn't that significant for processing time — even the fastest disks are still far slower than the slowest RAM. Leaving enough free space on your disk for **swapping** is important. Swapping means that when your computer doesn't have enough RAM for what you're asking it to do, it stores some of the data that it isn't currently using from RAM on to your hard disk. But that means it will have to go retrieve that data later on when we need it again. Moving data to and from your hard disk is a slow process (relatively speaking, compared to RAM access). Having a fast disk with enough free space so that the computer doesn't have to search around for swap space helps with processing speed.

How about the network? In terms of speed, the network doesn't really help you. The network is magnitudes slower than your hard disk. There are differences in network speeds that do influence your overall experience, but not necessarily the speed of processing on your computer. Wired Ethernet connections tend to be faster than wireless Ethernet connections. Modem connections are slower.

16.3.3 Display

How about the display? Does the speed of your display really impact the speed of your computer? No, not really. Computers are really, *really* fast. The computer can repaint everything on even really large displays faster than you can perceive.

The only place that one might imagine someone arguing that the display speed matters is with really high-end computer gaming. Some computer gamers claim that they can perceive a difference between 50 frames per second and 60 frames per second updates of the screen. If your display was really large and everything had to be repainted with every update, then *maybe* a faster processor would make a difference you could perceive. But most modern computers today update so quickly, you just couldn't tell a difference.

16.4   Concepts Summary

In this chapter we explained compilers and interpreters. We built a small interpreter for a graphics language. We talked about what makes computers fast and slow. We also talked about how to make your programs faster by using different algorithms. We talked about ways to determine and compare the speed of different algorithms.

Exercises

1. What are each of the following:
   - Interpreter
   - Compiler
   - Machine language
   - Java Virtual Machine (JVM)
   - RAM
   - Cache
   - Class P problems
   - Class NP problems

2. Find animations of different sorting algorithms on the Web.

3. Write a method to do a selection sort on an array of sounds. You will need to modify the Sound class to implement the Comparable interface. Compare two sounds based on their lengths.

4. Write a method to do insertion sort on an array of pictures. You will need to modify the Picture class to implement the Comparable interface. Compare two pictures first by width and then by height.

5. Write a method to do mergesort on an array of sounds. You will need to modify the Sound class to implement the Comparable interface. Compare two sounds based on their lengths.

6. How many times will the following code print out the message?
```
String message = "I will be good!";
for (int i = 0; i < 5; i++) {
   for (int j = 0; j < 10; j++) {
      System.out.println(message);
   }
}
```

7. How many times will the following code print out the message?
```
String message = "I will be good!";
for (int i = 1; i <= 5; i++) {
   for (int j = 10; j > 0; j- -) {
      System.out.println(message);
   }
}
```

8. How many times will the following code print out the message?
```
String message = "I will be good!";
for (int i = 1; i <= 5; i++) {
   for (int j = 10; j > 0; j-) {
      for (int k = 0; k < 3; k++) {
         System.out.println(message);
      }
   }
}
```

9. What is the Big Oh of the method `clearBlue`, which sets the blue value to 0 for all pixels in a picture?

10. What is the Big Oh of the method `negate`, which negates all pixels in a picture?

11. You've now seen some examples of Class P problems (such as sorting and searching), intractable problems (optimization of the song elements), and Class NP problems (such as the Traveling Salesman problem). Search the Web and find at least one more example of each class of problem.

12. Try something that takes a while in Java (for instance, chromakey on a large image) so that you can time it on a stopwatch. Now time the same task on several different computers with different amounts of memory and different clock rates (and different amounts of cache, if you can). See what a difference the different factors have in terms of the time it takes to complete the task.

13. Trace through the linear and binary search algorithms with a list of 10 items that you make up. Count exactly the number of times the loop is executed if the search string is (a) the first item in the list, (b) the last item in the list, (c) the middle item in the list, and (d) not in the list. Are there some situations where linear search is actually *faster* than binary search?

14. Don't actually trace it out, but imagine that the list has 1,000,000,000 items in it. Can you use your results from the last exercise to figure out the same loop counts for (a) through (d) for both linear and binary searches if you have a one billion item list?

15. Now assume that you're running a 2-*gigahertz* (roughly 2 billion instructions per second) processor, and you can run the whole loop, for either binary or linear search, in five instructions. Exactly how long, in seconds, will it take to obtain each of the results from the last exercise?

16. Recall that a linear search is $O(n)$ and a binary search is $O(log n)$. Let's imagine that we have two other search algorithms. The *Bad Search* is $O(n^2)$ — on average, it takes n^2 times through the loop to find the element. The *Awful Search* is $O(n!)$. Imagine that we have a 1,000-item list, and the same 2-GHz processor as before, and the loop takes five instructions to run. How long will it take, in seconds, for *Bad Search* and *Awful Search* algorithms to complete an average search? Notice that this is a 1,000-item list, not a 1-*billion* item list in this example.

17. Turing is known for another important finding in computer science, besides the proof that the Halting Problem is unsolvable. He gave us our test for whether a computer has actually achieved *intelligence*. Look up the "Turing Test" on the Web and see if you agree that that test would prove intelligence.

18. Define a `MoreMath` class that has a `factorial` method that takes an integer and returns the factorial of that integer. Make this method a class method by using the keyword `static` in the method declaration after the `public` keyword.

19. Create a new `linearFind` method in the `Searcher` class that works on any object of the type `Comparable` and takes a `List of Comparable` objects.

20. Create a new `binaryFind` method in the `Searcher` class that works on any object of the type `Comparable` and takes a `List of Comparable` objects.

21. If there are real problems that have such awful algorithms, and people really need solutions within their lifetimes, how *do* they solve those problems? Sometimes they use **heuristics** — rules that don't lead to a perfect solution, but they lead to a good enough solution. Look up "heuristics" on the Web. Find an example of a heuristic used in chess playing programs.

22. Another way around awfully hard algorithms is to use **satisficing** algorithms. There are algorithms that solve the Traveling Salesman problem (that is, find a route to all the cities) that run in reasonable time — they just don't guarantee the optimal (best possible) solution. Find an algorithm on the Web that does solve the Traveling Salesman problem in reasonable time, but isn't optimal.

17 Encoding, Manipulating, and Creating Movies

Goals of this chapter:

- To explain why movies take so much space to store.
- To add parameters to methods to make them more reusable.
- To reuse earlier methods to make movies.

Introduction

In this chapter, we're going to use the term **movies** to refer generically to **animations** (motion generated entirely by graphical drawings) and **video** (motion generated by some kind of photographic process). Movies are actually very simple to manipulate. They are a series of pictures (**frames**). You need to be concerned with the **frame rate** (the number of frames per second), but mostly the program code you will write is just things you've seen before.

Alice makes it easy to create short Disney™-Pixar™-like 3D movies. If you are using Alice 2.2, you can even export an Alice animation to a video file. Creating and exporting a movie in Alice is somewhat "magical" because Alice does much of the work for you, sort of like an engine in a car that does all the work of propelling the car along the highway (all you have to do is the driving). You may be wondering how Alice does this. In this chapter, we will "open the hood" of movie-making and work with the Java engine underneath so you can create your own movies in Java. In addition, you will be able to use Java to merge a live-action movie with an Alice movie. You will create frame-based animations (movies) with simple geometric shapes, text, and images. You will also use special effects like fade-out and chromakey.

What makes movies work is a feature of our visual system called **persistence of vision**. We do not see every change that happens in the world. For example, you don't typically see your eyes blink, even though they do it quite often (typically 20 times a minute). Our eyes retain an image for a short period of time. If we see one *related* picture after another fast enough, our eye retains the image and our brain sees continuous motion. If the pictures aren't related, our brain reports a **montage**, a collection of disparate (though perhaps thematically connected) images. About 16 **frames per second (fps)** is the lower limit for the sensation of motion.

Early silent pictures were 16 fps. Motion picture makers eventually standardized on 24 fps to make sound smoother. (Ever wonder why silent pictures often look fast and jerky? Think about what happens when you scale up a picture or sound—that's exactly what happens if you play a 16 fps movie at 24 fps.) Digital video cameras capture at 30 fps. How high is useful? There are some U.S. Air Force experiments suggesting that pilots can recognize a blob of light in the shape of an aircraft (and figure out what kind it is) in 1/200 of a second! Video game players say that they can discern a difference between 30 fps video and 60 fps video.

Movies are challenging to work with because of the amount and speed of data involved. **Real-time processing** of video (that is, doing some modification to each frame as it comes in or goes out) is hard because whatever processing you do has to fit into 1/30 of a second! Let's do the math for how many bytes are needed to record video:

- One second of 640×480 frame size images at 30 fps means $30(frames) \times 640 \times 480(pixels) = 9,216,000$ pixels.
- At 24-bit color (one byte for each of R, G, and B), that's 27,648,000 bytes, or 27 megabytes *per second*.
- For a 90-minute feature film, that's $90 \times 60 \times 27,648,000 = 149,299,200,000$ bytes—149 gigabytes.

Digital movies are almost always stored in a compressed format. A DVD only stores 6.47 gigabytes, so even on a DVD the movie is compressed. Movie format standards like **MPEG**, **QuickTime™**, and **AVI** are all compressed movie formats. They don't record every frame—they record **key frames** and then record differences between one frame and the next. In animation, key frames define the starting position and ending position of smooth transitions. The **JMV** format is slightly different—it's a file of JPEG images, so every frame is there, but every frame is compressed.

An MPEG movie is really just an MPEG image sequence that is merged with an MPEG (like **MP3**) audio file. We're going to follow that lead and *not* deal with sound here. The tools described in the next section *can* create movies with sound, but the real trick of processing movies is handling all those images. That's what we're going to focus on here.

17.1 Generating Frame-Based Animations

To make movies, we're going to create a series of JPEG frames and display them at a rapid frame rate. We have included a class `FrameSequencer` which will help you generate the frames. The class `FrameSequencer` also creates an object of the class `MoviePlayer` to display the frames. The `MoviePlayer` class also defines methods that let you save a directory of movie frames as a QuickTime or an AVI movie. You can also use tools such as Apple's QuickTime Pro (`http://www.apple.com/quicktime`) or ImageMagick (`http://www.imagemagick.org`), which can create QuickTime, MPEG, or AVI movies from individual frames (and go in reverse—burst a movie into a bunch of frames).

We'll place all of our frames in a single directory, and number them so the tools know how to reassemble them into a movie in the right order. We'll literally name our files `frame0001.jpg`, `frame0002.jpg`, and so on with leading zeros, so that the files are automatically in order when alphabetized by the computer's directory and file system.

Program 17.1 defines a class named `MovieMaker` that defines the methods we use to make movies. Our first movie-generating method is `makeRectangleMovie`, which simply moves a red rectangle down diagonally.

Program 17.1: Simple Motion of a Rectangle

```java
import java.awt.*;
/**
 * Class to create frames for a movie
 * @author Barb Ericson
 */
public class MovieMaker
{
  /**
   * Method to make a movie that has a rectangle moving
   * around
   * @param directory the directory to put the movie
   * frames
   */
  public void makeRectangleMovie(String directory)
  {
    int framesPerSec = 30;
    Picture p = null;
    Graphics g = null;
    FrameSequencer frameSequencer =
        new FrameSequencer(directory);

      // loop through the first second
      for (int i = 0; i < framesPerSec; i++)
      {
        // draw a filled rectangle
        p = new Picture(640,480);
        g = p.getGraphics();
        g.setColor(Color.RED);
        g.fillRect(i * 10, i * 5, 50,50);

        // add frame to sequencer
        frameSequencer.addFrame(p);
      }
      // replay the movie
      frameSequencer.show();
      frameSequencer.replay(framesPerSec);
  }

  // main for testing
  public static void main(String[] args)
  {
    MovieMaker movieMaker = new MovieMaker();
    String dir = "c:/intro-prog-java/movies/rectangle/";
```

```
        movieMaker.makeRectangleMovie(dir);
    }
}
```

■

You can change the directory that will hold the created movie frames from what is specified as the `dir` variable in the `main method`. Compile and run the `main` method for the class `MovieMaker`. You should see the rectangle move as shown in Figure 17.1.

The key part of the method `makeRectangleMovie` is the statement

```
g.fillRect(i * 10, i * 5, 50,50);
```

which draws a rectangle on a `Picture` object. Each time through the loop, we create a new `Picture` object and then draw the rectangle on it. The critical part is that the arguments given to `fillRect` use the variable *i*, which is the loop index, to determine where to position the rectangle. So, each time through the loop, the rectangle is drawn on the new `Picture` object at a lower position on the frame. Here are the first five values in the call to the `fillRect` method:

```
g.fillRect(0,0,50,50);   // i is 0
g.fillRect(10,5,50,50);  // i is 1
g.fillRect(20,10,50,50); // i is 2
g.fillRect(30,15,50,50); // i is 3
g.fillRect(40,20,50,50); // i is 4
```

When we add the `Picture` object to the `FrameSequencer` object, it writes out the frame to the directory. It also displays the current frame using a `MoviePlayer` object.

Debugging tip: Out of Memory Error

Working with the large number of pictures you have in a movie can cause Java to run out of memory and you can get an *out of memory error* (`java.lang.OutOfMemoryError`). When DrJava or some other Java IDE is started on your computer, the Java Virtual Machine sets aside some memory to work in and it has a limit of how much total memory it can use. You can change the amount of memory by adding some arguments for the Java Virtual Machine when you start it. In DrJava you do this by clicking Edit, then Preferences, which will display the Preferences Window. Click Miscellaneous under Categories on the left, and then change the maximum heap memory for both the main JVM and interactions JVM memory to 512 megabytes or more. Then click OK. Close DrJava and restart it.

You can also do this using the command-line tools from Sun:

```
java -Xmx512m -Xms128m MovieMaker
```

You can actually set the maximum to more RAM memory than your computer has. It will save some of the items in memory to disk and bring them back in when they are needed. This is known as **virtual memory**.

■

You may recall that `setPixel()` gets upset if you try to set a pixel outside of the bounds of the picture, but the graphics methods of the `Graphics` class `drawString` and `fillRect` don't generate these errors. They'll simply *clip* the image for the picture, so that you can create simple code to make animations and not worry about going out of bounds.

Figure 17.1
A few frames from the first movie: Moving a rectangle

This makes creating a tickertape movie fairly simple. Program 17.2 defines another method that you can add to the MovieMaker class to generate a movie with the text appearing on the right side of the picture and moving across to the left, similar to a tickertape.

Program 17.2: Generate a Tickertape Movie

```java
/**
 * Method to create a tickertape movie
 * @param directory the directory to write to
 * @param message the string to display
 */
public void makeTickerTapeMovie(String directory,
                                String message)
{
  int framesPerSec = 30;
  Picture p = null;
  Graphics g = null;
  FrameSequencer frameSequencer =
      new FrameSequencer(directory);
  Font font = new Font("Arial",Font.BOLD,24);

  // loop for 2 seconds of animation
  for (int i = 0; i < framesPerSec * 2; i++)
  {
    // draw the string
    p = new Picture(300,100);
    g = p.getGraphics();
    g.setColor(Color.BLACK);
    g.setFont(font);
    g.drawString(message,300 - (i * 10), 50);
    // add frame to sequencer
    frameSequencer.addFrame(p);
  }
  // replay the movie
  frameSequencer.show();
  frameSequencer.replay(framesPerSec);
}
```

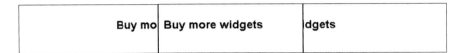

	Buy mo	Buy more widgets	dgets

Figure 17.2
Frames from the tickertape method

You can test this with the following `main`. You can change the directory that will hold the created movie frames from what is specified as the `dir` variable in the `main` method. The result of running this `main` method is shown in Figure 17.2.

```java
public static void main(String[] args)
{
  MovieMaker movieMaker = new MovieMaker();
  String dir = "c:/intro-prog-java/movies/tickertape/";
  movieMaker.makeTickerTapeMovie(dir,"Buy more widgets");
}
```

Can we move more than one thing at once? Sure! Our drawing code just gets a little more complicated. Program 17.3 defines a method `makeTwoRectangleMovie` that uses *sine* and *cosine* to create circular motion to match our linear motion we created previously in Program 17.1. You can add the method `makeTwoRectangleMovie` to the class `MovieMaker`.

Program 17.3: Move Two Objects at Once

```java
/**
 * Method to make a movie that has a two rectangles moving
 * around
 * @param directory the directory to put the movie
 * frames
 */
public void makeTwoRectangleMovie(String directory)
{
  int framesPerSec = 30;
  Picture p = null;
  Graphics g = null;
  FrameSequencer frameSequencer =
     new FrameSequencer(directory);

  // loop through the first second
  for (int i = 0; i < framesPerSec; i++)
  {
    // draw a filled rectangle
    p = new Picture(640,480);
    g = p.getGraphics();
    g.setColor(Color.RED);
    g.fillRect(i * 10, i * 5, 50,50);
    g.setColor(Color.BLUE);
    g.fillRect(100 + (int) (10 * Math.sin(i)),
               4 * i + (int) (10 * Math.cos(i)),
               50,50);
```

```
      // add frame to sequencer
      frameSequencer.addFrame(p);
    }
      // replay the movie
      frameSequencer.show();
      frameSequencer.replay(framesPerSec);
  }
```

You can test this with the following `main`. You can change the directory that will hold the created movie frames from what is specified as the `dir` variable in the `main` method. The result of executing the following `main` method is shown in Figure 17.3.

```
public static void main(String[] args)
{
  MovieMaker movieMaker = new MovieMaker();
  String dir = "c:/intro-prog-java/movies/rectangle2/";
  movieMaker.makeTwoRectangleMovie(dir);
}
```

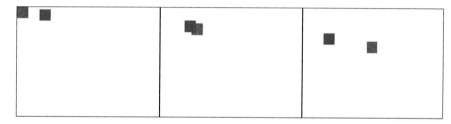

Figure 17.3
Moving two rectangles at once

We don't have to create our animations out of things that we can draw, like rectangles. We can copy `Picture` objects to different locations. Program 17.4 defines a method `moveMarksHead` that moves Mark Guzdial's head around on the screen. (Mark is the creator of the media computation approach.) This kind of code runs pretty slowly, so this method took over a minute to complete on a fast computer. You can add this method to the `MovieMaker` class.

Program 17.4: Move Mark's Head

```
/**
 * Method to move Mark's head around
 */
public void moveMarksHead(String directory)
{
  // load the picture of Mark
  String fName = FileChooser.getMediaPath("blue-Mark.jpg");
```

```
    Picture markP = new Picture(fName);

    // declare other variables
    Picture target = null;
    FrameSequencer frameSequencer =
        new FrameSequencer(directory);
    int framesPerSec = 30;

    // loop creating the frames
    for (int i = 0; i < framesPerSec; i++)
    {
      target = new Picture(640,480);
      target.copy(markP,281,164,382,301,i * 10, i * 5);
      frameSequencer.addFrame(target);
    }

    // replay the movie
    frameSequencer.show();
    frameSequencer.replay(framesPerSec);
  }
```

You can test this with the following `main`. You can change the directory that will hold the created movie frames from what is specified as the `dir` variable in the `main` method. The result of executing the following `main` method is shown in Figure 17.4.

```
public static void main(String[] args)
{
  MovieMaker movieMaker = new MovieMaker();
  String dir = "c:/intro-prog-java/movies/mark/";
  movieMaker.moveMarksHead(dir);
}
```

We can use image manipulations that were created in Chapters 10–12, over multiple frames, to create quite interesting movies. For example, we could renovate the sunset-generating code first presented in Program 10.3 for class `Picture`. The first step is to add a method that reduces the blue and green in the picture by a specified

Figure 17.4
Frames from moving Mark's head around

amount. Program 17.5 defines the method makeSunset that you can add to the Picture class.

Program 17.5: Make Sunset with a Parameter

```java
/**
 * Method to simulate a sunset by decreasing the green
 * and blue
 * @param the amount to multiply the original values by
 */
public void makeSunset(double reduction)
{
  Pixel[] pixelArray = this.getPixels();
  Pixel pixel = null;
  int value = 0;
  int i = 0;

  // loop through all the pixels
  while (i < pixelArray.length)
  {
    // get the current pixel
    pixel = pixelArray[i];

    // change the blue value
    value = pixel.getBlue();
    pixel.setBlue((int) (value * reduction));

    // change the green value
    value = pixel.getGreen();
    pixel.setGreen((int) (value * reduction));

    // increment the index
    i++;
  }
}
```

The next step is to create a new method in the class MovieMaker to make the sunset happen across many frames, as shown in Figure 17.5.

Figure 17.5
Frames from the make-sunset movie

Program 17.6 defines a method makeSunsetMovie for the MovieMaker class. The makeSunsetMovie method creates a Picture object of the beach one time and then repeatedly calls the Picture method makeSunset to keep reducing the blue and green color on the same picture.

Program 17.6: Make a Slow Sunset Movie

```
/**
 * Method to slowly create a sunset
 * @param directory the directory to write to
 */
public void makeSunsetMovie(String directory)
{
  // load the picture of the beach
  String fName =
      FileChooser.getMediaPath("beach-smaller.jpg");
  Picture beachP = new Picture(fName);

  // declare other variables
  Picture target = null;
  FrameSequencer frameSequencer =
      new FrameSequencer(directory);
  int framesPerSec = 30;
  frameSequencer.show();

  // loop creating the frames
  for (int i = 0; i < framesPerSec; i++)
  {
    beachP.makeSunset(0.95);
    frameSequencer.addFrame(beachP);
  }

    // replay the movie
    frameSequencer.replay(framesPerSec);
}
```

You can test this method with the following main method:

```
public static void main(String[] args)
{
  MovieMaker movieMaker = new MovieMaker();
  String dir = "c:/intro-prog-java/movies/sunset/";
  movieMaker.makeSunsetMovie(dir);
}
```

The swapBackground method, first presented in Program 12.11 can also be used to good effect for generating movies. Using the frame number as the threshold, we can create a slow fade into the background image. Figure 17.6 shows the effect.

Program 17.7 defines a method makeFadeOutMovie that creates the slow fade-out. The critical part of this method is the for loop, where we call the swapBackground

Figure 17.6
Frames from the slow-fade-out movie

method of the `Picture` class and pass in the frame number as the threshold. You can add the following method to the `MovieMaker` class.

Program 17.7: Fade Out Slowly

```
/**
 * Method to create a movie that fades out the person from
 * one background to another.
 * @param directory the directory to write to
 */
public void makeFadeOutMovie(String directory)
{
  // load the pictures
  String kidF = FileChooser.getMediaPath("kid-in-frame.jpg");
  Picture kidP = null;
  String wallF = FileChooser.getMediaPath("bgframe.jpg");
  Picture wallP = new Picture(wallF);
  String beachF = FileChooser.getMediaPath("beach.jpg");
  Picture beachP = new Picture(beachF);

  // declare other variables
  FrameSequencer frameSequencer =
     new FrameSequencer(directory);
  int framesPerSec = 30;

  // loop creating the frames
  for (int i = 0; i < framesPerSec * 2; i++)
  {
    kidP = new Picture(kidF);
    kidP.swapBackground(wallP,beachP,i);
    frameSequencer.addFrame(kidP);
  }

  // replay the movie
  frameSequencer.show();
  frameSequencer.replay(framesPerSec);
}
```

You can test this method with the following `main` method:

```java
public static void main(String[] args)
{
  MovieMaker movieMaker = new MovieMaker();
  String dir = "c:/intro-prog-java/movies/fade/";
  movieMaker.makeFadeOutMovie(dir);
}
```

17.2 Working with Video Frames

As we said earlier, dealing with real video in real time is very hard. We're going to cheat by saving the video as a sequence of JPEG images, manipulate the JPEG images, then convert the JPEG images back into a movie.

To manipulate movies that already exist, we have to break them into frames. The MediaTools application, shown in Figure 17.7, can do that for you, as can tools like Apple's QuickTime Pro™. The menu button in the MediaTools application lets you save any MPEG movie as a series of JPEG frame pictures.

17.2.1 Video-Manipulating Examples

On the website for this book is a brief movie of Katie dancing around. We used MediaTools on the original video to capture the frames and then stored the frames in a directory named `kid-in-bg-seq/`. Let's create a movie of Mommy (Barb) watching her daughter—we'll simply composite Barb's head onto the frames of Katie dancing, as shown in Figure 17.8.

Two important steps are needed to composite Barb's image onto the frames. First, we need to get the frames from the directory into an array:

```java
String katieDir = FileChooser.getMediaPath("kid-in-bg-seq/");
File dirObj = new File(katieDir);
String[] fileArray = dirObj.list();
```

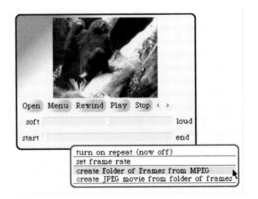

Figure 17.7
Movie tools in MediaTools

Figure 17.8
Frames from the Mommy watching Katie movie

Then, we need to loop through the array, one frame at a time and copy Barb's picture onto successive frames in a different location on each frame. We can use the loop control variable *i* to compute a new location for Barb's picture each time through the loop:

```
Picture currP = null;
for (int i = 0; i < fileArray.length; i++)
{
  if (fileArray[i].indexOf(".jpg") >= 0)
  {
    currP = new Picture(katieDir + fileArray[i]);
    currP.copy(barbP,22,9,93,97,i * 3, i * 3);
```

Program 17.8 defines a method makeMommyWatchingMovie that does this.

Program 17.8: Make Movie of Mommy Watching Katie

```
/**
 * Method to make a movie of Barb's head moving
 * and Katie dancing
 * @param dir the directory to read from and write to
 */
public void makeMommyWatchingMovie(String dir)
{
  String barbF = FileChooser.getMediaPath("barbaraS.jpg");
  String katieDir =
  FileChooser.getMediaPath("kid-in-bg-seq/");
  Picture barbP = new Picture(barbF);
  FrameSequencer frameSequencer = new FrameSequencer(dir);
  Picture currP = null;

  // get the array of files in the directory
  File dirObj = new File(katieDir);
  String[] fileArray = dirObj.list();

  // loop through the array of files
  for (int i = 0; i < fileArray.length; i++)
```

```
    {
      if (fileArray[i].indexOf(".jpg") >= 0)
      {
        currP = new Picture(katieDir + fileArray[i]);
        currP.copy(barbP,22,9,93,97,i * 3, i * 3);
        frameSequencer.addFrame(currP);
      }
    }
      // replay the movie
      frameSequencer.show();
      frameSequencer.replay(30);
  }
```

You can test this method with the following `main` method:

```
public static void main(String[] args)
{
  MovieMaker movieMaker = new MovieMaker();
  String dir = "c:/intro-prog-java/movies/mommy/";
  movieMaker.makeMommyWatchingMovie(dir);
}
```

We can certainly do more sophisticated image processing than simple composing or sunsets. For example, we can do *chromakey* on movies frames. In fact, that's how many computer-generated effects in real movies are made. To try this out, Mark took a simple video of his children (Matthew, Katie, and Jenny) crawling in front of a blue screen, shown in Figure 17.9.

Mark didn't do the lighting right, so the background turned out to be closer to black instead of blue. That turned out to be a critical error. The result was that the chromakey also modified Matthew's and Katie's pants and Jenny's eyes so that you can see the moon right through them, as in Figure 17.10. Black is another color that one should *not* use for the background when doing chromakey.

In Chapter 12, we wrote methods in the `Picture` class that do chromakey with blue and red backgrounds. In Program 17.9, we create another chromakey method that takes the `Color` to compare to and a distance to that color to use.

Figure 17.9
Frames from the original movie of the kids crawling in front of a blue screen

Figure 17.10
Frames from the kids on the moon movie

Computer Science Idea: Use Parameters to Make Methods Reusable
Notice that we are adding new methods that are like our old methods in that they have the same functionality, but they take more parameters. Adding parameters to a method will often make it easier to reuse. Remember that you can have many methods with the same name as long as the parameter list is different (method overloading). You can even have one method call another with the same name as long as the parameter list is correct.

■

Program 17.9: New Chromakey Method

```
/**
 * Method to do chromakey using the passed background
 * color and the distance to the color
 * @param newBg the new background image to use to replace
 * @param color the background color to compare to
 * @param dist the distance that limits the chromakey
 * it will happen if the distance is less than or equal
 * to this value
 */
public void chromakey(Picture newBg, Color color, double dist)
{
  Pixel currPixel = null;
  Pixel newPixel = null;
  // loop through the columns
  for (int x=0; x<getWidth(); x++)
  {
    // loop through the rows
    for (int y=0; y<getHeight(); y++)
    {
      // get the current pixel
      currPixel = this.getPixel(x,y);

        /* if the color at the current pixel is mostly blue
         * (blue value is greater than red and green combined),
         * then use the new background color
         */
```

```
      double currDist = currPixel.colorDistance(color);
      if (currDist <= dist)
      {
        newPixel = newBg.getPixel(x,y);
        currPixel.setColor(newPixel.getColor());
      }
    }
  }
}
```

We can use the new chromakey method from the Picture class to create a movie that looks like the kids are crawling on the surface of the moon. Program 17.10 defines a method makeKidsOnMoonMovie for the MovieMaker class that loops through the frames of a movie and invokes the chromakey method on each frame.

Program 17.10: Using Chromakey to Put Kids on the Moon

```
/**
 * Method to make a movie of the kids crawling on the moon
 * @param dir the directory to write the frames to
 */
public void makeKidsOnMoonMovie(String dir)
  {
    String kidsDir = FileChooser.getMediaPath("kids-blue/");
    String moonF = FileChooser.getMediaPath("moon-surface.jpg");
    Picture moonP = new Picture(moonF);
    FrameSequencer frameSequencer = new FrameSequencer(dir);
    Picture currP = null;

    // get the array of files in the directory
    File dirObj = new File(kidsDir);
    String[] fileArray = dirObj.list();

    // loop through the array of files
    for (int i = 0; i < fileArray.length; i++)
    {
      if (fileArray[i].indexOf(".jpg") >= 0)
      {
        currP = new Picture(kidsDir + fileArray[i]);
        currP.chromakey(moonP,Color.black,100.0);
        frameSequencer.addFrame(currP);
      }
    }

    // replay the movie
    frameSequencer.show();
    frameSequencer.replay(30);
  }
```

You can test this method with the following `main` method:

```java
public static void main(String[] args)
{
  MovieMaker movieMaker = new MovieMaker();
  String dir = "c:/intro-prog-java/movies/moon/";
  movieMaker.makeKidsOnMoonMovie(dir);
}
```

Mark took a video of fish underwater. Water filters out red and yellow light, so the video, seen in Figure 17.11, looks too blue. Let's increase the red and green in the video (yellow is a mixture of red and green light). We had a method in the `Picture` class that multiplied the red color at each pixel by 1.3. Program 17.11 defines a new method named `changeRedAndGreen` for the `Picture` class that will multiply the red and green values by passed multipliers. This way the same method can be used to increase or decrease the red and green values.

Figure 17.11
Some frames from the original too blue movie

Program 17.11: General Change Red and Green Values

```java
/**
 * Method to change the red and green values in the
 * current picture
 * @param redMult the amount to multiply the red by
 * @param greenMult the amount to multiply the green by
 */
public void changeRedAndGreen(double redMult,
                              double greenMult)
{
  Pixel[] pixelArray = this.getPixels();
  Pixel pixel = null;
  int value = 0;
  int index = 0;

  // loop through all the pixels
  while (index < pixelArray.length)
```

```
    {
      // get the current pixel
      pixel = pixelArray[index];

      // change the red value
      value = pixel.getRed();
      pixel.setRed((int) (value * redMult));

      // change the green value
      value = pixel.getGreen();
      pixel.setGreen((int) (value * greenMult));

      // increment the index
      index++;
    }
  }
```

Program 17.12 defines a new method in the class MovieMaker that will increase the red and green in each frame of the movie by calling the changeRedAndGreen method on the pictures in the frames of the movie.

Program 17.12: Change the Color in the Movie of Fish

```
/**
 * Method to change the red and green values in the frames
 * @param dir the directory to write the frames to
 */
public void makeFishMovie(String dir)
{
  String movieDir = FileChooser.getMediaPath("fish/");
  FrameSequencer frameSequencer = new FrameSequencer(dir);
  Picture currP = null;

  // get the array of files in the directory
  File dirObj = new File(movieDir);
  String[] fileArray = dirObj.list();

  // loop through the array of files
  for (int i = 0; i < fileArray.length; i++)
  {
    if (fileArray[i].indexOf(".jpg") >= 0)
    {
      currP = new Picture(movieDir + fileArray[i]);
      currP.changeRedAndGreen(2.0,1.5);
      frameSequencer.addFrame(currP);
    }
  }

  // play the movie
  frameSequencer.play(16);
}
```

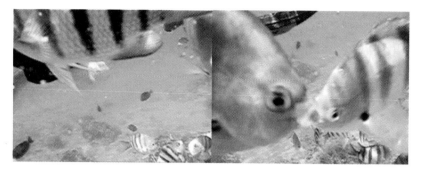

Figure 17.12
Some frames from the color-corrected movie

The result of executing the following `main` method is shown in Figure 17.12.

```
public static void main(String[] args)
{
  MovieMaker movieMaker = new MovieMaker();
  String dir = "c:/intro-prog-java/movies/fish/";
  movieMaker.makeFishMovie(dir);
}
```

17.3   Using Media Computation with Alice

You have been creating movies in Alice, and now you know how to create movies in Java. How about creating a movie that merges Alice characters with a real photograhic background? If you are using Alice 2.2, then you can export your animation to video. Alice 2.2 exports to video by first creating JPEG frames in a folder and then using the frames to create a QuickTime™ video file. After the video file has been created, Alice deletes the frames folder. However, it is possible to save the JPEG frames from your Alice movie by changing some of the export-to-video settings before you create the video.

First, in Alice 2.2 click **Edit** and then **Preferences** to bring up the preferences window. Then click the **Rendering** tab and uncheck the **delete frames folder after exporing video** checkbox as shown in Figure 17.13. This will stop the automatic

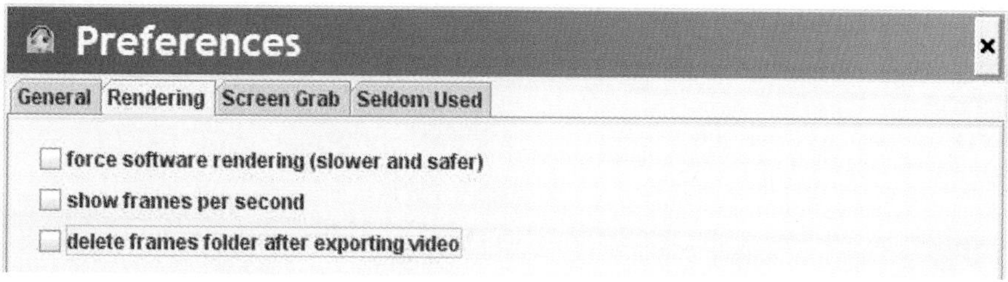

Figure 17.13
Stopping the deletion of the movie frames

deletion of the frames folder when you close the export video window. You can turn this off and on as needed.

Next, delete the ground from the object tree in your Alice world and set the background to green (just as we did in Section 12.8). When you are ready to save your Alice movie to frames, click File and then Export video. Alice will first ask you to save the current world, as shown in Figure 17.14. The directory in which you save the current world will also be the directory that will contain the frames subdirectory.

The export video window will appear as shown in Figure 17.15. (Your scene display will likely be different than the one shown here, but the export video window will have all the same buttons.) Click Record to start recording the movie to frames and then click Stop Recording to stop recording the frames. For our purposes, we only

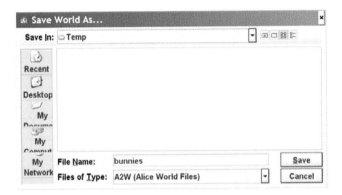

Figure 17.14
Saving the Alice world

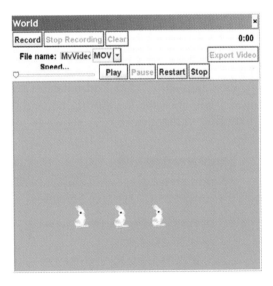

Figure 17.15
The export movie window in Alice 2.2

want the frames and so you can just close the export video window when you are done with it. If you want to actually create the video, however, you can click **Export Video** and then close the export video window.

If you check the directory in which you saved the Alice world you will find a `frames` directory that contains the frames from the Alice movie written out as a series of JPEG pictures. You can process these frames as you did with the fish movie in the last example, but you can use the `chromakey` method from the `Picture` class to copy only the non-green pixels from each picture to another picture (a picture of the real world). You did something similar to this in Program 12.12, where the background of one picture was changed to a different background. But Program 12.12 was using a blue background, and here we are using a green background.

This technique will make it look like your Alice characters are in the real world. You can delete the `frames` directory when you are done with it.

We can also merge live action and Alice characters. For example, we can merge a chicken dancing in Alice with the movie of Katie dancing. To do this, first remove the ground in the movie of the chicken dancing and set the background to green (just like we did in Section 12.8). We can use Alice 2.2 to save frames from an Alice movie. But, if you are using Alice 2.0 instead you can still save the frames using Java. To capture an Alice movie using Java, play the movie of the chicken dancing in Alice and pause it right away by clicking the **Pause** button, as shown in Figure 17.16.

Next, In DrJava double click `MovieCapture.bat` in the `bookClasses` directory. Then, specify the directory where you want to save the JPEG frames, as in Figure 17.17.

The Frame-based Movie Capturer window will appear. Move this to be outside the Alice window. Then click the **Capture Screen** button. This will capture the entire screen and show a scaled down version of it in the Frame-based Movie Capturer window, as shown in Figure 17.18.

We need to tell Java what part of the screen to capture (it doesn't know where the Alice window is). So position the cursor at the top left of the Alice window and then

Figure 17.16
Pausing the Alice movie

Figure 17.17
Specifying the directory to hold the movie frames

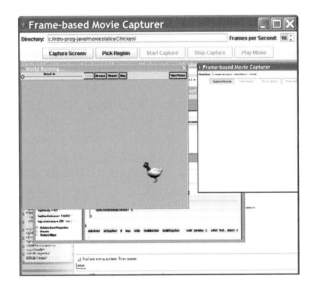

Figure 17.18
The Frame-based Movie Capturer Window after the screen has been captured

click and drag it to the bottom right of the Alice window as shown in Figure 17.19. You will see a black rectangle that shows the region you are picking. If you made a mistake, click the Pick Region button and try again.

Click the Start Capture button in the Frame-based Movie Capturer window and then go back and click the Restart button in the Alice window. You may need to click the top part of the Alice window first. The Alice movie will play again from the beginning. When it is finished playing, click the Stop Capture button in the Frame-based Movie Capturer window. Then click the Play Movie button in the Frame-based Movie Capturer. This will bring up the Movie Player window seen in Figure 17.20.

You can use the Next button to see each frame. Since you started the movie capture before you restarted the Alice movie, you may want to delete some of the early frames. Use the Next and Prev button to find the actual starting point and then click Delete All Previous. This will delete all the frames before the current one. If you have any additional frames at the end of the movie you can delete these by clicking Delete All After. This will delete all frames after the current one. Click Play Movie to see the current movie.

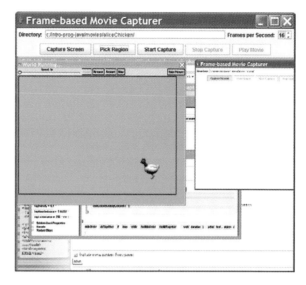

Figure 17.19
The black rectangle shows the picked region

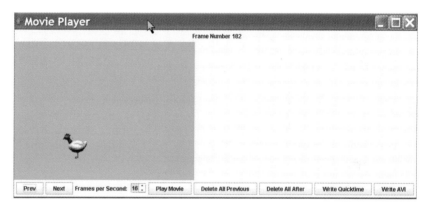

Figure 17.20
The Movie Player Window

Program 17.13 defines a method in the `Picture` class that will copy non-green pixels from each frame in the chicken movie to a frame of a live-action movie.

Program 17.13: Method to Copy the Non-Green Pixels to the Current Picture

```
/**
 * Method to copy from the passed source picture to the current
 * picture object
 * The copying will start at startX, startY, and end at
 * endX-1 and endY-1
 * The copy will be placed starting at targetStartX,
 * targetStartY
```

```
 * @param sourcePicture the source picture to copy from
 * @param startX the starting x value in the source picture
 * @param startY the starting y value in the source picture
 * @param endX the ending x value in the source picture
 * @param endY the ending y value in the source picture
 * @param targetStartX the x value to start at in this picture
 * @param targetStartY the y value to start at in this picture
 */
public void copyNonGreenPixels(Picture sourcePicture,
                                    int startX, int startY,
                                    int endX, int endY,
                                    int targetStartX,
                                    int targetStartY)
{
  Pixel sourcePixel = null;
  Pixel targetPixel = null;
  double distance = 50.0;

  if (this.getImage() == null)
     System.out.println(this.getFileName());
  //this.getWidth();

  // loop through the x values
  for (int x = startX, tx = targetStartX;
          x < endX && x < sourcePicture.getWidth() &&
                        tx < this.getWidth();
          x++, tx++)
  {
    // loop through the y values
    for (int y = startY, ty = targetStartY;
            y < endY && y < sourcePicture.getHeight() &&
                        ty < this.getHeight();
            y++, ty++)
    {
      sourcePixel = sourcePicture.getPixel(x,y);
      targetPixel = this.getPixel(tx,ty);
      if (sourcePixel.getGreen() < sourcePixel.getRed() +
            sourcePixel.getBlue())
          targetPixel.setColor(sourcePixel.getColor());
    }
  }
}
```

Program 17.14 defines a method in the MovieMaker class to merge the movie of the chicken dancing with the movie of Katie dancing.

Program 17.14: Method to Merge the Chicken Movie with the Movie of Katie Dancing
```
public void makeChickenMovie(String dir)
{
  String chickenDir =
        "c:/intro-prog-java/movies/chickenFull/";
```

```
    String danceDir =
            "c:/intro-prog-java/mediasources/kid-in-bg-seq/";
    FrameSequencer frameSequencer = new FrameSequencer(dir);
    Picture chickenP = null;
    Picture danceP = null;

    // get the array of files in the chicken dir
    File chickenDirObj = new File(chickenDir);
    String[] chickenArray = chickenDirObj.list();
    File danceDirObj = new File(danceDir);
    String[] danceArray = danceDirObj.list();

    int danceLen = danceArray.length;
    int chickenLen = chickenArray.length;

    // loop through the array of chicken files
    for (int i = 0; i < Math.min(danceLen,chickenLen); i++)
    {
      if (chickenArray[i].indexOf(".jpg") >= 0 &&
            danceArray[i].indexOf(".jpg") >= 0)
      {
        chickenP = new Picture(chickenDir + chickenArray[i]);
        danceP = new Picture(danceDir + danceArray[i]);
        danceP.copyNonGreenPixels(chickenP,
                                   158,122,798,599,0,105);
        frameSequencer.addFrame(danceP);
      }
    }

  // play the movie
  frameSequencer.play(16);
}
```

You can create the movie using the following main method in class MovieMaker.

```
public static void main(String[] args)
{
  MovieMaker movieMaker = new MovieMaker();
  String dir = "c:/intro-prog-java/movies/chickenDance/";
  movieMaker.makeChickenMovie(dir);
}
```

When you play the resulting movie you will see frames with both Katie and the chicken, shown in Figure 17.21. You can create a QuickTime movie from the resulting frames by clicking the **Write Quicktime** button. This will write out a QuickTime movie to the same directory as the movie frames. You can also click the **Write AVI** button to write out an AVI movie. (Note that writing AVI files may require you to install JMF, the Java Media Framework from http://java.sun.com).

If the video export in Alice is creating frames that are too large or too small, you can adjust the size of the Alice display window before creating the frames for use in a

Figure 17.21
The merged movie with Katie and the chicken

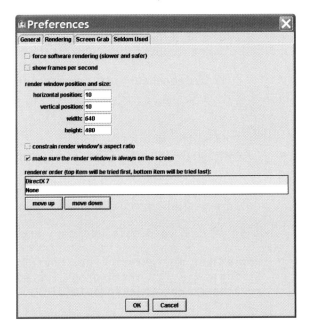

Figure 17.22
Setting the Alice display window upper left position, width, and height

live-action movie. First, click Edit and then Preferences. Then, click the Rendering tab. Set the position of the top left corner of the window, the width, and the height, as shown in Figure 17.22. Then click OK. Now, the frames you create should be an appropriate size.

17.4 Concepts Summary

In this chapter we explained how movies are stored and why they take up so much space. We created frame-based animations with simple geometric shapes, text, and images. We did special effects on movie frames, such as fading out and chromakey.

We created new versions of methods that take more parameters to make the methods more reusable. We also reused methods that we had created to work on `Picture` objects. When we program we try to create reusable parts. These reusable parts can be methods and/or classes.

Exercises

1. What are each of the following?
   - Frames per second
   - Frame-based animation
   - Persistence of vision
   - AVI
   - QuickTime

2. How many frames would you need for a two-hour movie with a picture size of 1,024 pixels width by 728 pixels height and 60 frames per second? How much disk space would this movie need?

3. Build an animation of at least 3 seconds (48 frames at 16 frames per second or 90 frames at 30 frames per second). Have at least three things in motion during the sequence. You must use at least one JPEG image and one drawn item (like a rectangle or oval or line). For at least one of the things in motion, change the direction that it is moving during the animation.

4. Create a movie that has the frames slowly becoming sepia-toned.

5. Create a movie that adds real people to an Alice movie. Film the people in front of a green background.

6. Create a movie that has a JPEG image rotating in it.

7. Create a movie that takes an image and slowly creates the negative of the image.

8. Create a new movie that shows the kids crawling on the beach.

9. Create a new movie like the `makeSunsetMovie` method that turns the beach black after the blue and green are reduced by a passed amount.

10. The site `http://abcnews.go.com` is a popular news site. Let's make a movie of it. Write a function that will input a directory as a string, then:
    - Visit `http://abcnews.go.com` and pick out the top three news stories headlines. They will often have some sort of text in front of them like `MainNewsHeadline`. Write a program to pull out the headlines.
    - Create a tickertape movie on the 640 × 480 canvas of all three news stories. Have one come across at $y = 100$, another at $y = 200$, and the third at $y = 300$.

Generate 100 frames, and don't have the tickertapes move more than 5 pixels per frame. (In 100 frames, you won't make it all the way across the screen—that's fine.) Store the frames to files in the passed directory.

11. Change the movie of the kid fading out. Instead of fading in the beach, fade in the original blank wall. The effect should be of the kid disappearing.

12. Remember the blending of pictures in Program 11.11? Try blending one picture into another as a movie, slowly increasing the percentage of the second (incoming) image while decreasing the percentage of the original (outgoing) image.

13. Create a movie of a turtle (`turtle.jpg`) crawling across the beach (`beach.jpg`).

14. Create a movie of the robot (`robot.jpg`) moving across the moon (`moon-surface.jpg`).

15. Create a movie with a filled oval moving up diagonally from the bottom left to the top right of the picture.

16. Create a movie with a filled rectangle moving diagonally from the top right of the picture to the bottom left.

17. Create a movie with text in a tickertape moving up from the bottom of the picture to the top.

18. Create a movie that changes the edge detection amount over time.

19. Create a movie that has the text in a tickertape moving diagonally from top left to bottom right.

20. Create a movie with the turtle moving across the frames of a movie of a blow-hole in directory `mediasources/blowhole`.

21. Create a movie that has two filled rectangles that move by a random amount in x and y ($<$5 pixels) each time. Make sure that they don't go outside the picture.

CHAPTER 18
Abstract Classes, Polymorphism, and Inheritance

Goals of this chapter:

- To give examples of object-oriented analysis and design.
- To explain why you need abstract classes and abstract methods.
- To give a detailed example of polymorphism.
- To show how to use inheritance to pull out a common parent class.
- To give an example of using a protected method.
- To explain the purpose of an interface and how interfaces and abstract classes are used.

Introduction

Java is considered to be object-oriented and Alice 2.0 is an object-based system. Why is that? Well, for a language to be considered object-oriented, it must implement and support encapsulation (classes and objects), polymorphism and inheritance. Alice 2.0 does have objects and classes but doesn't fully implement and support inheritance and polymorphism.

Alice 2.0 has a primitive version of inheritance. You can rename an object in the object tree and save it out, but this saves out a class with a new name rather than truly implementing inheritance. **Inheritance** means that fields and methods are inherited from a parent class, not copied to a new class. And, methods in Alice can't be overridden so you can't really do inheritance-based polymorphism. **Polymorphism** means calling different methods at run-time based on the type of object the method is called on. This is also called *run-time* or *dynamic binding*. We saw an example of this in Chapter 13, Section 8; when we ask an object of the `ConfusedTurtle` class to turn left, it actually turns right, and when we ask it to turn right, it will turn left. But an object of the `Turtle` class will turn correctly.

Java is fully **object-oriented** because it not only has classes and objects it also fully supports inheritance and polymorphism. These concepts are used in the analysis and design of software. They help make software easier to change, extend, and reuse.

18.1 Object-Oriented Analysis

Software engineers start creating new software by doing an analysis of the problem that is to be solved by the software. The goal of analysis is to understand objects in a context, determine how objects are classified, and understand the relationships between the classifications (classes). For example, if you are creating software to handle student registration for courses, you need to understand what is meant by student, course, teacher, room, class period, and more. If you are creating software to help diagnose a stroke in a medical patient, you need to understand signs and symptoms, patients, doctors, tests, findings, and more.

If you want to create software to make it easy to create comic strips in Java, you will need to know what is meant by a comic strip. Take a look at the comic section of a newspaper. What do the comic strips have in common? They usually have four comic panels, an author, and a name. What is a comic panel? It has a picture and can have speech balloons. A speech balloon has a tail that points to who is speaking and an ellipse with text in it, as shown in Figure 18.1.

What classes will we need to represent a comic strip? If we underline nouns in the description we get comic panel, author, and name. Both author and name are things that belong to a comic strip so they will be fields in the `ComicStrip` class. The author and the name of the comic strip can both be represented by `String` fields in the `ComicStrip` class, as shown in a UML class diagram in Figure 18.2.

What about a comic panel? It has a picture and speech balloons so it isn't just a simple primitive type or an object of an existing class. It will have to be a new class. Should the `ComicPanel` class inherit from the `Picture` class or should it just have a `Picture` object associated with it?

Beginners often make the mistake of using inheritance when it really doesn't make sense. Inheritance should only be used when the child is really a special type of the

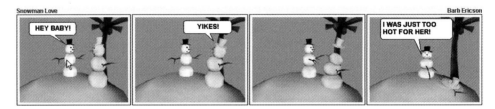

Figure 18.1
A comic strip with speech balloons

Figure 18.2
A UML class definition for the comic strip class

parent and an object of the child class can be substituted for an object of the parent class. For example, if you asked for a bear and got a polar bear that would be fine. A polar bear is a special type of bear having some characteristics that are different from other kinds of bears. The inheritance relationship is shown with a triangle pointing from the child class (`PolarBear`) to the parent class (`Bear`), as seen in Figure 18.3. This is also known as the **is-a** or more specifically a *is-a-type-of* relationship. If you asked for a bear, and got a circus, that wouldn't be correct. A circus is not a type of bear and shouldn't inherit from bear. It can have bears associated with it. The association relationship is shown with a line between `Circus` and `Bear` in Figure 18.3. This is also known as a **has-a** relationship.

What should a comic strip be able to do? We want to see it so it should be able to show itself. What should a speech balloon be able to do? It should be able to draw itself. In order to do that, it will need to know the upper left corner of the ellipse, the message or text to draw, and the end point for the triangular tail that points to the speaker.

A comic strip should know what comic panels it contains. A comic panel should know the picture in it and the speech balloons that are in the picture. The numbers at the ends of an association tell you how many objects of that class are associated with an object of the other class. A comic panel has only one picture and zero to many speech balloons. (The **0*** notation used in the diagram means "zero to many.") A comic strip has four comic panels. All of this information is shown graphically in the UML class diagram in Figure 18.4 on the next page.

Associations will become fields in one or more of the classes that are connected by the association. For example, a comic strip object will have four comic panels so we can represent this in the `ComicStrip` class using an array of `ComicPanel` objects, as shown in the following code:

```
public class ComicStrip extends JPanel
{
    //////////////////// fields ////////////////////////
    private String name;
    private String author;
    private ComicPanel[] panelArray = null;
}
```

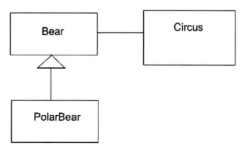

Figure 18.3
Shows an inheritance relationship and an association relationship

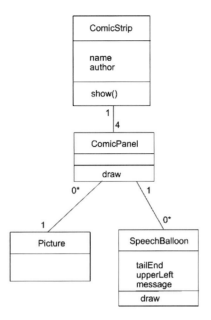

Figure 18.4
A UML class diagram for a comic strip

18.2 Generalization/Specialization

Some comic strips have thought balloons that show what some object is thinking. These are different from speech balloons in that there are small ellipses that connect the thinker to the thought, as in Figure 18.5.

How should we handle thought balloons? We could just add another class for the thought balloon. It would also need to have fields to track the end of the tail to the thinker, the upper left corner of the ellipse that encloses the text, and the text to display (message). One possible way to handle this is shown in Figure 18.6.

Figure 18.5
A comic panel with a thought balloon

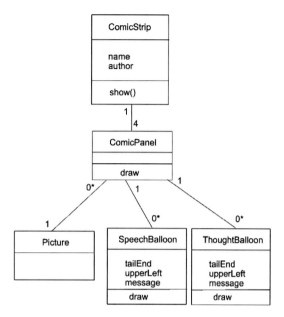

Figure 18.6
Comic strip UML class diagram with `ThoughtBalloon` added

But, if you look closely at the `SpeechBalloon` and `ThoughtBalloon` classes in the class diagram, you will see that speech balloons and thought balloons have all the same fields. The only real difference between the classes is in how the tail is drawn. In a speech balloon the tail is drawn as a triangle. In a thought balloon the tail is drawn as a series of ellipses. Some beginners might handle this by copying the `SpeechBalloon` class and saving it out as a `ThoughtBalloon` class and then just changing the code in the draw method. But, copying and pasting code multiplies the amount of work you need to do if you find a problem in that code.

A better solution is to pull out the common fields and methods and put them in a common parent class. In this case, we could create a new class `TextBalloon`, and move the common fields and methods into this class. Then both `SpeechBalloon` and `ThoughtBalloon` can inherit from `TextBalloon`. The relationship between a parent class and a child class is also known as **generalization/specialization**. The parent class is more general and the child class is more specialized.

Can you create an object that is just a text balloon? Would you draw the tail with a triangle or a series of ellipses? You know how to draw a speech balloon and a thought balloon, but not a text balloon. Actually we don't want anyone to be able to create a text balloon as an object. We only want to create speech balloon and thought balloon objects. To enforce this, we will create the class `TextBalloon` as an abstract class. An **abstract class** is a class that *does not* allow you to create objects, but you can use it as a common parent class. To make a class abstract, just add the keyword `abstract` before the `class` keyword in the class declaration.

```
public abstract class TextBalloon
```

In UML, abstract classes are shown with their names in italics as demonstrated with the class `TextBalloon` in Figure 18.7. Notice that we don't show the fields that are inherited from `TextBaloon` in the `SpeechBalloon` and `ThoughtBalloon` classes, but these classes will inherit these fields from `TextBalloon`. They will also inherit the `draw` method.

What will the `draw` method do in `TextBalloon`? It can draw the ellipse and the text, but it can't draw the tail until it knows if it is a speech balloon or a thought balloon. We will add an abstract method `drawTail` to the `TextBalloon` class. An **abstract method** is a method that doesn't have a method body — a block of code within curly braces that defines what actions should be executed when the method is called. Abstract methods are declared by adding the keyword `abstract` after the visibility and before the return type in the method declaration. Abstract method declarations end in a semicolon and cannot have a body for the method inside a pair of curly braces. The following shows the general structure of an abstract method:

visibility **abstract** *returnType methodName(parameterList);*

What should we use for the visibility for the `drawTail` method? The `draw` method should be public so that code in other classes can ask the comic panel to draw itself. But, do other classes need to be able to ask a comic panel to draw its tail? No, they

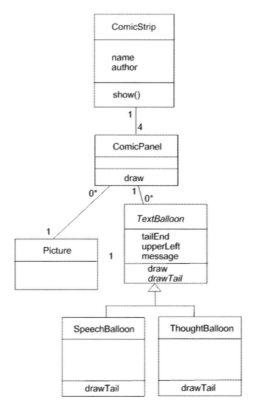

Figure 18.7
`TextBalloon` is an abstract class with an abstract `drawTail` method

shouldn't care how the comic panel draws itself. Does this mean `drawTail` should be a private method? Private methods can't be called by subclasses. So we wouldn't be able to override the `drawTail` method in the subclasses. The only option other than public or private visibility is **protected**, which means that subclasses can override it. Protected actually means that the method can be called by code in subclasses and also by code in classes that are in the same package, but not by classes outside the package. Recall that if you don't specify a package for a class before the class declaration, it is added to the unnamed package. So, the protected visibility doesn't really give all that much protection unless you are putting your classes in packages. But, it is still a little more protected than public, which allows code in any class to invoke the method. The complete declaration for the abstract `drawTail` method of the `TextBalloon` class will be:

```
protected abstract void drawTail();
```

18.3 Polymorphism

As you know, an object keeps a reference to another object that represents the class that created it. This is an object of a class known as `Class`. You can always get the `Class` object using the method `getClass()`. When a method is invoked on an object, it will first check with the class that created it to see if it has the method, and if so, it will execute it. If the class that created the object doesn't have the method, it will check the parent class of the class that created it. If the parent class doesn't have the method, it will check the parent of that class, and so on up the ancestor tree until it finds the method. It will always find the method since the compiler wouldn't have compiled the code unless the method was defined in a class somewhere in the ancestor tree.

To implement the comic strip example, you will need to create and display a `ComicStrip` object, and it will create and display the four `ComicPanel` objects. Each of the `ComicPanel` objects will have a picture and zero to many `TextBalloons` in it. The `TextBalloon` objects are stored in an `ArrayList` of `TextBalloon` objects. The field for an `ArrayList` of `TextBalloon` objects is declared in the `ComicStrip` class as shown below.

```
private List<TextBalloon> textBalloonList =
        new ArrayList<TextBalloon>();
```

Because we have a field `TextBalloonList` which is an `ArrayList`, the `ComicPanel` class will need methods to add and remove a `TextBalloon` object to/from the list `textBalloonList`. Since `TextBalloon` is an abstract class, we won't actually add `TextBalloon` objects to the list, but using the parent class `TextBalloon` will allow you to add/remove either `ThoughtBalloon` or `SpeechBalloon` objects.

The following code defines a method `getFinalPicture` that loops through the `textBalloonList` and draws each balloon on top of the picture in the comic panel to create the final picture to be shown.

```
public Picture getFinalPicture()
{
  // make a copy of the background picture
  Picture finalPicture = new Picture(picture);
  Graphics g = finalPicture.getGraphics();

  // loop through text balloons
  for (TextBalloon balloon: textBalloonList)
  {
    balloon.draw(g);
  }
  return finalPicture;
}
```

So, what happens when we create a comic strip? The following code is the main method in the ComicStrip class that creates a comic strip.

```
public static void main(String[] args)
{
  Picture p =
  new Picture(FileChooser.getMediaPath("MattJennyCorn.jpg"));
    ComicPanel panel = new ComicPanel(p);
    SpeechBalloon sBalloon =
      new SpeechBalloon(new Point(209,18),100,
                        new Point(218,149),
                        "It sure is corny in here!");
    ThoughtBalloon tBalloon =
      new ThoughtBalloon(new Point(14,60),100,
                         new Point(167,226),
                         "Oh, that was corny!");
    panel.add(sBalloon);
    panel.add(tBalloon);
    Picture finalPic = panel.getFinalPicture();
    finalPic.explore();
    finalPic.write(FileChooser.getMediaPath("comicPanel.jpg"));
}
```

This main method creates a Picture object and then creates a ComicPanel object with that picture. It creates one SpeechBalloon and one ThoughtBalloon and adds them to the comic panel by calling the add method. The add method takes as a parameter a TextBalloon, but since both SpeechBalloon and ThoughtBalloon inherit from TextBalloon, this means that they are also TextBalloon objects, so this is allowed. Next, it generates a new picture by calling the method getFinal Picture.

The method getFinalPicture loops through the list of TextBalloon objects and calls a draw method on each picture. Both SpeechBalloon and ThoughtBalloon inherit the abstract draw method from TextBalloon, as can be seen in Figure 18.8. So when the first TextBalloon object is told to draw, it looks for the draw method in

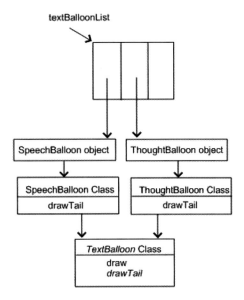

Figure 18.8
Objects in the comic panel

the class that created it, which is `SpeechBalloon`. Since it doesn't find a `draw` method there, it looks in the parent class, which is `TextBalloon`. It starts executing the `draw` method in `TextBalloon`. The code for the `draw` method is shown here:

```
/**
 * Method to draw the text balloon using the passed
 * graphics context
 * @param g the graphics context to draw on
 */
public void draw(Graphics g)
{
   // cast to graphics 2d and set colors
   Graphics2D g2 = (Graphics2D) g;
   Color fillColor = Color.WHITE;
   Color outlineColor = Color.BLACK;

   // get the font render context
   FontRenderContext frc = g2.getFontRenderContext();

   // get the attributed character iterator
   AttributedCharacterIterator attrCharIter =
        this.getAttrIterator();

   // get the height of the ellipse
   int ellipseHeight = this.getHeight(g2, attrCharIter);
```

```
                    // draw the balloon
                    drawBalloon(ellipseHeight,fillColor,
                            outlineColor,g2);

                    // draw the tail to the speaker
                    drawTail(ellipseHeight,fillColor,
                            outlineColor,g2);

                    // draw message
                    LineBreakMeasurer measurer =
                        new LineBreakMeasurer(attrCharIter,frc);
                    drawText(measurer,outlineColor,g2);


                }
```

When it gets to the line in the draw method that executes the drawTail method, it will first check for the drawTail method in the class that created the object, which is the class SpeechBalloon. It will find the drawTail method in SpeechBalloon and execute that one which draws the tail as a triangle. When the second TextBalloon object in the textBalloonList is asked to draw, it will also execute the draw method in TextBalloon, since there isn't one in ThoughtBalloon. And when it is asked to execute drawTail, it will check first in the class that created it, which is ThoughtBalloon. It will execute the drawTrail method in ThoughtBalloon that draws the tail as a series of ellipses as shown in Figure 18.9.

The execution of two different drawTail methods is an example of polymorphism, which means that the code that executes depends on what the type of the object is at runtime. At compile time all we know is that a ComicPanel can have zero or more

Figure 18.9
A comic panel with a thought balloon and a speech balloon

`TextBalloon` objects, and that these objects will know how to draw a tail. This compiles because the compiler can find a `drawTail` method in the `TextBalloon` class, even though it is abstract. But, at runtime the specific `drawTail` method executed is selected based on the type of the object.

18.4   Shape Example

Let's look at a different example of object-oriented analysis and abstract classes. If you want to create a simple drawing program that can draw simple two-point shapes by using the mouse, what classes would you need? With just two points you can define a rectangle, oval, or line. The two points represent opposite corners of the rectangle. For the oval, the two points represent the opposite corners of the enclosing rectangle. For the line, the two points are the end points of the line. These shapes are illustrated in Figure 18.10. What classes would you use to represent these objects?

By underlining the nouns in the problem description, we get rectangle, oval, and line. Each of these will need to keep track of the two points that define it. There is a `Point` class in Java that you can use to represent a two-dimensional point. You could create a UML class diagram like the one in Figure 18.11 on the next page.

You can pull out the common fields and method and put them in a parent class. What should the parent class be named? Well, rectangle, oval, and lines are all types of shapes, so let's create a `Shape` class. Figure 18.12 on the next page shows the diagram with the `Shape` class included.

Shapes should know how to draw themselves. You can draw a rectangle, oval, and line using the methods in the `Graphics` class. But, should you be able to create a `Shape` object and draw it? What would you draw? You shouldn't create an object of the

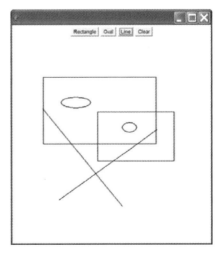

Figure 18.10
A panel that can be used to draw simple shapes

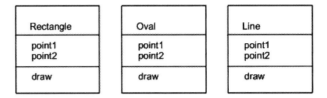

Figure 18.11
Class diagram for the shape example

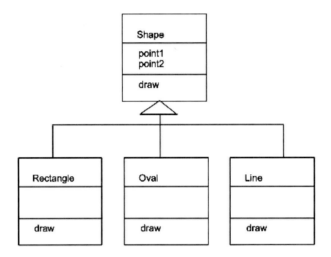

Figure 18.12
Revised class diagram for the shape example

class `Shape`, but only objects of the classes `Rectangle`, `Oval`, and/or `Line`. So the `Shape` class should be declared to be an abstract class, and the draw method should also be abstract, as shown below.

```
public abstract class Shape {
    // ... fields, constructors, and methods
    public abstract void draw(Graphics g);
}
```

The code for the `Rectangle` class will extend the `Shape` class and will override the inherited `draw` method to draw a rectangle:

```
public class Rectangle extends Shape
{
    // ... constructors

    /** Draw the shape
     *  @param g the graphics context on which to draw
     */
```

```java
    public void draw(Graphics g)
    {
      // set the color
      g.setColor(color);

      // draw the rectangle given the top left point and width
      // and height
      g.drawRect(getMinX(),getMinY(),getWidth(),getHeight());
    }
}
```

The code for the `Oval` class will extend the `Shape` class and override the `draw` method to draw an oval:

```java
public class Oval extends Shape
{
  // ... constructors

  /** Draw the shape
  * @param g the graphics context on which to draw
  */
  public void draw(Graphics g)
  {
    // set the color
    g.setColor(color);

    // draw the shape given the top left corner of the enclosing
    // rectangle and the width and height
    g.drawOval(getMinX(),getMinY(),getWidth(),getHeight());
  }
}
```

The code for the `Line` class will extend the `Shape` class and override the `draw` method to draw a line:

```java
public class Line extends Shape
{
  // ... constructors

  /** Draw the shape
  * @param g the graphics context on which to draw
  */
  public void draw(Graphics g)
  {
  // set the color
  g.setColor(color);

  // draw the line given the x and y value of one point
  // and the x and y value of the other point
  g.drawLine(p1.x,p1.y,p2.x,p2.y);
  }
}
```

You might wonder why you shouldn't just have one class called `Shape` that has a field that indicates the type and then use a conditional in the draw method based on the type. The code for such a method is shown below.

```java
public void draw(Graphics g)
{
  // set the color
  g.setColor(color);

  if (type == Shape.LINE)
  {
    // draw the line given the x and y value of one point
    // and the x and y value of the other point
    g.drawLine(p1.x,p1.y,p2.x,p2.y);
  }
  else if (type == Shape.RECTANGLE)
  {
    // draw the rectangle given the top left point and width
    // and height
    g.drawRect(getMinX(),getMinY(),getWidth(),getHeight());
  }
  else if (type == Shape.Oval)
  {
    // draw the shape given the top left corner of the
    // enclosing rectangle and the width and height
    g.drawOval(getMinX(),getMinY(),getWidth(),getHeight());
  }
}
```

The problem with the `draw` method that uses a conditional to determine the shape and then draws that shape is that if you want to add other shapes, you will have to edit existing code and change it and recompile. When you change code that is already working, you may accidentally break what was working. And, if you want to have other methods that do different things depending on the type, you have to add the conditionals there too. This makes the code more complex and harder to read, understand, and extend.

By having an abstract class and subclasses you can minimize the changes you need to make when you add a new type (subclass). You just create a new subclass that extends the abstract class and overrides the abstract methods. Polymorphism means that the subclasses can specialize their behavior by providing methods that override inherited methods. Using abstract methods means that subclasses won't compile unless they override the abstract method, or are also declared to be abstract.

18.5   Interfaces

We first introduced abstract methods in Chapter 14 where we looked at the `Comparable` interface in Java. You may recall that an interface is a special type of abstract class that only allows you to define public abstract methods and public constants. Interfaces define methods that are used to let class A communicate with class B without class A having to know the actual class name for class B, since it can refer to class B using the interface name instead. Without an interface, class A would have to keep a reference to an object of class B (called `bObj` in Figure 18.13) and use that reference to invoke a method or methods on class B (like the `notify` method shown in Figure 18.13).

Interfaces let you decouple classes. Think of train cars coupled together. If one car moves, the cars that are coupled to it also move. If you decouple the train cars, one car can move without moving another. One of the goals of object-oriented design is to decouple classes. This means that you can minimize the changes that you have to make if one class changes.

A variety of devices can be plugged into a USB port: an external hard disk, a camera, a flash drive, and more. How is this possible? All of these devices use the USB interface. As long as a device implements the USB interface the computer can talk to it. Java interfaces also allow you to plug in different classes that implement the same interface.

If class A wants to communicate with class B, and class B implements an interface, then in class A you can declare the field that holds a reference to class B to be of the interface type as shown in Figure 18.14. If you later want to swap out B and use C, and C also implements the same interface, you can do this without recompiling class A.

In the screen captured image that was shown in Figure 18.10, you can see buttons that allow you to pick what type of shape you want to draw. These buttons are fields in a class called `ButtonPanel`. But the class `ShapeComponent` needs to know which shape to draw. So the `ButtonPanel` needs to communicate with `ShapeComponent`. It

Figure 18.13
Classes communicating without an interface

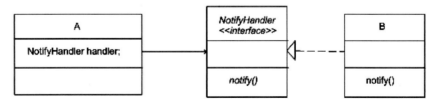

Figure 18.14
Classes communicating with an interface

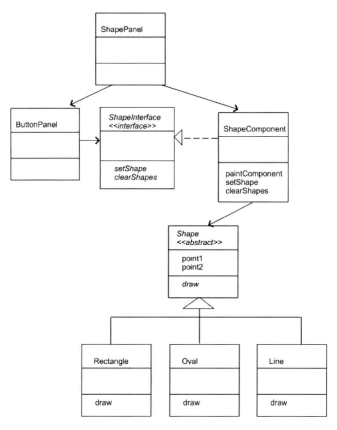

Figure 18.15
UML class diagram for the shape example

does this by using the abstract methods declared in `ShapeInterface` and implemented in `ShapeComponent`, as shown in Figure 18.15.

18.6   Interfaces and Abstract Classes

In chapter 16 the `Searcher` class had a method `linearFind` that took an array of
`Comparable` objects. The `Comparable` interface defines the method `compareTo`
which allows you to test if one object is less than, equal to, or greater than another. The
`Searcher` class uses the interface `Comparable` so that it doesn't have to know what
the actual class type is of the objects it is comparing. This makes it more general and
useful for objects of any class that implements the `Comparable` interface.

In object-oriented design you will often start with an interface which will define the
essential nature of a class, by declaring the abstract methods that are required for
classes that implement the interface. What can you do with a list? You can add items,
remove items, check and see if an item is on the list, and get an item at a position in the
list. The `List` interface (in the `java.util` package) declares methods for each of
these and much more. But an interface cannot have any fields or method bodies, so

common fields and methods must be defined in a class or abstract class. There is an abstract class, `AbstractList`, that implements the `List` interface. Since you can't create an object of an abstract class, you must create subclasses that inherit from the abstract class, such as `ArrayList`, `Vector`, and `LinkedList` which all inherit from `AbstractList` as shown in Figure 18.16. An `ArrayList` uses an array to store the items in the list and is not **thread safe**.

To describe what we mean by "thread safe," let's use an analogy. Have you ever had more than one person try to do something at the same time? How about if you have two people following the same recipe? This can be helpful if you break up the work and finish the recipe more quickly. One person can get the ingredients while the other is browning the meat. But you need to make sure that you don't both add the salt. Computers can also break up computational recipes so that parts (threads) can be done at the same time. Making a process thread safe means to prevent multiple threads from accessing a data structure at the same time and possibly messing it up (like adding the salt twice).

Because an `ArrayList` is not thread safe, it is best to use an `ArrayList` when you don't have multiple threads that might try to access the list at the same time. A `Vector` also uses an array to store the items in a list, but is thread safe. So, a `Vector` is what you should use if you have several threads that might attempt to access a list at the same time.

A `LinkedList` uses a structure of linked nodes where each node stores data and a reference to the next node in the list. This is different than an `ArrayList` which uses an array to store the list and the order of the items in the list is the same as the order of the items in the array. The next item in an `ArrayList` is the one at the next index (current index plus one).

When you declare a variable for a class that implements the `List` interface you should declare the variable using the interface name and just specify which class you want when you create the list, as in the following code:

```
List<Person> personList = new ArrayList<Person>;
```

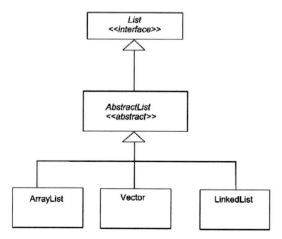

Figure 18.16
UML class diagram for classes that represent lists

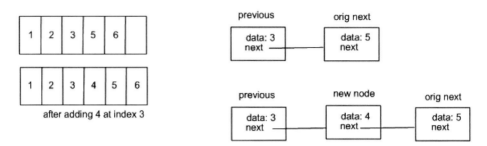

Figure 18.17
Adding at an index in an array (left) and in a linked list (right)

This declares a list of persons to be of the type `List` even though it is actually an `ArrayList`. Because `ArrayList` inherits from `AbstractList` which implements the `List` interface, an `ArrayList` is a type of `List`. The advantage of declaring variables to be of the interface type instead of the actual class type, is that if we later want to use a `LinkedList` instead of an `ArrayList`, we only have to change the line that creates the list.

Why would you choose to use a `LinkedList` instead of an `ArrayList`? An array list stores the data in the list in an array. It usually keeps track of how many items are being stored in the array, and if you use the add method that doesn't specify an index to add the new item, it adds the new item at the next open position in the array. But if you use the add method that specifies the index to add the new item, it must first shift right any items currently at that position or beyond. If you remove any items from the list, all items to the right must be shifted left. If you add items in a linked list, you simply find the previous item and set the new item's **next** field to the previous item's next, and set the previous item's next to the new item. The next field in a `LinkedList` data element (**node**) is a reference link to the next item in the list. Figure 18.17 shows how items are added to each type of list.

In addition, if you are using an `ArrayList` and you add many items to the list, the list may become longer than the array holding it. In this case a new, bigger array must be created, and all the items in the old array copied to the new array before the new item is added. If you later remove many items, the array may waste a great deal of space. But a linked list can grow or shrink easily. So if you will need to add and remove many items at specific indices in a list, or the list size can change dramatically, it is better to use a `LinkedList` instead of an `ArrayList`.

18.7   Concepts Summary

In this chapter we showed several examples of object-oriented analysis and design. We explained why we need abstract classes and abstract methods and showed detailed examples of how polymorphism works during run-time. This chapter also explains how interfaces are used in conjunction with abstract classes.

Exercises

1. Define each of the following.
   - Polymorphism
   - Object-oriented analysis
   - Object-oriented design
   - The association relationship
   - The inheritance relationship
   - An abstract class
   - An interface

2. If you were creating a simulation of traffic on a highway, what classes might you create? Would you have an abstract class? Why or why not?

3. If you were creating software for a bank that has checking and savings accounts, what classes might you create? Would you have an abstract class? Why or why not?

4. Does an abstract class have to have one or more abstract methods? If a class has an abstract method, does it have to be an abstract class? Can one abstract class inherit from another abstract class? Can an abstract class implement an interface?

5. Find another example in the `java.util` package that has an abstract class that implements an interface. What classes implement the interface? In what circumstances would it be best to use each implementing class?

6. Create a new type of text balloon such as a scream balloon that shows all the text in the ellipse in capital letters.

7. Create a new type of speech balloon that connects the speaker to the balloon using a straight line.

8. What is the output from the following?

```
> List<Integer> numList = new ArrayList<Integer>();
> numList.add(3);
> numList.add(10);
> numList.add(1,7);
> numList.add(2,4);
> System.out.println(numList);
```

9. What is the output from the following?

```
> List<Integer> numList = new ArrayList<Integer>();
> numList.add(2);
> numList.add(15);
> numList.remove(0);
> numList.add(5);
> numList.add(1,8);
> System.out.println(numList);
```

10. Create classes that represent types of books for a publishing company. Would the `Book` class be an abstract class?

11. Create a new type of text balloon such as a whisper balloon that shows all the text in a smaller font.

12. Create a new type of text balloon where the ellipse around the text looks like a cloud.

13. Extend the shape example by creating a new class `Polygon` that has an array of points. Can this class replace the `Shape` class in the Shape Example?

14. Extend the shape example by creating a new class `Arrow` that is a line with an arrow at one end. Have the arrow at the second point in the shape.

15. Extend the shape example by creating a new class `Arc` and have it draw an arc of the circle between the two points.

16. Extend the shape example by creating a new class `Star` that draws a star enclosed by the rectangle defined by the two points.

17. Extend the shape example by creating a new class `x` that draws an X between opposite corners of the rectangle defined by the two points.

18. What are the differences between interfaces and abstract classes? If you want to define object fields, which should you use? If you want to provide code in a method, which should you use? If you want to make classes as decoupled as possible, which should you use?

19. Create a UML class diagram for classes that represent money for an international bank.

20. Create a UML class diagram for classes that represent types of numbers including integers, floating point numbers, and complex numbers.

A Alice Tips and Techniques

A.1 Special Effects: Text and 2D Graphic Images

An important aspect of an animation is communicating information to the person viewing the animation (the **user**). Text, sound, and graphic images help you communicate. The following sections show how to add text and graphic images to your world.

A.1.1 3D Text

To add a 3D text object to a world, click on the Create 3D Text folder in the Local Gallery, as seen in Figure A.1.

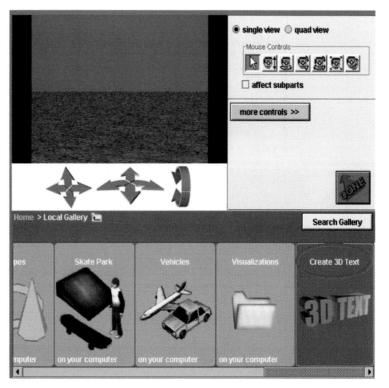

Figure A.1
3D text in the local gallery

A text dialog box pops up for entering text, as in Figure A.2. The dialog box allows font, bold, and italic selections, and a text box where words can be typed.

When the Okay button is clicked, Alice adds a text object to the world and an entry for the object in the Object tree. The name of the object is the same as the text displayed, as seen in Figure A.3.

The text object can be positioned using mouse controls in the same way as any other object. To modify the text in the object string, click on the text in the properties list of the Details area. Then, enter a new string of text in the popup dialog box, illustrated in Figure A.4.

Figure A.2
A text dialog box

Figure A.3
The text object is added to scene and Object tree

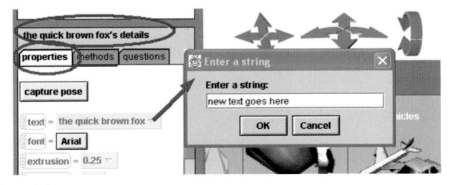

Figure A.4
Modifying text

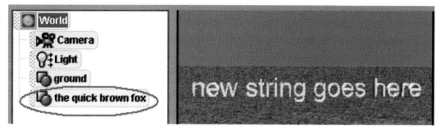

Figure A.5
The name of text object remains the same

Note that modifying the string in the text object does not modify the name of the object. The name is still as it was when the text object was originally created, as seen in Figure A.5.

A.1.2 Graphic Images (Billboards)

Although Alice is a 3D system, it is possible to display flat 2D images in a scene. Flat 2D images can be created in any paint tool and saved in GIF, JPG, or TIF format. To add a 2D image (Alice calls it a **billboard**) to your world, select Make Billboard from the File menu, as seen in Figure A.6. In the selection dialog box, navigate to the stored image and then click the Import button.

Alice will add the flat image to the world. The billboard in Figure A.7 illustrates one of the uses of billboards — providing information to the user about how to play a game or simulation. In this example, the billboard provides instructions for how to use the keyboard to control the motion of an object.

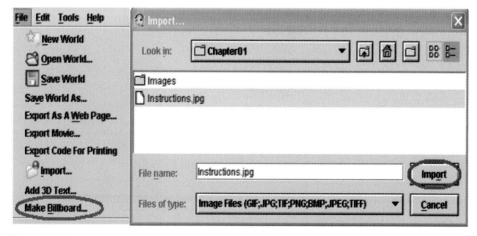

Figure A.6
Importing a billboard

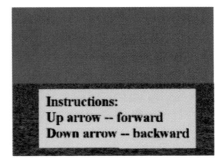

Figure A.7
A billboard to provide information

A.2   Orientation and Movement Instructions

To create your own animations, it is important that you have some understanding of where the center of an object is located. The center of the object is a reference point from which, and around which, direction and distance of a motion are measured.

One way to determine the location of the center of an object is to select the object in the Object tree and then view the axes within the bounding box that encloses the object. In Figure A.8, the monkey (Animals) object is selected in the object tree and a bounding box highlights the monkey in the world view. Within the bounding box, three axes are displayed as red, green, and blue lines. **The intersection of the axes is where the center of an object is located.** As illustrated in this example, the center of an object is NOT necessarily located at its center of mass. For objects that are bipedal (walk on two legs), the center is often located between the feet because that is a point of reference for the distance a biped moves.

The three dimensional coordinate system also provides a sense of direction — its **orientation**. Of course, the bounding box and the axes are not visible as an animation program is running. To illustrate the relationship of an object's motion to its

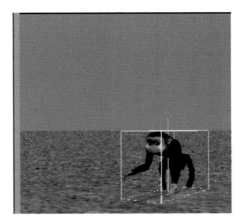

Figure A.8
Using a bounding box to view the center of a whole object

Figure A.9
The monkey's complete orientation

orientation as a program is running, we implanted a visible set of axes (Shapes) into the monkey, so the intersection of the axes is at the center of the monkey object. Figure A.9 shows the monkey with the intersection of the axes object positioned at the center of the monkey. The labels on the axes indicate the monkey's orientation (sense of direction).

A.2.1 The *move* Method

In an Alice program, an object's position in a world can be changed by calling a *move* method. In computer graphics, a *move* action is said to be **translational**, which is a motion on the horizontal or vertical plane. An object can perform a translational move in six possible directions.

move

- **left**
- **right**
- **up**
- **down**
- **forward**
- **backward**

The direction an object moves is ego-centric. That is, the direction an object moves is relative to its own orientation. To illustrate, an example world is shown in Figure A.10 where a chicken is facing a monkey. A tree is positioned in the background as a point of reference. The instruction in *world.my first method* tells the monkey to move left 2 meters.

Figure A.11 illustrates the scene after the world runs and the monkey has moved left 2 meters. Compare this "after scene" to the "before scene" in Figure A.10 above. As you look at the "after scene," it may appear to you that the monkey has moved to the right. Indeed, relative to the camera, the monkey has moved to the right. The

Figure A.10
A before scene: note the position of the monkey relative to the chicken and the tree.

Figure A.11
After scene: the monkey has moved left (relative to its own sense of orientation)

important thing to note, however, is that the monkey moves relative to its own sense of what is "left" and what is "right." Unless told otherwise, all objects in Alice move relative to their own sense of orientation.

A.2.2 The *turn* and *roll* Methods

While the *move* method causes translational motion, the *turn* and *roll* methods cause rotational motion. An object can turn in four possible directions (*up* and *down* are **not** included).

turn

- **left**
- **right**
- **forward**
- **backward**

A *turn left* or *right* is a motion similar to turning a door on its hinges. A *turn forward* or *backward* is a motion similar to lifting or closing a hinged lid, as on a jewelry box or a picnic basket.

An object can *roll* in only two directions (*up, down, forward* and *backward* are **not** included).

roll

- **left**
- **right**

A *roll left* or *right* is a motion similar to a clockwise or counter-clockwise twist of a door knob.

As with the *move* method, the motion for *turn* and *roll* are ego-centric and are relative to the orientation of the object. In addition, *turn* and *roll* are also relative to the center of the object or its sub-part's connection to the rest of the body.

If the whole object is rotating, the rotational motion occurs around the center of the whole object. For example, the instructions shown below make the monkey move up 1 meters and then turn forward 1 full revolution.

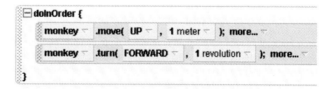

The images in Figure A.12 show the sequence of a *turn forward* motion, a somersault in mid-air. The screen shots were taken as the turn forward instruction was executing. As the monkey turns, the axes object turns with it and illustrates that the orientation of the monkey is consistent with the motion of the monkey. Because the center of the monkey object is between its feet, and the rotation pivot point is also between the monkey's feet.

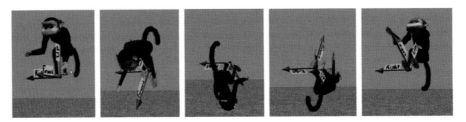

Figure A.12
A *turn* rotation for the whole monkey object

Likewise, a *roll* rotation for the whole monkey occurs around the center, at the monkey's feet. The following code moves the monkey up 1 meter and rolls the monkey right one complete revolution.

The images in Figure A.13 show the sequence of a roll right motion, a sideways cartwheel. The screen shots were taken as the roll right instruction was executed. Once again, the rotation pivot point is at the monkey's feet.

If a sub-part of an object is rotated (rather than a whole object), the rotational motion occurs around the joint where the sub-part is connected to the rest of the object. Think about a joint connection in terms of your own body. For example, your upper-arm is connected to the rest of your body by a skeletal joint at the shoulder. When your upper-arm rotates, it does so by rotating at the joint. For this reason, a joint connection may be thought of as a **pivot point**.

For Alice objects, the location of a joint connection for a sub-part can be found by selecting the sub-part in the object tree and viewing the intersection of the axes in the bounding box that encloses the sub-part. In Figure A.14, the monkey's left arm sub-part has been selected in the object tree and the axes intersect at the shoulder, the pivot point for rotating the monkey's left arm.

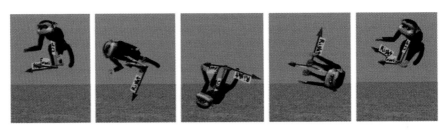

Figure A.13
A roll rotation for the whole monkey object

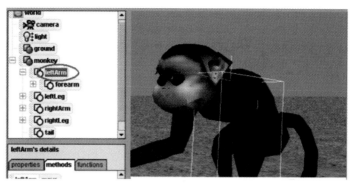

Figure A.14
Using a bounding box to view the pivot point for rotating a sub-part

To better illustrate the orientation of the left arm sub-part, we have imbedded an axes object at the pivot point, as shown in Figure A.15.

Figure A.15
The orientation of the monkey's left arm

In this example, the following code rotates the monkey's left arm 0.5 revolutions (one-half turn around) at the pivot point where the arm is connected to the rest of the monkey's body.

```
monkey.leftArm ▾ .turn( FORWARD ▾ , 0.5 revolutions ▾ ); more... ▾
```

The images in Figure A.16 show the sequence of motion. The screen captures were made as the *turn forward* instruction was executed. The rotation's pivot point is at the monkey's shoulder. And, the forward motion of the arm is relative to the orientation of the arm where it is connected to the rest of the monkey's body.

We recommend that you start Alice, add several objects to the world, and play around with *move, turn* and *roll*. There are hundreds of different models and the design of the internal skeletal structure of the body is **not necessarily the same** from one 3D model to the next. It is important to observe how the subparts are connected and what the orientation is at the joint connection, as the skeletal structure has a very real effect on how rotational motion is carried out when the program runs.

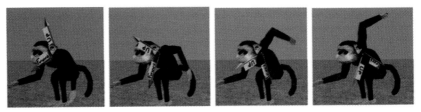

Figure A.16
A *turn* rotation for the monkey's left arm sub-part

One last word of advice regarding *move, turn*, and *roll*: A sequence of several motions, one after another, has a cumulative effect and can leave an object and its sub-parts in a twisted position. You may need to "unwind" some of the motion to return to the object to some more appropriate position.

A.2.3 The *orient to* Method

When two objects must move together, the orientation of the two objects must be synchronized. In the world shown in Figure A.17, we want the monkey to stay on top of the ball as the ball moves forward for a short distance.

The code we wrote to make the monkey and ball move forward together is shown in Figure A.18.

Figure A.17
The monkey jumps on top of a ball

```
doTogether {
    toyBall .move( FORWARD , 1 meter ); more...
    monkey .move( FORWARD , 5 meters ); more...
}
```

Figure A.18
Code to move ball and monkey forward together

Imagine our surprise when the ball moved in one direction and the monkey moved in a different direction, ending up well away from the ball, suspended in midair. Why did this happen? Well, the ball is an example of an object for which we can't tell (just by looking at it) which direction is forward and which direction is backward. Evidently, in positioning the ball and the monkey in the scene, we positioned the ball so its forward direction was not the same as the forward direction for the monkey, as illustrated in Figure A.19. So, when the ball and the monkey each move forward, they move in different directions.

The way to solve this problem is to synchronize the orientation of the two objects. In this example, we will use a *toyball.orient to(monkey)* instruction, as shown in Figure A.20.

Figure A.19
The monkey and ball move forward in different directions

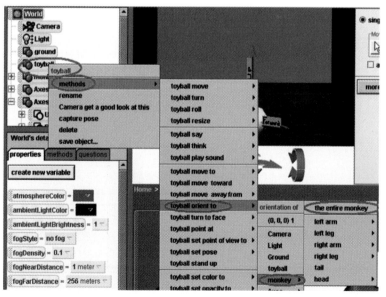

Figure A.20
Cascading menus for *orient to*

The result is shown in Figure A.21. Now, the toy ball has the same orientation (the same sense of direction) as the monkey. This means that the two objects will move in the same direction when a *move forward* instruction is given to each.

The *orient to* instruction may seem a bit weird, but it simply tells Alice that the first object should take on the same sense of direction as the second object. So, if we orient two objects to have the same orientation, then the two objects are synchronized — they have the same sense of up, down, left, right, forward, and backward.

Figure A.21
Now the monkey and the toy ball have the same orientation

A.2.4 The *vehicle* Property

Another way to synchronize the movements of two objects is to take advantage of a special property called *vehicle*. As an illustration of the vehicle property, consider a circus act where a chicken rides on the back of a horse, as seen in Figure A.22. As part of the circus act, the horse trots around in a circular path and the chicken rides on the back of the horse.

To synchronize the movement of the chicken and the horse, you can make the horse be a *vehicle* for the chicken. To create this special effect, select chicken in the object tree and then select the properties tab (under the object tree at the lower left of the window). Then click on the white tile to the right of the word vehicle. A list of possible vehicles is shown in a popup menu, from which horse can be selected, as illustrated in Figure A.23. Now, when the horse moves, the chicken will move with it.

Figure A.22
Circus act, chicken riding on horse

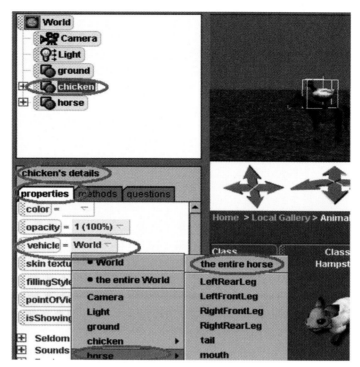

Figure A.23
Selecting horse as a vehicle for chicken

A.2.5 Arguments: duration, style, *asSeenBy*

Movement instructions (e.g., *move, turn, roll*) end with the editing tag "*more...*", as in Figure A.24.

When *more...* is clicked, a popup menu allows you to select from a list of three arguments:duration, style, and asSeenBy — as shown in Figure A.25.

The *duration* argument tells Alice an amount of time (in seconds) for animating the movement. (Alice assumes that the amount of time for a movement is 1 second.) A zero (0) duration is an instantaneous movement. Negative values are not used.

The *style* argument specifies the way in which one movement instruction blends into the next. The options are *gently* (begin and end gently), *abruptly* (begin and end abruptly), *begin gently* (and end abruptly), and *end gently* (and begin abruptly). To get the right degree of "smoothness" for a movement, it is often worthwhile to experiment with *style*.

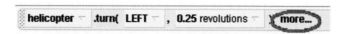

Figure A.24
The *more...* editing tag

Figure A.25
Popup menu for *more...*

Although each object in Alice has its own sense of direction (orientation), you can use the *asSeenBy* argument to tell Alice to use an orientation of one object to guide the movement of another object. This is best explained by using an example. Suppose we have a helicopter on a pilot training mission, as shown in Figure A.26.

The code in Figure A.27 is intended to roll the helicopter left and then move it upward.

Running the animation, we see that the result is not what we had in mind. When the helicopter moves upward, it does so from its own sense of direction, as in Figure A.28.

What we had wanted, however, was an upward movement with respect to the ground. To correct this problem, we clicked more... and then selected asSeenBy → ground, as in Figure A.29.

The resulting code, shown in Figure A.30, gives the desired movement.

Figure A.26
Training mission

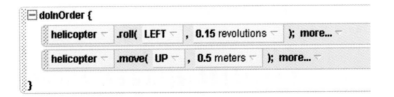

Figure A.27
Code to roll and then move upward

Figure A.28
Up — from the helicopter's sense of direction (orientation)

```
doInOrder {
    helicopter .roll( LEFT , 0.15 revolutions ); more...
    helicopter .move( UP , 0.5 meters ); more...
                                          duration        ▶
                                          style           ▶
                                          asSeenBy        ▶   • <None>
                                          isScaledBySize ▶
                                                              the entire world
                                                              camera
                                                              light
                                                              ground
                                                              chicken
}
```

Figure A.29
Selecting *asSeenBy* ground

```
doInOrder {
    helicopter .roll( LEFT , 0.15 revolutions ); more...
    helicopter .move( UP , 0.5 meters ); asSeenBy = ground more...
}
```

Figure A.30
The modified code

A.2.6 The *turn to face* and *point at* Methods

As discussed above, the *asSeenBy* argument in a movement instruction uses the orientation of one object to guide the movement of another object. Two special methods are also useful for making an object turn to "look at" another object. A *turn to face* method causes one object to pivot around until its front is facing some other object.

A second method, *point at*, can be used to align two objects from the *center* of one to the *center* of another. It is easiest to explain *point at* in an example. In Figure A.31, the rowers in the lifeBoat want to row toward the lighthouse on the island. An obvious first step is to have the boat and the rowers turn to look at the lighthouse on the island.

The *point at* method may be used to aim the boat at the lighthouse location. Then, movement instructions may be used to move the boat toward the island and the lighthouse, as in Figure A.32.

While this instruction does turn the lifeboat toward the lighthouse, it also has the effect of tipping the boat so it seems to be sinking on one end, as seen in Figure A.33.

The point at instruction aligns the center of the lifeboat with the center of the lighthouse, which is higher in elevation than the boat, as shown in Figure A.34. As a result, the boat tips.

Figure A.31
The lighthouse, island, and boat initial scene

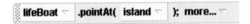

Figure A.32
Code to aim the boat toward the lightHouse

Figure A.33
The lifeboat tips on the *point at* instruction

Figure A.34
Alignment from center to center

You may, or may not, want the boat to tip. To provide some control of the *point at* instruction, additional arguments are available in the **more...** popup menu, as seen in Figure A.35. Selecting **true** for the onlyAffectYaw argument allows an object to point at another object without tipping (pitching). **Yaw** is technical term meaning a left-right turning motion, and pitch is a tipping, rocking-chair kind of motion. (When *onlyAffectYaw* is *true,* the *point at* instruction works the same as a *turn to face* instruction.) Note that in target games and flight animations *onlyAffectYaw* should be *false* (so as to align on the diagonal with a target object).

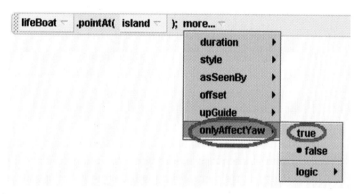

Figure A.35
Selecting onlyAffectYaw → true

A.2.7 The *move to* Method

A special instruction is useful for moving an object in relation to the location of another object. The *move to* instruction moves an object to a specific location in the world. Although we can tell Alice to move an object to a location by entering number coordinates, much of the time we use the *move to* instruction with the position of another object as the target location. (Alice knows the center location of every object in the scene and can move another object to the same location.) In the lighthouse and lifeboat example, we could write the code in Figure A.36.

Figure A.36
Code to *move to* the island

Figure A.37
Result of a *move to* the island

When this code is run, the boat moves to the center of the island, as seen in Figure A.37. Of course, the center of the island is located at its center of mass. So, the boat plows right into the middle of the island!

A.3 Camera and Animation Controls

Camera control is needed both at scene set-up and also while an animation is running. At scene set-up, positioning the camera eases the process of placing objects in a specific location. And during runtime, moving the camera adds a fun aspect to the animation itself.

The camera controls in the Alice scene editor, as in Figure A.38, allow you to move the camera position at the time an initial scene is being created. Of course, the camera controls are not available while the animation is running. In this section we look at a technique for controlling the movement of the camera at runtime. Also, we offer a tip on how to use the speed multiplier to speed up (or slow down) an animation at runtime.

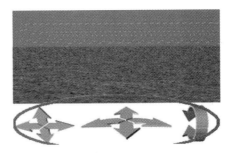

Figure A.38
Camera navigation controls in the scene editor

A.3.1 Setting *the Point of View*

One way to move the camera around a scene is to create one or more **dummy objects** that mark locations where the camera will be used during the animation. A dummy object is invisible and can be used as a goalpost — a target object to which the camera will move during the animation. Once a dummy object is in place, an instruction can be created to set the camera *point of view* to the *point of view* of the dummy object (essentially placing the camera onto a dummy tripod). At runtime, the *setpoint of view* method effectively moves the camera to the dummy object (similar to a *move to* instruction), and the camera viewpoint is now from that location.

This technique is best illustrated with an example. You may find it helpful to sit at a computer and try this out as you read the description. Figure A.39 shows an initial scene with the camera pointed at a skateboarder. From our perspective (as the person viewing the scene), the camera is allowing us to look at the scene "from the front."

We want to be able to move the camera around to view the skater's actions "from the back" of the scene while the animation is running. To prepare for this action, let's create a couple of dummy objects for the front and back viewpoints. First, drop a dummy object at the current location of the camera. To do this, click the **more controls** button in the scene editor, as in Figure A.40.

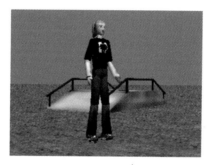

Figure A.39
Camera front view

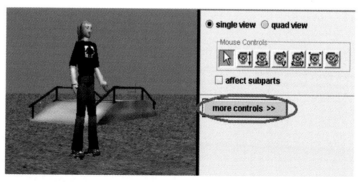

Figure A.40
The "more controls" button

The interface expands to show additional controls, including a drop dummy at camera button, seen in Figure A.41.

A click on the **drop dummy at camera** button creates a dummy object as a goal-post at the current location of the camera. The dummy object is added to the Object tree, as shown in Figure A.42. Alice automatically names dummy objects as *dummy, dummy2*, etc. In this example, we renamed the dummy object as *frontView* (a meaningful name makes it easy to remember).

The next step is to reposition the camera to view the scene from the back. One technique that seems to work well is to drag the camera's forward control (the center camera navigation arrow) toward the back of the scene. Continue to drag the forward control and allow the camera to move straight forward until the camera seems to move through the scene. When the camera seems to have moved far enough to be on the other side of the scene, release the mouse. Select the camera in the Object tree and select a method to turn the camera one-half revolution, as in Figure A.43.

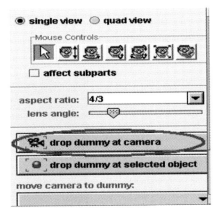

Figure A.41
The "drop dummy at camera" button

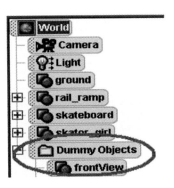

Figure A.42
Dummy object is added to the Object tree

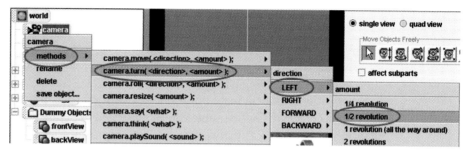

Figure A.43
Move camera to back of scene and then turn it around one-half revolution

The camera should now be facing in the opposite direction and you should be able to see the scene from the back. Click once more on the drop dummy at camera button. We renamed the dummy marker as *backView*. Two dummy objects should now be in the Object tree, *frontView* and *backView*.

Now you can write instructions to move the camera at runtime. Select camera in the Object tree and then drag the **setPointOfView** instruction into the editor. Select the particular dummy object for the point of view. Figure A.44 illustrates how to create the instruction.

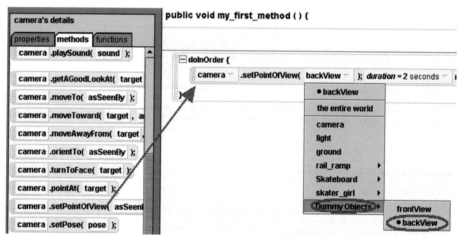

Figure A.44
Creating a *set point of view* instruction

A sample instruction is shown below. At runtime, this instruction will move the camera to **backView** and the camera's *point of view* will be from that location.

It is also possible to have the camera follow an object, by changing the camera's vehicle property. A fun exercise is to create a world with a skyride object (Amusement Park gallery) and then enter the program code shown in Figure A.45. In running this world, you will see the movement of a sky ride as if you were standing on the skyride platform for loading passengers.

To get a different sense of the ride, try also adding an instruction to change the camera's vehicle to the first cable car, as illustrated in Figure A.45(b). See the differences in what happens as the world runs. You may also want to experiment with "riding" some of the other amusement park rides.

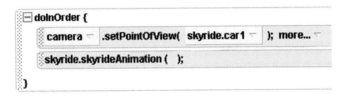

Figure A.45(a)
Setting the point of view to the skyride

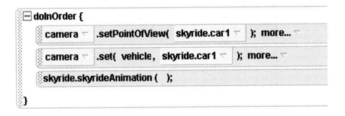

Figure A.45(b)
Specifying which vehicle in the skyride will be the point of view

A.3.2 Controlling the Runtime Speed

As you gain experience in programming with Alice, your animations will become more and more complex and the runtime longer and longer. Naturally, this means that testing your programs takes longer because the animation takes a while to run through the sequence of actions to get to the most recent additions.

A great way to "fast forward" through the actions you have already tested is to use the Speed Multiplier that appears in the Play window, as seen in Figure A.46. The Speed Multiplier is a slide bar with a thumb. You can grab the thumb with the mouse and slide it left or right while the animation is running to control the speed of the animation. (Sliding the thumb has no effect if the animation has stopped.) When you release the thumb, it snaps back to its original setting and the animation returns to normal speed.

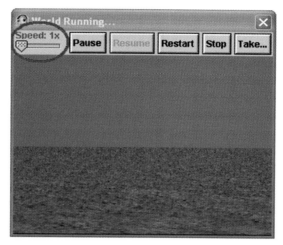

Figure A.46
The Speed Multiplier

As the animation is running, you may want to free up the mouse for other actions. You can temporarily lock the thumb at a particular speed. Hold down the Shift key and let go of the mouse. This locks the speed. Any readjustment of the thumb releases the lock.

A.4   Visible and Invisible Objects

Properties of objects are sometimes used in games and simulations to achieve a special effect, such as making an object visible or invisible. In this section we look at techniques and examples of changing the visibility of objects.

A.4.1 The opacity *Property*

The following example changes the opacity of a fish in an ocean world. (**Opacity** is how opaque something is, that is, how hard it is to see through.) Figure A.47 shows an aquatic scene. This world is easily created by adding an *oceanFloor* (from the Ocean folder in the online Gallery) and a *lilfish* (Animals).

The *lilfish* is swimming out to lunch, and her favorite seafood is seaweed. Instructions to point *lilfish* at the seaweed and then swim toward it are shown in Figure A.48(a). The *wiggletail* method, shown in Figure A.48(b), makes the fish wiggle its tail in a left-right motion.

As the fish moves toward the seaweed, she will also move away from the camera. So she should fade, because water blurs our vision of distant objects. We can make *lilfish* become less visible by changing the opacity property. As opacity is decreased, an object becomes less distinct (more difficult to see). To write an instruction to change the opacity, click on the *lilfish*'s properties tab and drag the *opacity* tile into the editor. From the popup menu, select the opacity percentage, as shown in Figure A.49.

The resulting code is in Figure A.50.

Figure A.47
An ocean floor scene with *lilfish*

Figure A.48(a)
Code to make *lilfish* swim toward the seaweed

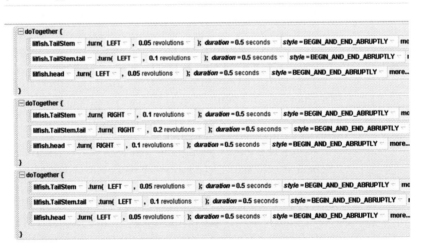

Figure A.48(b)
The *wiggletail* method

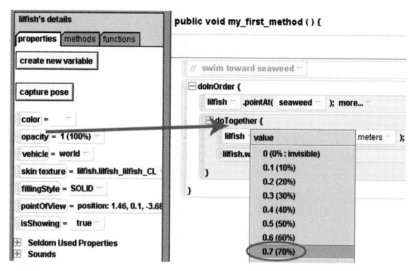

Figure A.49
Dragging the *opacity* tile into editor

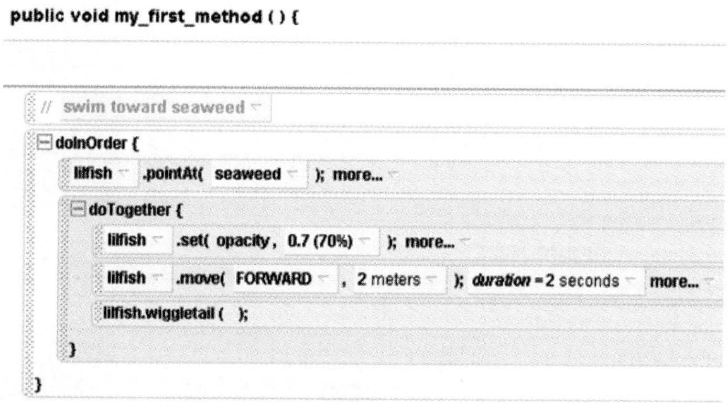

Figure A.50
Code now includes a *set opacity* instruction

When the world is run, *lilfish* will become less visible, as shown in Figure A.51. At 0% opacity, an object will totally disappear. This does not mean that the object has been deleted; it is still part of the world but is not visible on the screen.

A.4.2 The *isShowing* Property

Each object has a property called *isShowing*. At the time an object is first added to a world, the object is made visible in the scene and *isShowing* is set to *true*. Changing the value of this property is especially useful in gamelike programs where you want to signal the end of a game. Figure A.52 illustrates the *isShowing* property as *true* for

Figure A.51
The *lilfish* becomes more difficult to see as *opacity* is decreased

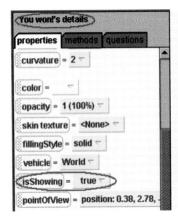

Figure A.52
isShowing is *true* and "You won!" is visible

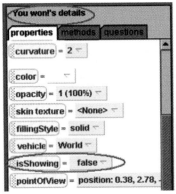
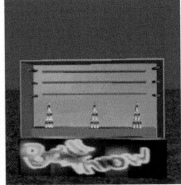

Figure A.53
isShowing is *false* and "You won!" is not visible

"You won!" Setting *isShowing* to *false* makes the "You won!" text invisible, as shown in Figure A.53.

When its *isShowing* property is set to *false*, the object is not removed from the world; it is simply not displayed on the screen. The object can be made to "reappear" by setting its *isShowing* property back to *true*.

In this example, we want the text to appear when the player wins the game. To create an instruction that sets the *isShowing* property to *true*, drag the *isShowing* property tile into the world and select *true* from the popup menu. The result is shown in Figure A.54.

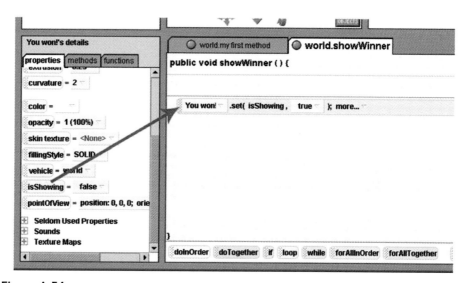

Figure A.54
An instruction to set *isShowing* to *true* at runtime

A.4.3 Relationship of *isShowing* and *opacity* Properties

The *isShowing* and *opacity* properties track different (though related) states of an object. *isShowing* is strictly *true* or *false* — like a light switch that can be either on or off. *Opacity* is a more sliding scale — like a dimmer switch that can adjust the brightness of a light. Though it is true that when *opacity* is 0%, the object is invisible, nonetheless when you make an object have an *opacity* of 0%, Alice does not automatically make *isShowing* false. Likewise, when you make *isShowing* false, Alice does not automatically make *opacity* 0%.

A good piece of advice is: "Be consistent." If you are using *isShowing* in your program to set the visiblity, then do not use *opacity* to check whether the object is visible. Likewise, if you are using *opacity* to set the visibility, then do not use *isShowing* to check whether the object is visible.

A.4.4 Rotating Around an Invisible Object

An invisible object is a good way to set up a stationary reference point for actions by other objects. Consider the world illustrated in Figure A.55. We want the pterodactyl to fly around the dragon.

Figure A.55
A dragon and a pterodactyl

The pterodactyl will fly around the dragon if we use *asSeenBy* = *dragon* in a *turn right* instruction for the pterodactyl object. (The *asSeenBy* parameter was described in Tips & Techniques 2.)

Suppose, though, that we want the pterodactyl and the dragon to both fly around in a half-turn relative to each other (facing each other down — sort of a bluffing technique). This would mean that the dragon should end up at the pterodactyl's location (facing the pterodactyl's new location), and the pterodactyl should end up at the dragon's location (facing the dragon's new location). A first attempt might be as follows:

```
doTogether {
    pterodactyl .turn( RIGHT , 0.5 revolutions ); asSeenBy = dragon      more...
    dragon .turn( RIGHT , 0.5 revolutions ); asSeenBy = pterodactyl      more...
}
```

When this program is run, each animal ends up where it started, facing in the opposite direction! The problem is that once each animal has begun to move, its location changes, so that further moves relative to each other lead to unexpected results! What we need is an object that does not move, located somewhere between the dragon and the pterodactyl. Let's add a sphere object between the dragon and the pterodactyl and make it invisible by changing its *isShowing* property to *false*. Now we can write the following code:

```
doTogether {
    pterodactyl .turn( RIGHT , 0.5 revolutions ); asSeenBy = Sphere      more...
    dragon .turn( RIGHT , 0.5 revolutions ); asSeenBy = Sphere      more...
}
```

When this code is run, the dragon and pterodactyl exchange places, as seen in Figure A.56!

Figure A.56
The pterodactyl and dragon change places

A.5   Creating Your Own People Models

The galleries provide hundreds of 3D models for use in building your worlds. Alice is not a graphics model builder, but two special people-building options (*hebuilder* and *shebuilder*) are available in the People folder of the Local Gallery, as seen in Figure A.57. A click on *hebuilder* or *shebuilder* will bring up a people builder window (Figure A.58), where you can select the desired body type, hair, skin color, eyes, and clothing. When you have completed your selections, click on OK to name the object and add it to your world.

A.5.1   Special Built-In Methods for Hebuilder/Shebuilder People

Alice automatically defines several built-in methods for the person object that you build. Figure A.59 illustrates those methods.

It is worthwhile to experiment with using each of these methods in your world. Many of these methods allow your person object to exhibit various emotions. The

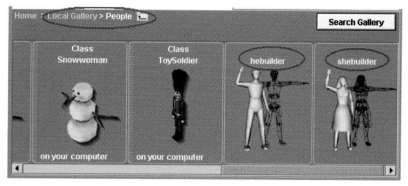

Figure A.57
The *hebuilder* and *shebuilder* model building utilities

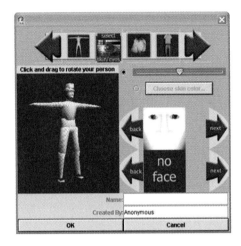

Figure A.58
People builder

Figure A.59
Built-in methods for people constructed using *hebuilder* and *shebuilder*

walk method is particularly worthy of your attention. This method provides a real advantage, because a *walk* method is difficult to write on your own. Note, however, that the *walk* method causes the person to walk "in place" – not moving forward. Thus, an instruction that calls the *walk* method should be paired with a *moveforward* instruction, in a *Do together* to have the person object walk forward. Figure A.60 illustrates the code to have the person Steve walk forward two meters.

Note: Alice uses poses when implementing these built-in methods. If an object is resized (either during scene set-up or at runtime) the built-in methods will not work properly. We recommend that you do not resize person objects constructed with the *hebuilder* and *shebuilder*. Instead, resize all other objects in your scene, as you are setting up the world.

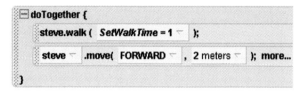

Figure A.60
Pairing the built-in *walk* method with a move forward

A.6   Random Numbers and Random Motion

A.6.1 Random Numbers

Random numbers play a big role in certain kinds of computing applications. For example, random numbers are used in creating secure encryptions for transmission of information on the Internet. An encrypting utility uses random numbers to create a code for scrambling the information stored in a file. Then the scrambled information is transmitted across the net. When the information arrives at the target location it must be decrypted (unscrambled). To decrypt the information, you need to know the code that was used. Various kinds of scientific simulations also make use of random numbers. For example, random numbers are used to create "what-if" situations in weather simulation programs.

To illustrate the use of random numbers in Alice, let's create an animation where an object's motion is random. A random number is created by selecting the world-level question *random number*, shown in Figure A.61.

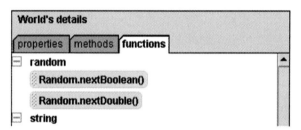

Figure A.61
World's *random number* functions

As an example, consider the world scene in Figure A.62. An Eskimo child and a penguin are playing together, sliding around on the ice.

Suppose you want to write code to make the penguin slide forward a random distance. This is easily accomplished by first creating a *move* instruction and then dragging the *random number* question tile into the distance parameter. The result is shown here:

Figure A.62
Pet penguin sliding on the ice

The *random number* question returns a fractional value between 0 and 1. When the above instruction is executed, the penguin will slide forward some fractional amount between 0 and 1. Although you know the range of values (somewhere between 0 and 1) you don't know the exact number. Also, each time the program is executed the distance is likely to be different. This unpredictability is what makes it random.

A.6.2 Selecting a Range for *Random Number*

The default range of values for *random number* is 0 to 1. Suppose you want a random number between 1 and 5, instead of between 0 and 1. To specify the range of numbers for the random number question, click *more* in the *random number* tile (purple) and select the *minimum* value. Then, do the same to select a *maximum* value. The instruction with a range of 1 to 5 is shown here:

Now, each time the program is executed, the penguin will slide forward 3.8 meters or 2.3 meters or some other random amount between 1 and 5. We suggest that you test this out by creating and running the world. Press the Restart button several times to observe the sliding motion.

A.6.3 Integers (Whole Numbers)

Sometimes you may want a random number that has no digits to the right of the decimal point. For example, instead of numbers such as 3.8, or 2.3 you may want whole numbers such as 2 or 3 or 4. Numbers that are whole numbers (have no digits to the right of the decimal point) are known as **integer** values. To use the *random number* question to obtain random integer values, click *more* in the *random number* tile (purple) and select *integerOnly* and *true* in the pull-down menu, as shown in Figure A.63.

Figure A.63
Selecting *integerOnly* for the *random number* question

A.6.4 Random Motion

If the *random number* question is combined with the *move* instruction, a form of random motion is created where objects move to a random location. Random motion is essential in many different kinds of games and simulations. As an example, consider the world in Figure A.64. The goldfish is to swim in a random-like movement. We want to restrict the movement to a nearby position. Otherwise, successive moves would make the goldfish jump around here and there on the screen — not at all like a goldfish swimming.

Figure A.64
Goldfish in a water world for a random motion animation

Because Alice objects live in a three-dimensional world, you can write a *move* instruction that moves the goldfish in any of six possible directions (*forward, backward, left, right, up*, and *down*). Combining the *random number* question with six *move* instructions might be a bit clumsy. Let's try to make our work easier by taking advantage of negative numbers. If a negative number is used as the distance in a *move* instruction, the object is to move in the opposite direction. For example, the instruction shown below is to *move* the goldfish *left* -1 meters. When executed, this instruction will actually move the goldfish *right* 1 meter.

If we use both positive and negative distance values, only three *move* instructions are needed. We will use *up, left*, and *forward* directions. With this idea in mind, let's write a storyboard for a *randomMotion* method:

---

fish.randomMotion:

Parameters: *min, max*
Do together
    fish move up a random number distance
    fish move left a random number distance
    fish move forward a random number distance

The *goldfish.randomMotion* storyboard contains a *Do together* block and three *move* instructions. In each move instruction, the random number question is called to generate a random distance. The parameters (*min* and *max*) are used to select the range of minimum and maximum values for the *random number* distance. In this example, we are going to use a *min* of −0.2 and a *max* of 0.2. So the *random number* question will return a value in the range of −0.2 to 0.2 for the move up and move left instructions. Note that *min* for the *moveforward* instruction is 0. This is because goldfish do not swim backward.

Now we can translate the storyboard into program code. The code for the *randomMotion* method is shown in Figure A.65. Think about how this method works. In each *move* instruction, the *random number* question is called to get a random distance. Let's say the *random number* question returns a negative distance for the *moveup* instruction; the goldfish will actually move *down*. A negative distance for the *moveleft* instruction will move the goldfish *right*. The distance for the *move forward* instruction will always be positive, so the goldfish will always move forward.

```
public void randomMotion ( Number [123] min , Number [123] max ) {

    doTogether {
        Goldfish  .move( UP  ,  Random.nextDouble() minimum = min  maximum = max  more...  ); m
        Goldfish  .move( LEFT  ,  Random.nextDouble() minimum = min  maximum = max  more...  );
        Goldfish  .move( FORWARD  ,  Random.nextDouble() minimum = 0  maximum = max  more...
    }
}
```

Figure A.65
The *randomMotion* method

The *do together* block executes the *moveup*, *moveright,* and *moveforward* all at the same time. As a result the goldfish will move to some random location within a cube of space defined by the minimum and maximum random number distances.

Once the *randomMotion* instruction has been written, it should be tested. To call the *randomMotion* method, *min* and *max* arguments must be passed to the method, as shown below. In this example, the *min* (-0.2) and *max* (0.2) arguments will restrict the movement of the goldfish to a random location near the current location.

```
Goldfish.randomMotion ( min = -0.2  , max = 0.2  );
```

A.7   Events and Repetition
A.7.1 The BDE (Begin-During-End) Event

In a *While* statement actions occur while some condition remains true. Sometimes, we would like to make an action occur when the condition becomes *false* and the loop ends. For example, consider the world in Figure A.66, where a helicopter has arrived to rescue the white rabbit. The helicopter is circling over the island. We want the rabbit to look at the helicopter and turn his head to keep an eye on it as long as the helicopter is in front of him. Of course, the helicopter is circling the island and will eventually fly out of sight of the rabbit. When the rabbit can no longer see the helicopter, we want him to look at the camera.

Figure A.66
The rabbit rescue scene

This animation has two repeated actions: a helicopter circling an island and a rabbit moving his head to watch the helicopter as it circles. Also, an action should occur as soon as the helicopter can no longer be seen by the rabbit: the rabbit looks back at the camera. The problem is how to make actions repeat (within a loop) but also make an action occur each time the loop ends. We have seen this situation before in working with interactive worlds and events. Perhaps we can create a solution to our problem by using events. In fact, Alice has a built-in *While* statement event for linking events to repeated actions. The event, highlighted in Figure A.67, is *While something is true*.

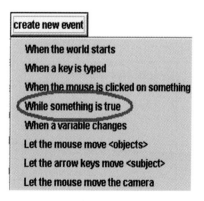

Figure A.67
Selecting *While something is true* in the Events editor

Selecting the *While something is true* event from the pull-down menu causes a *While* event block to be added to the Events editor, as shown in Figure A.68. The event block automatically contains a Begin-During-End (BDE) block that allows you to specify what happens when the loop begins, during the execution of the loop, and when the loop ends.

To create a BDE behavior, we need to specify up to four pieces of information (any or all may be left as *Nothing*):

A conditional expression/question (evaluates to *true* or *false*) — The *While* statement condition is *<None>* by default, but you must replace it with a Boolean expression or question.

Begin — An animation instruction or method that is to be done once, at the time the condition becomes true.

During — An animation instruction or method that is to be done repeatedly, as long as the condition remains true. Note that as soon as the condition becomes false, the animation instruction or method ceases running, even if it is in the middle of an instruction!

End — An animation instruction or method that is to be done once, at the time the condition becomes false.

In the above example, the helicopter is flying around the island. We would like to have the white rabbit's head look at (*point at*) the helicopter as soon as the helicopter is in front of the rabbit (Begin). Then, as long as the helicopter is still in front of the rabbit (During), we want the rabbit's head to continue to look at the helicopter. As soon as the helicopter is no longer in front of the rabbit (End), the rabbit should look back at the camera. The code in Figure A.69 accomplishes this task:

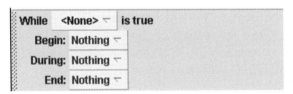

Figure A.68
While event with Begin-During-End (BDE)

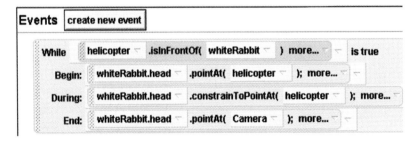

Figure A.69
While statement in an event link

The *constrain to point at* instruction is a built-in method that continuously adjusts the position of an object to point at some other object. In this example, *constrain to point at* is used to make the rabbit's head continuously point at the helicopter as long as the *While* statement condition (*helicopter* is in front of *whiteRabbit*) is *true*.

Note: Using multiple *do together* control structures within a BDE may cause a run-time error due to the immediate interruption that is triggered when the BDE ends but one or more of the *do togethers* are still trying to run.

A.8   Engineering Look and Feel

The phrase "look and feel" describes the appearance of objects. We often describe look and feel in terms of properties, such as color and texture. As an example, we might say that a sweater is "yellow and has a smooth, velvety texture." The topics in this section provide information on how to modify the look and feel of a world and objects within it.

A.8.1 *Texture Maps*

Objects displayed in Alice are covered with a texture maps to provide a sense of realness. For example, consider the plate on a table scene, shown in Figure A.70.

A texture map named *ground.TextureMap* covers the ground surface, and a texture map named *plate.TextureMap* covers a plate, as can be seen in Figure A.71.

A graphic file (.gif, .bmp, .jpg, or .tif) can be used to give an object a different look. The Internet is a good to place to look for graphic files — just be sure the images are not copyrighted! As an example, let's change the appearance of the plate to look like a cookie instead. Two steps are required. The first step is to import a texture map that we intend to use for that object. In this example, we selected the plate object, clicked the import texture map button, and then selected cookie.gif to be used as the texture. Figure A.72 illustrates the importing step. The second step is to set the skin property to use the new texture map, as in Figure A.73. The result is seen in Figure A.74.

Figure A.70
A plate on the table

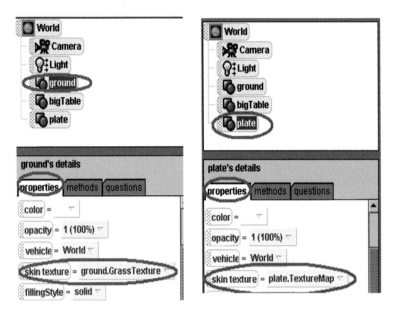

Figure A.71
Texture maps used as skin

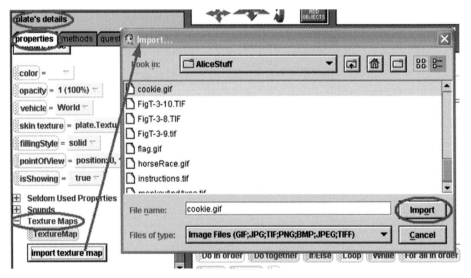

Figure A.72
Importing a texture map

A.8.2 Special Effect: Fog

In some worlds you may want to create a fog-like atmosphere. Consider the scene in Figure A.75. A knight is searching for a dragon in a forest. We would like to give the impression that the dragon is hiding from the knight. In most stories involving dragons, the weather is dreary and gray. Some sort of fog would make the knight's job (of finding the dragon) much more challenging.

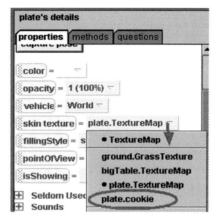

Figure A.73
Changing the texture map for the skin

Figure A.74
Cookie plate

Figure A.75
No fog

To add fog, click World in the Object tree and select properties, as shown in Figure A.76. Then, click the image to the right of fogStyle and select *density*. Density refers to the thickness of the fog. To adjust the fog density, click the *fogDensity* tile and adjust the density value to achieve the desired effect. A higher density value produces a thicker fog.

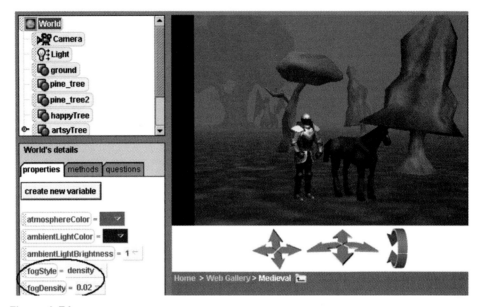

Figure A.76
The fogStyle and fogDensity properties are used to create a foggy scene

A.9   Poses

As you know, each Alice object has a center that marks its location. You may also have intuitively realized that an Alice object has the ability to remember the position of its component parts. We call the set of positions of the component parts a pose. You can think of a pose in the same way that a fashion model strikes a pose or a ballerina assumes a classic pose in ballet class. Figure A.77 illustrates a ballerina in a pose known as "first position." The ballerina's body is upright, the arms are outstretched, the feet are positioned with the heels together, and each foot is turned outward.

Figure A.77
A ballerina posing in first position

Suppose a program is written to have the ballerina begin in a first-position pose and then perform several ballet movements. Once the animation has been played (and the arms and legs of the ballerina are now in different positions), a click on the Restart button will cause the ballerina to resume her initial location and pose, so that the animation can play again.

You can use the Scene Editor to arrange an object in other poses and ask the object to remember them. Use the mouse and object methods to position the body parts of the object into the desired pose. Then click the capture pose button in the object's Details pane and enter a name for the pose. Figure A.78 illustrates the capture of an *onToe* pose for the ballerina.

Now you can write instructions to make the ballerina assume the pose during an animation. To create an instruction using a pose, drag the pose tile into the editor, as illustrated in Figure A.79.

A few words of caution about poses: resizing an object may have an unpredictable effect on poses. For this reason, we recommend that capturing a pose be the last step in creating an initial world. Also, we suggest avoiding poses if objects are being resized during the animation.

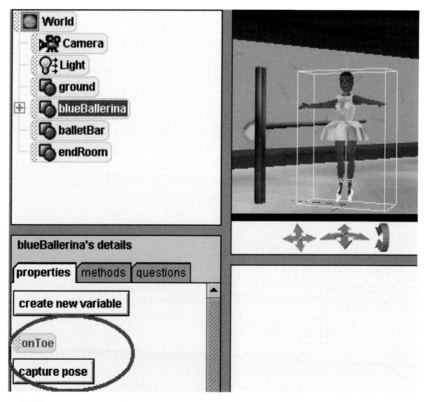

Figure A.78
Capturing an *onToe* pose

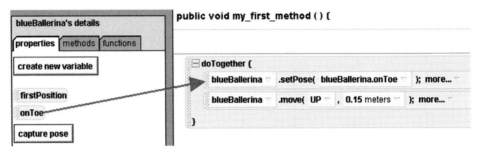

Figure A.79
Creating an instruction to have an object assume a pose

A.10   Debugging with Watch and Text Output

Throughout this text, we have encouraged an incremental development process. Write a method and test it (by running the animation) and then write another method and test it ... and so forth until the entire program is completed. Testing is a crucial part of program development. At each juncture, you can see the actions of the objects as the instructions are executed. In this way, you may find bugs in your program. This debugging process helps in building confidence that a program will work as expected each time it is run.

In this chapter we have introduced the concept of variables that store a value that can change as the program executes. The elusive thing about variables is that the values are changing "behind the scene" – somewhere in the murky depths of memory chips inside the computer. Variables are somewhat "magical" because, unlike the active objects we see in an animation, running the program does not allow us to view what is going on with the value stored in a variable. In this section, we look at two techniques that allow you to see variables in action as an animation runs: creating a watch and printing text.

A.10.1   Creating a *Watch*

Creating a *watch* is like hiring a private investigator to snoop on someone. The "private eye" sets a "tail" on that person and keeps a constant watch on his activities. In Alice, a *watch* creates a small window where the value in the watched variable is constantly displayed at runtime. Every time the value changes, it is immediately updated in the *watch* window.

As an example, let's create a *watch* on *direction* variable used in the Corvette steering example presented in this chapter. To create a *watch*, right-click on a variable and select *watch this variable*, as illustrated in Figure A.80.

After a *watch* has been created, a run of the animation is displayed in a split window. One pane displays the animation while another pane displays the value of the

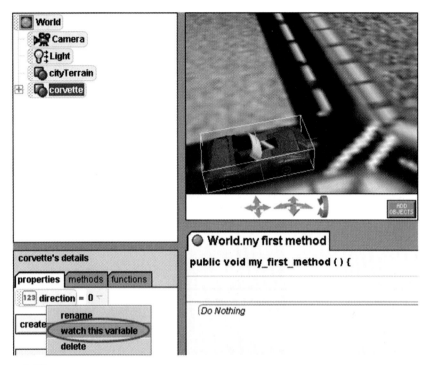

Figure A.80
Creating a *watch* on a variable

watched variable. You may recall that the *direction* variable is used to track the amount the corvette's steering wheel has been turned left or right. The *direction* amount is then used to guide the movement of the Corvette. In Figure A.81(a), the value stored in *direction* is 0, and the Corvette moves straight ahead. In Figure A.81(b), the value stored in *direction* is –2 and the Corvette is steering toward the left. Viewing the *direction* value and the resulting motion of the Corvette in the animation confirms that the animation is working as designed.

A.10.2 Text Output

The *print* instruction in Alice is another way to keep an eye on the value stored in a variable at runtime. As with the *watch* feature, the print instruction causes the animation to be displayed in a split window. One pane displays the animation, while another pane displays output in a text console.

As an example, let's modify the steering Corvette program to use *print* instructions to display the value in the Corvette's direction variable. In this program, the *direction* variable is incremented each time the right arrow key is pressed and decremented each time the left arrow key is pressed. All that needs to be done is to add a *print* instruction to the *corvette.right* and *corvette.left* methods. Figure A.82 illustrates dragging a *print*

Figure A.81
(a) and (b) Screen captures of a *watch* window at runtime

instruction into the *corvette.left* method. From the popup menu, we selected object →
expressions → corvette.direction.

The modified *corvette.left* method is shown in Figure A.83. A *print* instruction is
also created for the *corvette.right* method. After the *print* instructions are created, a
run of the animation and a text console are displayed in a split window. The first left or
right arrow press causes the text console to appear. Thereafter, the mouse can be used
to activate/deactivate the text console. Clicking the mouse0 on the animation pane
activates the text console; moving the mouse elsewhere on the screen deactivates the
text console. A sample run is illustrated in Figure A.84. (On some machines, the runtime window must be resized to make it large enough to view the text console.)

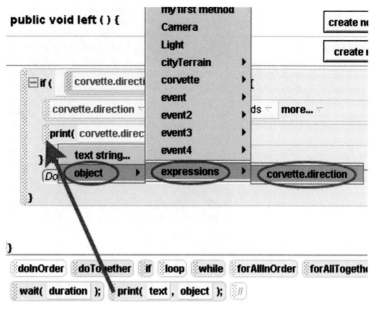

Figure A.82
Creating a *print* instruction

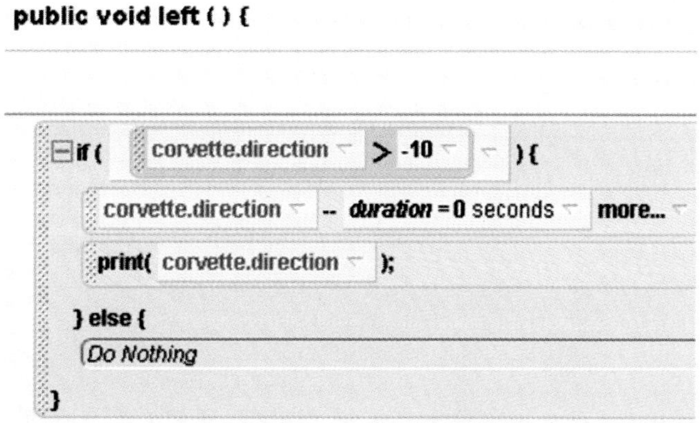

public void left ( ) {

> **if (** corvette.direction ▽ **> -10** ▽   ▽ **){**
>
>> corvette.direction ▽ -- ***duration*** **=0** seconds ▽ **more...** ▽
>>
>> **print(** corvette.direction ▽ **);**
>
> **} else {**
>> (*Do Nothing*)
>
> **}**

Figure A.83
The modified *corvette.left* method

If the text console is active, each left arrow or right arrow key-press causes the value stored in the *direction* variable to be displayed on the next line in the text console. In this way, a text console provides a history of the changes in a variable's value.

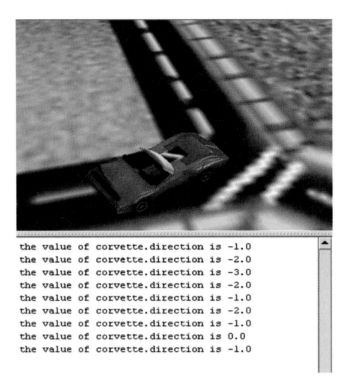

```
the value of corvette.direction is -1.0
the value of corvette.direction is -2.0
the value of corvette.direction is -3.0
the value of corvette.direction is -2.0
the value of corvette.direction is -1.0
the value of corvette.direction is -2.0
the value of corvette.direction is -1.0
the value of corvette.direction is 0.0
the value of corvette.direction is -1.0
```

Figure A.84
Runtime text console

APPENDIX B

Quick Reference to Java

B.1 Variables

Variables allow us to associate names with values. In Java you must declare a variable before you use it. To declare a variable you specify a type and a name followed by a semicolon.

```
type name;
```

You can also set the value of the variable when you declare it to the result of an expression.

```
type name = expression;
```

The type can be any of the primitive types (`int`, `boolean`, `byte`, `char`, `double`, `float`, `long`, `short`), a class name, or an interface name. The convention is to start variable names with a lowercase letter and uppercase the first letter of each additional word.

```
> int i;
> double totalBill = 32.43 + 20 * 32.43;
> String name = "Mark Guzdial";
> Picture pictureObj;
> List studentList = null;
```

Variable names can be made up of letters, digits, underscores, or currency symbols. They can start with any of these except a digit. Variables can be any word *except* the *reserved words*. The reserved words are:

abstract	assert	boolean	break	byte
case	catch	char	class	const (unused)
continue	default	do	double	else
enum	extends	false	final	finally
float	for	goto (unused)	if	implements
import	instanceof	int	interface	long
native	new	null	package	private
protected	public	return	short	static
strictfp	super	switch	synchronized	this
throw	throws	transient	true	try
void	volatile	while		

Most of the reserved words are also keywords. The only ones that are *not* keywords are null, true, and false. All of the Java reserved words have only lowercase letters.

We can use System.out.print or System.out.println to print the value of a variable. The second one will also force a new line after the value has printed.

```
> int x = 10
> System.out.println(x);
10
> String name = "Barbara Ericson";
> System.out.println(name);
Barbara Ericson
```

B.2   Method Declarations

Declare a method by specifying the visibility, the return type, the method name, and a parameter list. Method declarations are usually followed by code inside of curly braces which are the statements that will be executed when the method is invoked.

```
visibility returnType name(parameterList)
{
  // statements in the method
}
```

The parameter list is a comma-separated list of the parameters that will be passed to the method. For each parameter, specify a type and a name. Parameters are passed by value, which means that a copy of the value is passed to the method. So primitive variables passed to a method will not be affected by changes in the method after the return from the method, but because the value of an object variable is a reference to the object, a method can change the passed object, and such changes are preserved after the return from the method.

```
public void changeRedAndGreen(double redMult,
                             double greenMult)
```

The convention is to start a method name with lowercase letters and uppercase the first letter of each additional word. A method can return a value by using the return statement. The type of the value being returned must match the specified return type.

```
/**
 * Method to create a new picture by rotating the current
 * picture by the given degrees
 * @param degrees the number of degrees to rotate by
 * @return the resulting picture
 */

public Picture rotate(int degrees)
{
  // create a new picture object big enough to hold the result
  // no matter what the rotation is
  Picture result =
    new Picture((int) (Math.ceil(rect.getWidth())),
                (int) (Math.ceil(rect.getHeight())));
```

```
  // other statements in the method
  return result;
}
```

If a method doesn't return any value, the return type should be `void`.

```
/**
 * Method to decrease the green in the picture by 30
 */
public void decreaseGreen()
{
  // method statements
}
```

If you want all other classes to be able to invoke a method, make the visibility of the method `public`. If you only want to use a method in the class it is declared in use `private` as the visibility. If you leave off the visibility, then the method can be invoked by all classes in the same package. This is called *package visibility*. You can also use *protected visibility* if you want subclasses to be able to override an inherited method, but be aware that all classes in the same package also have access to the method.

B.3   Iteration (Loops)

If you are using Java 5.0 (1.5) or above you can use a for-each loop. The syntax for a for-each loop is:

```
for (type name : collection)
{
  // statements to execute
}
```

The type is the type of objects in the collection. The name is the local variable name to use. The collection is anything that holds a collection of objects, such as an array, list, or set. The following is an example of using a for-each loop:

```
// loop through all the samples in the array
for (SoundSample sample : sampleArray)
{
  value = sample.getValue();
  sample.setValue(value * 2);
}
```

If you know how many times a loop should repeat, then use a `for` loop. The syntax for a for loop is:

```
for (initializationArea; continuationTest; changeArea)
{
    // statements in the for loop
}
```

You can declare and initialize local variables in the initialization area. You specify a Boolean expression for the continuation test. The loop will continue while the test is true. The change area is where you specify how to change variables after each execution of the loop.

```java
// loop through all the pixels
for (int i=0; i < pixelArray.length; i++)
    pixelArray[i].setBlue(0);
```

If you don't know how many times a loop should repeat, then use a `while` loop. The syntax of a while loop is:

```java
while (continuationTest)
{
    // statements in the while loop
}
```

The statements in the curly braces will be executed as long as the continuation test is true. Often you will initialize variables before the while loop begins and change them just before the end of the while loop statements. But you can do this in the continuation test.

```java
// Loop while there is more data
while((line = reader.readLine()) != null)
{
    // print the current line
    System.out.println(line);
}
```

B.4 Conditionals

An `if` takes a Boolean expression and evaluates it. If it's true, the `if`'s block is executed. If it's false, the `else` block is executed, if one exists. If you have more than two possibilities, you can add `else if` for each additional one.

```java
// tint the shadows darker
if (redValue < 60)
{
    redValue = redValue * 0.9;
    greenValue = greenValue * 0.9;
    blueValue = blueValue * 0.9;
}
// tint the midtones a light brown
// by reducing the blue
else if (redValue < 190)
{
    blueValue = blueValue * 0.8;
}
// tint the highlights a light yellow
// by reducing the blue
else
```

```
{
    blueValue = blueValue * 0.9;
}
```

B.5   Operators

+, -, *, /, %	Addition, subtraction, multiplication, division, and modulus (remainder). Order of precedence is algebraic.
<, >, ==, !=, <=, >=	Logical operators less-than, greater-than, equal-to, not-equal-to, less-than-or-equal, greater-than-or-equal.
&&, ||, !	Logical conjunctives and, or, and not.

B.6   String Escapes

\t	Tab character
.\b	Backspace
\n	New line
\r	Return
\uXXXX	Unicode character, hexadecimal XXXX

B.7   Classes

Each class is usually defined in a separate file with the same name as the class name followed by `.java`. The convention is to uppercase the first letter of all words in a class name.

The syntax to declare a class is:

```
visibility class Name
{
    // fields, constructors, and methods
}
```

You can also specify the parent class using the `extends` keyword. If no parent class is specified, it will be `java.lang.Object`. A child class inherits public and protected fields and methods.

```
visibility class Name extends ParentName
{
    // fields, constructors, and methods
}
```

A class can also implement several interfaces. The list of interfaces is separated by commas and follows the specification of the parent class if given.

```
visibility class Name extends ParentName
  implements Interface1, Interface2, ...
{
  // fields, constructors, and methods
}
```

Here is an example class declaration. The Student class will inherit from the Object class.

```
public class Student
{
  // fields, constructors, and methods
}
```

B.8 Fields

Object fields are the data or state that each object of a class will have. Class (static) fields are in the object that defines the class so there is only one and all objects of the class have access to it. Fields are defined inside of a class definition. The convention is to start field names with a lowercase letter and uppercase the first letter of each additional word.

To declare an object field, use:

```
visibility type name;
```

To declare a field and give it a value, use:

```
visibility type name = expression;
```

The visibility for fields is usually private so that an object can protect its data from being directly accessed by code in other classes.

To declare a class field, use:

```
visibility static type name;
```

To declare a constant field, use:

```
public static final type name;
```

B.9 Constructors

Constructors are used to initialize the fields in a newly created object. The syntax for a constructor is

```
visibility ClassName(parameterList)
{
    // statements in the constructor
}
```

Constructors are usually defined with `public` visibility. Notice that they do not have a return type. The name on a constructor must match the class name.

B.10 Packages

The Java classes are grouped into packages. You can use any of classes in the package `java.lang`. If you wish to use classes in packages other than `java.lang`, you can use an `import` statement. Import statements go before the class declaration in a file. You can import all the classes in a package using:

`import` name.*;

or you can import just a named class using:

`import` name.ClassName;

To import all classes in the `java.awt` package use:

`import` java.awt.*;

To import just the class `java.awt.Color` use:

`import` java.awt.Color;

If you don't import the package or the class, you can use the full name, which is the package name followed by "." and then the class name (`java.awt.Color`).

Here is a table of some of the packages in Java and the interfaces and classes we have used from each of these packages. The interfaces are shown in italics.

java.lang	Basic classes in the language	*Comparable*, Object, String, Math
java.io	Classes for input and output	BufferedReader, BufferedWriter, FileReader, FileWriter, Reader, Writer, File
java.awt	Classes for drawing	*Paint*, Color, Font, Image, Graphics, Graphics2D
java.net	Classes for use with networks	URL
java.sql	Classes for use with databases	*Connection, Statement, ResultSet*, DriverManager
java.util	Utility and collection classes	*Iterator, List, Map*, ArrayList, HashMap, TreeMap

Index